THE EROTIC THRILLER IN CONTEMPORARY CINEMA

For Mark Kermode

THE EROTIC THRILLER IN CONTEMPORARY CINEMA

Linda Ruth Williams

EDINBURGH UNIVERSITY PRESS

Edinburgh University Press Ltd
22 George Square, Edinburgh

Typeset in 10/12.5 pt Sabon
by Servis Filmsetting Ltd, Manchester, and
printed and bound in Great Britain by
The Cromwell Press, Trowbridge, Wilts

A CIP record for this book is available from the British Library

ISBN 0 7486 1149 5 (hardback)
ISBN 0 7486 1148 7 (paperback)

CONTENTS

PART II   Suspense in Suspenders: The Direct-to-Video Erotic Thriller

          Introduction   249

      4   Softcore on the Sofa   253
          1. Video viewing   254
          2. Women and other audiences   258
          3. Softcore: 'Where adult meets mainstream'   266
          Interview: Director Gregory Dark   277

      5   The Bad and the Beautiful: Key Players in the Direct-to-Video
          Erotic Thriller   284
          1. B for Bad   286
          2. The Producers   290
          3. Video stars and moving centrefolds   294
          4. Genre Auteurs: Gregory Hippolyte and Jag Mundhra   305
          Interview: Director Jag Mundhra   322

      6   Uncovered and Undercover: Issues in the Direct-to-Video
          Erotic Thriller   331
          1. Sexual surveillance and female voyeurism   334
          2. Women's stories and lousy husbands   342
          3. The undercover heroine   353
          4. The strip-flick   359
          5. Sequels and repetitions   364
          Interview: Director Katt Shea   370

          Conclusion: The Erotic Thriller's Hybrid Children   377
          1. Sex, Zen and videotape: Hong Kong Category III Films 385
          2. Sexual melodrama   390
          3. The erotic thriller and the auteur   396
          Interview: Director and Editor Anne Goursaud   409

          Afterword on In the Cut: New Century, Old Sex?   417

          Bibliography   421
          Films Cited   444
          Index   456

ACKNOWLEDGEMENTS AND THANKS

This book would not be the book that it is without the hard work, ongoing enthusiasm and incisive interventions of a number of friends and colleagues. Peter Stanfield read all of it and Yvonne Tasker read substantial sections, and I am extremely indebted to them for insightful comments and encouragement. Thanks also to Michael Hammond and Mary Hammond for their perceptive readings of parts of the typescript. Participants at various scholarly gatherings – particularly at the University of Kent, the University of Keele and the National Film Theatre, London, provided useful feedback. In 2003 I was awarded AHRB-funded leave to work on this book, and I am grateful for the time this gave me away from my teaching and administration at Southampton University. I am also grateful for British Academy funding and my university's support, which enabled me to attend the Society for Cinema and Media Studies conference in Atlanta 2004. This book started life as a short article I wrote for *Sight and Sound* magazine in 1993, and since then various editors at that journal (Philip Dodd, Nick James, Ed Lawrenson) have commissioned pieces which have made me feel like *Sight and Sound*'s unofficial 'sex correspondent', allowing me to write about a number of films which I have gone on to engage with in a more scholarly fashion here. This book revisits some of these earlier pieces. My colleagues at Southampton University have also warmly supported this work throughout and have endured many renditions of draft chapters. I am grateful to Maitland McDonagh and Tim Worman for helping me with interview contacts, and to my occasional research assistant, Christine Cornea. Thanks also to Rebecca Feasey and Matt Hills, who generously gave me access to their unpublished writings. Some of the material on censorship and classification in chapter 1 originally appeared in 'Sex and Censoriousness: Pornography and Censorship in Britain' (Williams 2002).

Special gratitude goes to my interviewees, who were more than generous with their time, providing me with valuable information unavailable elsewhere and showing real interest in the project: Gregory Dark, William Friedkin, Andrew Garroni, Walter Gernert, Anne Goursaud, Frank Mazzola, Jag Mundhra, Brian De Palma, Katt Shea, Paul Verhoeven – thank you!

Finally, thanks, and love, go to Mark Kermode, to whom this book is dedicated, for his unfailing encouragement and good humour, and the hard work he put into helping me complete this project. Not only did he take on the lion's share of the childcare during this book's protracted gestation, he also transcribed the interviews for me, read through numerous chapter drafts and endured more Shannon Tweed movies than is good for any liberated man.

PREFACE

> Whole genres and styles of filmmaking arrive once and once only, never to be seen again, swallowing whole any actors or filmmakers who dare patrol their murky depths. One such inconstant genre is the erotic thriller.
>
> Review of John McNaughton's *Wild Things*[1]

There was a moment in one episode of the British soap *EastEnders*, aired in 2000, which convinced me that this book needed to be written. Long-suffering Natalie Evans (Lucy Speed) complains to her husband Barry (Shaun Williamson) (who had proposed that they lock themselves into his video store to get some privacy) that 'pinning me up against the erotic thriller section' was not her idea of a romantic setting for sex.[2] *EastEnders* has some of the highest viewing figures on British television. That Natalie could speak so casually of the genre (and its presence in video stores) and rely on her audience's understanding is ample evidence that the term 'erotic thriller' – like some of the lurid images and tropes which it has borne ('bunny boiler', for instance) – has a wide currency. Sex inspired by erotic thrillers is one lively audience response which this book touches on in a number of places (the sofa as viewing space is particularly interesting); but the erotic thriller itself as part-sex film, part-thriller, and much else besides, is my terrain.

So why write a book about sex films? Because, as Richard Dyer says, 'sexuality, both as knowledge and solution, is also the means by which men and women are designated a place in society, and are kept in their place' (1986: 26). Gregory Dark's seminal direct-to-video flick *Night Rhythms* (one of the first erotic thrillers I ever saw) begins with Martin Hewitt saying, 'Talk to me, Linda'. Erotic thrillers have been talking to me for some years now, and this book is where I talk back to and of them. *The Erotic Thriller in Contemporary Cinema* maps this genre, one which has made liberal use of softcore sexual display in the context of *noir*ish plots. It looks at sexy talking-point mainstream erotic thrillers (such as *Body of Evidence*, *Body Heat*, *Sea of Love*) alongside privately alluring direct-to-video formula works (*Night Eyes*, *Animal Instincts*, *Sins of Desire*). Some erotic thrillers are primarily thrillers, some erotic thrillers are primarily sex films. All contain sex and most use sex as a motivating nar-rative device. My terrain is quite precise: the films I look at are legally available at 18 certificate (or below) in Britain, or with (usually) an R-rating in the United States. Erotic thriller sex always remains *just* mainstream, available in high street video stores and at the multiplex – but *only just*. Many of my filmogra-phy texts have never made it into the academic pantheon of hip neo-*noirs* because most writers have never heard of them. Of the 300-plus films cited in this book, perhaps 250 are erotic thrillers (or conspirators, hybrids or near-relations of the erotic thriller). This very act of putting a figure on my filmog-raphy may mark me with what Peter Stanfield calls 'a collector's sensibility' (2002: 254), though this list is only a start. Of these, perhaps two dozen have been discussed in academic studies, a good many more on film websites, but a large remainder have never been addressed at all (and, I admit, will probably never be mentioned again). This book has partly been fuelled by the impetus to map this fast-fading film history before it is forgotten. Perhaps the Arthur Lyons of 2050, when writing *Sex and Death on the Cheap: The Lost B-Movies of the Erotic Thriller*, will use this book as her starting-point.[3] Of course, few films are now lost; databases such as the IMDb, video archives and DVD re-releases ensure that none of my sometimes obscure titles will ever be entirely gone. Looking at direct-to-video films alongside theatrically-released ones also means that I am at least not constrained by the choices distributors make about what constitutes a 'good' (that is, theatrically profitable) movie. It is still the case that the majority of academic film studies (and popular journalistic articles) look only at major, mainstream-released movies. This may be fine if your project is, say, the reception study of a blockbuster. But in a proliferating market which now includes straight-to-cable/made-for-TV and direct-to-video or direct-to-DVD films, any study which confines itself to movies which are defined by the mode of their opening release is allowing distributors to do its decision-making for it.

Furthermore, not only does this book look at the downmarket, low-budget direct-to-video world, it also investigates a number of films which were cele-brated flops. The erotic thriller spans the spectrum of success from titles which were amongst the highest earners in their year (*Basic Instinct, Fatal Attraction*) to those which courted large-scale success and bombed in a highly public way (*Showgirls, Jade*). Read textually, there is little to choose between them; indeed, Joe Eszterhas, who penned all but one of these films, is known for repeating the same sex-crime formula. *Jade* has a slick polish which might mark it out as a genre high point; instead, it was one of the worst received of the films I discuss. Read in a reception studies frame all these titles generated considerable critical heat, for very different reasons. Read as genre pieces they form distinct moments in the sweep of the erotic thriller's history, interesting as much in their market failure as their success.

But *how* to write a book about sex films? The history of the erotic thriller is the history of a genre as fantasy symptom: trace it through the last twenty years of the twentieth century and you get something closely approximating a story of the desires, fears, excitements and paranoias of these decades, at least as conceived by Hollywood and its fringes. *The Erotic Thriller in Contemporary Cinema* is, then, in part the history of a fantasy. But I have taken these two terms, history and fantasy, seriously in the approach I have fostered in this book, and each requires a number of different methodological lenses, lenses which other writers have preferred to keep separate. Rick Altman laments the fact that 'Genres were always – and continue to be – treated as if they spring full-blown from the head of Zeus' (1993: 28). This book discusses the history of this genre by mapping the ebbs and flows of this film form and looking carefully at a representative range of exemplary films and filmmakers who created that genre. In order to present the history of the genre as an interactive process between competing forces, I have maximised my approaches. Erotic thrillers are read not just as formal exercises in a particular type of filmmaking, but as economic exercises in audience attraction. As a genre the erotic thriller provides a resonant case study for understanding what audiences do to and with certain film forms, and how the agreed terms of a genre are established between audience and producer. I have supplemented this with original interviews with key personnel who have shaped the genre. I augment my readings with social and genre/production histories, approaching texts to show both how each individual film is an instance of its genre (and thus how it contributes to the history of that genre over twenty years or so), and how each film feeds into, and is informed by, wider debates about social definitions – under severe pressure in the 1980s and 1990s – such as sexuality, feminism and censorship. I also use the readings as frameworks to put to work some of the signal tenets of films studies (themselves also under pressure in the 1990s), such as auteurism, star studies and reception analysis. The erotic thriller requires a mixed methodological approach because in many ways it is an exemplary turn-of-the-century genre, the demon love-child of the popularisation of cultural theory on the one hand (postmodern identities; new celebrations of perversity; the feminist backlash), and, on the other, a canny approach to new forms of reception which have shifted world cinema into an entirely different gear (the rise of home viewing through DVD and video; the new respectability of porn; couples audiences). It would also be perverse *not* to turn to psychoanalytically informed theories of spectator and visual subjectivity given the erotic thriller's self-reflexive obsession with sexual spectatorship, its profound awareness of its own textuality and its sometimes blind, sometimes knowing, obsession with formations such as voyeurism, gendered identity and arousal.

But this is not at the expense of discussion of industrial practices which have brought this genre into being, or the observations of its personnel. I have also incorporated as much material from writers on the internet as I could garner – this, essentially, is where the paying viewer is represented in this study. The plethora of discussions and amateur reviews which have been posted on the Net since its popularisation (the rise of internet film discussion coincides with the rise of this genre as well as the rise of home viewing), through newsgroups and responses written for forums such as the Internet Movie Database, have provided rich source material.[4] Though this group of writer-viewers is highly self-selecting, I have preferred to incorporate this mode of audience discourse because, as well as avoiding the methodological problems bound up with empirical research, this form of writing is much closer to the published review in form and intention. I have also made ready use of popular reviews and print journalism on the erotic thriller, its texts, personnel and scandals. In bringing both forms of writing (professional and amateur, newsprint and webpage) into play I was able to draw on a cross-section of writings from the public arena, though each with different commercial intentions and contexts. Janet Staiger warns of the mediated nature of review material used as a source for reception work (it is 'no direct display of the reviewer's "response" to the film' [1989: 362]), but advocates its use in comparative contexts as a way of asking some of the key questions of reception studies, namely, 'What have been the receptions of cinema/genres/specific films/movements and . . . what explains these receptions' (1989: 354). Presenting a collage of such materials has allowed me to tackle these questions, though they are not the only questions this book is asking. I have also drawn on other published materials, like *The Wise Woman's Guide to Erotic Videos* and *The Psychotronic Film Guide*, which present video and DVD texts directly to the consumer with a strong sense of how materials target audiences, and what one should spend one's money (and one's desire) on. This cluster of sources forms a snapshot of the erotic thriller's contexts, and the debates it has engendered, across the two decades.

I have also kept my original interview material (largely) separate from my argument, though my meetings with filmmakers profoundly influenced my thinking on genre. These interviews are not the final story, the 'real' version of how the erotic thriller was born and nurtured; but they are one story. In researching this book I found that the history I had constructed, based on readings I had made about audience and address emanating from the film texts themselves, and information sporadically appearing in industry publications, was a very similar story to the one told to me by the filmmakers about what, when, how and why they were doing what they were doing, and who they thought they were doing it for. I hope that readers will use this primary interview material (unavailable elsewhere) as a supplement to the argument and history I put forward in my chapters, a fascinating set of material in its own right, and one starting-point for further work on this period of popular American cinema.

A word about titles: many of the DTV films discussed here were released in different territories under different titles. In the UK the thriller *I Can Make You Love Me* was released under the erotic thriller-inflected moniker *Fatal Proposal*. The UK's *Animal Instincts 2* was *Body of Influence* in the US, whilst the US *Animal Instincts 2* was the UK's *Animal Instincts 3*. Then there was

Animal Instincts: The Seductress. In the world of direct-to-video films titles are a primary element of film marketing; 'akas' ('also known as') thrive when a film has to hit the market quickly in a form that will maximise audience recognition. I will be saying more about titles in chapter 1; my filmography does, I think, tell a story about contemporary genre on titles alone. Where possible I have tried to include 'aka' titles, but if readers are interested in tracing any of the smaller films to see for themselves, it may be wise to cross-reference them on a film database such as the Internet Movie Database via other details provided, such as year and director.

NOTES

1 Adam Rivett, 'The erotic thriller, or how I learnt to love the erotic thriller' (review of *Wild Things*), from In Film Australia website, http://infilmau.iah.net/features/erotic/.
2 *EastEnders*, BBC1 television, Monday, 25 April 2000, written by Rob Gittings, produced by Richard Stokes.
3 Arthur Lyons, *Death on the Cheap: The Lost B Movies of Film Noir* (2000) has been one of my sources.
4 Matt Hills calls the IMDb viewer response sections 'an intriguing resource for academic study of film interpretation'; like him, I have found it valuable 'precisely because it is not wholly fan-centric, instead offering a more diffuse forum for film discussion that encompasses fan responses and those of more "generalised" moviegoers' (Hills, forthcoming).

1. INTRODUCTION
CARNAL CRIMES: THE EROTIC
THRILLER FROM *NOIR* TO THE 1990S

'What is a sex crime?'
'Not getting any!'

> An exchange between Sergeant Ray Duquette
> (Kevin Bacon) and a high school student in *Wild Things*

Although *Indecent Proposal* may have looked like contemporary cinema's answer to the game of 'Scruples', its source is a maligned direct-to-video genre, which thrived at many a local video store during the 1990s. The film that launched a thousand dinner-party conversations has lower roots than those who saw the movie but wouldn't dream of renting a B-class erotic thriller would imagine. Similarly, when Willem Dafoe posits the possibility that it's 'a crime to be a great lay' he situates *Body of Evidence* squarely alongside its sleazier, sexier genre sisters. High or low, blockbuster or denigrated exploitation video, the erotic thriller was one of the most prominent products in the late twentieth-century mainstream movie and video market, even though audiences and makers of films such as *Basic Instinct* or *Fatal Attraction* might have disputed their connection with 'lower' works such as *Animal Instincts* or *Basic Deception*.

Erotic thrillers are *noir*ish stories of sexual intrigue incorporating some form of criminality or duplicity, often as the flimsy framework for on-screen softcore sex. This is as true of the $45 million *Showgirls* as it is of the $1 million *Night Rhythms*. Despite the popular image that 'erotic thriller' is a blanket term for unchallenging sleaze, like any other genre there are good erotic thrillers and bad ones. Certainly, some of these films are simply feebly acted 1990s exploitation movies in designer underwear (or out of it; in *Acting on Impulse* – itself a direct-to-video erotic thriller – Linda Fiorentino plays an erotic thriller actress who spends her career having to, as she puts it, literally 'act my panties off'). Other titles are thematically as well as sexually provocative. The classic opening narrative runs thus: a neglected wife, some years into her lousy marriage, is advised by her female friend to find satisfaction with some new blood. Early scenes in which wives fail to get their husbands to come to bed are legion: the resolutely downmarket *Carnal Crimes* and *Secret Games* both boast key scenes of pleading in underwear, whilst even the relatively chaste blockbuster *Indecent Proposal* demonstrates its kinship to the B-erotic thriller when Demi Moore places the hand of her scribbling husband on her breast, only to have him remove it so that he can get on with his architecture. Careful viewers of the genre will spot this little gesture as the first step on the slippery slope towards erotic thriller unfaithfulness, and the perils as well as the pleasures of sex. Danger and sex combine in a format which is both thriller and skin-flick, often figuring a female protagonist who herself straddles the roles of sexual interest, enraged victim and vigilante survivor.

The purpose of this book is to map these lively film texts onto (and read them through) several parallel histories, which collectively chart changes in how we watch, enjoy and interact with popular films, and how these films are made and sold. This book thus partly looks at the meanings of a specific genre through the lens the marketplace. It asks what the erotic thriller has come to signify by thinking about how it achieved its position as 'the most popular genre of the 1990s' (Palmer 1994: 168). However we measure success, in the genre's high-water mark of the 1990s, erotic thrillers were *the* most discussed films and amongst the highest earners. Financial returns are impressive: *Fatal Attraction*'s domestic box office is $156 million, *Basic Instinct*'s is $117 million; both are amongst the top-grossing box office earners of all time.[1] One writer calls these 'the two most commercially successful films noirs ever made' (Naremore 1998: 263). Both were also the top opening films in their months of release, and *Fatal Attraction* – perhaps the definition of the 'word-of-mouth' film (it made more money in its second than its opening weekend) – played for thirty-nine weeks. Both films subsequently performed impressively on video and DVD, as they would be expected to after such major theatrical openings. But perhaps more impressive is the performance of a film such as the prototype direct-to-video title *Night Eyes*, which cost $1 million, and took $30 million on video alone.[2]

These are striking statistics for films almost entirely devoid of special effects whose subject matter militates against including lucrative family audiences. This book, like the films themselves, probes the conditions of the classification system which constitutes one form of public limitation: the genre's successes are achieved in spite of restrictive ratings – typically R or NC-17 in the US, 18 in the UK. Nor are erotic thrillers lucrative merchandise films: soundtrack CDs may be released, DVDs with 'making of' documentaries, but you won't see Glenn Close dolls for sale in Toys 'Я' Us, nor did McDonald's sell *Sliver* Happy Meals in 1993. The payoff for this exclusion is the cultural splash these films make as prime 'talkies', *the* sensational scandal flicks of their moment. They are as loud in the cultural 'noise' they generate as they are lucrative (the two being intimately connected) and that makes them especially interesting to anyone trying to get to grips with contemporary American cinema. Here, then, I will pose a set of interconnected questions: Why did these films appear when they did, and who are they made for? When contemporary mainstream sex cinema works to the limit of what it is allowed to do, what are we allowed to see? When such films target female as well as male viewers, are different visual pleasures the result? How important is classification to textual content, marketability and a film's potential for scandal? And finally, the question which shapes this introductory chapter, when mainstream film flirts seriously with the concerns and pleasures of the marginalised techniques of pornography and the narratives of *noir*, what genre is the result?

The 1970s and early 1980s were a seed-bed for the erotic thriller, with the basic formula developing through the sporadic release of some key titles (*Play Misty for Me*, *Looking for Mr Goodbar*, *Cruising*, *American Gigolo*), none of which would have appeared under this genre banner when released, but shift genre identities to trade on the new term when re-released. This was followed by a period of increased productivity which takes two paths. Genre formation is commonly understood in three phases: consolidation; 'a Golden Age'; followed by a period of decline, 'in which the played-out conventions dissolve either into self-parody or self-reflexivity' (Collins 1993: 246). This designation is only partly useful (I will open up a more complex view of genre below). Nevertheless, in the mainstream, theatrically-released arena, the 'Golden Age', beginning at the start of the 1980s with *Dressed to Kill* and *Body Heat*, also tracks the career of erotic thriller writer/pioneer Joe Eszterhas, especially the period from *Jagged Edge* (1985) to *Showgirls* (1995), and takes in the aforementioned genre high-points of *Basic Instinct* (Eszterhas' most visible, hyped work) and *Fatal Attraction* (not an Eszterhas screenplay, but a landmark in terms of representations, box office, and the involvement of Adrian Lyne and Michael Douglas). The architecture of the theatrically-released erotic thriller is the subject of Part One of this book. This period also overlaps the rise of home viewing through VHS and later DVD, and constitutes a significant history which runs parallel to the mainstream form. The direct-to-video (henceforth DTV) film has a distinct but overlapping history. The DTV is a film which has had no (or only a very limited) theatrical release prior to its appearance on video store shelves. In the UK the common term for this until recently was 'straight to video', but since DTV has a stronger international currency I will use it throughout this book. Some films are always destined for DTV status; others acquire it by other means. A kinder term is 'video premiere'. Films which went direct-to-video when video was the only available home viewing format may now also be going direct to DVD as well as or instead of VHS release. I am therefore using DTV as a catch-all or shorthand for such movies, whatever form they take when viewed in the living room, or, indeed, the hotel room. (Pay-per-view of soft-sex films is a lucrative revenue source for hotel chains.) The DTV erotic thriller might also have a number of other market destinations, and might be accessed via a cable or satellite channel as well as the video store. The 'Golden Age' of the DTV erotic thriller was the late 1980s to the mid-1990s. The form has its own discrete 'look', key players, production values and mode of marketing and distribution. Since then, with the video market saturation of the late 1990s, the DTV form has diminished, though a steady stream of iden-tikit texts continues to be released. My interviewees give evidence of a promised resurgence at the cheaper edges of the genre in the wake of new breakthroughs in the DVD market; brand-name directors Jag Mundhra and Greg Dark (aka Hippolyte) report that they are regularly approached to direct new projects.

At the same time, erotic thriller releases in the mainstream consolidated resources into fewer, bigger projects which play well internationally. The high-profile erotic thrillers which have appeared since 1995 have, however, had to navigate the wake produced by the critical failure of *Showgirls*, which caused the industry to lose faith in the new classification category of NC-17 (designed to enable a new wave of *adult* filmmaking: cinema for grown-ups which doesn't pander to the family market, as distinct from 'adult films' which pander to the masturbating market). Since the mid-1990s, a number of films have been pro-moted as 'steamy', though the trend is increasingly chaste, or rather the explicit has become implicit, and the mainstream erotic thriller has happily got into bed with other genres. Titles such as the costume drama *Original Sin*, or the erotic melodramas *Unfaithful* and *One Night Stand*, give a picture not of end-game or cycle-conclusion, but of a genre finally conforming to the Hollywood norm of saturation-opening, inflated star salaries and careful if over-resourced mar-keting strategies, as well as a willingness to hybridise further. There is also evi-dence that the erotic thriller has been annexed by the highbrow auteur, with a select series of prestigious or notorious titles emerging around the new century (Kubrick's *Eyes Wide Shut*, Campion's *In the Cut*). Such titles open a new chapter in the genre's story, of a form flourishing on mainstream and art-house screens, providing directors and stars looking for a new career trajectory with the chance to walk on the wild side. Émigré directors of esteemed 'foreign lan-guage' films (Chen Kaige, Volker Schlöndorff) have moved into English-lan-guage cinema by directing popcorn erotic thrillers (*Killing Me Softly* and *Palmetto* respectively, though Schlöndorff had directed *The Handmaid's Tale* in English in 1990, moving back to German cinema afterwards). Other 'names' have continued to produce interesting work in a genre they helped to forge – David Lynch's *Lost Highway* and *Mulholland Drive* are frequently read as neo-*noir* surrealism, though their cocktail of seduction and secrecy makes them interesting for this analysis. Abel Ferrara has also provided one independent pathway through the genre, from *Ms 45* to *Fear City* to *The Blackout*, whilst Brian De Palma largely mapped out the genre's basic co-ordinates in the 1970s and 1980s; his 2003 film *Femme Fatale* develops questions raised in *Dressed to Kill* and *Body Double*. High or low, seen at home or in the hotel room, in the multiplex or the art-house, this book discusses the erotic thriller in each of its multiple contexts.

1: CHEAP THRILLS AND EXPENSIVE EXPLOITATION

'It takes a lot of money to look this cheap.'

Dolly Parton

However much money you throw at an erotic thriller, it will always look like the sensational genre fare that it is, driven by the values of an exploitation potboiler, with its fingers in a blockbuster's expense account and its feet in the cheap shag-pile carpet. *Basic Instinct* cost around $40 million, with writer Joe Eszterhas getting the (then) highest ever salary for a screenplay ($3 million), and Michael Douglas bagging $14 million for his role. Although it is set in San Francisco, J. Hoberman reads the film as taking place 'in the realm of unfettered desire' in an 'atmosphere of super-consumption'.[3] Blockbusters are all too vulnerable to unfavourable comparisons with cheaper fare, or with each other, on the grounds that they deliver trash culture with a high price-tag. In 1995, reviewing the latest Joe Eszterhas-penned mainstream release, William Leith wrote: 'Unlike *Basic Instinct*, which was quite a good trashy porn thriller, *Jade* is quite a bad one' (1995: 38), whilst *Color of Night* was received as a 'so-bad-it's-good' festival of absurdity, and unfavourably compared to lower DTV genre and softcore works (e.g. Newman 1994b: 216).[4] Against this, B-class erotic thrillers made at one-fortieth of the price are all desperate to look classy, eking out micro-budgets into mini-simulations of *Jade*'s sleek *mise-en-scène*. Marketed as a form of 'quality entertainment' which is synonymous with high production values, massive budgets and stars who can open a movie, the respectability of theatrically-released films is equalled only by the tacky low-life image of the DTVs.

Whilst historically genres come in and out of fashion, some genres have lent themselves to cheaper forms of production than others; some have been consistently favoured for mainstream production (dramas, comedies, musicals), some have fared equally well as A- or B-movies (westerns, thrillers, melodrama), others have spent much of their history – certainly up to the mid-1970s – on poverty row (horror, science fiction, pornography). Sexy *noirs* have appeared across the strata of production and budget. Silver and Ward liken contemporary low-budget neo-*noir* production to classic B-*noir*:

> The plots of these pictures, all budgeted at under a million dollars, take only what they can afford from the classic tradition; but that is a considerable amount. All have enough money for a femme fatale, a hired killer or two, a confused and entrapped hero, an employer ripped off, a shake-down. . . . Like its antecedent, neo-noir and neo-B in particular makes few if any extravagant demands in terms of production value. (Silver and Ward 1992: 422)

Yet the high profile of the celebrated genre titles produced by New Hollywood has all but erased the barrel-scraping image of much genre cinema. 1975 is often cited as a watershed year, in that the phenomenal success of Steven Spielberg's *Jaws* blasted what was essentially an exploitation film into the main-stream, ensuring that many of the most successful titles from then onwards were good old-fashioned genre works wrought in epic proportions – creature-feature or alien invasion drive-in fodder injected with vastly expanding budgets and promoted to family audiences. This progressive 'mainstreamisation' meant that science fiction and horror in the 1970s and 1980s, and *film noir* (in the form of 'neo-*noir*' – sometimes called '*après noir*', or '*noir lite*') in the 1980s and 1990s, became genres with a wide audience base justifying larger budgets. The effects of this legitimisation of genre meant that filmmakers working at the bottom end of the market found that their stock-in-trade had been appropri-ated in a spectacularly inflated form on international mainstream screens. Veteran low-budget genre filmmaker Roger Corman, who helped establish the erotic thriller in the 1990s, said of this:

> The major challenge has been finding new markets and recouping costs while the majors have dominated the exploitation genres with budgets ten times higher than ours. . . . [I]t was Vincent Canby of *The New York Times* who once wrote, 'What is *Jaws* but a big-budget Roger Corman movie?' But when the Spielbergs and the Lucases make technically exqui-site genre films, they cut deeply into the box-office appeal of our kind of picture. (Corman 1998: xi)[5]

Thus it is fortunate for low-budget genre filmmakers that 1975 was also a watershed year in terms of diversity of film exhibition. This was the year in which Sony introduced Betamax, the first home video viewing and recording system, inaugurating an era in which viewers would gain some control over when, what and how they consumed films. Matsushita's VHS (video home system), which successfully competed with Betamax for the lion's share of the video market, was introduced in 1976 and – competitors such as DVD (digital versatile disc) and laserdisc notwithstanding – remained the internationally dominant mode of home viewing at the turn of the century. VHS also became a major format for the release of cheap genre films, including DTV films, which first made their appearance in the video boom of the 1980s when the supply of theatrically-released product (turned around onto video) could not keep up with consumer demand for films to view on those new living-room VCRs. Low-budget producers such as Corman responded to the challenge of the block-buster by diversifying their sales options, first taking up the opportunity of the expanding television market by selling to network television and the new cable channels also developed in the 1970s, then, as the VHS machine became an established feature of the domestic space, making films only or primarily for video release.

Given the gargantuan video and DVD rental and retail market of today, it is hard to remember a time when it was not possible to own one's own copy of a film to play when one chooses. The methods of interacting with films continues to change, as television, playback technology, PCs and the world wide web become increasingly interdependent; but as significant as any moment in cinema history (perhaps at least as important as the Paramount decrees) was the moment when it became possible to 'possess' a film for long enough to interfere with the shape of its time (through rewind, fast-forward, skip and pause functions, as well as simply choosing your moment to watch it). As I write in the early twenty-first century, this was still relatively recent history, but the notion of experiencing films *only* as and when an exhibitor determined at a place some distance from your home is now a fairly alien model of cinematic consumption. It is worth noting that both the DTV film and the video/DVD industry developed in the last quarter of the twentieth century. New viewing practices ushered in entirely new media industries. The rise of the erotic thriller is coterminous with the rise of these visual and industrial diversifications.

So what impact did these forces have on the erotic thriller? In its current form it did not exist prior to 1975 (though it has significant antecedents in *film noir*), and was therefore neither threatened nor saved in its low-budget format by the rise of the blockbuster or the development of video. Its exhibition history is much more intimately bound up with the new opportunities of home viewing, the development of the genre and the growth of the VCR happily progressing hand-in-hand. The early 1980s, which saw the release of my earliest examples of the genre, was also the period when the VCR became a familiar domestic item, and sales and rentals of tapes proliferated: '1984', reports Cahill, 'was homevideo's first "billion dollar year, in terms of the retail value of [prerecorded] videocasettes"' (1988: 137).

This was the culture into which the erotic thriller was born. The convergence of the two forms – genre and mode of exhibition – was particularly developed by the early 1990s, by which time the sexual potential of home viewing (you could watch whatever you wanted, whenever you wanted with whoever you wanted, in privacy) and the increasing sexual explicitness of the erotic thriller, met and married, all the better to exploit each other as far as sex and sales would take them. New media technologies are usually seen as affording new sexual opportunities: the sexual potential of the world wide web was manifest from the start. There is evidence that within seven years of cinema's watershed year of 1895 sexual intercourse had been filmed, though it is likely to be earlier than this.[6] The VCR has always been identified with the illicit.[7] The consolidation of the genre's and the format's distinct positions of dominance came in the early 1990s: by 1993, a year of peak production for the erotic thriller in cinemas and DTV, the total number of VCRs owned by American households was 80 per cent; this had risen to 88 per cent by 1997 (Friedberg 2000: 443).

As forms of consumption change due to shifting viewing practices, so too do patterns of production and distribution. It is now commonplace to budget filmmaking in light of significant returns from video revenue, but we should not forget how recent a phenomenon this is. Kochberg (amongst others) discusses the impact on a film's profitability which results from a film going direct to video: 'Apart from the lost revenue, a film that has not secured a theatrical release cannot secure anything but poor deals for the other windows, because video, TV, etc. rely on the publicity of a theatrical release to promote a film. Without one, the film is a far less valuable commodity.'[8] However, this gives the impression that all films are destined for theatrical release but only some make it, which is not the case. The production realm into which the majority of titles on my filmography are born is one in which budgets are cut to the desires and limits of the living room. Films in this category are able to spend on relatively cheap production areas such as location in order to achieve a 'quality' look whilst they save on marketing costs and star salaries.

It is also assumed that films which receive no theatrical release are inherently less challenging than mainstream movies (the entry on 'Straight-to-video' in Blandford et al.'s *Film Studies Dictionary* bears this out [2001: 227–8]). This isn't entirely the case, for a number of reasons. First, distribution is governed by the limited number of slots and outlets into which a large number of released films must be fitted, so sometimes there just isn't space to release a 'quality' piece into the cinemas, and this differs from country to country. Brian De Palma's *Femme Fatale* was theatrically released in the USA, backed by a 'quality' marketing campaign, but went DTV in the UK. *Killing Me Softly* was a video premiere in the USA, but theatrically released in the UK. John Dahl's *The Last Seduction* (1994), which made Linda Fiorentino a star, was funded by cable money and first aired on television in the USA, gaining a US cinematic airing following positive European responses. I discuss this film in chapter 2 as a mainstream erotic thriller and in chapter 3 as a star vehicle, but in terms of funding and distribution it looks more like one of the DTVs I discuss in Part Two, with (then) unestablished stars and – as at least one reviewer noted – a 'TV look' about it.[9] *The Last Seduction* challenges our judgemental categories which deem A-list good, B-list bad – or the reverse (the 'so bad it's good' subculture of B-movie veneration will be explored in Part Two). Whilst really big movies are usually guaranteed a theatrical slot, a smaller film aspiring to the cinema might never get there, for reasons entirely to do with what else comes out at the time of its release. The scaled-down sexy *noirs* Dahl made before *The Last Seduction* – *Kill Me Again* (1989) and *Red Rock West* (1992) – were initially forced down a narrow exhibition route. *Kill Me Again* did limited business at the box office, but gained in reputation after European festival success; *Red Rock West* did well at the Toronto Film Festival and in a San Francisco art-house cinema, prompting Columbia Tri-Star (who has 'quickly sold it to HBO and to video stores as an "erotic thriller"' [Naremore 1998: 165] – though it is the least sexual of these early Dahl films) to re-think, giving it a late theatrical release.[10]

Of course, whatever my claims below for the relative panache of films such as *Sexual Malice* or *Sexual Intent*, these are not near-misses hovering at the edges of the theatrical arena. Budgeted at a million or less and marketed almost entirely via their eye-catching exploitation video sleeves, they know what they are and who (or what) they're for.[11] The 1998 Shannon Tweed vehicle *Powerplay* has the words 'Erotic Thriller' printed on a red banner on the back cover of the UK video sleeve where one would expect the title to be. Inside the pre-release video trade version of the sleeve, dealers are wooed into buying this title for their rental stock with the lines 'Solid Rentable Genre! Eye-Catching Sleeve!'. Similarly, Jag Mundhra's early genre piece *Night Eyes* was marketed with the phrase 'An Erotic Thriller' so closely aligned to the film's title on the American video sleeve that it almost serves as a sub-title. Titles are a primary part of a film's branding, and are particularly important for DTVs which will have to do a lot of selling through a few boldface words in the absence of a large marketing budget. From *Acting on Impulse* to *Dangerous Indiscretion* to *Stripped to Kill* and *Victim of Desire*, here title speaks genre, not necessarily the individual characteristics of the film itself (though the first is about a movie actress and the third is set in a strip-joint, so there's some content clue there). Many titles marry two shocking elements into one come-on message, with the suggestion that any of these words could be remixed into a new combination (and have been). The erotic words tend to be adjectives, adding sexual emphasis to the nouns: instincts are basic, crimes are carnal, proposals are indecent, games are secret, intent is sexual. But this can be easily reversed, for just as dark thoughts are sexy, so is sex deadly, attraction fatal. Upon these banal reversals a whole genre rests.[12] Titles advertise sensations (pleasures, desires) yoked to judgements (illicit, scandalous), first experienced by the characters and then promised to the audience. The genre is, of course, entirely aware of these absurdities: '*Deadly Cleavage* – my favourite movie!' says a geeky fan to Linda Fiorentino in *Acting on Impulse*, 'I must have seen that thing twelve times!'[13] The titles also suggest direct reference back to those of classic *noir* – *Murder, My Sweet*, *Kiss of Death* and *Kiss Me Deadly* would all do brisk business as erotic thriller titles.[14] The repetition is mind-boggling: hard to remember but easy to categorise, films such as *Hidden Obsession*, *Naked Obsession* and *Blindfold: Acts of Obsession* may as well have called themselves 'Erotic Thriller 1', 'Erotic Thriller 2' and 'Erotic Thriller 3' for all the distinction the title gives as a designator of individuality (which may be why the DTV form of the genre became so fixated on sequels, more of which later). This is not (necessarily) to say that 'all erotic thrillers are the same', but that genre branding in title form is so strong they may as well be.

Titles can also be misleading, genre-wise. If the format says 'Erotic Thriller' but – by dint of sheer repetitiveness – this in itself makes the distinctions between films almost impossible to discern, it can also be used to sell as sexy films which are anything but. Following the success of *Fatal Attraction*, the word 'fatal' became synonymous with the genre and a metonym not for 'fate' (the inevitability of destiny), but deadly sex. Angela Martin reads the fatality of the *femme fatale* as underpinning the fatality of *film noir* itself: 'The femme fatale carries all . . . levels of meaning [of the word fatal], hence the easy slippage from deadliness to sexuality as weapon' (1998: 206). In the erotic thriller, however, the term 'fatal' has become most significant as a marketing hook, and the more the word is repeated, the more insistent 'fatality' becomes as a sales strategy rather than a simple description of (gendered) content. *Fatal Pursuit* (a Shannon Whirry vehicle), *Fatal Past* and *Night Eyes 4: Fatal Passion* are straightforward erotic thrillers, as are the two films released in 1991 and 1993 under the title *Fatal Instinct*, the first (a year before *Basic Instinct*), another story of a cop (Michael Madsen) falling for the suspect and subsequently branded as 'a sexy suspense-laced psychological thriller in the seductive style of *Basic Instinct* and *Sea of Love*'; the second, a star-studded, theatrically-released parody of the genre. Other 'fatal' films are hybrids or non-explicit thrillers which ride on the coat-tails of the sexier genre's success in suggestively aping its trademark title form. Of six such films released between 1988 and 1998 (though the list of 'fatal' films is far longer), *Fatal Secret* is an action film, *Fatal Image* a straight thriller, whilst *Fatal Temptation* and *Fatal Encounter* are American re-titlings of Italian and Hong Kong dramas respectively, both involving infidelity stories, the first a sexual melodrama, the second an AIDS saga. Two *Fatal Exposures*, from 1989 and 1991, are horror and made-for-TV mob-thrillers respectively, if with voyeuristic overtones. However, the first was re-released on video in the UK market in 1992 as a fully paid-up erotic thriller, its serial killer photographer-protagonist rebranded as a sexy *homme fatal*, with a video sleeve featuring a model's torso and legs in profile, clad only in strips of film wrapped around her breasts, groin and thighs.[15] The strong branding of the erotic thriller is thus used to sell adjacent or tangentially-related genres, perhaps to subsequently disappointed customers, who discover that *Fatal Deception* – a biopic of Lee Harvey Oswald's wife – is *not Fatal Attraction*. A similar tactic is the use of scantily clad models, who almost certainly won't appear in the film itself, the staple of DTV box-art. But whilst the DTVs *depend* on a genre-brand title, theatrically-released films deploy them too, even though they have other publicity tools available to them, to the point where title merges into high-concept encapsulation. *Body of Evidence*, slavishly title-led, offers everything in those three little words, as one of the highest of high-concept movies: Madonna kills men with her body, and her body is the evidence.

This deployment of an exploitation tactic is then another one of the cross-influences between 'high' and 'low' forms of the genre: both trade on sex from the title down. Yet the pervasive perception of video erotic thrillers as the poor cousins of the films is still predicated on the understanding that they exist for sex whilst theatrically-released films exist for story. Arousal is an index of marginalisation: 'in general masturbation is that rare thing in modern talk about sexuality', writes Thomas Laqueur, concluding his study of the cultural history of self-pleasuring: 'something best left unspoken and so discomforting that it can only be broached under the protection of a joke' (2003: 496). Video erotic thrillers *are* a joke in many quarters (they also frequently find themselves funny), and this may be linked to the fact that they also specifically set out to be sexually stimulating. In the sense that they operate with a constant cinematographic awareness of masturbation as a prime audience response and index of the film's success, they can openly flirt with pornography. Private viewing does, of course, change the nature of a film. However hot a blockbuster might become, masturbation in the auditorium is considered less of a 'danger' than in the living room, and it is the living room which is the DTV's primary screening room. Higher-end erotic thriller filmmakers don't see themselves as pornographers because they do not advertise themselves as arousing: 'The stuff that is shot and sold as porn is meant to get you aroused and climax', said Brian De Palma in 1984. 'I don't think my movies have people coming in their seats . . .' (Pally 1984: 14). This is despite the hope that they will arouse nevertheless: Michael Douglas says that he saw *Basic Instinct* as resembling 'the kind of detective novel you might read in the privacy of your own bedroom. Not really smutty but certainly stimulating!' (quoted in Lawson 1993: 211). However, films such as *The Last Seduction* have few sex-scenes to speak of, presenting just one set-piece scene (amidst a range of more fleeting moments) which follows mainstream softcore rules: a thunderstorm enables oscillating lighting, the camera slowly pans up and down naked bodies, gasping voices are woven into the ponderous jazz score. Two sex-scenes were cut;[16] *The Last Seduction* is not, textually speaking, a masturbation film.

But viewing context also determines what is considered 'dangerously' sexual. The Video Recordings Act was introduced in the UK in response to a moral panic about 'private home viewing', and was the first piece of British legislation specifically to take into account the criteria of 'suitability for viewing in the home'. What this has meant is that video certification in the UK is rather more draconian than cinematic certification, despite the persistent notion that sex films released into the home must be riskier, more explicit than anything that could show at your local cinema. The opposite is true in the USA, where more explicit 'director's cut' videos may be subsequently released with a 'stronger' rating (or more usually unrated) following a theatrical classification geared to the widest market (which might include teenagers and children). In theatres, blockbusters are often blander versions – anodyne remakes – of their riskier poor relations, such as the productions of the highly prolific Axis stable – brand leaders of the genre as it existed on video in the first half of the 1990s. *Indecent Proposal* was, after all, released in Britain with a 15 certificate (raising the question of what happens to a film which has its generic origins in pornography when you take out the pornography). Cleansing the plots of their raw, 'deviant' moments, the blockbusters have sanded off the genre's culturally revealing rough edges along with the sexually revealing softcore centres.[17]

The hierarchical differences which privilege the theatrically-released *Body of Evidence* or *Body Heat* above the DTV *Body of Influence* or *Body Chemistry* has meant that the latter have received little serious attention. Low budget does not necessarily mean low interest, and in many ways these rapidly produced, flawed works of schlock confront key sexual political issues in a far more interesting way than their mainstream counterparts. This is no accident, since a more intimate relationship of influence connects high and low. Carol Clover makes a similar point in her study of contemporary horror, *Men Women and Chain Saws*. 'When I see an Oscar-winning film like *The Accused* or the artful *Alien* . . . I cannot help thinking of all the low-budget, often harsh and awkward but sometimes deeply energetic films that preceded them by a decade or more – films that said it all, and in flatter terms, and on a shoestring' she writes (1992a: 20), a point which genre journalists and fans had long recognised, as they repeatedly saw 'their' films remade and blown up for mainstream audiences without a by-your-leave acknowledgement to the original. Maitland McDonagh's collection of interviews with off-Hollywood filmmakers picks open the intricate ways in which the boundaries between mainstream and fringe are blurred, arguing that 'exploitation movies and the people who make them' have changed the face of the mainstream (1995: xii). Clover returned to this issue:

> The case could be made that horror movies in general are the repressed of a fair share of American mainstream cinema. Scratch the glossy surface of *The Silence of the Lambs* and you have a slasher film . . . Scratch *Pacific Heights* and you are in an economy of bloodsucking that looks like nothing so much as a vampire film. . . . Even a cursory glance makes it clear that the direction of trickle here is up, not down . . . today's 'meat movie' is tomorrow's blockbuster. (1992b: 18)

This pattern of authority also marks other genres: today's scuzzy skin-flick is also tomorrow's supermovie. But equally, today's 'classy' blockbuster erotic thriller is also tomorrow's lower-class DTV: here influence flows (at least) two ways. Thus, whilst Kim Newman's comment, 'Almost all video genres are cutdowns of big screen trends' describes the prevailing view ('the erotic thriller certainly seems to owe its existence to a handful of 80s hits', he continues [1996a: 112]), this is not always so; DTV erotic thrillers frequently function as the disavowed but influential underbelly of sexy blockbusters. Individual film cases from the late 1980s onwards evidence a 'trickle-up' as well as a 'trickle-down' effect, with the exploitation fringes providing as much raw material for the theatrically-released blockbusters as vice versa. Sometimes the theatrically-released stories get there first and spawn a spate of DTV clones; some low-budget erotic thrillers are so inventive that the mainstream movies follow their lead (hoping, perhaps, that since the originator of an idea was a small circulation DTV, most mainstream audiences won't have seen it anyway). Whilst everyone compared *Basic Instinct* to *Jagged Edge*, also written by Joe Eszterhas, an even less flattering comparison could be made with a number of more disreputable films. Sharon Stone as Catherine Tramell is perhaps a more expensive version of erotic thriller video-queen Delia Sheppard as Bridget the avenging lesbian of *Night Rhythms*, who at least sticks to her sexuality and cannot be swayed by the charms of the first man who crosses her path. *Basic Instinct* is surely *The Other Woman* in reverse; instead of the cop falling for 'the wrong woman' and in the process persuading her away from lesbianism, *The Other Woman* presents a female heroine turning towards another woman, challenging in part the notion that all women ever need is a good heterosexual seeing to. Individual scenes demonstrate most clearly the exchange between small and big screen. Greg Dark/Hippolyte certainly kept an eye on his classic precedents: *Mirror Images II* boasts a staircase descent which echoes Phyllis's in *Double Indemnity* and a scene in which a woman watches someone having sex through a cupboard door (cf. *Blue Velvet*). But surely Joe Eszterhas – described as the '*meister* of porno-*noir*' (Hirsch 1999: 202) – was taking notes for *Sliver* when *Animal Instincts* was released, since it seems an even more significant influence than Ira Levin's novel. Scratch the surface of *Basic Instinct* and you have a straight-to-video erotic thriller with a bigger budget, whilst *Indecent Proposal* looks rather like *Secret Games* with most of the sex taken out. The soundtrack might tell us that this is 'no ordinary love' as Demi Moore and Woody Harrelson fuck on their bed of money, but it is the love that erotic thrillers are made of. It is also a love prefigured by Jag Mundhra three years earlier. Compare sex on a bed of dollar bills *circa* 1990 in *Last Call* with sex on a bed of dollar bills *circa* 1993 in *Indecent Proposal*. In the former it is Shannon Tweed who revels naked in the dosh; in the latter it is rising thespian Demi Moore. Compare, also, Tanya Roberts dripping candlewax on Andrew Stevens' chest *circa* 1990 in *Night Eyes*, with Madonna doing the same for Willem Dafoe three years later in *Body of Evidence*. The former Mundhra films are cheap DTV, the latter are glossy talking-point blockbusters, the images are nearly identical – it's just that Mundhra got there first (*Mirror Images II* also shows sex with hot wax).[18] Many of these images are born of a real desire to innovate on a budget.

One textual influence I do not have the space to examine in any detail here is hardcore, perhaps even 'lower' in cultural estimation than DTV genre films. Though throughout this book I show how aspects of the hardcore revolution fed into the softcore revolution, providing a parallel history (the VCR as exhibition platform; the rise of the couples audience; porno-chic in popular and academic arenas), I have not looked at how individual hardcore texts form blueprints for later softcore ones. Since some erotic thriller players previously worked in hardcore (the 'Dark Brothers', for example, were central to Axis – producer Walter Gernert and director Greg Dark aka Hippolyte), this may be a fertile area of enquiry. There is, of course, a lively sub-industry producing explicit parodies of mainstream movies, enabling the porno-trainspotter to compile an obscene comedy of titles such as *Shaving Ryan's Privates*, *Forrest Hump* and *Saturday Night Beaver*. This sub-genre might be seen as a witty formation of Clover's 'trickle-down' factor. However, my discussion of the erotic thriller in mainstream markets focuses on the cross-fertilisation between theatrical and DTV forms. There is another story which still needs to be told about hardcore erotic thrillers (the term is used, for instance, in *Adult Video News'* review of *The Fashionistas*), and hardcore narrative inventions crossing over into softcore movies for mainstream markets.

There also remains a problem in seeing either low- or high-budget erotic thrillers (or any genre) as the primary repository of ideas and interest, occupying the moral or inventive high ground. No film form is essentially more liberating or progressive simply because it is cheaper or less processed (to say so would be rather like sanctifying poverty). Noting that 'many of the best noir films were B film', Paul Schrader observes the opposite phenomenon when he notes:

> This odd sort of economic snobbery still lingers on in some critical circles: high-budget trash is considered more worthy of attention than low-budget trash, and to praise a B film is somehow to slight (often intentionally) an A film. (1972: 62)

Nevertheless I have found that perhaps because the DTVs I am considering haven't undergone the same processes of smoothing over the cracks that their generic big sisters have, they often contain revealing and contradictory moments, even a twisted kind of feminism, which many viewers have been hard-pressed to find in blockbusters like *Fatal Attraction*. In saying that the paths of influence between the DTVs and the blockbusters run both ways, I hope to give credit where credit is due, but I also want to acknowledge that Hollywood and its fringes operate rather like a sea of sharks: everything is food; every narrative idea, marketing technique and talent resource is up for grabs, and available to the highest bidder (or whoever is willing to buy). Filmmakers and sellers will exploit what the other has to offer as far as they can. Whilst the small films might function like a pre-emptive test screening, trying out ideas to see if they work before studios invest, the big films also provide a cosy context of expectation into which the smaller films can nestle. Andrew Garroni says that *Basic Instinct* did not give Axis content ideas (they had already honed their signature product two years before Verhoeven's monster came along), but it did give them a sales hook, making their risky-looking commodities a safer bet. High-gloss blockbuster erotic thrillers 'were advertisements' which helped producers to reassure tentative distributors that their product was dependable: '*Basic Instinct allowed* the middle managers that run the outlets of distribution to be able to point to [a similar film and say] it's like *Basic Instinct*. It just has David Carradine instead of Michael Douglas in it!' (see below, p. 69). This is also evident in the customary trade press and video sleeve technique of comparing like with (almost) like, using a range of other titles as market orientation co-ordinates – if you bought *that*, then buy *this*. Roger Corman reports that he put the 'New' into New World Pictures because he had read that 'New' was one of the seller's best allies (1998: 179), but genre viewers want the known as well as the new. The trade press understand that they will get nowhere if all they have are genuinely original products; the new must be introduced with reassurances of the old. If likeness is a hallmark of genre, then genre is still primary in the marketing of movies as safe, known commodities.

At one point, of course, the term 'erotic thriller' itself was new. 'Erotic' started being used as an adjective to give a particular emphasis to the established term 'thriller' during the early 1980s; by 1990, just after the success of *Night Eyes*, a number of my interviewees claim to have invented, or consolidated, the concept and the term (Gernert and Garroni, Mundhra, and Dark all tell similar versions of the same story). The video sleeve blurb for one 1993 DTV reads: 'When the instincts are this basic, the attraction this fatal, there's no escape for a beautiful college professor who becomes drawn into a wildly sensual relationship with a dangerous prisoner in the high voltage erotic thriller, "Over the Line"'.[19] *Dangerous Touch* was reviewed in *Video Home Entertainment* (the UK's foremost trade journal from 1992 onwards) through a framework of familiarity, a combination of like-films and known (if has-been) near-stars: 'A truly erotic thriller in the *Fatal Attraction*, *Basic Instinct* mould. With a strong sleeve and a cast led by Lou Diamond Phillips of *Young Guns* and *La Bamba* fame this latest PolyGram release should be a dead cert for excellent rental business' (11 December 1993, p. 22). Similarly, the video sleeve for the Zalman King-produced *Business for Pleasure* contains the legend 'From the Creator of "9½ Weeks" and "Wild Orchid"', suggesting that the film is directed by King, perhaps even by Adrian Lyne. *Weekend in Vegas* trades on a DTV ancestry ('From the producers of "A Woman Scorned"') and puns on a mainstream connection (tag-line: 'An indecent proposal. Too tempting to resist!'), whilst *A Murderous Affair* insinuates itself into the camp of both the true-life story and the biggest title in the genre ('A woman scorned is a deadly enemy. The true story of a "Fatal Attraction" killing'). This is one fertile road in the formation of genre: *Deceptions* – to pick one example from many – helps to consolidate its category as well as situating itself within one when it advertises itself as 'In the tradition of *Body Heat* and *Jagged Edge* . . . a provocative thriller, intense in passion and seething in sexuality'.[20]

2: GENRES AND DEFINITIONS

Genres do not consist solely of films. They consist also of specific systems of expectation and hypothesis which spectators bring with them to the cinema and which interact with films themselves during the course of the viewing process.

Steve Neale (2000: 31)

We didn't get up every day and repeat the mantra of the genre that we were in. Once we made the decision we understood the realities of the market place. . . . We understood what we were making.

Andrew Garroni

So how do these thoughts on the erotic thriller as a marketable genre feed into more formal models of genre? Erotic thrillers became so lucrative because they offered 'a financial guarantee: generic movies are in a sense always pre-sold to their audiences because viewers possess an image and an experience of the genre before they actually engage any particular instance of it' (Maltby 1995: 112). Genre theorists have often complicated an area of cinema which audiences and the industry have approached rather more bluntly and have adopted a number of different methodologies to address film categories. Genre study began in earnest in the 1970s as a way of engaging with popular Hollywood cinema, sometimes as a challenge or a supplement to auteur theory. This work has too frequently been led by theoretical models which have had little purchase on how the industry itself has made and marketed different types of films, the historical fluidity of key categories and audiences' use of genre – perhaps because of the prestige of the formal over the historical. For instance, in the introduction to an important collection of essays which read genre through, for example, the filters of structuralism, auteur theory, models of ideology, narrative, psychoanalysis, stylistics and formalism, Barry Keith Grant briefly mentions genre's primary commercial function:

> Stated simply, genre movies are those commercial feature films which, through repetition and variation, tell familiar stories with familiar characters in familiar situations. They also encourage expectations and experiences similar to those of similar films we have already seen. . . . Traditionally, Hollywood movies have been produced in a profit-motivated studio system which, as the result of sound business practice, has sought to guarantee acceptance at the box office by the exploitation and variation of commercially successful formulas. In this system, praised for the 'genius' of its efficiency by André Bazin, genre movies are the Model T's or the Colt revolvers with interchangeable parts. (Grant 1986: xi)

Yet the fact that genre films are mass products marketed to particular audiences, the parts continually interchanged to maximise even wider audiences, is discussed in only a few of the essays which follow this statement (and even then, these think about audiences only as an effect of implied textual meaning). If critics have read movies as celluloid Model T's, it is often only in order to produce a kind of cinematic owner's manual for identifying how they work and categorising their ideal form.

Neale begins his study *Genre and Hollywood* with the definition: ' "Genre" is a French word meaning "type" or "kind" ' (2000: 9). Formal approaches, pursued with what Maltby calls 'a cartographer's concern with defining the exact location of the boundary between one genre and another' (1995: 107), have included the identification of motifs, foregrounding the iconographic elements of *mise-en-scène* which characterise a genre, or identifying a set of what Tom Ryall writing in 1975 called 'family resemblances' between members of a genre.[21] Thus genre theorists have engaged in a kind of cinematic genome project, identifying typical characteristics in order to pinpoint the essence of genre via fixed components.

Colin McArthur's *Underworld U.S.A.* (1972) was a pathbreaking categorisation of what now looks like a rather loose genre, running against the grain of the then dominant auteurism, and has been seen as more important for the principles of categorisation it introduced rather than for its definitive statements about 'the gangster film/thriller' (1972: 8). Written before the important wave of work on *film noir* got under way in the 1970s and 1980s, *Underworld U.S.A.* is both definitive and unwieldy, proposing that key elements which define a genre offer a 'continuity over several decades of patterns of visual imagery, of recurrent objects and figures in dynamic relationship. These repeated patterns might be called the iconography of the genre' (ibid.: 23). This iconography is, however, only meaningful to audiences who have been widely exposed and sensitised to a range of different but similar examples of related 'icons'. A seasoned erotic thriller aficionado will recognise, for instance, the 'Fredricks of Hollywood' co-ordinated underwear, the security camera with sexual potential, the half-hidden gun in a lingerie drawer. He or she might also expect a mild lipstick-lesbian performance, a murder or financial double-cross, a scene in a strip-joint. Perhaps a courtroom sequence. A lousy or a dead husband. A *femme* or *homme fatal(e)*. However, these elements are not present in their varying measures because some transcendent generic structure called 'erotic thriller' deems them to be crucial components. They are there because they provide opportunities for innovative variations on dependable staples, satisfy the filmmaker's sense of interesting workmanship, and sell the films to their target audiences. The drives of genre are primarily industrial, and genre films lay bare the poetics of the marketplace. For all the textual complexities individual films might display, a clear generic structure reveals the simple truth that genre is one way of targeting a film to a guaranteed audience sector, an audience that must be reassured by familiarity whilst being entertained by innovation. Genre films thus hang on a dynamic interchange of sameness and distinction, or, as Krutnick puts it, 'genres serve as frameworks for mediating between repetition and difference' (1991: 11). They are repetitive whilst at the same time no two films can be exactly the same – the audience seeks the same but wants it differently encapsulated. This makes sexual genre cinema the perfect partner for sexual behaviour, which also balances the desire for familiar and repeated satisfaction with the excitement of experiment. Sexual genres are perhaps amongst the most successful in cinema because sex itself combines the novel with the known.

So just as genre cannot by definition inhere in any one work (it exists in the repetition/difference between films) so generic hallmarks do not exist as isolated textual phenomena, understood only when the formal analyst magically unlocks them with her critical key. Genres 'are public and institutional – not personal or critical' (Neale 2000: 42). The dynamic interplay between a genre film and its audience means that an element of iconography – the 'tools of the trade' (Buscombe 1986: 14) – such as a murder weapon like *Basic Instinct*'s ice-pick, or an item of voyeuristic technology such as *Sliver*'s sex-cam surveillance system – signifies not just as a formal component in an individual film's visual patterning, but has a more fundamental social currency which the film 'knows' its audience will read for its familiarity and innovation (so that the ice-pick is lined up alongside Phillis's revolver [in *Double Indemnity*], Angela's blowtorch [in *Exception to the Rule*], Rebecca's sexual skills [used to kill men in *Body of Evidence*]).[22] Iconography can also be used by films to signal a genre's apprehension of social change: Stone's climactic act of reaching for the ice-pick under the bed is referenced when Linda Fiorentino seems to do the same one year later in the DTV *Acting on Impulse*, but pulls out a condom instead, the contextualising of safe sex also shifting woman from *femme fatale* to good-bad girl (I will explore her below); prototype psycho-*femme* Evelyn in *Play Misty for Me* also has a key scene with an ice-pick. The sex-cam is aligned with Rebecca's home porno-movies (again in *Body of Evidence*), the multiple viewing positions and apparatus of *Body Shot*, or the reflective surfaces of *Mirror Images*. Guns are also allied with the intimate fabric of fetishism in the erotic thriller (Fig. 1): in *Night Eyes 3* DTV erotic thriller diva Shannon Tweed plays a B-actress playing a *noir*ish TV cop who tucks her revolver inside her stocking-top. In *Body of Influence* Lana (Shannon Whirry) orders a dominatrix to have sex with a man at gunpoint. Dolly (Virginia Madsen) holds a gun to the throat of fall-guy Harry (Don Johnson) whilst giving him a blow-job in Dennis Hopper's *The Hot Spot*, whilst a psychotic female patient of Bruce Willis fellates a gun at the start of *Color of Night*. When prostitute Rain is fucked by a murderer in Greg Dark's *Undercover*, the killer places his gun next to her face on the red, crushed-velvet pillow. The combination of sex, flesh, gun, fabric and colour is a classic erotic thriller conjunction, like the accidentally spilt (ejaculated?) bag of blood which Val Kilmer sprays across *femme fatale* Joanne Whalley-Kilmer as she lounges expectantly on a bed, waiting for her death to be faked in Dahl's *Kill Me Again*. Soft S&M is suggested across the genre, such as when Nick Cassavetes give Shannon Whirry roses in *Body of Influence* – she cuts her breast with a thorn and he licks the wound. The aphrodisiac of violence is foregrounded in a number of places, such as when, excited by their conspiratorial amorality, Frank and Cora fuck on a hillside next to Cora's dead husband in *The Postman Always Rings Twice* remake. Repetition itself builds the viewer into an intelligent (in the sense of one who renders a code intelligible) genre reader, the cumulative effect of repeated exposure to a number of similar products producing a genre sensitivity borne of saturation. The genre viewer is thus perfectly placed to do justice to the dynamic of knowing 'nods' across and between films. This is an intertextuality which both nourishes and feeds from the knowing audience, involving them in the complex process of signification. Genre films and generically clued-up audiences are made for each other, and the genre critic must operate with an awareness of both.

This book does, then, address the erotic thriller as a body of texts ripe with a highly charged and abundantly signifying iconography, not in order formally to set in stone a picture of generic hallmarks, but because repetition tells us something about viewing pleasure. Any first attempt at mapping a genre is vulnerable

Figure 1: Guns and sex in the erotic thriller: Shannon Whirry and Maxwell Caulfield in *Animal Instincts*. Courtesy of Upcoast Film Consultants, Inc.

to the charges of exclusivity and canon formation: because genre is repetitive, textual analysis will reveal regular or obsessively returned to motifs which may amount to an iconography, and any collection of similar texts will equally exclude others. Perhaps the trick is not to be exclusive in this pragmatic exclusion (this book is therefore a starting-point not a sewn-up definition), and to read icons not as fixed elements in a transcendent pattern but tools in a film-maker's armoury, image templates for the poster designer, moments of genre familiarity which the fan can congratulate herself on recognising.

Many of my films are also, quite frankly, fun films to read: drenched with resonant images, sparking off haphazardly witty screenplays, knowing their own silliness and absurdity, they present a vocal set of cultural symptoms. What viewers do with and to these films – and how far filmmakers and distributors can comfortably rely on this understanding – is central to this study. I am one such viewer, but I am also interested in a complex of other viewers, such as the implied viewer positioned by the film's address (heterosexual men hoping to get off, the girlfriends of those men hoping for 'something for the ladies', other illicit viewers such as lesbian spectators who enjoy sexual spectacle against the grain and through the cracks), and viewers traditionally associated with reception approaches – critics, internet writers, fans.

I also want to think about the erotic thriller as a genre in a rather more pervasive way. Andrew Tudor writes,

> Genre notions . . . are not critics' classification made for special purposes; they are sets of cultural conventions. Genre is what we collectively believe it to be. (Tudor 1986: 7)

This 'collective belief' has important implications for how we interpret the 'interplay between filmmaker, film and audience' (ibid.). That genre exists both inside and outside of films is taken up by Richard Maltby:

> We know a thriller when we see one. Indeed, we know a thriller before we see one, and to some degree we also recognize that, beyond describing the obvious content of a movie, these generic categories have a broader cultural resonance. (1995: 107)

How, then, does the erotic thriller as a genre inhabit a culture wider than that occupied by the films themselves, their producers and their viewers? Would it, indeed, be possible or legitimate to discuss the erotic thriller without looking at a single film – or without reference to audience or industry? This book partly takes as its brief the question of whether we do indeed know an erotic thriller before we see one, or *without ever* seeing one. We all know what a 'bunny-boiler' is regardless of whether we've seen *Fatal Attraction*. Whether or not we've seen *Basic Instinct*, we probably know about Sharon Stone's crotch-flash. Elements from the mainstream form of the genre have pervaded popular culture. But beyond this we may be drawn to, or we may shun, the top shelves of our local video store; we may use the distributor's label 'erotic thriller' printed on the video sleeve as a reason to rent or to put the video back on the shelf. Ann Gray found in her study of female video users that 'the video library is a particularly interesting site for the circulation of meanings about genres' (1992: 230–1). Video dealers operate in a world only partly supported by mass advertising; a small proportion of DTV titles may do well because of a TV commercial campaign, but hundreds of others must stand or fall on how well they are presented in the video store. Even if we've never seen an erotic thriller, the 'promise' of explicitness or the attraction of a thriller plot presented by the sleeve design informs our choices. We may also understand the listing in this week's TV guide, telling us that on Friday night in the UK Channel 5 will show yet another Shannon Tweed erotic thriller. Regardless of whether we know who Tweed is, we understand enough to make us tune in or turn off. Beyond the semantics of the term 'erotic thriller' (partly descriptive but, as I'll discuss below, also promising a whole lot more), we might also be influenced by the style of description adopted by the listings writer (and the many listings writers before her), by whether we knew about Tweed's *Playboy* centrefold career, or even by how we read her name.

Fluid Genres: Mutants, Hyphenates and Amoebae

If McArthur traces a consistent strand running through the forty years of film-making which he analyses, he is also open enough to the possibility of difference within this identification of sameness to deem the thriller 'a constantly growing amoeba assimilating the successive stages of its own development'; it is a form the limits of which are 'fluid' (1972: 8). This adaptable (perhaps unstable) notion of genre is useful for thinking about the fluid mutation of *noir* into neo-*noir* into the erotic thriller, an interconnected chain of categories which, through the 1980s and 1990s, fed in and out of each other. Overlapping and cross-fertilisation between predicated groupings extends the market and enables individual films to exploit a wider range of generic influences. This is not a recent phenomenon – Hollywood has long exploited the fact that hybrid genres maximise box office receipts. Genres are less categorical and more open-ended than the critical taxonomist would have us believe. Indeed, the most interesting recent work on genre has endorsed this, emphasising not the purity of categories but genres as mobile groupings. This may be particularly true, or self-consciously deployed, in contemporary cinema. Jim Collins makes a case for a reinvigorated genre theory which can account for the media-aware environment within which contemporary films operate, with genre cinema since the 1980s responding in complex ways to a media-sophisticated cultural landscape. In particular, he discusses a number of 'eclectic, hybrid genre films' which 'engage in specific transformation *across* genres' (Collins 1993: 245). Krutnick advises that 'the boundaries between genres are by no means fixed and precise, and moreover a genre cannot simply be defined in terms of the elements it contains':

> Rather than seeing genre as a strictly rule-bound context, then, one should stress that any process of generic designation locates very broadly defined sets of discursive configurations, narrative procedures and stylistic emphases. (1991: 8)

Whilst other writers have addressed the historical sweep of a genre in terms of 'cycles, runs or sets'[23] – shifts in emphases across the developmental history which allows for a certain fluidity or hybridity between categories – Neale is not even particularly rigorous about the differences between genres and sub-genres.[24] Genres are then drawn with wide strokes rather than fine cartographer's lines, and should be viewed by theorists as openly as they are by studios. This is borne out by a number of recent writers. For Janet Staiger, the fact that 'Hollywood films have never been "pure" – that is easily arranged into categories' (1997: 6) – almost constitutes a definition of Hollywood itself: hybridity is endemic to the classical form. For Maltby, 'a broad generic category such as the romance can be understood as a field containing a large collection of more or less familiar elements: stars, settings, plot events, motives, and so on', and reminds us that 'generic hyphenates' (he also calls them generic mutants) are common: 'musical-comedy, comedy-adventure, Western-romance', emphasising the fact that 'most movies use categorical elements in combination' (1995: 108). Elizabeth Cowie sees a 'major aspect of genre and hence of genre study [as] therefore the extent to which any particular work exceeds its genre, how it reworks and transforms it, rather than how it fits certain generic expectations' (1993: 128). Christine Gledhill bears this out when she writes that all films '"participate" . . . in genres of one kind or another – and usually several at once': 'Most texts, and most films, are multiply generic: *Star Wars* and *Body Heat* . . . are, simultaneously, "films", "fiction films", "Hollywood films" and "narrative feature films"; the former is also "science fiction", "space opera" and/or "action-adventure", and the latter a "thriller" (and possibly also "neo-noir")' (1999: 147).

The erotic thriller (another of *Body Heat*'s subsequent labels) ought, then, to be seen as a prime example of Maltby's generic hyphenate. Yet like the marketers of these films, I do not hyphenate the term. This is because a hyphen suggests two separate categories welded together, almost as if two different films politely cohabit a category, but play out separate stories and styles in parallel across their ninety minutes of shared screen time. *Oklahoma!* may be a musical-western, but on some level it remains discretely *both* a musical and a western. The hyphen, then, serves to divorce the two terms, as well as marry them. '[M]any Hollywood films – and many Hollywood genres – are hybrid and multi-generic', writes Steve Neale, endorsing the practice of approaching films 'under a number of different generic headings' (2000: 51). There are very few entirely uncontentious genres, and for most recent writers the more promiscu-ous a genre term becomes, sliding into bed with any and perhaps all of its neigh-bours, the more interesting it is. Neale's discussion of the fluid and ubiquitous nature of the term 'melodrama' ('mello' or 'meller' in *Variety*-speak), challenges the now accepted use of the term as a synonym for 'woman's film' (character-ised by the analysis of only a limited range of films made in the 1940s and 1950s). 'Melodrama' has lent itself to a number of unholy alliances: there are domestic melodramas, full-blooded melodramas, vivid melodramas, even virile melodramas, not to mention a 'cactus country meller with an all-male cast' (2000: 179–204). The softcore melodrama will also be discussed in this book.

The erotic thriller is a textbook case of a form which 'participate[s] . . . in . . . several [genres] at once'. In particular, the term 'erotic' taken as an adjective is itself highly promiscuous and resonantly trans-generic. It functions in some ways like the term 'adult', used by the industry to designate content (adult = sexual) and to target a limited but dependable audience ('For Adults Only' promises something, like 'Men Only'). Read the erotic thriller as an 'adult thriller' and it becomes more of a Harley Davidson than a Model T: a sexy pleasure model marketed to a wide public, but with no room for the children or the family dog: this is a couples-only, grown-up ride, but no less a mass-pro-duced product for all that. The successes of New Hollywood are predicated on the catchment of a multi-generational audience, the prime age target being PG13 (in the US) or 12 (in the UK) rather than the 18/R/NC-17, which an erotic thriller would attract (the largest single certification category in the UK is 15, however). To work, this exclusion of children must become a virtue: 'Adults Only' is most obviously a term which shuts out a large sector of ticket-buyers, so it must deliver to those who *can* buy. 'Adult' also functions as a metonym for 'erotic' (Adult Drama, Adult Comedy, etc.; the 1990 women-in-prison film *Caged Fury* is labelled an 'Adult Thriller'). But, like melodrama, 'erotic' is also a mobile term, which can form allegiances of description with more distinct and uncontested genre categories. It attaches itself not only to the thriller noun, but to vaguer generic terms. *Feminine Chemistry* (the English title of a 1990 Italian film) plays safe by branding itself an 'Erotic Feature'. The *Wild Orchid* films are described by those marketing the videos as 'Erotic Dramas', and are listed as such in the *Radio Times* when the TV franchise spin-off series is aired in Britain. *The Wise Woman's Guide to Erotic Videos* sexualises soap-opera by referring to *The Red Shoe Diaries* as 'Made-for-TV Soft-Core Suds' (Cohen and Fox 1997: 172).[25] In its most parodic formation the erotic thriller can be exces-sive in its hybridisation; Roger Ebert reviewed the hysterically misanthropic *Wild Things* as a 'three-way collision between a softcore sex film, a soap opera and a B-grade noir' (1998b). *Caged Women* (like *Caged Fury*, another varia-tion on Demme's classic *Caged Heat* theme) is called an 'Erotic Prison Thriller', whilst *Beach Beverly Hills* is given the genre label 'Erotic Adventure' on the video sleeve. Dealers are also advised in the promotional material that this is a 'Mega Commercial Genre', comparing the film to more straightforward genre pieces: 'Essential viewing for everyone who enjoyed "Basic Instinct", "Night Rhythms" and "Animal Instincts"'.[26] Perhaps the allegiance between Eros and Comedy is the least contentious pairing, possibly because of our willingness to laugh at sex – and particularly for British viewers in light of the history of the British sex comedy, hence the 'Erotic Comedy' label on the UK-released video of hardcore cut-down title *The Erotic Adventures of The Three Musketeers*. Yet 'erotic' can also render uncontested terms such as horror much harder to pin down: *Embrace of the Vampire* is described as an 'Erotic Horror' (begging the question of what horror film *isn't* erotic, and thus what this one does that the others don't). The English title of one film starring the queen of Hong Kong Category III films, Amy Yip, was *Erotic Ghost Story*, a sexually explicit Category III films (more of which later), which has spawned four sequels.[27]

During the 1990s, also as an effect of the form's widespread success, a number of films came to be marketed in a way which suggested a relationship to the erotic thriller whilst not quite committing to it as a genre. This has often happened in the re-release of a film onto video, in the wake of the success of the genre. A cult film which was first received as a work of art-house science fiction, *Liquid Dreams* (1992), was re-categorised for its video release as an erotic thriller. Jim McBride's 1986 corrupt cop thriller *The Big Easy* relied heavily on the sexual chemistry between its stars Dennis Quaid and Ellen Barkin in its marketing, even though the sex-scenes, whilst suggestive, are few and hardly explicit. The UK video-box text, from 1998, uses 'erotic' as an adjective, calling the film a 'humorous, stylish and erotic thriller'.[28] Similarly Dennis Hopper's *The Hot Spot* was described as 'a torrid erotic thriller' in its 2003 US DVD sleeve blurb, but the voiceover on its original theatrical trailer called it 'Film Noir for the 90s' (though against a series of images which repeatedly juxtapose tantalising sexual snippets with violent outbursts). The Checkout.com retail website lists Gregory Hippolyte's *Undercover* (aka *Undercover Heat*) under 'Genres: Mystery, Suspense, & Horror', whilst an IMDb reviewer called it 'a very nice Erotic-Thriller'. Though the British video packaging (unusually) doesn't claim a genre for this film, its plot-blurb covers all the bases: 'She's young, beautiful and with a body to die for. She's also a cop . . . . But as night falls in the city, detective Cindy Hanen swaps her police blues for black lace.' The basic elements of crime and sex are advertised upfront, with the promise of criminal thrills and sexual spectacle set against a dangerous cityscape (which actually hardly features in the film itself – and as a detective Cindy never dresses in police blues either).[29]

'Erotic' is, then, no more or less of a firm genre label than melodrama (which is etymologically simply the conjunction of music [melos] + drama). Erotic means sexual love, but the word is also defined by the *Oxford English Dictionary* as 'a doctrine or science of love'. The term thus has a cultural association with sexual material, as well as a long (if fraught) history distinguishing it from pornography ('science of *love*', not sex). In practice, 'erotic' as a genre term has meant something less explicit than 'adult', with the former frequently standing in for 'softcore' and the latter doing service for 'hardcore'. For almost all of my filmmaking interviewees this was an understood working definition which means something very specific to audiences and classifiers. It is this which guarantees the erotic thriller a place alongside other feature films in mainstream videostores such as Blockbuster, staying out of the designated hardcore terrain (the backroom of 'mom and pop' video stores in the USA; the UK sex shop licensed to sell R-18 films). The erotic thriller is therefore purposely not called the sex thriller (which might be a more accurate term), though not because it is a particularly 'loving' form. It does not cherish tender and respectful sex, nor does it strive to be aesthetically subtler or more suggestive. Like its hardcore bad twin it prefers contextless and often consequenceless sexual display, anonymous encounters, a variety of sexual scenarios and as much diversity as it can get away with within the confines BBFC or MPAA certification. It often sets its narrative clock by the requirement of having a sex-scene every ten minutes, like a production number in a musical (as Linda Williams describes hardcore sex-scenes). A number of key DTV erotic thrillers are extensively pornographic, in the sense that the screen-time taken up by sexual spectacle frequently exceeds that taken up by thriller plot. The spectacle itself may not contain the hardcore checklist of penetration or cum shots, but it pervades the film nevertheless. Yet by calling itself an erotic thriller rather than pornography, a film can advertise itself to those who would avoid the top shelf. That women have been understood as traditionally preferring the 'erotic' over the 'pornographic' (a moot point to which I will be returning in Part Two) only reinforces the need to deploy a term which targets women too, or which at least will not alienate heterosexual women when they join their (male) partners on the viewing-sofa.

Thus 'erotic' is used as both a description of content and a promise of effect: if the film contains erotic scenarios, it ought to produce an erotic response in its viewer. This is also to some extent true of 'thriller'. These are not simply erotic films which hang on a thriller plot, nor are they simply thrillers with a high sex quota. Perhaps this is partly because of the pun on 'thriller': a term which is commonly used as a loose synonym for a *noir* or crime film has been extended to include the thrills of sex as well as suspense. Whereas the musical and the western began as terms of description based on the text's content, the terms 'erotic' and 'thriller' are also terms of response: the erotic thriller should thrill its viewers in a uniquely two-edged way, through narrative suspense and engagement, and through sexual delivery. Each component ('erotic' and 'thriller') is, then, more intimately bound to its other than a hyphen would allow (in 'erotic-thriller' the hyphen serves to separates as well as unite). This interplay between popular terms is reinforced by the fact that erotic thrillers are often referred to by popular journalists as 'suspense in suspenders'[30] films (or sometimes as 'tits and terror' films, a term which would also do service for a number of horror flicks; 'cops and copulation film' is also doing the rounds). Here, says the label, you will be erotically thrilled as well as criminally thrilled, with the former (sex) taking precedence as long as the latter (suspense) is available to viewers who prefer to think of themselves as narratively – rather than sexually – buying into the film. Wrote *Empire* in 1994, 'Gregory Hippolyte makes "erotic thrillers", those top-shelf titles that pretend not to be sex films because they have ridiculous murder conspiracy plots between the shagging scenes'.[31] The term erotic thriller thus promises not just thriller plots, soft-porn spectacle, but an intimate marriage of the two – and somehow more than the sum of its parts. In the erotic thriller the thrills are *in* the sex, the sex drives the thriller action, but the more traditional sense of the term 'thriller' strings it all along. Sex and crime are often interdependent, such as in the genre staple when the cop fucks the suspect (in *Sea of Love* the cop's partner asks him, 'Should we dust your dick for prints?'). B-*noir*'s time-honoured (and cheap) strategy of deploying chiaroscuro lighting also weds one form to another, literally mapping the 'look' of *noir* onto sexual action, such as when the naked bodies of (suspect) Shannon Tweed and (cop) Gary Hudson are liberally striped by Venetian blind shadows in *Indecent Behaviour*. The more recent trend to ring the changes in genre labelling thus misses the opportunity provided by the use of Erotic, which is used both to describe and to promise. Distributors have begun to replace 'Erotic' with 'Exotic': for their DVD reissue *Sexual Malice* and *Body of Influence 2* were relabelled 'Exotic Thrillers'. Having done so much to establish the term erotic thriller as a recognisable brand in the 1990s on video, a different but related term was needed for the new world of DVD release to give the same films a fresh twenty-first-century marketable edge. But unlike the selling of kinky lingerie (when exotic passes muster as erotic), the exotic thriller cannot promise its audience feelings of exoticism (whatever they may be – though in *Boogie Nights* porno-auteur Jack Horner says he makes 'exotic pictures'). As an *erotic* thriller *Sexual Malice* can makes powerful suggestions about response as well as content to its potential viewer. DTV auteur Jag Mundhra has suggested the 'Erotic-Exotic' as a new marketable development of the earlier form (see interview below, p. 324), trading on elements of travelogue and spectacle which have characterised his Indian-set features.

It may, then, seem that at times in this book I play fast and loose with genre. I read the erotic thriller as a fluid, often hybrid genre, perhaps at its 'purest' in the most formulaic DTV examples, bleeding into and out of adjacent forms such as classic *noir*, neo-*noir*, porn, the woman's film, serial killer and horror films, and the auteur-led art-film. It may also be that film historians will ultimately frame the erotic thriller as a production cycle rather than a fully paid-up genre. Krutnick defines a cycle as 'a short-term attempt to rework a proven success' (1991: 12). The parallel histories of mainstream and DTV erotic thriller production do look rather like production cycles linked by proximity under a wider generic umbrella, but a more convincing example would be films such as the female revenge story which sprang up in the wake of *Fatal Attraction*, or the (related) killer nanny psycho-sexual-thriller which sprang up in the wake of *The Hand that Rocks the Cradle*. The erotic thriller must be distinguished from this in that its variants are less disciplined, more prone to further hybridisation, and have bled into forms such as the woman's film or the TV serial. I also use some terms interchangeably with the term 'erotic thriller', largely because this generic cycle is nothing if not fluid and hungry to cross-breed with adjacent genre tendencies, creating such variations as erotic melodramas, sex-musicals and sex-romances. In chapter 2 I discuss films which range across the sexually-driven or sexually-explicit spectrum from *Jagged Edge* to *Body of Evidence* to *Guilty as Sin*. If pushed into bald categorisation I might call each of these a courtroom drama. But the central focus of each is sex crime, sexual culpability, erotic implicatedness and guilt; the narratives focus on a *homme* (or a *femme) fatal(e)*, seducing and exploiting the fall-girl or guy. It is much more useful to read these films in terms of the cinematic representation of sexual rather than legal practice, and to read them off and against each other rather than, say, against *The Juror* or *Twelve Angry Men*. It is also far more productive to read Joe Eszterhas (writer of *Jagged Edge* and the similarly inflected courtroom drama *Music Box*) in the context of *noir* novelist James Cain than to compare *Jagged Edge* to the legally obsessed adaptations of John Grisham.

Yet happy as filmmakers might be to feed off any and every genre influence, writers often reflect this as a critical confusion, which itself tells a story about genre. A good example of how this bears on the reading of a distinct text is found in the case of *Basic Instinct*. A film's failure to fit neatly into place is often what makes it most interesting for genre analysis (it is this that has kept the *film noir* debate going for so long). In the case of neo-*noir* films, their generic eclecticism has been read almost solely in terms of their postmodern relationship to *noir* itself; Fredric Jameson's early discussion of *Body Heat* as a nostalgia film is perhaps responsible for this all-pervasive notion that deployment of multiple generic techniques is primarily meaningful as stylistic pastiche, a nostalgia of film history (as well as – for Jameson – a more serious incapacity in 'dealing with time and history' [1983: 117]). More straightforwardly, '*noiring*'[32] makes sense as marketplace strategy: *noir* sells, particularly when used in conjunction with (and in justification of) sex. *Basic Instinct* has also been vulnerable to this approach. Arguably the most written about erotic thriller of all, both the scandal of its release and the slippery nature of its material have made it attractive to academic and journalistic writers alike. *Variety* called it 'grade-A pulp fiction' and an 'erotically charged thriller', the UK's *Financial Times* called it a 'sexual aggression thriller' (Andrews 1992: 21), whilst Chris Holmlund read it as 'a thriller cum soft core porn film, containing elements of both the slasher and rape-revenge subgenres of horror' (1994: 32). In production Paul Verhoeven was happy to call it an erotic thriller, but, as my interview below evidences, he deployed *noir* and anti-*noir* strategies as an exercise in intellectual play as well as generic branding. It is also true that the genres which the erotic thriller 'participates in' – *film noir*, neo-*noir*, thrillers, women's films, comedies, action-adventure and dramas about the sex industry – are themselves unstable. I now want to turn to the two genres which feature most prominently in the erotic thriller's ancestry: pornography and *noir* (which itself has fed or bled into neo-*noir*), both of which bring with them their own bank of iconography and audience expectation.

Underwear USA: From Film Noir *to Erotic Thriller*

Somebody has to die.

Crime writer Catherine Tramell in *Basic Instinct*

In many ways, the video or blockbuster 'erotic thriller' is the direct descendent of *film noir*: *Body Heat* (and any number of subsequent erotic thrillers) explicitly references *Double Indemnity*, *Jade* replays elements of *The Lady from Shanghai*, and both *The Postman Always Rings Twice* (1981) and *Diabolique* (1996) show the genre's propensity for sexing up a classic period original as a hotter softcore product (1946, and *Les Diaboliques*, 1955). Though a relatively chaste psychological thriller, the latter film was marketed as lesbian titillation for heterosexual men ('Two women. One man. The combination can be murder'); the inclusion of Sharon Stone as a murderous bisexual drew marked comparisons with her *Basic Instinct* character. The second *Postman* emerged in that *Body Heat* moment when the genre was gathering itself, though what most viewers remember of it is the steamy kitchen table sex-scene (and Jack Nicholson's alleged proclamation that he did it because he always wanted to be in a porn movie; there is, indeed, something beyond verisimilitude in the way he kneads Jessica Lange's crotch). The remakes (and there are others – see Schwartz 2001) remind us (if we needed reminding) that *film noir* was and is centrally about sex anyway, but the erotic thriller, in its confusions and fascinating self-betrayal, also shows *noir* to be at the heart of a certain form of (increasingly mainstream) pornography, albeit one overlit with the bright opulence of Californian primetime soap. Crucially, *noir* lends softcore an aura of psychic and narrative complexity, which justifies its sexual excesses to timid buyers. How ironic that a genre (*noir*) originally associated with the pulpiest of pulp fictions should now lend its new-found respectability to an even more debased form.

If ever any category was heterogeneous it is *film noir*, both as a body of films and in its critical reception. The sheer promiscuity of the term is astonishing. It is no wonder that feminist critics have found it so seductive; not only does it celebrate the bad girl in its images, it is itself a 'bad girl' category which has become all things to all critics, refusing fixed definitions along the way. For Elizabeth Cowie, the term is a critical fantasy which meets a need for genre writers:

> Unlike terms such as the 'western', or the 'gangster' film, which are relatively uncontroversial . . . film noir has a more tenuous critical status. This tenuousness is matched by a tenacity of critical use, a devotion among *afi-*

cionados that suggests a desire for the very category as such, a wish that it exist in order to 'have' a certain set of films all together. Film noir is in a certain sense a fantasy. (Cowie 1993: 121)

Yet as psychoanalysis has suggested, to say that something is a fantasy is not to say that it isn't real, but that it is – to paraphrase Juliet Mitchell – 'real as fantasy' (1984: 299). In this case *noir* functioned first as an interpretative structure: perhaps the one thing that is 'known' about it is that it is a critical rather than an industrial category. Critics have variously described it as a mood, a style, a movement and a perspective. Generally associated with a series of films made between 1941 (*The Maltese Falcon*) and 1958 (*Touch of Evil*) (though this periodisation is disputed), it is known for its presentation of the alienated city, a symbolically coded 'look' which through its use of high-contrast, low-key lighting and disorienting cinematographic styles, draws parallels between unsettled ways of seeing and uncertain moral positions. *Film noirs* are often, though not always, crime films. Their exploitation of sex may be central; indeed, early French critics, who first gave *film noir* its name, identified the erotic in *noir*, the obsessive forms which its central sexuality took. Jean-Pierre Chartier, writes James Naremore, 'suggested that the puritanical Breen Office had deflected the characters' sexual motives into an "obsessive criminal fatality"' (1998: 16). By 1978, nine years before Adrian Lyne's film, James Damico had described the crux of *noir* as the hero's meeting with a 'non-innocent woman . . . to whom he is sexually and fatally attracted' (1996: 103).

From the title down, the erotic thriller signals its debt to this *noir* of fatal attractions. *Noir* is as inherent in an erotic thriller's marketing strategies as it is in its textual content, since in this sex/death combo it is death (or violence or thriller-suspense) which is the more 'respectable' pairing, the side of the genre mix which enables it to occupy the shelves of Blockbuster. The tag-line of the starry, $26 million *Original Sin* is 'Love is a killer', echoing *Black Widow*'s 'She mates and she kills' and *Sea of Love*'s 'In search of a killer, he found someone who's either the love of his life . . . or the end of it'. *Cruising* gives this a gay spin: 'Al Pacino is cruising for a killer' (Fig. 2). DTV promotion reproduces – or perhaps initiates – this rhetorical pairing of sex and death: *Sins of Desire* offers 'The height of Ecstasy. The depth of Murder . . .'; *Animal Instincts II* asks 'Would you lie? Would you cheat? Could you kill . . . for love?', whilst *Indecent Behaviour* tells us that 'Sex this good is murder'. The Debbie Harry vehicle *Intimate Stranger* plays on arousal and aggression with 'She just turned on the wrong guy!' All of these *noir*ish promises (a number of which could do brisk business for *Double Indemnity*, which would undoubtedly be marketed as an erotic thriller were it released today) are about sex as death, though only the DTVs are brazen enough to promise open explicitness ('Sex can be an act of murder', says Nick Cassavetes in *Body of Influence*). Clearly, these examples are prime fodder for cultural psychoanalysis; this is Eros-as-Thanatos thrown to the marketplace. Perhaps the death drive was never put to work in a more

Figure 2: One of *Cruising*'s posters puts a gay spin on the genre's heated mix of
sex and death. Lorimar/The Kobal Collection.

debased form than this. Foster Hirsch, however, reads all this sexy death in a
very historically-specific way, as a counter-erotic message about unsafe sex –
'the traditional link in noir narratives between sex and catastrophe is no longer
merely symbolic or moralistic' [1999: 9] he writes, before attributing the
success of the erotic thriller to the AIDS crisis: 'erotic thrillers of the 1980s and
1990s are metaphors for the dangers of sex in the time of AIDS. A simmering
offstage "noise," like World War II in 1940s noir, AIDS is a significant struc-
turing absence' (ibid.: 188–9). Thus whilst classic *noir* sex-crime films are
underpinned by historical trauma, contemporary erotic thrillers are underpinned by sexual catastrophe.

Much of this fatal sexuality is focused on the figure of the *femme fatale*, a
film noir stalwart and manipulative dominatrix into whose trap the duped hero
falls. A number of key *noirs* were based on hardboiled thriller novels, and in
particular the men and women of James M. Cain's work gave *noir* its prime
sexual icons, established through the films of Cain's novels *The Postman
Always Rings Twice*, *Double Indemnity* and *Mildred Pierce*. Michael Walker
sees the Cain story as paradigmatic because of its focus on 'the femme fatale
[as] the key figure who lures/tempts/seduces the hero into the noir world',
ensuring that 'the hero becomes a "victim" of his own desires'. For Walker, the

Cain male is 'the hero [who] becomes so obsessed sexually by a woman that he is persuaded to murder her husband, and the *noir* world which he enters is psychological rather than physical, characterised above all by corrosive guilt and the fear of discovery' (1992: 12). The first shot of Tay Garnett's *Postman* is of a sign outside *femme* Cora's diner, reading 'Man Wanted'; Frank (John Garfield) becomes the wanted man both sexually and criminally. This duped male is still with us, prototype also for Willem Dafoe in *Body of Evidence*, Peter Berg in *The Last Seduction* or Ed Harris in *China Moon*, as well as Jack Nicholson in the *Postman* remake and William Hurt in *Body Heat*. As the low-budget counterpart of these characters, Will Griffith in *Night Eyes* (the ubiquitous DTV star Andrew Stevens) says at the moment he grasps his own ignorance, his own danger and just how deep in the *femme fatale*'s trap he is caught, 'Someone either tried to kill me or frame me – I can't figure out which'. If 1990s *noir* is primarily a (postmodern) quotation from a (modernist) 1940s source, this male figure, along with his female antagonist, is its clearest reference-point: John Orr sees the plight of the fall-guy as 'pre-ordained as much by film history as by plot' (1998: 210). In Part One of this book I will be discussing this fall-guy more fully, as sex-object and as masochistic figure to which Michael Douglas returns in *Fatal Attraction*, *Basic Instinct* and *Disclosure*.

The *femme fatale*, for Walker, occupies a range of positions in a continuum of deadliness, from ruthless killer to sympathetic if sexualised heroine – the good-bad girl I will discuss in chapter 2. The contemporary erotic thriller trades in femininities positioned across the range of these possibilities, from the extremes of deadly sadism to a more sympathetic position of sexual self-discovery – Orr also sees the 1990s *noir* woman as ambivalently oscillating between aggressive competitiveness and exultant victimhood (1998: 211). Rarely is she an entirely reprehensible spider-woman; if she is deadly she is also funny (Linda Fiorentino in *The Last Seduction*), or poignantly tragic (Madeleine Stowe in *China Moon*, or Kathleen Turner in *Body Heat*, sitting on a tropical beach staring blankly at her losses). More often, this neo-Cainian *femme* has female friends, understandable motives or is an action-heroine-investigator who herself refuses to be duped. Steve Neale has traced the *femme fatale*'s ancestry through a much wider range of films and types, including the 'Inscrutable Female', 'The Evil Woman' and 'murderous ladies';[33] the female forms played out in the contemporary erotic thriller have a multifarious genetic heritage. Stephen Farber's 'Bitch Goddess' would also need to be added to this list. The Bitch has taken on popular currency more recently with the publication of Elizabeth Wurtzel's flimsy but widely publicised celebration of the icon, *Bitch* (1998), followed by *The Bitch Rules* and Camille Paglia's *Vamps and Tramps*. The Bitch has become ever more explicitly sexualised in her passage from *noir* to pomo/porno/neo-*noir*, now not only an exocitised formation of desperate – and excluded – avarice, but achieved pleasure in a position of presumed control over the Symbolic. Whether or how she is a figure of and for post-feminism is central to most writings on films such as *Basic Instinct*, and to this study.

The erotic thriller is however only selectively neo-*noir* and only partly a crime film; a useful identification text is Charles Derry's *The Suspense Thriller: Films in the Shadow of Alfred Hitchcock* (1988). Of the six categories of thriller which Derry identifies, four are useful here. For instance, what Derry calls 'the thriller of murderous passions, organized around the triangular grouping of husband/wife/lover' (1988: 72) might describe *A Woman Scorned*, *Poison Ivy* and its sequels or *Sexual Malice*. Derry's chapter on this begins with a lengthy quotation from *Body Heat*. The 'thriller of acquired identity', which is 'organized around a protagonist's acquisition of an unaccustomed identity, his or her behaviour in coming to terms with the metaphysical and physical consequences of this identity, and the relationship of this acquisition to a murderous plot' (1988: 175) describes a number of erotic thriller twin or *doppelganger* films, including James Dearden's *A Kiss Before Dying* and Tom Berry's *Twin Sisters*, and the Hippolyte films *Mirror Images* and *Mirror Images II*. Noir's *doppelgangers* are legion, from the two Albert Dekkers in *Among the Living* (1941), through the two Olivia de Havillands in *The Dark Mirror* (1946) to the two Bonita Granvilles in *The Guilty* (1947). In *A Kiss Before Dying* Sean Young plays both the murdered twin, Dorothy, and the investigating twin, Ellen; Matty sacrifices her lookalike in an elaborate murder-fraud plot in *Body Heat*, whilst in the first *Mirror Images* Delia Sheppard plays sexual and repressed twin sisters Shauna and Kaitlin, the good sister taking the place of the bad. In the sequel, Shannon Whirry plays another set of good and bad twins, but after the bad twin's (faked) death the good twin begins to question her own identity. This is a doubling which liberates, whereby one woman might fetishistically shadow her mirror-image. The twin theme is potent enough for Carl Reiner to incorporate it into his parody, *Fatal Instinct*. For reasons of sexual psychosis or duplication the erotic thriller also trades in situations in which a woman finds herself sexually vulnerable because she is foreshadowed by her (now dead) lookalike. In *Sliver*, for instance, Carly (Sharon Stone) 'replaces' a murder victim who could be her clone, whilst the heroine of De Palma's *Femme Fatale* takes over (or saves, depending on which part of the film you're viewing) the life of her double.[34] *Basic Instinct*'s use of doubling is more characteristically *noir*, with female replication used to underpin women's demonism. Catherine Tramell's familiars, Roxy and the older Hazel, all look similar. Lynda Hart notes that 'All three women are of similar build, have long blond hair, and manifest the stereotypical physical attributes of upper-class white women. The threesome resonates with the doubling effect that is characteristic of the lesbian as autoerotic/ narcissistic' (1994: 129). The copycat behaviour between Elizabeth (Jeanne Tripplehorn) and Catherine (Stone) through which one dyes her hair and dresses like the other, also constitutes for Hart a 'diabolical doubling'. This is not unlike the other-replication which takes place between 'bunny-boiler' Jennifer Jason Leigh and her victim Bridget Fonda in *Single White Female*. Jag Mundhra's reincarnation erotica *Monsoon* and *The Perfumed Garden* puts a different spin on this, featuring contemporary multiracial couples replaying the sexual Romeo and Juliet sagas of ancient forebears, with doubled identities displaced across time, racial and cultural difference.

Derry also discusses 'the psychotraumatic thriller', which 'is organized around the psychotic effects of a trauma on a protagonist's current involvement in a love affair and a crime intrigue. The protagonist is always a victim – generally of some past trauma and often of real villains who take advantage of his or her masochistic guilt'. Derry cites *Body Double* (1984) as a psychotraumatic thriller, but various 'Out of the Past' films in which a *femme fatale* manipulates a hero through knowledge of his past could also be included here, such as *Body Heat, The Last Seduction* or *Body Shot*. Finally, Derry's 'thriller of moral confrontation' describes erotic thrillers which blur as well as distinguish the moral ground between villain and hero/heroine. Any number of erotic thrillers feature attraction, sex and clearly drawn similarities between criminal (or suspect) and his or her pursuer/detective/victim: the juxtaposition of sex and danger on which these films rely so heavily is often played out in a sex-scene between good girl and bad guy, or vice versa, the moment of highest erotic charge being also the moment of most extreme moral culpability. *Cruising, Bodily Harm* and *Love Crimes* all deploy this motif. Yet useful as Derry's categories are, they must be taken as basic templates which an individual film will deploy but to which it will only intermittently stay faithful. Perhaps the reason that a film like *Basic Instinct* was so successful as a thriller is because it combined a number of tropes: a film of undeniably murderous passions, it flirts with the acquired identity issue, Douglas is manipulated by Stone because of what she knows of his cocaine-fuelled and trigger-happy past, and the confrontation between Douglas and Stone is moral as well as sexual – one of a long line of 'detective as the flipside of villain' films. In a number of DTVs this becomes a scenario extended through an undercover theme: cops masquerading as hookers, strippers, models, with the new, sexually performing self as the underside of the repressed, everyday one.

A similar proto-Proppian character taxonomy is enacted by Foster Hirsch in his study of *film noir*. Here Hirsch classifies *noir* protagonists into three types: investigators, victims and psychopaths (1981: 167), a model which was supplemented in his follow-up study of neo-*noir*. Whilst films like *Original Sin* or *Night Rhythms* feature all of Hirsch's types (Antonio Banderas or Martin Hewitt as investigator-victims; Angelina Jolie or Delia Sheppard as *femme fatale* psychopaths), *Black Widow* features a female investigator who desires and identifies with the *femme fatale*, whilst *Dressed to Kill* develops into a story in which a female investigator confronts a *femme fatale*, who is a man in drag. As in both of these cases, whilst Hirsch's victim-heroes are 'stained and transformed' (1981: 178) by 'a dark and capricious fate', the erotic thriller's female protagonist can be empowered by her encounter with the dark side.

Yet whilst the erotic thriller draws on some key *noir* tropes, the question of whether *noir* ever existed as a genre remains open. Richard Maltby prefers to see *noir* as 'a fluctuation in the more persistent genre of the crime film . . . its specific characteristics could be related to the historical circumstances of the period 1945–55' (1995: 122). For Neale, *noir* 'as a single phenomenon . . . never existed. That is why no one has been able to define it and why the contours of the larger noir canon in particular are so imprecise' (2000: 173–4). In particular, Neale argues that writing on *noir* has tended to stress its hardboiled heritage rather than its relationship to Gothic romance, even though it is difficult to make a clear distinction between *noir* and the gothic women's film. Both forms

> frequently centre on an element of potentially fatal sexual attraction; they stress the risks, emotional and physical, this may entail for the central protagonist; they lay a great deal of emphasis on the protagonist's perceptions, feelings, thoughts and subjective experiences; and they share the context of a culture of distrust. (ibid.: 164)

Some of these terms will become useful as I open up the different directions or emphases taken by the erotic thriller, which plays out *noir*'s multiple identities, including female Gothic. I want now to consider the erotic thriller as a branch of the much more certain generic category, neo-*noir*.

Cops and copulation; censorship and classification

You gotta decide if you wanna book me or fuck me.
Nora 'Hugs' Hugosian (Gina Gershon) in *Black & White*

In thinking about the generic ancestors of the erotic thriller I have tended to privilege a thread running from the contested genre of *film noir*, largely because this is the genre most overtly acknowledged in the self-consciousness of the films themselves, and because of the erotic thriller's kinship to neo-*noir*. Indeed, a number of films I read as erotic thrillers are more commonly grouped by critics as neo-*noirs*, even when marketing and filmmakers say otherwise. The Hippolyte title *Object of Obsession* was, for instance, made by the dominant DTV production house Axis Films International and branded alongside its stablemates as an erotic thriller, yet one of the few published references to it calls it an 'unusually well-crafted neo-Gothic' (Rubin 1999: 177)·. This seems to be a prime example of how 'serious' critical recognition effectively renders examples of this discredited form more respectable by refusing (or forgetting) the industry-designated category 'erotic thriller', renaming favoured works with more esteemed academic categories such as neo-Gothic or neo-*noir*. 'Neo-*noir*' sells films to one kind of audience; 'erotic thriller' to another. Neo-*noir* is also written about by one sort of writer (academic), erotic thrillers by another (largely only by reviewers of schlock cinema on websites, or cult movie reviewers). Neo-*noir* has consumed gallons of scholarly ink in its dissemination, erotic thriller very little. Despite the significant overlaps and exchanges between the two forms, and despite the fact that some films can be interchangeably deemed both neo-*noir* and erotic thriller, neo-*noir* remains the generic respectable big sister.

Neo-*noir* is, however, a tricky genre to define in that as exemplary postmodern pastiche its relationship with and to *noir* as cinematic past is complex.[35] It has also had the effect of retrospectively securing the categorical status of *film noir* in claiming it as its antecedent: 'The films made "after noir",' writes Foster Hirsch, 'may well constitute the strongest case for noir as a genre' (1999: 4; see also Krutnick 1982: 16–17).[36] Neo-*noir* is consolidated in the practice of film-makers, the strategies of marketers and the responses of fans. But the relationship of *noir* to neo-*noir* is also bridged by television. Steven Spielberg has said that 'my stepparent was the TV set' (McBride 1997: 63), a statement as much about the ubiquity of television in the early lives of movie-brat filmmakers as it is about the postwar nuclear family. From the 1950s onwards *noir* viewing and *noir* memory became primarily televisual. This is why Brian De Palma opens his 2003 erotic thriller *Femme Fatale* with the spectacle of a woman watching *Double Indemnity* on TV: 'You're trying to tell the audience you're going to see a *film noir* dream', he told me. 'Late at night you're watching *Double Indemnity* on television in bed, and you fall asleep and you *dream Double Indemnity*' (p. 142 below). The televising of *noir* as a central part of the biographical memory of filmmakers constitutes another layer in the story of home viewing, and one which requires further work.[37] Whether made to be viewed on television sooner (as DTV, cable or pay-per-view) or later (after a theatrical release), neo-*noirs* were also constructed by filmmakers who first met *noir* on their childhood televisions. As a genre first (or most regularly) digested via a small cathode-ray-generated image augmented by the surrounding ephemera of domestic and 'private' life, it is also appropriate that a new formation of *noir* swept back into the living room on the crest of the home viewing revolution.

Neo-*noir* has also bled into adjacent genres and formulated some significant tributaries. The third edition of Silver and Ward (1992: 398–423) cites thirteen different 'neo' forms, a mixture of recurrent narratives and modes of production, only three of which ('Victims of Circumstance 1 – Love with an Improper Stranger'; the discussion of women directors of neo-*noir*; and the useful analysis of low-budget neo-*noir* B-productions) share significant common ground with this analysis. But whilst not all neo-*noirs* are erotic thrillers, many erotic thrillers are shot through with a postmodern *noir* or 'white *noir*'. The erotic thriller is also (albeit rarely) cited as part of the success story of *noir* style in contemporary cinema (see, for instance, Palmer's final sentence [1994: 187]), or derided as a quickie exploitation of the now more respectable neo-*noir*. Clearly, there are key areas of cross-fertilisation between neo-*noir* and the erotic thriller. If *noir* used sex to make a political point, the erotic thriller uses noir to contextualise its pornographic tableaux, consolidating a set of issues and representational possibilities bubbling under into a distinct marketable form. It draws on a selective *noir* history – predicaments of desire rather than 'tough-guy' films or *policiers*. Titles such as *LA Confidential* or *Mulholland Falls* may hang on sexual scandals and deploy *femme fatale* figures, but they are not primarily sexually driven, nor do they take elaborate detours into sexual spectacle. The emphasis rests on the extent of sexual content – to paraphrase my Gina Gershon epigraph, the genre question is also whether to book her or fuck her (*Black & White* teeters over into erotic thriller terrain by plumping for the latter).

When, then, is a neo-*noir* an erotic thriller? In both forms, sex and crime are liberally mixed, but each prefers to foreground one or the other. Sex as crime, or sex so foregrounded that it overwhelmingly subordinates crime to the minimal status of sub-plot or narrative pretext, distinguishes the erotic thriller (and, for Hirsch, separates it from *noir*).[38] This is not to say that narrative is not important: it is crucial in securing the film's market niche. 'Stories were porn's original alibi', writes O'Toole (1998: 209). Some filmmakers – including those I interviewed – argue that sex scenes are, or should be, an integral part of storytelling. David Cronenberg opens *Crash* with three sex scenes in a row, to which objectors have argued, 'A series of sex scenes is not a plot.' Cronenberg responds, 'Why not? Who says? . . . In *Crash*, very often the sex scenes are absolutely the plot and the character development' (Rodley 1997: 199). For neo-*noir*, as with its 1940s and 1950s antecedents, sex might be a tributary traversed on the route to criminality, crime's vehicle rather than its object (whilst also providing a handy promotional angle).

Censorship issues also dominated how sex was treated in *film noir*. Post-Hays Code, post-1970s porno chic and post-BBFC's 2000 classification changes, it *is* possible to show explicit sex in cinema below the confines of the R-18 certificate in Britain or NC-17/unrated in the US. Yet many critics make the mistake of assuming that whilst classic *noir* had to be sexually restrained and implicit, 1990s *noir* could be as explicit as it wanted to be.[39] But in aiming for a mainstream audience both *film noir* and the erotic thriller must still restrict their sexual representations in historically specific ways. Frank Krutnik writes that both *The Postman Always Rings Twice* and *Double Indemnity* were 'written fictions which in their sexual orientation in particular seemed almost unfilmable' (1982: 31).[40] In the frenzy of bidding which accompanied the studio's attempt to get *Postman* onto the screen originally, the Motion Picture Producers Association censors (the Breen Office) had 'warned studios that they were unlikely to approve any adaptation of *Postman*, no matter how it was scrubbed up' (Schickel 1992: 24); and it took twelve years to come into production. It is hard to imagine such a panic surrounding the adaptation of a novel in the late twentieth century, however explicit its content, although contemporary mainstream erotic cinema has its scandals – perhaps *Crash* comes closest. The process of accentuating explicitness whilst minimising cuts and maximising audiences has animated the history of sex on screen; films in which sex is central have had to be particularly tenacious in their methodology. The history of sexual representations has developed in tandem with mutating moral, public and industrial codes. Sex and violence continue to be the key anxieties of the censor. Like *noir*, the erotic thriller has both. Like *noir*, the erotic thriller mixes sexual spectacle with violent thriller plots, and combines neo-*noir* narratives with extended moments of explicit eroticism. As Catherine the novelist says in *Basic Instinct*, 'Somebody has to die' – murder is the 'commercial and generic necessity' (Wood 1993: 50) of the crime story. Sex also functions in this way for the erotic thriller: somebody has to fuck, then somebody fucks up. Sexual murder? Even better. These edgy generic necessities mean that the story of the shifting of censorship boundaries in the 1980s and 1990s can partly be told through the erotic thriller and its close relations, from *Cruising* (an alleged forty minutes of gay S&M cut, but hardcore subliminals inserted instead to cock a snook at oblivious censors) to the steamy *Body Heat*, through the crotch-flash of *Basic Instinct* to the extensive simulation of the NC-17 *Showgirls*. It might then be said that neo-*noir* and the erotic thriller are mirror-images of each other. Each deals in sex and crime but prioritises one over the other, and each chooses differently. The closer to the wind of censorship a film sails, the more primary sex becomes at the expense of crime.

I do not, however, propose to labour away at a generic taxonomy of the erotic thriller, certainly not at the expense of presenting new information. I have said that the term began to be used regularly only in the late 1980s and early 1990s. It could therefore be argued that the relationship between the 1980s erotic thriller (prior to the term becoming fixed) and the 1990s erotic thriller (by which time the term had stuck) is like the relationship between *noir* and neo-*noir*: the erotic thrillers of the 1980s become understood as such only when seen as the 'parent' of those of the 1990s, and when re-released on video or DVD with the term attached. Neo-*noir* has also segued with horror, particularly following the success of dark serial killer titles like *Silence of the Lambs* and Michael Mann's original *Manhunter* (1986). Whilst films such as *Kiss the Girls*, *Along Came a Spider* and *The Bone Collector* are more horror-thriller than erotic thriller, they fashion pornographically aligned suspense narratives, in their obsession with sex crimes and *femmes-* or *hommes-fatal(e)s*, and bear a common ancestry with the erotic thriller through early glossy sex-shockers such as *Eyes of Laura Mars* or De Palma's 1970s and 1980s porno-slashers. *Kiss the Girls* echoes a number of erotic thriller titles ('. . . and make them cry' completes the phrase, a spooky nursery rhyme rendition of sexual violence),[41] whilst its theme could be that of any number of DTV erotic thrillers (two sex fiends – 'Casanova' and 'The Gentleman Caller' – 'collect' women through kidnap and murder), flirting with the morality and spectacle of S&M along the way. Despite its calibre cast (the double act of Morgan Freeman and Ashley Judd also featured in *High Crimes* [2002]) this is an expensive exploitation film, which has shifted its emphasis towards the spectre (if not the spectacle) of sexual violence. The widely discussed recent move away from explicit sex in Hollywood which greeted George W. Bush's election and the new century's dawn may account for the desexualisation of such overtly sexual subject matter, or the sublimation of sex by sexual horror: a backlash against sex which 'say artist-managers, producers and studio executives, is partly to do with Washington's assault on Hollywood

55555555555
555555555555555

of a few years ago over targeting young audiences with sexual content. Violence is still OK, sex isn't' (Helmore 2003). The explicitly sexual erotic thriller is thus a rare bird in twenty-first-century Hollywood, though not unseen. I now want to open up a discussion of the pornographic in the erotic thriller as one of the forms which pornography takes when it is subject to the constraints of the mainstream.

3: PORNOGRAPHY – THE FORGOTTEN GENRE

Pornography is the bastard child of entertainment.

Al Goldstein[42]

If it makes your dick hard, it's a weakness.

Bad girl Lana/Laura (Shannon Whirry) in *Body of Influence*

Pornography is the genre that dare not speak its name – or so you might think if you only read genre theory. Steve Neale mentions it once in his whole book on genre, but only as a genre which has merited having its own specialist cinemas (2000: 40). He does not mention the erotic thriller at all in his long list of thriller subdivisions and hybrids. Pornography is also entirely excluded from Wes D. Gehring's *Handbook of American Film Genres* (1988), as well as from the other studies Gehring seeks to supplement with his expanded discussion of eighteen genres.[43] Gehring himself only goes as far as noting his exclusion when he admits that 'additional genres not included but worthy of possible further consideration would include disaster films, sports movies, and erotic films' (1988: xi). It seems that despite the wave of porno chic which swept academia in the 1990s, only a handful of texts – Linda Williams' *Hardcore: Power, Pleasure and the 'Frenzy of the Visible'*, Kipnis's *Bound and Gagged* and O'Toole's *Pornocopia*, for instance – get close to discussing porn as a genre. Williams in particular sees its place after legalisation as a 'genre-among-genres' (1990: 121), but however much pornography may see itself in these terms, other genres (and those who write about them) would rather keep their distance. More prominent is discussion of porn's relationship to feminism and representations of women, its potential harm and realised pleasures to audiences or readers, its impact on sex workers. These elements are clearly important, but comprise only part of the picture. Fashionable as pornography has become as an area of academic interest, it has rarely been presented alongside the western or the comedy film, despite the fact that in terms of all criteria such as form and iconography, audiences and effects, production and marketing, it is a classic genre case.

This critical omission becomes even more stark when it is considered that porn is one of the most widely consumed genres on the planet. Kipnis writes that in the USA pornography's 'annual multi-billion-dollar sales rival the gross revenues of the three major TV networks combined' (Kipnis 1996: ix). In 1997 *U.S. News & World Report* testified that in the previous year American consumers spent 'more than $8 billion' on sex industry products, 'an amount much larger than Hollywood's domestic box office receipts and larger than all the revenues generated by rock and country music recordings' (Schlosser 1997). The bulk of this revenue comes from video. According to the pornography trade journal *Adult Video News*, 28.7 per cent of all videos sold or rented in the USA in 2001 were adult.[44] It is also the case that softcore cinema and mainstream representations of sex not accounted for in those 'adult' statistics have expanded in quantity and explicitness alongside the increasing acceptance of hardcore since the 1970s. For some viewers, significant swathes of that non-adult 71.1 per cent of the market will also be too pornographic for their tastes, supporting the argument that sex cinema is a broad church, requiring more significant work as part of a wider understanding of American genre cinema. Clearly, bracketing 'erotic films' alongside sports movies as genres 'worthy of possible further consideration' is a ludicrous underestimation of their cultural prominence.

It is tempting to argue that the exclusion of sex cinema from genre analysis is another form of censorship, given the centrality of censorship and classification systems to the history of the form. If pornography has readily taken up the cue offered to it by available technology, censorship has just as quickly dogged its production and distribution. 'Wherever films were made or shown censorship boards sprang up', writes Philip French in his survey of 100 years of British film censorship (1997: 23). For the campaigning group Feminists Against Censorship, 'until feminism entered the debate, pornography and censoriousness were an inseparable couple' (Rogerson and Wilson 1991: 25–6), although some forms of feminism have encouraged this coupling. The dynamic between the production and the prohibition of pornography is a complex one, to which academia's ambivalent relationship of exclusion/fascination might be added. Definitions of pornography are, however, notoriously problematic, and cultural critics are no more capable of giving clear explications than are legislators. Erotica has been cast as 'the rich person's pornography',[45] but differentiation between 'soft' erotica and 'harder' pornography is particularly difficult, since it generally rests on subjective judgements of personal disgust or arousal, making one person's soft another person's hard. 'Soft' is often understood as mainstream material distributed with an R or NC-17 rating in the USA or with a 15 or 18 certificate in the UK, whilst 'hard' is that which is obtainable only in sex outlets in the USA and UK, though much hardcore which can legally be rented or bought in the USA still remains beyond the pale of even the R-18 certificate in the UK, and is thus illegal. Hardcore, of course, primarily features images of real sex performed by porn actors, whilst softcore 'erotica' shows simulated sex performed by movie actors. The fact that those actors simulated sex in films oriented towards orgasmic relief (the alibi of plot notwithstanding) only blurs an already dubious distinction. The fact that some of these actors were also former 'glamour' models further obfuscates the distinction between porn and erotica, and supports the idea that perhaps the only tenable way of distinguishing 'soft' from 'hard' is by reference to the 'reality' of the filmmaking situation: were they really doing it or not? Does the film strive to show us the intimate details of this reality, or does it want to arouse without explicit disclosure? In mainstream cinema this distinction is also complicated by the suggestiveness of 'leaks' in the PR campaigns of mainstream films that the actors were indeed 'really doing it'. Some commentators feel that the possibility of an A-list actor doing hardcore is not far away.

For the feminist writer Andrea Dworkin these definitions need to be radically politicised. In *Pornography: Men Possessing Women* Dworkin cites pornography's etymology: 'The word *pornography*, derived from the ancient Greek *porne* and *graphos*',

> does not mean 'writing about sex' or 'depictions of the erotic' or 'depictions of sexual acts' or 'depictions of nude bodies' or 'sexual representations' or any other such euphemism. It means the graphic description of women as vile whores. (1981: 200)

Pornography is then defined by the way a film, image or text represents women as victims of the 'hit-and-run sexuality' (ibid.: 134) of men which is both aggressively controlling and out of control; as a genre it is the textual proof and culmination of the 'seedy pact' men have made 'with and for male power' (ibid.: 66).[46] Written at the same time and emerging from the same feminist moment, Susan Griffin's *Pornography and Silence* (1981) deploys a similar argumentative armoury, although her conclusions are rather more mystical. For Griffin, 'Not women, but feelings, are the object of sadistic fantasy', and pornography's prime sin is the separation of 'culture from nature. It would desacralize matter' (ibid.: 55; 49). As prone to sweeping generalisations as Dworkin, Griffin argues that,

> One can look at the whole history of civilization as a struggle between the force of eros in our lives and the mind's attempt to forget eros. We have believed pornography to be an expression of eros. But we find that after all, pornography exists to silence eros. (ibid.: 255)

According to these writers, pornography must be distinguished from erotica in order to rescue the latter from the debasing influence of the former: eroticism encourages soulful, holistic sexuality, pornography indulges power and violence. Dworkin has no truck with Griffin's attempt to rescue the highbrow term 'erotica' from its debased sister 'pornography', arguing that sexuality in its publicly expressed form is dominated and dictated by male power, so any sexual materials will be infected by this contaminating influence. For Dworkin porn is not representation, it is act; it does not just depict violence to women, it *is* violence to women. Or, in Robin Morgan's (in)famous phrase, 'pornography is the theory, rape is the practice'.[47] And so the writings of the Marquis de Sade are placed alongside *Hustler*, gay male pornography alongside girlie magazines, literary texts alongside images, *Emmanuelle* alongside *Snuff*, all of them actualised forms of violence.

Dworkin's *Pornography* had enormous currency when it appeared in the early 1980s. More than separating the ostensibly erotic/holistic/feminist sheep from the pornographic/exploitative/sexist goats, I am interested in looking at the influence of porn (like *noir*) as a genre (or a set of interconnected genres – printed, cinematic, hardcore and soft) on the development of the erotic thriller. The popular influence of this brand of pro-censorship cultural feminism certainly had an impact on the reception of a number of texts central to this study, including street protests against Brian De Palma's *Dressed to Kill* and Ken Russell's *Crimes of Passion*. Gay opposition to the filming of *Cruising* and *Basic Instinct* tells a different story of popular involvement in film representation, though the PR coup is the same: public scandal can rebrand a film as prime 'watercooler' fodder and hugely maximise its box office. These are particular cases, which show the erotic thriller to be the genre most likely to stir up the extremes of audience response. At the same time, the period covered by this book demonstrates a steady increase in sexually explicit spectacle on mainstream screens and a seismic shift in hardcore representations on pornographic screens – both trends, perhaps, exemplified by the career of Greg Dark, who, as the directing side of the 'Dark Brothers', made exemplary nasty hardcore (mostly) in the 1980s and, as Gregory Hippolyte, made exemplary DTV erotic thrillers in the 1990s. Both career paths were enabled by increased liberalisation in legitimate sexual representation, and the vast profit opportunities afforded by a VCR in (almost) every home. Dworkin's work must therefore be seen as a counter-argument to the more powerful convergence of currents comprised of more pervasive sexualisation on hardcore and mainstream screens (at least until the late 1990s) on the one hand, and the technology which enabled this on the other.

Dworkin's work, though popularly read as anti-sex, was primarily anti-sexism, and the politics of representing the sexualised woman remains a nagging question for the erotic thriller, foregrounded by Odette Springer's 1995 documentary on women in B-movies, *Some Nudity Required*, which presents women as intrinsically exploited in image and on set. *Pornography: Men Possessing Women* is essentially a crystallisation of a number of ideas already in circulation, concerning the political power of the pleasurable image, the male gaze, the problem and representation of female masochism. An argument posited by many feminists of Dworkin's generation saw pleasure and its representations as key signs or symptoms of wider sexual politics. Laura Mulvey's agenda-setting *Screen* article of 1975, 'Visual Pleasure and Narrative Cinema', argued that classic Hollywood film had 'coded the erotic into the language of the dominant patriarchal order' (1999: 60); its pleasures were guided and guarded by male desire targeted on the fetishised female object of the gaze. Mulvey's cinematic women were inherently imbued with '*to-be-looked-at-ness*': 'Woman displayed as sexual object is the leitmotif of erotic spectacle: from pin-ups to striptease, from Ziegfeld to Busby Berkeley, she holds the look, and plays to and signifies male desire' (1999: 63).[48] Thus the pornographic bleeds into the everyday in the way in which women's represented bodies are shaped to the pattern of male fantasy; this 'to-be-looked-at-ness' holds true whether women are posing for *Playboy* or performing in features. It is an argument to which the erotic thriller is particularly vulnerable, since mainstream Hollywood is still animated by this familiar view of woman (Brian De Palma said to me, 'Women have always been a visual mystery to men, and that's why they've been used so relentlessly in advertising. They don't have to say anything – they just *look*' [p. 146 below]). However, though it might seem from these feminist perspectives that women become more objectified the more sexualised they are, this is not the case: many of my films, especially the cheaper ones, manage to be women's films as well as sex films, or perhaps because they are sex films (unthinkable for many 1970s and 1980s cultural feminists). At one extreme (art-house feminism) Campion's *In the Cut* gives Meg Ryan her most sexualised as well as her most feminist role; this is also the one recent erotic thriller which shows the erect male organ (or at least a highly realistic prosthetic) in full close-up, but avoids the same view of woman. At the other extreme (DTV exploitation) Gregory Hippolyte fashions sometimes sympathetic women's stories from an unpromising tapestry of human absurdity and T&A. The rise in female/feminist porn also contributes a small but significant voice to this debate. To counter this, Springer's documentary argues that it isn't possible to participate in exploitation cinema without being actually and figuratively exploited. *Some Nudity Required* brings together a variety of industry talking heads in support of her conclusion, delivered in voiceover, that 'It became clear why these images so repulsed, and so attracted me. Degradation, pleasure, fear: that's the basic formula for an erotic thriller', which also, she maintains, underpins her own experience of childhood abuse. What should have been a cogent analysis of how and why exploitative images prevail (and the moments at which alternative readings leak out through the cracks) becomes instead primarily an agent of sexual self-analysis. Nevertheless, voices such as Maria Ford's report on her experiences as a softcore actress trying to break through into films in which nudity is *not* required are important for a wider understanding of women in contemporary Hollywood. My interviews with both Anne Goursaud and Katt Shea below also develop some of these questions about how female filmmakers who establish their reputations working with sexual material then fare in the mainstream.

So can a genre which is primarily marketed for the male heterosexual eye have any interest for heterosexual women? A version of the argument that low-budget/non-mainstream is intrinsically exploitative whilst the high-budget glossies are less so also operates in perceptions of the sexual relationship between the 'low' DTVs (understood as more sexually and politically extreme because they're cheaper) and the 'high' movies. Backing this up is one particular cultural feminist line on pornography, that the further away from the mainstream (in cinema or magazines) sexually explicit material gets the more pernicious to women it becomes. Whilst it is true that many DTVs have appeared with some of their sexual riskiness intact, sexiness is not necessarily an index of sexism. Despite compulsively repeated images of naked women's bodies, the erotic thriller's sporadic sexism is no more heinous than the majority of Hollywood fare; indeed, because it needs to show ample samples of T&A it gives some of the owners of those tits and asses the chance to tell their stories. Some filmmakers I interviewed saw this as an irrelevance or a lucky accident; others value the opportunity to do something relatively complex within the strictures of the minimum which genre template and audience appetite required them to do. In a BBC Radio 5 interview from 1993, Dave Lewis of Medusa Pictures called the films his company distributed 'good quality B movies – B for beer, biriani and bonking', which would appeal primarily to 'young guys aged between 18 and 30'.[49] He added, however, that 'these are films that look at sex from a woman's angle', and it is true that the pleasures for women here are substantial. The discourse of male ownership, for instance, permeates the fabric of the DTV *Secret Games* and the star vehicle *Indecent Proposal*, but it is arguably only the former which challenges it at all. Where Julianne (Michele Brin), heroine of *Secret Games*, independently capitalises on her role as her ghastly husband's prize possession by selling herself in a ritzy brothel for millionaires (and enjoys it too), Demi Moore's Diane in *Indecent Proposal* is traded from husband to lover, protesting both that she did it for her husband and that she could not make the decision alone. Women from both films might go back where they 'belong' in the end, but only the DTV version presents the man who says, 'You're for sale – and I'm going to buy you' as finally dangerously objectionable. 'You collect things, don't you?' asks Demi Moore of Robert Redford as she is herself acquired, but Redford emerges as a benign figure who, having 'collected' her, lets her go; *Secret Games*' Eric (Martin Hewitt), on the other hand, is finally defeated by a group of women working together. Furthermore, male threat to the DTV heroines overtly lays bare the oppositional nature of relations between the sexes and the danger, as well as the desirability, of men. Sex is both the answer to and the cause of women's problems, and in presenting sexual relations as threat as well as indulgence, erotic thrillers, for all their glossy post-feminism, are still dramatising a battle in the sex war. There is little fudging the issue of sexual conflict by presenting men – as the blockbusters do – who are nothing worse than likeably confused, misguided or simply blinded by desire (Douglas in *Basic Instinct*, Hurt in *Body Heat* or Joseph Fiennes in *Killing Me Softly*). The husbands of the DTVs are at best unpleasantly indifferent to their women, at worse aggressive, whilst lovers are frequently murderous. In *Carnal Crimes* the heroine's vile husband and feckless lover enter into a pact against her, whilst in *Sexual Intent* the tale of the villain who systematically defrauds women is spliced with a series of candid female vox pops elaborating with personal relish on an 'all men are bastards' theme. It is easy to see the pleasures for women in this film, not only from the to-camera testimonies, but as it turns from erotic thriller to feminist-revenge narrative when three of the women overcome their sexual rivalry by getting together, rounding up the villain and shooting him in the desert, only so that a fourth can run him over. Even the less liberated *Carnal Crimes* has its revengeful heroine redistribute her husband's money to the servants.

This is not to say that the simple presentation of men as villains constitutes a feminist move, even in tandem with a barrage of soft-feminist points – Madonna's line in *Body of Evidence*, 'I never know why men lie – they just do' is the faint, mainstream echo of many angrier voices in the videos. Nor could it be said that these are unambiguously misogynistic works. In films which are so overtly directed towards male heterosexual desire, the narrative attack on masculinity presents something of a problem, so that whilst on one level the images are specifically tailored to male pleasure, the patterns of identification for the male and female viewer aren't simple. A scene in *Secret Games*, for instance, in which a group of women discuss the inadequacy of men ('Women are more considerate', says one, whilst another protests that 'Men don't know what women want') takes place with the women lounging topless around a swimming pool: the soft-porn spectacle and women-only confidences suggest male-fantasised lesbianism, but the talk itself takes the scene elsewhere. Earlier, three women try on their raunchiest underwear for each other in a scene which manages to combine the pleasures of shopping with the pleasures of sex in an atmosphere which is part-tupperware party, part-orgy.

The form which the softcore takes is also rather more inventive in the low-budgets, including soft forms of sadomasochism or other gratuitous 'perversions'. The *film noir* seductress with a pearl-handled revolver is succeeded in the erotic thriller by the Beverly Hills housewife with an appetite for sexual danger or the 1990s adventuress with a way with candle-wax and a damn good lawyer. The ponderous sadomasochism of *Body of Evidence*, so desperate to shock, entirely lacks the routine nonchalance of the numerous scenes of three-way sex, voyeurism and domination of the DTVs, which is all the more surprising since, as I said above, *Body of Evidence*'s sexuality is second-hand. The heroine of *Carnal Crimes* is initiated into infidelity as she drips blood from her wounded arm onto another woman, as a man – the film's 'purveyor of perversions' – takes pictures; the glamorous female shrink in *Sexual Intent* masturbates over videos of testifying women. Before their own lesbian encounter in *The Other Woman*, Jessica watches a man pouring milk over Traci's breasts, whilst the madame of the high-class brothel of *Secret Games* masturbates over the remote camera images of her girls getting it on. The spectacle of female pleasure, particularly pleasure which excludes men, is central. There is little moral gloss, and women are seldom the villains, and even less often the villains by virtue of their sexuality.

Erotic thrillers seem, then, to have almost done away with the *femme fatale*, or at least have dissociated her sexuality from her villainy. The pornography of the erotic thriller allows sex to be separated from punishment. However sexually audacious the B-women are, they don't get punished for it, and, having enjoyed the sex, they can switch roles as the films begin to slip genres towards female revenge. Compare this to the familiar track-record of the blockbusters, at least those mainstream critics have most readily labelled 'softcore' (this was even said of the relatively chaste *Fatal Attraction* in 1987): Glenn Close in that film is dispatched in perhaps the most notorious female death in 1980s cinema; in *Body of Evidence* Madonna is put on trial, shot and then drowned; Stone's *Basic Instinct* character is deemed 'the devil' by Verhoeven. If *Fatal Attraction* had gone direct-to-video, avoiding the infamous preview screenings in which audiences, enraged by the original suicide ending, shouted 'Kill the bitch!', the Close character might have escaped such lurid retribution, and might have had more fun than just a quickie in the washing-up. The incredibly pernicious conclusion of *Night Rhythms* gets close to this, as Bridget is carted off to prison with Nick accusing her not only of killing her lover Honey, but of being lousy in bed, a frustrated dyke and an ambitious career woman who has stolen his radio show. Bridget, however, does spend most of the film with her clothes *on*; contrary to the *Scream* generation truism that it's the sexy ones who die (in horror at least), the more explicitly eroticised bodies (in the erotic thriller) are also those that survive.

If these films offer pleasures between the lines for female viewers, this is not because they are deliberately feminist in project or programme. But that they are male products focused on female stories makes them surprisingly interesting. We might also get further with this understanding of the politics of the erotic thriller as porn or otherwise if we shift analysis from image to effect, from the exploitation of women to the arousal of men – and women.

4: SEXING THE AUDIENCE

Everything I learned about porno, I learned at McDonald's.
Porn producer Russ Hampshire

What, then, is this genre supposed to do to its viewer? At the most explicit end of production, the DTV erotic thriller must provoke sexual response. There are fourteen full sex-scenes or briefer sexual spectacles in *Mirror Images II*, an 88-minute film. Though these aren't evenly spaced, that's roughly one scene every six minutes, far too often for even the most energetic onanist to keep up with. Actually, the scenes come in bursts, presumably because the average length of self-pleasuring stretches beyond the duration of one individual scene: there are two scenes/spectacles around the 2–3-minute mark, another two around the 12–14-minute mark, three around the 25–30-minute mark, and another two around the 65–70-minute mark. Others are spaced out across the duration of the film.[50] In interview in 1996 DTV siren (and *Mirror Images II*'s star) Shannon Whirry acknowledges that 'in erotic thrillers a lot of it [the sex] is somewhat gratuitous anyway, that's the point' (Salisbury 1996: 111). Whirry's fans agree: 'Shannon Whirry delivers again in another direct-to-video erotic thriller', says one. 'She looks incredible and she has a lot of nude scenes, and that is the whole idea of this movie.'[51] This is efficient genre filmmaking: soft-core producer Russ Hampshire supplements my epigraph with a comment which does service for both porn and McDonald's: 'Everything was timed. Little margin for deviation' (Gaffin 1997: 151).

Films that *do* have audiences 'coming in their seats' (to recall that De Palma quote) have been theorised by Linda Williams in *Hard Core*, where it is argued that bodily response in the audience effectively mirrors the spectacle of bodily response and action on screen. Porn is not just an issue around the body (and how bodies are represented), it moves the body (to arousal), just as other low cultural forms provoke tears (melodrama or romance) or screams (horror) (as Williams also discusses elsewhere [1991]). This suggestion that genre is partly definable through effect, or intended effect, has also found its way into British legal-political polemic. Mandy Merck points out that Dawn Primarolo's 1989 Location of Pornographic Materials Bill first introduced the term 'pornography' into British legislative discourse. Primarolo's definition runs:

> 3 (1) Pornographic material means film and video and any printed matter which, for the purposes of sexual arousal or titillation, depicts women, or parts of women's bodies, as objects, things or commodities, or in sexually humiliating or degrading poses or being subject to violence.
> 3 (2) The reference to women in sub-section (1) above includes men.[52]

This is interesting (and disturbing) for a number of reasons. Point one targets the question of the reception of and audience response to sexual material, as well as attempting to speculate about the intentions of filmmakers ('for the purposes of sexual arousal or titillation'). The definition then tries to focus a kind of legislative textual analysis in its listing of potentially pornographic depictions of women (with men included as an add-on). Clearly, Primarolo hasn't learnt from the notoriously worded Obscene Publications Act (OPA) of 1959, which defined obscenity as a 'tendency to deprave and corrupt' and which has proved a sticking point for the legal profession, local councils and pornographers in the UK ever since. In the face of a failure on the part of cultural critics to define the pornographic, it has been left to the censors, legislators and cultural police to produce a negative definition of its generic qualities. Pornography, and the presumed effects of pornography, have effectively become bound to a set of inappropriate definitions set by legal practitioners, politicians and censors in a polemic of opposition.

But even if cultural critics have defined the genre in terms of the moral aesthetics of the sexual image, at least legislators and filmmakers seem to agree that its function lies in how 'effective' it is. In *The Philosophy of Horror* Noel Carroll writes, 'Works of horror teach us, in large measure, the appropriate way of responding to them' (1990: 31). To be successful, sexual cinema must *do* to us before it *teaches* us, though sexual response may be another form of teaching. Certainly, repeated genre experiences also teach us how genre must be read. Although some attempt has been made to map the thriller's primary generic characteristics (as *noir*'s umbrella genre; as a subset of the crime film), it is harder to say how and why we are thrilled: what it is to be *thrilled* by cinema is not something that can be discussed only through textual analysis or through a rigorous definition of generic terms. Similarly, what is erotic is not ontologically given, and, like that thorny use of the term 'obscene' in the OPA, the erotic is never intrinsically so; images become erotic in their activation by a paying spectator, and this, as Elizabeth Cowie points out, is a profoundly psychically complex process:

> Sexual arousal is not merely a bodily affair but first and foremost a psychical relation so that it is not a matter of nature but of signification. What arouses is already a highly coded entity. However, this signifying process is not a set of contents – of socially learned conventions of sexuality – rather it is what psychoanalysis has termed fantasy. (1997: 170)

How this can be put to work in analysis of the genre's arousal potential requires a particular kind of textual analysis. Exotic lingerie may be to the erotic thriller what the Stetson is to the western, but it does not guarantee the production of erotic response in the viewer. The genre, and its name, were formed as a kind of promise to its audience which is delivered (or not) through their response in the cinema or on the sofa. It trades in images and stories more complex than is initially apparent – appropriate to their gripping obsession with sex and transgression, erotic thrillers can be multiply inflected films, encouraging identification with a range of contradictory positions. As we will see, numerous softcore cinema websites judge films primarily in terms of their ability to excite (which usually means no more than the self-evident statement of which particular starlet gets naked in which film, though 'neither erotic nor thrilling' is a common criticism of the worst genre performers). But they do not say how this arousal emerges from the particularly fantastic psycho-sexual coordinates of the text. Writing about the sexuality of erotic thrillers thus requires a rather mixed methodology, combining the ability to look historically at the genre's development and its reception with a critical view of the psycho-poetics of the image.

What, then, makes a film a sex film? To call a movie a sex film is no more definitive than to call it a war film. Jeanine Basinger proposes that 'The war film does not exist as a coherent generic form', emphasising context as the key element of definition:

> 'War' is a setting, and it is also an issue. If you fight it, you have a combat film; if you sit at home and worry about it, you have a family or domestic film; if you sit in board rooms and plan it, you have a historical biography or a political film of some sort.[53]

A similar case might be made for sex – as a spectacle and an issue and a motivating principle, sex's very pervasiveness is intrinsic to its incoherence. If sex is the motivating narrative force but is not explicitly presented on screen, the film might be anything from a sex comedy to a farce to a woman's film to a romantic comedy to a classic *film noir*. A form of mainstream pseudo-pornography also recently emerged in a small sub-genre of films about the sex industry. Features such as *Boogie Nights*, *Dancing at the Blue Iguana*, *The Players Club* and *Striptease* present softcore spectacle for mainstream audiences (all were theatrically released in Britain). Whilst there may be a case for regarding the first three films under the loose auspices of the erotic thriller (they all have criminal sub-plots, yet each also presents its sex-scenes for the sheer pleasure of contemplation as well because they contribute to narrative and character), they might more properly be called erotic melodramas.[54] They also sit well alongside the DTV 'strip-flicks' I discuss later, which are both more sexually explicit and more likely to be animated by a murder-mystery scenario. There are also, of course, documentaries about sex, how-to-do-it or sexual tableaux non-fiction videos, and films of sexual performance art. Anything else should probably not be called a sex film, but all these forms of cinema which focus sex so centrally need to be qualified with particular reference to the specific way in which sex features as spectacle or issue. The documentary *Sex: The Annabel Chong Story* might be called a female sexual-quest film, a significant thread running through the erotic thriller. Thus sexual content *per se* does not (necessarily) buy a thrill. But can the erotic thriller arouse its audience in other ways?

Fatal Attraction*'s murderous audience*

Don't just watch me, *discuss* me.

> Valerie Grove reviewing *Fatal Attraction* (1988: A12)

Someone once defined a psychiatrist as a guy who goes to a strip show and looks at the audience.

> Jonathan Brooks (Nick Cassavetes) in *Body of Influence*

I want to close this introductory chapter by looking at the case of one film, the erotic thriller's 'ur-text', *Fatal Attraction*, to set up a range of key issues which will bear fruit in the remainder of this book. One precedent for this methodology might be Janet Staiger's work on *Silence of the Lambs*, which takes on the cultural meanings surrounding the film, responses to its homophobia and the 'outing' of Jodie Foster around its release, in the context of its media reception. Just as *Silence of the Lambs* foregrounds an unease about the relationship between the insides and the outsides of women's bodies (through the killer's acts of skinning his victims and placing a moth in their throats), so Staiger's essay moves deftly across the boundary between the (insides of the) film as text and the (outside of the) film as signifier in a cultural history. Through this move the film is read not (just) as a text but as an 'event', a focus for a set of interpretations (here journalistic reviews and popular print responses) which speak to the cultural history of a particular moment. This method (historical reception studies) aims 'to illuminate the cultural meanings of texts in specific times and social circumstances to specific viewers' (1993: 143). In a sense, then, she rewrites arguments about the prioritisation of textual or contextual material by presenting the film 'event' as an interplay between inside and outside. Staiger's analysis of the anxieties and repressions which leak out through the terms of the writers she analyses are underpinned by cultural theories of transgression, psychoanalytic theories of totem and taboo, and anthropological theories of dirt and cleanliness. Nevertheless, as she wryly notes in conclusion, 'Interpreting interpretations is viciously circular' (1993: 153).

When such provocative texts as erotic thrillers are in debate, the effect of reception analysis can mimic the psychiatrist's view as described in Greg Hippolyte's *Body of Influence*, looking at the audience instead of the strip-show. I want to ask whether looking at the audience *also* shows us the show (what kind of show does it become?), and whether looking at the show also reflects the audience. In this way, by looking at film in relation to review and back again we might pinpoint how the intersection between cinema and wider cultural anxieties are articulated. This book combines analysis of the erotic thriller's historical components (production, exhibition and reception) and contexts (historical issues informing each of these), with its fantastic components (how films function in our fantasy lives, affecting our models of subjectivity and sexuality). Perhaps its most revealing discoveries lie in the contradictions which are set up between what the films seem to be doing and how they are received; what filmmakers hope they have produced, what emerges in the text and the contradictions which spark off when production, aspiration and received film 'event' rub together. My interview with Paul Verhoeven, for instance, shows a director genuinely shocked at the hostile reception which met *Showgirls*, and he reflects that his and Eszterhas' big production mistake was a genre error: add a murder, turning the film therefore into a fully paid-up erotic thriller, and he would, he now feels, have got away with it.

If *Showgirls* exhibited to Verhoeven a body of critics out of control ('I was clearly amazed about it, the *violence* of the reviews . . .'), one anxiety which characterised the release of *Fatal Attraction* was that of the power of an audience out of control, but it was also one of the most controversial talking-point films of recent times, a major cultural and sexual milestone. The story of a weak married man's fling with a single woman (Michael Douglas as Dan, Glenn Close as Alex), who then violently pursues him and his family after he tries to end the relationship, *Fatal Attraction* was the cinematic 'event' of its year. However skilfully it was marketed, the hysteria it generated formed a lucrative box office/public response feedback-loop: vociferous audience reaction generated box office, and the more people saw the movie the more people talked about the movie, which in turn generated more box office. Douglas said, 'I've never

before been involved in a picture that emotionally hits people like this . . .
Women are dragging their boyfriends or husbands to see it. It's sort of unre-
lenting' (Lawson 1993: 176). This 'unrelentingness' may be one definition of
the long-playing sleeper hit; it also aligns the film itself with the unrelentingness
of its anti-heroine Alex, as if what she is doing to Dan mirrors (or sets a precedent for) what the film did to the public, which I want to return to later. 'It's
become Americans' favourite nightmare', wrote Mike Bygrave in *The
Guardian*: 'the subject of magazine covers and TV talk shows, the spur to all
sorts of instant sociology and a huge hit movie, grossing over $100 million to
date' (1987: 11). Under a headline which asked 'Is this the end of one-night
stands?' the *Daily Mirror* reported that marriage guidance counsellors hoped
the film would make their jobs easier.[55] New York critic George Gordon wrote:

> In the first week, seven out of ten patients with marriage problems were
> discussing the film on the couch of a prominent Manhattan psychoana-
> lyst. The intriguing aspect of *Fatal Attraction* is that everyone who sees it
> can attach their own theories, find motivations that are unvoiced in the
> film and, above all, relate it to personal experiences. (1987: 7)

The film's huge box office success, its 'talkability' and its topicality, made an
irresistible package for writers who were as interested in cultural impact as narrative content ('the most boring and inescapable topic in town' [Burchill 1988:
18]). 'Don't just watch me, *discuss* me', wrote Valerie Grove in *The Sunday
Times* (1988: A12). But critics also ended up discussing the discussions, and
becoming the hysterical audience's audience. The cultural meanings of *Fatal
Attraction* were debated so explicitly that in effect the writers themselves
became their own historical reception critics. Directed by the 1980s' key director of daring sex scandal films, written by a man who would go on to direct a
key erotic thriller *noir* remake (James Dearden directed *A Kiss Before Dying* in
1990), *Fatal Attraction* also initiated the mainstream erotic thriller's leading
man, Michael Douglas, into a series of similar roles. But perhaps more than
anything its title, as well as paying lip service to a *noir*ish blend of lethal erotics
(a kind of *Kiss Me Deadly* for the 1980s), could have advertised subject matter
appropriate to the AIDS age, when sex could well mean death. For Charles
Laurence, 'The key to its success appears to be a subliminal translation of the
title from *Fatal Attraction* to *Lethal Sex*' (1987: 13).[56] Though the film does not
mention AIDS, it dramatises the consequences of sex, and as an anti-sex sex
thriller *Fatal Attraction* spoke to a number of positions.

Fatal Attraction seemed to encourage *zeitgeist* statements, and its success
became part of the story which was told about it.[57] I have said that genre pre-
exists particular genre works, and that you can know an erotic thriller without
necessarily having seen one. Since *Fatal Attraction* was the first in one cycle of
erotic thrillers which subsequently used it as their blueprint, and was not called
an erotic thriller by any contemporary reviewer, I am not suggesting that it was

yet a recognisable 'type'. Writers picked up on Glenn Close's involvement in *Jagged Edge*, predicting that it would 'cut a wide and prosperous "Jagged Edge" at the box office', and noting that Close 'displays the dark flip side of the career woman she depicted' in the previous film (Hutchinson 1988: 38). This critical categorisation relies on both an awareness of generic type (which *Fatal Attraction* was only just helping to originate) and a recognition of star-typing. Yet generically, except at a few moments of sex or suspense, *Fatal Attraction* looks more like director Adrian Lyne's glossy British advertising work than a *noir* or neo-*noir*. Usually it is simply a thriller, though writers who stress the impact of the ending call it a horror film and writers who stress Alex's story and the family narrative call it a melodrama. How we read Alex is, then, partly an effect of how we categorise the film, the genre shift enforcing a reinflection of gender and star.[58] Retrospectively, it can be seen as the perfect erotic thriller blueprint, hinging on sexual obsession and ending in murder. J. Hoberman called it 'bedroom horror rather than farce' (1987: 68), which may be another way of describing the erotic thriller. *The Hollywood Reporter* also anticipated that its success would spur an upsurge in the fortunes of the thriller. More recent films have been marketed for their *Fatal Attraction*-like qualities.[59]

Genre issues aside, the publicity campaign which foreshadowed it did give audiences and critics the sense that they had seen *Fatal Attraction* even before it had been publicly screened. Sue Heal in the UK newspaper *Today* wrote:

> The pre-release hype has been mind-numbing: I felt I knew the film from back to front before the opening credits rolled. But cast aside the head-lines, sweat-shirts, commemorative mugs and *Fatal Attraction* pregnancy kits. Does the movie live up to the hype? (1988: 26)[60]

UK audiences – and indeed most non-American audiences – rarely receive an American film in pristine ignorance. Any film which is publicised and reviewed has a pre-life before it is seen, but non-American audiences of American films are particularly exposed to pre-screen hype. Such was the intensity of this that writers on *Fatal Attraction* made American responses part of the subject of their own response, with New York audiences and critics particularly targeted by British audiences and critics partly because the film is set in New York, and New Yorkers' reactions were deemed the most authentic response to the film's issues. New Yorker Michael VerMeulen used *Fatal Attraction* as an excuse to meditate on sex and cinematic passion in the city, reporting to the British *Sunday Telegraph* that in New York the film is taken both 'as acute social commentary' and 'wild roman[ce]' (1988: 21). Most British reviewers also start with an account of the film's astonishing US box office, as well as the changed endings and hysterical preview screenings. An uncanny sense pervades the press material, that everyone is watching everyone else watching the film, and that the film 'event' of *Fatal Attraction* is partly the fact that it was such a publicly debated commodity, an event with no obvious fixed beginning.[61]

The spectacle of audience response became as fascinating as the spectacle of the film itself, a festival of bloodlust most notoriously focused on the *femme fatale*. Regina Nadelson reported on New York's response for *The Guardian* just before the film opened in Britain:

> 'Kill the bitch! Kill the bitch!' The audience was getting into it now, the walls of the theatre alive with the noise of New York at holiday time. (1988: 1)

However, a number of critics argue that the success of *Fatal Attraction* is not attributable to wholesale demonisation of Alex, but reflects the fact that it is all things to all sectors of the audience, whereby the film offers multiply identifiable, multiple entry-points. Alongside an interview with the film's producer Sherry Lansing, Sue Summers wrote that

> The film has been seen in America as a warning against the dangers of casual sex. 'If Aids doesn't stop you, this movie will,' said one critic. Another wrote that every married woman in America should take her husband to see it. 'And they are,' says Ms Lansing, sounding understandably pleased.
> 'Everyone seems to identify with one part of the triangle,' she says. 'People will tell you Michael Douglas is 100 per cent right or wrong. I believe that dialogue reveals as much about us as it does about the movie'.[62]

But these diverse interpretative and identificatory positions also seem capable of eliciting and reinforcing a range of different audience positions, and this is a good case of the promotion machine providing critical respondents with their interpretative terms. 'There are as many theories as audience responses', wrote Charles Laurence, echoing Lansing:

> To some, the film is an injunction against philandering in an era when sex can be deadly; to others it is a feminist tract – the exploited woman fights back – or even an anti-feminist diatribe against sexually willing women. It can be 'He deserved it' or 'Poor fellow, you can't even risk a fling in this day and age' – or even, in the droll words of a young woman outside a cinema in Manhattan: 'Everything is fatal these days'. (1987: 13)

Although collectively the interpretations are multiple, critics seem to want individual viewers to line up behind one character or another, rooting for Dan (the husband) or Beth (the wife) or Alex (the lover), whilst *they* (the discerning critics) – like the exemplary psychoanalytic fantasist as described in Freud's 'A Child is Being Beaten' – are capable of sympathy across the board, in particular in relation to Alex as both used woman and psycho-*femme*. Gordon reported that how viewers behaved corresponded to who they were viz. *Fatal Attraction*'s love triangle:

> When it was first shown in Manhattan, women jumped to their feet cheering and applauding. In the final Psycho-like minutes, married women screamed 'Kill the bitch'. Single women watched in horror – and men in general left the cinema chastened, stunned and plagued by guilt. (1987: 7)

This is a film which thus polarises through the instinctive response it elicits – if we take Gordon's word for it. *All* men are philanderers as an effect of their 'chastened' response. *All* single women are Alex. *All* married women, like Beth the wife (Anne Archer, who finally dispatches Alex), kill the bitch every time the film is screened. And if *Fatal Attraction* offered married women a revenge opportunity against the Other Woman, it also gave them the chance to warn their errant husbands. In an article reassuring women readers of the *Daily Mirror* that this is 'The movie that shocked American men into being faithful', Noreen Taylor wrote:

> Wives sit in the cinema with their husbands screeching and booing at the screens, and no doubt, using the chilling plot of the film to say: 'Look what happens when you play around, sweetheart'. (1988: 1)

Barbara Amiel uses personal witness as evidence of the sensible non-feminism of average audiences:

> 'Get her, get her,' muttered the woman next to me, as Alex stalked the family home. The audience knows internally that this ideal [Alex's feminism] is not theirs, and by Heaven, they want to see her comeuppance. And by Hollywood, they get it. (1988: 11)

Amidst headlines which lauded this as a film which would *both* end infidelity *and* punish feminism, *The Guardian*'s Nadelson overheard a young woman saying to her date after the film, '"If you ever have an affair, I'll cut your balls off".' *Today*'s Daphne Lockyer uses the narrative of a horrified male viewer's response to reinforce the sense that the film will teach men a lesson.[63] The fascination of the spectacle of audience response to *Fatal Attraction* is in part augmented by the fact that, as a result of negative audience reactions at preview screenings, Paramount had to spend an alleged $1.3 million shooting a new ending. Before release the rumour went out that the newly cut version of the film was simply more violent, but not specifically misogynistically revengeful (Kasindorf 1987: 7). Then the 'kill the bitch' stories emerged, and Alex as target came to the fore. 'More and more today commercial cinema looks to its audience to tell it what it would like to see', wrote Iain Johnstone in *The Sunday Times*, reporting that Paramount shot the film with two versions of the ending, both of which featured Alex committing suicide with a knife: 'a fully frontal suicide and a tamer version with the suicide off-screen'. This is inaccurate: the 'tamer version' was never shot, though what Johnstone is referring to is the ending Dearden wrote for the original screenplay. In both versions Dan's fingerprints are found on the knife; in the first (screenplay) version he's sent to prison for her murder and that's that; in the second (filmed – the 'original' ending) his wife finds evidence which frees him (I will discuss these different endings in chapter 3, when I look at their impact on the character played by Douglas). Johnstone writes that 'preview audiences gave both endings the thumbs down and what we now get is their preferred, quite different version', in which the wife kills the lover (1988: C6). Lyne says of this: 'I thought the suicide was fabulous, but it didn't work with an audience. By the end, they hate Close and you've got to give them a release' (Bygrave 1987: 11).[64] Lyne then relinquishes his control and buries his preferred ending for the sake of box office, passing to the paying viewer some artistic control over the film. In this way audiences effectively rewrote *Fatal Attraction* to produce an experience which would elicit the most excited subsequent audience responses: the preview audience became the author not just of the new film ending but of the hysteria of future viewers. As the next link in the chain, reviewers then became the audience's audience – watching their response alongside the film and reporting back on it. Viewers screamed 'Kill the bitch!' at the version previous viewers had ensured *did* include the murder (rather than the suicide) of the bitch.

But why did this film provoke such passion? What the audience's critics were witnessing was a curious repetition of Alex's craziness by her viewers. In that *Fatal Attraction* was read as an AIDS parable about the consequences of casual sex, it casts Alex as the contagious agent – both the channel of contagion and the location of the symptom. But she is perhaps most worrying because of the way she demonstrates the ease with which violent emotional response is passed round, not just between characters within the diegesis, but across the boundary of the screen and into the auditorium. Quoting George Gordon earlier, I said that if single women respond 'as' Alex, married women respond 'as' Beth, but in that both must be characterised as variously avenger and quarry, and both take their own revenge, it may be that there is little to divide them. This fluidity of character positions also informs an audience-identification which is more fluid, as women oscillate between 'being' these positions on screen. That this is a film which also cannot decide if its anti-heroine should be a suicide or a murder victim compounds these resonant confusions. However, in all its versions *Fatal Attraction* is sure that it's Alex who 'started it', dramatising the way in which the contagion of violent craziness passes from Alex to infect first Dan and Beth, and then the audience. Despite the fact that Beth has been characterised as always cool, never crazy, it is nevertheless Beth (in the theatrically-released version) who finally shoots Alex. Alex is out of control, and through her wayward impulses she is able first to strip Dan of control, then turn him and his wife into revenge figures, by which time the audience has been infected

too. First Alex, then the Gallaghers, then the viewers, 'catch' a form of responsive rage. Lockyer reports that the audience she saw the film with 'oohed and
ahhed and gasped like asthmatics'. Denby argues that audience bloodlust had
in effect destroyed the film by ensuring that it would pander to their most reprehensible misogynistic impulses – a liberal rendering of Amiel's position:

> The filmmaker's way out is to withdraw all sympathy from the character,
> which means trashing their own work. The awful thing is that in box-
> office terms, they aren't wrong. When I saw the picture (on opening day
> at the Loews Paramount), the audience, cheering on any sign of crazed
> possessiveness, was obviously longing for Alex to go nuts. They wanted
> excitement, of course, but they also wanted a release from the burden of
> caring for an exasperating woman. I'm not immune to that feeling – I
> wanted Alex to get lost. Still, the filmmakers' cop-out is enraging, an all-
> too-explicit example of the way giving in to the audience can make a
> movie worthless. (1987: 118)

The relationship between a film text and its audience's response is, then, two-
way, and there are at least two ways to read Alex's relationship to her viewers.
For Denby an audience-driven film will cater to the lowest common denominator in the viewer. But taking the idea of the film as an AIDS tract as a way of
thinking about the exchange across the auditorium, we might also say that if
Alex infects her viewers with her murderousness, then the interrelationship
between narrative and reception is much more intimate. Audience does not
destroy character, but rather is the logical conclusion of its construction: Alex's
infectious rage loads the dice of reception against her. Alex represents a plague
born of passion (she 'carries madness, disease, the unknown' [Kael 1987: 106])
which is capable of being transmitted across the divide between audience and
image. Alex wants blood (Dan's), and so does the audience (Alex's). The interplay between character, narrative and its reception is uncannily symbiotic; by
these accounts, the audience, in hating Alex, *turns into* Alex.

Reception here becomes an agent of pathologisation: Alex's sickness is passed
on to audiences, but it is the critics who read the aberrant symptoms those audiences betray. At the front of the audience viewing queue is Lyne himself, who
'wasn't prepared for how much of an audience-participation movie it was going
to be' (Lawson 1993: 176). Lyne has testified a number of times to his pleasure
in standing at the back of cinemas after his film opened to revel in the hysteria:
'I went to a cinema where the film was playing and recorded the audience. It's
terrifying to listen to. They're screaming and shouting "Kill the bitch". It's total
hysteria' (Bygrave 1987: 11).[65] He also notes changes in the response as the
film's run extends: 'people who saw the movie the first week are going back and
dragging their friends. "The reactions are louder and there's a knowing quality"
he said' (Harmetz 1987: C17). Are these just the words of a man translating
the sounds of impassioned involvement into the ringing of the cash register, or

is Lyne a director who lives to serve his audience? Suspense cinema, sexual cinema, sex-crime cinema, *require* the viewers to experience a raised heartrate or arousal, edge-of-seat or damp-seat bodily responses. What the disappointed preview audience experienced was a kind of cinematic coitus interruptus. Of the original ending Lyne said: 'I adored the ending . . . It was totally horrifying. She's got him from the grave! But audiences in this country would have thrown rocks at the screen. If you really don't care what an audience thinks, make a home movie and show it on your wall' (Harmetz 1987: C17).

The hysteria of *Fatal Attraction*'s reception was not to be repeated with subsequent erotic thrillers, though through the late 1980s and 1990s the genre did produce more scandal movies than any other. In this sense *Fatal Attraction* is a singular exception to the genre rule – its biggest hit, its liveliest reception and exhibition scandal. But as a set of textual genre conventions it is exemplary, a high-profile formation of motifs and types later present across a range of similar films. Part one will lay out in more detail the genre history of which *Fatal Attraction* is a part, a history it also helped to make. It will analyse the basic co-ordinates of the theatrically-released erotic thriller – the antithesis of 'showing a movie on your wall' – made for the widest of adult audiences, presenting its nefarious vices and violences in the most popular arena.

NOTES

1 *Fatal Attraction* at number 52, *Basic Instinct* at number 119 according to *Variety*'s 'Films Grossing $100m-Plus in the U.S.' list (*Variety* 1999: 65).
2 A statistic which even compares well to top earners such as *Titanic*, which cost $200 million and took $4 billion. However, director Jag Mundhra quoted me a different figure from that which appears in other press materials. According to him it cost '$750,000 dollars, and it did twenty million dollars worldwide', but he also told me that there were 'five sequels after that' (there were three sequels; four films including the first).
3 Hoberman (1992: 55). This is despite John Orr's point that 1990s *noir* is 'the one genre that challenges the continuing power of money in the mythology of the American Dream' (1998: 210).
4 Criticising *Palmetto*, internet critic James Berardinelli makes explicit the connection with DTV works: 'This is the kind of movie I've seen on a cable movie channel late at night, although it usually shows a lot more skin and features names like Andrew Stevens and Shannon Tweed rather than Woody Harrelson and Elisabeth Shue' (1998).
5 See also Neale (2003: 52–3) for a discussion of this.
6 Schaefer quotes exploitation pioneer David Friedman as saying, 'After Mr. Edison made those tin-types gallop, it wasn't but two days later that some enterprising guy had his girlfriend take her clothes off [for the camera]' (1999: 6)).
7 The 1997 *U.S. News & World Report* cover-story 'The Business of Pornography' (Schlosser 1997) argues that 'hard-core films on videocassette were largely responsible for the rapid introduction of the VCR'. For Friedberg, 'VCRs became an easy "open door" for cultural contraband', associated with 'banned material: Indian films in Pakistan and Bangladesh, Western films in Eastern Europe, pornography everywhere' (2000: 444).
8 See Searle Kochberg, 'Cinema as Institution', in Nelmes (1996: 30–1). Video remains

one of the most profitable distribution modes, even for large-scale theatrically-released productions. James Schamus writes that cinema 'is simply an advertisement for what you in fact financed – a television and video programme', and '[F]or the vast majority of films an exhibition run in cinemas is simply an advertising campaign that lends an aura of cinematic legitimacy to the "back end" ancillary exploitation of the film on various forms of television and other media – video rentals and sales, pay and basic cable, broadcast television and satellite transmission, aeroplane and cruise ship projection. This "back end" long ago became the front end in terms of financing and ultimate revenues' (in Neale and Smith 1998: 94). Tim Ritter describes how it is possible to secure a limited theatrical showcase for even the cheapest and most resolutely 'DTV'-looking movie (Ritter, in Lindenmuth 2002: 216), and Corman uses the limited theatrical release as his primary form of publicity, greatly reducing his distribution costs (1998: xii). Elsaesser calls theatrical release 'merely a billboard stretched out in time, designed to showcase tomorrow's classics in the video stores and the television reruns' (in Lewis 2001: 11).

9 'It just feels small and cramped, looking more like a TV movie. Everything is framed so that it can be cropped for the small screen. Every scene opens, Dallas style, with an establishing shot' (Duane 1994). Dahl's films had, by the time of *The Last Seduction*, also encountered classic small-scale indie funding and distribution problems, proving themselves in the US market only after foreign successes or a 'sleeper' build-up of interest, so they cannot be read as assured blockbusters.

10 Dahl himself says that *Kill Me Again* 'was pulled almost immediately at theatres. The reviews came out, we went back to the moneymen. It was released in Los Angeles, where it ran for eight weeks. *Red Rock West* was a sleeper. Columbia TriStar couldn't find a distributor for it. It did well in Europe. It was saved by a Canadian distributor who saw it in France. *The Last Seduction* was taken up by HBO after high praise at Berlin's Film Festival' (Tanner 1995: 34).

11 A useful historical comparison is Elizabeth Cowie's formulation of the distinction between different kinds of B-features in classic Hollywood: B-pictures were either those films destined only for the B-slot (second feature on a double bill) and 'sold on the basis of a flat rental fee . . . [it] thus had a very reliable return, but could never become a blockbuster for the producers', or they were production category B-pictures (one-off productions which simply had a smaller budget), which might cross over into A-exhibition if pre-audience reports were favourable (1993: 164–5). The DTV film corresponds to the first form of B-picture, whilst low-budget sleepers such as John Dahl's early films correspond to the latter.

12 One reviewer of the Sean Young vehicle *Motel Blue* (1999) writes that an investigator has been warned 'not to get involved in Young's life, but like everyone else in every erotic thriller ever made, she cannot stay away, and soon finds out that Young is involved in erotic deceptions, illicit pleasures, scandalous desires, and many other two-word phrases that could double as video-titles' (Rabin 2003).

13 However, the fan is perhaps more of a horror geek than an erotic thriller aficionado, and cannot speak the sexual: 'You know that scene where she takes that guy's face and kind of stuffs it between her – her –', he hesitates, leaving Fiorentino to interject 'Tits'.

14 However, *Kiss of Death* and *Murder My Sweet* were both remade (the latter as *Farewell My Lovely*, its original US title and that of Chandler's novel) as rather chaste but tough neo-*noirs* in 1994 and 1975 respectively.

15 *Fatal Exposure* (dir. Peter G. Good), distributed in the UK by Rio Pictures, a prolific erotic thriller video distribution house.

16 'In one', reports Tanner (1995: 35), Bridget seduces Mike 'in a school gym. In the second, she handcuffs him to a bed, seduces and abandons him.' According to Dahl the cuts were made for reasons of narrative economy rather than classification.

17 Kim Newman discusses this in the context of a history of traffic between exploitation and mainstream cinema. The sanitisation which accompanies the transition of

18 Greg Dark reminded me that Rollergirl (Heather Graham's character in the mainstream sex-melo-saga *Boogie Nights* [1997]) is also the name of a character in his hardcore *New Wave Hookers* (1985).

19 *Over the Line*, dir. Oliver Hellman and Robert Barrett, 1993, Cannon Pictures Inc.

20 US video sleeve burb for *Deceptions* (1989), Republic Pictures Home Video.

21 'Genre criticism has confined itself to producing taxonomies on the basis of "family resemblances", allocating films to their position within the generic constellation, stopping short of what are the interesting and informative questions about generic groupings' (Tom Ryall, 'Teaching through Genre', *Screen Education* 17, 1975/6, 27–33, p. 27, quoted by Neale 2000: 12).

22 See Mark Kermode's discussion of horror aficionados for an analysis of how genre devotion produces learned readers engaging with movies which 'seem acutely aware of their audience' and which in turn 'feed upon the knowledgeability of their fans' (1997: 60). Matt Hills (2002) discusses this extensively.

23 See Christine Gledhill's discussion of Laurence Alloway's 'On the Iconography of the Movies', *Movie* 7, 1963, 4–6; Gledhill, in Cook and Bernink (1999: 138).

24 For instance, he refers to musical comedy as 'a genre – or sub-genre' (2000: 107).

25 *Feminine Chemistry*, distributed by Guild Home Video/Rio Pictures, is further described as 'Coupling the erotic power of *Bedroom Eyes* with the promiscuity of *9½ Weeks* and *Basic Instinct*'.

26 Taken from promotional video sleeves distributed to press and video dealers by British film distributors. *Caged Women*, an Italian film directed by Leandro Lucchetti, was a Rio Pictures film distributed by Guild Home Video in Britain. *Beach Beverly Hills*, dir. Jonathan Sarno, was distributed in Britain by 20:20 Vision.

27 Taken from the UK promotional video sleeves of *The Erotic Adventures of The Three Musketeers*, Rio Pictures/Guild Home Video; *Embrace of the Vampire*, Medusa pictures; *Erotic Ghost Story*, Media Asia Distribution.

28 *The Big Easy*, released in Britain by 4 Front Video 1998.

29 See Checkout.com review of *Undercover Heat* at http://www.checkout.com/movies/title/info/0,7695,899148,00.html. The video sleeve blurb continues: 'But for Cindy the twilight world of hookers and thrills for money is more dangerous than for most. She's on the trail of a brutal killer and the deeper undercover she goes the more she becomes entwined in a tangled web of sex and erotic desires that threatens to run out of control' (*Undercover*, distributed in Britain by High Fliers Video Distribution).

30 'Suspenders' in the UK are garters used to hold up stockings – rather sexier than the braces used to hold up American stockbroker's trousers.

31 Newman and Crook (1994: 62). Newman and Crook also list what they consider to be the key DTV erotic thriller motifs: 'Endless saxophone-scored moaning, writhing and gasping, with anatomically improbable breasts on the bounce and finger-sucking aplenty. All the women seem to have profited from a trip to Silicone Valley . . .'

32 Following Erickson (1996: 308), Helen Hanson (2000) proposes '*noiring*' as an aesthetic process, in an argument discussing the importance of the Gothic woman's film in the formation of dark aesthetics usually associated with classic *noir*.

33 Neale (2000: 162–3), quoting Martha Wolfstein and Nathan Leites, *Movies: A Psychological Study* (New York: Atheneum Press 1977), and Michael Renov, *Hollywood's Wartime Women: Representation and Ideology* (Ann Arbor: UMI Research Press 1988).

34 De Palma is fond of *doppelganger* narratives, and revisits them partly in homage to Hitchcock (*Vertigo* in particular), preceding *Femme Fatale* with the identity conundrums *Sisters* and *Raising Cain*.

35 Some writers who are confident in their designation of *noir* as a genre see recent *noirs*

as a genre in decline, an occasional trickle from an established source rather than a new form. Writing in 1988 Jack Nachbar saw *Chinatown*, *Taxi Driver* and *Blood Simple* as new formations of *noir*, but read *Body Heat* as only a non-innovative remake of *Double Indemnity* (Jack Nachbar, 'Film Noir', in Gehring 1988: 74).

36 By the early 1980s the term *film noir* had assumed such widespread cultural currency, and its neologistic form was used as a common marketing label; writers commonly cite *Body Heat* as a watershed in explicit neo-*noir* labelling. Hirsch (1999: 182) sees it as the start of neo-*noir* proper; he also argues that it was only with *LA Confidential* that *noir* had 'escaped the historical vise' and could be used 'without any disclaimer' (1999: 5).

37 Naremore also touches briefly on this point (1998: 212), but it requires further development.

38 Hirsch argues that because the sexuality in classic *noir* is repressed, *noir* and sexual spectacle are mutually exclusive: 'Prolonged sex scenes are narrative and visual distractions, not only unnecessary but, in fact, a betrayal of the pinched, essentially straightlaced bourgeois ideology from which most noir stories were written' (1999: 57).

39 For instance, Christopher writes: 'It is not so much that the neo-noirs are graphically explicit in the bedroom – few of them are – as the fact that they could be. There's no need any more for those lingering kisses or cigarettes passed in a darkened room to denote sexual intercourse. The vast range of suppressed subject matter in the 1940s and 1950s is not on the table, to be dealt with as directly as one wishes' (1997: 242). However, censorship and classification constraints continue to determine filmmaking parameters. Furthermore, when a seductive woman tries to woo John Garfield into her car in Tay Garnett's *Postman* with the line, 'It's a hot day and that's a leather set, and I've got a thin skirt', it is debatable how covert the sexuality is. We may not see what happens on that leather seat, but the line in itself will have been as boundary-challenging as any crotch-flash in 1990s cinema.

40 Krutnik also writes that Cain's 'crime-and-passion stories *The Postman Always Rings Twice*, which MGM bought for filming in 1934, and *Double Indemnity*, acquired for adaptation by Paramount in 1936 . . . were secured by the studios because of their success, but they had to wait twelve and eight years respectively before the representational context was favourable for adaptation to the screen'(Krutnik 1991: 36).

41 The title comes from the James Patterson novel on which the film is based. Patterson also wrote the novel and screenplay for *Along Came a Spider* (also featuring the Morgan Freeman serial detective character Alex Cross), and specialises in titles which evoke the uncanny of childhood. See, for example, *Pop Goes the Weasel* (2000), *Four Blind Mice* (2002) and *The Big Bad Wolf* (2003).

42 Quoted in Gaffin (1997: 112–13).

43 Gehring explicitly expands the terrain covered by Schatz's *Hollywood Genres*, Barry Keith Grant's *Film Genre: Theory and Criticism* and *Film Genre Reader*, Stuart Kaminsky's *American Film Genres* and Steven Earley's *An Introduction to American Movies*.

44 See 'Annual Sales/Rental Charts', *Adult Video News*, December 2001, archived at www.adultvideonews.com/cover/cover1201_05.html.

45 Chris Bearchall, quoted by Dyer (1990: 208–9).

46 The book itself is largely a series of readings of sundry sexual materials strung together by an uncompromising polemic which defines men as objectifying sexual monsters and women as their objectified victims, who live frightened lives 'circumscribed by the sexual sadism of males' (Dworkin 1981: 136). 'Force is intrinsic to male sexuality', she writes (ibid.: 198); in Dworkin's later book *Intercourse* (1987) she argues that the act of penetration itself embodies this aggressive sadism, with the penis as mutilating weapon.

47 Dworkin's book set the agenda for a whole programme of action in the campaigning

political arena: 'We will know that we are free when pornography no longer exists', she writes in her conclusion (224). For a further discussion of Dworkin's attempts to influence US legislation, see Linda Ruth Williams (2002).

48 As has often been pointed out, Mulvey's argument is indebted to an earlier text, John Berger's challenge to the history of art, *Ways of Seeing,* which reads a number of images of women through an embryonic theory of the power of the gaze: 'To be born a woman has been to be born, within an allotted and confined space, into the keeping of men. . . . *men act* and *women appear.* Men look at women. Women watch themselves being looked at. . . . Thus she turns herself into an object – and most particularly an object of vision: a sight' (1972: 46–7).

49 Dave Lewis of UK video distributors Medusa Pictures, feature: 'Erotic Thrillers – Art or Agony?', on *A Game of Two Halves* presented by Mark Kermode and Caron Keating, BBC Radio 5, Wednesday, 21 April 1993.

50 Hardcore films contain longer, and fewer, sex scenes: Winks quotes an average of five or seven, and 'you may wonder why the sex scenes are so long. The director's expectation is that you're masturbating or having sex while watching' (1998: 2).

51 Cal-5 of Manteca, California, writing to the IMDB User Comments section, http://us.imdb.com/CommentsShow?0110529.

52 Merck (1992: 50); this is also quoted and discussed in Rodgerson and Wilson (1991: 27–8). Merck also quotes Annette Kuhn's important point that pornography is largely defined in common-sense terms 'whose reference is not specified representations, but the effects that representations may be thought, in certain circumstances, to produce.'(ibid.: 51).

53 Jeanine Basinger, *The World War II Combat Film: Anatomy of a Genre* (New York: Columbia University Press 1986), p. 10, quoted by Neale (2000: 125–6).

54 Though at least one – *Boogie Nights* – is a faithful disciple of hardcore, and another example of 'high' drawing from 'low'.

55 'The people who really know about fatal attractions are hoping the film does make an impact. Zelda West-Meads, of the National Marriage Guidance Council, says: 'It could make men think twice before having a one-night stand or an affair' (Taylor 1988: 1).

56 Further to this Valerie Grove, writing in *The Sunday Times,* summed up the anti-sex interpretations which had been made by various reviewers: ' "Why *Fatal Attraction* hates women," *The Listener* promises to tell us. "Is *Fatal Attraction* part of a sexual hurricane that is devastating sexual tolerance?" asks the *New Statesman. Time* magazine says the film taps "the current mood of sexual malaise". David Mamet, the playwright, finds it anti-women, fearful of sex; *Vogue*'s critic sees male paranoia; the American feminists see anti-feminism' (1988: 12).

57 For example, Rod Lurie wrote in *Spotlight,* that it 'grossed $8 million its opening weekend – a figure almost unheard of for a film making its debut in the fall . . . . Since then the film has flattened box office records with steamroller efficiency' (1987: 68). Writers trot out box office statistics with relish, the size of the sums testifying to the importance of the film as subject matter and jacking up the hyperbole of the surrounding piece. Donna Leigh-Kile reported to the *Sunday Express* that 'it made $17.5 million in its first month' (1987: 13), whilst Charles Laurence had reported to the *Daily Telegraph* a month earlier that 'it grossed $76,461,481 in the first 46 days of its release, putting it on target to be the year's biggest hit' (1987: 13). This success was repeated in Britain, particularly remarkable for an 18 certificate film (see 'Attraction Makes a Killing in the UK', *Screen International,* January 1988, p. 1).

58 *Fatal Attraction* is a good case of a multiply genred film which produced a range of categorisations from critics, who responded in a similarly multiple fashion across the US/UK divide. *Variety* called it a 'suspenseful meller', and praised Lyne's anticipation of audience response: 'Lyne very adeptly jangles the viewer's nervous system on his way to the big payoff scene, which will produce plenty of screaming, screeching and arm-grabbing, just the ticket for an audience pleaser' *Variety,* 16 September

1987, p. 13. David Denby pondered: 'At first, we can't tell whether the picture will be a shrewdly observed domestic drama of New York life and manners, a soap opera with stars – or what the trade papers call a "psycho thriller"' (1987: 118), whilst Pauline Kael called it 'a gross-out slasher movie in a glossy format' (1987: 107). In the UK, Derek Malcolm wrote, 'It's the very stuff of melodrama, and skilfully organised melodrama is exactly what *Fatal Attraction* is' (1988: 25). Alexander Walker saw horror and melodrama as part of the same commercial package when he called it 'a horror story wrapped up in a commercial for family togetherness'.

59 *Obsessed* (Jonathan Sanger, 1993) was called 'A "Fatal Attraction"-style thriller' on its video release by Imperial Entertainment UK, whilst *Double Jeopardy* (Lawrence Schiller, 1992) was called '"Fatal Attraction" meets "Final Analysis"' by CBS Video.

60 Heal also stressed the irresistibility of the film: '*Fatal Attraction* is the movie magnet that has drawn American punters like iron filings to the flicks' (Heal 1988: 26).

61 James Deardon's script had had a previous outing on British television as a short play entitled *Diversion*, screened in 1979. *The Sun* reported that 'Movie bosses have burnt every copy of the original film on which the steamy blockbuster *Fatal Attraction* is based. Paramount producers Stanley Jaffe and Sherry Lansing paid $5,000 for all 60 prints of the British movie *Diversion*, released in 1979' (*Sun*, 13 January 1988, p. 15).

62 Lansing sold the movie as a multiply identifiable entity, telling the *Daily Mail*: 'The reason for the success of *Fatal Attraction* is that everyone identifies with one side of the triangle in the story. Glenn Close is unrequited love; Michael is the nightmare; and his wife is the best part of us all – she is the only innocent' (Lewin 1988: 13). She told *The Guardian* that *Fatal Attraction* 'is a Rorschach test for everyone who sees it' (Bygrave 1987: 11).

63 'The man in the seat next to me had slipped out of the office on his secretary's advice. "That's right" he uttered smugly. "Silly cow said *Fatal Attraction* would change my life. I ask you? Change my life. It's only a sodding film now isn't it?" Later he claims to have "been reborn"' (Lockyer 1988: 9).

64 The 'suicide version' (as opposed to what *Variety* called 'the "horror" version') was, however, released in Japan, with substantial box office success, because, it is argued, 'The alternative version has a more Japanese flavour' (Bailey 1988: 10).

65 In the video version of *Fatal Attraction* released with extra footage under the 'Paramount Directors Signature Series' distributed by CIC Video, Lyne plays a tape he made of the audience reacting to his film, on which it is impossible to hear the soundtrack of the film above the rise and fall of gasps and screeches.

INTERVIEW: PRODUCERS ANDREW GARRONI AND WALTER GERNERT

Linda Ruth Williams (LW): You set up Axis Films International and it became the foremost producer of direct-to-video erotic thrillers. How was it formed, and how did you view its potential market and target audience?

Andrew Garroni (AG): We got into this business because we loved movies. I started in the industry in the early 1980s as a one-off producer for a number of successful genre pictures (*Maniac, Vigilante*). That was an exciting time for me, but creatively I was looking for a home. The formation of Axis was that home – all we needed was to find our niche market. In our hearts we were filmmakers first and businessmen second – but the business side of the process is a vicious cycle. The whole process of running around and raising the money for the budget, to shooting the film and eventually selling it, had become very anti-climatic and draining. We needed to find a way to make it more exciting and rewarding. Blockbuster Video had inadvertently carved out a market for us. Throughout the early to mid-1980s, every town in America had a 'mom and pop' video store. Almost overnight, Blockbuster Video began buying up commercial real estate as fast as they could – building these giant videos stores with ten times the inventory as the smaller stores. Most independent stores couldn't compete and were forced out of business. The only hold that the small video stores had in terms of being able to compete was that they carried adult videos. Blockbuster had made a very vocal pronouncement that they would never carry X-rated or adult, sexually explicit tapes in their stores. They were all about apple pie and American values. Meanwhile, Showtime and HBO, the pay-TV channels, were showing late-night films from the 1970s like *Emmanuelle* – old erotica: looks like a movie, walks like a movie, talks like a movie, sometimes has recognisable former movie stars. So they could say that yes, it's got titillation aspects, but it's still a *movie* like any other movie – they just happen to put it on at one in the morning.

Walter Gernert (WG): I myself had come from the porno industry where we did do everything in series. You set up the factory to do this – that was the informing idea. There were a lot of guys making exploitation, action and horror for a lot of money, but there was a need for adult programming in the mainstream market.

AG: So we sort of talked about what kind of company you could start that would be viewed as a supplier of more than a one-off. And *Night Eyes* had come out and was very successful on video. So we came to see that there was a genre that we could build a company around. You could sort of specialise if you will.

LW: So was *Night Eyes* the beginning of all this?

AG: That could be right. It was a big deal from a commercial video standpoint.

LW: So this softcore niche, adult films that weren't sold through the back rooms of the mom and pop stores, was really defined by a gap in the market?

WG: Well, we were also finding more and more TV stations with cable systems around the country who were wanting to buy softcore – this was in the days when you still spent a hundred thousand dollars to make a porno film, and you shot enough coverage to have something that didn't show penetration. So there was a growing market for these hackneyed 'neither fish nor foul' things.

AG: But some countries prohibited the programming of even cut-down versions of hardcore films. So we jumped in. Greg Brown [aka Gregory Dark and Gregory Hippolyte] and Walter had worked together in both the adult and non-adult world, they had made a couple of films that Walter produced and Greg directed, and they were neighbours. I was crashing at Walter's place downstairs, because I didn't have the money for an apartment, and we all started talking about how it would be great to get back into production. Greg was working on television projects at the time; he made a sci-fi film, and he'd done *Dead Man Walking* and *Street Asylum*, and then he went off to work on television projects. And he wasn't all that crazy about things – working within Hollywood is difficult; when you go to them to finance something you have to work by their rules and it can be extremely frustrating.

WG: This, by the way, is how Greg Brown became Greg Dark and then Greg Hippolyte something . . .

AG: The fear was that there would be a mark against these films if they were seen to be done by somebody who had done adult movies.

WG: It was two-fold; on the one hand, everybody was trying to escape their porno past because there was no way you could go and work for the studios if you had that mark. And at the same time, you didn't want it to look like a bunch of pornographers were making films and trying to trick the honest guys who didn't want to have anything to do with pornographers.

AG: So yeah, that was the start of Mister Hippolyte. And *Carnal Crimes* was the first film we made.

LW: How did you divide up your different roles?

AG: Greg would be the creative force, he was going to bring in writers and develop material and direct it. I came up as a nuts-and-bolts production guy. I was production assistant, production manager, line producer. And then because I had morphed into actually producing, raising some money and then having to sell it, that was my role too. The sales activity I guess was Walter's and mine. But having said that, everybody crossed over. We'd sit around Walter's office and say, 'Do we make a movie like *this*?' and everybody would say, 'What about making a movie like *that* . . . ?' Incidentally, I should say, as a sort of teaser trailer to your meeting with Mr Dark, that I think you're gonna find that his version of the 'birth of Axis' films is going to look entirely different, like he did everything and we sort of assisted him.

WG: It's an affectionate recollection. We haven't seen Greg for years, but there are some rather pronounced qualities that I think won't have changed over the years.

LW: So what happened when you got in people like Jag Mundhra to direct Axis films?

AG: Truly, honestly, what we wanted to happen was that Greg would act like the executive in charge of production from the standpoint of supervising other directors, making sure that they were developing scripts that fit within the genre and the budget that we were making. That was the purity of what we were looking for, and Greg would fulfil that role. He's a very creative person, has a lot of creative ideas, and he'd be able to talk on a creative level to other directors and their writers. But it didn't turn out that way. He didn't like the fact that other directors were being brought in. Perhaps if I have a regret it would be that I was hoping that Axis was going to be a Roger Corman-style company. You'd make this deal with the devil that said 'You're a young creative film-maker and you can come here and we'll let you do it', you know. In the back of my mind, when I talked to Walter we knew what we were hoping it would evolve into. And it didn't.

LW: So who did you imagine your target audience to be?

WG: Well, what we were doing was really a type of bait and switch, which never made us very happy because we knew in fact that the typical guy that wanted to get excited would rather watch hardcore sex. We were really a kind of poor man's substitute in terms of the limitations built into the distribution system. So the audience obviously was a couple at home who were either ashamed to rent pornography or needed to carry on the persona of 'we're not that kind of a person'. But the films were clearly a sort of aphrodisiacal experience.

LW: But you had your eye on the female part of that couple too?

WG: I think that was more a thing that would have been in the head of the director than in ours at that point. And it's funny because while we're talking I have some recollections of having these sexual politics discussions about it, but I don't remember what they were. Greg had a rather involved worldview of that, but you'll have to talk to him about it personally.

LW: I think what's interesting about these films is that they're often women's stories – that's surprising.

WG: Well, it's not surprising because you need to keep the women in front of the camera. The guys are incidental, the guys are appendages.

LW: Yes, but you don't need to keep the woman in front of the camera saying, 'I'm having problems with my life and these are the choices I'm making', which surprisingly your films did. So from the viewer's perspective, I'm reading these as stories about women's lives as well as stories showing their T&A. And part of the purpose of this interview is for me to find out whether you meant it like that.

WG: No . . .

AG: I can't say for myself that I was particularly going out to make films for the female audience or make them empowering. Although as the father of a fifteen-year-old girl, I very much do feel like that. I think realistically what happened was that we took the films deadly seriously. We worked on the scripts. We had script meetings and story conferences and we truly tried to make the films as entertaining for ourselves as possible. I think if you can make it entertaining for yourself you can ultimately make it entertaining for a wider audience. I mean, we did spend time on it, we did, to the best of our abilities, try to make the characters as complex as we could, especially psychologically, because it complemented the genre that we were in. But was that the primary motivation? I think the answer's 'No'. Was it the outcome of the process? I think the answer is 'Yes'. They're more interesting women. Like when Shannon Whirry played two characters in *Mirror Images II*, it made it *much* more interesting. It

65

got into the psychological aspects of the character and still the sexuality came out. But I was always the one in the story conferences saying, 'Couldn't she have this conversation in the shower?'

WG: *You know, I'm feeling more and more base as you describe how inane we were.*

AG: But the women are the strong assertive characters who are driving the story, who are manipulating . . . the men are dancing on the strings.

WG: *Which is a reflection of real life, after all . . .*

LW: Exactly. And it's interesting to hear you say that you took your filmmaking so seriously.

AG: Very much. Our collective interests – Greg's, mine and Walter's – was to make films as interesting as possible. We didn't want to go broke though. We didn't get up every day and repeat the mantra of the genre that we were in. Once we made the decision we understood the realities of the marketplace. We were respectful of the genre, we understood what we were making. Occasionally we strayed, like when we made *Stranger by Night*. We thought that was an interesting film to make for perhaps a bigger cast with a little bit more money. It wasn't 100 per cent successful as a psychological drama, and it certainly didn't have the sexuality, but it was good enough for us to sell to HBO as a world premiere. So there were times when we strayed, but certainly when we knew we were making an erotic thriller we knew the elements that needed to be in there. So we didn't need to constantly have that discussion. But we *would* constantly have the discussion about how to make it more interesting. Can we make the characters' motivations in these sexually titillating situations be a little bit more rooted in reality?

WG: *They were also informed by current events to a certain degree . . .*

AG: Yeah, like *Animal Instincts*. Somebody read the story of this husband and wife somewhere in the South who were in court, and the defence was that she was a nymphomaniac. He was a local sheriff who couldn't satisfy her, and so he was doing the right thing by his wife by allowing her to be a prostitute. And we were like, 'This is cool!'

WG: *At the same time, Andy and I were trying to buy the rights to the* Weekly World News *which we wanted to make a TV series out of. It was a tabloid whose typical headlines were 'Baby Born With Wooden Leg' or 'Hitler's Daughter Dancing in the Follies'. The question was, how could we do this and not offend the buyer at HBO?*

AG: My own predisposition: I *love* the *Secret Games* idea. The bored Beverly Hills housewife is forced to become a highly paid courtesan in the afternoons in a beautiful Beverly Hills mansion. And then she meets a dangerous man who she falls in love with, but you know she shouldn't. And bad things happen, but it really is OK in the end. I would have made that film – I *did* make that film – over and over again! I could *watch* that film, just with a different fix, over and over again! And I'm honest about it! But Greg, really early on, wanted to move away from the genre. And given the opportunity, or if you left the office for too long, he would. Because he was looking to push the envelope in other directions to stretch himself as a filmmaker. And I certainly would have loved to do that, but I'm going to lose money. Our thing was, you don't lose the rent, right? You don't let the kid drive the Cadillac.

WG: Jag was a perfect case of this. Everyone really liked Jag – he was great. Yet if you'd have let him, he would have done everything for double the budget . . .

AG: . . . and with much less sex . . .

WG: . . . and the second half of the budget would have been absolutely useless for our needs.

LW: Would he really have had less sex?

AG: Absolutely. Jag, and oddly enough in the latter stages of the company Greg as well. Greg's interest was to push beyond the confines of the genre of the erotic thriller and I think that's probably the nature of a director who's done it over and over again. We should have pushed for other directors to come in. My hero when I was growing up was Roger Corman. I think Walter admired him as well. Because he'd let the filmmaker make the films they wanted to make as long as they fit in a particular genre.

WG: What was that famous line? 'If you do well, you'll never have to see us again'.

AG: Precisely. You're exploiting them, you know, so that they can achieve what they need to achieve, which is to get in some practice.

LW: Was that the case with Wally Pfister, the cinematographer?

AG: The *famous* cinematographer of *Insomnia*? Yeah, Wally is the perfect example of what we were talking about. Wally is a very talented director of photography. He used to work as a camera operator on bigger Hollywood features, but his goal was to become a director of photography in his own right. Wonderful personality, great guy. Really an artistic type of person. But he understood what we were doing. It was never a question that we had to have long drawn-out discussions about 'these films are these films and those films are those films'. He understood it. And what he tried to do within the confines of the budget and the genre – he pushed it. He's the perfect example. And so eventually he made *Memento*.

LW: The Axis films did look great, which is not surprising.

AG: I give it to Greg one hundred per cent. He understood that very early on.

WG: His low-budget porno films looked great too. He's got a great eye. He came out of a fine-art background. He didn't know from the beginning to the middle to the end of a story, but he could really light a scene.

AG: The look was everything, and I think to a great extent that helped the commercial outcome of the films as well, because they *did* look good.

LW: So where did you sell internationally? Where were your best markets?

AG: Germany was a big market.

WG: Wherever the Allies occupied after World War II, we did well. It's true.

AG: Our biggest sales were US video, Germany, South Korea, South America, Mexico, UK.

LW: Were they sold in what would be the R-rated versions available here?

WG: Well, we made available to them whatever they liked. A lot of people would do the same thing – they'd have a TV-restricted and they'd have a video version as well. That's axiomatic – the harder you could push it, the better your customers liked it.

AG: Blockbuster's edict was that it had to have an R-rated version – that sort of squared with their stated philosophy of the kind of films they were carrying. So you had to get the MPAA to rate it R. Initially they would say, 'It's an NC-17', and we were clearly looking to achieve an R-rating from them. And we would just cut the film until they gave us an R-rating. And so it was a give-and-take. You'd literally cut frames.

WG: Grind 'em down, as it were.

LW: But did you deliberately go over the wire of what you thought they'd accept in order to be able to cut back?

WG: Oh, for sure. Because you actually never knew what they'd accept. And at the same time that this was going on the MPAA and the studios were really conflicted because they needed to push that boundary themselves . . .

AG: With films like *Basic Instinct* . . .

LW: And *Showgirls*.

WG: And in the middle of this whole thing they created the NC-17. So after five years of living with the system, we still didn't understand what was going on.

LW: In terms of your relation to the studios, it seems to me that there were two kinds of erotic thrillers running in parallel. On the one hand, you had what you guys were doing. On the other, you had studio films like *Body Heat, Jagged Edge, Fatal Attraction, Basic Instinct, Jade*, which were doing the same thing but with huge budgets and overinflated stars. So did those big movies threaten your province at all?

AG: No. Just the opposite. If anything, those were advertisements which helped us. *Basic Instinct allowed* the middle managers that run the outlets of distribution to be able to point to our films and say 'It's *like Basic Instinct*. It just has David Carradine instead of Michael Douglas in it!' We used to put out the casting director's instructions as 'Whoever's just got out of rehab – book 'em!' We got David Carradine just before he went up to Canada to do the new *Kung Fu* series. And we got him for 10,000 dollars a week, which for us on our budgets was a lot of money. So he straddled two films. He did the last week of *Night Rhythms* and the first week of *Animal Instincts*. Those are all Corman tricks – we didn't invent any of that stuff.

LW: So what went wrong? Why didn't the genre thrive?

WG: Well, if you look at the history of sex on film, there's been this slow but steady concentration of what is it really there for. And in the end, what it was there for was titillation. The more you dress the pig up like a lady the less the people liked it. And now, the porno industry went from six-figure budgets shot on 35-mm film with horrible scripts but attempts at filmmaking, to today where probably the average budget is a tenth of that and it's simply nothing but sex. The same thing gradually was happening with erotic thrillers. The pretext of real storytelling and filmmaking gradually gave way to what the viewer really wanted to see, which was an excuse to be titillated.

LW: So, are you seeing the thriller narrative as *just* a pretext for getting the sex in?

AG: Let me tell you what it is – it's all about hypocrisy. Nobody that I've ever met outside of the adult entertainment industry has ever watched a porno. I mean, *ask* them! Nobody watches it, but its a multi-million dollar industry. Nobody wants to think that they're making a softcore porno. So when, for example, we worked with Jag Mundhra, we had this conversation. We said, 'It needs to hit these marks'. If you compare Jag's films with Greg's films, Jag's are not as sexually explicit. So we had to work with him at the comfort level that he was in. If it was up to him he would try and make, ultimately, a thriller, only. With probably *no* sex.

LW: So in the checklist of scenes that had to be in an Axis erotic thriller, why was there always a lesbian sex-scene?

AG: Because it's a guy's fantasies. Because you don't have to perform. You can just simply watch. And I absolutely introduced it in every story meeting we *ever* had on *any* project that, when we got the script, did *not* have a lesbian scene, I introduced it in *every* conversation. Wher*ever* I could win the argument, it existed. And the directors understood exactly what it is. It's a male fantasy. If it only was to succeed on *that* level, sexually and commercially, you have to have *that* element.

WG: I think in our case it was that you get two girls naked in the same scene. The guy just gets in the way.

AG: That's the truth. And if you're asking what's the fascination, especially in pornographic films, for lesbian scenes, it's because I think you can just simply *watch* it and you don't have to perform. Men always have those performance anxieties: did I satisfy the woman, did she think I was really good?

LW: So the answer to that is to just not be there at all? To be aroused by absenting yourself?

WG: We're getting really deconstructive here, aren't we?

AG: But it's right. How many guys get to actually live out the fantasy of being in a *ménage-à-trois*? Very few. That's why it's in *films*. You're working in a factory in Detroit – how many times do you *get* that? You don't have the money to buy that fantasy, and you're not good-looking enough to be able convert the fantasy like, say, Charlie Sheen or Matt Damon or any of these other guys. So when do you have that fantasy? Never, ever. So yeah, part of it could be that living *in* there . . . but the truth is, your fear is that the women don't really want you, 'cos they really *don't*. Well, you know that's just one humble opinion.

LW: So since you had figured out this successful formula, and you were getting the films into Blockbuster, why did you stop making them? What happened towards the end, the mid-1990s?

WG: The same thing that was going on to every type of genre filmmaking; there was a general shift from video sales to TV sales, and as TV sales narrowed, pornography opened up in more and more markets and eroded that. For example, Scandinavia went hardcore over the airwaves, and there just was no space for us at all. A number of factors affected all genre filmmaking to a certain extent, but more particularly us.

AG: I remember in 1995, I had pre-sold the US video distribution rights to a title, and I got a call from the president of the video label in New York, who said that he was disappointed in the acting ability of the lead of the film. At which point – I think at that moment – I knew that we should stop making these films. Because the second that I want some video distributor giving me an opinion on acting in a genre film, this simply meant to me that he was playing the Hollywood game and not understanding the commercial expediency of the product. So I told Walter, 'We're in trouble.'

WG: You have really two ways to judge whether you should make films, I guess, besides whatever non-economic reasons you might have. One is how much you make in relationship to your budget, and the second is how long it takes you to get the budget back in to make more. And both of those things started to be negatively affected. The money started coming in slower and came in less and our first response was to start to drop the budgets. And we ended up dropping the budgets dramatically; I think at the end we were shooting for probably 30, 35 per cent of what we started to shoot for.

AG: And we had other interests that sort of came about at the same time. We'd been with a couple of studio-level projects that we owned the rights to. We'd been in those kinds of Hollywood meetings with the rich and the powerful, and you really don't wanna be there if you're just regular guys. You just don't wanna be there; it's kind of repulsive. But we could have adjusted the budgets downward and made a different kind of film, or just continued to make the elements, just make a number of sexual interludes. And it certainly wouldn't have been what the earlier films were. But it was the people, I think, for me. Walter's much more analytical than I am. I was on the phone with them and the idea that every time I'm gonna have some sort of creative discussion with an idiot is . . . well *I'm* an idiot. Why don't I talk to myself?

LW: So had something shifted in the home viewing market at that point?

WG: No, what shifted was completely distribution.

AG: It had *nothing* to do with the audience. The audience is still there to this day. There are erotic films on whatever level that are still made to this day. We created some people's businesses because of the fact that we started Axis. We were in a groove for about three years or so, that we could almost do no wrong. Because truly with very, very little ego, you know, we solidified the genre. I don't think we created it, but we certainly made it more pronounced. We really liked the fact that once Walter said I'll risk the money, we didn't have that bullshit, the Hollywood bullshit. We just had to make the movie. I love being on movie sets. I probably feel somewhat nostalgic about it.

WG: *And in retrospect, I guess it's true whenever these things happen, like the writers in Paris between the wars didn't know that that was the place to be and write, and we didn't realise how fun it was to have that liberty to make, not a personal film, but a film that you can actually put your hands on and say, 'I want it to turn out different'. And you could actually make it turn out different without having to answer to any powers. That was a really good deal.*

AG: That's what I truly think from *our* perspective was in retrospect the greatest part of it. We didn't have to deal with those idiots – they're the worst scum of the earth. The way that you make films in the Hollywood system today is that you go to Harvard, and then you go to the mailroom at William Morris. All we did was we got these young kids come in the door, and we'd go just 'Write this, make sure it has this, and other than that . . .'

WG: *And what could be more fun?*

LW: **That is how the films have always looked to me. That they're not going through this anodyne process of streamlining and sawing off the rough edges, so the interesting things remain.**

AG: And having truly never articulated it, until you're here sort of pressing me to do so, if anything I would say *that* was it. It was like we had none of the bullshit – except our internal bullshit that we had with Greg always wanting to go over budget and make something different, and keep people out. . . .

WG: *It would be 9 o'clock in the office and Andy would come charging in with the budget going 'He wants FIFTEEN THOUSAND dollars to do a crane shot! It wasn't in the budget YESTERDAY!' But there was also about that period of time, '94, '95, there was a Springtime in Düsseldorf in 1944 feeling in the film industry. Every one of the big players that had raised money was going broke, and there was no way to continue to make a living in the independent film business. And it's surprising that while none of the production companies exist any more, some of the distribution companies that handled the licensing still managed to survive here seven or eight years. But it was like you'd get a call from an old friend saying, 'Oh man, I'm going to be in the neighbourhood can I come by?' And you'd sit down and say, 'Well, what do you think, CD-ROM, is it the future? And we heard about this thing called the internet, think there's room for us?' But there was no discussion like, 'We'd better make better films'. Because there just wasn't a way. The door was shut.*

AG: In retrospect we *could* have continued and re-envisioned or refocused the business end and had we had no other choice we probably would have. But for the most part we had a lot of fun doing it. Truly, it was a great time. In fact, in retrospect, although I never thought it at the time, we could do no wrong.

PART I

BLOCKBUSTER THRILLS: EROTIC *NOIR* IN THE MAINSTREAM

DEFINITIONS AND PRECURSORS

Part One of this book discusses how mainstream cinema embraced neo-*noir* in the 1980s and 1990s, threading the sexual through contemporary thriller narratives to form the theatrically released erotic thriller. Through analysis of films such as *Body Heat, Sea of Love, Body of Evidence, The Color of Night, Killing Me Softly* and *The Hot Spot,* I discuss how some significant *noir* character staples – the *femme fatale* and the fall-guy; the good-bad girl; the *homme fatal* and the female investigative heroine – are sexually reinflected to become key props of the genre. Building on this in analysis of some of the genre's biggest titles, chapter 3 addresses the popularisation of the genre in the mainstream through the work of some key figures, first a screenwriter, a director and an actor whose work has crossed and overlapped in a set of significant interconnected films (Joe Eszterhas, Paul Verhoeven and Michael Douglas collaborated on *Basic Instinct*); I will also look at other key titles which developed the genre profiles of these figures, particularly *Fatal Attraction, Showgirls, Jagged Edge, Jade* and *Disclosure.* Finally, I will develop earlier discussions of the *femme fatale* through analysis of three other stars whose star iconography was bound to their erotic thriller roles: Sharon Stone as the devil; Linda Fiorentino as the bitch; and Gina Gershon as a mainstream lesbian icon.

Because the brief of this book is wider than many cinema studies, encompassing the broadest spectrum of US films from independent and DTV works through to high-end theatrically-released A-movies, a definition of terms might be helpful. The films I discuss here date roughly from a period marked by the release of *Body Heat* in 1981 through the high-water mark of *Basic Instinct* ten years later, into a more consolidated period from 1992 onwards. If we choose to understand the period of the erotic thriller hitherto as a genre cycle, I would characterise it in these two arcs: building up from the early 1980s to the peak period of production in the first half of the 1990s (when the biggest theatrical releases appeared, and the DTV version of the genre boomed), then waning as the video industry stepped down production in the late 1990s, when the erotic thriller became a more consolidated choice for studio productions. As the century closed, fewer but bigger star-name productions established the genre as a safe commercial bet: *Eyes Wide Shut* (1999), *Original Sin* (2001), *Unfaithful* (2002) amongst others.

But these films have a complex ancestry, not least in a range of risky semi-exploitation movies from the 1970s, usually now remembered as precursors to neo-*noir* or as specific inspiration for later films. Clint Eastwood's *Play Misty For Me* (1971), a man-in-peril psycho-*femme* flick, was much cited in the reception around *Fatal Attraction* as a revenge saga charting the dangers of fooling around with unstable women who take their sexual rights too seriously (see Knee 1993: 91–2). In many ways it is a deeply problematic misogynist tract, drawing from *Psycho* and bleeding into the horror/slasher film as much as the sex-thriller. As a fable of the dark side of sexual liberation it also set running a social-political thread which is coterminous with the development of the genre: women's liberation brings sexual freedom (and censorship shifts enable its representation), but it also brings potentially violent demands and an exploration of the psychic fragmentations which underpin calls for subject-sovereignty. This was explored a little later in the decade in *Looking for Mr Goodbar* (1977), a female sexual-quest film in which Diane Keaton breaks free of her repressed home and throws herself onto the swingers scene, picking up a number of desirably dangerous men in the process. She is both the film's point-of-view focus and its eventual woman-in-peril, caught in an arousing conjunction of exploration and risk. Richard Gere, who features in an early role as one of the psycho-lovers Keaton samples, is a name that recurs across the genesis of this genre: In *Goodbar* he is a dangerous love object, a profile which is developed in Paul Schrader's *American Gigolo* in 1980, where he plays a male prostitute accused (and perhaps guilty) of murdering a client.[1] This sets rolling a number of fertile erotic thriller conventions, including the sex-worker in jeopardy, sex as a statement of style and class, and it foregrounds women as (potentially endangered, but enthusiastically participating) active sexual consumers of men (the promotional tag-line is a genre classic: 'He's the highest paid lover in Beverly Hills. He leaves women feeling more alive than they've ever felt before. Except one').[2] *American Gigolo* also tells the male sex object's side of a familiar erotic thriller story – the 'bored housewife' who strays into the arms of illicit pleasure. Perhaps the most fertile DTV narrative thread, this also manifests itself in a number of films about respectable women who moonlight as high-class hookers, a trope with its roots in another of the genre's disparate cinematic grandparents, Luis Buñuel's *Belle de Jour*.

More recently, Gere has taken on the role of spurned spouse who – like Anne Archer in *Fatal Attraction* – keeps the home fires burning when his wife strays, before killing her lover in *Unfaithful* (both films were directed by Adrian Lyne, the second perhaps answering some of the ideological problems posed by the first in its gender reversal and shift from erotic-*noir* into erotic-melodrama). The murderous though wholesome family man is prefigured by a darker role, bad cop family man Dennis Peck in Mike Figgis's *Internal Affairs*. Though the whole film is haunted by male anxieties about female infidelity and unfulfil-ment, it is Dennis who emerges as its sexual villain, killing and swindling in order to provide for the excessive needs of his proliferating family (nine chil-dren and four wives, three ex-, one current). Dennis's traditional paternalistic sense of duty is inextricably bound to his corrupt authority; his women are fucked and goaded into complicity with his criminality: there is a chilling machismo about his sexual incontinence. What seems at first like a standard *policier* becomes a twist on the *noir* staple of 'absent families' (Harvey 1998): here too much family has rendered Dennis pathological, an over-controlling working-class provider who can only be felled by the yuppies (as he calls them in his bitter dying speech) from internal affairs – a childless man (Andy Garcia's Raymond) and a childless lesbian (Laurie Metcalfe's Amy). If Dennis's sexual-ity is excessive, Raymond's becomes insufficient as the film proceeds, turning him into a classic erotic thriller bad husband ('We don't even fuck anymore' says his wife, a line written for her DTV sisters). Here, then, the good guy is anti-domestic and sexless, the bad guy over-familial and oversexed, a monster of polygymy. Two years later Gere was back in erotic thriller mode with a role as a duped male victim to a *femme fatale* double-act in *Final Analysis*, which I will be discussing below.

Eyes of Laura Mars (1978) also has an impressive production pedigree and an important role in the pre-ancestry of the erotic thriller. Its star, Faye Dunaway, had previously played the *femme fatale*-apparent in *Chinatown*, a crucial milestone in the development of neo-*noir* and, though not an erotic thriller, a retro-*noir* which replays the regular motif of cop/detective/law repre-sentative falling for the wrong woman.[3] *Laura Mars* also featured an up-and-coming Tommy Lee Jones, a big theme song by Barbra Streisand, risqué photographs by Helmut Newton (who provided Laura's photographic work), and stylish direction by Irvin Kershner, which deployed gloss and a veneer of erotic 'classiness' to deflect attention away from its sheer exploitation nastiness (it was written by king of slash John Carpenter). But its themes – chic voyeur-ism, dead sex-models, women imperilled by the sexualised gaze – feed straight into the genre. The blurb for the 2000 UK DVD release reads: 'Fashion photog-rapher Laura Mars (Faye Dunaway), world-renowned for her erotic portraits of transparently-gowned models in settings of urban violence, becomes the focal point for a series of bizarre murders.' Substitute the name of a DTV starlet (perhaps one of the Shannons: Whirry or Tweed) for Dunaway, and this would sit perfectly on the jacket of a 1990s low-budget erotic thriller. The original theatrical poster relied simply on a horror-inflected image of Dunaway's face,[4] suggesting that a DVD released in the wake of the erotic thriller trades off a more recent history than that which the film originally occupied. In its themes of visionary blindness (photographer Mars, though sighted, has her vision blanked out by a point-of-view image of the murderer committing his crimes as they happen) also feeds into films such as *Blink* and its DTV predecessor *Eyewitness to Murder* (1991),[5] as well as countless DTVs which feature

Peeping Tom-esque kinky glamour photographers as murderers or victims (*Die Watching, Body Shot, Carnal Crimes*).

More problematic – and indeed more interesting than all of these – is William Friedkin's *Cruising* (1980), arguably the erotic thriller's clearest starting-point. It was also the 'opening act in a decade-long controversy over sex and violence in the movies, particularly in films where the sex and violence were conjoined with each other' (Prince 2000: 343). Though *Cruising* was not called an erotic thriller on release, and has been called a whole lot of other things since ('leather-queen serial killer thriller' is a pretty accurate description [Burston 1998]), it is essentially an A-feature sleeper which critics only started waking up to once the gay political scandal had faded and the film came to be reassessed late in the century (see Kermode 1995; Burston 1998). In 1980, however, *Cruising* gave the genre its first headline-calibre scandal, and it gave American cinema a radical form of audience response – gay demonstrators targeted the location shoot in an unprecedented protest based on suspected homophobia in a film which hadn't yet been made.[6] Friedkin's cut was then savagely hacked in order to secure an R-rating, and cinemas were picketed by gay activists when the film was released. Though protests against *Cruising* concentrated on the bad press which would be visited upon gay culture in general by dramatic exposure of a violent sub-culture (the film is set in New York's S&M club scene), subsequent protests against other erotic thrillers took a similar form – this pattern of bad publicity (which does nothing but good for box office returns) was to be repeated with *Dressed to Kill, Crimes of Passion* and *Basic Instinct* in various measures. Only the perceived sexual blasphemy of *The Last Temptation of Christ* rivals the public outcry provoked by erotic thrillers in this period.

The (now) familiar story of a cop (Al Pacino) who goes sexually undercover, here posing as gay to infiltrate the S&M club culture and track a killer, *Cruising* is remarkable for a number of qualities, not least the fact that what has since become a heterosexual genre staple had a homosexual origin – the potential for the erotic dark side to transform its participant: Pacino's character discovers both his queer potential and his own potential murderousness ('a man becomes his own Nemesis' [Roberts 1980]). This motif was transformed into a straight fable in films such as Katt Shea Ruben's *Stripped to Kill* (female cop goes undercover as a stripper to track a murderer preying on strippers and discovers a new sexual potential), Greg Hippolyte's *Undercover* (female cop goes undercover as a hooker to track a murderer preying on hookers and discovers a new sexual potential), Harold Becker's *Sea of Love* (also starring Pacino, as a male cop who goes undercover in the lonely hearts singles scene and discovers a new sexual potential). None of these more recent titles put the undercover cop under suspicion of murder (as does *Cruising*), but all of them put him or her into dangerous if heterosexual scenarios – *Black Widow* is unusual in formulating an undercover story which is hesitantly lesbian. It is therefore all the more remarkable that in 1979 the gay community should be so vehemently opposed to the film simply on the grounds that it depicted a killer as gay, since it also did such interesting work with its uneasy star (as Friedkin testifies in his interview below), and established a genre blueprint. Indeed, the genre necessity that (to quote Catherine Tramell once again) 'somebody has to die' also means that somebody has to kill, and if a film is set in a gay sub-culture that somebody has to be either gay, homophobic or both. 'That bulge in your pants ain't a knife. Why don't we take a walk?' asks a guy as a pick-up line (the erotic thriller's version of Mae West's 'Is that a pistol in your pocket, or are you just pleased to see me?'). The penetration of sex and the penetration of knives in death is made particularly explicit in one subliminal shot Friedkin inserted, which juxtaposes a hardcore image of anal intercourse with a knife hitting a victim between the shoulder-blades. Whilst this might support one view of the film as equating homosexuality with pathology ('its lurid storyline suggests that gay sexuality is part of a milieu of violence, exploitation, and perversity' [Prince 2000: 344–5]), it also makes explicit the repeated dance of danger and desire in the genre as a whole. Friedkin justifies the subliminal as a way of ridiculing the ratings system – it was inserted, unseen by the censors, after they had demanded an alleged 40 minutes of cuts. The same might be said of another moment in the film, when a victim's blood splatters across a cinema screen onto which a porno film is being projected, at which point another subliminal, a close-up of a penis, is inserted into the film's fabric. If all of these interpretations of such outrageously salacious moments are equally valid, they reinforce the notion that this is a genre which can stir up a frenzy of opprobrium and censoriousness. For Friedkin, prohibition provokes, and though pornography is not his prime agenda, he will use it both to tell his story and offend his critics. He still relishes the extremity of the film and its response (even the final, R-rated cut was generally agreed to be nearer to an X film in content),[7] and has no truck with a notion that screen depictions of gays should 'demonstrate what nice people homosexuals really are' (Burston 1998: 24). The same could be said of Verhoeven discussing *Basic Instinct*, which twelve years later depicted a killer as bisexual. *Cruising* threw down a provocative gauntlet, suggesting ways in which the thriller could develop at the edges of a blockbuster-saturated market and beyond the bounds of family audiences. It is unfortunate that this remained largely unseen for a considerable time, with audiences blinded by the glare of its censorship and sexual scandal. Though pre-dating more high-profile erotic thrillers by up to a decade, *Cruising* signalled that the genre's criminal-sexual inflections, its sporadic flirtation with taboo, its obsession with the cinematic foreplay of voyeurism, were set to roll. These were tendencies which another major New Hollywood auteur, Brian De Palma, had begun to develop in his 1960s and 1970s work. I want briefly to pause on his 1980s films in order to trace one significant trajectory in the early development of the genre.

BRIAN DE PALMA: 'SEX IS TERRIFYING'

'Brian De Palma' as brand name and organising principle for a style and compulsively repeated set of cinematic obsessions underpins discussion of his films
in popular, critical and journalistic writings. One tag-line for *Dressed to Kill*
read 'The Style is Shocking/The Cut is Classic/The Look is De Palma' which
'insists upon De Palma's possession of the film' (Bryant and Pollock 1981: 25);
De Palma *means* classic (cutting?) shock to his purchasers. However, he certainly does not make 'just one film', in the formulation of Bertolucci, describing the ideal auteur figure: 'If we . . . put the films [of any single director] all
together we will have the figure of one man, of an auteur, the life of an auteur,
transferred in many different characters naturally. But the film is one film'
(quoted in Gelmis 1970: 171). (I will return to questions of auteurism and genre
when I look at the erotic thriller as an art-film later.) There are at least two De
Palmas, and various stages in a career trajectory: the post-Hitchcockian 'master
of suspense', director of genre works (mostly horror and thrillers, all amply
infused with overheated sexuality, which I read as proto-erotic thrillers), and
lately the studio hired hand, producing formula work such as *Mission:
Impossible*, *Bonfire of the Vanities* and *Mission to Mars*. As a genre director he
is something of an enigma: a consistent interest, for instance, in 'nightmares of
the soul' (as the *Dressed to Kill* Production Notes put it) is seen as auteurial
rather than generic. He wavers between, and exploits, suspense, thrillers,
horror, all frequently with the word 'sexy' thrown in; when critical categories
fail, writers fall back on the generic generalisations 'shocker' and 'chiller', both
– like thriller and erotic – terms of response, terms which promise some sensa-
tion-experience to a potential viewer. Movies which in another director's hands
would unproblematically be deemed erotic thrillers are here 'Brian De Palma
films'. Brown (1980) reads them as an effect of personal narcissism. For Pauline
Kael, a long-time supporter, genre facilitates directorial genius: 'He doesn't
have to move away from thrillers to prove he's an artist. In his hands, the thriller
form is capable of expressing almost everything – comedy, satire, sex fantasies,
primal emotions' (Kael 1980). Librach calls his films 'highly personal thrillers'
(1998: 171), and refers to a 'personal stamp of stylized erotica' (1998: 172);
these are genre films which manage to be *both* auteurial vehicles *and* cogent
sexual/political statements.

As Hitchcock's most celebrated son, De Palma obsessively reworks and revisits issues of voyeurism, psychic fragmentation and sexual fixation. Around the
time of *Body Double*'s release he told *Esquire* magazine, 'Sex is terrifying' (Pally
1984: 12), a concern which also underpins the anxieties of Hitchcock's work.
It is through De Palma's pervy, self-reflexive sex-crime films that we see most
clearly the debt the erotic thriller owes to Hitchcock. Though De Palma is frequently read as a genre auteur, none of his films up to *Femme Fatale* in 2003
had been explicitly packaged as an erotic thriller, though the UK press notes for
Body Double promised 'action, sensuality, suspense and entertainment', as well

as 'everything that people expect from a Brian De Palma movie'.[8] When he is ascribed a genre it is usually 'thriller' (though sometimes the Hitchcockian obsessiveness of his work seems to constitute itself as a genre category in its own right).[9] One writer called *Dressed to Kill* 'De Palma's most erotic film so far and . . . more to do with sex than murder' (Brosnan 1980: 15); another celebrated his penchant for 'erotic Grand Guignol' (Bilbow 1980: 17); a third termed his signature films 'unique black-humorous thrillers about the corrosion of sociosexual relations' (Librach 1998: 171). When he is directing at his most auteurist (in films such as *Sisters, Blow Out, Obsession, Dressed to Kill, Body Double, Femme Fatale*), he consistently links the violently sexual with the sexually violent, weaving scenarios of secrecy and neurosis through intricately twisting plots. His fascination with voyeurism spans his directing career, and though it no doubt underpins elements of his self-reflexive postmodernism (self-interrogating his position as controlling seer) as well as his left-liberal politics (surveillance as a formulation of political control, post-Kennedy, pre- and post-Watergate, as in *Greetings* and *Blow Out*), it is also a crucial prop of his psycho-sexual filmmaking. *Sisters* begins with a parodic female spectacle/male spectator scenario, which turns out to be a gameshow called *Peeping Toms. Hi Mom!* and *Greetings* feature Robert De Niro as an overt voyeur figure setting up sexual-visual scenarios – *Rear Window* revisited as pornography. De Palma has also occasionally encountered classification problems because of the way he pushes his scandalous subject matter to the fringes. One writer rather ambitiously claimed that he 'may be the first director to use pornography as a way of dramatizing the unconscious' (Denby 1980: 44). *Body Double* 'involves voyeurism, sexual paranoia, violent death, pornography, misdirection, and murder' (Hogan 1985: 45), a series of cinematic misdemeanours and connections which collectively come close to a definition of the erotic thriller. De Palma positions himself at the point where thrillers and pornography meet, a master-controller of suspense strategies who shows a developing interest in sexual difference, sexual violence and the sex industry itself.

This cluster of lurid concerns underpins De Palma's position on women. He is consistently charged with a redolent misogyny, largely because his female deaths look rather like punishments for sexual appetite: the question of whether he simply dramatises or positively relishes the uneasy position of women in sexual culture particularly taxed readers around the release of *Dressed to Kill*, which became something of a crisis text in issues of represented sexual violence, a *cause célèbre* for 1970s cultural feminism (see MacKinnon 1981; Ryan 1981). One (male) reviewer worried that 'women in the north of England [would] find little in it to entertain them, a feeling borne out by recent demonstrations of protest' (O'Sullivan 1981: 31) – *Dressed to Kill* signifies in a culture overshadowed by the spectre of the Yorkshire Ripper, a serial killer who preyed on women during the early 1980s. Another argued that *Dressed to Kill*'s heroine is really 'looking for the fatal Mr Goodbar' (Brien 1980). This was echoed by a gay male writer, who saw the film more as a critique of straight masculinity than a punishment of voracious femininity, though both were implicated in the generalised message about sexual peril: 'From *Anna Karenina* to *Looking for Mr Goodbar*, from the Bible to *Cruising*, society has taught us one lesson that continues to affect us even – and perhaps particularly – when we reject it: fucking around is dangerous' (Aitken 1981: 22). De Palma understood the cinematic potency of dangerous fucking, perhaps earlier than his feminist detractors.[10] This also became increasingly important to film studies in the AIDS-shaded culture of the late 1980s. Yet the auteur-inflected rhetoric of critical discourse often positions the director as murderer, holding him personally responsible for the deaths of his women (Brown 1980: 181). De Palma reports that his films' savage though sporadic violence towards women articulates a crisis moment when 'Women aren't going to make the terrible bargains they made in the past', whilst at the same time men 'find women's intelligence and aggression, their ambition, threatening' (Pally 1984: 14). Women are sliced with razors (*Dressed to Kill*), skewered with drills (*Body Double*), kidnapped and blown up (*Obsession*), strangled with wires and then 'decorated' with knife wounds in the shape of the Liberty Bell (*Blow Out*). He admits that part of the crime is opportunity – what one writer calls 'a kind of vulnerability that calls for abuse' (Matusa 1977: 33): 'I don't particularly want to chop up women but it seems to work,' he has said (Pally 1984: 17). Yet this exploitation strategy doesn't detract from his reputation as a serious director with a consistent set of cinematic concerns.[11] Whether his films expose or exploit the mechanisms of misogyny is debated in contemporary review material (Andrews 1985); De Palma justifies his work via genre history: 'I'm basically making . . . theatrical melodrama!' he says; 'I'm using a conventional genre – women in peril – which goes back to *The Perils of Pauline*!' (quoted by Librach 1998: 169). He is also fascinated by the control, and its lack, which is at the heart of sex and filmmaking: 'Sex is out of control,' he has said, but he also admits to being a director because it gives him control: 'I don't like to be out of control. I don't see scary films. . . . Why put yourself in a situation where you were out of control?' (Pally 1984: 14). This is De Palma the terrified masochist-turned-controlling monster, who fends off his fear of letting go by obsessing over his own control, and dramatising the plight of other men who have already lost it. The feminised/manipulated hero of *Body Double* was received as 'a loser, a *schlemiel* . . . a sucker' (Gill 1985), having 'a helpless, masochistic quality' (Denby 1984: 47) and compared to 'Hollywood's perennial fall-guy Elisha Cook Jnr' (French 1985b). The flip-side of sexism is then De Palma's interest in the demasculinised male as patsy or out-and-out gender-bender.

A number of these issues are crystallised in *Dressed to Kill*, a movie as problematic for censors as it was for feminists. It also occupies generically ambivalent territory: marketed as a 'classily' erotic suspense thriller (largely due to the presence of Angie Dickinson, returning to cinema after a decade spent as TV's *Police Woman*,[12] and the call-girl character played by Nancy Allen, who invests her earnings in shares and art-works), and received as a sexualised slasher-movie, it slips between marginally distinct critical categories such as horror and thriller, exploitation and art-cinema, exploration and arousal. Its opening sequence is a blueprint for an erotic thriller genre staple: the bored housewife neglected by her lousy husband. In De Palma's hands the spectacle of Kate (Angie Dickinson, with a body double) in the shower lustfully ogling her indifferent husband (and fantasising into existence his more interested substitute) becomes a partial tribute to Hitchcock; but shower scenes as sites of fulfilled lust or displayed frustration for women have also become a prime DTV erotic thriller motif. Kate offloads her sexual disappointment on to her shrink Dr Elliott (Michael Caine), has a brief hot fling with a stranger in a taxi, then at his apartment, and is slashed to death in an elevator. Having witnessed the aftermath of the murder, high class hooker Liz (Allen) teams up with Kate's son, a whiz at constructing surveillance systems, and catches the killer, who turns out to be Elliott in the guise of 'Bobbi', a blonde, bewigged female *alter-ego*. This shrink-killer of *Dressed to Kill*, a man-woman, Norman/Mother Bates character was, for Robin Wood (1986), symptomatic of a pervasive castration anxiety, and is a figure De Palma worries over throughout his directorial career.

Critics almost unanimously picked open *Dressed to Kill's Psycho* references (Dickinson in the shower; Dickinson the star being murdered halfway through; Allen as the Vera Miles figure, sorting out the mystery) and the *Rear Window* allusions (Kate's son spying on Liz and Elliott/Bobbi from across the distance). Hitchcock tropes characterise the history of De Palma's films (*Dressed to Kill* and *Sisters* 'are' *Psycho*; *Obsession* and *Body Double* 'are' *Vertigo*), but more interesting than ticking off the homage/plagiarism is examining the way in which De Palma shows a different route through from Hitchcock into contemporary cinema from that which has already been mapped. Whilst openly forging an equivalence between slashing and seduction, *Dressed to Kill* is not born of the same school as its 'teen scream' contemporaries working in the tradition of Mario Bava (such as *Halloween* or *Friday the 13th*). The stalk-and-slash film is usually read as emanating from *Psycho*, but it is only one of Hitchcock's 1980s generic legacies: Norman Bates' cinematic children may have found a logical home in the surreal horror of the 1970s and 1980s (with cult-killers such as Freddy Kruger, Jason Vorhees, Michael Myers), but his offspring also infiltrated neo-*noir*'s sexual thrillers. In fact, the sexual murders of the erotic thriller look far more like Hitchcock than does the high school mayhem of John Carpenter or Wes Craven. In Caine's Elliott/Bobbi, Norman Bates' natural heir comes out of the closet, but even before this what we might call a *Psycho*-sexual serial killer thread develops in the 1970s prototypes I discussed earlier (*Looking for Mr Goodbar, Eyes of Laura Mars, Cruising*). And later there is the serial killer in *Blink*, seeking to reassemble the donated organs of his dead love; or Anthony Perkins' own homage to his most famous character in *Crimes of Passion*. Even the butch/*femme* killer-women in *Basic Instinct* have something of the Norman Bates about them. Unlike the calculating lover-killers of *A Kiss Before Dying*, or *Jagged Edge* or *The Postman Always Rings Twice*, these figures murder (or seek to kill) out of incoherent sexual rage, often born of gender confusion. Such formations of chaotic passion do not sit happily alongside the slasher film's suburban horror fairy tales featuring comic monsters like Kruger, Vorhees or Myers – figures sent up in the parodic B-films on which John Travolta works in *Blow Out*. The sexual *Psycho*-killer lives and breathes the generic elements of erotic suspense/melodramas. As different as Norman Bates, 'Bobbi' and Catherine Tramell are, they are all murderers of (and in) the sexual revolutions of feminism and gay rights, and they all inhabit urban *noir*-scapes. Their motives concern sexual fury, not avarice or supernatural retribution. The slasher film makes Norman Bates' legacy demonic; the erotic thriller makes it sexual-political, especially in De Palma's confused visions.

De Palma's films have also become ready props for the cultural scandals of their day, which makes the discourses of reception material particularly interesting – *Dressed to Kill* and *Body Double* run a close second to premiere scandal movies such as *Basic Instinct*, *Cruising* or *Fatal Attraction* in their ability to push a culture's rawest buttons. The director has said that he made *Body Double* deliberately to up the ante following the infamy of *Dressed to Kill*: 'So after the battles, which had started with *Dressed to Kill*, I said, "OK, you want to see violence? You want to see sex? Then I'll show it to you," and I went out and made *Body Double*!' (Boorman and Donohue 1996: 32). *Body Double* takes *Vertigo* and *Rear Window* and puts them to work in the context of a 1980s dark satire on the movie industry, incorporating horror B-movies and hardcore filmmaking in its investigation of sexual obsession. Down on his luck actor Jake Scully is first seen losing his starring role in the kind of sexy B-movie I will discuss in Part Two (a film-within-a-film called *Vampire's Kiss*), when his claustrophobia gets the better of him (a fatal flaw like James Stewart's vertigo in Hitchcock's film). A fellow actor, Sam Bouchard, offers him the use of a ritzy panopticon-like flat in the Hollywood hills ('What a set-up!' he exclaims, impressed at the revolving circular bed, though of course it's him who's being set up). From here he spies (*à la Rear Window*) on a sexy female neighbour, Gloria Revelle, who does a masturbation dance in front of her window every night. Lured by the view, he subsequently witnesses Gloria being impaled by a drill, a witness position for which he was being set up all along.[13] But viewing a late-night porn cable channel, he discovers that a porn actress (Holly Body, played by Melanie Griffith) masqueraded as Gloria in the sexy dancing scenes in order to get Jake visually hooked so he would be in prime position to witness Gloria's death (Holly is therefore a kind of hardcore version of Judy in *Vertigo*). Scully pursues Holly into the porn industry and does a brief turn as a hardcore actor, catches the murderer and cures his claustrophobia so that he can return to B-acting. It's all very contrived and highly charged, the thrill resting more in set-piece scenarios than plausible narrative.[14]

Body Double takes De Palma most securely into erotic thriller terrain. 'This is going to be the most erotic, surprising and thrilling movie I know how to make,' promised the director in the press pack. 'It's a wild, erotic rollercoaster ride with many twists and turns' (Murrey 1985). The discourse of sexual thrill (promising a cinema of attractions) is reproduced by contemporary reviewers: one described it as a 'surreal sex thriller' (*Video Business* 1985); one headline ran 'Fatal Allure' (Barkley 1985). For Ackroyd it incorporates softcore pornography, elements 'of the "horror film" and of any cheap detective series' (1985: 34). Erotic thriller staples which De Palma bequeaths to the genre's DTV form include an interest in the culpability of voyeurism, which functions as a sly interrogation of the film's own form. If everybody in *Dressed to Kill* was watching everybody else (Ryan 1981), in *Body Double* voyeurism becomes a form of self-critique, which also takes on the audience's viewing position. A cop says to Scully after Gloria's death, 'As far as I'm concerned you're the real reason Gloria Revelle got murdered': anyone who looks with pleasure, including the film's own audience, is culpable. Looking but not acting is presented as a dangerous compulsion, a message which resounds throughout Hitchcock (think of Grace Kelly's critique of 'Rear Window ethics' in *Rear Window*, later parodied in a Jim Wynorski film), as well as a powerful sub-genre of voyeur-horror following *Peeping Tom*. But *Body Double* makes voyeurism also reflect on the process of filmmaking, which for one critic makes it the exemplary LA movie, dramatising the bleeding of Hollywood into architecture and psyche:

> *Body Double* is about Los Angeles, about the eroticized way of life, partly created by the media culture, in which exhibitionist and voyeur are linked by common need. The people live in houses with huge windows; they cruise one another insolently, unafraid of being watched as they watch; privacy is meaningless – there is only the sexiness of endless scrutiny and quick encounter. (Denby 1984: 49)

De Palma's appropriation of *Rear Window*'s visual ethic thus enacts a number of critical shifts: if *Rear Window* is New York, *Body Double* is LA, not the *noir*-LA of shadows, but a neo-*noir* plate-glass formation of over-illumination and exposure, facilitating the encounters Denby describes. This is, as Robin Wood puts it, De Palma making 'the connection between voyeurism and the visual media explicit' (1986: 142): if *Rear Window* is photography, *Body Double* is cinema, cable TV and video; Jake is a B-film actor, a voyeur in a number of technologies (with his telescope, his cable channels and his VCR rewind/fast-forward functions; he even features in the musical sequence which forms a brief surreal break in the middle of the movie, Frankie Goes to Hollywood's 'Relax').[15] The whole premise of *Body Double* is inspired by the situation De Palma encountered in *Dressed to Kill*, when Angie Dickinson had a body double standing in for her in the nude scenes. De Palma concludes the film squarely in exploitation territory, when Scully, back on set as a vampire, shoots his shower scene with a body double, whose close-up bloodied breasts form the film's final shot. This follows a series of scenarios dealing with fakes and mimicry, the fake standing in for the real and revealing the real to be fake, which contemporary critics foregrounded as a central issue for the film as exemplifying De Palma's postmodernism.[16] Holly masquerades as Gloria; the killer – Gloria's husband – masquerades as an actor in order to lure Jake into the position of witness, then masquerades (wearing the mask of) an Indian thief in order to kill his wife. The fictionalisation of self is underlined when, in an absurd 'Scooby Doo' moment of revelation, the mask is pulled off and he complains, 'You've ruined my surprise ending!' But we might also see the film as a form of De Palma 'body doubling' for Hitchcock, taking his premises into more sexually explicit territory. *Body Double* is an exercise (as Jones puts it) in 'watching De Palma plagiarise himself plagiarising Hitchcock' (1985: 17); 'De Palma will become Hitchcock will become De Palma, *ad infinitum*', writes another UK critic (Combs 1980: 213). Plagiarism itself becomes a form of masquerade (De Palma becomes Hitchcock), and – ironically – takes on the aura of an auteurial badge of recognition.

Like *Body Double* after it, *Dressed to Kill* courted controversy by presenting the MPAA Ratings board with images and dialogue which suggested an X-rating rather than the box office-friendly R-rating: De Palma submitted to cuts in order to secure the latter (see Lucas 1980; Frederick 1980). *Body Double* was yoked to two prominent mid-1980s issues, pornography and video viewing of violent material, though reception discourses differ between the UK and the USA. It was released in the UK simultaneously on video and in cinemas,[17] with a slight cut made to the video version. UK critics therefore saw it as a test-case for the recently passed Video Recordings Act (VRA), which sought to control the classification and availability of controversial materials for home viewing, particularly by children (see Perry 1985, Waymark 1985; Walker 1985b). Andrews, addressing the uneasy mix of lurid content and auteurist reputation, suggested that 'with De Palma . . . a video nasty becomes a *thinking* man's video nasty' (1985: 27). Two discussions yoked *Body Double* with Russell's *Crimes of Passion* (placing two films together in this way aids 'moral panic' discourses by giving the illusion of a rising tide of filth); one reflecting not on the VRA but similar anxieties in the USA about cable channels piping sexual violence direct into people's living rooms for a fee (Campbell 1985: 7), the other – written for *Time* Magazine – calling for 'a new rating, between R and X, for serious nonporn sex films. How about an S?' (Corliss 1984: 36).[18]

But if the VRA focused critical attention in the UK, the Minneapolis Ordinance, which was passed in 1984 and sought to make pornography prosecutable under human rights legislation,[19] formed a context for discussion of De Palma in the USA. Inspired by *Body Double*, *Film Comment* ran substantial pieces in two consecutive issues, the first containing excerpts from the film's screenplay ('Brian's Body', *Film Comment* 20, 5, Sept./Oct. 1984: 9–11) plus an interview with the director focusing largely on questions of pornography and liberty (Pally 1984); the second containing responses from fourteen critics, pro- and anti-censorship feminists, pornographers and lawyers, to the porn industry in general and *Body Double* in particular. The question of whether works of art-cinema could also be prosecuted under the Minneapolis ruling was at the forefront of these discussions, foregrounding issues around the judgement of mainstream cinema's pornographic content. For his part, De Palma refutes the link between pornography and violence to women, with reference again to the self: 'I've seen a lot of movies and a lot of porn, and it's not made me violent to women in *any* way' (Pally 1984: 14). Clearly the sexual politics of violent and erotic movies is rather more complex than this. De Palma has also said that he doesn't think his films are going to provoke arousal, though at least one critic went beyond generalised gestures towards his deployment of softcore technique in *Dressed to Kill* to argue that he 'is exploring the very experience of movies, recognizing . . . the eroticisim of the cinema and its invitation to voyeurism and masturbation' (Mackinnon 1981: 45).

Yet rare now is the kind of political arousal discussed above; though tabloid moral panics against particular films are still relatively commonplace, members of the public seldom stir themselves to picket a cinema or a film set. *Femme Fatale* (2003) is arguably De Palma's most explicit film, at least in one sequence, when Rebecca Romijn-Stamos strips and has sex on a pool table, which is much more revealing than comparable sequences in his earlier films. But it is not a scene of sexual violence, and audiences have changed: De Palma could be confident that he would face none of the protests which greeted *Dressed to Kill*, and the sexuality is legitimised by the ultimate knowledge that Romijn-Stamos is cavorting in fetishistic underwear as part of her own self-made fantasy. The relative cases of *Dressed to Kill* and *Femme Fatale*, as texts and events pitched at either end of the erotic thriller's history hitherto, tell a significant story of shifts in tolerance and classification boundaries.

A number of issues raised by De Palma's profile – about genre and auteurism, about generic hybridity, about shock – run through this book. Until the DTV release of *Femme Fatale* in the UK in 2003, De Palma was also a resolutely mainstream director, and his work in the genre has done much to position it on theatrical screens. But are these films blockbusters? I have called this section 'Blockbuster thrills' even though none of the films I will discuss below are strictly speaking blockbusters in the critically debated sense of the term, and this is as true of the mass-marketed *Basic Instinct* as it is of small-scale movies like *Romeo is Bleeding*. In fact, as mainstream films dealing with adult subjects, these might be said to be anti-blockbuster. None of these films commands the vast budgets required by special effects technology as an action adventure title would, nor have their stars demanded salaries at the very top end of the scale for these roles. They are not 'front-loaded' as blockbusters, with the expectation of vast returns on the opening weekends, nor are they what Schatz calls 'super-blockbusters'; most are mid-range films, 'mainstream A-class star vehicle[s] with sleeper-hit potential' (1993: 35).[20] Wyatt's definition is more broad church, and goes some way towards supporting my title. For him a blockbuster is 'a pre-sold property (such as a best-selling novel or play), within a traditional film genre, usually supported by bankable stars (operating within their particular genre) and director' (1994: 78). This certainly defines some of the A-movies I discuss here, though not all. Wyatt also calls *Fatal Attraction* and *9½ Weeks* high-concept blockbusters, though this may be retrospectively predicated on their subsequent success. Yet both films, by virtue of their sexual content, also specifically exclude the market central sector, teens and children. Even if an erotic thriller is contractually bound to conform to an R-rating for its US theatrical release, it is still not mainstream teen fare. Unlike front-loaded blockbusters, erotic thrillers are also relatively cheap to make; a blockbuster proper would demand a return on the massive investment of its creation by 'aiming at not just the largest possible audience . . . but *all* audiences' (Corrigan 1998: 47).[21] By their very nature, sexual films can never reach all audiences, which makes their story of limited, specifically targeted material securing the attention (and affection) of its viewers (albeit over a longer time-scale), especially fascinating in a Hollywood enthralled by the lure of opening weekend lucre. *Cruising*, then, also might be said to have carved out the niche the theatrically-released erotic thriller came to occupy, developing Friedkin's interest in making adult films dealing with tough subjects (X material in all but rating – *The French Connection*, *The Exorcist*), which then find a wide audience for new dark sexual stories (even if this is not the universal audience of the light family story).

The baseline definition of an A-list film, for the purposes of this discussion, therefore, derives from mode of distribution (though this eventual destiny determines everything about a film's scale of budget, production practices and its nature as text). The world and cultural work of theatrically-released erotic thrillers is in itself a broad church (from expensively formulaic studio fare to cheap or innovative indies), but it provides a basis for comparison with the direct-to-video films I will look at later. A film which is destined for a theatrical release is formally as well as economically a particular kind of film: it will generally have spent a long time in pre-production; is perhaps based on a script which has either been produced by a name writer (in the erotic thriller's case, this is Eszterhas) or has been subject to extensive development; will secure appearances by established stars who work in a variety of genres and could command some control over the final cut; and it may be promoted in terms of the director's name rather than as a genre product. It may be subject to saturation booking and marketing, guaranteed a large-scale national release, all predicated on a budget which can run to striking hundreds if not thousands of prints and expensive advertising campaigns, with a view to getting as many people as possible past the box office for the opening weekend figures. The DTV film is none of these things. In its 'purest' form it 'knows' from the moment of its short pre-production phase (DTV films often dispense with script-doctoring and other preparation) that it will never achieve a theatrical release, video copies will proliferate, but prints will not be struck, marketing will be targeted at the video trade so that the videos walk out of the rental shop door. A has-been star on the video jacket might help to drive it on its way.

Eventually, DTV stars, directors, video genres emerge within this specific market (fuelled by an enthusiastic web-based fan culture, rather than serious analysis in print film journalism), again giving the DTV film form a different tone and quality. As we have seen, films which consumers think of as DTV (because they were unaware of them until they appeared on the video store shelves) *have* been granted a very limited theatrical release, which functions solely as a publicity platform. For the purposes of Part One, however, I am not including these as mainstream theatrically-released products, as – save this small cinematic exposure – they do not operate primarily in the mainstream market: production budgets and time-scales are generally lower than the films I am considering here, they draw on B- rather than A-list actors and directors, and are often not reviewed in the week of release by the mainstream press. A-list erotic thrillers expect a serious return at the theatrical box office (even if their primary revenue eventually comes from video and other ancillary sales), and operate in a mainstream media reception context. B-movie erotic thrillers operate in a different reception environment, are marketed to video dealers and are reviewed in only a few print media contexts (*Sight and Sound*'s 'Video Premiere' column; Kim Newman's Video Dungeon in *Empire* in the UK) or on dedicated film websites. One honourable exception to this is *The Last Seduction*, which premiered first on TV, for various funding reasons. Despite this technicality (which denied Linda Fiorentino the chance of an Oscar nomination for what most reviewers regarded as 1994's powerhouse female performance), *The Last Seduction* has been received as the exemplary 'quality' mainstream erotic thriller. However, few critics explicitly compared it to its high and low stablemates. Kim Newman was unique in pinpointing what distinguishes its director's fascinating neo-*noir* portfolio:

> John Dahl has developed an interesting sub-category of medium-budget, moderately starry trick thriller. Without the baroque overkill of *Basic Instinct* or the top-shelf sleaze of Gregory Hippolyte's direct-to-video silicone slashers, Dahl redeems the 'erotic thriller'. (Newman 1994a: 44)

Though Newman's is primarily a judgement of quality and taste, it is also a useful identification of the genre's stratification, how similarly sexy *noirish* thrillers are nevertheless separated across zones of distribution, budget, star prominence, into categories we take as innate but which prove more slippery the closer you look. In 1993 I wrote that *Basic Instinct* is a DTV film with lots of money thrown at it; some DTV films are also clearly blockbusters in disguise and on the cheap. *The Last Seduction* is neither – and both.

The erotic thriller runs across and through all of these forms. 'Mainstream' or 'big budget' does not necessarily mean 'quality product' or 'original script'. Mainstream genre works can be (perhaps must be) remarkably repetitive; changes of director or cast seem to make little difference to the cocktail of sexual tropes, visual obsession and narrative twists. A figure such as Joe

Eszterhas has made a vast fortune identifying these elements and putting them repeatedly to work. Eszterhas writes the most successful sex-crime films for an age of softcore acceptability, and he has most recently re-read his own erotic thriller work as the most appropriate entertainment form for an age dominated by political sleaze. All of the films I look at in Part One are directed, written by and usually star men. A small proportion of these theatrically-released films centre if not on women's issues, then on women as the focus of narrative identification and sympathy. Such is the condition of new Hollywood that the biggest films I discuss are male-helmed (though there are singular cases, such as Paramount's Sherry Lansing, in which a woman produces or executive produces). However, I hope to redress this balance by looking later at the erotic thriller also as a form in which women writers, directors and stars have excelled, and at the genre as (sometimes) a new form of women's cinema.

The mainstream erotic thrillers I discuss here are seldom what Thomas Schatz calls 'the high-cost, high-tech, high-stakes blockbusters, those multipurpose entertainment machines that breed music videos and soundtrack albums, TV series and videocassettes, video games and theme park rides, novelizations and comic books' (1993: 9–10). Though a few of them (such as *Dressed to Kill*) *become* amongst the biggest films of their year, this is usually achieved by good word-of-mouth and by press discussion yoking a film to a key talking-point issue or scandal. However, erotic thrillers are also a riskier investment as far as the international marketplace is concerned: though action thrillers are good international sellers, the erotic thriller's sexual content means that sometimes, however stringently films are censored, they will not be acceptable to some cultures. So what makes them 'talkies' in one culture (*9½ Weeks'* refrigerator sex, for instance, or *Basic Instinct* crotch-shots, or *In the Cut*'s fellatio) may make them unmarketable uncut elsewhere. Nevertheless – as we saw in relation to *Fatal Attraction* – highly public scandal (and the accompanying high box office returns) has favoured (or dogged) mainstream erotic thrillers in a way which smaller straight-to-video productions could never hope for. Writers such as Wyatt (1994) and McLean and Cook (2001) have shown how movies court controversy and become vivid conduits for cultural contention, functioning to expose the relationship between film text and social context in a blazingly public fashion. Perhaps more than any other genre, 'talking point' erotic thrillers attract hot contemporary issues: yoke your erotic thriller to a sexy cultural anxiety, or authenticate the sex in your movie with reference to supposedly 'serious' social concerns and you have a marriage of image and issue made in PR heaven. Though few mainstream erotic thrillers start life as high-concept movies in the strict sense outlined by Wyatt, a good number of them shape up into prime 'talkies' – films which through their 'discussability' achieve the heady position of being debated in newsprint in places other than the film review columns (one measure of a film's success as a 'talkie'). *Disclosure* rode its steamy sexual promises on the back of a serious issue about reverse sexual harassment, its PR campaign targeting women's' magazines as much as film journalists. *Indecent Proposal* spawned discussion about how much you would charge to wreck your marriage and sleep with Robert Redford – Diane (Demi Moore) charges $1million (though UK comedian Jo Brand quipped that she'd shag him for a tenner), as is appropriate to the high-stakes spending pattern of the blockbuster in content (looks expensive) and receipt (becomes lucrative).[22] *Indecent Proposal* makes it into *Variety*'s $100 million-plus grossing movies list at number 143, on the strength of its talking-point issue-tainment value. *E.T. the Extra-Terrestrial*, *Ghostbusters* or *Batman* may have been bigger films in terms of budget, synergistic potential and promotional campaigns than *Fatal Attraction*, *Basic Instinct* or *9½ Weeks*, but it is the latter films which have generated the most copy as vehicles for burning concerns. Of course, *E.T.* and its brethren made more money: if the 'talkie' status of a film doesn't follow through at the box office, it may as well not be talked about at all. The chances are, however, that the more a film becomes 'discussable', the bigger its returns will be: *Basic Instinct* was the sixth biggest movie of 1992, a strongly sexual title competing at the top of its game with the big boys of sci-fi and family-fare action-adventure.[23] Also known as 'watercooler movies' (so called because – as with hot TV episodes from the night before – they are discussed the next day at work over the watercooler), talk-issues turn films into slowly gestating 'sleepers'. In the US and the UK the most successful theatrically-released erotic thrillers have been 'sleepers', films which don't necessarily command a huge opening weekend (as a calculated blockbuster must), but which end up with sustained cinematic runs generated by audiences who come back for repeated viewings (*Fatal Attraction* and *9½ Weeks* all benefited from viewers returning with spouses or friends).[24] Perhaps the single exception to this is *Basic Instinct*, which is the nearest the erotic thriller gets to blockbuster status. With a massive publicity campaign fuelled by Joe Eszterhas's record-breaking fee, Michael Douglas's return to the genre and ample scandal surrounding its production (picketed by both women and gay activists), *Basic Instinct* was the kind of film which could justify blockbuster distribution strategies and expense. In its mainstream form the erotic thriller is not usually born high-concept, but rather it becomes so through the process of release and reception. This is one area which makes the erotic thriller so rewarding for reception analysis, and one reason why I am interested in what these films have come to signify culturally in the context of a history of the genre.

The erotic thriller is well positioned to exploit this extra-cinematic promotional potential, with its mixture of sex, violence and gender concerns. Cases of films associated with the genre which were promoted or received more as examples of 'issuetainment' than as key marks of cinematic quality provide interesting slices of contemporary cinema history: 'talkie' erotic thrillers have been linked to contemporary debates around the dangerous influences of pornography and cinematic violence (*Dressed to Kill*, *Crimes of Passion*); the 'mainstreamisation' of sadomasochism (*Body of Evidence*, *9½ Weeks*); vanilla lesbianism (*Basic Instinct*, *Bound*); the failing or shored-up family unit

(*Unfaithful* and *Fatal Attraction* again). Action-adventure may be the genre guaranteeing most dependable box office returns, but the erotic thriller, with its ability to prise open our niggling anxieties about sexual identity and its uneasy challenge to work, family and power, has produced some of the most cogent debates in a wider, extra-cinematic arena.

I want now to set out some of the prime constituents of the mainstream erotic thriller, before proceeding to a closer look at the Eszterhas–Verhoeven–Douglas constellation, and then engaging in an analysis of three key erotic thriller female stars: Stone, Fiorentino and Gershon.

NOTES

1 *American Gigolo* makes play of the frame in which Julian (Gere) is caught ('I think I'm in a frame . . . All I see is the frame') – he asks Leon why *him* and is told, 'Because you were framable, Julian. You stepped on too many toes.' However, Julian asserts an *übermensch* quality which suggests he is also above morality: 'Some people are above the law,' he tells the police, and when his confidant says, 'You did it, didn't you? The Ryman killing. Don't worry . . . it doesn't matter', he neither denies nor affirms his innocence. Julian may then be feminised in his ambivalent relationship to guilt; like the women of *Basic Instinct*, though innocent he may be sexually guilty anyway.

2 See poster reproduction, and discussion of its negotiating of *noir* and style, in Wyatt (2003: 121, 119).

3 *Chinatown* is also a film which – like the more recent *Mulholland Falls* (1996) – seems to be about one thing but is actually about another: though it foregrounds a mystery about water supplies (in *Mulholland Falls* this is an investigation of a dead woman who slept with important men), it is really about illicit, incestuous sex (*Mulholland Falls* turns into a fable about atomic experimentation).

4 See Wyatt (2003: 136–8) for a reproduction and discussion of this.

5 In Jag Mundhra's *Eyewitness to Murder*, which Joe Bob Briggs inimitably refers to as 'the first erotic thriller for the handicapped', a woman (Sherilyn Wolter) goes blind at a crime-scene, and then has an affair with the investigating cop (Andrew Stevens). In *Blink* Madeleine Stowe's blindness is cured, but her view of the killer is subject to a movie disease which distorts and delays what she sees.

6 Protests against both *Cruising* and *Basic Instinct* targeted the illusion-making processes of Hollywood: in production *Cruising* protestors 'did everything in their power to disrupt filming, blowing whistles to interrupt the sound takes and shining mirrors to break up the lighting scheme' (Burston 1998: 24). *Basic Instinct*'s opponents picketed cinemas with signs designed to dispel the production of suspense, reading 'Catherine did it!'

7 The MPAA 'effectively admitted that an X-rated film went into national release with an R-rating' (Prince 2000: 348); *Variety* wrote: 'To put it bluntly, if an R allows the showing of one man greasing his fist followed by the rising ecstasy and pain of a second man held in chains by others, then there's only one close-up left for the X', *Variety*, 13 February 1980, p. 16, quoted by Prince (2000: 345–6).

8 UK press notes, archived at the BFI Library (Murrey 1985).

9 Almost every reviewer of De Palma since the early 1970s has noted the Hitchcock connection. One reviewer of *Sisters* insisted that it was impossible to make thrillers without visiting Hitchcock first: 'De Palma is merely showing us that if one wants to make a first-rate thriller, one <u>must</u> imitate Hitchcock, for he is the very definition of the genre' (McCarty 1973: 28, underline in original). Debates around his genre packaging seem to say more about the slipperiness of genre than the consistency of

De Palma: MacKinnon, for instance, writes: 'If *Carrie* and *Dressed to Kill* are of the horror genre, too violent and dark to be classified with the more extrovert "thriller," much of their force lies in those passages where a quite different tradition, that of romantic melodrama, seems to be invoked' (1981: 43).

10 This was two years prior to the important feminist collection, *Pleasure and Danger* – papers from the 1982 conference 'Towards a Politics of Sexuality' at Barnard College, New York – which developed influential arguments around perversion and consent.

11 Pally notes that even though De Palma's films are 'redolent with the bouquet of sex and violence' they nevertheless attract 'the serious discussion of critics' (1984: 12). Others, such as Malcolm (1985c) and Perry (1985b), still protest that his films nevertheless present a manifest dislike of women. Asselle and Gandhy (1982) report on the various protests against *Dressed to Kill* which accompanied its release, at the National Film Theatre in London and marches in New York. Charles Hirsch, a long-time collaborator and the producer of De Palma's 1968 film *Greetings*, justified its themes thus: 'We [Hirsch and De Palma] both like to screw girls, so the girl-chasing part of the three guys' obsession in *Greetings* was easy enough. And I'm a bit of a voyeur. But Brian's the real voyeur – so that element was Brian's contribution' (Gelmis 1970: 57) Asselle and Gandhy do give De Palma the benefit of the doubt, however, preferring to read his sexual violence generically rather than personally, and seeing *Dressed to Kill* as a crisis-text provoking 'urgent discussion of the problematic connection between sexuality and aggression' (1982: 143).

12 It hardly needs saying that the move back to film from TV is for Dickinson a move from authoritative agent of the law (as *Police Woman*) to sexual victim.

13 This lurid death is sent up in Reiner's *Fatal Instinct*, which promises a more customary erotic thriller murder (Kate Nelligan 'doing' Barbara Stanwyck says to her lover, 'Maybe I'll just screw you to death') before she kills him with a drill.

14 De Palma aficionados and critics read this complexity in terms of the auteur-genre brand. One reviewer notes that, as in Hitchcock's films, 'the story, although important, is secondary to the bizarre situations created within that narrative' (Baxter 1985: 36); another finds that 'the pleasure is in watching [the films'] construction rather than in their believability' (Hugo 1989: 60).

15 As a coda to some of the censorship questions the films under question here have raised, 'Relax', as a single and a music video, were both also banned from airplay by the BBC at the time of their original release because of their sexual content. J. Hoberman sees the inclusion of 'Relax' in *Body Double* as part of a generalised obsession with video 'as form, technology, and consumer item. De Palma makes witty use of the fast-forward scan mode, sets a comic scene in the adult section of Tower Records' (1984: 67).

16 See Hoberman (1984); Gill (1985) and Usher (1985).

17 Distributors sometimes release a film simultaneously on video and theatrically, or on dates very close to each other, when it is thought that although a film might bomb theatrically, a limited theatrical release will publicise video sales. According to Malcolm (1985c), there were no press preview screenings of *Body Double*, a strategy usually adopted to minimise negative press prior to the opening weekend.

18 This was answered in 1990 with the introduction of the NC-17 rating.

19 For a discussion of the Minneapolis Ordinance and its significance for feminism, see Williams (2002). As with a number of filmic investigations of the porn industry which aren't in themselves pornographic, liberal critics generally concluded that (in Hugo's words), '*Body Double* is not a pornographic film but it does . . . cause the audience to think about the fact of what attracts some of us towards pornography' (1989: 61).

20 Schatz defines 'super-blockbusters' as huge hits which, particularly in the early 1980s, 'tended to dominate the marketplace doing well over $100 million and far outdistancing other top hits': 'From 1986 to 1990, however, the number of super-

blockbuster hits dropped while the number of mid-range hits earning $10 million or more in rentals increased significantly, as did the number returning $50 million or more – still the measure of blockbuster-hit status' (1993: 26).

21 Corrigan continues: 'With blockbusters, what begins as an attempt to target the teenage audience quickly becomes an attempt to absorb as many other groups as possible within that mass; it becomes the only methodology that makes sense to a conglomerate's bottom line' (1998: 47). Big erotic thriller titles need a different strategy, since they cannot depend on teenage audiences, even though most must first of all secure at least an R-rating in the US.

22 *Indecent Proposal* also spawned at least one DTV imitator, *Sexual Roulette*, which reverses the prostitution pact by featuring a rich woman (Tane McClure) in the Robert Redford role, and a man (Tim Abell) as the husband who has to perform sexual favours in order to have his gambling debts paid off.

23 The five titles which grossed more were resolutely family fare: *Batman Returns*, *Home Alone 2*, *Lethal Weapon 3*, *Sister Act* and *Waynes World*. See '92's Pix: Putting it in Gross Terms', *Variety*, 4 January 1993, archived at www.variety.com.

24 In his brief discussion of 'sleepers', Schatz (1993: 27) predicts that surprise hits will inevitably mutate into blockbuster sequels on the basis of proven popularity. In the case of the erotic thriller, however, the sequel has only thrived in DTV form; *Basic Instinct 2* has been in discussion since *Basic Instinct 1*; Verhoeven is no longer involved, but *Risk Addiction* is in pre-production as a stand-alone project with a newly named main character.

2. *FEMMES FATALES*, FALL-GUYS AND PARANOID WOMEN: SEXUAL AND NARRATIVE BLUEPRINTS

1: Neo-porno *femmes fatales*

In many ways the *femme fatale is* the erotic thriller, central to a sexual-action-oriented genre focused on spectres of violent, eroticised death. Erotic thrillers may be organised around the point of view of a male victim (like the 'victim *noir*' narratives of the 1940s and 1950s [Horsley 2001: 69]), but if one had to choose they are more sadistically than masochistically focused. Even when a film's point of view is the manipulated male, its point of interest is sexual activity rather than passivity: sexually aggressive characters usually eclipse the sufferings of the target, becoming the prime figures of interest. In this sense erotic thrillers are grosser, simpler, more open (and perhaps openly sadistic) sexual fantasies than their more twisted, self-denying or despising *noir* antecedents; unlike 'victim *noir*', the erotic thriller seldom wallows in the gutter of abjection with the male protagonists discussed by Frank Krutnick. The *femme fatale* may be multi-generic, having, as Chris Straayer puts it, 'the ability to contribute a *noir*ish quality to any genre' (1998: 161), but her role in sex-thrillers is historically determined. In classic *noir* she was 'a kind of visual shorthand for dangerous attraction and steamy corruption' (Horsley 2001: 130); in the newly undefeatable incarnation she often takes in the erotic thriller, she intensifies a potent cocktail of sex and crime. In her most aggressive, amoral incarnation she is more post-*femme* than classic *femme fatale*.

Discussions of *film noir* frequently conflate analysis of key narrative tropes with a taxonomy of character types, and contemporary sex-*noirs* have rearranged the stereotypical sexy, hardboiled usual suspects. Not surprisingly for a book which discusses sex thrillers featuring aroused and arousing heroines or anti-heroines, I will continue to worry away at the term *femme fatale*, which has never been an easy one for film theorists. Key writings on this figure include the pathbreaking British Film Institute collection *Women in Film Noir* (re-edited with neo-*noir* inflections in 1998), which set rolling a number of crucial debates for feminist film theory as well as for *noir* analysis; also useful are Mary Ann Doane's *Femme Fatales*, and more recent post-neo-*noir* contributions, including Elizabeth Cowie's essay 'Film Noir and Women', and Jans B. Wager's comparison of *noir* to the Weimar Street Film, *Dangerous Dames*. Julianne Pidduck's discussion (1995) of *femme fatale* films which form a cycle across genres such as horror, noir, suspense, romance and melodrama is also useful. Though many of these critiques concentrate on producing psychoanalytic or socially informed analyses, they often cannot resist the impulse to taxonomise *noir* women, a trait embedded in wider *noir* theory. Indeed, for a genre renowned for its ambiguity, *film noir* seems to invite excesses of categorisation – perhaps critical morphography is one way of shoring up the anxiety of generic (and gender) diffuseness: pin it down to a list or it will dissolve into unknowability. Women are prime targets for this: catalogues of motifs, icons and character-types abound, and are one way of defining the multifarious women (and men) of *noir*. Some writers keep the types simple: Janey Place (1998) posits a primary dualism between the spider woman and the nurturing woman, sometimes recoverable as positive images for female viewers, whilst for Michael Walker (1992: 23–5) the *femme fatale* and the 'domestic woman' circulate primarily in their relationships to male figures. Reading such women against the grain is central to both editions of the *Women in Film Noir* collection. But more insistent is reading the *femme fatale* as a sign of social, feminist and masculine unrest. Gender and sexual relationships are destabilised in *noir*, becoming 'symptomatic of a larger social disorder' (Belton 1994: 200), particularly in relation to the family. Sylvia Harvey reads the absence of family in *noir* as a subversive seedbed for the production of counter-ideologies (1998: 45); Belton – who divides *noir* women into 'Women as Social Menace' and 'Women as Psychological Terror' (198–9) – sees the family, neglected by women, as a site of pathology and violence. Postwar changes in the position of women

> pose a threat to traditional values, which are seen as centred on the institution of the family. Film noir registers the antifeminist backlash by providing a picture of postwar America in which there is no family or in which the family exists chiefly as a negative phenomenon. . . . Film noir dramatizes the consequences of this neglect [of men, of the family] transforming women into wilful creatures intent on destroying both their mates and the sacred institution of the family. (ibid.: 198)

For Doane (and others) the *femme fatale* is 'not the subject of feminism but a symptom of male fears about feminism' (1991: 2–3); Straayer sees her as a site of 'gender turbulence' (1998: 151). This seems to make fixed categorisation all the more urgent for some writers. Mitchell Cohen argues that 'The genre's women – les femmes noirs – basically came in three types: the girl next door,

Figure A *Film Noir* Character Types

Spicer's Types	Martin's Types
The Male Victim	
Damaged Men: Maladjusted Veterans and Rogue Cops	
The *Homme Fatal*	
The Private Eye	Female investigators
The *Noir* Criminal and Psychopath (Spicer calls him a 'tough guy')	Female killers (a) victims deciding to kill (b) accidental murder (c), suicide (d)
The *Femme Fatale*	
	Female mental instability
The Nurturer/Homebuilder: The Girl Next-Door	
	Good women turned temporarily bad
The Good-Bad Girl	Women investigated by men in authority – the police, lawyers, doctors or psychiatrists
	Bad blood relatives
The Female Victim	Victims of psychotic males
	Women who choose the wrong man
	Witnesses to murder
	Female voiceover
	Confiding/confessing to a man

Spicer's men are in bold.

the deceptive seductress, and the beautiful neurotic'. Wager replaces the female nurturer with the '*femme attrapée*, or woman trapped', though here both female types are covertly or overtly trapped by patriarchal authority, 'the *femme fatale* by her resistance, the *femme attrapée* by her acquiescence' (1974: 15). Andrew Spicer includes nine prominent representative characters in his survey of *film noir*, all of which are variously manifest in the erotic thriller. Angela Martin, in her essay on central women in 1940s *noirs*, identifies eleven female types (**Fig. A**; Martin 1998; Spicer 2002: 84–104). In Spicer's list the *femme fatale*, though important, is one of only four possible female types. Martin refuses a formation as broad as *femme fatale*, identifying more subtle characterisations. Almost all these types feature in the erotic thriller at some stage in its development, with some individual films containing multiple and hybrid characterisations. Later in this chapter I will find Spicer's *homme fatal* and good-bad girl, and Martin's female investigator, particularly useful.

Neo-*noir* showed the *femme fatale* to be an unsettled figure ripe for reinvention, but perhaps it is useful to begin here with some of the few contemporary incarnations which present her in her 'purest' form. The manipulative – though for some women positively powerful – spider-woman, the *femme fatale* whose meaning derives from her relationship to the men around her, is rare in contemporary cinema. As defined by Andrew Dickos (amongst others; Dickos essentially distils existing critical positions), the *femme fatale* is motivated by 'a lust for exciting sex, a desire for wealth and the power it brings, and a need to control everything and everyone around her' (2002: 162); the power she wields lies in her ability to 'disorientat[e] the male object' (2002: 156). She 'must inevitably die – or, at the very least, be mortally injured or be arrested for her crimes' (2002: 162). When such a figure appears in 1980s or 1990s cinema (or appears to appear, she is often not what she seems) she is usually a figure of pastiche and parody, or turns out to have twists of complexity, hybridised with other elements of characterisation, such as those from Martin's list. Many writers see her as a post-feminist figure of postmodern 1990s *noir* (see, for example, Hirsch 1999: 56). Following Barbara Creed, Kate Stables argues that the neo-*noir* femme is 'almost exclusively "castrating," rather than "phallic"' (1998: 180): these women's weapons symbolise not strong pseudo-masculinity but the *vagina dentata* permanently hungry for male fodder.[1] We might, then, see them as reactive rather than active, and determined wholly by the male point of view which frames their films. A contemporary sex/crime thriller such as *Palmetto* features an overambitious and oversexed Elisabeth Shue ensnaring ex-con Woody Harrelson into a kidnap-fraud scam. Though Harrelson controls the male-sap voiceover, Shue is the film's sexual centre: her last scene, as she descends the stairs into the arms of the police (a parody of Gloria Swanson getting ready for her close-up at the end of *Sunset Boulevard*), positions her as the film's real star, with Harrelson as merely – in the title of the novel on which the film is based – *Just Another Sucker*.[2] Though he survives, the implication is that, like William Holden, he was prime dead meat for the *femme fatale* from the start. This strategy, of reading the punished but briefly glorious woman as the film's real focus of energy, is common in feminist analyses of classic *noir*. Another formation is Suzie (Neve Campbell) in *Wild Things*, a figure whose manipulation of every twist of the switch-back plot is revealed only in the final scene, before which she was positioned as either victim or dead: the 'truth' of her avaricious ruthlessness is only actually shown in the scenes accompanying the end-credits (a self-reflexive space reserved in contemporary cinema for real or fictive 'outtakes'). Suzie is then a retrospective *femme fatale* in a film dominated by lesser *hommes fatals* played by Matt Dillon and Kevin Bacon.

Body of Evidence is a textbook case of a mainstream erotic thriller, presenting its female star as iconic spider woman. In this it is rare for a genre which often melds its *femmes fatales* into good-bad girls, refusing to see them 'inevitably die', or channels female strength through a female investigative lead. Narratively and stylistically it sticks close to the *noir* template, ticking off the iconographic motifs of the genre as it goes. It also features some big names, including the most famous American of 1993, Madonna, so was guaranteed publicity and extensive worldwide distribution on its theatrical release. Yet even calibre actors like Joe Mantegna and Julianne Moore are hard pressed to do anything convincing with the poor script, though somehow this determined drive to mediocrity serves only to emphasise the film's formulaic qualities, its dogged allegiance to generic mode. Essentially a replay of *Jagged Edge*, *Body of Evidence* features Willem Dafoe as lawyer Frank Dulaney defending Rebecca Carlson (Madonna), who is accused of murdering her lover. 'Trial's over, Frank', says state prosecutor Bob Garrett (Mantegna) as the film draws to a close. 'Walk away.' But when faced with a *femme* like Rebecca, no *noir* male ever does, however separately they are positioned on opposite sides of the law. Like *Jagged Edge*, the courtroom drama gets under way fairly swiftly, but unlike *Jagged Edge*, which is non-explicit in its exploration of the romance developing between defendant Jeff Bridges and defence lawyer Glenn Close, the sex between Rebecca and Frank is extensive and graphic – a naked Madonna going where few *femmes fatales* had gone before was a prime selling point. *Body of Evidence* also unashamedly replays the opening of *Basic Instinct*, except that here the copulating couple whose sex act results in the death of the man are seen on video playback, which the corpse lies in bed and 'watches' as he waits for the police to discover him. This victim, an elderly man with a heart condition who has been murdered with a cocktail of strenuous sex and cocaine, has made Rebecca the sole beneficiary of his generous will. The sex features more luridly than the drugs in the prosecution's case, with extended examples of Rebecca's sadomasochistic techniques as the relationship with Frank develops, including the famous sequence of hot candle wax being dripped onto his genitals, and sex in a public car park on a bed of broken glass. *Body of Evidence* thus allows us to open up one of the ongoing questions of this book, concerning the extent to which the hybridisation of porn and *noir* which culminates in the erotic thriller – particularly its direct-to-video form – constitutes a shift from the implicit to the explicit. The neo-*femme fatale* makes explicit what was only ever implicit for the *noir femme fatale*: it might be said that she keeps open the bedroom door which was firmly closed by the production codes surrounding classic *noir*. She also, as Straayer points out, demands sexual satisfaction as well as financial gain, one of many 'orgasmic *femme[s] fatale[s]*' who have 'become a staple of neo-*noir*' (1998: 153).

In this way *Body of Evidence*, in an efficiently porno-*noir*-by-numbers fashion, ticks off its genre motifs with the enthusiasm of the club member. A figure of self-invention such as Madonna 'doing' the *femme fatale* is a particularly resonant example of neo-*noir* as a pastiche of *noir*, a performance of *noir*.[3] Indeed, *Body of Evidence* positively revels in its own unoriginality: the classic *femme fatale* is defended to her acquittal by her duped lawyer, who then discovers that she is guilty as sin and $8 million better off as a result of his efforts. Her partner in crime, the victim's doctor who testified against her at the trial in a complex process of set-up, shoots her when she threatens to leave him, culpable, at the film's conclusion. Thus the guilty woman is punished, but the straying man is offered absolution as the film closes, with the image of Frank's (working and therefore neglectful) wife (Moore) walking towards him as Rebecca's corpse is taken away ('Corpse and wife cross paths,' as Tasker puts it [1998: 125]). The family has been disrupted by his dalliance, but, as with the closing image of the happy domestic unit at the end of *Fatal Attraction*, it offers the most legitimate form of closure once the *femme fatale* has been dispatched. Like many classic *noirs* in which the victim-hero survives the *femme*'s machinations, *Body of Evidence* presents a dark passage which the straying male briefly traverses before returning to mainstream normality. So it fulfils many of the requirements of its genre: beginning with a sex crime and underpinned by a criminal conspiracy which demands that the bitch erotically implicates a man on the other side of the law, connecting sex and danger in every way it can. The only thing it lacks is a lesbian sex scene.

Body of Evidence also has a particular chiaroscuro *noir* look, more so than many of its hyper-illuminated contemporary stablemates – think of Dahl's desert-*noirs Red Rock West* and *Kill Me Again*, Verhoeven's white *noir* or James Foley's bleached *After Dark, My Sweet* (in which, as one reviewer put it, the loser-protagonists are put out 'to rot in the desert sun' [Travers 1990]). The courtroom sequences are all dusty beams of light shafting down from high windows, Venetian blinds filtering horizontals of light, and cavernous ceilings dwarfing the participants. Rebecca's opulent boat-house is enshrouded in voile drapes, through which Frank can gaze at her revealed but concealed body, and through which we also spy on the sex between them. An ocular flirtation characterises the sex scenes, with the camera and *mise-en-scène* giving and taking away the image in the same fluttering diaphanous frame. The film's self-reflexive obsession with voyeurism also demands a lighting set-up which is low-key, high-contrast. When Rebecca has acupuncture Frank watches through a chink in the bamboo screen, concealing him but enabling his gaze to make just enough visual sense. Sex in the car park is preceded by Rebecca smashing the light with her high-heeled shoe, creating a lighting context appropriate to both *noir* and porn. Rebecca is also costumed to ape her blonde *femme* forbears: classic black or white, sharply cut suits, pearls, severely pleated hair in the courtroom but sexually tousled locks in the bedroom. Her lipstick is never less than vividly sharp; her shoes click as she walks. Not only is she a vamp, she may also be a vampire: Frank's wife asks if the marks on his chest (burns from the hot candle wax) are bite marks. As Breathless Mahoney in *Dick Tracy* Madonna had tried out this heartless role, justifying her visible indifference to mourning her dead lover with 'I'm wearing black underwear'. In *Body of Evidence* we witness, as it were, the evidence of this on a number of occasions; here the 1940s *femme fatale* underpins her wardrobe with the lingerie of the 1990s porn star. Contrast this with *Red Rock West*, at the other end of the genre spectrum's reassessment of the *femme fatale*: here Lara Flynn Boyle's Suzanne, no less deadly, comes on like Snow White – white gowns (like her 1940s antecedents), black hair and eyebrows chiselled into shape, ultra-pale skin forming a veil of vulnerability.

So far so formulaic. But it is one of *Body of Evidence*'s more ludicrous emphases that marks it out as interesting. On most counts a low point in 1990s mainstream cinema, the film notches up one generically useful achievement, which is to crystallise and then render utterly explicit a notion bubbling under the history of *noir*: that women are dangerous not because of what they do, but because of what they are, and thus they do not need pearl-handled revolvers to dispatch their victims – their sexualised bodies will do quite nicely. Rebecca is accused of 'fornicat[ing] Andrew Marsh to death'. From this springs the film's title: Rebecca's body is all the evidence needed to prove her guilt. Just look at her, the film says, and you'll see what she's capable of doing: 'She's not only the defendant, she is the murder weapon itself', says Garrett at the trial,[4] a notion bequeathed to/by the Hong Kong Category III film, which often figures women celebrating their bodies as weapons. 'I am a killer, not a hooker,' says Kitty in *Naked Killer*, made the same year as *Body of Evidence*. 'It's the same,' replies Sister Cindy. But though Frank had argued to the conviction-hungry cops before Rebecca's arrest, 'What're you gonna do? Tag the body as a murder weapon? . . . It's not a crime to be a great lay,' *Body of Evidence* argues that it *is*, whilst simultaneously revelling in the spectacle by repeatedly returning to the 'crime-scene' as Frank and Rebecca get it on. Although we have been introduced to Rebecca as a successful art dealer, her concluding career statement makes clear that her business is more sexual than aesthetic: 'I fucked you, I fucked Frank – that's what I do. I fuck. And it made me $8 million.' But with a body like Rebecca's you don't need to kill someone when you fuck them to be a threat; the mere presence and potential of Madonna's/Rebecca's body is threat enough and renders her almost the definition of deadly flesh: 'When this trial is over you will see her no differently than a gun, or a knife, or any other instrument used as a weapon', says Garrett to the jury. Whilst this is one of the erotic thriller's clearest instances of Barbara Creed's *femme castratice*, it also demonstrates how open the 1990s genre became to increasing sexual explicitness.

Fucking may be what Rebecca does and what she is, but avarice is usually key to the *femme fatale*'s motivation, with films such as *The Last Seduction* and *Body Heat* developing the *Double Indemnity* fraud/double-cross blueprint. Here it is more appropriate to look back to Wilder's precedent than more recent neo-*noirs* shorn of sex as set-piece and subterfuge, including Dahl's *Red Rock West*. Both *Body Heat* and *The Last Seduction* use sex as weapon and strategy as well as spectacle; both pit dauntingly intelligent women against dim men. 'You aren't too bright. I like that in a man', says Kathleen Turner's Matty Walker in *Body Heat*, whilst the male quarry of Linda Fiorentino's Bridget Gregory in *The Last Seduction* asks her to 'stop reminding me that you're bigger than me'.[5] It is also said of Suzie in *Wild Things* that 'her IQ was way up there. Around

200 or some such shit.'[6] Curiously, *Body Heat*'s tag-line also rests on women's superior knowledge, but implies that they give generously: 'She taught him everything she knew – about passion and murder'. *Femmes fatales*, however, hardly ever tell the full story, and one wonders that, by the 1980s, their prey have not seen enough 1940s *noirs* to alert them to this. Matty lures Ned Racine (William Hurt) into a plot whereby she defrauds her husband, murders him and makes Ned take the fall, whilst in *The Last Seduction*, having stolen the proceeds of her husband Clay (Bill Pullman)'s drug deal, Bridget uses sex to frame archetypical fall-guy Mike (Peter Berg) for Clay's murder. Distinct differences divide *Body Heat* and *The Last Seduction*, the most obvious being point of view. *The Last Seduction*, notwithstanding fine performances from Pullman and Berg, is Fiorentino's film, and her perspective orchestrates our view of events. Matty appears in *Body Heat* through the lens of Hurt's fantasy-scape, which might enhance the sense that she is a vision of a vision, a 'hyperbolic' pastiche of a 1940s precedent (Grist 1994: 272–4). *The Last Seduction* is a *noir* comedy in which sex as tool is deployed; *Body Heat* is tragi-melodramatic in tone, and indulges in extensive and (then) cutting-edge explicitness, whilst *The Last Seduction* had some of its sex-scenes cut by Dahl prior to release. *Body Heat* also developed a distinct steamy Southern sexual style, which permeates other films spanning the range of overheated, oversexed southern Americana: *Zandalee* (New Orleans), *China Moon* (Florida) and *Palmetto*, which critic Roger Ebert called 'the latest exercise in Florida *Noir*, joining "Key Largo", . . . "A Flash of Green", "Cape Fear", "Striptease" and "Blood & Wine"' (Ebert 1998a).[7] Whilst these span a huge range of American cultural histories from Texas to the Panhandle, 'heat' – whether the humid Deep South or the parched South-West – connotes sexual opportunity, but also combines eroticism (overheated) with violent, armed threat. 'Heat' has a number of slang connotations, which make it the perfect erotic thriller climate: definitions include 'intensive police activity' and making 'sexual advances'. 'Heater' is also US slang for the female gentials (see Green 1998: 583). It is no accident that a number of erotic thriller titles contain synonyms for high temperature (*The Hot Spot* and *Warm Texas Rain*, as well as *Body Heat*); Carl Reiner's genre parody *Fatal Instinct* features a bar (Le Hot Club) with the motto: 'No air conditioning and proud of it!' Turner's characterisation also plays on different connotations of 'hot', a sexual wildcat overheating the atmosphere.[8]

But there may also be a feminist moralism embedded in these performances (remember Rebecca's 'I don't know why men lie. They just do'). Matty is poignant if uncompromising; Bridget has no conscience, no emotional fissures, and does what needs to be done. Both enjoy sex along the way, and the film's lack of retribution has contributed to a sense of the genre's inconclusiveness. Mayer reads *Body Heat* as a 'stepping stone between *Double Indemnity* and *Basic Instinct*' (1993: 28), in terms of women finally being let off the hook (Phillis is punished; Matty gets away with it; Catherine Tramell is positively rewarded) and in terms of the progressive undecidability of the films' conclusions: the final shot of *Body Heat* is significant for its 'slow tilt towards the blue sky over the beach where [Matty] sits, refus[ing] to resolve the future of each character' (1993: 28) (the ice-pick shot at the end of *Basic Instinct* has a similar function). Whilst Rebecca is ragingly sinful, Matty and Bridget court admiration. *Kiss Me a Killer*, a quickie remake of *The Postman Always Rings Twice* set in Hispanic Los Angeles, is also interesting here. Whereas in Garnett and Rafelson's versions of *Postman* it is Cora who dies, here Theresa survives both husband and lover, economically independent. *The Last Seduction* even provides a justification. Early on Clay hits Bridget, and though this never marks her as victim, it forms a clear validation for subsequent actions.[9] Fiorentino performs Bridget as a woman coolly thinking on her feet to keep one step ahead of her pursuers – she teeters on the brink of losing control, but never a flicker of remorse crosses her face. Matty seems to steel herself to do what she does, whilst Bridget is amoral and purposeful, though holding fast to the morality of 'It's mine. You hit me.' Bridget was received as one of the 1990s best bitches, but the fact of theft also being a form of revenge might locate her closer to the 'good-bad girl' I will dissect below. With a questionable pulse (she is asked, 'Anyone check you for a heart-beat lately?') Bridget is no tart with a heart (nor is she the heartless tart found ultimately *not* guilty like Fiorentino's other *femme* incarnation, Trina in *Jade*).

If *The Last Seduction* presents the *femme fatale* as feminist icon, two early 1990s star-vehicle 'shrink-films' refract her through a popular image of mental illness, reworking her as more mad than bad. Via a sub-Hitchcockian fascina-tion with the sexual-criminal potential of the psychoanalytic scene, both *Final Analysis* (1992) and *Color of Night* (1994) feature Richard Gere and Bruce Willis, respectively, as duped males floundering in their inability to know their dangerously sexy female patients (a similar scenario was revisited in the DTV *Body of Influence*. Female shrinks, usually of the sex-therapist variety, are more likely stars of the DTV shrink-flick erotic thriller – see *Sins of Desire, Sexual Intent, Night Eyes 4*). Gere and Willis both replay the 'cop-falls-for-suspect' trope; if cop-in-analysis Michael Douglas in *Basic Instinct* is doubly unprofes-sional in having an affair with his own shrink *and* with his own suspect, Gere and Willis are just one step behind: Gere transgresses with a patient's sister; Willis with a patient in disguise. Gere, as we have seen, is something of a genre regular; this is Willis's only foray into sex thrills, and his film's key selling point was the post-*Basic Instinct* promise that, in such scenes, you would finally witness full-frontal A-list male nudity (a brief underwater glimpse of Willis's flaccid member, cut in the US for an R-rating but not in the UK for an 18). Both films also have their *Vertigo* moments, mixing the saxophone-drenched sex-scenes of the erotic thriller with Hitchcockian staircases and towers ('Instead of Kim Novak in a church tower, it's Kim Basinger in a lighthouse' [Howe 1992]). Using Hitchcock as a stick to beat the inferior (because contemporary) erotic thriller is a reception position regularly taken, as we have seen, in rela-tion to De Palma.[10] Both films also play with the psychotic disorders which justify either unknowing culpability or the inability to see the truth, inventing preposterous movie diseases (*Final Analysis* 'pathological intoxication', *Color of Night* shock-induced colour blindness; *Jade*, featuring another erotic thriller shrink [Fiorentino], also invents 'hysterical blindness').

But it is the ambivalently fatal *femmes* who are of interest here. *Final Analysis*'s Heather Evans (Kim Basinger) is set up as villainess (red lips, red coat, dark shadows), shifting briefly into good-girl mode in contrast with her abusive gangster husband, before manoeuvring her lover, Gere, into testifying on her behalf in a murder trial and allowing her to pocket her husband's legacy. Her treachery is contagious; when she dies her sister (and accomplice, played by Uma Thurman) takes her place. As we shall see later in relation to Linda Fiorentino, bitchhood is a communicable disease amongst *noir* women. *Color of Night* collects a roomful of varying loonies and asks us to pick which one did it. It turns out to be the boy who's really a girl (Rose, played by Jane March) who's also the mysterious creature ensnaring Willis, whilst at the same time sleeping with everyone else under the guise of different identities. When the relationship with Willis is consummated, the film slides into a sexual montage (of the kind beloved of DTV auteur Jag Mundhra) which involves the inventive conjunction of naked, writhing bodies and opulent interior design: here the aspirational images presented for the audience combine the lifestyle ideals of gorgeous homes and uninhibited women. The colour-blindness is another carnal-criminal motif: Willis cannot see March/Rose's scarlet lipstick (nor the significance of her red name – his disability sets him up to both see and not see her), and he misses key bits of evidence (blood stains, red cars). The film touches base with its genre stablemates in the customary sex-in-the-shower scene and a moment of light lipstick lesbianism. However, unlike *Final Analysis*, *Color of Night*'s apparent *femme fatale* is not *fatale* at all, as March's Rose emerges as an innocent set up to be multiply culpable but ultimately more sinned against than sinning. Her 'crime' is finally her manipulability and her prolific promiscuity, which has implications for the way in which Willis – the male manipulatee – is read. Though sexualised in his relations with March and his genital flashing, it is still March that the camera loves and lingers over, in its familiar complicity with Willis's point of view.

I want now to look at the genre's development of a more explicitly sexualised male figure, still 'owned' by a canny post-*femme fatale*, but interesting for two reasons: his potential appeal to female heterosexual viewers, and the way his overcharged sexuality effectively 'unmans' him.

2: HUNG LIKE A HORSE AND NOT TOO SMART: THE SEXUALISED FALL-GUY

'He fed the hole, and kept the hole happy.'
Voiceover in *Romeo is Bleeding*

'I'll tell you about what you need to know when you need to know it.'
Uncle Bud (Bruce Dern) in *After Dark, My Sweet*

If the woman's body was ample confirmation of guilt in *Body of Evidence*, the man's ownership of a penis is foregrounded in *The Last Seduction* as evidence of his willingness and complicity. Bridget explicitly uses men's sexual equipment to get them where she wants them: the penis, with its culpability and manipulability, becomes a willing adjunct of the *femme fatale*'s avarice. She is not, then, a phallic woman only because of her aggression and firearms confidence; she also appropriates the members of her male targets and uses them like a switch, reading arousal as weakness. Penises are more effective tools even than pearl-handled revolvers: the erotic thriller portrays them as entirely stupid organs, given to 'monkey see, monkey do' erectile response which can be activated at the whim of the woman's will, unarguable and unignorable for the man, who is victim of his own member's propensity to respond to the *femme*'s bidding. Though 18, R-rated or NC-17 films cannot generally show erections,[11] their existence is evident as narrative effect: men are acted upon and are made to act because of their implied arousal. In one of the few direct references to an erection in the genre – *Color of Night* – manipulator March passionately kisses manipulatee Willis in a secret corner of a public space, then walks away with a glance down at his groin, literally putting him in his place because he cannot follow her into the open without exposing himself. Thus the erection hovers somewhere between spectacle and narrative – unseen but with a story to tell, or perhaps driving the story we see. Like female response in hardcore, it cannot be shown, but it can make men *move*. Mike's charming come-on line 'I'm hung like a horse' in *The Last Seduction* may have been delivered in the hope that his weapon would tempt and then fell Bridget, but it is received as a suggestion that he can be useful and used. Bridget procures his services with her sexual favours (which he reads as love), her first action in this transaction being to feel the contents of his underwear to see if he delivers on his promises ('I never buy anything sight unseen'). If avarice is her motivation, her discourse constantly reveals an awareness that all contracts are sexual: ignored by a bartender, she yells, 'Who's a girl got to suck around here to get a drink?' We might read this as a further sexualisation of the woman – any male action requires women to put out first. But Bridget treats sex as the quickest route to money, male service and male weakness focused through an efficient manipulation of the male member (Mike's friend reports that 'She went for my fly and said she wanted to suck it [information] out of me'). Trapped in a car with a black private eye, Bridget cajoles him into showing her his dick ('Is it true what they say? . . . You know – size?'),[12] and takes advantage of his preoccupation with his zipper to crash the car and propel him through the windscreen.

But there is another story to be told about the fall-guy, which is not simply that of manipulable penises as tools of female greed. The primacy of Richard Gere's body in Schrader's *American Gigolo* (Fig. 3) introduced the possibility of the eroticised male eclipsing the female,[13] confirming theories of masculine spectacle which were to emerge in the 1980s (see Neale 1983; Dyer 1992; Cohan and Hark 1993; Kirkham and Thumim 1993; Lehman 2001). Gere's

Figure 3: The eroticised man's body eclipses the woman's: Richard Gere in *American Gigolo*. Paramount/The Kobal Collection.

Julian Kaye is a man who pleasures women (in one speech he details the care he takes getting them off, his full-body nudity divided by *noir*ish shadows as he speaks). Yet as sexual spectacles women are peripheral, taking second place to Gere's body and his Armani wardrobe. His is a universe of homoerotic narcissism, policed first by him ('This is *my* apartment,' he says. 'Women don't come here') and then by the state (he ends up in prison). Thus *American Gigolo* sets up its (perhaps) framed hero as vulnerable (and odious to the heterosexual men around him) because of his sex-work. In the developed erotic thriller, such a spectacular male figure is explicitly reformulated as a sexualised fall-guy – a 'sexual winner as *noir* loser' also found in Gary Oldman's Jack Grimaldi in *Romeo is Bleeding* and Don Johnson's Harry Madox in *The Hot Spot* – 'a failure at anything other than sex' (Hirsch 1999: 224). Crucially, as John Orr suggests, this also reaches out to women in the audience: 'the fall-guy as explicit object of desire' attracts 'not only the *femme fatale* but . . . the gaze of the female spectator' (1998: 191). Mike's complaints in *The Last Seduction* that Bridget treats him like a sex-object will clearly be read differently by heterosexual women and men: a fantasy for men, but an opportunity for women. So might we read Johnson's muscled torso and Oldman's feckless romanticism as 'something for the ladies' in the context of a softcore couples market and the mainstream film's need to please all audiences?[14]

The Hot Spot and Romeo is Bleeding are significant both as genre pathbreakers and pastiches. One *Washington Post* reviewer of the former film, apparently unaware of the emergence of neo-*noir* (such films as *The Hot Spot* 'almost constitute a new genre – let's call it nouveau noir'), criticises it for being too sexed-up, making pulp-*noir* too 'voluptuous' (Hinson 1990). Clearly, Dennis Hopper knew where the genre was driving, as is borne out by later stablemates. *Romeo is Bleeding* also ticks the genre boxes (though it strays into gangster territory) through moments of raunchy titillation which signal the sexual fecklessness of the hero (he watches three-way sex through a neighbouring window with binoculars, and plays cards with a nudie-motifed pack). *The Hot Spot* similarly picks up on a number of crucial hallmarks – its strip-joint scenes, with twists of narrative manipulation taking place against a backdrop of table-dancing, its lesbian sub-plot, its sexual blackmail and its story of sexual danger culminating in a sexualised death scene, which was to be revisited in numerous films, including *Basic Instinct* and *Body of Evidence* (*femme fatale* Dolly Harshaw [Virginia Madsen] reports that her husband 'had his first [heart] attack the first day he met me', then, when the time suits her, she straddles him, gags him, makes him snort amyl nitrate and proclaims, 'I'm fucking you to death, George'). It is tempting to discuss the importance of these films via their sensational *femme fatale* figures – Mona Demarkov (Lena Olin) in *Romeo is Bleeding* takes Bridget Gregory's humorous amorality to monstrous proportions, outrageously cavorting in front of her prey, legs akimbo to form the claws of a trap. In an athletic take on the *vagina dentata*, at one point she even tries to strangle Jack with her thighs as he drives a car ('"Romeo"', wrote *The Washington Post*, 'is most notable for being the first film of the year to cash in on post-Bobbitt fears of castrating (and worse) females' [Brown 1994]). In her bid to be a mob supremo, she happily cuts off one of her own forearms (by contrast Jack is unmanned by the mob's amputation of just one toe), and then asks Jack if he wants sex 'with or without' (he plumps for without, so she unstraps her prosthetic arm and flings it away). The film's rich confusions of sex, violence and greed are focused particularly acutely on Mona: when she talks wistfully about 'the first time' she means the first time she killed someone.[15]

Sensational as their *femmes fatales* are, these films are essentially about desire-fuelled male failure, at times spectacularly sexualised. Both Jack in *Romeo* and Harry in *The Hot Spot* are bad-boy fall-guys because they simply aren't as good as those around them ('You're the tough guy. I'm much worse than that', says one of Harry's [male] opponents). Jack is a cop who informs on informers to the mob, but is outwitted by Mona. That he survives and she doesn't only reinforces his mediocrity; whilst Mona's death is luridly cinematic (a very *red* action sequence constituting the film's climax), Jack ends up in a witness protection programme in bleached-out Nowheresville, without the wife he loves but has repeatedly cheated on – a post-climactic wraparound which explains how Jack lost his identity. After Mona's sensational demise, male survival seems anti-climactic; it is almost as if the film is positively showing off how female spectacle (albeit the spectacle of her death) can eclipse man's ability to keep the narrative going at the expense of fascination. How much of a woman

Mona was is also questionable, given that persistent impotence has so unmanned Jack. Here, then, feminisation is an effect of both the sexual glamourisation the fall-guy undergoes and his systematic disempowerment. Fall-guys can also be 'the most hysterical character – the most "feminine",' as Larry Wachowski described the fated Caesar in *Bound* (in Lippy 1996: 93).

The Hot Spot's Harry is cut from the same cloth as Jack, a drifter who falls into a job selling cars in a small town (the kind of town Jack ends up in), gets involved with both Dolly and pure teen good girl Gloria (Jennifer Connelly – a vision of the unobtainable, just as Jack's wife is a vision of the lost), robs a bank and ends up as Dolly's slave. *The Hot Spot*'s final thought is of Harry accepting his fate as Dolly's sex-object and lap-dog: 'I found my level, and I'm living it', he says in voiceover. Grist reads this as 'fatalistic' (1994: 285), though why acceptance of a woman's mastery should constitute a *noir*ishly downbeat conclusion rather than a happy ending is a matter of opinion. For her part Dolly is only ever seen engaging in sex and scheming, but she excels at both, and is particularly fond of the back-seats of cars (luring him in by lying back, kicking the door open and opening her legs), suggesting an understanding that Harry the drifter-turned-salesman is a fall-guy refugee from a road movie (perhaps this is why he fails to read the genre signs which surround him). But selling cars in this movie also becomes a commentary on sexual commodification, including Harry's own at Dolly's hands, with car dealership forming a witty sub-text to the sexual text. Harry's getaway car from a murder scene is one of the car lot's products, still bearing a sticker on its windscreen which reads 'Killer Deal'. Harry's sales job is first advertised on a sign which reads:

Red Hot Deals
Salesman
Needed

inviting a vertical as well as a horizontal reading. Later the sign has mutated into 'Hot Deals New Salesman', to which the silhouette of a naked woman has been added, purloined from nextdoor's strip-joint sign. (Is he now the seller or the sold?) It is, then, not true that he is 'a failure at anything other than sex'; he's a pretty good used car salesman, his 'red heat' extending from the bedroom to the forecourt.[16]

This is a buyer's market, in which woman picks and man is purchased. Dolly's powers of consumption are, however, predicated on nothing: her pathological wantonness seems to be organised around a social absence (at least in Harry's view), a blissful lack of productivity. Dolly is a pariah. The desperate Harry at one point diagnoses her drivenness in remarkably Freudian terms, with cure coming through the traditional routes of productive pursuit or motherhood: 'You're too worked-up, you're off your head', he says. 'You better find something to do . . . get a job, a hobby, have a kid.' Though the list of female possibilities had by 1990 extended beyond postwar *noir*'s prescription to return women to the home, the impulse is still the same: Dolly must attain a level of feminine acceptability through socially sanctioned activity, because her limit-lessness (endless days; too much money) has created an aberration. This is the *femme fatale* as, in Mary Ann Doane's words, 'the antithesis of the maternal – sterile or barren, she produces nothing in a society which fetishizes production' (1991: 2). Except that Dolly *does* produce something – Harry's desire is her creation, and Dolly's labour in this department is no different from Violet's feigned heterosexuality read as a form of sex-work in *Bound*. Indeed, sexual production is presented as the only form of tolerable industry in *The Hot Spot*'s pervasive heat: here sexual heat is both an effect of climatic temperature and the indolence it produces, charged up by numerous scenes of listless time-wasting (even the film's paid workers succumb to the torpor of living in burning, boring, small-town America, where the only events are buildings catching fire). Desire emanates from a nothingness born of boiling ennui and women with too much time on their hands. 'There are only two things to do in this town', says Dolly. 'Have you got a TV?' 'No', Harry replies. 'Well, now you're down to one.' At least, we might say, Dolly's sexual avarice is an index of her refusal to submit to daytime soaps, though Harry becomes the thing Dolly wants to 'do'. Dolly is said to have 'happened' to her husband like a force of nature, and though Harry recognises that she is also 'happening' to him (it is he, after all, who says that 'the smart thing would've been for [Dolly's husband] to get the hell out of there and let her happen to someone else'), he becomes the done-to, (merely) that 'someone else'. Dolly's house is full of stuffed carnivores, suggesting its hostess's predatoriness as well as the fact that Harry is next.

Gary Oldman's Jack presents a different kind of spectacle. Johnson's Harry says at one point, 'My life's been a succession of jams over floozies of one kind or another', but this is even more relevant to Jack's predicament, as his wife's photo album of his infidelities attests. Jack is led and felled by the activities of his over-enthusiastic dick, but his relationship with his wife also promotes him as an 'unmanned' romantic, weeping over her loss, trying to fill her absence with hallucinatory images. What makes Jack most like Harry is not their sexual incontinence, but the way in which their subjectivity is formulated through the desires of others. Barbara Kennedy argues that Jack is disoriented by the 'array of feminine identities' which impinge upon him, destabilising him to the point of madness (1999: 136–7). Indeed, we might go further and say that all male masochistic victim-*noirs* which continue to fragment women across figures such as the *femme fatale* and the nurturing virgin are also exploring the impact of this fragmentation on the desiring male psyche. Women live with their impossible divisions; men are destroyed by them. Yet Jack's instability is a product not just of competing female demands, but of the way he rationalises these through an economic discourse. (*The Hot Spot* also shows this in its rear-ranging sales boards – men as commodity.) In Jack's universe, money must be earned, sometimes paid for by bodily damage, and sex occurs in a marketplace of credit and debt (his wife receives a gift with the line, 'Either I was really good, Jack, or you were really bad' – this is giving as reward or recompense). *Romeo is Bleeding* formulates desire into a singular image not of lack, but of an entity with a substantial appetite which sucks at him. Jack buries his stash in a hole under a drain cover in his garden, and his relationship with this is articulated as like an exhausted gigolo endlessly servicing a rapacious client: 'He fed the hole,' says the voiceover, 'and kept the hole happy.' The hole also speaks back to him: everytime he fills it up, it seems to sigh its gratitude. We hear a small feminine gasp as he drops the money in – the same erotic noise which Mona makes when they have sex towards the end of the film (her name does, of course, suggest sexual moaning). Though Jack comes on like a Jack-the-Lad in his dirty deals and dirty sex, he is a figure of male masochism, driven to fulfil desire as a demand to which he is subject: both Mona's and the money-hole's appetites come to determine his actions. He is even subject to his own control-ling romantic feelings (the hackneyed formation of his monologue sentiment, 'What makes love so frightening is that you don't own it. It owns you', is sup-plemented by the sense that this is part of a wider network of claims on him). In Jack's dreams even his wife contributes to his fantasies of subjection and sub-mission, as *femme fatale* and wife tie him at gunpoint onto Coney Island's big wheel and let him go (a gender reversal of a similar scene in *9½ Weeks*, when it is Mickey Rourke who suspends a terrified Kim Basinger on the same ferris wheel). Jack's masochistic relationship to desire and money becomes the formula of self-definition, but in the Nowheresville anonymity of the film's con-clusion he all but ceases to exist: no women, no deals, no money-hole to satisfy and no subjected self.

By contrast, the drama which ensnares Harry as character is also connected to the way in which Don Johnson is positioned to play him. Though Harry is a no-hoper, Don Johnson was then an established TV star (starring in *Miami Vice* from 1984 to 1989), giving credence to the character's arrogant self-assurance (Harry may not have a TV, but Johnson knows all about it). If Harry is Dolly's possession, purchased through blackmail and blow-jobs, Johnson is the viewer's, framed as the film's prime beefcake. Repeated shots show him – more pumped-up matinée idol than the quirky-looking thespian Oldman – on display alongside the cars he (as Harry) is trying to sell: white vests frame his muscles, his tan, even his erect nipples, suggesting sexual readiness to his spectators as well as his co-stars (Fig. 4). As the film's active point of view this combines fall-guy/protagonist with visual focus, his sexuality activating both narrative and spectacle. One effect is therefore to align viewers' response with the arousal of the *femme fatale*, an identification which shifts the customary 'sympathy for the devil' support for the predatory woman ever further into sexual objectification, as the genre slips from crime to carnality. Richard Dyer discusses male specta-cle as promising activity: 'Even in an apparently relaxed, supine pose, the model tightens and tautens his body so that the muscles are emphasized, hence drawing attention to the body's potential for action' (1992: 270). However, for

Figure 4: Muscled-up Don Johnson, *The Hot Spot*'s 'red hot' car salesman.
Orion/The Kobal Collection.

Dyer the more muscular the body, the more it draws attention to masculinity's constructedness ('muscles that *show*' are not natural but achieved [1992: 274], signifying both work and a form of corporeal dressing up). But muscularity for the erotic thriller's male does not necessarily underpin his power. When viewed from the perspective of a Dolly Harshaw or a Bridget Gregory, biceps are metonymic of the penile tissue which, when flooded with blood, produces an erection. What Dolly sees in Harry's pumped-up arms is the fallible sap he could become when pumped up otherwise.

The conundrum for gender analysis is how we read the centrality of these male figures. Sexual objectification also serves to reinforce these men's importance: to become a sex-object here ironically reinforces cinema's customary balance of power, making men not just the sexy spectacles, but also the narrative activators (having their cake and eating it). The 'masculinity as spectacle' movement in 1980s and 1990s cinema (which literalised and rendered ever more self-conscious a trend in cinema at least as old as Valentino)[17] served therefore to reinforce the male protagonist's advantage with the aura of sexual power – even if, in the plot itself, this is rendered through a story of the man's sexual manipulability. *Femmes fatales* may pull the strings (more so in *The Hot Spot*, less so in *Romeo*, though Mona is the more powerful figure), but they are doing so from the wings rather than centre-stage. These stories of male manipulability offer sexualised updates on the *noir* fall-guy which retain male prominence even as men are objectified. Though Harry ends up most subjected by this, he is also more cinematically spectacular than Jack – perhaps because of Don Johnson's physical glamour as compared to Gary Oldman's, perhaps because his sex scenes are more sustained, perhaps because the nihilism of Jack's fate, removed from the defining desires of women and his sucking pit, leaves him uneasily positioned in relation to his audience.

3: GILDA'S DAUGHTERS: THE EROTIC THRILLER'S GOOD-BAD GIRLS

'So which category do you think you fall into – the good girl or the bad girl?'
Gregg Henry on Linda Fiorentino's ambivalent cop character in *Bodily Harm*

'You want her to be guilty. Why do you want her to be guilty?'
Rory Cochrane on Gina Gershon's tough cop character in *Black & White*

If films such as *Romeo is Bleeding* and *The Hot Spot* revisit the *noir* anti-hero through female desire both inside and outside the story, the *femme fatale* also needs to be supplemented by a figure who challenges traditional sexual moralities of punishment. In *LA Confidential* Kim Basinger plays Lynn Bracken, a specialist whore/star-lookalike who is part of a stable fashioned (literally 'cut' into shape) by an upscale pimp (Pierce Parchett) who deals in 'High-class porn, drugs, hookers that look like movie stars', and 'bankrolls B-movies under the table'. Lynn 'is' classic *noir* leading lady Veronica Lake, whilst as a whole *LA Confidential*'s plot revolves around the death of the whore version of Rita Hayworth (who played a *femme fatale* in *The Lady from Shanghai*, and a *femme fatale* revealed as good-bad girl in *Gilda*).[18] As they fuck in the cinematically glamorous room where paid sex takes place – a literal *mise-en-scène* of desire (Cowie 1984: 71) – the johns watch movies starring the women's *alter-egos*, imagining themselves as their tough-guy screen counterparts. *LA Confidential* is not an erotic thriller, even though, like its near-contemporary *Mulholland Falls*, its complex corruption plot is fuelled by sexual scandal. Nevertheless, its enigmatic female lead comes on like a *femme fatale* (she is first seen enshrouded in a hood and cloak, vivid red lips surrounded by milk-pale skin and hair, ordering booze for a party), and reads off a female *noir* heritage just as the film as a whole reads off a male one. Finally, Lynn is a good-bad girl, sexual but sympathetic, skilfully negotiating the intricate games her roles make her play with sexual and personal identity, foregrounding the parodic formation of the neo-*noir femme fatale* by performing and commodifying prior cinematic figures in sexual scenarios. Basinger (veteran of *9½ Weeks* and *Final Analysis*) thus plays Lynn as sometimes simultaneously playing Lake, whilst Lynn distinguishes her manufacture from that of the other whores who have undergone plastic surgery: 'I'm really a brunette, but the rest is me', she says (Basinger herself is 'really' a blonde). The overall effect is of slippage between the two identities, as good/real girl Lynn and bad/fake whore Lake slide into and out of each other in a fantasy role for which Basinger won an Oscar.

In many ways Lynn is a 1990s revisiting of *Chinatown*'s Evelyn Mulwray (Faye Dunaway): though Evelyn has herself been read as 'a "correction" of the misogyny inherent in the characterisation of the *femme fatale*' (Grist 1994: 270), her formulation is perhaps not entirely 'corrected' until the 1990s. Here in an era and a genre in which sexuality is no longer automatically punished, Lynn can be rewarded with the 'happy ending' of a long-term relationship with a damaged cop (Russell Crowe) and the promise of a future outside the sex industry. The triumphantly sexualised, usually surviving *femme fatale* I discuss above may be legion in contemporary cinema, but so is her more sympathetic screen sister, the good-bad girl. I turn to Gilda because (along with Jane Fonda's Bree Daniels in *Klute*) she is one of the few bad girls revealed as good which feminist criticism recognises, embodying a positively charged sexual charisma which is attractive to a wide audience base ('she could be a sex-symbol for servicemen without offending the women back home' [Kobal 1977, quoted by Martin 1998: 202; see also Dyer 1998]). These simple facts of woman appeal cheek-by-jowl with active sexuality usually go unnoticed, such as in Kate Stables' insistence that non-deadly *femme* figures are synonymous with killer-women just because they come on with the same sexual bravura (Linda Forentino's Jade/Trina in *Jade*, despite her ultimate innocence, is judged by

Stables a 'postmodern *fatale* [who utilises] sex to deliver death' [1998: 172]). To paraphrase my epigraph, it is not only the demonising patriarchy of traditional *noir* which 'wants her guilty'; feminism also seems to have a stake in bad girls. This is not dissimilar to the misogynist critical opinionating of the writers with whom Angela Martin takes umbrage, such as Maxfield (1996), who reads any female character as a *femme fatale* if anything about them (however innocent) turns out to have 'a devastating effect . . . on the hero of the film'.[19] Even a woman's own death will be more 'fatal' for the man she upsets (by dying) than it is for the (dead) woman herself. For Chris Straayer 'film noir's femme (sexualised woman) today always connotes deadliness until proven otherwise' (1998: 161). Woman is guilty if she does, and guilty if she doesn't – even for feminism. The story is different in the erotic thriller, however. Here if her only 'sin' is sex, the genre will usually acquit her.

As a regular player in the erotic thriller the *femme fatale* is more likely to be proved innocent than her male counterpart, the *homme fatal*, to whom I will turn in a moment. Outside of the erotic thriller, however, the good-bad girl is discussed by Lee Horsley as more of an invention of fiction than film. Whilst classic *noir* cinema almost without exception punished its *femmes fatales* and distinguished its good girls from its bad ones in the strongest black-and-white terms, *noir* fiction from the same period played

> *against* stereotype, often setting up plots that initially lead us to judge according to stereotype and then reversing our expectations, or complicating our judgements and in the process establishing strong female figures who, though sexual, are admirable and/or indomitable. The literary as opposed to the Hollywood femme fatale is less likely to be repressed, killed or otherwise punished for her strength and transgression. (2001: 130–1)

Thus when filmic *femme fatales* die, literary *femmes fatales* survive (the same character may even survive in the novel but die in its cinematic adaptation).[20] Whilst Laura and Gilda – as Martin points out – were important female creations (scripted, co-scripted or produced by women in collaboration with their stars), Lynn Bracken and Daphne Monet (from *Devil in a Blue Dress*) were originally literary creations (from books by James Ellroy and Walter Mosley respectively). The erotic thriller might then be seen (unknowingly) to take its cue from this fictional tradition Horsley lays out.

A prime example of this process of reversing expectations and complicating judgements is a big star vehicle given a wide theatrical release in 1989. *Sea of Love* traded on the steamy sexuality between its stars Al Pacino and Ellen Barkin, marrying the terms of pleasure and danger in its publicity ('In search of a killer, he found someone who's either the love of his life . . . or the end of it', runs the video tag-line). For Silver and Ward, the focus on the unreliable male detective rather than the *femme fatale* makes it a neo-*noir* (although it was 'sold to audiences as [an] erotic thriller' [1992: 404]). Like many of its stablemates, *Sea of Love* starts with a sex crime: in the first scene a naked man is forced to cavort sexually before being shot, all by an unseen assailant. This is soon followed by another genre regular, the 'sexual scene-of-the-crime scene'. *Jagged Edge*, *Basic Instinct* and *Body of Evidence* all open with the abrupt image of a sex crime (or its aftermath – the violated body in its crumpled bed, recently pleasured in the case of the latter two films), followed by a sequence when the cops set the film's agenda by laying out the crime's sexual co-ordinates. This introduces a parallel discourse of explicitness, in which telling replaces showing. In *Jagged Edge* the jagged nature of the knife wound is discussed; we see 'BITCH' written in blood above the woman's corpse. In *Basic Instinct* the forensic light cast across the sheets causes semen stains to take on a magical luminescence, and one cop utters the immortal lines of the victim's sexualised death, 'He got off before he got offed.' In *Body of Evidence* Bob Garrett gestures towards a knowledge of sadomasochistic practices by identifying a nipple clamp. *Sea of Love* has a rather different take on this tradition, with cop Frank Keller (Pacino) discussing his ex-wife whilst examining the corpse and noting the lipstick-stained cigarette butts in the ashtray. Here Frank develops his theory of the murderess as avenging *femme fatale*: 'I admire this woman . . . for her directness. I mean the guy fucks around on her . . . Bingo! Pop him in the head – it's over . . . No walking wounded.'

If the murder is sexual, so will be the manner of detection. Frank and his new partner Sherman (John Goodman) discover, after a second murder has been committed, that the victims both placed lonely hearts verses in newspapers, so they place one themselves and then set about trapping the respondents through a series of dates until they get the killer. Helen (Ellen Barkin), a siren who picks her dates on the basis of 'animal attraction', soon emerges as prime suspect, and prime target for Frank's obsession, following a night of hot sex. As a type, Frank (damaged goods) is ripe for this form of sexual transgression: 'She's the friggin' suspect, Frank,' says Sherman. 'Walk away.' But Frank Keller can no more walk away than Frank Dulaney could (why are they all called Frank? Does this signify some element of openness in their personalities to contrast with the women's scheming?), setting up a web of implicatedness which makes Frank sexually enslaved and a paranoid wreck by turns. Layered into this is the sense that Pacino's performance also recalls his work as the implicated New York cop who gets sexually involved with the suspects in *Cruising*.

Yet Helen is not what she seems. Her name suggests classic female trouble, Helen of Troy in Manhattan inviting us to 'put the blame on' her (Hinson 1989 – just like Mame). If the twist in *Body of Evidence* and *Jagged Edge* is that the suspects *did* do it after all despite their acquittals, the twist in *Sea of Love* is that Helen is innocent, exposing just how reliable the iconography of *noir*'s bad girls is at establishing guilt. Through its manipulation of a fantasy of the *femme fatale* (finally absent from the film), *Sea of Love* sends both its audience and the detectives down the wrong road. Neither Helen nor any other woman is murderer here. In contrast with *Basic Instinct*, in which, as Lynda Hart argues, on some level all the women did it,[21] here the spectre of the *femme fatale* conceals a banal figure of evil, Helen's ex-husband who shadows her dates (he does not even have the dangerous glamour of the genre's darker *hommes fatals*). Like a range of finally sympathetic sexualised *noir* heroines, Helen leaves a trail of signs of innocence in her wake which we assume are red herrings, but which turn out to be more credible than the signs of murderousness. Though dressed like danger (scarlet jacket, tight suits, high heels) she provides a place of safety for her family. She looks like trouble but acts like a devoted mother, for this is not a neo-*noir* of absent families. Harvey's 'terrible absence of family relations' in classic *noir* (1998: 45) might also be read as the context for the anti-family rages of neo-*noir*'s *femmes fatales* but here this is not the case. Helen, it turns out, is devoted mother to a small daughter and protective daughter to a live-in elderly mother. Here it is not family which is 'the locus of [*this* woman's] particular oppression' (ibid.), but rather that which is outside of family, or at least beyond blood relationships. Matriarchal single motherhood may not be what classic Hollywood propounded as 'normal' (think of the consequences for Mildred Pierce or Stella Dallas), but *Sea of Love* presents it as more acceptable than Frank's choice.[22] The most dysfunctional element of Helen's scenario is her ex-husband. Yet as with *Internal Affairs*, this very *present* neo-*noir* family does not overtly implicate the film in strategies of melodrama. The strong message spoken by costume and sexual appetite makes Frank read the names of the murder victims pinned on Helen's fridge door as signs of her culpability, despite the domestic context, and we follow Frank. *Sea of Love* exposes our expectations through a process of playing tricks on them. Writing on the early neo-*noir* *Klute* (perhaps the ur-text for good-bad girl analysis, as its prominence in *Women in Film Noir* evidences) Christine Gledhill underlines *noir*'s ambiguities for its audience when aligned with the male protagonist against the woman: 'not only is the hero frequently not sure whether the woman is honest or a deceiver, but the heroine's characterization is itself fractured so that it is not evident to the audience whether she fills the stereotype or not' (1998: 31). Hirsch reads *Klute* as a female point of view film, which pierces 'the mask of the fatal woman . . . to reveal her own awareness of how and why she exploits her looks' (1999: 150–1). 'Bree is a sexual woman who is innocent,' continues Hirsch; a figure he calls a *noir* 'genre rarity', though she is an erotic thriller commonplace. Helen does and doesn't fill the stereotype; she is both good-bad girl and nurturer/homebuilder, though for women rather than for men. Through a set of recognisable motifs, *Sea of Love* positions itself in a long history which it simultaneously challenges, demonstrating to both Frank Keller and the film's audience that seeing is not believing.

In renegotiating the deal sexuality delivers in contemporary cinema, the good-bad girl reassesses what it is to be victim or avenger. One refusal of this aggressor/victim economy which articulated understanding of *noir*'s women (homemaking madonnas or murderous whores) is Chris Holmlund's illuminating paper, 'Cruisin' for a Bruisin': Hollywood's Deadly (Lesbian) Dolls' (1994). This reads two very different films, *Basic Instinct* and *Fried Green Tomatoes*, as examples of 'deadly doll films', accounting for the genre confusion which they spark when read together through an analysis of the slippages of race, sex and age. Listing a diverse body of texts ranging from *Aliens* to *Surf Nazis Must Die*, all of which contain 'deadly dolls' who damage ('cruise') and are themselves damaged ('bruised'), she writes:

> That these deadly doll films constitute a cinematic cycle cannot be appreciated within the framework of classical film genres like film noir and melodrama, however. In such genres cruising is too often made synonymous with aggression and bruising too often conflated with victimization: film noir's bad girls appear primarily as predators, while melodrama's good girls are seen mainly as martyrs. (1994: 31)

For Holmlund, this new form focusing on murderous women makes them all simultaneously 'bruised' and 'cruising', damaged and violently active, but not necessarily in a causal relationship. By sitting *Basic Instinct* (aligned to *noir*) alongside *Fried Green Tomatoes* (aligned to melodrama), she challenges models which would see women as doers or done-to according to their genre. The 'deadly doll film' thus suggests that 1980s and 1990s cinema has produced a new interdependence, or mirroring, of *film noir* and melodrama. Figures such as *LA Confidential*'s Lynn and *Sea of Love*'s Helen are neither predators nor martyrs; they cruise and bruise, injecting traces of melodrama into their sexually dangerous *noir* city stories.

A rather different figure is the character played by Angelina Jolie in *Original Sin* (produced by Ashok Amritraj, a prolific figure behind a plethora of DTV erotic thrillers who has since ascended to the mainstream), at first glance a characteristic erotic thriller double woman. Arriving in Cuba as good girl Julie, the bought bride who travels from the US to marry coffee baron Luis (Antonio Banderas), Julie soon emerges as a masquerade. Underneath she is Bonny Castle, who deceives a series of men and approaches crime with a cold practicality (and lacks an 'original' identity: a pauper prostitute, she took her name from a Scottish postcard with a picture of a Bonny Castle on it). A wedding is arranged for the day Julia and Luis meet which recalls the hasty marriages of 1940s female Gothic (more of which later), but here it is Luis who is conned, becoming victim to Julie/Bonny as the marriage proceeds. Though a nineteenth-century set costume drama, *Original Sin* develops as a fully-fledged mainstream erotic thriller, based on veteran pulp author (and perhaps the most filmically adapted of *noir* writers) Cornell Woolrich's 1947 story *Waltz into Darkness*, and is a remake of Truffault's *La Sirène du Mississippi*. Woolrich's literary *femme fatale* is, as Horsley argues, marked as thoroughly modern (despite the heritage backdrop) in the '"slips" she makes by smoking or by displaying her more sexual side' (2001: 137) (Fig. 5). *Original Sin* then runs early twenty-first-century star

Figure 5: Angelina Jolie as scheming, smoking Bonny/Julia in *Original Sin*.
MGM/The Kobal Collection.

Jolie through a 1940s *femme* filter into nineteenth-century costume (which readily comes off for the film's requisite steamy sex-scenes between its glamorous stars).[23] For Horsley, Woolrich's novel explores feminine masquerade through the multiple scheming characters its female protagonist inhabits (Bonny plays Julia, but also various other entrapping personae), representing 'a woman's apparent nature not as a product of inherent traits but as something constructed', and implying that 'a "bad" or "good" role can be assumed by any woman' (2001: 137). Bearing this out at first, *Original Sin*'s (anti-)heroine hovers on the brink of undecidability. To paraphrase Simone de Beauvoir, one is not born, but rather becomes, a *(fatale)* woman – and one can unbecome her too. Good and bad or neither, when Julia leaves Luis, taking all his money, his servant says, 'She was never here – you were married to a dream.' Bonny/Julia makes this plain in her fondness for the melodrama actors performing in a travelling theatre, particularly the Satan figure. But according to Horsley, Woolrich, who 'pays close attention to the subjective experience of his women' (2001: 137), does not see masquerade as liberating; Bonny/Julia is 'a woman trapped by the roles she plays' (2001: 138) (we are still in the territory of existing *noir* categories here – remember Wager's *femme attrapée*). In reworking *Waltz into Darkness* as a twenty-first-century costume erotic thriller, *Original Sin* must break with this, shifting into a genre which values the drama of role-playing, and particularly sees performance as the tool of avarice and desire.

But it is also confused by its double point of view: on the one hand, its wraparound voiceover by Bonny on death row implies that the *femme fatale* is the film's focus, and, as with the nearly-dead storytellers of *Double Indemnity* or the 1946 *Postman Always Rings Twice*, is about to embrace her punishment (now wouldn't *that* be an original neo-*noir* stroke!). But much of the action is also presented from victim Luis's progressively implicated position – *Original Sin*'s confusion of focus bleeds into how it plays its characters and how it utilises its stars. Bonny's voiceover is contradictory and unsympathetic, more like the fragmenting voiceovers of *noir* which Hollinger (1996) discusses.[24] Luis forgives her because he is sexually obsessed with her, and the film forgives her because she is Angelina Jolie, its (in 2001, highly bankable) star. The ghost of female complexity is implicit in the multiple identity of the character, and her willingness to inhabit and use a range of others, and selves. But *Original Sin* denotes 'good-bad' credentials on Jolie only because it doesn't have the courage to condemn or entirely vindicate her: it hasn't the imagination to frame her sexuality in anything other than bad girl terms, and hasn't the complexity to see her cipher past as anything other than a formation of victimhood. Her namelessness could have finally signified nihilism; her masquerading escapology could have tackled the problem of punishment. Instead, the film plumps for the solution Hollywood knows best: switch genres and you might find a way out of the problem. Escaping death row with Luis, *Original Sin* fashions a melodramatically inflected happy ending. Love redeems her, dispelling the *noirish*-ness she brought into the film, dissolving the story, with the credits, back into a heaving-bosomed costume drama. Imagine William Hurt escaping with Kathleen Turner to the tropical beach in *Body Heat*, or Linda Fiorentino waiting until Peter Berg gets out of prison at the close of *The Last Seduction*, and the enforced conclusive 'goodness' of Jolie's character becomes clear. If, as Dyer (1998) argues, Hayworth resists Gilda's fatalism because of Hayworth's own star charisma, Jolie resists Bonny's nihilism because contemporary stardom on this scale requires halfway happy endings. Perhaps Jolie didn't relish the career implications of being so irredeemably unsympathetic; perhaps the producers relished even more the open-endedness which would allow for the development of *Original Sin 2*.[25]

So is the good-bad girl a development or a refutation of the *femme fatale*? Debates have often crystallised around the pros and cons of the *femme fatale* as either prime symptom of male anxiety about female power or glorious celebration of female appetite and potency. If either of these positions was ever a useful engagement with the 1940s incarnation, their tenability in relation to the female figure of neo-*noir* seems to me to be at best stretched. Readings of films such as *Basic Instinct* with central prime bitches calling the shots and 'failing' to be punished like their *noir* grandmothers have extended the old model, celebrating the excesses of the Catherine Tramell blueprint, or reading her as symptom of another age of male anxiety around post-feminist female power. It is as if it has been agreed that the *femme fatale* can *only* signify male anxiety (whether postwar or postmodern) and consequently any time she pops up she must be a sign that men are worried. I find these positions as unconvincing as they are unoriginal. The *femme fatale* is a handy, available trope, part of a bank of genre images the sex-thriller could happily feed off in its mission to maximise publicity and rentals. Filmmakers are not in the business of alienating filmgoers, not least the lucrative 50 per cent of the cinema audience which is the female population. The bitch stepped elegantly from *noir* to porno-*noir* because she fulfilled a range of genre requirements. Not only is she sassy, strong and spectacular, epitomising avarice and lust in a way which appeals to an international audience, this focus on money and sex means that she readily lends herself to a cross-fertilisation of *noir* and porn, leading female viewers into new generic territory. She is a handy genre trope which has continued to sell – the covert pleasures women have found in the 1940s punished *femme fatale* have mutated into the overt saleability of the 1990s get-away-with-it version. The 1990s good-bad girl is what happens to the *femme fatale* when she gets bored with demonisation, when she wants to come in from the cold but still gets the hots, appealing to a wider audience base and avoiding the moral dichotomies of classic *noir*. Chris Straayer suggests 'femme' rather than *femme fatale* to characterise such an icon: 'Whereas the femme is defined as sexual, femininity requires domestication', so the femme is *not* the nurturer or home-making 'good girl'; the femme is an 'actively sexual woman whether straight or lesbian', but she is not necessarily 'fatale' (1998: 162). For the femme, sex does not elicit punishment. However, the erotic thriller is even more confident with this sexual woman than Straayer suggests; often they are 'feminine' as well as femmes, coming and going into the domestic space. In this formation the good-bad girl might be read as one of Yvonne Tasker's 'working girls', oscillating at times between female hero/investigator, female revenger and plain old good-time girl. Sometimes (as in *Sea of Love*) she also manages to be a homemaker/nurturer, though usually to other women (mothers, daughters) rather than to men. It may be that this hybridisation of *noir*'s female types into a more multifaceted woman acceptable to female audiences is itself Hollywood's response to women's past readings of the punished dangerous dame. Straayer sees her lack of punishment as the film's 'superego . . . lighten[ing] up' (154; who cares now if she gets away with it?). Though Hollywood remains a largely male workplace, a form of soft popular feminism (particularly in the wake of *Thelma and Louise*) sells films to women. To read this figure as solely a symptom of anxiety seems to miss the point of her celluloid centralisation and audience-pleasing qualities.

But this argument might also expose the limitation of iconography studies. In her illuminating analysis of a number of contemporary horror-melodramas, Deborah Jermyn sees the 'bitch from hell/victim-wife' dyad 'as a symbiotic relationship of the conflicts of womanhood' (1996: 253): externalising woman's limited choices. A heartless whore such as *Body of Evidence*'s Rebecca might be read as abject in the sense that Jermyn argues: 'The female psychopath is woman's abject since she crosses the borders other women are forced to maintain' (1996: 255). Helen in *Sea of Love* seems to combine these positions rather than challenge them – suspected of psychopathology, she also has a victim-wife backstory. The question which a writer such as Nickolas Pappas asks, however, is whether her final refusal of the bitch/victim dichotomy constitutes a liberation. Though 'the film's *dénouement is presented as* a rehabilitation of the woman' (1990: 16; original italics), and Helen is neither victim-wife nor psychokiller (instead, she is one of the genre's 'sexy mothers'), she still, for Pappas, fails to achieve full cinematic subjectivity. Instead, *Sea of Love* prefers to agonise over *Frank*'s neurosis, making Helen a mere function of his homosocial networking ('Helen is only a means by which he communicates with other men in general' [1990: 17]). This was borne out in the film's critical reception, which almost unanimously saw it as a Pacino vehicle, with Barkin as a feisty handmaiden to the actor's career. In *Sea of Love*, then, the good-bad girl functions as conduit for male–male relations, making its sexual-political gains limited:

> The story of the film has been the story of Frank's fear of women, so the film can only end when he overcomes that fear. On this reading, the film criticizes the social relations between the sexes, and asks for a new male attitude toward women which does not reduce them to a supporting role in some male strategy. (1990: 21)

One film which *does* achieve this, at the same time scrambling Jermyn's 'bitch from hell/victim-wife' dyad and reorganising it into a double good-bad figure, is *Black Widow*. As the title suggests, this sets up a classic *femme fatale* figure as a starting point for an extended deconstruction of female villainy and heroism, as embodied by murderous bad girl Theresa Russell and her nemesis, cop Debra Winger. Here the good-bad girl is divided into two women who connect in an increasingly symbiotic (and implicitly lesbian) relationship – Winger's fascination with Russell replays any number of cop-as-flipside-of-killer-flicks, though usually the symbiosis/mirroring is either a form of black/white buddy story (*Manhunter*, *Heat*) or a dark romance (*Silence of the*

Lambs), or one of the classic *noir* 'twin' films I discussed earlier, in which distinct identities are dark and light sides of each other (if performed by a single actor). Neo-*noir* 'twins' may be less distinct entities, more likely to function as problematisations of psychic unity or individuality than to shore up a Manichean opposition of good (girl) and bad. At one point Winger justifies her obsession with Russell with 'She's not about guns. You wanna catch her, you gotta think like she thinks,' to which a male colleague retorts, 'She's obsessed with killing and you're obsessed with her' (interest between women is, it seems, almost as bad as murder). Winger also goes undercover to befriend Russell (posing as a holidaymaker in Hawaii), like a range of asexual female figures of authority who forge new sexual pathways through disguise in the 1990s DTV. Here the good girl's increasingly sexual obsession with the bad girl reveals the bad girl as potentially lovable and the good girl as potentially corruptible. It is Winger's character who activates this, and the Russell character who accepts it, seemingly relieved that a 'real' relationship, rather than one in which she has to 'work' (i.e. marry and then murder for money) is being offered. Early on in her investigation, Winger arrays large images of Russell on a wall and positions herself amongst them, an image which functions as emblematic of *Black Widow*'s uneasy interconnections between its double hero/villain. The women do a scuba diving course together, practising mouth-to-mouth resuscitation on each other, before Russell saves Winger in a dive which goes wrong. Winger's wedding gift to Russell, a bejewelled black widow brooch, is as much a love token as it is an open acknowledgement that Winger the investigator is on the trail of Russell the murderer, and Russell accepts it as such, initiating a passionate kiss between the two. *Black Widow* has been read as a film lacking the courage of its lesbian convictions (engaging in a hasty 'process of recuperation, almost as if it doesn't know how to – or is afraid to – develop the inherently oppositional structure it has established' [Grist 1992: 284]). Yet it does extend the favour *noir* offers its flawed male villains and their equally flawed pursuer/investigators – that of problematising the moral absolutes by which they are judged – to a female duo. The spectacle of female desire may be withdrawn as soon as it is mooted, but the judgements of female evil are also questioned by the film's narrative of sympathetic obsession.

4. FEMALE POINT OF VIEW AND THE *HOMME FATAL*

'I could break your neck, I love you so much.'
  Adam (Joseph Fiennes) to Alice (Heather Graham) in *Killing me Softly*

Winger's good-bad girl also embodies another crime cinema characterisation central to the erotic thriller, the female investigator – a figure sometimes associated in heterosexist cinema with asexuality or lesbianism (Laurie Metcalfe in *Internal Affairs*, Alison Eastwood in *Black & White*). Winger is unusual in being pitched against a woman, though Theresa Russell is not so unusual in being given a sympathetic hearing as a *femme fatale*. The *homme fatal*, another stalwart of the erotic thriller, is a rather different matter, since he is rarely vindicated and provides the basis for a shift in generic emphasis and influence, from the characteristic male-focused point of view of *noir* to a female sympathy which looks more like 1940s female Gothic. The female investigators and victim-heroines of a number of films need to be viewed in rather different terms, drawing on a tradition which often looks and plays like *noir*, but takes the pursued, professional woman as the focus of sympathy and point of view (in theatrically-released products she is likely to be a cop or a lawyer; in DTV films she might also be an expense account housewife, inhabiting a 'private' life rather than a public role). Elizabeth Cowie disputes the male-focused image of *noir*, pointing out that many *noir*s were animated by female investigators, a number of *noir*'s *femmes* were not so *fatale*, and that it would be mistaken to read 'the women's picture melodrama' as parallel to 'the "tough thriller"' (itself 'a form of "masculine melodrama"' [Cowie 1993: 130, quoting Krutnik 1991: 164]). Instead, Cowie re-situates female-focused melodrama into the heart of *noir*. I want here to look at the female sympathies and structural point of view of these sexy neo-*noir*s as further unsettling the notion that the erotic thriller is a men-only preserve.

One such film is *Guilty as Sin*, released in the same year as *Body of Evidence* and playing rather like its smarter twin, which places Rebecca De Mornay as ambitious attorney Jennifer Haines in the Willem Dafoe position, and Don Johnson as David Greenhill in the Madonna role. If *Body of Evidence* is all sex and no screenplay, *Guilty as Sin*, written by Larry Cohen and directed by Sidney Lumet, is a crisply photographed '*noir* lite', in which the heroine manages to resist the *homme fatal*'s villainous seductiveness in order professionally to negotiate the thorny path he lays out for her. What Cowie calls the 'duplicitous man' of 1940s melodramatic *noir* ('similar to the "spider-woman" figure in that he uses his sexuality to prey on women' [1993: 136]) is no less threatening in the erotic thriller, though his sexuality is more explicit (dangerousness may then be both undercut and augmented by his role as spectacle for audiences as well as the heroine) and he is often played with a comic relish which exudes a knowingness of his *noir* antecedents. As befits a man who has thrown his rich wife out of a window, Greenhill is performed by Johnson with a polished balance of slimy smooth and self-parodying self-aggrandisement, his *homme* comic as well as *fatal*, appropriate to an era in which – in horror at least – monsters are self-reflexively witty. Greenhill matches *The Hot Spot*'s Harry for arrogance, but twists his sexual skills into manipulator rather than manipulatee. Harry acquiesces to becoming Dolly's kept man; Greenhill actively pursues the role (boasting, 'I don't do anything. Women support me'). Once more sex is central, though here not explicit: when asked towards the end of the movie why he risked fingerprint detection and took his gloves off to kill his wife, Greenhill makes explicit the genre's fascination with the sexuality of murder: 'Because it felt better', he says. 'Killing with gloves on would be like fucking with a rubber.' If *Basic Instinct* and *Body of Evidence* (as well as other films such as the art-house *Matador* or *Ai No Corrida*, or the DTV *Last Call*) conflate sex and death in the same murderous moment of orgasm,[26] a number of films in this genre take their tip from the sadomasochistic sexuality of the stalk-and-slash film and make murder a sexual act. Carol Clover has argued that the female focus of the slasher film problematises the trajectory of identification engaged in by the male viewer. Jennifer may be Greenhill's prey, but like the slasher heroine she is also his nemesis: though stretchered off in a neck brace at the end of the film following Greenhill's violent death, she is still able to say, 'I beat him – tough way to win a case!'

Jennifer is more multiply positioned than her fall-guy male counterparts like Frank Dulaney or Ned Racine. If she is marked out as Greenhill's ultimate victim, she is also the film's articulate heroine and guides its organisation of the spaces of power. The iconography which positions Jennifer as an effective working woman whilst also – for reasons of suspense – suggests her potential victimhood, relies on the way she occupies her work environment. Not so much a streetwalking *flâneuse* as a creature of corporate interiors, her smallness is repeatedly emphasised by the relative size of the *mise-en-scène*. Christopher argues that postwar skyscraper architecture is the prime context for *noir* alienation filtered through the impotence of the workplace, overpowering and suffocating: 'The noir city, in life and death, is never far from the metaphorical city-as-human-giant' (1997: 86). Though often framed in a way which emphasises her vulnerability (dwarfed at one end of a long, shiny corporate meeting table, or striding through empty, labyrinthine interiors), Jennifer negotiates this landscape with a sense of ownership. Once in the courtroom she is 'a real killer'. Jennifer as subjective focus thus inflects not only how we read the narrative (did he do it and will she fuck him?) but how we read *mise-en-scène*. Yet *Guilty as Sin* is also a rather chaste film. Though early on we see her striding alone, after hours, through the long corporate corridors of an office complex, only to arrive at her lover's glass suite, instantly disrobe and initiate sex (and all because she has just won her case), eroticism develops as covert implication rather than overt explicitness, an effect of the tendrils of sexual and moral insinuation which bind its leads through a complex of culpability. As Jennifer's defence of Greenhill proceeds, he begins a systematic process of intimidation by confessing to her in the privileged space between attorney and client that this wife-murder was not the first, and that each time he has not only enjoyed it but has benefited greatly from killing rich women. Like Glenn Close's Teddy Barnes in *Jagged Edge*, Jennifer finds that she is defending a man who manipulates his sexuality in order to win his case, but unlike Teddy she never submits. When asked why he is sexually harassing her, he replies, 'Because if you loved me, you'd do a better job of defending me.' Her sexuality is, then, not an excuse for vulnerability, and since she maintains that her involvement with David will always be professional, she is never cast as a loser (unlike his bill-paying victims).

Guilty as Sin was received as both a confused genre piece and as Don Johnson's film (Ebert, Howe, both 1993); though De Mornay's Jennifer is its star, Johnson's hammy rendition of malice is the film's central spectacle, like *noir*'s *femme fatale* but connecting to a *noir*ish tradition of male menace ('Johnson might as well hand out pens, "Courtesy of Mr. Goodbar"' [Kempley 1993b]; 'an update on Robert Walker's gentleman rogue in "Strangers on a Train"' [Howe 1993]). Nevertheless the primary emotions in which the film trades are those of entrapment and threat, all Jennifer's responses to her demonic client, responses we are encouraged to share. *Guilty as Sin* is Jennifer's story. How then is she, occupying the film's privileged point of view position, characterised as victim or survivor? Greenhill's performance is played out for her eyes and her benefit, and with her we watch him. This must be set against the contrary drive of the film which positions Jennifer as Greenhill's prey, an object marked out for his use. In the opening sequence, in which Jennifer's rhetorical skills are demonstrated, Greenhill watches from the audience day after day like a legal groupie or voyeuristic stalker. This is another 'Out of the Past'-influenced story. Like Matty's manipulation of Ned in *Body Heat* which was based on prior knowledge of his mistakes, Greenhill, it turns out, planned his latest murder with Jennifer as potential defence attorney in mind, knowing her legal passions and her past successful acquittal of a wife murderer. 'You know what the problem is with committing perfect murders?' says Greenhill, confident of the confidentiality of his relationship with his attorney; 'You can't tell anybody about them.' More frightening to Jennifer than what Greenhill will do to her is what he will say to her; more threatening are his words than his actions, since in the passing on of knowledge lies the involvement of culpability. Enforced by her profession into occupying the woman's traditional position of listener (the space of client–attorney confidentiality becoming rather like a confessional), the trap into which Jennifer falls is primarily aural and epistemological; what she hears and what she knows (too much rather than too little) becomes the issue. If Greenhill's performance is an attempt to seduce Jennifer, this is only so that he can eventually 'play'/author Jennifer's performance: 'You wrote this entire scenario', she says when she realises the extent of her manipulation. 'We just played out our parts.' And the film excuses its absent on-screen sex via the way it conceives the legal process: what we have been watching is one long sex-scene between Jennifer and Greenhill articulated through the rise and fall of courtroom discourse and thriller tension, with the woman as a most unwilling partner: 'We've been close, haven't we, Jennifer?' says Greenhill. 'Closer than most people who fuck.'

The fatal man is clearly a trope common to a number of other contemporary genres, though films which pitch a strong central heroine against an *homme fatal* are not the same as slasher-features incorporating the multiple deaths of scream-queens, even if they die at the hands of fatal men. Films like *Guilty as Sin* are more like thriller versions of Carol Clover's 'final girl' horror films, driven by a central female protagonist who makes choices and outsmarts the dark and deadly male. The erotic thriller's female investigative heroine is then a hybrid figure, part *noir*ish detective woman, part horror final-girl, dominating the film's primary point of view and eliciting sympathies appropriate to both hero and quester. Whilst scream-queen/slasher fare insidiously centralises the killer (Freddy Kruger, Jason Vorhees and Michael Myers all eclipse their various victims),[27] female hero/*homme fatal* films align us with the stalked woman and either keep the killer male largely in the shadows, or make his threat play second fiddle to her fear, which quickly becomes fearless giant-killing ingenuity. *Blink*, for instance, offers limited insight into the killer's motivation, focusing more on the perception tricks which the formerly blind heroine Emma's eyes play on her regarding her visions of the killer. This makes for an unreliable view, crucial to the film's suspense strategies. Centralisation of the heroine also means that the *homme fatal* is finally interesting only to the film and its audience in the way he threatens our (female) object of sympathy. Here, then, is a sexualised *noir* form in which the man is a function of the woman's story.

A Kiss Before Dying occupies all these positions and provides cross-references to a range of other erotic thrillers. Its writer-director is James Dearden, who penned *Fatal Attraction* four years earlier; it is also a remake of a *noir*ish original based on a novel by Ira Levin, author of a number of imperilled women tales adapted for the screen, including *Sliver* (which I will look at in relation to Joe Eszterhas). Its *homme fatal* is Matt Dillon, one of the duplicitous males in *Wild Things* later in the decade, and its heroine/victim (it's a 'twin film') is played by Sean Young, a veteran of the erotic thriller, star of a number of lower-budget DTVs (*Exception to the Rule* [1997], *Motel Blue* [1999], *Night Class* [2001], *Threat of Exposure* [2002]) as well as the parody *Fatal Instinct* [1993] and the important female-helmed analysis of sexual-criminal collusion, *Love Crimes* [1992], in which she plays a complicit investigator-detective). In *A Kiss Before Dying* she is both the female-victim Dory Carlsson (dispatched by Dillon in the first few minutes) and the investigative-avenger Ellen Carlsson (Dory's twin), who marries Dillon then uncovers his treachery, consolidating the genre's pleasure/danger fascination by making the imperilled/investigative woman the wife of the killer. Dillon's character is, however, also given some sympathetic screen-space: vowing one day to own the fleet of trains marked 'Carlsson Copper' which pass by his childhood window, he determines to insinuate himself into the family and their fortune by marrying a daughter – either, Dory or Ellen, will do. His poverty and her wealth are therefore given as some kind of justification for murder, whilst Dillon's villain at times threatens to eclipse Young's female hero.

Other formations of the *homme fatal* in the erotic thriller still rely on the centrality of the female protagonist, but the motivations and desires which underpin male threat are different and recall what Mary Ann Doane calls the Paranoid Woman's Film more than classic *noir*. If *Guilty as Sin* and *A Kiss Before Dying* make their female heroes investigative subjects in relation to the dark men who pursue them (reversing the pursuer/pursued dynamic at the end), the mode of male fatality in *Killing Me Softly* and *Fear* takes the genre elsewhere. Both feature men who are dangerous to the women with whom they are involved, not because of greedy murderousness but because of obsessive love or jealousy. In the case of *Killing Me Softly*, this 'romanticises' the genre. Later, I will look at some examples of the erotic thriller metamorphosing into erotic romance (particularly in the films of Zalman King), creating a distinct genre more squarely aimed at female audiences, or at least inclusive of watching women. Films like *The Red Shoe Diaries* or *Two Moon Junction* look like nothing so much as sexed-up Harlequin romances for softcore mixed-gender consumers. In general they ditch the murder-mystery quest of the erotic thriller in favour of a romanticised female sexual quest, so that the woman's story usually rests on a 'will she/won't she?' issue regarding partners and choices. Both *Fear* and *Killing Me Softly* have much in common with these titles as stories of women finding sexual fulfilment with excitingly dangerous men. In the latter American *ingénue* adrift in London Alice (Heather Graham, a wide-eyed innocent in what becomes a dangerous European wonderland) meets primal-male mountaineer Adam (Joseph Fiennes) and starts a passionate affair which rolls into what looks like one of 1940s female Gothic's 'hasty marriages'. Sean Young's Ellen enters into such a marriage with Jonathan (Dillon) in *A Kiss Before Dying*; Ellen's twin Dory avoided it by being murdered practically on the registry office's doorstep. Doane reads these hasty marriage stories (*Rebecca* [1940], *Suspicion* [1941], *Secret Beyond the Door* [1948]) as hinging on the question 'Is the husband really what he appears to be?' (1987: 124); if not, then murder may be the underbelly of marriage. Like a number of Doane's 1940s heroines, Alice has no family or connections of her own (Adam entirely envelops Alice in his world); her dominant point of view, which we share, is more that of romantic fiction's unknowing woman, the woman in peril because she is denied the truth. Once married, Alice becomes the investigator of her husband's dark secrets, ensnared and spurred on by his possessive love and denial of knowledge. But what makes this a twenty-first-century erotic thriller and not a 1940s Gothic romance is the sex, which starts as a kind of 'Last Tango in Bloomsbury' anonymous tryst and metamorphoses post-wedding into bondage, an erotic representation of the tie to which she has succumbed (Fig. 6). With a scarf round her throat during one episode Alice's voiceover tells us, 'I let him decide when I could breathe and when I couldn't and I loved it.' Adam seems to be a Bluebeard – How did his first wife die? Why does Alice keep getting warning letters? Most significantly, what is hidden in his padlocked cupboard? – a trope common to the paranoid woman's film, many of which feature 'a room to which the woman is barred access' (Doane 1987: 134). If Adam sexually has unlocked Alice, narratively he denies her knowledge of the secret past locked beyond the door. Like a Mills and Boon heroine,[28] Alice is trapped by the way knowledge is denied her, and energised by the investigative thread she follows when snooping. Adam is not finally revealed as a murderer (Alice is endangered by his psychotic incestuous sister instead); his weird behaviour is an effect of his damaged past and his wild passions. But *Killing Me Softly*'s absolute adherence to Alice's blinkered point of view ensures that we ultimately

Figure 6: Alice (Heather Graham) succumbs to the bonds of wedlock in erotic melo-thriller *Killing Me Softly*. Montecito Picture Co/The Kobal Collection.

care less about the causes that impel Adam and more about the effects that petrify and motivate Alice. For all its flaws, this makes *Killing Me Softly* a woman's erotic thriller.

In *Fear* (directed by *After Dark, My Sweet*'s James Foley) Nicole (Reese Witherspoon) is the object of David (Mark Wahlberg)'s obsessive attention. Nicole isn't charged with investigating his mystery, however, but with escaping his irrational violence when she tries to leave the relationship and her lover turns nasty. *Fear* then metamorphoses into an exploitation siege-movie like *Straw Dogs*, foregrounding a family-versus-outsiders dynamic, which was also present in *Fatal Attraction*[29] (and underpinning the Oedipal relationship between Nicole and her father). David moves from seductive lover to rampaging psycho with very little explanation; all Nicole can do is *react*, struggling, once again, to be the film's final girl. This itself begs a deeper question about the potency of the woman whose point of view we share in these erotic thrillers. If *Guilty as Sin* and *A Kiss Before Dying* are erotic thrillers because the defining male desire which drives them is murderously avaricious, *Killing Me Softly* and *Fear* are erotic romances or melodramas because the defining male desire which drives them is obsessive passion. Narratively, these are female point of view films, but their genre tone is dictated by what the men do to their women. How, then, to read their interest for women, given that male desire here still determines what women do? How to understand our own alignment with the female point of view, given that it too is determined by the machinations of male desire? I will return to these questions when I look at the erotic thriller's female stars and at the DTV erotic thriller as woman's film. In the meantime, chapter 3 investigates how the genre has been shaped in the mainstream by some of its key players.

NOTES

1 For Stables, however, the *femme fatale* subsumes all other female types: 'Long gone is the "nurturing woman", representing a wholesome alternative in classic noir. Instead, the fatale is now surrounded by women who mirror and double her effects, as they too are discovered to be duplicitous sexual transgressors as the narrative unfolds. . . . the femme fatale has come to stand in for all women – once the figure of woman is comprehensively sexualised on screen, all females are reduced to form and (fucking) function' (1998: 170; 179). As this chapter and chapter 6 will show, this is not the case; nor is it true that the contemporary *femme fatale* 'signifies nothing but sex' (1998: 179).

2 James Hadley Chase published *Just Another Sucker* in 1974.

3 For John Belton neo-*noir* is a conscious performance, or rather a conscious reconstruction of what is unconscious in *film noir*: 'Stylistic elements which, in the 1940s and 1950s, were part of a strategy to disorient spectators have been refashioned, in the 1970s, into a systematic, carefully tailored "look" . . . The overall effect of these allusions to earlier films noirs upon contemporary audiences is more reassuring than unsettling' (1994: 192).

4 In this Rebecca seems to be the cinematic descendant of Clara in Duke Linton's 1950 novel *Crazy to Kill*, as discussed by Horsley: 'She is a woman whose softly feminine attractions are themselves a deadly weapon: "Clara with two ivory-hued mounds of feminine dynamite exposed . . . to an inch above the hard, detonating nipples"' (2001: 132). This also recalls two Chesty Morgan films in which the well-endowed star smothers men with her breasts (*Deadly Weapons* [1971]) and in which breasts double as 'photographic weapons' (*Double Agent 73* [1974]) (see Gorfinkel 2000: 157–69 for a discussion of this). This is the female body on the attack; the tag-line of *Stripped to Kill* makes it aggressively defensive: 'A Maniac is Killing Strippers. Detective Sheehan Has One Weapon to Stop Him. Her Body'.

5 Sean Young's *femme fatale* Lola Cain in the parody *Fatal Instinct* reiterates the sentiment: 'You really are incredibly stupid, aren't you? I like that in a man.'

6 Brains alone are not enough, though – as the 154 IQ Sharon Stone told *Rolling Stone* in May 1992 as part of a strategy of self-mythologisation which effectively elided the distinction between star and the role of Catherine Tramell – 'If you have a vagina and a point of view, that's a deadly combination' (quoted in Campbell 1994: 58).

7 Ebert (1998a) writes: 'Noir is founded on atmosphere, and Florida has it: tacky theme bars on the beach, humid nights, ceiling fans, losers dazed by greed, the sense of dead bodies rotting out back in the Everglades. (Louisiana has even more atmosphere, but noir needs a society where people are surprised by depravity; Louisiana takes it for granted)'.

8 This was a focus in the film's reception. One critic saw Turner as 'the ultimate, phosphorescent *femme fatale*, her temperature always a few degrees above normal, her dress sense evocative of a sultry cinematic past' (Duane 1994).

9 Though some (usually male) critics choose to forget the fact that she was hit first, or at all, preferring to read her as an image of untouchable amorality – see e.g. Spicer (2002: 165).

10 One review of *Killing Me Softly* even argues that 'Alfred Hitchcock may be the father of modern suspense, but he's also the father of the genre's redheaded stepchild, the erotic thriller' (Rabin 2003). Friedkin reiterates this lineage in my interview.

11 In 2000 the BBFC relaxed its criteria for allowing 18-certificate films to contain explicit sexual content, so whilst prior to that erections had occasionally been visible in art-house movies, post-2000 they are a more common spectacle.

12 The detective responds to the racism of the question, 'Is it true what they say about white women . . . No ass?', and Bridget then engages him in a 'you show me yours and I'll show you mine' temptation exchange.

13 Though Richard Dyer would perhaps see this as a development of a trait in classic *noir*, according to his reading of Johnny (Glenn Ford) in *Gilda* as equal to Gilda herself in being 'visually constructed as an object of desire' (1998: 118).

14 One viewer of *The Hot Spot* called it a 'Good couples movie for a hot summer night': 'This movie has someone for everyone to like and almost everyone to hate. Between Don Johnson, Virginia Madsen, and Jennifer Connelly, there's a romantic interest for both you and your sweetie' (IMDb user comments contribution, www.us.imdb. com/CommentsShow?0099797).

15 Though Jack's voiceover echoes this sense of killing as sexual consummation: 'Whoever you shoot, you may as well marry 'em, 'cause you're tied to them for life'.

16 The sign may also reference the 'Man Wanted' sign which opens Garnett's *Postman*.

17 See Hansen (1991), who discusses the spectacular nature of Valentino for early female audiences.

18 The 'real' Lana Turner is also encountered in one comic scene, when she is mistaken for a lookalike whore. Of Gilda's relative innocence Martin asks, 'What exactly has she been guilty of – apart from the "stupidity" of marrying "two insane men in one lifetime" and trying to make the best of it by *enjoying* herself' (1998: 218).

19 'Without intending to be femmes fatales, Evelyn [from *Chinatown*] and Judy [from *Vertigo*] nevertheless qualify as "fatal women" in my terminology because of the extremely destructive effects they have on the male protagonists' (Maxfield 1996: 9, quoted by Martin 1998: 226). Both Evelyn's and Judy's deaths are, then, significant only for the effect they have on their men.

20 'Literary noir . . . in fact offers ample opportunities for the survival and even the prospering of the tough, independent, sexual woman' (Horsley 2001: 134). One of Horsley's examples is Jacques Tourneur's *Out of the Past*, based on Geoffrey Homes' *Build my Gallows High* (and a source for *Body Heat*): in the novel the *femme fatale* survives; in the film she dies.

21 'When we ask the film to tell us who did do it, the only answer it can give us is that the *women* did it, which is to say, ~~The~~ Woman did it' (Hart 1994: 130).

22 Though divorcé Frank also shows an unusual devotion to family structures which cuts against the hardboiled cop stereotype. His widowed father stays at his flat some-times, he hankers after the stability which Helen's child-centred unit provides and wants her to move in with him, and the poem he places in the lonely hearts column was written in the 1930s by his mother for his father. It is when Helen finds out that the poem was his mother's creation that she decides to develop their relationship.

23 Banderas's clothes also come off, fulfilling the genre's function of providing eye candy for heterosexual female audiences; one viewer read the film, for all its faults, as perfect 'couples viewing' fodder. Banderas's speech (as Luis) which concludes the film, when he talks straight to camera about his love for Bonny, also seems to cut through the artifice of the narrative and directly address the female viewer.

24 'In *film noir* a narrational hierarchy fails to establish itself and a proliferation of point of view dominates the texts. While first person voiceover can act as an author-itative evocation of the power of the text's implied author, when it is combined with certain elements in *film noir* . . . it loses control of events, which seem inevitably to escape the voice-over narrator's power' (Hollinger 1996: 247).

25 Tasker argues briefly that the *femme fatale*'s survival at the close of the narrative is attributable to 'the demise of the Production Code, together with the desire to build in a sequel if possible' (1998: 125).

26 Michele Aaron's work on self-endangerment and the sexuality of risk is useful here.

See the essays in her 1999 collection for further discussion of the culture of 'perilous pleasures'.

27 Though not so in more recent serial killer tales such as *Scream* (1996) or *Taking Lives* (2004), in which investigative/pursued heroines (Neve Campbell and Angelina Jolie, respectively) are far more central than their objects/ pursuers.

28 At least two internet critics notice this; *Killing Me Softly* is both like 'something straight out of a Harlequin romance' (Mr Cranky; http://www.mrcranky.com/movies/killingmesoftly.html) and 'a sexually liberated version of Hitchcock's *Rebecca*' (http://www.moviemartyr.com/2002/killingmesoftly.html).

29 Both films suffered from the negative comparisons to genre stablemates. *Variety*, for instance, called *Fear* 'a gender-reversed *Fatal Attraction*, with a strong measure of *Cape Fear* thrown into the formulaic mix'. And of *Killing Me Softly*: 'Bad acting, worse script and ludicrous sex scenes . . . suddenly *Body of Evidence* doesn't look all that bad' (Young 2002); *Killing Me Softly* resembles 'a soft porn Brian De Palma pastiche' (The Wolf 2002).

INTERVIEW:
DIRECTOR WILLIAM FRIEDKIN

Linda Ruth Williams (LW): I'm interested in *Cruising* as a starting-point for the erotic thriller.

William Friedkin (WF): Let me say that *Cruising* shows *everything*, or as much as it could at the time; there was 40 minutes on the cutting-room floor. My own personal taste, frankly, is for those films that showed less. For example, the sexiest scene I've ever seen in a film was in *Indiscreet* with Cary Grant and Ingrid Bergman. A shot of the two of them talking, then they stop talking. The camera follows them into an elevator to her floor, they get off the elevator, they say goodnight. She goes into her apartment and closes the door. Then she opens it, and he goes in. And then the door closes and the camera just backs away. To me that's the most erotic scene I've ever seen in a film to this day, because it leaves everything to the imagination. Two beautiful people, the audience shared their intimacy. In my own mind's eye what went on in that apartment is far richer than anything that can be shown.

LW: But in *Cruising* you go *through* the door and you show us what's on the other side.

WF: I don't know that I would make the film in the same way today. When I made *Cruising* I was still very much enamoured of trying things out. Getting away with stuff in a way that most people at the time weren't getting away with. I wanted to see how far I could push the envelope. Today, I don't think that pushing the envelope is any great shakes. You can see everything in pornography. And you always could. In out-and-out pornographic films you could always see everything. And because there's no storyline in pornography with rare exceptions, such as that great film, *The Devil in Miss Jones* – Gerard Damiano was a terrific, underrated filmmaker – it became boring, unless you are totally into voyeurism. But *Cruising* was not pure pornography, though it resembled pure pornography in many ways.

LW: But since you are documenting a subculture in *Cruising*, it's necessary to show something to audiences who have no knowledge of it.

WF: But you understand, Linda, that that world was only background to a murder-mystery. I never really intended to make a statement about gay life or the gay world. It just was an exotic background that mainstream audiences had not seen – those people who didn't go to see pornography.

LW: And what was in the forty minutes that you had to cut?

WF: Absolutely graphic sexuality. Many of the people in that film were not actors, with the exception of Pacino and one or two others in major roles. The guys in the clubs where most of the film is set, and where the plot took mysterious twists and turns (which it no longer takes), were not actors; it was real – these guys were not simulating. And that material showed the most graphic homosexuality with Pacino watching, and with the intimation that he may have been participating. But you never get that clearly now. So it becomes a gap in the film because at the end of the film there is the suspicion that he may in fact be a murderer himself, and that was set up in those forty minutes a lot better. It was less ambiguous, and somehow *more* ambiguous at the same time.

LW: How did you research the sub-culture of *Cruising*?

WF: Most of the stuff in the film is set in these clubs which I got permission to go into from the guys who owned them – the Mafia, with members of the New York City Police Department as silent partners, moonlighting on the side, owning these clubs. Periodically, they were forced by their superiors to go in and bust these clubs when things got a little strange. There were actual murders – body parts found in the 'Mineshaft' for example, which is one of the places we shot. That was all documented by Arthur Bell who wrote for the *Village Voice*. He was one of the few to write about the gay subculture, as a gay man, and his articles about what was going on in these clubs – the deaths and the murder and the violence – were what inspired me. There was a novel by Gerald Walker, a *New York Times* reporter, called *Cruising*, which had only a scant resemblance to what we did. The film's producer, Jerry Weintraub, owned that book; he brought it to me, but I thought this is not really very interesting, and I *know* that this isn't what's going on. But I liked the title, and so I spun a completely original film out of it based on Arthur Bell's articles in the *Village Voice*. Later, when the film came out, Arthur Bell went crazy, denounced and attacked the film, provoking numerous attacks from other gay journalists, who suddenly came out of the closet to attack *Cruising*. Arthur Bell had been alone in writing this stuff, but saw it as a warning to gay men, as something which was going to lead to trouble. The playfulness of it was getting out of hand, the drugs that were being consumed, and it was just on the cusp of AIDS – there were these mysterious deaths as well. Bell wrote these graphic, warning articles. Then when he saw it on film he went crazy, because he never intended for the straight world to see it like that. His articles were directed at gay people, and he had no idea that straights would even be interested in this stuff.

LW: So was the problem that something that he felt should have been a dialogue between different factions of the gay world was being represented in the straight world?

WF: A *monologue*, not a dialogue – a monologue by Arthur Bell. He saw himself as a provocative pamphleteer, writing screeds about what was going on in the clubs. Now he sees it in a mainstream film with Al Pacino, and cameras in these places, and something else kicked in for a lot of gay people at that time. It was the beginning of gay rights, and the Stonewall movement – gays were still being widely discriminated against everywhere, but especially in America. He realised, as did a number of other gay writers, that this was not putting the best foot for gay rights – he saw that the strides that were being made were going to be set back by this, and to some extent they were. There were those who said, 'This is exactly what it is, and we ought to face it', and there were others who said, 'This shouldn't be seen – it's only going to cause more, and perhaps violent, discrimination'.

LW: What about the picketing of *Cruising*?

WF: The pickets would throw cans and bottles at the set and the crew and at us when we were filming, sometimes at three in the morning in Greenwich Village, and we started to throw stuff back. It was like a war zone. And then the police would break everything up. There's one shot in the movie when you see Pacino walking down a street late at night coming away from one of the clubs, and it's dead silent. We filmed it at three in the morning, and all you can hear are his footsteps on the street. But at the time we filmed it there were thousands of gay men out of shot shouting 'Pacino you little faggot! You little cocksucker! You motherfucker!' And he had to walk down the street as if there was nobody there. He really freaked out during the making of the film. He had no idea what had been unleashed.

LW: But he really wanted the role, didn't he?

WF: Yes, but there were several guys who lobbied hard for it. Richard Gere, Treat Williams. We had actually started negotiating with Richard Gere, who was really desperate to do it. Then one day I got a call from my agent at William Morris, who was also Pacino's agent, and who said, 'I'm sure you'll want Al'. I actually didn't want Al that badly. I leaned much more towards Richard Gere, because of the androgynous thing that he represented. Pacino's image was totally macho whereas Gere's was not. And so he was far more interesting to me.

LW: Were there moments in the middle of the flak when Pacino regretted doing the film?

WF: Oh sure. He had no idea what he was involved in. It's only in hindsight that I can be somewhat glib about it.

LW: But Pacino is terribly interesting in the film. He's obviously a character who's struggling with his own desire, but he's also the object of desire in a way that he's not anticipating. It's a really interesting role for a guy to be taking on at that point.

WF: But it largely grew out of his difficulty with playing the part. You very often as a director have to use what you've been given. Had Richard Gere played that part it would have been completely different. But I don't think Pacino ever understood any of the subtext of the picture, so I never even talked to him about subtext. Gere might have telegraphed certain things that Pacino never telegraphed because he didn't understand these levels. Gere did. Gere understood *all* the levels, and Pacino understood none of them, not even the surface level. He wanted to work with me, and he understood that it was a cop undercover in homosexual clubs story. When we took him into places like the 'Mineshaft' he wasn't acting, he was scared, he was really scared. So what comes off is the guy also afraid of what's going on with his own problems.

LW: Is that why he's reluctant to talk about it?

WF: It was a very traumatic experience for him. He had done some great and challenging parts, and other films that were dreadful, and he was a big American star, and in control of his work as an actor. After *The Godfather*, *The Godfather Part II*, *Dog Day Afternoon* he had become a force to be reckoned with as an actor, and he *chose* his own roles, and he *chose* this role. But that meant he was completely out of control. He had no control over this character or this part whatsoever.

LW: But that is exactly why it's interesting – that sense of a world out of control and a character out of control, and Pacino is locking into that.

WF: I never talked to him about the possibility that he was also a killer, but I shot it that way. At certain points, like when he's lying in bed with his fiancée Karen Allen, and she's asking him some questions, and his answers are kind of hooded, they're without energy but there's an inner masking going on with his emotions.

LW: There's a wonderful shot when you take the point of view of Al Pacino in the club, and a whole bunch of guys parade in front of him and size him up . . .

WF: One of them's the so-called killer . . .

LW: . . . yes, but we at that point we are explicitly identified with his perspective, and we are also being scrutinised by this parade of guys. One of the things it made me think about was how the film would play to different audiences. I know some very straight guys who find those club scenes very erotic. So these displays of male sexuality are pressing people's buttons in different ways, especially when as audience members we are explicitly the scrutinised object of the desire looking back from the screen.

WF: Well, it's true that audiences were very upset when the film came out – they didn't know *how* to take it. It's easier to reject it and denounce it than to embrace it. *Cruising* scratched something in audiences that was disturbing and disgusting. I thought that was great. I was delighted about that. I had fulfilled my purpose to an extent that was beyond my own imagination – being able to get to that in a film. What led me to make films originally was the notion that they *could* change people's lives, one way or the other.

LW: I wondered what you thought of the similarities between the protests against *Cruising* and what happened many years later with *Basic Instinct*.

WF: The picketing of *Basic Instinct* came from people who were disturbed by the fact that the film was suggesting that a woman who was gay was also a killer. A part of the gay movement jumped on that kind of stuff, and that morphed into political correctness, which we have on almost every level of entertainment and media. But whatever protests there were against *Basic Instinct* were far overwhelmed by the very famous shot of Sharon Stone, which drew people to the cinema as never before. So the protests were by the usual suspects, and by that time people weren't paying that much attention.

LW: Joe Eszterhas talked to the protesters at the time of *Basic Instinct* and he claimed he wanted to change some things afterwards, although Verhoeven didn't. I was thinking back to the disclaimer at the beginning of *Cruising* which says: 'This film is not intended as an indictment of the homosexual world'.

WF: That disclaimer we had to put in because of the ratings board. Saying that 'Not all gays are like this' was part of the dark bargain that was made to get the film released at all. It was a sap to organised gay rights groups. You gotta say somewhere that this is not typical of all gay people – like we thought it was! But Joe Eszterhas has been known for some very boneheaded things, and one of them was to make peace with the gay groups in San Francisco, because I think he lived there at the time. He didn't want them at his door. What's in *Basic Instinct* is exactly what he wanted to be in that film.

LW: He did a similar thing in *Showgirls*. He has said that he regretted the rape scene in that movie.

WF: Joe lives his life constantly falling all over himself and then regretting it. Joe is a very interesting guy, to a large extent because of that mighty dollop of guilt that he carries around. Joe is a guy who sampled or tried on everything and then was sorry about it. He went to the extremes, every possible way you could abuse yourself, and then spent his latter years doing *mea culpas* about it, which is interesting.

LW: Let's talk about *Jade*, which you directed from an Eszterhas script. How did that start?

WF: Joe had written a script and gave it to me and I virtually rewrote it. I loved the central notion, the idea behind Joe's script, but Joe was not interested in doing any sort of rewrites.

LW: So his involvement with the project ended when you picked it up?

WF: Basically, yes. We talked a few times, and then he came to some screenings and made a few suggestions. But he was never on the set.

LW: So what did you like about his script?

WF: The idea of the masks that we all live behind. Basically, when I say I changed it, I mean that his original architecture remains intact. It's a rip-off of *Belle de Jour*, and that's what attracted me to it – I still think that *Belle de Jour* is one of the greatest films ever made. You talk about sex in the cinema, it begins and ends there, in terms of all the levels that's going on in that. So I thought that this was similar to *Belle de Jour*, which was good for me. A woman who is not finding satisfaction in her marriage decides to experiment on the outside. Now melodrama gets introduced by Eszterhas in the form of a couple of murders that take place, and it turns out ultimately that it's the husband, who knew all along what his wife was doing. When it looked like it was going to get exposed, that's when he decided to kill some people. So I thought that was a wonderful conceit, for a movie based on *Belle de Jour*.

LW: So we're in erotic thriller territory again in that it's a crime narrative that's being intimately married to a sexual melodrama. Could you have imagined doing *Jade* without the criminal thriller thread running through it?

WF: Yeah, sure. But the changes would have meant that it would not have gotten made, except as a French movie (laughs). Buñuel's film is so anarchistic and so outrageous. There's a slight crime element in *Belle de Jour*, in that two of the guys that get involved are thieves and hit-men, and one of them achieves a fatal attachment to the Catherine Deneuve character. But *Jade* had to be masked as a crime melodrama, with the secret life of a woman as the background. It would only get made in America as a crime melodrama, as a thriller. It would not get made if it was just a pure examination of a woman's sexuality.

LW: It's interesting that, although the story shifts away from Jade herself and onto the crime narrative, Linda Fiorentino still took it on because she thought it was such as strong female role.

WF: Well it's really a triangle, which is also what I liked about it. And because it's Joe Eszterhas, and my own sensibilities were similar at the time, the woman could only be presented as a sex-object, and as the threatening element from the Garden of Eden; the cause of the serpent's appearance, and of the ultimate fall from grace. So it's still one of those films that's in that category, where the woman is seen as a sex-object and a troublemaker who's come between the two guys. And that's not only a common underlying theme in the films that I've made (including *The Exorcist*) but also of most American filmmakers. It's completely different in European films, where the women are much more complex and they don't just play that one role as being the object of sin and desire. I have to tell you that *Jade* is the favourite of all the films I've made. I think, though it seems like one of the most simplistic, it's really one of the most complex, and it still carries its secrets with it.

LW: When you're directing sex scenes, do you want them to be arousing? And if so, to whom?

WF: That's a really good question. I'm not aware that they are arousing. I don't know if they are. Everyone has their own fantasy. Generally, the scenes I've done are more Boschean than erotic. They're only erotic in the sense that they are terrifying and threatening to the characters in the film and very possibly to the people watching the films. Bosch shows the most outrageous imagery, often sexual, but it works on a level that is more deeply psychological than sexual. Dark fantasy – that's what interests me.

LW: One last question: to what extent do you think that genre labels like 'erotic thriller' are useful for audiences or filmmakers?

WF: I doubt that any filmmakers who are known for particular genres, with the possible exception of Hitchcock, were consciously aware that that's what they were doing. In fact, the great American filmmakers, like John Ford, or John

Huston, worked in *every* genre. Those guys were under contract, the studio handed them a script, and they worked all the time. Nowadays, no one is under contract and people develop their own stuff. To me, a genre director is Dario Argento or Mario Bava – guys who set out to make horror films. But Hitchcock was the master of the erotic thriller, period. All one needs to do is look at those films, and they are a veritable catalogue. Even though most of them don't go as far as *Psycho*, a film like *Vertigo* is in its own way much more disturbing as an erotic thriller than *Psycho*. And *Psycho* is *definitely* an erotic thriller. If you read Donald's Spoto's *The Dark Side of Genius*, and you chart Hitchcock's repression, leading up to his physical assault on Tippi Hedren (which she told me about herself), then you see that following her rejection of his advances, the next film he made was *Psycho*, where the blonde gets cut to pieces. So I think Hitchcock is the only guy I know who is literally transcribing his fantasies on film. Perhaps Buñuel, in a different way. Or Henri-Georges Clouzot, where you're talking about an almost sadomasochistic approach to filmmaking. There's so much going on in *Les Diaboliques*, for example, beyond the central story. It's so wise about men and women – about jealousy and revenge and masks. I take it that Clouzot, who did not make many films, really *intended* to do pictures like that, as did Hitchcock. And as I said, Hitchcock *is* the master of the erotic thriller.

INTERVIEW:
DIRECTOR BRIAN DE PALMA

Linda Ruth Williams (LW): *Femme Fatale* is an erotic thriller about time, and a film which reaps different rewards on second or subsequent viewings and requires a very precise camera language. I know that you've done interesting work around going back to different points of view to see what really happened, a thread which runs through your films.

Brian De Palma (BP): Time, yes. But because the movie is driven by this subconscious dream sequence a lot of it is things which happen in your life, which connect to your subconscious in a way which you logically can't explain. And that's what's unique about movies; images which go right past consciousness, and you're kind of obsessed by them, but you don't quite know why. What's going on in this movie is that structurally it's a heist movie, but then there's a long dream sequence when the woman steals the identity of the woman in Paris who looks like her, and then she reflects on what she dreamt and changes her life.

LW: But this film is also about cinema. It starts with that amazing opening with *Double Indemnity* being watched on television – classic *film noir*, watched from your generation onwards, on TV.

BP: For me it sets out a schematic of where the film's going. You're telling the audience, 'You are going to see a *film noir* dream'. It's late at night, you're watching *Double Indemnity* in bed, you fall asleep, and you *dream Double Indemnity*! That's what you're setting the audience up for.

LW: But you're also watching *Double Indemnity* with the heroine, and the camera pulls back and you realise she's watching it with French subtitles, and it displaces you. Like one film revealing something about another film, a layering in cinema history.

BP: The whole first sequence is about cinema, the Cannes film festival layering dramatic reality onto movie reality.

LW: You watch it, obviously, from A to Z, but then you have to revisit it and think about it in reverse. But I was also thinking about it in relation to fantasy, imagined realities and sexual fantasy as well. The heroine, played by Rebecca Romijn-Stamos, gets to play out different versions of herself.

BP: Absolutely.

LW: Bad girl, girl who makes good, girl exploring different sexualities.

BP: Walk into anybody's closet and they've got all kinds of different versions of themselves.

LW: So she's trying on other personalities?

DP: Absolutely. She's having this obsessive pursuit dream: They are coming for her. Somebody is chasing you for something that you did wrong.

LW: But it turns into a fairy tale. She says, 'I'm your fucking fairy godmother' towards the end.

BP: That was a very instinctual idea. Most *noir* ends very badly. And once I had finished off the *noir* dream I said, 'Well, what would happen if I turned this around 180 degrees?' Things that we learn in our lives, if we know the history, are we doomed to repeat them? Well, I don't feel that. I think you learn from your experiences; that's what wisdom is supposed to be about. That seemed very right to me, though very unconventional in terms of what you would call twenty-first-century cinema story-telling, but I thought, let's just go with what I feel here.

LW: It was marketed in the UK as an erotic thriller, but there's a danger that viewers are going to think it's one kind of film and then realise it's another kind of film, which for me was part of the pleasure of it.

BP: Especially with me they try to connect everything to thrillers or mysteries or horror pictures. When you read reviews like that it looks like they've never even seen the movie. They're just replaying everything they've ever seen written about me over the last three decades.

LW: Did you think of it as an erotic thriller, and are you conscious of genre? Is it meaningful or helpful in the filmmaking process?

BP: You make educated guesses about how a picture should proceed. We had a very inventive trailer that won all kinds of prizes. It gave you the idea. I don't know how you sell movie like that. The most innovative ones like *Mulholland Drive* and *Momento* – they're unique. They don't fit into a marketing niche; but the distributors do the best they can.

LW: I'm interesting in the scandal and reception around *Body Double* and *Dressed to Kill*, particularly the feminist picketing, and there are elements in *Femme Fatale* which are in many ways more explicit, more overtly sexual, maybe to some minds more problematic, than anything that appeared in those films. But of course time has moved on and there's none of the scandal attached to what you're doing with the female character here.

BP: That's the problem with whatever mores are going on in your particular culture at the time you're making these movies. But the movies have an integrity and honesty and if they do, they will live through the maelstroms when they come out. There are so many ways they sentimentalised *Dressed to Kill*. Twenty, thirty years away nobody even mentions the political issues that it was up against when it came out.

LW: Would you prefer to be the scandalous filmmaker who's provoking those kind of responses?

BP: I don't think you approach it that way. You approach it like something that makes perfect sense to you, and I seem to have always swum against the stream; I've done that all my life. But it's not something I feel uncomfortable with. Is it difficult? Is it unpleasant? You bet. But what can you do? You have to do what appears to be the truth. You have to live through it and hopefully continue working. (Laughs)

LW: So do you feel that you've consciously got a stake in making adult films for adult viewers?

BP: That's another interesting thing that as I've gotten older you become very aware of. The subject matter that's flooding the American cineplexes is completely of no interest to you. Well, why should it be? You're over sixty. You're not really interested in how you're going to get laid this Friday. It's not at the top of your priorities. And I guess at sixty, if it were, that would be a sad comment. So yes, you are drawn to more adult stuff. I watch a lot of French movies because they seem to deal with adult situations and obviously being an adult you'll relate to that.

LW: *Femme Fatale* seems to me to be an American in Paris story, like *Obsession* in Italy – it's thinking about an American relationship to Europeanness.

BP: Again, it's something that's been done across the history of the creative arts. An English artist goes to Venice – what's surprising about that? But I'm living in America in an era which has become completely isolated. Not only are they not interested in what's going on in the world outside the United States, they're antagonistic about it!

LW: So how does that affect the way that a film like this played to American audiences?

BP: Not very well. At first they thought it was a foreign film. And the fact that it had subtitles really confused them. The concept that you can't have a film with subtitles on without killing it in the marketplace! I was brought up on films with subtitles!

LW: So to the question you're always being asked about your relationship to Hitchcock – clearly *Femme Fatale* is also revisiting that voyeuristic, stalking sequence in *Dressed to Kill* and *Vertigo*.

BP: To answer this question for the hundred thousandth time. Hitchcock discovered a lot of pure cinematic tools in a vast and brilliant career. The point-of-view shot followed by the close-up is a basic building block of cinema. It's what makes cinema unique because it shows audience and character the same precise visual information. That's what brings you into the movie – you're seeing the same thing Jimmy Stewart's seeing in *Vertigo*. So that's why this experience goes beyond somebody retelling a story. This is *your* story.

LW: But this story is also about the female protagonist's point of view.

BP: It's her dream. That's something I had to explain to Antonio [Banderas] all the time. Your [character is] a paparazzo only because she *dreams* you as a paparazzo.

LW So he's a function of her desire and her fantasy?

BP: Absolutely. A complete projection of her subconscious. But it's kind of difficult to explain to an actor that you're a figment of someone else's imagination!

LW: She's also much taller than him. Did you want that?

BP: Yes, I wanted her to be overpowering, certainly in her dream of herself.

LW: How did you handle the look of her?

BP: Well, first you have this fantastic, beautiful girl, who can carry all kinds of clothes and looks. That's what models do even better than actresses in some ways. They really transform themselves. That's what makes the mystery of the woman, which is interesting for film directors because it's a visual mystery. Women have always been a visual mystery to men, and that's why they're used so relentlessly in advertising. They don't have to say anything – they just *look*.

LW: This is a cinematic film in the best possible sense. But people repeat-view on DVD or video now. That's clearly a shift in cinema culture.

BP: That's true of any lasting work of art. What books do we keep on our shelves? I don't think it's the latest potboiler mystery that sold seven million copies that you keep. You keep *War and Peace* on your shelf – things you can re-read and as you grow older you find different things in them. I haven't got a vast DVD collection because I try to only keep things that I will in fact look at again.

LW: So when you're making films, are you thinking of it as a cinematic film or have you got your eye on that afterlife?

BP: No, no, no. You are who you are as a filmmaker. I'm sure Hitchcock never thought that we'd be studying his films in the way we so obsessively do. He was just making a good mystery story, a suspense story. Artists don't really think about that. They just go out to make things that make sense to them and are very straightforward about it. It's a job. And to connect with something that's particularly truthful, which seems to last if your perceptions are particularly unique. In movies I feel close to Hitchcock because I'm driven by the eye, much like he was.

3. 'MEISTERS OF PORNO-NOIR' – KEY PLAYERS IN THE CINEMATIC EROTIC THRILLER

This chapter develops work on the mainstream erotic thriller by discussing some key genre players. Writer Joe Eszterhas is almost entirely identified with his prolific work on the genre, the '*meister* of porno *noir*' (Hirsch 1998: 202), having penned four of its biggest titles (*Jagged Edge*, *Basic Instinct*, *Jade* and *Sliver*) as well as a key scandal of mainstream softcore, *Showgirls*. Eszterhas is interesting for a number of reasons, not least that he is an exemplary genre player, repeatedly recycling formulaic erotic thriller fare. He is also responsible for making the screenwriter a public figure, an adept self-mythologist whose image is of 'the poor immigrant boy who grew up to sell multimillion-dollar scripts' (Holub 1991: 82). As a star writer in the 1990s Eszterhas was in a league of his own, able to command huge salaries precisely because across the erotic thriller's high-point period his name attached to a film guaranteed a certain level of box office interest: 'the talent I have is to write audience movies', he has said (Grove 1992a: 10).[1] This ensured that with a few peak films, the mainstream erotic thriller became one of the most publicised of contemporary genre forms. One internet writer lamented, 'The superb films of noirmaster John Dahl play in art-houses and drive-ins and on cable television, while virtually every premise that Joe Eszterhack touches evolves into cultural symbolism.'[2] Whilst audiences loved being driven hard by the rollercoaster of the James Dearden-penned *Fatal Attraction*, the most frequent criticism of Eszterhas is that he is too much of an audience manipulator. In this he is abetted by sensationalist director Paul Verhoeven, a renowned genre player, also known for his work in fantasy-science fiction (*Robocop* [1987], *Total Recall* [1990], *Starship Troopers* [1997], *Hollow Man* [2000]). However, the focus here will be Verhoeven's sexual material, including *Basic Instinct* and what we might call its 'pre-make', *De Vierde Man* (*The Fourth Man*, 1983) – a Dutch title which looks very much like a try-out of the *Basic Instinct* scenario, only seen by wide audiences outside the Netherlands once Verhoeven had made it in Hollywood. The Verhoeven-directed and Ezsterhas-penned *Showgirls* will be discussed as blighted through genre, a critical and box office failure partly because it abandoned tried-and-tested erotic thriller co-ordinates in order to develop a new generic hybrid, the porno-backstage musical. In it, however, Verhoeven continued to develop a set of positions on the pornographic, pushing the envelope of explicitness as the next stage in his engagement with censorship and American popular genre. The third part of this chapter will focus on Michael Douglas, who has become perhaps *the* leading man of the mainstream erotic thriller, the initially hapless but finally revengeful dupe of *femmes fatales* from Glenn Close (*Fatal Attraction*) through Sharon Stone (*Basic Instinct*) to Demi Moore (*Disclosure*). Although his star image has been shaped across a range of different products (*The War of the Roses*, *Wall Street*, *Falling Down*), one strong career thread runs through his erotic thriller work. He is, I will argue, a contemporary incarnation of the 'Cain male' victim of desire epitomised by the men of hardboiled writer James M. Cain. Through the image of Douglas we might address the effect of identification with genre on star persona.

Though Douglas is my focus, throughout this book it will be noted that, such is the dominance of the erotic thriller in 1980s and 1990s cinema, a number of stars recur in different guises in different titles, though none is as consistently identified with the genre as Douglas or the women I will come to later: Sharon Stone (also an Ezsterhas collaborator in *Basic Instinct* and *Sliver*), Gina Gershon (who was in Eszterhas'/Verhoeven's *Showgirls*) and Linda Fiorentino (who was in the Eszterhas-penned *Jade*). But other stars are significant to the genre. Glenn Close preceded her vengeful prototype *femme fatale* role in *Fatal Attraction* with a female form of the Cain male in *Jagged Edge*, playing the lawyer-dupe of an archetypical *homme fatal*. (Perhaps *Fatal Attraction* can be seen as Close's revenge on the role she was dealt by Eszterhas in *Jagged Edge*, though the duped – usually male – victim is distinct from the female victim of classic *noir* and the horror film's woman-in-peril.) Tom Berenger's profile has also partly been forged through work in erotic thriller-influenced films (*Sliver*, *Someone to Watch Over Me*, *Body Language*, *The Substitute*, *An Occasional Hell*, *Fear City*), though he is not as consistent a male-type as Douglas. Mickey Rourke's career plummet too can be traced in his work in softcore sex films, from mainstream success like *9½ Weeks* and *Angel Heart*, to the DTV work of *Love in Paris* (aka *Another 9½ Weeks*), *Wild Orchid* and *Exit in Red*. Only the last two are erotic thrillers; the *9½ Weeks* films are erotic melodramas, whilst *Angel Heart* is a horror film. All have strong softcore elements running through them which sexualise Rourke (though he is seldom a beefcake equivalent of the female cheesecake), making him a fascinating figure for discussions of contemporary masculinity and performance, shot through with an existential aloofness, and lately a beaten-up quality. Sean Young and Madeleine Stowe, despite high-profile work as sometime A-listers, have both appeared in a number of erotic thriller-related titles. Young's move from mainstream to DTV work bears out that old dictum, that in B-movies you're either on your way up or on your way down – now the latter, but at least she's still in work. High-profile mainstream productions such as *A Kiss Before Dying* and *Love Crimes* were followed by the genre spoof *Fatal Instinct*, and then more than her fair share of DTV fare. Madeleine Stowe appears in *Blink*, *China Moon* and *Unlawful Entry*, like Young varying her input as good girl or bad, avenging woman or woman in peril. Other stars who have been more regular habituées of the erotic thriller become significant for the final part of this chapter, when I look at figures most closely identified with the mainstream *femme fatale* – Fiorentino as bitch, Gershon as lesbian icon, Stone as devil.

1: WRITTEN BY JOE ESZTERHAS: *JAGGED EDGE*, *SLIVER*, *JADE*

'You don't like sex and violence? It sells, you know.'

Jack Lansford (Tom Berenger) in *Sliver*

Many critics have been quick to point out that screenwriter Joe Eszterhas has made a lot of money writing the same film several times over.[3] This makes him the exemplary formulaic genre player, with a long (if not honourable) tradition of repetition behind him. Richard Maltby tells the story of 1930s Warner Brothers producer Bryan Foy, 'known as the "keeper of the Bs"':

> He is supposed to have kept a pile of about 20 scripts on his desk. Each time his unit completed a movie, its script would go to the bottom of the pile. Over a period of about a year, it would gradually work its way back up to the top. Then it would be dusted off and given to the scriptwriter to rewrite: a crime story would become a Western, the sex of the leading characters would be changed, the location moved. In due course, the new script would return to the bottom of the pile to be recycled in the same way. (Maltby 1995: 112–13)[4]

Whilst Maltby admits that this story may be apocryphal, at the very least, 'it illustrates the cost-effectiveness of Hollywood's system of constructing familiar fictions that fulfilled their audience's requirement that movies be "just like . . . but completely different" from each other'. Joe Eszterhas, however, does not even inject the difference of a change of genre into his repeated narratives, though the good guys and bad guys do sometimes switch sex between shoots. If Foy produced a version of the same movie eleven times over, Eszterhas has written the same film as an erotic thriller four times over (*Jagged Edge*, *Basic Instinct*, *Sliver* and *Jade*), but he has also twice given us that same plot in another thriller form (*Betrayed*, *Music Box*), and has supplemented his erotic thriller work with an ongoing interest in the sexuality of America (*Showgirls*, the unfilmed screenplay *Sacred Cows*, his Clinton-era prose work *American Rhapsody*, and his 2003 autobiography *Hollywood Animal*). Reviewing *Jade*, one internet writer mirrors reception of a number of Eszterhas products when he writes, 'Eszterhas simply stacked one cliché on top of the next, turned out generic Hollywood product, and cashed an enormous check'.[5] 'Sooner or later', wrote Adam Mars-Jones reflecting on how *Basic Instinct* follows its female-lead predecessors but with a male protagonist, 'sitting in front of his gold-plated word processor with nothing in his head but the need to repeat a past success, Eszterhas was bound to transpose the genders in the story that had served him so well' (1992: 18).[6] Thus the story of Ezsterhas' repetitions becomes the story of the films' reception.

In July 1993 American *Premiere* magazine ran a competition asking readers to create their own version of the Eszterhas story, accompanying this with a comically neo-Proppian chart mapping out the repetition of types from five films (*Jagged Edge, Basic Instinct, Sliver, Betrayed* and *Music Box*). In each film there is an Imperilled Protagonist who has a Memorable Trait, who is usually the lover of the Suspect who also has a Memorable Trait (though in *Music Box* the suspect is the Father). Each film also contains a Decoy Suspect, a Lethal Weapon and the killer (who usually turns out to be the Suspect, the Decoy remaining just a decoy) displays a range of often kinky Homicidal Refinements. It is also animated by the suspense-fuelling Burning Question: 'Did Jack carve up his rich wife?' (*Jagged Edge*); 'Did Gary murder talk-radio shock-jock Sam Karaus?' (*Betrayed*); 'Is Mike "Miska", a war criminal?' (*Music Box*); 'Did Catherine murder "civic-minded" rock star Johnny Boz?' (*Basic Instinct*); 'Is Zeke murdering the tenants of his building?' (*Sliver*) (Hoffman 1993: 40). *Jade* was written after *Premiere* prepared its chart, but it is easy to imagine Eszterhas dusting down his *oeuvre* (and perhaps even consulting *Premiere*'s tropes) to help him pose the next question in line, 'Is clinical psychologist Trina also exotic prostitute Jade, and did she kill politically connected businessman Kyle Medford?' (or as one internet writer put it, 'Was it Jade? Was it Trina? Or was it someone we would never suspect, because Eszterhas couldn't be bothered to plant some damn clues?').[7]

What *Premiere*'s chart doesn't include is an intimation of the sexual tropes which drive the Eszterhas fantasy-factory, though this is foregrounded else-where (French 1995b).[8] William Leith (1995) noted:

> Raymond Chandler once said that if he felt his plot was ever in danger of sagging, he'd make a man walk into the room with a gun. Eszterhas does the same sort of thing – a man walks into the room with a stack of porn.

In 1997 *Neon* magazine followed *Premiere* with a shorter version of the 'all Joe's screenplays are the same' story, under the heading 'Join the Plots: The Inventive Storylines of Joe Eszterhas'. This sat brief synopses of Eszterhas's more sexualised films next to each other (*Jagged Edge, Basic Instinct, Sliver, Jade* and *Showgirls*), demonstrating that though the first is called a Murder Mystery, the second, third and fourth are called Erotic Murder Mysteries and the latter is called an 'Erotic Why-was-this-made? Mystery', they all contain a subplot which relates characters sexually across a divide of power or criminality, plus a 'brutally realistic' sequence (usually of S&M, rape or stripping – some kind of sexual spectacle which is justified as slice-of-life rather than salacious voyeurism), whilst the last four are notable for their gratuitous sex (Mitchell 1997: 17). Andy Spletzer, of website Film.com, identified the characteristic Eszterhas tropes: 'A hyper-masculine writer, Eszterhas is famous for his strong, sexual, often sexually ambiguous, female fantasy-figures who stalk, control, and often kill their weaker male counterparts. That and taking adolescent boasting and cursing out of the boy's locker room and applying it to the male-dominated workplace.'[9] Eszterhas' version of hardboiled dialogue is to throw in as many expletives as possible in a desperate attempt to display the writer's liberated attitude to permissive issues as well as a neat way of jacking up a film's controversy quota (Stables reads this explicitness as neo-sexism). Moral minder internet site kids-in-mind (www.kids-in-mind.com) regularly rates popular films for their levels of sex/nudity, violence/gore and profanity, also commenting on a film's adult issues and its overall message. Not surprisingly, Eszterhas' screenplays usually merit high scores on kids-in-mind's 1–10 system of 'Movie Ratings That Actually Work'[10] (clearly, this could also provide an efficient form of recommendation to certain sections of the audience, as a neat way of calculating a film's quota of transgressive elements): *Jade* scores 8 all round, *Basic Instinct* between 8 and 10; *Showgirls* gets 9 for sex and 8 for profanity; *Sliver* gets a high score for sex but lower for violence.

Although Eszterhas had already penned the enormously successful proto-musical *Flashdance* for Adrian Lyne, the first try-out of this formulaic plot was the 1985 film *Jagged Edge*, the contemporary blueprint for the characteristic story of sexual involvement with 'the wrong guy' (or woman), coming several years before other mainstream versions of the same narrative (*Sea of Love*, *Body of Evidence*, *Someone to Watch Over Me* et al.). That it contains only 'plot-relevant sex' makes it a prototype mainstream erotic thriller which does not hinge on softcore spectacle.[11] Here high-powered female lawyer Teddy Barnes (Glenn Close) falls for the suspect, Jack Forrester (Jeff Bridges), whom she is defending on a murder rap, just as Nick Curran (Michael Douglas) will fall for the murder suspect (Sharon Stone) he is pursuing in *Basic Instinct* seven years later, just as Carly Norris (Sharon Stone) will fall for her landlord Zeke Hawkins (William Baldwin) whom she suspects of killing women in *Sliver*, two years after that. In *Jade*, detective David Corelli (David Caruso) investigates a woman with whom he had an affair several years earlier, now married to his best friend, a lawyer, but this doesn't stop investigator and suspect having a brief sexual tryst. In between, *Betrayed* sees Debra Winger as an FBI agent falling for the man she is investigating for murder. If Jessica Lange's involvement with the man she is defending in court in *Music Box* is familial rather than sexual (he's her father), this is nevertheless a version of the favourite Eszterhas story tracing personal implication between a couple on different sides of the law.

Since the narrative point of view of each of these films is that of the law rather than the suspect, the emphasis is on the pleasures of transgression for the law's tainted representative. What is also significant is that Eszterhas's deployment of powerful female protagonists diminishes as his career progresses and his pay-packet grows (it was probably all downhill after the female welder of *Flashdance*). Of these similarly plotted thrillers, all three 1980s scripted films focus on a strong heroine in an authoritative job (*Jagged Edge*, *Music Box*, *Betrayed*); of his 1990s thrillers, only one (*Sliver*) deploys a female protagonist and privileges her point of view (combining this with an unironic fetishising male gaze almost entirely absent from the 1980s thrillers), whilst the other two (*Basic Instinct* and *Jade*) deploy the traditional gender mix of male investigative protagonist and apparently demonic *femme fatale*. From the 1980s to the 1990s an escalation in the salacious sexual detail of Eszterhas' films has accompanied a regression into the traditional types of male hero/female other. Set against this, and perhaps contrary to some feminist readings of the period such as Susan Faludi's (who sees 1980s Hollywood as regressively 'silencing' women as part of a backlash against feminism [1992: 140–70]), viewers writing about Eszterhas' work have become increasingly impatient with his sexual stereotyping, which may also account for the diminishing box office returns for his work after *Basic Instinct*. It therefore could not be said that the sexism of Eszterhas' 1990s work reflects 1990s sexism, for his viewers are telling a different story – by *Jade* at the decade's mid-point the stupidity of the role Linda Fiorentino is given is one of the prime criticisms of this Eszterhas rewrite number 6, by writers in popular and broadsheet papers as well as on the internet. The cycle from *Jagged Edge* to *Jade* plots the gradual disparity between Eszterhas' interpretation of the sexual attitudes of his times, and his audience's increasingly critical reading of his sexual vision. The interplay between text and its reception context is marked, after *Basic Instinct* at least, by a widening gap between what he thinks audiences want and what they will actually tolerate. His legendary talent for writing 'audience movies' carries him through to *Basic Instinct* only. Though he casts himself as a liberal, by the mid-1990s Eszterhas was writing ill-judged, sexually conservative scripts which failed to meet the much more liberal expectations of his viewers.

Jagged Edge might then be read as a high-point. It opens, like John Carpenter's *Halloween*, with an unknown killer, whose point of view we share, enacting a sex-murder. *Basic Instinct* opens similarly (minus the point-of-view cinematography), and is also followed by a lurid cops-at-the-scene-of-the-crime scene. Such scenes, along with Eszterhas favoured police interrogation sequences, frequently descend into an exchange of cod legalese clichés and hardboiled retorts, making it difficult to distinguish between characters in each particular scene, and between the same scenes across different Eszterhas films. Both *Jagged Edge* and *Basic Instinct* also chart the sexual involvement of law-keeper and (suspected) law-breaker: in both films the lawyer/cop becomes vulnerable to the charms of the suspect because of a prior professional misdemeanour which gives the villain maximum powers of manipulation. Sexual implication also makes Teddy a female version of Nick Curran in that she, unusually for a mainstream erotic thriller woman, becomes hormone- rather than reason-led – a colleague asks, '[is it] your head talking or another part of your anatomy?' Nick is equally led by a woman who is able to deploy sex in order to screw 'with your head', using that 'magna cum laude pussy' – this became a much-replicated line for the genre, such as when cop Linda Fiorentino's partner in *Bodily Harm* comments, of Fiorentino's foolish defence of the handsome suspect, 'If you were a man I'd say you were talking with your dick.' Desire-led justice and sex-skewed investigation are something to which both men and women are prone.

This is standard Eszterhas fare. But in its focus on and through the perspec- tive of a central female character the film also confronts women with their own 'jagged edge' of identification. One characteristic Eszterhas contradiction is an ability vividly to present misogynistic spectacle and then contextualise it through a gesture of feminism, implicating a female character in such a repre- sentation then drawing back from it himself by claiming that he's just the mes- senger. *Showgirls*, for instance, contained a rape scene which Eszterhas later came to regret: 'We should not, I feel now, have shown [it], although I do insist that to show such a scene does not imply any complicity in it' (Vulliamy 2000: 2). This presentation and disclaimer usually happen at one and the same time, however, as when Teddy, *Jagged Edge*'s heroine-in-control, is misogyny's ambivalent target. In a scene of astonishingly salacious misogyny, one female witness is made to report her mutilation by an assailant, which Teddy, and her viewers, must watch. The spectacle of her horrified absorption in the descrip- tion becomes as central as the telling of the story itself.[12] This focus on Close's face and her performance is clearly more directorial than scripted, but it rein- forces an earlier scene when, cross-examining a male witness, Teddy becomes the target of his hatred. An atmosphere of tension emerges from the screenplay which frames misogyny from both sides, exposing its effect on its victim but also revelling in the sexual malice as a high point in the thriller rollercoaster, typical of the genre's wider ambivalence about its own misogyny. It may be that a balanced screenplay will present both sides of the story, but Eszterhas' inabil- ity to decide between misogyny or feminism marks his work in a much more fundamental way.

This is particularly true of *Sliver*, Ezsterhas next venture after *Basic Instinct*, a film in which the heroine Carly (Sharon Stone) is caught in a vicious scopo- philic network, living in an upmarket apartment block shot through by a myce- lium of video surveillance networks through which the building's owner (Carly's neighbour Zeke [William Baldwin]) watches his tenants from a panop- ticon-like viewing room, bedecked with numerous monitors. A series of murders take place as Carly's sexual relationships with two men, both suspects, unfolds; voyeurism may or may not be implicated in the crimes (the film's stra- pline was 'You like to watch, don't you?'; the live-action footage Zeke obsesses

Figure 7: 'No more private moments': Carly (Sharon Stone) on *Sliver*'s bank of
surveillance monitors. Paramount/The Kobal Collection.

over looks remarkably like the content of an average DTV erotic thriller). *Sliver*
was received as a kind of sexualised update of Hitchcock – *Rear Window* in
particular (Hirschhurn, Kempley, Walker, Hutchinson, all 1993). If a string of
horror films have taken their 'murderous gaze' cues from *Peeping Tom*, erotic
thrillers have developed the sexual undercurrents of Hitchcock into extensive
sexual-criminal opportunities. *Sliver* engages in a cod psychoanalytic justification of perversion which (like *Peeping Tom* before it) effectively blames aberration on one's parents (Zeke's fascination with TV monitors comes, he says,
from seeing his soap-star mother more often on TV than in the flesh).[13] The
complex of criminal pretext and psycho-sexual intrigue provided by infant
trauma in the backstories of dodgy characters is a gift to the erotic thriller, not
just those which unfold on the shrink's or the sex therapist's couch (*Body of
Influence, Sexual Intent, Threat of Exposure*). *Last Call* begins with a flashback
of mother-murder which justifies the daughter-heroine's retribution; *Mirror
Images II* is predicated on a convoluted web of rivalry and lust between good-
bad twins and their father. *Sliver* doesn't dwell on Zeke's pathology except by
sharing it; its all-pervasive voyeurism, which the press notes claim generates a
sense of unease as well as eroticism ('I wanted to give the sense of looking
through a lens at all times', says production designer Paul Sylbert) aims to evoke
the feeling that, as director Phillip Noyce says, 'there are no more private
moments' (Fig. 7).[14] One scene, in which Carly is watched by Zeke through surveillance equipment as she masturbates in the bath, will be examined later in

relation to the erotic thriller's widespread neo-scopophilic sexual interest in voyeuristic women. The problem for *Sliver* was how to do this whilst maintaining some sort of consciousness of (paying lip-service to) the feminism of a portion of the target audience (and, in Sharon Stone's case, the lead performer). The DTV erotic thrillers I will turn to later make a virtue of female visual pleasure, seeming to cock a snook at male-gaze theorists by including women as active scopic participants (typically in these films women masturbate whilst watching video footage of sex acts). At the same time these DTV films award their own audiences pole position for securing a good look at those women in the act of sexual looking. But the DTV film also knows itself to be exploitation cinema of the highest/lowest order; any empowering arguments about women taking control of the gaze which the DTVs might make come after the fact of pleasing the core male heterosexual audience with sexy images of women taking secret pleasure. *Sliver*, on the other hand, wants to be something else, a higher-budget erotic essay on contemporary sexual power, perhaps, with a classier pedigree than, say, Hippolyte's voyeuristically similar *Animal Instincts* or Mundhra's surveillance-obsessed *Night Eyes*. One way of creating a gap between high and low comes, of course, with cast and crew: Stone was at the top of Hollywood's A-list tree *circa* 1993, Eszterhas was its highest paid screenwriter, Robert Evans came back from a legendary fall to produce (with the pedigree of *Rosemary's Baby*, *Chinatown* and *Marathon Man* underpinning his new venture). Eszterhas' script here is also based on a novel by Ira Levin, which ought to separate it from the common Eszterhasian plot junctures outlined above. Narratively, *Sliver* promises a woman's story, which ought, with one significant genre-shift, to distance it from exploitation: Carly gives us a sympathetic point of view, the woman-in-peril with a sensitive back-story and a questing trajectory. Though it shows her becoming increasingly interested in Zeke's surveillance equipment (women can do it too; 'I love the view,' she says early on), it tries to disavow an undercurrent of salacious glee in peeping with a final critique of visual obsession: Carly walks out of Zeke's visual eyrie, passing a violent moral judgement on his fascination with the live-action footage of his tenants' lives (she shoots his bank of TV monitors). This seems to be Eszterhas having his cake and eating it, typical of a writer who undercuts his own exploitation instincts with a later bleeding-heart retraction or disavowal. *Sliver*, it seems, wants both to indulge in its own barefaced voyeurism and give itself the alibi of mild feminist critique of male-gaze obsessions. Thus we get the exploitation spectacle (scopophilically-framed views of Carly, and views of Carly viewing) and we get the critique of exploitation spectacle (Carly's suspicion and dismissal).

Sliver was not the box office success of *Basic Instinct*, though it performed decently, faring worst with reviewers on both sides of the Atlantic (it grossed $35 million in its first five weeks and was number one in the box office for its first two weeks). Though one reviewer, reading it in a tradition of voyeurism movies (*Blue Velvet, Sex, Lies and Videotape*) criticised it for 'an *excess* of vision' (Romney 1993), most UK reviews criticised its excess of sex, suggesting that in mainstream cinema at least something was beginning to shift *circa* 1993, a pre-echo of the reception of *Showgirls* two years later. With *Sliver* it became smart for journalists to adopt a neo-puritanism regarding mainstream sexual images. The same tone was taken in reception material surrounding *Body of Evidence* also released in 1993, with both films allowing writers to focus on the limited acting abilities of their female leads, whose performances were eclipsed by their general images as sex sirens (Madonna's *Sex*, a book of erotic photographs of the star, had been published in 1992). Stone seems to have partly seen their point: originally sold to her as 'an equal-opportunities revealer' (McGregor 1993: 20), *Sliver* was re-edited to cut out the frontal nudity of Baldwin but retain Stone's nakedness ('I just hope the audience give me the benefit of the doubt', Stone said. 'At least my character, a book editor, is a woman with some intellectual life' [quoted in Davis 1993: 39; see also Lyttle 1993: 18]). However, these early signs of an impending backlash against the erotic thriller's eroticism (in its A-movie form at least) may be symptoms of its prescience in other ways. In particular, it may also be that films like *Sliver* paved the way for later popular forms of the female sexual quest narrative such as *Sex and the City*. Whatever else it is, *Sliver* is another female sexual-quest tale; recently single Carly – like Carrie Bradshaw (Sarah Jessica Parker) and Samantha Jones (Kim Cattrall) some years later and in a more comedic television genre context – is in search of satisfaction in New York, 'new orgasms' as Ezsterhas' screenplay puts it.

But a specific critical indignation is reserved for Eszterhas as author of *Sliver* (Levin's more oedipally-charged original novel hardly gets a mention and certainly attracts no blame), largely because of how much he is supposed to have been paid. Below I will discuss how difficult it is for female erotic thriller stars to escape the sex-star label once it has stuck. Eszterhas' star-trap was formed when he cashed his pay cheque for *Basic Instinct*; his salary became the reported fact about him, the standard by which everything he subsequently did was judged. Phillip Noyce, director of *Sliver*, gets hardly a critical glance amidst the barrage of opprobrium poured on Ezsterhas ('The movie's main liability is its woeful script' [Amidon 1993; see also Brown 1993; Malcolm 1993]). Most reviews of the film start from the premise of Eszterhas' salary for his *previous* film; critical judgement becomes, then, a question of assessing cost-effectiveness, with screenwriting quality reflecting (or not) screenwriter's salary.[15] This is a charge which followed Eszterhas through into another project (*Jade*) with a different director (William Friedkin).

Jade: 'I do the fucking – I never get fucked'

That Eszterhas' next screenwriting outing after *Sliver* and *Showgirls* was a flop is also generally attributed to the writer rather than the director. *Jade* opened in America three weeks after *Showgirls*, and with Eszterhas already in the firing line, the latter film also carried some of the cultural flak attracted by the former.

Director William Friedkin gamely tries to inject some *noir*ish style into the same old story: the opening sequence, a long take with the camera wandering through an opulent, art-filled house towards what turns out to be a murder, committed just as we arrive, replays *Jagged Edge*, except that here the camera point of view is that of the omniscient narrator rather than the killer. The film also nods to its genre heritage with a 'Lady from Shanghai' sequence (a chase through a Chinese theatre, building on the film's obsession with oriental exotica underpinned by the sexual pseudonym Jade), as well as some stylish *noir*ish deployments of shadows, mirrors and characterisation: at one point Linda Fiorentino's face is exactly cut in half by a shadow cast by her husband, but the film shows that it's not the divided woman but the shady man whodunit. Friedkin also makes ample use of the subliminal inserts he had first deployed in *The Exorcist* to evoke an unsettling sense of seeing and not seeing a thing at the same time, provoking an ocular uncertainty which prefigures the film's psychological theme of 'hysterical blindness' (psychologist Trina's specialist subject).[16] Yet despite this stylistic '*noiring*', *Jade* remains a curious mix of the formulaic and the impenetrable, almost universally condemned for its reliance on the writer's previous scripts. Indeed, Eszterhas is often blamed so that his director can be exonerated; one internet reviewer wrote of *Jade*: 'there is nothing anyone could have done with this material. Orson Welles, Brando, and Larry Olivier in their primes could only have made a screwed-up movie out of this script.'[17]

After *Cruising*, this is not entirely unfamiliar territory for Friedkin; but *Jade* also hits all the usual Eszterhas buttons fairly efficiently. Friedkin's intermittent *noir* style, crisp cinematography and an innovative use of music consequently do battle with a strong injection of pornographic voyeurism featuring extended sequences of powerful men having kinky sex with classy prostitutes, caught on secret video. The story is familiar: clinical psychologist Trina Gavin (Fiorentino) is suspected of killing San Francisco millionaire Kyle Medford, who has been facilitating the sexual escapades of a number of powerful men (including the Californian Governor) by providing them with prostitutes and a house by the sea (equipped with the kind of sexual paraphernalia which brings out Eszterhas' most lurid dialogue tendencies). Here Medford videoed them in action (in order to blackmail them), also capturing on film the mysterious 'Jade', a pot of whose pubic hair was in his collection of trophies. Jade turns out to be Trina, moonlighting in the sex industry both for her own pleasure and to revenge her philandering attorney husband, Matt Gavin (Chazz Palminteri), who it turns out killed Medford. A number of other criminal and sexual sub-plots generously pattern the story with red herrings, one of which concerns Assistant District Attorney David Corelli (David Caruso), best friend to Gavin and ex-lover of Trina. At one point Corelli and Trina begin to have sex, and Corelli's investigation is haunted by the sense of his implicatedness with the suspect through their shared sexual past. This may sound like any other Eszterhas plot: a *femme* who may or may not be *fatale*, an implicated cop smitten with the suspect, a crime which uncovers a labyrinth of weird sexual practices underpinned by political corruption, all laced with the usual profane hardboiled Eszterhas language (it is the sex-hungry Governor Edwards who says, 'I do the fucking – I never get fucked'). But critics evidence a frustration in the combination of repetition and confusion which *Jade* delivers.[18] Why, then, given that Eszterhas has had so much practice in reshuffling the narrative pack, should *Jade* have been almost universally received as a failure?

If the seven years from *Jagged Edge* to *Basic Instinct* chart Eszterhas' most culturally successful period (when 'virtually every premise . . . evolves into cultural symbolism'), the three years after provide a series of critical and/or box office failures (*Sliver*, *Showgirls*, *Jade*) which evidence a decreasing ability to track the pulse of his times. Since his focus has been so sexual, it is appropriate that his most fundamental misunderstanding is about his audiences' acceptance of feminism. Running through *Jade* is the issue of pinning a woman to a sexually inflected homicide which then turns out to be not her doing. As with *Basic Instinct*, the woman's guilt pervades *Jade*, and even though in this case she isn't actually guilty, she is somehow guilty anyway (this erotic thriller staple is common across the genre in its many forms: the tag-line of Jim Wynorski's *Body Chemistry 4*, also released in 1995, might serve to summarise a number of Eszterhas plots: 'Guilty or not, there's no way she's innocent').[19] Indeed, even when her innocence is revealed, Gavin arranges the visual spectacle of her guilt – photos of her sexual escapades – around her dressing table, as a visual frame to his *own* confession. In *Jade* Eszterhas once again airs his fascination/phobia for beautiful but brainy women, a combination as manifestly deadly to the genre as the blonde broad with the smoking gun. He is also fond of female shrinks: Jeanne Tripplehorn's Beth is a police psychologist in *Basic Instinct*; Tramell took a psychology degree. This enables women to 'pull your strings', as one character in *Jade* puts it, all the more efficiently. Female viewers often seem to be that bit more vehement about Eszterhas' textual sexism: Monica Sullivan, for instance, laments the premise which sees woman as guilty even if she *didn't* do it ('Spotlight wanker Eszterhack fearlessly strikes a blow for nineteenth-century domestic morality when he implies that none of these bad things would have happened if only Linda had stayed at home and worked a little harder on her sex life with [her husband]').[20] I will return to the implications of this bitch-type-casting for Fiorentino's stardom later. Eszterhas' ambivalence towards women is also amplified by his ambivalence about sex. We saw that *Fatal Attraction* was marketed, and received, as all things to all viewers. Somehow *Jade* managed to be received, in the UK at least, as both too tame and too extreme: although Steve Wright in the mass-market *Sun* tabloid thought it was too strong, Nigel Andrews in *The Financial Times* wrote that '*Jade* calls itself an "erotic thriller", but you should check your rights under the Trade Descriptions Act' (Andrews 1995). For Anne Billson it was 'nothing more than a megabudget porno movie, not because the sex scenes are particularly *outré* (they're not) but because plot and characters are every bit as perfunctory as the plot and characters in, say, *Naughty Blue Knickers*' (1995: 10). *Jade* also revisits some of the voyeurism of

Sliver, but here at least surveillance functions to make something *noir*ish of sex. The secret video cameras which record the sexual shenanigans of the rich and powerful turn a brothel into a B-movie studio. 'It's not just a fuckhouse,' says a cop in another scene-of-the-crime scene. 'We've got a nice little camera over here. And there's another one up here. Low light – high density.' The kind of camera, in other words, which can record the dark spectacles of *film noir* as well as the shady spectacles of surreptitious sex.

Eszterhas' ideal viewer

'Wouldn't it just be an awful goddam shame if one hairy little pussy and a thimbleful of sperm were to affect the future of this great state of ours?'
Governor Lew Edwards (Richard Crenna) in *Jade*

At worse, then, by the mid-decade Eszterhas is presented in the reception of his films as, on the one hand, repetitively consistent yet, on the other, simultaneously contradictory and confused, an ostensible liberal who pens conservative sexual tracts, writer of erotic films wherein the explicitness somehow defuses the sexiness. These curious political/aesthetic conflicts make him a very specific symptom of his post-1960s moment, an era he meditates on at great length in the political memoir of 2000, *American Rhapsody*. Yet he has also penned some remarkably resonant scenes dramatising female point of view which speak particularly sympathetically of the dilemmas of the single female in the late twentieth century working city. Sharon Stone's first film assignment in *Stardust Memories* features her as a blonde party-goer watched by a dreaming Woody Allen, positioned across a space he can't cross, in a land of pleasure he'll never belong to. By *Sliver* it was the turn of the single girl to represent the existential loneliness of contemporary life: Carly looks at party-goers in an adjacent apartment building, and reflects on her apartness. In *Jagged Edge* Teddy, as a divorcée who has custody of the children, sits in her bed late at night looking through grim pictures of murdered women, but has to put this aside in order to comfort her daughter who interrupts the late night work by insisting on the safety provided by Teddy as mother. In an age which cast dark cinematic suspicion on the career woman (most notoriously, Close's later *Fatal Attraction* character, *not* penned by Eszterhas), these heroines are never singled out for choosing to work outside the home – indeed, they all *do* work outside the home (with the exception of Catherine Tramell, who works on her novels *at* home, despite her significant private wealth).

This focus on the woman's perspective is effectively an extension of another aspect of the Eszterhas persona, that of champion of the underdog: 'Nothing could be more Eszterhasian', it has been said, 'than to rush to the defence of a downtrodden minority' (Holub 1991: 104). Indeed, in an interview Eszterhas repeatedly presented *Showgirls* as a film which dramatises the difficult life of an ex-street girl working as a lap-dancer, a version of the marginalised figure otherwise represented as union leaders (*F.I.S.T.* [1978]), gays (the controversy over the homophobia of *Basic Instinct* notwithstanding),[21] and the whole Jewish nation (*Music Box* [1990]).[22] In this left-liberal gesture of siding with the disenfranchised, he (sometimes) includes women, even (as we saw from his regret about that *Showgirls* rape scene) occasionally sliding into a pale version of feminism. He is also prone to moral pontification on the subject. Of *Music Box* he has said, 'We do indeed have moral and social responsibility to stand up against what's wrong,'[23] but it has also been said of him that 'when he gets into a brawl, he turns it into a morality play. Starring Saint Joe.'

This intermittent moral soapboxing must, however, be set against the seriously sleazy sexism which also characterises Eszterhas' work. *Showgirls* is a particular offender on this score. Unchecked by the demands of a thoroughgoing thriller plot, here Eszterhas had *carte blanche* to explore more regressive fantasies about women's sexuality. Most irritatingly, *Showgirls* follows an adolescent desperation to shock with a total failure even to surprise, pornographically. Its 'adult' pretensions notwithstanding, it is written in the spirit of lascivious amazement which accompanies a schoolboy's first erection, animated by a misguided assumption that the images are arousing enough to sweep the viewer across the manifold absurdities of plot and characterisation. The prevalence of menstruation as an issue of shock is not presented in a spirit of bodily liberation but a tone of self-congratulation. This accompanies each of the film's so-called excesses, underpinned by an apparent certainty that the writer knows what male heterosexual desire is, and is meeting that desire head-on.[24]

Eszterhas' erotic thrillers are thus the forum in which a singularly contemporary set of contradictions can be played out, contradictions which are resonant of a man who – rather like Michael Douglas – started as a 1960s radical, came to epitomise the liberal establishment of 1980s/1990s Hollywood, but singled out political correctness and political hypocrisy as the evils of his age which must be exposed or defied (Nixon is his arch-demon ['Nixon was a liar and the sixties was about telling the truth']; Clinton disappoints because following his sex allegations he responded by 'jabbing his middle finger at us with a great big fucking lie' [Vulliamy 2000: 2]). One form of this contradiction lies in Eszterhas' gender representations: the hostile targeting of feminism as theory and ideology combined with a powerful respect for working women combined with a keen eye for a commercially lucrative angle on woman as succubus. His men are no more straightforward: led by desire (or their dicks) and thus weakened by their own heterosexuality (this is the image Michael Douglas has perfected), unable to speak in anything but hardboiled clichés, lurching between perversion, liability and sleaze-ball repulsiveness. And if Eszterhas' women are superbly honed players at the cutting edge of their profession and in complete control of the Symbolic Order, his men are seldom seen doing their jobs even adequately, paradoxically rendered impotent in the public sphere by a desire which drags them in pursuit of sexual satisfaction in the private.

The image of the prime Eszterhas male which emerges from *American Rhapsody* is Bill Clinton (perhaps a more publicly successful version of the Michael Douglas rendition of the James M. Cain male, which I will unravel below).[25] *American Rhapsody* doubles as a critique of contemporary American politics and a world for which the author's own movies are entirely appropriate. With *American Rhapsody*, Eszterhas' national critique and a personal/career self-examination come together in a curious way. However contradictory Eszterhas is, this very contradiction is also something he has already diagnosed in himself, via an analysis of the erotic thriller's place at the heart of debased American culture. *American Rhapsody* is a Clinton-era fantasy/kiss-and-tell text which both dishes the dirt on key players with whom Eszterhas has worked (including Sharon Stone, Michael Douglas and Gina Gershon) and imagines the sex-mad Clinton (or perhaps 'the postmodern star text of Bill Clinton' [McLean and Cook 2001: 4]) being transplanted to Hollywood in order that his generous carnal appetite can finally find satisfaction. The Clinton Eszterhas feels most let down by is thus the ideal inhabitant of the world Eszterhas has helped to create. In the chapter 'Bubba in Pig Heaven' he writes to Clinton:

> You've got to move out here, Bubba. You don't belong in Washington or Little Rock or Chappaquiddick – Hollywood is the place for you. 'Addicted to the sexual excitement . . . more and more sex and a higher intensity.' This place reeks sex from its celluloid pores. (2000: 207)

The ironic critique of Clinton as fallen president thus also becomes a backhanded career self-appraisal. If Clinton has been undermined by his unchecked appetites, Eszterhas is the court jester who has stoked those appetites to burning point. Yet in this Eszterhas does not entirely take the backtracking *mea culpa* position he adopts in relation to smoking in *Hollywood Animal*. He both abhors and relishes his move from self-proclaimed laureate of downtrodden minorities to porn-panderer to the president. Whilst self-consciously positioning himself as a left-liberal in relation to some social issues, Eszterhas is not above providing for the sleazy sexual peccadilloes of those he is also opposing. He wryly notes that 'O.J. is a fan, too; the first thing he did after his acquittal was to see *Showgirls* and *Jade* back to back' (2000: 222). Whether or not this is true, it speaks eloquently of Eszterhas' own view of where his work is most appropriately placed in American culture.

American Rhapsody thus reads the erotic thriller as a genre cut to the measure of its corrupt moment, with its author, Joe Eszterhas, as prime architect of America's decadent fantasy landscape. At the same time as Clinton is savaged, he is also enshrined as Eszterhas' ideal viewer:

> *Basic Instinct, Showgirls, Sliver, Jade, Flashdance, Jagged Edge* . . . I know you've seen all of those. I know you're a fan. . . . If I have a core audience for those movies, I know you're a hard-on hard-core, Bubba. (2000: 206)

As 'Bubba in Pig Heaven' proceeds, the interplay of influence between Eszterhas' scripts and Clinton's sex life becomes increasingly intimate. Just as preview audiences of *Fatal Attraction* created their consummate ending to the film, so Eszterhas has fantasised the object of his objection as also the ideal viewer of the erotic thrillers he has written. But it also seems – according to Eszterhas' fantasy – that Clinton has partly drafted Eszterhas' scripts. (This may be one way of passing the buck.) *Basic Instinct* becomes the blueprint narrative for political corruption through sex; and as the dick-led male undone by his hyper-heterosexuality Clinton has a hand in helping Eszterhas draft that compulsively repeated sexual storyline:

> This is what Gennifer [Flowers] said: 'One night Bill asked me to put on a short skirt with no underwear, then sit in a chair and cross and uncross my legs while he watched. He became so aroused just watching me, it was a thrill. He said he read about that move in a magazine, long before Sharon Stone wowed audiences with it in *Basic Instinct*. His fantasy was to have that scenario actually take place in a meeting someday.'
>
> Of course you liked that movie, Bubba. It's about you and Gennifer, isn't it? Some of it is a direct homage to your relationship. You had Gennifer tie you to the bedpost with silk scarves – the opening scene of my movie. (2000: 206–7)

The castigated Clinton then doubles as co-author of Eszterhas' landscapes of lust, the bane of the screenwriter's moral polemic but one who is called upon to provide sexual titbits, which then feed into Eszterhas' feverish scenarios. Clinton thus becomes not just a passive ideal audience member, but a role-playing (re-)activator of cinematic sexual scenarios, doing for *Basic Instinct* what other audiences did for *The Rocky Horror Picture Show* or *The Blues Brothers*:

> Gennifer describing her relationship with you is Gennifer describing the subtext of not only *Basic [Instinct]* but also *Sliver* and *Jade*: 'All I could think about was our sex games! What we had done to each other the night before and what we might do the next day. I spent my days in a trance, pretending to work and function like a normal person, but all the while being obsessed with what we were doing.' (2000: 207)

Genre – and a genre in which Eszterhas has been the major player – thus functions as more than a framework for political critique (as it had with Brian De Palma's Chappaquiddik/Zapruda footage essay *Blow Out*). It becomes the language through which political scandal is spoken. The genre flick is elevated to the status of motivation and prime signifier for the riskiest of political moments. In Eszterhas' self-aggrandising reading of Clinton's sexual misdemeanours as softcore theatre, the erotic thriller becomes the fantasy architecture within which secret thrills and humiliated men are constructed, consumed – and lamented.

2: DIRECTED BY PAUL VERHOEVEN

There we were, making what was meant to be a little psychothriller and all of a sudden we were of sociological importance.

Michael Douglas on *Basic Instinct*

There is a sense in which the mainstream erotic thriller reached its apotheosis in Paul Verhoeven's *Basic Instinct*, which honed traits developed through a number of films from the 1980s (not least those penned by Eszterhas, and Verhoeven's own *Fourth Man*), into a film the legacy of which would be seen throughout the following decade and beyond. *Basic Instinct* is one of the definitive films of neo-*noir*, as well as being a crucial moment in the erotic thriller's passage from sleeper surprise hit to secure bankable movie commodity. In production Verhoeven reported that 'he was going to make the ultimate sex thriller' (Hutchinson 1992); my interview below confirms a continuing interest in pushing the parameters of the sex scene. *Basic Instinct* is by far the most academically analysed erotic thriller of the several hundred films I am looking at in this book, the *Hamlet* of its genre. For J. Hoberman it was 'a movie that's been refracted through the American media for so long, it seems to get off on watching itself' (2003: 14), and the second wave of reception – academic engagement – has extended this beyond the media frenzy of the moment of release. That it was the most mass-marketed of its form may account for why academics have been more interested in writing about *Basic Instinct* than many other possible candidates from the genre's parade of expensive blockbuster exploitation, leading one to conclude that academics are as vulnerable to the lure of film scandal and hype as any other audience sector. Stables (1998) takes the film as her main focus, producing a reading of the contemporary *femme fatale* which is completely skewed by Catherine Tramell. Lynda Hart (1994) uses *Basic Instinct* to describe a state in which all women are eternally culpable: It is not that Beth or Catherine 'did it', or even that they did it together: The Woman did it. This, for Hart, is revealed by *Basic Instinct*'s lazy (or typically Verhoevian?) inability to resolve its plot points (which amounts to the message that 'they' – women, lesbians – are all the same). Celestino Deleyto argues that the film is a symptom of male paranoia about female power, exploring Nick and Gus's homosexual/homosocial relationship, and concluding that, because of this pattern established in *Basic Instinct*, the very genre of the 'erotic thriller in general becomes . . . a space in which contemporary patriarchal American culture both flaunts – female independence and sexual activity, lesbianism – and represses – male homosexuality' (1997: 36). Working from my earlier paper on erotic thrillers, Feasey sees *Basic Instinct* as the moment when the genre is liberated from the implications of its potentially 'top-shelf soft-core' material, legitimised by promotional strategies 'as suitable for the mass audience' (2003b: 169). Most writers – academic and journalistic – concentrate on two dominant areas, both of which were already in place as a result of the film's own marketing campaign: Sharon Stone as devil woman, and the film's dubious gay politics. I will look at the Stone issue later. Here I consider how Verhoeven handled the public scandals of both *Basic Instinct* and *Showgirls* as sex films (or films about sex), contributing to his career-long challenge to censorship, but I also want to think about why *Basic Instinct* has come culturally to signify so much, and why it is largely the beginning and end point of the limited scholarly interest in the erotic thriller hitherto.

Verhoeven affirms that American movies played a huge part in the cultural life of post-Occupation Holland (where he grew up and established his directing career), with an emphasis on B-movie genre cinema[26] (Hoberman has noted Verhoeven's tendency to place 'Hollywood genre between quotation marks' [2003: 15]), and *Basic Instinct* was received as the next stage in two distinct genre trajectories: the development of neo-*noir*, and of Verhoeven's playful engagement with American genre. Thus the exemplary film of its genre is also a parodic interrogation of that genre. This may be as much an effect of the film's émigré direction as it is of its postmodernism, and would not be the first time that a European working in Hollywood had developed American genre whilst also bending it. Verhoeven has said that Hollywood represented a fantasy opportunity for him, not just in terms of funding and technical opportunity, but as an imaginative space, the move from Europe to the USA forming a shift to fantasy genres. He has characterised his style as hyper-realism, anchored by 'the need to show everything so explicitly: the fucking and the pricks and the shit and the drugs and the violence' (Scheers 1997: 58). This tendency runs across both his European and American films, in varying censorship contexts.[27]

Basic Instinct was received as a fantasy of amoral sex, which effectively whipped up a frenzy of divided response, dependent upon the primary allegiance of the respondent: gays, feminists and moralists hated it differently, but in similar measures. Sexual fantasy wrought for the public space of the mass market clearly brings significant problems of licence and legitimacy. It offered Verhoeven the opportunity to push the envelope of mainstream sexual acceptance. But it was significantly prefigured by *De Vierde Man* (*The Fourth Man*), which complicates some of the strategies of its more famous Hollywood remake (though it is not, strictly speaking, an English-language version of the Dutch original – Eszterhas' script is as 'original' as ever). This was the last Dutch movie Verhoeven got financed 'after a lot of rejections', and it was 'considered extremely decadent because of the homosexual items that are in the movie' (Shea and Hennings 1993: 7). In both films the *femme fatale* is overtly demonically shaded, even if a strict reading of each narrative leaves open the question of female guilt. Verhoeven has a longstanding obsession with Christian symbolism, and his *femmes fatales* are not merely metaphoric devils. Promoting *Basic Instinct* he said, 'It's a sexy, erotic thriller, that's how you sell it. But for me it's more about sympathy for the devil. . . . Catherine is the devil, that's why she is bisexual' (McGregor 1992: 18–19).[28] But in this devilishness Tramell was foreshadowed by Christine, *De Vierde Man*'s *femme fatale* and object of fascination for protagonist Gerard. Christine's three previous lovers have died in mysterious, possibly accidental circumstances for which she may or may not be responsible; Gerard perceives himself as the 'fourth man' in line. Whether or not she is guilty, Verhoeven targets her in a kind of cinematic witch-hunt:

> In my view, if Christine had not been there those accidents would certainly not have happened. Her charisma is so strong that she does not have to lift a finger to influence events – she only needs to look in order to pull the characters into her Dark Realm. If you look at it that way, Christine is a reincarnation of the Devil. (Scheers 1997: 158)

Verhoeven has her lie down on a piece of glass, which she does not feel ('According to medieval superstition, this was one of the ways to recognize a witch' [Scheers 1997: 158]). We might recall that Rebecca in *Body of Evidence* fucks on a bed of broken glass, a trait which suggests a streak of demonism in her deviousness, whilst Mona, *femme fatale* of *Romeo is Bleeding*, crawls unflinching through the jagged edges of a shattered car windscreen flashing her stocking tops. Dolly in *The Hot Spot* (at one point called a 'lousy little witch') initiates sex on gravel, whilst teen-*fatale* Ivy (Drew Barrymore) in *Poison Ivy* grinds glass under her stiletto, which her male prey (Tom Skerritt) then caresses. Verhoeven also underscores his explicitly Christian reworking of *noir*'s *femme fatale*/nurturing woman dyad by contrasting Christine with a mysterious madonna-icon who functions as Gerard's hope-figure. 'Mary' (Scheers' '*femme céleste*' [1997: 160]) is the nurturing counterpart to the *femme fatale*.

Basic Instinct is predicated upon no such binarity of female archetypes – its women (and men) are all as multiply culpable as they are multiply sexed: by the 1990s Verhoeven seems to have dispensed with good guys almost entirely (hence the bleak amorality of *Starship Troopers* and *Showgirls*). Not for nothing did Anne Billson (1992: 29) argue that *Basic Instinct*'s homophobia is the least of its problems; it is also voraciously sexist (unfair to both men and women), developing Verhoeven's trademark obsession with 'sexandviolence' (see also Mars-Jones 1992). If *The Fourth Man* posits women as both/either guilty as sin or innocent *and* sexualised, *Basic Instinct* is populated only by sinners, countered by no image of redemption and unthreatened by spectres of retribution. The film's theology is then either hyper-moral or post-moral, depending on how you view the absence of *noir*'s retributive framework, its redemptive, nurturing home-makers, its justice through death. It removes the good girl figure from *noir* and frees its demon-heroine from the possibility of punishment. Its nasty fall-guys (here all men arc fall-guys, just as all women did it), squirm abjectly in their own desire with no vision of the sublime, as is vouchsafed to *The Fourth Man*'s hero. On this hinges *Basic Instinct*'s contradiction for feminism: as female demon Catherine is prime exhibit in Verhoeven's *Malleus Maleficarum*, and evidence for feminism's case against him; but as demon in a universe which primarily values the demonic, she rules supreme, thus also functioning as celebratory role-model. Pressing his theology beyond good and evil, Verhoeven also pushes the genre beyond the bourgeois neurosis and pacts of *noir* into an unsettling, post-social, post-empathic universe. The question he hoped he could pose in *The Hollow Man* was, what amoral freedoms could invisibility offer you, if you know you won't get caught given that cinematic justice depends on specular proof? Yet it seems to me that this is also a question he had already asked in *Basic Instinct*, where everyone does what they want in full view of each other (in Jan de Bont's blazing white light of spectacular visibility), with consequences coming only occasionally and arbitrarily (Beth's and Rocky's deaths, for instance). Eszterhas, as we have seen, emerges as a moral man who writes (apparently against himself) questionable tales he them comes to regret, in dialogue with moral and political campaigning objectors. He then tries to redress his scripts' political shortcomings with retractions, apologies, requests to rewrite. The conflict over whether to reshoot sections of *Basic Instinct* pinpoints issues of control and authorship regarding aspects of the film's sexual-political vision: Eszterhas comes to have sympathy with gays and feminists, so asks for rewrites; Verhoeven refuses, and continues to pose similar questions of sexual and existential morality in subsequent films. If *Basic Instinct* makes feminism interrogate its own morality (Catherine as victim of Verhoeven's demonising or victor in a Machiavellian game feminists are tricked into applauding – because, of course, many women *did* applaud Catherine),[29] it is Verhoeven's *Basic Instinct* rather than Eszterhas' which poses those questions. This is not simply because of an auteurial profile which insists on nasty questions, picking away, across a range of films, at the scabs of US heroism and morality, but because explicit exposure of scenarios of appetite (violence, lust) are an effect of direction: the visual orchestration of Roxy's death, Catherine's crotch-flash and its reception, the four-minute sex-scene between Catherine and Nick which threatens to mutate into murder.

Basic Instinct is, then, a discomforting film, not because it demonises Catherine as a woman, or a bisexual woman, but as an affluent desiring American. She is simply better at the game everyone is playing than they are. What, then, can the gay lobby's lengthy campaign against the film tell us about the specific reception of erotic thrillers as cultural sore spots? The campaigns (one attempting to disrupt the location shoot, the second picketing cinemas on release) pinpointed a set of sexually controversial issues which raised the film's profile and guaranteed its discussability, for scholars as well as popular audiences. As with *Silence of the Lambs*, a popular campaign designed to sink the film or defuse its power has contributed to its academic interest value as well as its box office. 'Talkies', it seems, are equally talkable, whether the discussion takes place over the workplace watercooler, at the academic conference table or indeed on the picket-line. Yet there is nothing essentially more pernicious here which distinguishes *Basic Instinct* from, say, *Black Widow* or *Jade*, both of which foreground similar 'sexandviolence' moments, or raise questions about gay sexuality and crime, or problematically refract women. But whereas these were solid mainstream sexy thrillers, the PR capital made out of the protest campaign in turn made *Basic Instinct* an *event*. As Michael Douglas bears out in the epigraph to this section, vociferous political opposition catapulted the film from A-list mainstream thriller to something which could be marketed using the most aggressive high concept selling strategies.

On one level the *Basic Instinct* protests took at face-value a primary equation between on-screen villain and off-screen social image. Queer Nation activist Annette Gaudino argued that Tramell 'continued a long line of lesbian psychotics on film' and once again 'an open gay community was used as the backdrop and the colour'.[30] Verhoeven has countered this with the observation that he has generally given gays an even hand and a broad canvas, especially in his Dutch movies.[31] But the protests were also generically canny. On release gay activity developed through naming a protest group 'Catherine Did It', an attempt at stymieing the whodunit issue ('You can know that Rosebud is a sleigh and still think that *Citizen Kane* is a great film. If giving away the ending [of *Basic Instinct*] takes away its value that's really not our fault,' says Gaudino of 'Catherine Did It's' actions). The dominant reading of the film which has emerged argues that whilst all of the murder suspects are female (Verhoeven's 'there are two or three possible suspects – they are all women, in fact' [Shea and Hennings 1993: 20]), no single woman can be definitively indicted (though Stone performed the opening [disguised] killing, and maintains – with those gay protesters – that Catherine Did It). Yet the text leaves it open: like Christine, Catherine may not be culpable. Verhoeven calls *Basic Instinct* the third film in his 'psychosis trilogy', also comprising *Robocop* and *Total Recall*, so-called because each explored parallel or ambiguous realities, both of which may be true, or real (Scheers 1997: 234–5; although when I interviewed him Verhoeven even suggested that this uncertain tendency is itself uncertain). In *Basic Instinct* Douglas is the psychotic subject, unsure of the truth of his experience in relation to Stone's *femme*. Verhoeven's loose use of the term psychosis here becomes a postmodern stand-in for the anxious terminal uncertainty of the sexualised neo-*noir* hero: no pillars of justice descend to provide him with a deathbed moral certainty, as in *noir* – death may or may not come; right and wrong are irrelevant. The director attributes this interest in undecidable realities to his émigré status, and his PhD in mathematics. '[M]ultiple universes and multiple reality' (Scheers 1997: 234) characterises his experience of 'my coming here from Holland and having two realities myself'. Verhoeven's sexual-devil discourse may, as I have argued, be a way of resolving the matter (but it may not). His response is disingenuous: he claims still to provide the audience with space to negotiate a range of possible interpretations, whilst simultaneously asserting a preferred theological/misogynist conviction: 'The viewer had to decide, although Verhoeven never had any doubt. Catherine was the murderer because Catherine was the Devil' (Scheers 1997: 255).

Showgirls: *promises and confusions*

I should have protected myself better and gone back to genre.

Paul Verhoeven

Verhoeven's next film had a less secure generic foundation, and its manifest sexual ambition was to cause its director and studio significant problems. *Showgirls* is also another episode in the translation of B-feature motifs into A-feature fare. Marketed as a truly pathbreaking and 'honest' exploration of human sexuality and a positive image of a strong heroine, its sexual pretensions amazed those already familiar with the rougher charms of its cheaper antecedent, the strip-flick (more of which in chapter 6). Certainly, it staked its importance on the small piece of distribution history it made, being the first American film to be given a wide release in the States with an NC-17 rating, suggesting unprecedented explicitness, and marketed as an *adult* film for all adults. Verhoeven himself had welcomed the rating: 'I think adding NC-17 to the rating is probably a step forward', he said in 1993 when it was pretty much untested, though whether the category 'will be accepted by the majority of the media or not' remained questionable (Shea and Hennings 1993: 14). Though it was the mainstream art-sex biopic *Henry and June* which was first in line for the MPAA's new classification, Verhoeven's work has tested the limits of what could be done within R- and NC-17 ratings. Prior to the introduction of NC-17 in 1990, adult-oriented films had to be able to achieve an R-rating for a lucrative theatrical release. By the 1980s the X-category was reserved for hardcore pornography; an X-film would be excluded from mainstream cinema chains, so could not attract the large box office required of studio films. Contracts commonly compel a mainstream director delivering sexually inflected work to cut for an (at most) R-rating to maximise box office. NC-17 was introduced ostensibly to signal to an audience that the material was not suitable for children but was not pornography, enabling mainstream cinemas to screen NC-17 films without the hardcore taint. Though NC-17 had just been introduced by the time of *Basic Instinct*, Verhoeven was bound by his contract to deliver an R-rated film; material was then reinstated for a subsequent unrated US video release. Video and DVD as the destination market for controversial films has thus enabled filmmakers to go closer to the wire with their representations, and has meant that erotic material can be available in various 'strengths' in different formats and for distinct audiences. This practice is widespread across the strata of theatrically-released and DTV movie-making. But with his next film, *Showgirls*, Verhoeven set out to see if sexual material could be treated in an adult fashion with a large-scale theatrical release.[32] However, classification issues only partly explain why such an overtly sexual film should fail in the mid-1990s, at the crest of a wave of successes in mainstream, explicit cinema.

The story of Nomi (Elizabeth Berkley), a young woman who arrives in Las Vegas, becomes a lap-dancer at the Cheetah Club, then star of a more respectable erotic revue show at the Stardust, *Showgirls* reunited Verhoeven with Joe Eszterhas and upped the ante in mainstream sexual shenanigans. It explicitly cashed in on the lap-dancing/striptease vogue of the mid-1990s: Eszterhas acknowledges his bandwagon jump: 'In the 1990s especially, clubs featuring lap dancing are very successful across the country. . . . That is an interesting phenomenon, and one that is worth exploring artistically' (Grimes 1995). The lap- or table-dance was also promoted as central to the 1990s sexual agenda, its no-touch spectacle and avowal of masturbation consolidating a form of voyeuro-safe sex (see, for instance, Katz 1995; Ezterhas' screenplay pays lip-service to this: 'You fucking without fucking', someone says to Nomi). Reports of stars stripping for real, for kicks, were commonplace: Drew Barrymore told the *New York Times*, 'It wasn't a sex thing, it was a freedom thing,' echoing the discourses of female empowerment peddled by sexual filmmakers, high and low. Demi Moore and later Daryl Hannah both frequented or performed in strip-joints in a peculiar form of T&A method preparation, gearing up to roles in *Striptease* and *Dancing at the Blue Iguana*, respectively, and one writer reported in 1995 that 'In the past month Naomi Campbell and Sharon Stone have given impromptu shows at different clubs' (Jeffreys 1995; see also Katz 1995). The strip-flick sub-genre had by the mid-1990s been doing brisk business at the exploitation fringes, its genre ur-text being Katt Shea Ruben's *Stripped to Kill*, made for Roger Corman's Concord-New Horizons company. This is a form which has predictably flourished on DTV (where it is understood that disrobing women is primarily exploitation, and only secondarily a form of cultural political critique), yet it has largely undersold in the mainstream. This might partly be because it has become a vanity sub-genre, a forum for A-list performers to show off their worked-out commodity bodies and extend their acting portfolios. It is also, in the mainstream, a genre in search of an identity, or rather one trying to escape its inherent softcore tinge. *Striptease* was announced as 'a political comedy' (Jeffreys 1995), whilst *Showgirls* overtly traded on what it would show rather than the story it would tell, at the same time promising that it would all be in the best possible taste.[33]

Another problem is the representation of hardcore subject-matter in softcore frameworks. The A-list strip-flick is one element in Hollywood's brief 1990s infatuation with the porn industry as manifest in films such as *The People vs Larry Flynt* or *Boogie Nights*, both interesting examples of what mainstream, mass audience filmmaking does to risqué subject-matter. Neither film is an erotic thriller (the first is a biopic, the second a feel-good erotic drama), and each acquires its eroticism from some tangential relationship to a specific historical moment, airbrushing hardcore material to within an inch of its life. Laura Kipnis discusses Larry Flynt as a pioneer of political pornography (1995: 122–60), but her Flynt is not Milos Forman's. Though both read Flynt as a libertarian freedom-fighter, Kipnis's is Rabelaisian, whilst Forman's is cut to the measure of a free speech-endorsing Hollywood, presenting mainstream softcore spectacles rather than the hardcore with which Flynt's prime publication

Hustler flirts. It is no accident that *The People vs Larry Flynt*'s female lead, Courtney Love, had featured in *Playboy* rather than *Hustler* itself. When *Hustler* comes to mainstream cinemas it must therefore be rendered through the filter of a view which is more Hefner than Flynt.

Larry Flynt and *Boogie Nights* avowedly draw back from explicit spectacle; *Showgirls'* first mistake was the promotional boast that it would push beyond the audience's wildest imaginings. Pre-release, the trailer declared it to be 'the most controversial film of the year', but one irony of this is that it became so largely because of its inability to fulfil this promise. If a film cannot deliver on its assurances, the controversy becomes its failure to do so. The production notes given to the British press by distributors Guild built extravagantly on a discourse of unflinchingness and the much-hyped category of 'honesty', which rewrites sensationalism as realism: 'This project really required a director like Paul who wouldn't shy away from the highly-charged sexual reality of this world' bragged the blurb; the lap-dancing sequence alone was allegedly 'one of the most compelling and provocative scenes ever committed to the screen'.[34] This line extends a familiar view of Verhoeven, endorsed in a number of promotional interviews – that he is the director of mainstream excess and will push the envelope, sexually or violently, or through generalised shock, as far as he can, and then a bit further. In a 1995 British television documentary about the director, Joe Eszterhas cites *Basic Instinct*'s crotch-flash as prime example of this: we know from the previous scene that Tramell isn't wearing any underwear, so the leg uncrossing could have been done from another angle and the effect inferred from the diegetic male spectators' responses. But Verhoeven has to *show* us, peering in when mainstream cinematic convention would dictate a discrete cut away (Sharon Stone has a different take on this shot, of course).[35] The crotch-flash does not appear in Eszterhas' shooting-script; Verhoeven attributes it to a biographical experience of his own (see my interview below, pp. 246. Eszterhas, as we have seen, reads it as the cinematic consummation of Clinton and Gennifer Flowers). Excessive as Eszterhas is, he meets his match in Verhoeven and offloads excess onto a director who ultimately refuses to pull back.

Trading on this backstory of excess, a film called *Showgirls*, directed by Verhoeven and set in excessive Las Vegas, could almost market itself ('Verhoeven will Show us Girls' is the high concept encapsulation). Because of the difficulty NC-17 films face securing conventional advertising space, *Showgirls'* backers, MGM/UA, had to follow different promotional routes, which they did rather inventively. In a (then) unknown practice, they sent out half a million eight-minute long preview tapes, containing many of the film's more explicit moments, to be given away at video stores in the US. They also deployed on-line publicity opportunities, in a very early use of web-based film marketing. But the film's most visible iconography, deployed in massive, extravagant billboards in prominent, highly populated locations, became its brand, a visual formation of the sexual promise it makes to its audience. The film's poster (which has remained the central design of the video and DVD jacket –

see reproduction in Figure 8) features a slice of star Elizabeth Berkeley's naked body, seeming to step from between two black curtains, which function both to conceal what is 'too much' (nipples and pubic hair) whilst exposing the fact that she is naked. An image of brazen disavowal, it plays with what is there and is not there, managing to sell whilst also negotiating censorship codes and conventions of decency by being simultaneously explicit and discrete. It is a prime fetish image, put to work in the marketplace. A similar image lent itself to a horizontal alternative, when billboards took a landscape rather than a portrait format: here the Berkley figure seems to lounge, lying across from left to right, more passive but ready for sex. In the vertical/portrait version of the poster (and the video jacket), she is more active, stepping towards her viewer/purchaser, but she also functions as a grapheme in the layout of lettering. Her sliver of flesh, from head to painted toe, becomes a slinky 'S'-shape ('S' also for sex), mimicking the letters which bookend the film's title (Showgirls). But the body/letter also splits the word in half, the woman's figure dividing the two syllables: she splits 'Showgirls' into 'Show /S/ Girls'. A noun becomes a verb; a statement of content (this will be a movie about showgirls) becomes a promise (this movie will show us girls, revealing what's hidden behind the poster's black concealments). A simple masterpiece of exploitation design, the image exemplifies a moment when Hollywood's strategies of high-concept marketing served a climate of liberated sexual openness, unmatched since.

If this image promises nudity, the film delivers in abundance: Verhoeven directs like a man with a permissive mission, seeming to rewrite the terms of explicitness between *Basic Instinct* and *Showgirls*. What was shocking about the former's crotch-flashing wasn't what you saw, but the fact that it was there: shadowy and fleeting, Stone's pudenda were most significant as presence rather than spectacle. By the time of *Showgirls*, however, explicitness is judged as an effect of quantity rather than quality, with a profusion of G-stringed nubiles in incongruously composed tableaux around every backstage scene and every on-stage pageant. This is a 131-minute testament to Roland Barthes' famous 'Woman is desexualised the moment she is stripped naked'. In its effort to do female nudity to the point of overkill, the film also comes near to perversely confirming the Mulveyite notion that female spectacle freezes the flow of the action; nakedness is often so incongruously at odds with the tone of the scene played out around it, it becomes an irritating distraction from the narrative. The almost universal critical opprobrium on release made reference to too much nudity, but it is also stringently patrolled for unwelcome corporeal excesses. Here, perhaps, *Showgirls* is no different from any other mainstream sexual product: the erotic thriller is a generic celebration of thin, white, frequently blonde bodies (I will look at the more recent development of the black erotic thriller in my conclusion). Dark secrets have no bearing on the body, which is always, manifestly, a temple of health and efficiency; blemishes, rampant pubic hair undisciplined by wax, signs of unfitness or – horror of horrors – cellulite itself, these do not even exist as shameful traces at the margins of the genre. *Showgirls*, then, tells an old story of body fascism clothed in the message of a openness about the *right* body, or at least its matter-of-fact role in the industry (Las Vegas as a metaphor for Hollywood, for the USA). The riskiest figure thus becomes the rotund comedienne, Henrietta Bazoom, a kind of Chubby Brown earth-mother, who does a turn at the Cheetah Club, hiding her breasts behind a comedy bust which pops open as a carnivalesque punch-line.

Ubiquitous nudity is substituted for extreme sexual action, and herein lies one of *Showgirls'* most significant problems. The nude female icon stepping out between the film's title on the poster was augmented by a series of provocative straplines which promised something 'beyond'. Audiences are invited across the film's new erotic threshold with the pre-release come-on 'Leave your inhibitions at the door – The show is about to begin' – a dare more than a promise (muster your sexual courage before entering the cinema), but not one underpinned by the truth of the film. The video/DVD jacket is bolder, boasting: 'Beyond your wildest dreams . . . Beyond your wildest fantasies.' According to producer Alan Marshall in the press notes, one musical number 'is going to be wilder than anything seen on screen',[36] which only begs the question of *which* screen – the screen on which one might see, say, *New Wave Hookers*, or even *Debbie Does Dallas*? Clearly there is wild, and *wild*, and all *Showgirls'* promises must be read in a delineated distribution context. Undoubtedly excessive (excessive bad taste, performances, excessive budget), *Showgirls* is nevertheless not a film which exceeds mainstream tolerance (even if NC-17 'exceeds' the R-rating), since NC-17 levels of explicitness (all simulated) had been within rather than beyond the pale for five years by 1995. *Showgirls'* first mistake, therefore, was vociferously to promise 'more than' so much, when it was also 'less than' a whole lot else. This is not to say that here Verhoeven should have bitten the bullet of hardcore, but rather that since *Showgirls* had purloined hardcore terrain, it was foolish for its promoters to present its greatest virtues as those 'beyond', exceeding, supplanting the sexual mainstream. Perhaps, then, the film's most telling line is Al Torres' (Robert Davi's) to Nomi, when he observes that in her new line of respectable sex-work at the Stardust, 'It must be weird not having anybody cum on you'. *Showgirls* is a film in which no one cums on anyone, ever; yet it was promoted as an experience in which everyone does everything constantly.

If *Showgirls* does not present previously unseen qualities of sexual action, it does, however, push other buttons. First, the characteristic profanity of Eszterhas' script seems to provide a verbal substitute for what the visuals leave out. In Eszterhas' hands, the erotic thriller becomes the genre in which the bald hardboiled talk of the detective thriller is metamorphosed into graphically profane sex-talk. In the erotic thriller, hardcore acts occupy an 'obscene' off-stage space which can only be suggested verbally. Another moment suggests other contradictions of the unseen, when a Japanese punter at the Cheetah Club observes that 'In America everybody's a gynaecologist', as a woman crouches on all fours in front of him. In the rude language of this film, the private gaze of the clinician becomes the erotic aspiration of the peep-show punter. Yet if sex audiences crave the view of the gynaecologist, they will not find it in *Showgirls* (it does not show us *that* much of its girls). This is softcore which talks the talk of hardcore, but cannot walk the walk. 'Everybody in America', that line should run, '*except Showgirls*' audience'. The vulgarity of the commentary exceeds the explicitness of the image: Verhoeven goes no further than he did in *Basic Instinct* (perhaps not as far – Stone did offer the glimmerings of the gynaecological view).

And then there is the uneasy suggestion that the thing we *don't* see is the only thing we *ought* to be seeing, the only thing worth seeing, posed in one of the film's most telling moments of obscenity, which expresses both its anxiety about feminism and its crisis of the unshowable. Henrietta Bazoom's concluding 'joke' stands uneasily alongside the gynaecologist line: 'You know what they call that useless piece of skin around a twat? – a *woman.*' If the woman is useless, undesirable and seen everywhere in this film, the twat is desirable but unseen, unseeable in this context. The audacious sexism of the line (one of the vile truths the film – and its culture – suggests and then fails to dispel) is matched by the breathtaking self-critique it suggests: *Showgirls*, like the woman, takes on the 'uselessness' of being the context, the frame, the piece of celluloid skin which surrounds the 'real thing' it then cannot show. Perhaps this is another instance of Verhoeven's characteristic moral and semiotic undecid-ability. If women are useless apart from their twats, *Showgirls* must also be useless, for it can show everything of a woman *except* this. Or perhaps it is the opposite: since the film itself is a fetishised reification of the woman, both work together to disarm the joke.

Showgirls' less than obvious gender discourse thus emerges through some unexpected routes. Also at stake is its investigation of male heterosexuality. If all looking is ultimately gynaecological (that is, if America gives us the logical conclusion of voyeuristic pleasure, the thing we are purported to be *really* after), sexuality becomes a question of genitality, which is certainly one posi-tion *Showgirls* is testing in terms of how it represents male response. Do (American) men want to be gynaecologists in the bedroom (or the strip-club)? And is the simple vision of a woman enough to produce straight male reaction? It may be that *Showgirls* is getting both male and female sexuality seriously wrong, but it may be that it is simply following through the cultural chestnut that if women want relationships, men want gross physical stimulation.

Actually, Verhoeven and Eszterhas are hardly interested in Freud's question, what do women want? Female sexuality is not at issue here; in *Showgirls* sexual women are always at work,[37] never at play or in love (like obscenity, these too exist beyond the film's cynical boundaries). Female sexuality for *Showgirls* is only a function of commercial ambition. The greater mystery is what *men* want, and whether they find it here. I have said that the film is driven by (and was marketed in terms of) a relentless will to exposure which it cannot follow through. A further question it poses is whether, indeed, showing is enough, for male viewers and their protagonist-representatives on screen. Proceeding with all the crudity of a Pavlovian experiment, the certainty which justifies this plethora of nipples and waxed pudenda is that image will produce reaction, effect will follow from cause, response from stimulus. Show a man enough and he will react, he will deliver (this is also the tactic of a number of erotic-thriller *femmes fatales*: Mona only has to open her legs in *Romeo is Bleeding* to get what she wants). When Nomi performs her lap-dancing routine on Zack, the result (his arousal and ejaculation) is deemed inevitable: she acts and he reacts, as surely as night follows day (what is interesting about this scene is that Cristal [Gina Gershon] watches). And what Nomi does to Zack the film might also do to its audience: what goes in through the eye will come out through bodily arousal. Thus *Showgirls* overtly reads sexuality as commodity, never as romance, which perhaps accounts for its lack of suggestiveness and its plenitude of angry bravura. Yet where films such as *Romeo is Bleeding* equate sexual satiation with financial greed (with crime connecting the two), here the relationship seems to be not primarily focused on consumption (man defined by consuming women, and women consuming him) but on commodity as producer of sexual effect. Perhaps the most shocking thing about *Showgirls* is the sheer crudity of the erotic economics upon which these images rely: sexual charge will produce sexual discharge which will accrue a profit. Show (a man what he wants to see), and (his body will) tell (it will give itself away). The visual becomes a conduit through which bits of bodies are bought and sold. In the post-theological landscape of *Basic Instinct*, sex and power circulate in a *noir*ish free-for-all. *Showgirls* humanises this, becoming an exemplary Verhoeven piece not on the level of visual extremity but on the level of human nastiness as explored in its voyeuro-exhibitionist contracts. The question remains whether women are as prone to this as men. Perhaps it is a question which only the DTV erotic thriller answers, as I will explore below.

Interestingly, Verhoeven now feels that the problem with *Showgirls* wasn't the quality or quantity of the nudity, or the cynical sexual content, or even that it attracted the wrong classification. Rather, its prime error lies in the fact that it was anchored to the wrong genre(s). From the studio's point of view, not only did *Showgirls* fail artistically, it failed as an NC-17 test-case, exposing NC-17 as the pariah category, lacking a significant market, and aligned ever nearer in the public mind to the pornographic X-certificate it was created to escape. In fact, as my exploration of the DTV erotic thriller below shows, there is a significant market for mainstream softcore, but saturation booking and innovative mass ad campaigns are not the way to address that market. As a theatrical-release category, NC-17 is neither fish nor fowl – not able to deliver hardcore, not satisfied by softcore. With appalling press, *Showgirls* failed to muster any significant box office interest, but it has since acquired cult classic status[38] and amassed decent video and DVD sales, which indicates that its material is far more suited to home viewing (where viewers can respond like Zack at a lap-dance). A 2003 magazine advertising campaign for MGM Home

Entertainment LLC (promoting the video and DVD release of five erotic thriller titles, *Showgirls*, *Killing Me Softly*, *Wild Orchid*, *Body of Evidence* and *Original Sin*) makes this explicit. 'All Praise the Inventor of "Slo-Mo"' reads the copy over a still image of Elizabeth Berkley fellating a pole (Fig. 8); 'Enjoy. You have our permission', the message continues, begging the question of who the 'you' and the 'we' are here. All of this sits incongruously beneath the MGM logo (and claim to cine-heritage, with its slogan, 'MGM Means Great Movies'). This is the 1980s promise of the home video revolution made good through early twenty-first-century technology with (mostly) 1990s titles. *Showgirls* is revealed as made-for-the-living room masturbation fare which briefly tries to pass itself off as theatrical-class. Even Verhoeven seems to have always been aware of this: 'The only thing I could imagine with regard to *Showgirls* is that part of the audience will go home in a state of excitement and, thinking of the film, make love or masturbate' (Scheers 1997: 271). For MGM as video distributors, you don't even need to go home because you are already there, ready with the freeze-frame button.

Home viewers may also be less fussy about genre blancmanges as long as the sexual content is intense enough. As my interview below and my epigraph above attest, Verhoeven now feels that his (and Joe Eszterhas') error lay in hitching sex to melodrama (the film replays *All About Eve* in Las Vegas) rather than to the thriller, as *Basic Instinct* had done. Add a murder or two, and perhaps *Showgirls* would have been as redeemed at the theatrical box office as it has been rehabilitated in the video store. Atom Egoyan's *Exotica*, a film which, in its similar focus on lap-dancing, might be unkindly read as the art-house version of *Showgirls*, foregrounds a central energising question crucially absent from Verhoeven's film. 'You have to convince yourself that this person has something hidden that you have to find' are the first lines of Egoyan's work, offering one key to his central fascination with complex forms of ritualistic sexuality. *Showgirls* disappoints partly because as a non-thriller sexual set-piece it hides nothing, so there is nothing to find. Perhaps the history of the NC-17 category would also have been different had Verhoeven 'hidden' something, preferably something criminal. 'Basically to make that movie more successful we should have just had a murder mystery and situated it in Vegas, and it would have been fine,' says Verhoeven. 'And we would have got away with everything that people got so angry about. I should have protected myself better and gone back to genre' (p. 242 below). Perhaps the charges of extremity and excess would have been the same; perhaps a thriller-*Showgirls* would have brought criticisms of repetition, charging Verhoeven with an inability to develop beyond the success of *Basic Instinct*. There are many 'perhapses' here, but the survey of mistakes made over the marketing and content of this film charts another chapter in the story of genre in general and the erotic thriller in particular. Perhaps *Showgirls*' final problem is that, however raunchily you revisit it, the adult, live-action musical is dead, whilst, at least in 1995, the erotic thriller was alive and well, and the obvious vehicle for sexual innovation.

Figure 8: The theatrical erotic thriller explicitly marketed to the home viewer. Promotional advertisement: Copyright MGM Home Entertainment LLC, 2003, including images from *Showgirls* (1995, Caralco Pictures Inc/Chargeurs/United Artists, Vegas Productions); *Killing Me Softly* (MGM/Noelle Entertainment Ltd/The Montecito Production Company); *Wild Orchid* (1990, Vision PDG); *Body of Evidence* (1993, De Laurentiis); *Original Sin* (2001, DiNovi Pictures/Epsilon Motion Pictures/Hyde Park Entertainment/Intermedia Films/MGM/UGC International/Via Rosa Productions).

Nomi leaves Las Vegas, departing under a sign pointing her to Los Angeles. I like to think that she is heading for a career in B-scale erotic thrillers at the fringes of Hollywood, the obvious trajectory for a strip-circuit veteran (DTV divas Delia Sheppard and Kira Reed both started as showgirls). If she's lucky she may (unlike the hapless Berkeley who performed her) use soft-sex cinema to climb the A-scale, like some of the stars to which I now turn.

3: STARRING MICHAEL DOUGLAS

Michael Douglas spends most of *Fatal Attraction*, *Basic Instinct* and *Disclosure* running, either away from a woman who is pursuing him, or towards a woman who is running away from him. His moments of achieved arrival in satisfaction or ownership of his object are all but nonexistent; he is almost never safe. This has ensured that he is often figured as *the* representation of flawed, crisis-ridden masculinity and the concomitant decline of male cultural and social authority. He is the male version of Wager's *femme attrapée*. Michael Douglas is *the* leading man of the erotic thriller, the initially hapless and sometimes revengeful dupe of *femmes fatales* from Glenn Close through Sharon Stone to Demi Moore. His work on four key issue-led films has also made him a target for a range of liberal political groups; his erotic thriller work is highly charged with unsettling sexual-political uncertainty. In 1995, *Empire* magazine called him 'chief minority provocateur' because of his willingness to take on roles which target contemporary political positions, and a year earlier the *Washington Post* had called him 'Hollywood's designated point man for Zeitgeist issues' (Hinson 1994). *Fatal Attraction* was read as anti-feminist, *Basic Instinct* as anti-gay, *Falling Down* was anti-minority (the plaintive voice of the beleaguered white male), *Disclosure* was read as anti-powerful women, highlighting the issue of reverse sexual harassment. In each, Douglas relishes his anti-PC stance;[39] in all, Douglas has honed a star image which combines a challenge to authority (the targeted 1980s/1990s 'authority' being powerful women) with troubled male victim (he has also been excessively well paid for this public victimisation).[40] What is surprising is that his image of singular white masculine voice in the wilderness comes from a range of films which identify him squarely with weakness. Early in the production of *Basic Instinct* Douglas is known to have complained that his character, Nick Curran, was 'way too wet and weedy compared with the powerhouse of the female lead' (Cooney 1992: 56). Nick was then strengthened a little, but even in the empowered version he still falters, flawed and failing to control his own impulses. That Douglas's alignment of masculinity with deficiency predominates in the cultural image of the star over figures of sovereign power embodied by roles such as Gordon Gekko in *Wall Street* and what Douglas has called 'Prince-of-Darkness characters in *A Perfect Murder* and *The Game*' (Berk 2000: 56) is testament to the power of the roles he took on in sex thrillers rather than other genre films. Male failure/retribution essays such as *Falling Down* and *Wonder Boys* only seem to underpin what has been etched out in the erotic thriller.[41] And if female strength necessitates male weakness, he has made a virtue of his position relative to his leading ladies: 'I don't think anybody in Hollywood has a history of making more films with stronger roles for women than I have', he bragged in 1992 (Cooney 1992: 60).

I want to address the interplay between star and genre, the two-way traffic of influence which constitutes, on the one hand, Douglas's role in the development of the erotic thriller, and on the other, the erotic thriller's influence on the creation of Douglas's star persona in the 1980s and 1990s. Douglas is particularly interesting because, without being entirely typecast, he has chosen roles which overlap, presenting a continuation of contemporary issues which develop certain character types. Schatz plays with the possibility that stars can be genres, when he suggests that the A-list male stars of the 1980s and 1990s (he includes Douglas in his list) have become 'not only genres but franchises unto themselves' (1993: 31). 'A Michael Douglas film' is thus a specific category, with star and genre becoming interdependent, risking, perhaps, the loss of star identity in the wider concerns of genre. The pay-off has been that the actor has had a key role in the development of the genre, comparable perhaps with James Cagney's work in the gangster film or John Wayne's work in westerns. In *Basic Instinct*, writes J. Hoberman, Douglas 'synthesizes all previous roles from *Fatal Attraction* and *The War of the Roses* to *Black Rain* and . . . *The Streets of San Francisco*' (2003: 15), but by the release of *Disclosure* reviewers had noticed the reappearance of a type. *Time* magazine wrote: '*Basic Attraction*? No. *Fatal Instinct*? No. It's *Disclosure*, in which Michael Douglas again plays the victim of one hot broad' (Schickel 1994).[42] Film form and star development are thus intimately bound together. How a star's work impacts on the process of genre definition is a question which is crucial to both genre and star studies, and which forms the basis for later discussion of stars who are identified with DTV erotic thrillers (Shannon Tweed, Delia Sheppard, Shannon Whirry, Andrew Stevens, Martin Hewitt) or, like Douglas, with mainstream formations of the neo-*noir* sex film (Linda Fiorentino, Gina Gershon, Sharon Stone). This conjunction of genre (as an arena for public debates around gender-shifts), and a problematic male star image, is the subject of this section on Michael Douglas.

The contemporary Cain Male

The Douglas characters' relationship to authority has never been easy. From rookie cop in *The Streets of San Francisco* to alienated cop in *Black Rain* to jaded, disgraced cop in *Basic Instinct*, his representation of problematic relationships to the law, even when ostensibly upholding it, has been developed through various forms of the thriller, from TV crime thriller to police drama to corporate thriller. The Douglas image in *Basic Instinct* is both a distillation of the decadent masculinities represented by the culpable victim-turned-avenger figures in *Fatal Attraction* and *Disclosure* and an echo of what Frank Krutnick describes as the transgressing, castrated male of *film noir*. Douglas is a contemporary incarnation of the Fred MacMurray character in *Double Indemnity* (the 1944 film based on one of James M. Cain's novels), except that MacMurray moves from adventurer to fatally wounded, whilst Douglas (in *Fatal Attraction* and *Disclosure* at least) does nominally survive, albeit as damaged goods.[43] In a climate in which a crisis of masculinity is presented as a widespread cultural, economic and social problem, New Hollywood cinema needed a figure like Michael Douglas and was ripe for a revival of what I will call the 'Cain male' (developing Frank Krutnik's discussion of filmic adaptations of James M. Cain's hardboiled novels which formed the building blocks of *film noir*). Douglas (like Cain's males) is an exemplary 'Everyman' figure; or to put it the other way round, it is perhaps Douglas's claim to be a contemporary Everyman which makes him a Cain male. In her essay on Cain's fiction, Joyce Carol Oates writes that his literary method 'is to single out an ordinary human being, centre upon him with every acknowledgement of his still being ordinary, and bring him to an encounter with his "fate"' (Oates 1968: 112). This is Douglas, tied to the tracks and waiting for the female train to run him over. Once desire is set running (one explosive episode at the start of *Fatal Attraction* and *Disclosure*, or a series of moments throughout *Basic Instinct*) Douglas runs through the film panicking over its consequences. Douglas, and indeed *Fatal Attraction*'s producers, testify in a number of interviews to the fact that in the lead-up to that film he had just wanted to make a movie about how lust 'can destroy a man's life' (Leigh-Kile 1987: 13). Douglas ends up making (at least) three.

Desire is also the problem for the original Cain male, but it is primarily the man's lack of control over his own desire, not necessarily his inability to control a desiring woman. Krutnik stresses the problem of a male desire which threatens male power as one side in a tense exchange of passion between desiring male and desirable female, the two being eternally balanced in mutual destruction. Lurid as Cain's stories are, their focus on a punishable transgression serves to uphold the pillars of the law as well as any judicial system. Krutnik sketches out the basic co-ordinates of a Cain tale:

> Cain himself saw his early works as 'intense tales' dealing exclusively with 'one man's relation to one woman' . . . They begin with the eruption of desire at the sight of the woman, an eruption that displaces the hero and locks him within a trajectory leading to transgression – most often through the crimes of adultery and murder, the murder of the woman's husband – and ultimately to catastrophe. Gratification and survival are mutually exclusive, something that is stressed through the fatalism of the first-person narration which continually locates desire as illicit and stresses the 'inevitability' of its repression. (Krutnik 1982: 31)

Consistent to Cain's work is an obsession with the 'recurrent, neuralgic' (Krutnik 1982: 32) repetitive male desire which victimises its subject (the man) via his involvement with a deadly object (the woman). The Cain male is thus victimised not just because of but *by* his desire. Krutnik continues:

> The Cain-mode . . . features a much more precarious hero, a lapsed hero who is subject to internal as well as external pressures – the latter a seeming result of the former. (1982: 42)

Although none of the Douglas texts I am discussing is a Cain adaptation, this does not mean that they do not contain a Cain character, activated by the impossibility of forbidden desire, damned by the consequences of its pursuit. Michael Douglas plays lapsed heroes for the blockbuster market of the 1980s and 1990s. He has said that he is 'interested in people who are flawed', who have 'a dark or degrading truth or edge to them' (Lawson 1993: 178). He struggles to survive the desires of women either to have him or to destroy him, desires which are only sometimes matched by his own. But he is not a Cain male primarily because of desire (despite *Basic Instinct*), but because of his pathological lack of control. Douglas's characters are ruined by, and predicated upon, lack in its various forms: incompetence, ignorance, impotence – symbolic forms of castration which mark him as damaged. In the voice-over dominated hardboiled text, this loss of control manifests itself through the signs of 'the telling of the story' – for Krutnik: 'the voice-over commentary oscillates between misogyny, self-pity, and sheer redundancy' (1982: 39). The Douglas character's lack of control over the narrative in which he is embedded is manifested not through the discourse of voiceover but through other symptoms, though misogyny, self-pity and redundancy still mark his response to his own victimhood and impotence.

As I discussed in my definition of neo-*noir* in chapter 1, since sex is not the prime explosive issue in the era when softcore spectacle is possible, other areas of life must come to the fore to spark the dynamic between Cain male protagonists and their antagonists, as endangered and desired, tempting and lacking. Oates describes the Cain universe thus: 'It is as if the world extends no farther than the radius of one's desire', but if we accept that desire is predicated on lack, this radius also describes the shape of one's emptiness. In *Basic Instinct* Douglas's character is driven by a desire which represents him as aching absence and '*victim* to desire' (Krutnick 1982: 39), though his failures are not as marked nor as interesting as in the two other films analysed here. For *Village Voice* writer Georgia Brown, the prime charm of *Basic Instinct* was that Stone and Jeanne Tripplehorn spent most of the film leading 'Michael Douglas's lustcrazed detective around the Bay Area by his dick' (1995: 80). *Fatal Attraction* and *Disclosure*, however, are not predicated on man's desire for the woman he lacks, but more diffuse, worrying and, perhaps, even less controllable forms of lack: security, power, knowledge, privacy. Because he cannot control the women with whom he had his explosive sexual encounter in the first act of the film, he loses control over these things too. Sexual failure or transgression are just items in a list of uncontrollables for Douglas's men, who come to have so little command over *any* aspects of their universe. Nor are these *noirs* of the absent family; Douglas's men are not loners but fathers and husbands, and it is the revered family which they stand to lose most dramatically. Whereas in *Postman* and *Double Indemnity* the woman's husband is murdered, in both *Fatal Attraction* and *Disclosure* it is the man's relationship with his wife that is jeopardised, for revenge in the former film, for the sake of corporate ambition in the latter. Douglas's characters are thus sketched through slightly different co-ordinates of failure from Cain's: it is not desire which disrupts the hero's control, but a panoply of threats which systematically render him impotent. Lee Horsley discusses *noir*'s male victim figure who says to himself – in the words of another pulp writer, Horace McCoy – 'I should have stayed at home' (67). Michael Douglas's career in the erotic thriller moves from home-leaving to a protracted process of return (perhaps he should have stayed at home too).

Douglas's relationship to authority is also an issue which distinguishes him from the classic Cain hero, and this underpins his penchant for survival. Cain's heroes must be explicitly punished for their transgression. Douglas's failed male characters precariously survive when his more successfully Machiavellian characters often die (such as Steven Taylor, the *homme fatal* of the *Dial M for Murder* remake *A Perfect Murder* [1998]). If, as Krutnik argues, 'the power of Law [is] fundamental to both *film noir* and the Cain-text' (1982: 44), it is much more problematic in neo-*noir* and the contemporary police, sex-crime or erotic thriller. Here, authority is severely undermined and villains are not necessarily punished. *Fatal Attraction* was indeed seen as a Cain-like cautionary tale (remember those responses detailed in chapter 1 – 'Look what happens when you play around, sweetheart'), but *Fatal Attraction*'s Dan is also a highly culpable and sexually seducible lawyer, like cop Nick Curran. Yet if the law's representatives are flawed, they also survive despite their transgression, fractured by new vulnerabilities. Cain's originals never survive; for them the law is inevitable, the postman who always comes, always rings twice.[44] Whilst the future of Nick at the end of *Basic Instinct* is uncertain (like Frank Chambers [Jack Nicholson] in the remake of *The Postman Always Rings Twice,* though on a different side of the law), the conclusion is at least open. Yet even when Douglas's Cain men survive, they still have that 'aura of doom about them' (Oates 1968: 113). This does not come from the effect of 'finishedness' achieved by retrospective narration,[45] for the films are still suspenseful – you want to see just *how* he survives. Rather, it comes from the sense of inevitable humiliation about to unfold parallel to the whodunit story. The paradox of identification with his point of view, a point of view which is also discredited, wrongfoots the viewer: you just know your respect for Douglas's men will diminish not increase as the film rolls on, yet you also want them to win. Nevertheless, whilst Douglas's career-lurch from one fall-guy to another traces a downward trajectory in masculine representations, so his bankability as a star has rocketed. Douglas's men are resilient, which might prove that the mainstream erotic thriller cannot bear to present a finally defeated or punished masculinity, unlike its generic predecessor. This phenomenon of Douglas as the wounded survivor is interesting for signalling a regressive political shift in the move from classic *noir* to this formation of neo-*noir*, even if the 'elements of masochism, of self-loathing' (Spicer 2002: 85) which characterise the Cain male also mark the aggressive passivity of Douglas's men. I now want to look at the particular forms this inadequate or castrated masculinity has taken in three films.

Infidelity and incompetence: Fatal Attraction

According to Tom Hanks' character in *Sleepless in Seattle*, *Fatal Attraction* 'scared the shit out of every man in America', but it was Michael Douglas's Dan Gallagher who got scared first. *Fatal Attraction* tells the deeply problematic story of a man's brief infidelity followed by his extended intimidation. Whilst his wife Beth (Anne Archer) and his daughter Ellen (Ellen Hamilton Latzen) are out of town, lawyer Dan has a brief steamy affair with editor Alex Forrest (Glenn Close). 'I don't think having dinner with anybody is a crime', says Dan, to which the predatory Alex replies, 'Not yet', setting the scene for the proto-type erotic thriller dangerous liaison, the criminality of seduction itself. The line prefigures the repeated genre sentiment, that sex itself is deemed a crime even before a crime is committed – remember *Body of Evidence*'s suggestion that it's 'a crime to be a great lay'. Trina in *Jade* also protests, 'I cheated on my husband one time – I didn't know I could be arrested for it.' Dan thinks he can get away with it and breaks off the relationship when Beth returns, but Alex pursues and then terrorises him. When Alex finally breaks in to the family home armed with a knife, Dan tries to drown her in the bath but she is shot dead by Beth. Dan, then, is on the run for around sixty minutes of the film's duration, after a first act in which the good times are briefly enjoyed, including hot sex on Alex's kitchen counter, fellatio in an elevator (accompanied by steamy, *noir*ish light filtering through the grilles) and an operatic pasta dinner. As Dan and Alex enter and leave her apartment we see that she lives in the meat-packing district, envisaged as Hell: butchers carry animal carcasses, there are fires everywhere. The *mise-en-scène* marks Alex as shadowed by death and with a nose for blood, and Dan is her quarry. [46]

Dan's family was a prime focus for critical discussion of *Fatal Attraction* on its release – a near-perfect unit briefly disrupted by the avenging angel of the single, childless, career woman, and reunited in the final frame when the camera rests on a photo of all three embracing for eternity. Dan has strayed, but the film, and its audiences, absolve him. Nevertheless, Alex's role is by no means straightforward (as we saw in chapter 1). On the one hand, Dan's brief transgression is presented as forgivable, the unity of his family as entirely desirable, Alex's pursuit as monstrous. On the other hand, *Fatal Attraction* is careful to present Alex's side of the story too: she declares herself pregnant, forcing Dan to confront the consequences of his actions: 'You're not gonna run away', she insists. 'You thought you'd have a good time – you didn't stop for a second to think about me.' Screenwriter James Dearden gives her all the best lines. Though she acts crazy she speaks sense ('You play fair with me, I'll play fair with you'), and she has to confront the oldest responses misogyny can throw at her in her justification of her pregnancy: 'How do you know it's mine?' asks the repellent Dan. 'Because I don't sleep around', she replies[47] ('I'm just asking you to acknowledge your responsibilities. Is that so bad?' she says on a crazed tape-recording). But sensible as this sounds, the combination of Close's performance and the way that *Fatal Attraction* inflects Dan's response casts Alex as always and entirely insane. It is testament to the power of point of view in Hollywood narrative that these words cut no mustard in shifting our sympathy away from the Gallaghers and towards Alex. Adrian Lyne discusses his film in an introductory section which appears on the reissued video version of *Fatal Attraction* released under the 'Paramount Directors Signature Series', where he says of Douglas that 'it was a considerable achievement that he managed to still be sympathetic at the end of this movie'.[48] However sensible Alex's words are ('You thought that you could just walk into my life and turn it upside-down without a thought for anyone but yourself'), we are so swept away by our allegiance to Dan's perspective on events that conclusive sympathy for 'the bitch' would be reading very hard indeed against the grain of the narrative point of view (nevertheless, some writers did manage this, as we saw earlier).

If American's everyman Tom Hanks identified so strongly with Douglas, it seems inevitable that every other man would too. Yet review material offers a more contradictory set of positions, which do not necessarily see male viewers lining up behind Dan and female viewers lining up behind Alex; *Fatal Attraction*, as we saw in chapter 1, strives to be all things to all sectors of the audience. Structural identification with his point of view is not the same as sympathy, and reception material evidences a strong case against Dan-as-character coexisting with support for Dan-as-survivor. George Gordon in the *Daily Mail* writes that 'Dan . . . is loathed by women for his casual hit-and-run attitude to a night of love'; producer Sherry Lansing speaking to the *Independent* attributed sympathy for Alex to women having been badly treated by men, but she also saw Dan as highly sympathetic (Summers 1988: 44). This final allegiance to Dan's perspective is particularly striking considering that he is such a loser. Many contemporary critics stressed Dan's dim-wittedness versus Alex's smartness – the mismatch of intellect and cunning;[49] he is 'the sheep in wolf's clothing' who only 'rises to adequacy' (Hutchinson 1988: 38). Lyne saw Douglas as a brave man for taking on the role: 'Michael had a huge problem in that he was playing a man who was weak, who was vulnerable, and who essentially wasn't a winner for two hours. . . . This was kind of difficult for Michael. Michael is the son of Kirk Douglas and he had been used to kind of winning in movies.'[50] Yet this was to be a role to which Douglas would return. From his first formal introduction to Alex when he gets cream cheese on his nose, to the lunch date when he can't attract the waiter's attention but Alex can, to his final failure to kill her, Dan's impotence is marked out – he, as Douglas himself notes, 'doesn't have a sense of his own dignity' (Lawson 1993: 181). Most critics likened Alex's corkscrew locks to Medusa's snakes, which might account for Dan's inability to act – he is turned to stone. Valerie Grove saw Dan as 'softened and trapped by his own passive complacency', whilst Ellen Willis attributes his passivity wholly to the presence of women:

> His car doesn't crash into anything – it gets trashed by Close instead. His dominant emotion is fear, not only of Close but of his own wife, who is Mommy at her warmest and sexiest: he doesn't dare tell her he's been bad. (1987: 85–6)

Though he's a lawyer he can't make the police do anything to help him or to restrain Alex, but if his powers as a professional male fall short, his sensory powers as a competent human being do too. Alex assaults him through his ears, but his ears also fail him. Listening to the threatening tape she sends him becomes an act of self-torture. And at the film's climax Dan has been sent to the kitchen, where the domestic sound of the whistling kettle makes him oblivious to the noise of his wife being attacked in the bathroom. The ringing of phones terrifies him: Alex has the right to invade his aural space at any time of the night or day. If he hears too much and too little to be in control of events, he also sees too little and is seen too much. Dan is afflicted by a certain blindness which often strikes the erotic thriller victim. Because he is Alex's visual prey often he cannot see her – he cannot look back. She chooses him, pinning him with her gaze first erotically and then aggressively, seeing him before he sees her, peeping in through the windows of his life. This ability of the seeing woman to strike her prey blind is both a classic attribute of the phallic *femme fatale* and a symptom of the fall-guy's innate incompetence.

Fatal Attraction thus exposes the splitting which takes places when we view, perhaps particularly when we view thriller material. If the drive of the film enforces identification with Dan as protagonist, the film also provokes a contrary response to its politics. Viewers wanted the bitch to be killed, but also recognised, and debated, her point of view. Disliking the feckless philandering male, they also rooted for his survival. Identification with the loser is thus complex, compromised and incomplete, operating not just (perhaps not even primarily) unconsciously but at all levels of response from visceral thrill to conscious recognition. Carol Clover discusses the problematic relationship of male viewers to the slasher film, and writers on male spectacle from Steve Neale onwards have read men's relationship to men on screen as part of a process of identification bound up with narcissism. Although equally problematic, identifying with monsters who eventually get slain by chainsaw-wielding 'final girls' is not the same as identifying with failure, nor with despising the failed, but also wanting them to redeem themselves in the final reel.

Sherry Lansing attests that it took so long for *Fatal Attraction* to come to the screen (it was four years before it went into production with Paramount) because studios were wary of making a film which represents such a problematic masculinity: 'They didn't want to do a movie where a man cheats on his wife for no reason,' says Lansing. 'They were afraid the Michael Douglas character would be unsympathetic.' This remains true of the film in its finished form, but the question of how to read the failed male and what audiences want from their protagonists is made more acute by the issue of *Fatal Attraction*'s famously changed ending. Preview-screened to audiences who demanded not that Alex (as it were) 'gets away' with/by committing suicide, but that she is forcibly dispatched by the wronged wife Beth, the producers listened and responded. Yet in the video reissue of *Fatal Attraction* from which I quoted earlier, Lyne discusses not one alternative ending but two, one of which was never filmed. In James Dearden's original script (then called *Affairs of the Heart*), Dan is charged with 'Eve's' murder (as Alex was then called),[51] because his fingerprints are on the knife which Eve has used to kill herself. Dan argues that Eve was suicidal, but Detective O'Rourke replies, 'In my experience a woman who wants to kill herself doesn't do it by sticking a nine inch knife in her gut . . . The fingerprints on the handle are yours.'[52] The film ends in the darkest of *noir* modes:

> THE CAMERA TRACKS TOWARDS [Dan]. He is trapped.
>> DAN
> I'm innocent. I swear to God, I am innocent!
> INT. PRISON CELL. NIGHT
> DAN stands in the doorway of a small cell. He turns to face the
> CAMERA.
>> DAN
> I am innocent!
> The cell door slams in his face.
> CUT TO BLACK
>> THE
>> END

Here, Alex has committed suicide but Dan has gone to prison for her murder. Dan has been punished for his transgressions, but Eve/Alex has also paid the price of self-violence; getting some kind of revenge from the grave, she takes Dan down with her.[53] Lyne reports that he thought this ending was powerful because 'it's black – it's Hitchcockian'.[54] It would certainly have made *Fatal Attraction* a far less mainstream film, more in line with the ambivalent endings of American New Wave cinema of the late 1960s and early 1970s, or some of *film noir*'s bleaker moments. And it would perhaps have defused some of Susan Faludi (1992) and others' arguments against the politics of the film. In *Affairs of the Heart* no one wins, making it more a work of black nihilism than of anti-feminism.

Lyne argues now that in mainstream cinema you can't ask an audience to identify with a family for two hours and then expect them to accept its total destruction in the last frame, so a decision to find a way of helping the Gallaghers to
survive united was agreed in pre-production. In addition to this unfilmed ending,
there are also two different filmed endings in existence, both of which have significant differences in consequence for Dan and for women. The ending which
was preview-screened (*Fatal Attraction* version 1) features much of the above
(Alex kills herself and Dan is arrested for her murder), but then Beth discovers
a tape of Alex vowing to 'cut deeper next time – I'll kill myself', which gets Dan
off the hook. The politics of this are still dubious (Beth breathes 'Oh Thank God'
as she hears Alex's promise), especially the film's last (flashback) image of Alex
triumphantly slicing her throat to the accompaniment of *Madame Butterfly*. In
both *Affairs of the Heart* and *Fatal Attraction* version 1 Dan really is the fall-
guy; if he survives in *Fatal Attraction* version 1 it is only because one woman
finds a tape with another woman's voice on it, and then goes with her daughter
to the police to vindicate him. *Fatal Attraction* is a film, wrote George Gordon,
'in which women had the macho roles. Dan is simply swept along by events,
putty in the hands of two women.' Gordon also notes that Alex is more afraid
of Beth than of Dan. But in this dénouement, not only does Alex get Dan from
the grave, she also presents Beth with the evidence to save him. The wife must
find the solution left by the lover, for the man cannot save himself.[55]

Fatal Attraction version 2 (the version which was generally released) was
made because preview audiences wanted a much more graphic form of revenge
to be heaped on the *femme fatale*. If she has controlled most of the action of
the film (pulling Dan's strings), she should not be allowed to control her own
death. The *Fatal Attraction* which cleaned up at the box office features wife
Beth shooting Alex after she has supernaturally risen from her own death by
drowning (at Dan's hand). Alex's termination is thus left as a matter between
women (a fatal version of a mud-fight), with Dan deprived of the opportunity
for conclusive action (he wasn't even strong enough to drown her properly). So
what was taken as pandering to the worst desires of popular reactionary audiences has interesting implications for masculinity in mainstream cinema. What
they wanted was a confrontation between women, and a spectacular death for
a grand *femme fatale*, which effectively excluded the enfeebled man.

As many reviewers pointed out, *Fatal Attraction* is about the consequences
of sex – as much a morality tale for the age of AIDS as a film targeting the rise
of the childless career woman. Alex is Dan's retribution: in the face of her
actions he is powerless. She acts; he cannot even effectively react. Oates'
description of James M. Cain's morality looks remarkably like *Fatal
Attraction*'s ethics:

> Cain's parable, which is perhaps America's parable, may be something
> like this: the passion that rises in us is both an inescapable part of our lives
> and an enemy to our lives, to our egoistic control of ourselves. Once

unleashed it cannot be quieted. Giving oneself to anyone, even temporarily, will result in entrapment and death; the violence lovers do to one another is no more than a reflection of the proposed violence society holds back to keep the individual passions in check. (1986: 127–8)[56]

But this is a violence which targets men and women differently. In *Fatal Attraction*, Douglas is even excluded from this traditional male pursuit.

The Femme Fatale *writes the Castrated Cop:* Basic Instinct

Basic Instinct has been read as a film which demonises both women and gays in its representation of the violently vengeful woman, but it is also a film about men as victims, specifically straight men as victims of their own heterosexuality.[57] It offers another stage for Michael Douglas's humiliated male, developing his take on the jaded contemporary cop. Its opening scene poses the whodunit question in relation to the ice-pick-wielding blonde, but it also sets an agenda for radical (fatal) male subordination. As the police scour the scene, one notes that the victim and his partner 'got his and hers Picassos', but 'hers is bigger'. If all *Basic Instinct*'s women are actual or potential villains, all its men are actual or potential victims; here men will always be weaker and stupider, and all as liable as each other to be women's meat. This is a curious effect for a film which graphically displays the deaths of both Roxy and Beth, yet leaves the impression of male corpses piled up after a holocaust of female vengeance (one writer even reported, entirely erroneously, that 'Everyone who dies, notably, is a straight white male' [Holub 1991: 82]). Perhaps the film's resounding misogyny lies in its insistence that men's deaths (and male victimisation) matter but women's do not. The sexual balance of violence insinuates that if women do it, men are done to, and then mourned.

As *Basic Instinct*'s hero, Douglas as Nick Curran carries the responsibility for the deficiencies of his sex. His story progresses through systematic entrapment in the spider-woman's snare, accompanied by a regression into professional inadequacy (the etching on Catherine's door is of a spider's web, but Nick still walks through it). He carries the nickname 'Shooter' because of a trigger-happy episode when he shot some tourists for which he was disciplined, after which his wife committed suicide. In a quirk of film referencing, this moniker also sexually unsettles the Douglas character: 'The Shooter' is also the name the cops dub the killer in *Sea of Love*, presumed for much of the film to be a deranged woman, but ultimately revealed as a man who sexually humiliates other men before he kills them. As Nick becomes implicated in the murders which surround him, he even has to relinquish his gun – and the very basis of that name. Catherine then takes his story and fashions it into her new novel. This book, she tells him, is about 'a detective – he falls for the wrong woman'. As Nick loses his gun and his name, Catherine appropriates it as the title of her novel, *Shooter*.

The castration of Nick is slow but thorough. As Tom Sanders in *Disclosure* also learns, one effective means of ensuring impotence is through ignorance: 'You won't learn anything I don't want you to know,' says Catherine to Nick, as she lures him through the narrative with the bearing of the mistress leading her dog on a chain. Like Frank Dulaney and Frank Keller in *Body of Evidence* and *Sea of Love,* respectively, Nick cannot walk away. The cat-and-mouse interview scene in which the famous Stone crotch-flash takes place hinges on the way in which the spectacle of woman not only subordinates men but also has the power to turn them into biddable sexual captives. This is a film in which men's eyes are explicitly rendered their organs of vulnerability: look at a woman and you're lost, for where the eyes are led the penis must follow. For Frank Krutnik the Cain male is 'frozen passively in the act of looking' (1981: 38), and so are Douglas's men. The police then proceed to formalise their relationship of visual subordination to Catherine (she shows, they look; she wins, they lose) by giving Nick the job of following Catherine to 'see where she leads'. From then on his view of her, and her display of herself, are the prime means through which she ensures his co-operation. Yet this visual tracking prevents Nick from seeing the consequences, becoming, for Robert E. Wood, a 'blind plunge into the unknown' (1993: 45). Wood also argues that in its obsession with voyeurism *Basic Instinct* finally renders the visual void, and shows the sexual act to be never enough for desire: '*Basic Instinct* begins with the exhibition of the body and ultimately exhausts voyeurism'. Nick as desiring subject is doubly wanting, first lacking his object, then, once he's had her, finding that having will never be enough. *Basic Instinct* thus offers one rejoinder to critics who argue that the move from the implicit sexual desire of *noir* to the explicit sexual spectacle of neo-*noir* presented a defeat or deflation of desire. However often and in whatever ways Nick has Catherine, he still emerges as desire's Cain-like victim: congress with the woman just proves how much he is wanting.

Wood also suggests that Catherine's power lies in word as well as look. Though it is the spectacle of her – and of Sharon Stone – which focused most viewer's attention, Catherine's control might be primarily narrative, with Nick's impotence an effect of the fact that he is her character – not just her biddable object, but her linguistic invention. What Catherine writes, Nick acts out; the more she writes him into her book, the emptier he is in the flesh, like a kind of novelistic vampirism. This seems like a marriage made in pulp-fiction heaven: 'Nick's susceptibility to being narrated by others,' writes Wood, 'dovetails with Catherine's propensity to narrate' (1993: 49–50). Consequently, the end of writing terminates the relationship: 'Your character's dead – goodbye.' Wood's reading limits itself to an analysis of Catherine as abstract generator of Nick's narrative, with Nick as her creation. Nick is defined by his complete absence of individuating characteristics, which makes him a conduit of other people's stories, rather like the Thompson character in *Citizen Kane*: 'As a result of this absence, the protagonist is a nexus for the narratives of others, narratives he seeks rather to channel than to contest' (1993: 44). Wood's reading is also predicated on the idea that the whole film, and the fantasy of a woman who 'writes' you, is actually Nick's solipsistic nightmare.[58] Nick imagines Catherine imagining him – a masochistic fantasy in which the man finally controls the woman's control, dramatising his passivity as a way of enjoying the effects of her authority. The Douglas character's passivity is therefore an active passivity.

But Nick's drama also hinges on genre. Despite the fact that he's a cop, he fails to understand that he's participating in Catherine's style of thriller. For Wood the empty Nick has 'a remarkable inability to generate his own language. He echoes language, often language of extreme banality' (1993: 49). Director Paul Verhoeven has explained the special effects-heavy *Robocop* and *Total Recall* as an effect of the new émigré's lack of confidence with the English language.[59] By the time of *Basic Instinct*, having been in America since 1986, he felt that he could take on something which was 'much more based on dialogue than anything I've done before' (Shea and Hennings 1993: 12). Perhaps, then, Nick becomes a figure for Verhoeven, struggling with a foreign discourse (America's, women's) which he can't quite master. But Nick is not just confused by the fact that men and women speak different languages in this film, but that Catherine is most familiar with the genre they both inhabit (writers understand thrillers more than cops do). As writer of a sex-crime thriller in which Nick is a character, she is the puppeteer not just of his desire but of his plot. Wood writes that 'Catherine's narrative is central to the threat of death she poses. Catherine can make Nick cease to exist in three ways: she can kill him; she can cease to love him; and she can cease to imagine him.' Nick's existence is then textual, but not self-authored.[60] It is, of course, as I argued earlier, also a text written by Eszterhas, and so the whole narrative of Nick as written must also be read as the fantasy of a man who compulsively repeats the same sexual story, trying out men and women in the fall guy roles as he goes along. As with the film which saw Douglas in a similar position two years later, his role as figure manoeuvred on someone else's chessboard was assured.

'When did I have the power?': Disclosure

Douglas's erotic thriller specialism reaches new lows of exclusion and humiliation in *Disclosure*. Though Tom Sanders (Douglas) eventually wins his case of sexual harassment against his boss, Meredith Johnson (Demi Moore), his character and performance are framed by an ambivalence towards personal authority. The film's first plot-point is Tom's failure to be made a Vice-President of DigiCom, the computer company for whom he works, but even before we see him (at home) we witness that he cannot so much as control his small daughter. Like *Fatal Attraction*, the film opens inside the family and we hear Tom reminding his daughter, 'Liza, I am your father. When the father says put your jacket on you, Put Your Jacket On!'[61] In one of the film's shrewdest lines, his wife Susan points out to him a little later, 'You're the only person I know who sucks up to the people below you.'[62]

Disclosure partly positions itself in the erotic thriller tradition in that it is about a sex crime and develops some key genre threads (culpability and sexual guilt, the *femme fatale* versus the castrated male, sex as power), but it is also a corporate and cyber thriller. Indeed, it shifts genre halfway through after its one forceful sex-scene has established the film's erotic co-ordinates, from a very dialogue-heavy, character-led thriller to a visually futuristic techno-adventure (including a virtual reality sequence animated by Industrial Light & Magic). As most of its reviewers pointed out, it sits neatly alongside *Fatal Attraction* and *Basic Instinct* in that Douglas is playing essentially the same part, but it also builds on the themes of victimised but avenging white masculinity which had been established in *Falling Down*, the 1993 film which separates *Basic Instinct* from *Disclosure* in Douglas's career filmography (*The Washington Post* called Douglas 'Angry Male Voter Poster Boy' [Howe 1994]). When a female friend in *Disclosure* reiterates the 'fact of life' that women are oppressed, Tom responds with '80 per cent of the suicides are committed by men. They're dropping like flies with heart attacks.' And when his wife urges him to back down from his sexual harassment charge, he retorts, 'I've got a better idea – why don't I just admit it? Why don't I be that . . . evil white guy you're all complaining about? Then I could fuck everybody.' What in a pre-PC age would have denoted power (white masculinity) becomes, in the paranoid world Tom inhabits, the prime location of his guilt. In *Disclosure*, all that white men have is responsibility without power, and certainly without pleasure ('When did I have the power?' laments poor Tom).

Tom develops as a kind of Kafkaesque protagonist, surrounded by ominous talk of redundancy which goes beyond a state of employment towards an existential condition (an ex-IBM employee friend reports that he has been 'surplussed': 'Boom – no more room for you. Smaller, faster, cheaper, better'). Tom's own surplus-potential becomes the film's key spectacle: his colleagues talk of little other than how he is responding as the threats close in. His boss Bob (Donald Sutherland) says that taking the transfer he is offered would be like a duck accepting a transfer to orange sauce;[63] though Tom refuses the job, the image lingers of Douglas trussed up. If Nick the Shooter is deprived of his gun in *Basic Instinct*, Tom – working at the cutting-edge of information technology – loses his access to knowledge. Meredith berates him for being afflicted by that typical masculine trait of fearing the exposure of ignorance, and praises the strength of owning up when one doesn't know something: 'You can't say you don't know because, in your mind, that means you lose, you're worthless. Men!' But when Tom admits in a corporate meeting that he doesn't know something, he is humiliated for it. Later Meredith identifies Tom's ignorance as the crux of his impotence: 'Poor Sanders. You have no idea what you're up against – as usual.'[64] Tom's attorney in the harassment case says to him, 'Sexual harassment is not about sex. It's about power. She has it and you don't.' Tom's impotence is underpinned by knowledge and its absence – everyone else has it and he lacks it. After his files have been confiscated he discovers that his privileged access to the company's database has been revoked, which is accompanied by a very *noir*ish overhead shot of Tom at his desk, revolving back and forth on his chair, his crumpled suit and face half-lit, his forehead lined, his hands nervously placed over his crotch. Soon after he invokes Bob's image again when he laments to his attorney, 'I'm like a sitting duck . . . I feel like one of those people out there walking around like a ghost with a résumé.'

The conspiracy against him grows, and the more paranoid he gets, the more fascinating he becomes as his pursuer's object. If *Fatal Attraction*'s Dan is assaulted through his ears and *Basic Instinct*'s Nick is blinded by sights, Tom is the unseeing seen. The glass palace of a corporate building he works in becomes a *Rear Window* panopticon, but with Tom in his transparent eyrie as more surveyed than surveying. When anonymous emails arrive for him he looks round to see who's watching him. In this conspiracy of disenfranchisement even cinema history is deployed to comment on his condition. As he and his wife lie in bed following Tom's assault by Meredith, Billy Wilder's *The Apartment* plays on TV. Crucially, we see not a scene of hapless Jack Lemmon as employee Bud Baxter taken advantage of by all his superiors in the insurance company he works for, but a scene which features a justification of infidelity made by his boss, played by Fred MacMurray. If in 1944's *Double Indemnity* MacMurray was the exemplary Cain male and an insurance company employee, by 1960 he is running the show and in sexual control. A scene which represented the struggles of the embattled Baxter would have given Tom a comic mirror for his own tragedy; instead, the TV confronts him again with an image of the power he lacks (as well as commenting on his sexual waywardness). That it is MacMurray who presents this to him provides a moment of great cinematic irony.

The scene in which Tom explicitly becomes Meredith's sexual victim is the culmination of a number of threads running through *Disclosure* which position him as someone who is literally being 'fucked' by the company. Tom dreams of being in a lift with boss Bob; the camera adopts Tom's point of view as Bob advances, open-mouthed and tongue out, in an astonishing attack of French kissing.[65] Bob's desire for Tom's demise is expressed as a literal castration as the harassment case develops: 'I want you to cut his balls off', he says to a colleague. When Meredith forces herself on him in the seduction scene, the film's tag-line ('Sex is power') is woven into the discourse of rape: Tom's 'No' she takes to be a 'Yes', before amplifying their employment positions into sexual role-play: 'You just lie back and let me be the boss,' she says (Fig. 9). That said, the female rapist must elicit from her male victim a sexual response which will ensure performance, so Meredith, like all good sadists, relies on the desire of her victim. 'I like to keep the boys under me happy', she says, and as much as admits that her desire for him denotes power onto him: 'Why don't you just lie back and let me take you?' she says. 'Now you've got all the power.' In this world of erotic power-exchange, sex is a dangerous place in which male impotence can be either redressed or accentuated.

Figure 9: 'You just lie back and let me be the boss': Michael Douglas is obliterated by the superior Demi Moore in *Disclosure*. Warner Bros/Baltimore/Constant/The Kobal Collection.

Sexually, Tom is also his own worst enemy; it is not only his crisis of self-authority which positions him as Meredith's target. *Disclosure* strongly suggests that there is something about masculine heterosexuality *per se* which makes all men potential prey for a woman like Meredith, as if she were a Dworkinite porno-spectacle and he were the stimulated consumer. Ellen Willis wrote that sex with Alex in *Fatal Attraction* could only be justified as a vestigial male reflex he 'can't be expected to account for' (1987: 85); male sexual incontinence is thus read as weakness. Tom also is not just victim of others' desires, he is victim of his own hormones. If Meredith's black stilettos symbolise the new power on the block (they are the first thing we see of her), the erect penis signals not sovereign authority but men's lack of self-control. One of Tom's colleagues reminds him that he has 'a sexual urge every twenty minutes. It's a physiological certainty . . . you can't fight it', and later, when Tom is cross-examined by Meredith's lawyer about whether he responded to her advances, he justifies his erection with 'She had her top open. It was an involuntary reflex.' Even his own attorney can only come up with (as her best shot at defending his response) 'What he did, he did out of weakness.' In a film which abounds with discussion of hard-ons, the erection seems to be (pardon the mixed metaphor) the rope with which men hang themselves.

Tom's return from the brink is accompanied by a costume change. He started the film with egg on his tie, but concludes it wearing a masculine version of Meredith's dark suit (has he learnt how to power-dress by copying women?). He also adopts the discourse of the hunter: 'There's a real talent to fishing', he says. 'First you've gotta choose the right bait. Then you have to know when to reel it in.' Nevertheless, the whiff of orange sauce still lingers round the edges of even this sharper image. When he asks Meredith if it ever occurred to her that maybe *he* set *her* up, the camera lingers on her doubtful face for a moment to give Tom's point some credence, but really this could never seriously occur to anyone, because it could not occur at all. Douglas's men are set up, not the other way round. Tom's small victory in hanging on to his job notwithstanding, *Disclosure* doesn't seem to want to break the habit of humiliation it has established, and even the cinematography joins in. Meredith's replacement is announced and once again Tom fails to get the job (his being passed over is thus the starting and end-point of the film); instead, he finds himself under another female boss (albeit a benign one this time). When the announcement is made the camera cruelly focuses on Tom's face (Douglas in best disappointed Oscar-nominee mode) as he has to absorb the information that he's failed again, then master himself and congratulate the victor. It's a spectacularly public passing-over, with Tom once again visibly disempowered at the centre of the scene: all DigiCom's employees look down on him from the upper levels of the building, ringed in tiers floor by floor above the hall, like spectators at the Circus Maximus. It is not enough for Douglas's men to be humiliated, they must diegetically be *seen* to be humiliated, the public gaze as agent of male shame.[66]

This might serve as a fitting image of the mainstream erotic thriller's damaged

men. The spectacle of their lack of authority is perhaps more perversely compelling than is the seductiveness of the *femme fatale*. Even sexual success is
seldom cast as the controlled desire of the male subject: they are chosen not free,
manipulated not authoritative, abject-object not sovereign subject. At this
Michael Douglas excels. Yet discussing *Fatal Attraction*, Sherry Lansing argues
that the Dan/Alex positions are gender-neutral: 'I feel the sexes could have been
reversed. We chose to make the Glenn Close character a woman, but her problems are not gender-related. We could just as easily have made her a man.'
Given the violent furore surrounding the politics of Alex's representation is
predicated on her deranged feminist femininity, this seems unlikely. Alex, for
all the masculinity of her name, is a specifically female revenger. But this is not
to say that Dan/Douglas is not feminised. Even in the version of *Fatal Attraction*
which exists, it may be perfectly possible to read Dan as a women though he is
a man – his incapability and lack of authority all point to this, a troubled
version of the more positively celebrated 1980s New Man. Michael Douglas
deals with this representation through roles which show men to be struggling
with their impotence but still failing fully to overcome it. If nothing else, they
know that they can never return to the searing authority of the flawless masculinity embodied by Douglas's father's star image. In interviews, Michael
Douglas often stresses his closeness to his family and his enjoyment of childcare, stressing the amount of time he spent bringing up his first son whilst his
first wife worked. In 2000 he testified on The Michael Douglas website that he
planned to do the same following the birth of his second son, enabling his wife
to make the movies so that he could become 'Mr Mom' (Palta 2000: 128). The
ambivalence which Douglas's characters display on-screen towards adopting
positions traditionally associated with femininity does not seem to have
affected his embrace of the caring, domestic persona in his personal life. That
he has returned to the anxious positions of the erotic thriller male rather than
embrace an on-screen New Man-ism such as that played out by the pregnant
Arnold Schwarzenegger in *Junior* or the child-rearing men in *Three Men and a
Baby* makes him acutely symptomatic of the masculinities of his moment.

4: THE BITCH, THE DEVIL AND LESBIANISM FOR MEN

Earlier I asked what has become of the *femme fatale*? Three further answers
might be Sharon Stone, Linda Fiorentino and Gina Gershon. This section looks
at how the interconnections of stardom, sex and genre impact on the public and
screen images of these women through the framework of the erotic thriller.
Much of the viewing pleasure of cinema for audiences is bound up with the star:
star awareness enhances what we take away from film, and film (in conjunction with other media factors) reinforces star awareness. Visual pleasure in the
body of the star is particularly crucial for the erotic thriller, given its enhanced
sexual focus: the star's body is the erotic thriller's trump card (or, as DTV director Jim Wynorski so inimitably argues, breasts are his best and cheapest special

effects). But the star's sexual private life is also in play here. Richard deCordova argues that even as early as 1909, with the emergence of the 'picture personality', 'there was an intense proliferation of knowledge' about the real lives behind the images which played on screen (1991: 24), and with the emergence of the star in a recognisably modern form some years later 'the question of the player's existence outside his/her work in films entered discourse' (1991: 26): stars have always been 'characterised by a fairly thoroughgoing articulation of the paradigm professional life/private life'. Fascination with the boundary between star identity and real self focuses particularly on the intersection or separation between sexual image and 'real' sexual practice. This is particularly acute as it pertains to women in the industry. However weak the Michael Douglas persona in *Fatal Attraction*, *Disclosure* and *Basic Instinct* might be, his off-duty persona as a heterosexual regular guy and a good father is never in question. Even when he played a gay man in a 2002 episode of the NBC sitcom *Will & Grace*, the effect was comic, his macho-camp policeman character playing off real-life knowledge of his heterosexuality, as well as his erotic thriller heritage (the episode was entitled 'Fagel Attraction').[67] His handling of publicity around his marriage to Catherine Zeta-Jones promoted an image of ageing potency and devoted paternity. Female erotic thriller stars have, however, been much more vulnerable to an intimate identification between star-turn and real self: as icons, playing out the most masochistic of male desires (bitch, ballbreaker, and – as lesbian – not necessarily even interested in men), they have struggled to differentiate self from role, even though their careers (the chance to play a variety of roles) depend on it. The erotic thriller therefore informs and inflects the star's story, especially if she is a woman. Douglas has overtly identified himself with his roles at least as much as a star like Stone did with hers (the slippage between Stone/Tramell was particularly marked, and stuck), but no one came away from *Fatal Attraction* thinking that Douglas *was* Dan despite the fact that he said, 'I think *Fatal Attraction* was the closest to who I am. I remember first looking at the script and saying, "Wait a minute, I could have been him!"' (Lawson 1993: 178). Why, then, should women be more prone to this interdependence of star-profile and role-quality?

Sharon Stone's career arc is particularly contradictory in this capacity: posing in 1990 for *Playboy* to get attention ('I had to do something and the *Playboy* spread seemed like the most efficient thing' [Cooney 1992: 60]), flashing her genitals in the most famous shot of the decade, then striving to desexualise herself by reiterating her denial of consent to the crotch-shot through a series of dowdy, 'actorly' roles. Much of this was driven by her desperate need to escape the B-movie ghetto in which she languished during the 1980s (one journalist even misread her 1980s films as blanket 'porno' simply because they were B-features [Young 1993: 4]). Though now established stars, each of these women revisits the industry adage that in B-movies you're either on your way up or on your way down. However, the careers of each also serve once again to complicate the strict division between A- and B-film as perceived in the popular view. One model, for instance, is that A-movies are star-led whilst DTVs are has-been-led (or vehicles for the up-and-coming). Stone's ascent to movie deity is the most clear-cut rise-and-rise pattern, beloved of star hagiographies: with *Basic Instinct* behind her, there was no returning to DTV work. Fiorentino's 1990s films were variously released theatrically and as DTVs, and though post-*Last Seduction* she bags starring roles, she is also a regular co-star, and by the new century was forging a second career as a screenwriter. Gershon has had more variable success, with lead roles in smaller films and supporting roles in larger ones, but still working in low-to-mid-budget productions some of which may not secure theatrical release. Stone's mainstream erotic thrillers *Basic Instinct* and *Sliver* were preceded by the resolutely DTV *The Calender Girl Murders* (aka *Victimised*) and *Scissors*. Fiorentino is best known for the mainstream *Jade* and *The Last Seduction*, yet though the latter has mainstream sleeper-hit written all over it, it in fact premiered on TV in the USA. Fiorentino's erotic thriller work – *Acting on Impulse* and *Bodily Harm*, for instance – both precedes and postdates her biggest theatrical successes. Gershon's release story is more complicated again, pitching her right across arbitrary lines drawn by distribution deals: a mainstream star who nevertheless makes films which get released DTV, a fate from which the high profile of her stardom post-*Showgirls* and *Bound* could not protect her. It would thus be too easy to perpetuate the notion that once you've arrived in the heady realms of theatrical release you will never return to DTV or low-budget: both Gershon and Fiorentino have actively courted smaller, more interesting films, though not because they are (yet) on their way down. It is also the case that three of these stars' most prominent roles – in *Jade*, *Basic Instinct* and *Showgirls* – were penned by Joe Eszterhas. It may well be that Eszterhas emerges from this study not only as the genre's most consistent key player, but also as a central figure shaping the iconography of Hollywood's women as the century closed. How all three female stars developed their sexual personae on the ladder from low to high (or high to low), and how this icon identification has affected their stardom, is the subject of this section.

Gina Gershon and lesbianism for men

Gina Gershon's star profile has been largely constituted in the public mind with reference to sexual cinema, particularly what she refers to as her 'trilogy of perversion' (Logan 1997: 7), *Showgirls* (1995), *Bound* (1996) and *This World, then the Fireworks* (1997). The first (a porno-musical) cast her as a bisexual sex performer, the second (an erotic thriller) as a butch-lesbian ex-con, the third (an erotic melo-*noir*) as an incestuous sibling-lover. Although by the end of the 1990s she had appeared in more than forty films and TV shows, her image was constructed through this alignment of *Showgirls*' Cristal, *Bound*'s Corky and *This World, Then the Fireworks*' Carol: together, this triptych cast Gershon's smouldering inflection of the *femme fatale*/good-bad girl, and justified a blizzard of press coverage. The sexually assured tone of these performances ('A vixen, every inch the celluloid sack artist' was how one magazine presented her [Powers 1999]) is augmented by a cluster of lesser-known thriller-inflected films, particularly *Flinch* (1994), *Palmetto* and *Black & White* (both 1998). She also starred as a private eye in the ABC TV series *Snoops*, which ran for one season (1999–2000). The Gershon star persona is predominantly defined through her negotiation – in performance style, role choice and publicity strategies – of a sexual/subjective ambivalence which has maximised her appeal to both genders. Profiles touch on her valley- and surfer-girl background, her penchant for psycho-babble, but focus most squarely on the question of her sexuality, the 'real' of what she does in bed distinguished from the fiction of Corky or Cristal or Carol. Like Stone, Gershon was launched into the mainstream by *Showgirls*' director Paul Verhoeven; he allegedly tried to get her to enact an explicit Verhoeven-esque sign of self-reference by repeating Stone's leg-crossing gesture from *Basic Instinct*. (Did he like the idea of visible vulvas becoming his directorial trademark?) Gershon demurred, either out of modesty or a refusal to become the next (brunette) incarnation of Verhoeven's *femme*. Instead, she became a prime lesbian icon, apparently bucking good box office sense in embracing gay roles. Yet this image is largely based on a conflation of lesbian-inflected iconography in only two images – Cristal's femme bisexual and Corky's butch dyke – as well as the 1997 'coming out' episode of the ABC TV series *Ellen,* which contained a dream sequence populated by dyke-fantasy squeezes of choice, including Demi Moore and k.d. lang, as well as Gershon. How these images play to and are read by heterosexual and lesbian audiences might provide a microcosm for understanding contemporary Hollywood's strategies for maximising exposure to different markets.

'Stars are involved in making themselves into commodities', Richard Dyer tells us. 'They are both labour and the thing that labour produces' (Dyer 1986: 5). But bodies displayed and simulating sex in pristine 35 mm are so close to the 'real thing' it becomes hard to tell the difference: to those who have adopted Gina as lesbian poster-girl, would a naked Gershon making love to Jennifer Tilly look any different from a naked Corky making love to Tilly's Violet in *Bound*? In the spirit of the age-old image of actress as whore, the labour of producing a sexualised star image seems very close to the labour of sex work. There are, of course, a number of places where a star can promote (labour at) 'the thing that labour produces' (her own star image), whilst preserving a self beyond publicity. Stardom partly negotiates a balance between so-called 'ordinariness' and unavailability of star identity (Ellis's 'The star is at once ordinary and extraordinary, available for desire and unattainable' [1992: 91]), and this is nowhere more manifest than in the public/private encounter of the star interview, a useful primary reception material. The interview also frequently negotiates the territory of how wider celebrity culture focuses on sexual practice. Promoting the fantasy that here fans touch some semblance of the real behind the celluloid, the interview is central to film promotion and sales. For the star it might augment what he or she has constructed on screen, but it might also be a moment at which self, role and sexuality are seen to separate as well as to fuse.

A staple of the interview-based profile is the cat-and-mouse game in which the interviewer tries to get the star to disclose 'real truths' of her life, and the star either refuses point-blank or feeds a modicum of pseudo-information to bolster that 'aura of the star constructed outside the film', uneasily straddling the public, private and publicised. Gershon is adept at sidestepping the interview's risky will-to-exposure. 'We all know how the studios build up star images, how stars happen to turn up on chat shows just when their latest picture is released, how many of the stories printed about stars are but titillating fictions; we all know we are being sold stars,' writes Dyer again. 'And yet those privileged moments, those biographies, those qualities of sincerity and authenticity, those images of the private and the natural can work for us' (1986: 15). A typical piece appeared in, of all journals, *Cigar Aficionado* (Gina loves cigars), beginning with discussion of the clothes she is wearing on the day of the interview (do they reinforce or contrast her screen personae?) and her reluctance to discuss her private life, before proceeding to a typical interview juncture: 'As you watch her over tea and sandwiches, the question only deepens: behind her many professional masks, who is Gina Gershon?' (Chutkow 1998). Gershon's response gives little away but still manages to be all things to all audiences: 'For everyone I've ever lived with, it's like the big joke: who's going to come home today? I'm like a split personality. My face changes, my voice changes, my personality changes. . . . I have no personality!' She also frequently deflects a question with a question, thus flattering the interviewer with the illusion that she is equally interested in who *they* are. Gershon's interrogation of the interviewer thus deflects the interviewer's personal interrogation of her, a reverse-scrutiny which enables her to evade more personal revelations and spout off about her belief in dream analysis, causing one interviewer to reflect, 'Crumbs. I've been deconstructed by the star of *Showgirls*' (Logan 1997).[68] Sex still signifies, even over tea and sandwiches, and Gershon will ever be 'the star of *Showgirls*'.[69] This is developed further in a *Sunday Times* interview in which 'every time [the interviewer tries] to get biographical, she gets psychological', and 'instead of telling me more about herself, she's telling me more about Cristal' (Iley 1997: 24), which serves primarily to identify Gershon *as* Cristal. The interviewer nevertheless conveys a sense that she has breached a private frontier, with star becoming friend. The star interview scenario reaches a bizarre apotheosis in a piece which ran in *Interview* magazine in 1997 when Gershon was publicising *This World then the Fireworks*. Having been paired with erotic thriller veteran Nick Cassavetes in supporting roles in *Face/Off*, *Interview* ran what is basically a transcribed conversation between friends masquerading as a transgression of the public/private boundary, with Cassavetes playing the prying journalist and Gershon playing the evasive star. At one point she says, 'Regular reporters don't ask me those things, so you can't either', to which Cassavetes responds, 'Are you crazy? You have to talk about your personal life. There's no other reason to do publicity' (Cassavetes 1997). Nick Cassavetes has a rare cinematic pedigree (son of John Cassavetes and Gena Rowlands), he is also a DTV erotic thriller regular who works in the B-sector presumably in order to fund his more prestigious projects. Part-chat between friends (to which we lucky readers are privy), part-promotional exercise, the dynamic is of a woman (Gershon) fostering stardom and a man (Cassavetes) as jobbing actor. That it is Cassavetes playing interviewer and Gershon playing star rather than the other way round may also reflect his lowlier ranking some way down the ladder which leads from B to A.

The 'real' these interviews are seeking to reveal has been generated by a series of sexy roles, the most talked about being Corky in *Bound*. It is interesting that *Bound* itself pivots around questions of real sexuality, that of Jennifer Tilly's character Violet, a gangster's moll who seduces butch 'handy-dyke' (as *Girlfriends* magazine called her [Crockett 1997]) Corky into bed and partner-ship to do the Mafia out of $2 million. Part of *Bound*'s cleverness as both an erotic lesbian wish-fulfilment tale and a heist thriller is the way its narrative is predicated on the supposed imperceptibility of lesbianism.Violet is a lesbian passing as straight, and the film's play on character, as well as its most signifi-cant narrative twist, is enabled by the interplay of Violet's real dyke sexuality and her assumed heterosexual performance (which she calls her work). The women's sleight-of-hand is predicated on Violet slipping from the appearance of heterosexuality into the practice of lesbianism, and forging criminal alliances in the process, without her man suspecting. Caesar thinks there is no way she could be double-crossing him with a woman, so fails to see the double-cross at all and pays for this heterosexist oversight with his life (Fig. 10). The man's not-seeing what is overtly displayed makes lesbian desire here something like Poe's purloined letter, concealed in the very fact of its being on show, in its place. Ellis Hanson begins the collection *Outtakes: Essays on Queer Theory and Film* with a eulogy to this aspect of the film:

> Much of the plot hinges on lesbian invisibility, and yet the film uses the whole gamut of classic scopophilic lures – carefully staged sex scenes, fet-ishistic costumes, killer cosmetics, shadowy lighting, voyeuristic point-of-view shots, and so on – to help us to recognize the sexual intensity of the relationship between the two female leads, Violet and Corky. Theirs is a desire that the men in the film cannot see, though the women hide it in plain sight. (Hanson 1999: 1)

Bound was shot directly after *Showgirls*, and though both films are pre- and postdated by a full roster of roles where Gershon is as heterosexual as they come, the notion that role and life mirror each other lingers: the lesbian friend of one interviewer is reported as saying, 'Definitely she does it with girls. I want her. Bring her back for me' (Iley 1997: 18). Gershon absorbs compliments on her courage for actively choosing lesbianism as her career launchpad, given the

Figure 10: Lesbian desire passes between Corky (Gina Gershon) and Violet (Jennifer Tilly), unseen and unsuspected by heterosexual men in *Bound*. Dino De Laurentiis/Summit Entertainment/The Kobal Collection.

climate of pervasive homophobia which still guides the 'carefulness' of key players' public sexual choices: 'Everybody told me not to do a script with lesbians. But I really wanted to do it' (Iley 1997: 23).[70] However, the coincidence of these breakthrough, high-profile films presenting her as non-straight belies the dozen or so films before *Showgirls* and even more since *Bound* which have featured her as straight (or presumably so). The hybrid erotic thriller/comedy, *Flinch*, for instance, requires Gershon to be the heterosexual love-object leading its romantic thread: as 'a living mannequin' posing stock still in a shop-window display, she witnesses the murder of a glamour model by a deranged artist in the street in front of her (another instance of her absolute visibility – she is on display – making her own gaze invisible). The role oscillates between woman-in-peril and justice-seeker, contributing to the film's confused critique of imagistic objectification, particularly of women (at one point Gershon's character 'kills' some female torso sculptures with a baseball bat). *Palmetto* pushes this even further, with Gershon the faithful girlfriend figure betrayed by ex-con Woody Harrelson: Elisabeth Shue, not Gershon, is the *femme fatale* here. Like Sean Young in *Exception to the Rule*, Gershon stays at home making an honest living selling her sculptures, whilst Shue (like Kim Cattrall in *Exception to the Rule*) makes a dishonest one scheming for profit by implicating weak men. Classic *noir* comparison is a common discourse for situating neo-*noir* stars, and critics saw *Palmetto* as miscast, even if it is a perfectly workmanlike sexy *noir-*

by-numbers. One reviewer thought Gershon 'looks too evil to play a good girl' (Schulgasser 1998) and unfavourably compared its stars with classic *noir* equivalents (Shue should be Rita Hayworth; *homme fatal* Michael Rapaport should be Robert Mitchum), a strategy also followed by Roger Ebert:

> Gina Gershon and Elisabeth Shue are the wrong way around. Gershon is superb as a lustful, calculating femme fatale (she shimmers with temptation in 'Bound' and 'This World, Then the Fireworks'). Shue is best at heartfelt roles. Imagine Barbara Stanwyck waiting faithfully behind the easel while Doris Day seduces the hero, and you'll see the problem. (Ebert 1998a)

If nothing else, this is evidence that a tradition of genre as star limitation also characterises the relatively short history of the erotic thriller. Gershon has one moment of determined aggression in the film, but otherwise *Palmetto* conforms to her post-*Bound* roster of supporting female roles. However proficient her performances elsewhere, lack of *noir*ishness or sex appeal will make them deficient star-turns. Since *Palmetto* Gershon has been strenuously trying to play against type, a calculated strategy for widening a role portfolio, but particularly difficult to pull off when such a strong star image has been established. It is far easier to form a brand than it is to break it, particularly so when a star uses genre to coalesce image. In this case it is not only Gershon's own history of roles which fixes her to a type; here genre history also seems to be ganging up on her, militating against her efforts to be Doris Day rather than Barbara Stanwyck. This is surprising given that her two most prominent vehicles (*Showgirls* and *Bound*) are generic hybrids. In the mid-1990s there was a strong feeling that *Showgirls* would be the platform for Gershon's jump into megastardom, with *Bound* confirming the move. So was her willingness to play dyke a career weakness or a strength? Or did she play too close to genre?

If Gershon's image is fixed as a *femme fatale*, it is also rather more sexually ambivalent than her straight (or gay) roles would suggest. In particular, given her strong lesbian following and willingness to suggest a less than straight sexual predilection, the heterosexual roles have only provided extra copy for lesbian fans to use and read against the straight grain. Moreover, Gershon's brand of lesbian chic was never a threat to male and heterosexual box office. She capitalised on *Bound* (which 'whipped up a froth of interest in Gershon's sexuality') with a teasingly non-committal strategy regarding her own sexuality ('"I got really used to kissing girls. They're much gentler and have sweeter breath"' [Logan]), and responded to the question 'Sexually speaking, can too many cooks spoil the sauce?' posed in *Playboy*'s '20 Questions' with 'It depends what kind of sauce it is' (Crane 1999). Speculation about her real sexuality is nourished by snippets which swing both ways. *Bound* co-star Jennifer Tilly reported that Gershon frequented 'lesbian clubs trying out Corky's lines' (Fuller 1996: 40). This is countered by (heterosexual) tattle about her relationship with a prominent (male) LA restaurateur, and her teenage obsessions with bad boys (though even this becomes somewhat ambivalent): 'I went out with surfers before I started falling in love with gay men', she has said, and, 'Lately, I've been a little sad that I'm not a gay man' (Powers 1999). An enticingly confused profile emerges of a beautiful straight woman who might obligingly fulfil any red-blooded man's lesbian fantasies, and – for lesbian fans – a straight woman happy to be lesbian-identified, or else a mainstream icon who 'definitely does it with girls'. One compromise Gershon reached when asked how it felt to be a gay icon was the response, 'I feel like a professional lesbian' (Hensley 1997), an alignment at one remove from either sexual or political lesbianism (the female equivalent of Eric McCormack, the real-life heterosexual who plays gay Will in *Will & Grace*).[71] Her presence on the internet is phenomenal, largely due to the enthusiasm expressed at numerous lesbian fan-sites.[72] *USA Today* called her 'an Internet goddess, worshipped by millions on Web sites devoted to her' (Graham 1999), thus establishing Gershon as a specifically end-of-century star. The fact that she is a Net icon becomes a central aspect of her stardom, or – to put it another way round – prominence in one current location for the dissemination of stardom becomes one of the singular facets of the Gershon star brand. The Net makes stars (especially sexual ones), and Gershon's stardom takes on a particularly edgy appeal, acquiring a hot up-to-the-minuteness by virtue of its proximity to both lesbianism and new technologies ('I remember thinking, Wow, like, I'm so hip', she has said. 'Then I realized, No, I'm just trendy at this point because there are so many lesbian movies coming out' [Fuller 1996: 40]. The same could be said of her Net ubiquity). Stardom is, of course, not the same as celebrity, but Gershon is/has both.[73]

Bound may be prime lesbian chic but *Showgirls* is a curious text to look at in terms of gay representations. Its hysterically thrashing sex-scenes are most interested in eliciting male performance, and most obsessed with selling women to both diegetic and non-diegetic male audiences. Yet Gershon's input to the film identifies that it is uneasy in a number of areas. Sexually, its spectacles are generically confused, featuring on-stage 'erotic' performances which include choreographed striptease and 'classier' set-pieces through which *Showgirls* bizarrely manages to 'exploit' both the plot conventions and clichés of erotic thrillers *and* 1930s musicals. Generally considered as the performer who emerged from *Showgirls* with her career intact, Gershon camps it up with an apparent sense that it's all an excess of nonsense. And just as the film is split across its genre allegiance, so it is split in the way it represents Gershon, who is pivotal to the 'classier' showpieces as both musical and softcore spectacles. Two Gina Gershons emerge from *Showgirls*, one heterosexually- and one homosexually-inflected. Although playing the bisexual lover of a man (Zack [Kyle McLachlan]), all of Gershon's scenes relate her sexuality to that of women, primarily Nomi (Elizabeth Berkley), whom she watches, flirts with, manipulates, purchases and finally kisses. It is through this female focus that she becomes the prime spectacle for heterosexual men as well as gay women.

Indeed, *Showgirls*, despite its title claim that it *shows girls* and tells their stories, is almost hysterically obsessed with the processes and responses of male heterosexuality. Yet it presents straight male response as both easily evoked on the one hand (press a button and you'll get a response), and most grossly provoked by non-heterosexual images (all straight men really want to see two women together) on the other. In this sense it is the fitting successor to *Basic Instinct*, in which Catherine Tramell as designer dyke is not so much bisexual as hetero-lesbian, putting her lesbianism on show primarily as a foreplay spectacle for the eyes of a man, the primary weapon of heterosexual enticement. Tramell manages to alienate women not only by virtue of her final indifference to them as sexual partners the minute Michael Douglas's cop waves his magic wand, but by her use of them to appear more alluring to him in the first place. In this light, the spectacle of Tramell and her psycho girlfriend becomes that of a pair of entwined Playmates of the Month, maybe a bit murderous, but still looking fixedly into the male eye, which is finally more interesting. Cristal is thankfully somewhat more girl-friendly for all her absurdities; when she lasciviously declares to Nomi 'You've got great tits – I like nice tits', she seems to mean it. Still *Showgirls* is a fully paid-up male heterosexual film, telling its story about heterosexual men almost entirely through the tales of women, using women to speak to male desire.

Bound's Corky built on the bisexual brazenness of Cristal, for lesbian viewers bringing Gershon – as a fantasy figure at least – further out of the closet. Gershon's tomboy tool-wielder is resolutely butch, whilst Tilly's femme, all blonde locks and flirty frocks, is identified as such even before we see her (the shoes, skirts, feminine paraphernalia of her closet are revealed before she is. Queer theorists [such as Hanson above] make much of the film's 'in the closet' sartorial opening). Chris Holmlund (1994) sketches cinema history as system-atic 'delesbianisation', yet *Bound* – to the delight of queer and lesbian critics – is a 're-lesbianisation', particularly of *noir* itself (often read for its homophobic disavowals)[74] for mainstream audiences. The marriage of sexual and criminal is as manifest as in other neo-*noirs*, but whilst the crime is the same, the sex is not (Corky says stealing is a lot like her kind of sex: 'Two people who want the same thing . . . talk about it. . . . [T]he more they talk about it the wetter they get'). Violet is both femme and *femme fatale*, modelled on the classic *noir* anti-heroine, which by definition casts Corky as its sexually dazzled duped Cain male (like the scheming seducers of the dumb-ass fall-guys I have discussed, Violet it also 'a lot smarter' than Corky.). There is, however, a happy ending; *Bound* rewrites *noir*'s moral fatalism through neo-*noir*'s ambivalence about punishing women, pathologising the straight (male gangster) character and seeing its gay women prosper, smart and free.

Nevertheless Gershon sold *Bound* to the press junkets as a classic *noir* struc-ture all but unaltered by lesbianism: 'It's like those old Robert Mitchum movies when he gets out of jail and some femme fatale seduces him. Only I'm the ex-con and Jennifer is the femme fatale. . . . I get the girl. I get the cash' (Svetkey

1996). This may reinforce her image as prime fantasy material, the literally bi- or hetero/multiply/sexed woman who can be sold to a range of desiring positions,[75] which is indeed overtly foregrounded in reception material: 'Treading a razor-thin line between feminist-lesbian correctness and straight-male-slob lasciviousness,' wrote *Entertainment Weekly*, 'it may be the only movie ever made that both Howard Stern and Valerie Solanas could love' (Svetkey 1996). Clearly, it is in Gershon's box office interest to refuse a resolution of these fragments of star iconography: this way she gets the girls *and* the guys in the audience as well as the girl and the money in the story. An interesting diegetic comment on this situation comes in the predicament of her good-bad girl character, seasoned tough cop Nora 'Hugs' Hugosian in *Black & White*. This is one of those efficiently executed erotic thrillers which fell through the net of distribution – a mainstream, medium-budget star vehicle for Gershon which ended up going down the DTV/cable route rather than getting a theatrical release in some countries, the UK included. *Black & White* takes its feminism for granted, and takes its cue from Kathryn Bigelow's *Blue Steel* (the presence of Ron Silver is an active reminder of the earlier film). In *Blue Steel* we saw the feminine underwear beneath the cop's uniform; in *Black & White* Hugs initiates her new partner by making them both strip naked so they won't be curious about what's underneath their clothes ('uniforms aren't bathing suits,' says Silver later. 'Everyone looks the same sex'). Hugs may be the psycho cop responsible for the rising body count, or she may be simply sexualised and aggressive, and innocent of murder. At one point she confronts a range of cop colleagues who may or may not be framing her for the murders, picking out each and every character's potential individual reason for making her the fall-guy. Hugs flails angrily around the room, surrounded by accusers like a caged animal, talking fast, hunted but aggressive. Motives for her framing rest in thwarted desire – 'Is there anyone in this room who doesn't want to fuck me?' she says. 'Everyone if you look hard enough, dig deep enough, everyone has a motive.' The woman's predicament in being multiply desired also means that she is multiply identified as guilty, a sexualised good-bad girl read through the filter of others' nefarious desire for her as guilty. The screenplay gives Hugs full consciousness of this, and Gershon's performance shows a certain conviction in the belief that sexual and social freedom do not designate guilt. Her penchant for walking at night (Hugs is an ex-New Yorker) places her under suspicion for murder (she is also mistaken for a prostitute, recalling earlier *flâneuse* figures), to which she retorts to her accusing colleague, 'I was lonely. And I like to walk. Which one is illegal?' Being a desirable woman (on the loose) and being guilty are here the same thing: Hugs is 'wanted' in more ways than one.

Black & White is, then, a film in which Gershon's propensity for getting the girls and the guys diegetically designates her as guilty, whilst her presence gives the film a wider sexual audience potential. Included in Hugs' diatribe against those who find her desirable/guilty is detective Lynn Dombrowsky (Alison Eastwood) ('How do you want me Lynn, huh? I know you do. What do you want, a little one-on-one action? . . . Sorry you're not my type. Will you feel rejected? . . . Maybe you're setting me up') and Sergeant Wright (James Handy) ('Oh I'm sorry Sarge – is this getting you hot? All this girl talk? Don't worry – I'm into guys'). This begs a further important question, which is why it is that such 'girl-talk' gets guys hot – why it is that in getting the girls Gershon *also* gets the guys. Why do soft-*femme*, mainstream images of lesbian sex form such a central part of heterosexual men's fantasy repertoire? When asked if *Bound* is 'really a lesbian movie for men', Gershon replied, 'Will guys watch it and get turned on? Absolutely. Every guy who sees it goes, "Oh, my God, that seduction scene is so hot!" . . . Guys just get into that for some reason. I don't know why.' Tilley then interjects an interpretation which also marked readings of *Basic Instinct*, 'They think they're going to get in the middle of it. They're like, "Oh, those two poor girls. What they need is" – and Gershon finishes the sentence – "something in between 'em".' Reviewers were divided on whether this is a heterosexual fantasy or lesbian wish-fulfilment, or whether it can be both. Noble reads it as deploying 'the simulacra of film noir to stage a femme coming-out quest' (1998: 32): is it 'a million miles' from being 'a lesbian movie . . . pure gloss and style in the mainstream tradition' (Gray 1997/8: 21) or does it present – as the lesbian press put it – 'sexy and surprisingly authentic lesbian love scenes' (Halberstam 1997: 14)? Are the sex-scenes 'cartoons of heaving passion, which the [Wachowski] brothers linger over with unabashed heterosexual glee' (Matthews 1997: 43) or did the filmmakers and performers try to avoid eroticising the love-scenes 'in the traditional male pornography vision of lesbians, because we felt it wouldn't be authentic' (Tilley in interview, Applebaum 1997: 75)? Or is *Bound* a 'clever, eye-catching, highly stylized, faux-chic caper featuring: (a) Coen brothers-style gore; (b) Scorsese-style mob double-crossings; (c) Candida Royalle-style erotica; (d) Joe Eszterhas-style lesbians? Schwing!'[76] If all of the above, then *Bound* is the perfect vehicle for a star whose image is nothing and everything, both lesbian *and* heterosexual, and therefore pleasing all audiences.

Male heterosexual pleasure in lesbian spectacle has become a lynchpin of the erotic thriller, both dismissed and deemed transparent because of its clichéd status as one of the bedrocks of male heterosexual fantasy (the scene from *Wild Things* which everyone remembers and many men cite is sex between Neve Campbell, Denise Richards and Matt Dillon. Websites positively salivate in their enthusiasm for prominent key lesbian scenes).[77] Chris Holmlund sees the lesbianism of cinema's 'deadly dolls' as the central element of their sinister murderousness: 'a murmured fear of lesbianism lurks beneath the general discomfort with violent women,' she writes (1994: 32). Nevertheless, she acknowledges that Catherine Tramell's lesbianism is part of a cocktail of come-ons designed to appeal to Nick's male masochism: '*Basic Instinct* casts Catherine's lesbian affairs as titillating and temporary phenomena played out for Nick's staunchly heterosexual gaze' (1994: 38). But is it this straightforward? One-time editor of American lesbian porn magazine *On Our Backs*, Susie Bright (also *Bound*'s lesbian consultant, who makes a cameo appearance as Corky's bar pick-up) has made the point that the sexual imagination is adept at appropriating material from a variety of sources, and that lesbians have long used male heterosexual porn, viewing against the grain of the text's heterosexual message to find other pleasures through it, including the stock images of lesbian sex such as those which appear in numerous erotic thrillers. However, many lesbians, especially those involved in producing pornography for women, have a problem with the male enjoyment of lesbian images, and it is probably true that the most widely 'disseminated' images of lesbianism are those familiar tableaux set up to titillate heterosexual men. Nevertheless, no one is really very clear about what *is* going on when men enjoy images of lesbian sex, or why it should be problematic for women themselves. Richard Dyer once called for a more critical consciousness about heterosexuality: 'we do need to try to see it, not just move within it as the air we breath,' he wrote in *The Matter of Images*, advocating 'mak[ing] hetero-sexuality strange' (1993a: 134). Lesbianism as male heterosexual titillation is a widely accepted form of 'normality', yet it does have some significant strange-ness built into it. 'The baffling question is the one that Freud unaccountably never thought to ask,' continues Dyer: 'what do heterosexuals want?' (1993a: 135). One strangeness of male heterosexuality is that sometimes, it seems, men want to be excluded from the sexual scene entirely.

Yet lesbians have seen men as both hostile to their sexuality's exclusivity, whilst male visual participation in a lesbian scene, their inclusion even as voyeur, is also politically problematic. This is partly because heterosexual enjoyment of homo-sexual images is read as a devious form of sexual appropriation, with men being able to enjoy women even when those men are irrelevant to women's enjoy-ment.[78] Gina Gershon complicates this argument, as does *Bound* itself. Whilst the average DTV erotic thriller (which I will analyse in Part Two) cannot unprob-lematically be called lesbian porn (even though at least one such sex scene is obligatory in each of them), as we have seen, at least one of Gershon's erotic thrillers has received warm lesbian responses. A number of critics picked up on the common model that lesbianism is appealing to heterosexual men precisely because it excludes them, 'a male fantasyland of beautiful, bisexual, bloodthirsty vixens'[79] which threatens and beguiles, but mostly threatens (the male heterosex-ual fantasy of three-way action is reworked as a typical erotic thriller strapline, attached to the Sharon Stone vehicle *Diabolique*: 'Two women. One man. The combination can be murder'). Wallace suggests that the *noir* potency of lesbian-ism as radically violent male exclusion is framed by 'the question of Violet's sexual allegiance, whether she goes with men or women', a question which is answered by 'homicide, by the chill expedient of having her wipe out Caesar. His pulpy, slow-motion death stands as a displaced yet unequivocal testimony to lesbian desire' (2000: 385). So is Tramell positioned as threat or come-on? If les-bianism, which ought to exclude men, is tantalising, then so is the possibility of murder, which ought to do away with men altogether. Female murderousness is a partner in crime with hetero-lesbianism, a man's exclusion guaranteeing his enticement. We are faced, then, with a number of paradoxes: male sexual exclusion becomes the most exciting possible thing, as does the risk of total annihilation. In both cases the male role is more central the greater the risk it takes, the more sexually and fatally threatened it is. The less a man seems to be needed in the sex-scenes of these films, the more you can be sure the whole is being played out for his benefit. So when a character such as Tramell turns to women as she is turning on men, she may suggest the possibility of the man being done away with altogether; but this is a stylised ritual of taboo-breaking at which erotic thrillers are adept. Madonna's body-as-murder weapon – 'no different from a gun or a knife' – is precisely what Willem Dafoe wants, even though, or perhaps because, he risks being its victim. This, then, overtly presents lesbianism (like death) as the final come-on, with men as sexually central as they are apparently excluded: exclusion becomes an index of involvement, with men's marginality a sign of their importance as choreographers of desire. Violet's murder of Caesar may be a more than unequivocal 'testimony to lesbian desire'; it may be the ultimate male-masochistic come-on. As Andrew Garroni suggests in my interview above, the thrill for men is that of not having to take responsibility for female pleasure (lesbian spectacle frees men from the spectre of performance anxiety).

Equivocally hetero-lesbian or unequivocally gay, this question of lesbian spectacle in mainstream thrillers may not be resolvable. The importance for opening both a movie and a star image to the projections and desires of the biggest possible audience may lie in not fixing a spectacle as primarily homosexually or heterosexually inflected. Yet does this openness of identification (like most other things) finally serve male heterosexuality? Adrienne Rich's seminal 'Compulsory Heterosexuality and Lesbian Existence', as B. Ruby Rich puts it, 'formalized what had always been felt: that the boundary between heterosexual and lesbian was not fixed but fluid, that a woman could cross over at unpredictable moments, and that sexual identity in this sense was not necessarily stable' (1998: 357). How ironic that the most common cinematic manifestation of this should be the ease with which heterosexual female icons slip into bed with women, and then back into bed with men, all for the titillation of a primarily male audience and – if you're lucky – their girlfriends too. Invisible as the charge of lesbianism is to the male heterosexual protagonists *within Bound*, it is highly visible to the male heterosexual spectators *of* it; clearly Caesar, who misses the sexual charge between Violet and Corky entirely, cannot have seen many erotic thrillers. To male heterosexual audiences, the *noir*ish twists of the women's criminal progress may be all but irrelevant. Key to Gershon's appeal to lesbians is the conviction with which she performed sex scenes with Tilly; key to her appeal to heterosexual men is the formation of her body (particularly her lips), obsessively salivated over in the press material in a way which recalls writing on Monroe: 'Her mouth, so sultry and pillowy, seems to be a sexual icon all on its own. . . . One man explained her as "unbelievably attractive . . . it's raw beauty, it defines sex, it exudes sex. Her face is so predatory looking"' (Iley 1997). Website AskMen.com rated her lips as prime feature: 'She can twist and turn those strawberry *labias* into positions that make grown men's knees buckle.'[80] *Esquire* magazine dedicated a whole article to Gershon's 'Lips like Mating Snakes', justified by the argument that 'Box-office returns and careers [are] sometimes made or broken by a few seconds of extreme close-up' (MacGregor 1999). This prime physical detail animates the aspect of the 'Gina Gershon' brand which straddles the public/private divide: in the absence of definitive (or unwelcome) information about what she does in bed, writers will focus on the body instead. It may be too simplistic to say, however, that lesbian fans enjoy the way she acts whilst heterosexual men enjoy the way she looks, especially given the numerous lesbian websites dedicated to the dissemination of still images of Gina. Kelly Kessler persuasively analyses the sexual dynamics of *Bound* as enabling 'entry' by any kind of viewer because of its oscillation between point-of-view and voyeuristic shots, avoiding forcing 'one single type of visual identification' (2001: 25); *Bound* uses 'strategies of heterosexual pornography and lesbian erotica to draw in both audiences' in a way which is 'at once empowering to lesbians and titillating to heterosexual men' (2001: 24, 19). The viewer, therefore, can insert him- or herself into the scene as third party, rewriting it as a lesbian or straight *ménage-à-trois,* according to his or her own sexual persuasion (or the fantasy of the moment).[81] But it may go even further than this. Susie Bright has written in celebration of dyke daddies, 'lesbian-identified men' who 'don't want to *save* the lesbians' (the man getting, in Gershon's words, 'in between 'em'), 'they want to *be* the lesbians'. Thus male heterosexual response may not be as straightforward as even Kessler's model proposes, with more radical cross-identifications going on in the pornographic scene, for men as well as for women. Kessler argues that lesbians want to see one thing and male heterosexuals another, so you have to find a way to do both. It may be, however, that male desire is omnivorous enough to mean that what works for lesbians will almost certainly work for male heterosexuals (Kessler says that lesbians wanted 'sweaty, slippery, body-grinding, bed-squeaking lesbian sex',[83] but this is surely also a successful male heterosexual recipe). Evidence of autonomous female appetite may be more appealing to men than feminism has hitherto acknowledged – the hope that female desire (of whatever persuasion) is also desperately obsessive. Perhaps, sexually speaking, men and women don't part company over heterosexual/homosexual differences (especially not now that we have readier access to each other's porn), but over degrees of sexual readiness. The question then might be not which way you want it, but how much you want it. This has implications for the view of erotica encountered so far in this book. The notion that women need porn augmented (or diluted) by story may be more important than it seems. It may be that, for (some) men, the story makes sex less sexy, so whether that story is gay or straight is less central than its 'strength' or 'weakness' relative to its sexual intensity and spectacular energy.

We might also ask why it is that Gershon rather than Tilly has inherited the lesbian icon legacy of *Bound* (notwithstanding the eulogy to Tilly's femme authored by Noble [1998: 31]). Perhaps one reason is that *Bound* frames Gershon with the same magnetic potency that a number of *noirs* and neo-*noirs* deploy to 'set up' their sexualised fall-guys, as I discussed above in relation to *The Hot Spot* and *Romeo is Bleeding*. (Although it is a man in *Bound* who says that women 'make us do stupid things', this could equally be Corky's line.) Perhaps the eroticism of the doomed sucker who just can't help it is more unique than the ubiquitous significations of female fatality. When fall-guy erotics are borne out by Gina Gershon's body, augmented by memories of her *femme* incarnation in *Showgirls*, the charge is potent. It may also be that it is Gershon's perceived bisexuality (the inheritance of *Showgirls*), rather than her either/or-hetero/lesbian qualities, which have inflected her stardom. One of the most interesting models of stardom to appear recently is Marjorie Garber's notion that stardom and bisexuality are intimately bound in their mutual bid to be omnivorously attractive:

> Whether it is actualized in sexual relationships or remains on the level of elusive attraction, this heightened performative state, this state of being simultaneously all-desiring and all-desired, incarnates in the celebrity the two, sometimes apparently conflicting, definitions of bisexuality: having two genders in one body, and being sexually attracted to members of 'both' sexes. (2000: 140)

By this account, Gershon is a star because 'she' is bisexual (at least in terms of audience appeal), and she is bisexual because this is in the very nature of stardom.

This is only reinforced by the slippage of public/private discourse, also present in lesbian writing. *Bound* explicitly sets up Gershon/Corky as the desired object; as Straayer argues, 'Corky's body is repeatedly put on erotic display, for example, in an overhead shot of her lying on her bed in jockey shorts and a side view of her modelled statuesquely while painting the ceiling. Like Johnny in *Gilda*, the camera finds Corky beautiful' (1998: 159). In the sex-scene it is Violet who masturbates Corky, and here too 'the breasts we finally see' are Gershon's (ibid.). In general, actors who take their clothes off seem to be more prone to the belief that they have laid bare part of their real self in baring their physicality: nudity and apparently authentic sexual performance suggest a breach of the gap between public and private self. Discourse around star bodies becomes a close second-best to 'real truths' about the star's sexual behaviour. The star body, however honed, bronzed, augmented by surgery it has been, seems to invite us a step closer to the real behind the persona. Between the sexual personae of *Showgirls* and *Bound* (images from both films enrich many a Gershon website, gay and straight) Gina/Cristal/Corky seems not only to be able to straddle the hetero-bi-lesbian divides but also – in her lesbian for-mation – to move with ease from femme to butch. Perhaps this doubling of sexual predilections defines her stardom for lesbians.

A similar phenomenon seems to have stricken male responses to the star. Gershon's complicity in lesbian titillation has attracted men, but they also like her butchness in *Bound*, her suggestions of masculinity within her suggestiveness to it. This seems to go beyond the stylised butch-dyke swagger in which she was tutored by Susie Bright. *Esquire* implicitly suggested that she might be positioned as a mediator of homosocial if not homosexual desire for male viewers: 'With her wary, half-mast Mitchum eyes and a come-hither smirk nearly Elvine in its rude hunger, Gershon slouched the outline for a new kind of postmod/altsex fem*noir*' (MacGregor 1999). Woman, then, mediates for the straight male desire for both Robert Mitchum and Elvis Presley. As the female-to-male transvestite scene in *9½ Weeks* evidences, even the most red-blooded heterosexual man can desire a man if he is really a woman. Of course, butch lesbianism is not intrinsically masculine, but it might be the closest the erotic thriller's male heterosexual viewer gets to crossing a border.

Linda Fiorentino as screen bitch

Bitch. n.
1.a. the female of the dog
b. The female of the fox, wolf, and occasionally of other beasts . . .
2.a. Applied opprobriously to a woman; strictly, a lewd or sensual woman. Not now in decent use; but formerly common in literature. In mod. Use, *esp.* a malicious or treacherous woman; . . . (see also SON OF A BITCH.)
b. Applied to a man (less opprobrious, and somewhat whimsical, having the modern sense of 'dog'). Not now in decent use.

Oxford English Dictionary [83]

Women *are* bitches! . . . Woman is the bitch goddess of the universe!

Camille Paglia (1994: 489)

Though one common connotation of 'bitch' is of a masculinised woman who is at the same time a threat to men (the woman with balls as a ballbreaker), the *Oxford English Dictionary* identifies the bitch as both animalistic and femininely sexual. The bitch is first a female animal, and second an indecent term for lewd, sensual or treacherous women. Of course, to call a man a bitch is 'less opprobrious', even though to call him that now would be to feminise him. Linda Fiorentino has been identified as prime screen bitch largely because of her performance as Bridget in *The Last Seduction*. We may go further and say that bitchness has stuck because of a single line she delivers when, during energetic sex in a car, Mike says, 'I'm trying to decide whether you're a total bitch or not', to which she emphatically replies, 'I'm a total fucking bitch', laughing and slapping the ceiling. That this takes place with Bridget on top in the 'cowgirl' position, straddling him with her rear facing his face, is a double reinforcement of her mastery and his submission. Further proof of bitchery comes when she stubs out her cigarette in one of his grandma's homemade pies, and bakes cookies for a detective who's staking her out as a cover for puncturing his tyres. Bridget's bitchness combines conniving with coldness; it is an intelligent callousness, more superhumanly unnatural (in the sense that the unfeminine has been thought unnatural) than subhuman and animalistic (the woman as dog). The intelligent bitch is therefore both insufficiently and excessively womanly, yet as Bridget, Fiorentino manages to master the mysogyny of it (perhaps the cinematic counterpart of feminism's reappropriation of the term).[84] Certainly, she *is* 'lewd', but the lewdness is almost accidental; that she enjoys the sex she deploys to manipulate the bigger picture is a secondary effect of bitchness, not its source or core.

There is a lot we can learn about the erotic thriller from bitches, as word and cultural-sexual formation. The adjective 'bitchily' is defined by the *OED* as 'sensually; also, maliciously', a pretty close linguistic approximation of the genre's carnal–criminal combinations, though in the erotic thriller all genders perform equally bitchily. 'Bitch' has also long been a synonym for *femme fatale*, at least since the first publication of Stephen Farber's 'Violence and the Bitch Goddess' in 1974 (Farber 1999), though Farber discusses the bitch as a prominent element in the woman's picture rather than *noir*. Farber's focus on women is, however, a refinement of a larger argument linking 'the bitch-goddess SUCCESS' (1999: 48, original emphasis) to violence in American culture; if the American success story 'is most often told as a story of destruction and betrayal' (1999: 48), then women are a convenient way of displaying that destructiveness. Yet this in turn means that only when success becomes destructive are women allowed to get a piece of it. Farber slides from the bitch-goddess success (the female deity of avarice) to the bitch-goddess as avaricious woman, in a definition which takes in a range of deadly sins: 1940s bitch goddesses are 'monsters and harpies, hardened by greed and lust, completely without feeling for the suffering they caused' (1999: 49). Bitchness is also matrilineally genetic, it seems, capable of being passed as an hereditary disease between female relatives. Martha (Barbara Stanwyck) catches it from her aunt in *The Strange Love of Martha Ivers*, whilst Mildred (Joan Crawford) in *Mildred Pierce*, a saintly victim for some feminist critics, is, for Farber, a contaminating force, passing bitch qualities on to her daughter Velda (Ann Blyth) (Velda has 'absorbed the poison from her mother's success drive . . . Mildred's values have noirished murder' [1999: 52]).[85] *Noir*'s bitches are, then, daughters, if not sons, of bitches.

Bridget has no diegetic female ancestors or descendants; she is the *noir*-woman with an absent family, like Catherine Tramell (who has, of course, killed her family, and publishes under the pen-name Catherine Woolf – the female writer as bitch). If anyone has contaminated Bridget with greed it is her husband, who also casts the first blow. She is, then, the wife of a male bitch, and true to the *OED*'s sense of such figures as more whimsical, roguish, dog-like entities, Bill Pullman's Clay was received (and performed) not as monstrous but 'funny, touching, creepy' (Newman 1994a: 44). Bridget was, on the other hand, 'diabolical' (*Variety* – Stratton 1994) or morally reprehensible (Thompson 1995), though not for all. Feminism's bitch may be a justice-seeker or a woman who exceeds all justification: that Clay's domestic violence not only motivates Bridget's theft but also her acts of murder only enhances her potential as feminist icon. Elizabeth Wurtzel's lightweight (and often misguided) polemic *Bitch* reiterates how female assertiveness inevitably attracts the charge of recalcitrance: 'as soon as she [woman] lays down the option of my way or the highway, it's amazing how quickly everyone finds her difficult, crazy, a nightmare: a bitch' (1998: 30). Nothing so very remarkable in that, except that Wurtzel also elides the distinction between cultural artefact (or role) and public self (and actions). Here bitchness can stick, whether you mean it or just played it:

> The few women who manage to completely spit in the face of such an arrangement are naturally heroic. The appeal of films like *The Last Seduction* and *Basic Instinct* and *Thelma & Louise*, . . . the reason the bad behaviour of Shannen Doherty and Naomi Campbell and Courtney Love is so intriguing is that you don't get the feeling these girls are reading *The Rules*. (ibid.)

Yet for all Wurtzel's desperation to fix her heroines as postmodern self-determinists, the language used to describe Fiorentino's power is more in line with Farber's fantasies. Certainly, a quaint sense of déjà vu marks the marketing of her films and her wider star profile, suggesting that Linda Fiorentino is not a unique film bitch. Her screen sexuality may be foregrounded as prime exhibit in a marketing strategy, but in a discourse which falls back on an earlier film iconography. We have seen that films are often discussed with reference to other films (usually negatively – *Basic Instinct* wasn't *Fatal Attraction*, *Showgirls* wasn't *Basic Instinct*, as Feasey noted [2003: 169, 173]), but bitches are also often described with reference to earlier incarnations, which suggests that extra-textual discourse around the bitch sees it/her as an eternal form – a filmic Lilith or Eve or Medusa (figures evoked remarkably commonly in contemporary reception material). Thus not only does *film noir* form a template for the neo-*noir*ishness of the erotic thriller, and the 1940s *femme fatale* give birth to the 1990s harpy, but critical and reception discussions around the films also deploy an established language of sensation. 'She's sultry, she's sexy and she's a screen siren', wrote the *Daily Telegraph*. 'This class act inherits the mantle of Mae, Barbara and Bette with the modern twist of amorality' (Mather 1994: 11). Fiorentino herself told director John Dahl of Bridget, 'There are only two women who can play this role, me and Barbara Stanwyck – and as she's dead you'll have to take me' (ibid.). This is the cue for *Jade* co-star Chazz Palminteri, writing up a celebrity interview, to describe Bridget as 'a vulgar, callous phantom of tormented male desire harking back iconographically to the great Joan Bennett in Fritz Lang's *The Woman in the Window* (1944) and *Scarlet*

Street (1945)' (Palminteri 1995). The same position was adopted by a different *Telegraph* journalist, discussing *Jade*: 'Fruitless to look at her contemporaries for comparisons', wrote a gushing David Gritten, 'you can't imagine another actress of today coming close to capturing her smouldering malevolence. Instead, we must delve back 40 or 50 years, when stars such as Bette Davis, Barbara Stanwyck and Joan Crawford held sway' (1995: 33). Here, then, Fiorentino's uniqueness can only be described with reference to the precedents set by an earlier school of 'greats', making her a one-woman refutation and confirmation of the commonplace that 'they don't make stars like they used to anymore'. Fiorentino is both a repetition and a one-off, an exception to and confirmation of the rule that stars now are but glimmers compared to the blazing deities of old. She is, somehow, a unique reproduction, as if the language of journalistic praise can only apprehend distinction in a way which makes it somehow less distinct. This is a classic star paradox, but it too is underpinned by bitchery; bitches usually work alone, malevolent individualists, but they also bear out the notion that they are following a female blueprint. It is also no accident that these antecedents are primarily associated with *noir* and the woman's film: despite the contemporary performer's best efforts to differentiate her spectrum of roles, some genres stick faster than others.

Fiorentino is an interesting case for testing the various methodologies of star studies. She has attracted some fan interest, but is not the internet goddess that Gershon has become. Dyer distinguishes between star images produced by stars who are at one with their public image, and those star images produced through a 'tension between screen image, manufacture and real person' (1986: 6); Fiorentino exemplifies the latter, though this has served only to reinforce the bitch-tag at all levels. Her 'failure' to toe the line in promotional work has also reinforced comparisons to star system rebels such as Bette Davis; she balks at the film promotion system, which in turn becomes one aspect of Fiorentino's star textuality. Stories circulate in celebrity forums about ludicrous star demands as a symptom of disconnected primadonna-ishness, but Fiorentino is known not for demanding on-set comforts, but for her 'difficultness' in taking direction and challenging the way in which she must fit into the machine of production. This in turn is read as an adjunct of the roles she chooses: 'People hire me to play these sexy bitches, and they don't expect a little bit of that to rub off,' she has said (the contagion of bitchness, again) (Gritten 1995: 35). This is not unlike the ambivalent heterosexual/lesbianism of Gershon, suggesting the 'real' private as part of the public game. Christine Geraghty has argued that star studies have emphasised 'the polysemy, contradiction and instability of the star-image', deploying extra-filmic discourses at the expense of performance and acting within the film text (2003: 105). Fiorentino's case invites a combination of these approaches, though performance itself rewards close analysis. Fiorentino plays Bridget as a woman who knows she is infinitely brighter than her male victims/accomplices, and is constantly engaging in a scheming form of multi-tasking – thinking ahead to push forward her plans, but with one eye on the progress of the men she is pursuing or those who are pursuing her. There is a 'quickness' about the style she adopts, a readiness to move on to the next level when necessary and a constant sense of a character thinking on her feet. This is often a question of the subtle ways she angles her body – leaning over desks, holding on to the phone whilst doing something else – a busyness which conveys in gestures of irritation and mild impatience the fact that she is waiting for men to catch up. Her delivery is clipped, resisting the temptation to camp it up (her complaint that the banknotes she subsequently steals are 'soft – I thought they'd be hard' is passed off, but could have been played for all its available sexual innuendo). Fast-paced exchanges such as the initial conversation with a divorce attorney ('Still a lawyer Frank?'/ 'Still a self-serving bitch?') do recall the *tour de force* ping-pong dialogue of hardboiled *noir*. If the screenplay repeats the bitch message as the film's baseline mantra ('Anybody check you for a heartbeat lately?' – the bitch is not just a sexual dog but an undead one), Fiorentino augments this in her precise ability to do cold calculating *and* to masquerade caring. Yet Bridget is also a comic performance, which ought to suggest a self-conscious distance between self and role. Unfortunately, her sheer skilfulness in the bitch's execution ('note-perfect thesping' as *Variety* judged another role [Eisner 1993: 25]) hooked Fiorentino ever surer onto the part. *Empire* read the blurring of role and self as an effect of effective performance: 'when you have played a part so well . . . people believe you *are* that person' (Trower 1994). Newman (1994a) used the term 'effortless' to describe the performance; if you can't see the gap between performer and role, you might assume that there is no gap.[86]

Yet Fiorentino also performs herself even when she is not, as it were, strictly acting, another source of her apparent through-and-through bitchness. Interview reception material often presents her as engaging in an anti-sales pitch, which in turn constitutes part of the substance of how she is represented. Writes Gritten:

> The folks at Paramount pictures, who know star quality when they see it, have been promoting her as the Next Big Thing: all she has to do in return is undertake an exhausting round of press interviews, smile sweetly, look ravishing and coo pleasantries about their film's virtues. This is something Fiorentino is pathologically incapable of doing: she is a woman who cannot help but speak her mind. (1994: 35)

Furthermore, Fiorentino does not think it is a star's job to promote films: 'Studios have a gun at your head. Somehow they came up with the idea that you're not only an actor in their movie, you're a salesperson for it too' (Gritten 1994: 37). To discuss this as an aspect of Fiorentino's star textuality is also to shed a particular light on her starring roles and performance style. How she sells herself (and is sold) as bitch has a significant bearing on how her performing bitchness is read, as does her rebellion against the studio promotion-machine. Journalists also seem to enjoy casting themselves as the off-screen counterparts to her on-screen victims: 'The 34-year-old Fiorentino will slap you around, figuratively, as part of her personal style' writes one reporter (Thompson 1995). Fiorentino's case also tells another story about the erotic thriller, its marketability and its feminine fantasies.

One effect of this confusion over self and role is that Fiorentino's struggle to distinguish private from public becomes one of the discourses which permeates her publicity. As with Gershon, this slippage is sexual, *about* her sex: in their fantasy of what she is, journalists read Fiorentino's performance as infusing 'her' innate sexuality into a like-minded character: 'Even in mediocre material . . . she brings her sensational, femme fatale aura: insolent, carnivorous, a sexual athlete and nobody's baby' (Guthmann 1995). She is both 'the heartless sex kitten in *The Last Seduction* and . . . a no-nonsense interviewee who can be as nasty as she wants to be with unsuspecting reporters'.[87] One interview reported that 'Linda Fiorentino's ideal man is one who knows she is not the diabolic temptress from *The Last Seduction*, who does not sleaze after her because she is an actress, and who sees her for who she is' (Berens 1997: 40). One critic predicted that Linda Fiorentino, *not* Bridget Gregory, 'is going to be the bitch of the century' (Duane 1994). Fiorentino (sometimes and ambivalently) reinforces this, describing the filming of *The Last Seduction*'s most notorious sex-scene as her creation rather than Bridget's act, and one in which she plays it like a man:

> [T]he role-reversal that happens in the film was actually happening on set. Peter Berg was very concerned about the scene being pornographic and he spent hours talking to John Dahl . . . about how he was going to shoot it. Usually it's the woman who's doing that. Finally, I got sick of them arguing about it and I just threw Peter against the fence. Then I climbed on him and said, 'Let's shoot!' (Palminteri 1995)

Here, then, Fiorentino's marketing of self and film supports the collapse of self into role. But whilst her involvement with Bridget has been viewed in a frame which includes Stanwyck, Crawford and Bennett, it also needs to be seen in a more intimate tradition of Fiorentino's history of roles – as she puts it – 'in the bargain basement of the movie business' (Palminteri 1995). Unlike Gershon, who has acquired a lesbian patina despite a plethora of heterosexual roles, dark women predominate in Fiorentino's work prior to *The Last Seduction*, most notably Alan Rudolph's *The Moderns* (1988), an arty period melodrama which features her as Rachel Stone, an enigmatic seductress for whom men will die. In Scorsese's *After Hours* (1987) she plays a sadomasochistic sculptor, whilst the Zalman King melodrama *Wildfire* (1988) featured her as an impulsive wild-child torn between an old returning lover and her new family. There is something of the bitch in all of these women, even *Wildfire*'s young mother: Fiorentino doesn't do apple pie very easily, if at all.

Acting on Impulse (1993) is perhaps the most interesting screen formation of the on-screen/off-screen pact. Here Fiorentino is Susan Gittes, a B-movie actress with a full-on *femme fatale* persona on-screen and off (at one point Gittes' face is featured on the cover of the horror fanzine *Femme Fatales*). Susan's vampishness is literalised when, wanted for murder, a policeman holds up a movie still featuring her with vampire teeth ('Is this an accurate likeness?' he asks), and the name she assumes when checking into a hotel is D. D. Slaughter. *Acting on Impulse* plays with its many genres – any aficionado will tell you that a woman who looks this guilty is inevitably innocent. Yet whilst the diegetic film-world Susan inhabits is erotic horror (Brinke Stevens' terrain – Gittes stars in the kind of films Jim Wynorski would routinely direct), *Acting on Impulse* itself plays like a comic-erotic thriller, featuring the usual cocktail of lesbian friction (scenes in which Fiorentino and Nancy Allen perform for the male eye), violence-inflected sex (Fiorentino pushes C. Thomas Howell up against a wall and feels him up and down as if enacting a strip-search) and parodies of moments from more famous genre products (a *Basic Instinct* moment when a condom is found under the bed instead of an ice-pick). It is also, perhaps, a double-B movie; a low-budget movie about low-budget movies (the kind I will discuss in Part Two), which itself failed to 'slash its way out of the midnight-cult ghetto' (Eisner 1993), and therefore locked its star into the bargain basement for a little while longer.

Another title in Fiorentino's erotic thriller portfolio is the post-*Jade*-by-numbers genre work, *Bodily Harm*. This owes a heavy debt to *Jagged Edge* and replays the cop-falls-for-suspect template, with Fiorentino as cop Rita Cates and Daniel Baldwin as Sam McKeon, an ex-cop-(and Cates' ex)-turned-strip-joint-owner (Cates, as *Variety* put is, tosses 'professional detachment to the wind and her clothes to the floor' [Leydon 1995: 102]). The film is replete with loaded lines underpinning the eroticism of danger ('the riskier it was the more turned on I got . . . I knew it was bad, that's what made it so good'; 'Any woman attracted to this man would have to have a sick flirtation with self-destruction'). It trots out a number of genre staples – strip-joint scenes, dead and murderous strippers, scene-of-the-crime scenes, ambivalence about its good/bad girls and its *hommes fatals*, its cop-heroine's guilty back-story (Cates' husband committed suicide after discovering her affair with McKeon; she frequently flashes back both to the husband's death and heady, mirrored sex with McKeon). But *Bodily Harm* also gives its female hero the luxury of manipulating the suspect/sex-object in the way that female suspects in a similar position have been manipulated (think of Fiorentino herself as Trina/Jade). Using a private sexual encounter to get what she wants professionally, she persuades McKeon to come to the lab to give a sperm sample (having collected her own in sex). Yvonne Tasker argues that *Bodily Harm*, along with *Impulse* and *Blue Steel*, involves 'an exploration of the sexuality of the female investigators alongside, and complexly entwined with, the central case itself' (1998: 93). But, as Tasker goes on to argue, this is a reversed version of the usual male cop/female suspect 'equation between investigation, desire and sexuality' (1998: 103; though 'role reversal . . . is not straightforward' [1998: 104]). Tasker argues that the film's foregrounding of Cates' sexuality as part of her investigative strategy makes her as much working girl (prostitute) as working woman (professional investigator). It also, as I argued with reference to Gina Gershon, risks sexual screen self becoming confused with private sexual persona. Michael Douglas may not risk being mistaken for a gigolo just because he performs sex with Glenn Close or Sharon Stone or Demi Moore, though in each of these instances pervasive sexual obsession and compromised sexual identity are at stake. Because Fiorentino is, however, such a powerful, sexually-charged female performer, she also – to extend Tasker's model into the area of stardom – risks attracting the 'working girl' charge attached to many an actress.

Fiorentino's negotiating of this is, of course, itself subject to the confusion of persona involved in the interview process, a performance which can reinforce or challenge the star/role axis and which, as we have seen, some writers prefer to read as a sadomasochistic opportunity. But she is also read occasionally as an anti-bitch, and victim of the feminism of her roles. One *Scotsman* interview headline muddles public and private in a single phrase: 'The Sex Bomb Who Can't Get a Date' (Sorensen 1997: 9). Bridget and Trina are the sex bombs; Fiorentino, according to the interview copy, can't get a date. In 2000 *The Guardian* described her as 'femme fatale Linda Fiorentino', despite the fact that in the interview which follows this slippage of self into role she says, 'I'm not so sure I'm as attracted to dangerous women as people are attracted to me playing those parts' (Strauss 2000: 15). The customary motif which authenticates an interview as a private meeting, even though it is one cog in the industry's publicity machine (which Fiorentino often rejects), is the attention to clothing detail, usually deployed to distinguish the 'real star' sitting at the restaurant table with the interviewer from the 'picture personality' on-screen. Different roles give variance to picture personalities (*Men in Black* gave Fiorentino 'breathing space from the vampy roles for which she is most famous' [Sorensen 1997: 9]), but different clothes give the impression that a real self has made herself available for analysis: 'In a trouser-suit and prim white blouse reminiscent of her Catholic upbringing, she seems more the vulnerable girl next door than the emasculating vixen' (Sorensen 1997: 9; the vixen, of course, is another bitch-formation). Nevertheless, as self-promoter, Fiorentino wants to have her cake and eat it, lamenting the fact that 'here I make a living as a screen siren and I'm the shyest person on Earth. Most expect me to be aggressive, and then they're disappointed' (Sorensen 1997: 10). Interview materials also present Fiorentino incoherently as ambivalently feminist, yet women's responses to her films have been informed by the assumed feminism of the star herself, provoked by such lines as 'I would rather be poor and live on my own than depend on a man', and 'I don't have a husband, I don't have children, I don't even have a cat. I don't want to be tied down to real estate' (Berens 1997: 43). The ambivalence perhaps rests on how she partly welcomes her status as feminist icon (she hoped that *The Last Seduction* would play well to female audiences – 'I thought from the outset if we did this right, it would touch a nerve in a lot of people . . . Especially women' [Gritten 1995: 35]), at the same time as distancing herself from it. 'I hope people see it as a fantasy', she told *Empire*. 'The problem I'm having is all these women saying they want to emulate me' (Trower 1994). Emulation is, however, one side-effect of admiration, and this is in keeping with the general sense that bitchness is contagious and can be passed between women. The *OED* defines one original connotation of the verb 'to bitch' as 'To frequent the company of lewd women'; associate with bitches enough (as Fiorentino has done in her performances, and as audiences do when they frequent the celluloid company of women like Bridget or Susan or Jade) and something of the bitch may rub off, but also the very fact of association is itself 'bitching'.

This 'problem' of emulation has also produced one of the most interesting fan-responses to the erotic thriller. Though *The Last Seduction* largely deals with Bridget's attempt to divorce Clay and escape with the cash, along the way she also hatches a scheme to make money from female vengeance, cold-calling women whose husbands have been unfaithful and proposing hit-man solutions. This strangely revisits the philosophy of *Acting on Impulse*'s Susan Gittes, who, when told of Cathy's husband's philandering and violence, prescribes death: 'Should've killed him the first time he laid a hand on you. One shot point blank, right between the eyes.' In homage to Bridget's version of this, a website was established in the mid-1990s 'dedicated in honor of Linda Fiorentino' called 'The Last Seduction Club', with a philosophy which counsels: 'We believe that women should be more like Bridgette [*sic*] and less like helpless little fools.' Key to the club is its customised *Sex and the City*-infused version of 'The Rules' (which includes 'I could blame it on PMS, but I'm really just a bitch'), all predicated on the notion that 'LSC is more than just a forum to bash men and all the stupid things they do. . . . LSC is designed to bring the power back to us women' (President's Greeting Letter). However, The Last Seduction Club is primarily reactive, reading its source-text as a revenge drama[88] (which recasts Bridget as avenging justice-seeker) rather than a greed fantasy (greed, remember, underpins Farber's bitch analysis). In interview, Fiorentino also notes that what we might call 'the last seduction syndrome' has also been reappropriated as a male fantasy. 'I never saw that character as a role model for little girls,' she has said,

> But I've had women come up to me and say, 'I saw your movie and I've been walking around like a bitch ever since, and I'm driving my boyfriend crazy. It makes me feel really strong and really great.' (Palminteri 1995)

This is bitch, then, as male aphrodisiac – the bitch version of lesbianism for men, perhaps. If women have cast Fiorentino as patron of The Last Seduction Club, men primarily remember the fence sequence (Palminteri interviewing

Fiorentino: 'I just have to speak for all the men on this planet. When I say "I'm working with Linda Fiorentino from *The Last Seduction*," they go, "Oh God! The fence!" . . . Maybe that's a secret passion of men: they want to be thrown up against a fence'). Perhaps this is another instance of the incoherent star as all things to all audiences, though Fiorentino's image seems to have resolved into two sides of the same bitch coin: feminist icon and/as fantasy dominatrix. Which brings us to Sharon Stone.

Sharon Stone: white devil or bedevilled blonde?

Lillian Gish could be considered the supreme instance of the confluence of the aesthetic-moral equation of light, virtue and femininity with Hollywood's development of glamour and spectacle. . . . Very soon the radiance of femininity came to be seen as a trap for men, not a source of redemption – Louise Brooks in *Pandora's Box*, Rita Hayworth in *Gilda*, Sharon Stone in *Basic Instinct*.

(Dyer 1993b: 4)

'Talk of the devil.'
Glamour model speaking about Cassie Bascomb (Sharon Stone) in *The Calendar Girl Murders*

Like stars, blondes are ambivalent creatures. Blonde stars carry with them a physical signification of both virtue and demonism, sexuality and innocence. The equation of fairness with goodness has a long cultural and religious history: blonde hair, Marina Warner reminds us in her book on the history of fairy-tales, 'has naturally enciphered female beauty – inner as well as outer' (1995: 366). From the seventeenth century onwards the word blonde suggested

> sweetness, charm, youthfulness; only in the 1930s and 1940s, under the influence of Hollywood, did the word emerge as a noun, and acquire its hot, vampish overtones, based in the jaunty ironical reversals of meaning cultivated by popular media this century. (Warner 1995: 363)

As a hair colour and moral disposition, twentieth-century blondeness must therefore be distinguished from 'fairness' which, as Warner points out, has long been 'a guarantee of quality' (and, supporting Richard Dyer's later [1997] argument about the morality of whiteness, fair is opposed to 'foul', 'it connotes all that was pure, good, clean' [Warner 1995: 364]). Hollywood's blonde *femme fatale* is instrumental in making blondeness, as it were, the dark side of fairness; the blonde devil is the foul underbelly of the fair maiden.[89]

Sharon Stone has reminted the currency of blondeness. Dyer places her in a tradition including Louise Brooks and Rita Hayworth, but though Stone's blondeness signifies a recognisable though updated version of cinematic female evil, it also (as she tries to diversify roles) does double-service as a more regular victimised 'fairness' (a late twentieth-century version, perhaps, of the early century 'devil or angel' debate).[90] Blondeness specifically identifies Stone as a consummately *white* star (pale 'as a snake's belly' [Gristwood 1998: 25]). As the foremost blonde icon of the 1990s (hardly a profile passes without eulogising her blondeness),[91] her star persona borne out by her roles and her wider cachet in celebrity culture both epitomise and challenge the contradictions of blondeness, as not-so-dumb blonde, as ice-cool villainess, as the thriller's formation of the pursued pure maiden, the woman-in-peril. These are all feminine permutations in which the erotic thriller (with which Stone is largely identified) came to excel. If classical Hollywood preferred these forms (endangered or endangering women) separated into different star incarnations (narcissists or nice girls like Marilyn Monroe or Doris Day, sadistic nasty girls like Barbara Stanwyck or Lana Turner), contemporary Hollywood 'allows' someone like Stone to straddle the good/bad divide as long as her blondes are sexualised. More Monroe than Day (Marilyn was her adolescent idol), her first film appearance was as a Monroe look-alike, pouting, blowing kisses to the audience like the original wowing the troops in Korea, in Woody Allen's dream of exclusion from *Stardust Memories*. Her enigmatic character in *The Specialist* (written, incidentally, by the Wachowski brothers) is called May Munroe. But this is a play, an echo: the eroticism of Stone's persona is self-gratifying, positioned in a two-way economy in which sexual generosity is a bargaining chip. If there is a narcissism about her image, it is active, aggressive, sadistically self-referring, not Monroe's passive, touch-me sensuality.[92] Dyer's analysis of Monroe as not just blonde but white identifies her as 'fair' in a very ethnically specific, and morally weighted, manner. Though 'overdetermined in terms of sexuality', Monroe is nevertheless 'not an image of the danger of sex'. For Dyer, this is the reason that *Niagara*, featuring Monroe as *femme fatale*, was finally unconvincing. Sharon Stone's stardom post-*Basic Instinct* brings a number of these co-ordinates – blonde-whiteness, good-bad sexualised femininity, the trace of demonism – together in the consummate form of 1990s celebrity.

As a blonde/white female star Stone also – like Fiorentino – inherits the mantle of Hollywood sirens before her. 'Not since Marilyn Monroe has a Hollywood star been as completely identified with sex as Sharon Stone', eulogises one journalist (Young 1993: 4) – a comparison to a classical Hollywood 'great' which has both served and stunted Stone's star-image. As a neo-*femme fatale*, like Gershon and Fiorentino she also risks the role-play of evil sticking to her stardom and consequently she either cannot escape the mode of sexy blonde beast, or has to work to embody its opposite, sexy blonde innocent. But add to that the key line which was taken by both Stone herself and her director Verhoeven, that she *was* Catherine Tramell and Catherine Tramell *was* the devil, and you have a particularly insistent version of star-as-role, of the private self identified via the public persona (Eszterhas' screenplay reinforces this: 'You're dealing with a devious diabolical mind,' we are told). Feasey attributes

Stone's persistent sexualisation to the rare 'perfect fit' between the actress and the character in question; review material attest that 'the two women do not simply share character traits, but that they are actually to be read as a single persona' (2003a: 144). That this was Stone's breakthrough role is enough to suggest that she sold her soul to play Tramell, who, as Verhoeven wickedly suggests, is the devil herself.

Stone is the starriest of the three A-list female stars I am considering here, exemplifying (in proportion to the size of her biggest film) the pattern of sexual/genre typecasting discussed in relation to Gershon and Fiorentino. She is often characterised as the exemplary *zeitgeist* feminist ('her aggressive show of sexuality was on schedule, in terms of the culture's shifting sexual politics' [Lahr 1996: 75]). Perhaps because she is the biggest star, hers is the starkest case of self/role interdependence (Catherine is demon, therefore Sharon is demon) whilst also foregrounding the sheer constructedness of stardom. Like Fiorentino Stone has propounded her own version of feminism, informing her role-choices[93] and broadening her appeal to women (she wants to make 'women feel championed' [Andrews 1994: 78]; Austin [2002] also discusses Stone's appeal to women). However a sense of her monstrousness informs much of what is said about her: 'Stone is a kind of Frankenstein goddess,' wrote *Time Out* magazine.

> Built in a Hollywood laboratory from spare parts lying around central casting: Jean Harlow's hair-do, Grace Kelly's wardrobe, Carole Lombard's wise-cracks, Arnie's personal training schedule and Madonna's material gal manifesto on becoming a millionairess. (Chaudhuri 1993: 22)

The female reference points here are all iconic blondes, though Stone is most usually mentioned in the same breath as Madonna, rivals for the 'blonde of the 1990s' title (in interview Stone is scathing about her *Body of Evidence* rival). But both are also remarkable for the way in which they foreground the manufacture of stardom and/as idealised femininity. Probing into 'what she's like when she's not playing the movie star', one interviewer gets the answer, 'I can do glamour; I can make glamour happen, turn the volume up and down, but it's not real' (Hayward 1993: 9). Glamour, the *Oxford English Dictionary* tells us, also has something demonic about it, defined both as 'magical or fictitious beauty' and the power devils use (casting 'glamour o'er the eyes of the spectator') when engaging in visual trickery.[94]

There is, of course, something intrinsically 'starry' about visual brightness itself. Stars, as Richard Dyer famously wrote, 'are things that shine brightly in the darkness' (1993b: 1): astral bodies shining down on us from above, film bodies shining into the darkened auditorium. In *White* Dyer describes how Western culture idealises the 'angelically glowing white woman' (1997: 127) so that she seems to 'glow rather than shine. The light from within or from above appears to suffuse the body' (1997: 122). This is facilitated by 'Northern' lighting techniques which are ideally suited to making whiter-than-white figures like the blonde Stone pop out of the darkness in a way which makes it hard to look at anything else.[95] Blonde stars are therefore doubly bright; more starry in Western cinema than their black or Caucasian-brunette counterparts. Unlike a figure such as Gish, Stone is known primarily not as fair angel but as white devil. Cinematographer Jan de Bont reports that in *Basic Instinct*'s disco scene he deployed techniques that would pick out Stone and Douglas in the throng of dancers: 'I wanted an eye or light of God to shine on them, to select them out of the crowd' (Pasquariello 1992: 46). God's eye may never catch her (she is unrepentant, an unpunished devil), but ours do – or rather are caught by her. The question of specularity (is she/are we victim or manipulator of the gaze?) and a question of star-as-brand (is she victim or manipulator of her sexual image?) converge in Stone.

A self-consciousness regarding her own performativity has characterised Stone's relationship to stardom, perhaps emphasised by her willingness to play to the look. Blondes have long been dogged by the spectre of the lookalike; Fiorentino may be read as a reflection of her bitch predecessors, but blondes, perhaps because of the proximity of peroxide, stand in for other blondes. Grace Kelly, who was a natural blonde, may have lent Stone her wardrobe sense, but Harlow's trademark platinum blonde shade was manufactured not God-given. Furthermore, the hairdo was itself a simulacrum: Harlow cut off her own hair and performed for much of her career in a ready-made Jean Harlow wig (Evans 1995: 43). The woman who inspired a national rash of peroxide demands at beauty parlours was her own lookalike (1995: 39). Whilst Gershon practically denies her own existence as a fixed identity, Stone, like Monroe before her, discusses her star persona in public as if 'Sharon Stone' were a separate person ('it pretty much has its own life now. It doesn't include me anymore. It's as if she lives in another house. I don't know her' [Campbell 1994: 62]). This is a distinction (me/her; real/role) enabled perhaps by the glamour of a blonde image you can 'put on', necessitated by the intense sexualisation which followed *Basic Instinct*. No such sense of a psychotic performativity seems to pervade the Michael Douglas who persists behind the roles, closely identified though he may be with the victim-*noir* males of the genre. Stone's interview persona fluctuates wildly, and may reflect the wide oscillations in the roles she took on in the 1990s (and the films the interviews are selling), part-confirming, part-distancing her from Tramell's demonic legacy. If Stone used the erotic thriller as a springboard to stardom, she is also disingenuous in complaining about the constrictions of sexual typecasting which bound her to a particular form of femininity and a particular marketplace after *Basic Instinct*.

So what kind of sexuality does the Stone-brand speak? If Stone's blonde-whiteness is the visual bait, her lines often reinforce the come-on by paradoxically warning men away. 'I'm not a woman you can trust,' May writes to Stallone's Ray in *The Specialist* (in the film's twist this ironically becomes the most trustworthy thing she utters). May's body is a double trap; ensnaring the man who shot her father with sexual favours so as to get her revenge (using Ray as her hit-man), she is in fact luring Ray to his doom too. Though the blonde danger of this strategy is undone when May, after extensive athletic sex with Ray, turns out to be a loyal girl after all (the pair drive off into the sunset and even Ray's cat is saved), it only takes a few iconic images to remind us of the star persona we are dealing with here. Attending her own fabricated funeral in black veil, black stockings and short skirt (the blonde deploying darkness as disguise), May breathily embraces Ray at the back of the church, who discovers the revolver hitched into her stocking-top. However, the first three times we see her in *The Specialist* she is wearing white, the preferred colour for Catherine Tramell's key scenes.

Tramell is white (a blonde white woman) but has a black heart, a function of her white-blondeness and femininity. But, as Beth also points out, her demonism (like Lucifer, who's name means light-bearer) is an effect of her dazzling qualities, intellectual and otherwise. 'She's evil! She's brilliant!' Beth cries (brilliant as both deviously clever and 'Brightly shining, glittering, sparkling, lustrous', one of the *Oxford English Dictionary*'s defininitions of brilliant; stars – like Lucifer – are, of course, also brilliant in this sense). Contemporary *film noir* (the white Stone's genre) has been identified by Christopher (1997) as predicated on the slippery etymology of 'black blurring into white'. '[I]n Middle English' he notes, 'black and white become "distinguishable only by the context, and sometimes not by that"' (1997: 267), whilst monochrome classic *noir* is 'Black on a white screen, projected by white light' (1997: 268). Jan de Bont describes *Basic Instinct* as 'a *film noir*, but it's not *noir* that much. We always wanted it to be more white than black' (Pasquariello 1992: 44). In interview with me, Verhoeven described his vision for the film as dazzling, Hockneyesque: 'there's a lot of blue there, bright blues and whites . . . countering *film noir* by making *film clair*'. If *film noir* is black film, *film clair* is light or bright film. De Bont, Verhoeven adds, created visual unease not through deep shadow, but by bouncing light off broken mirrors (see below, p. 241).

Stone's work, and the 'dark' blonde star persona she brings to her films (many of which deal squarely with the conjunction of crime and sexuality), can be considered in two phases, the first leading up to *Basic Instinct* (*The Calendar Girl Murders* [1984], *Cold Steel* [1987], *Where Sleeping Dogs Lie* [1992] and *Scissors* [1992]), the second following on from *Sliver* (primarily *Intersection* [1994] and *Diabolique* [1996] – I will not discuss other genre diversifications such as *The Quick and the Dead*, though other feminists have [Tasker 1998: 51–64; Feasey 2003a]). *Sliver* and *Basic Instinct* form a switch-point, not only because they are the two films for which Stone garnered most marquee space (*Sliver* 'opened' on Stone's presence), but also because they crystallise her two primary genre positions. *Total Recall* was preceded by a slew of B-movies, two of which positioned Stone across the *noir*/female Gothic divide as *Basic Instinct* and *Sliver* respectively would do later in her career. Indeed, Stone's preblockbuster B-movie and bit-part career was built largely on the legacy of hair colour – the 150 IQ-er slid into the dumb blonde stereotype with an ease that confirmed the truth that pigment (whether from nature or a bottle) as well as anatomy are destiny in Hollywood. Eight years before *Basic Instinct*, *The Calendar Girl Murders* positioned Stone as a kind of B-list version of the *femme fatale* of the later film, if somewhat less programmatically demonic. Her conniving character in the 1984 *Irreconcilable Differences* also 'drew hisses from audiences'.[96] Yet, *Scissors* casts Stone as a Gothic paranoid/pursued woman, just as *Sliver* would three years later. These are significant shifts for the Stone character, which require us to read her as operating from B- to A-list and from aggressor to victim/revenger and back again. Yet even when she has risen to the A-list, a trashy sexuality imprints her films, for some critics, with the memory of the B-flick ('Twelve years it took for her to get that *Basic Instinct* break,' wrote Anne Billson in the UK broadsheet the *Sunday Telegraph* of *Sliver*, 'and now she ends up trapped in a big-budget version of the sort of exploitative rubbish she thought she'd left behind' [1993: 7]). A- or B-movie, sexual or chaste, Stone's screen stardom (pervading her extra-filmic publicity) seems to exude overt sexuality despite the demands of the screenplay, even as her celebrity stardom (that which pervades her extra-filmic publicity) achieved an image of classy Hollywood royalty. The shift of acceptability which has accompanied her 'real-life' star persona has apparently had no bearing on how we read her performances: the snippets propounded by celebrity organs have systematically presented her more sympathetically as time has gone on, from the bad girl marriage-breaker in her thirties who screwed Joe Eszterhas, to the mature woman in her forties, with a string of miscarriages, broken relationships and a successful baby adoption trotted out for the public. As Feasey has argued, Stone has been partly rehabilitated beyond the erotic thriller-bequeathed image of sex-star bimbo by her relationship to high fashion,[97] which in turn has been articulated through a discourse which makes reference to classic Hollywood. This aspect of her star persona, Feasey argues, connects her to female audiences (countering erotic thriller performances which connected her primarily to male ones) and back to a long tradition, discussed by Stacey, which sees glamorous female stars as the objects of female visual pleasure in the 1940s and 1950s. Here, then, the star image has shifted; image-change may be acceptable in real life, but it has eluded Stone's screen life, suggesting a dissonance at the heart of her star profile: in *OK* magazine she may be a charming, multifaceted woman, but on film she can only be good or bad blonde, failing if falling somewhere in between, but always sexualised. Stone's stardom rests on the knickerlessness of *Basic Instinct*;[98] Stone as actress tries to revisit and retake that scene, but fails to rewrite its significance. Only Stone as celebrity attains a more complex image of womanhood.

As we have seen, much has been written about *Basic Instinct* as key neo-*noir* text, as neo-*femme fatale* vehicle, as postmodern; and I am positioning it as the A-form genre's highpoint. Readings of *Sliver*, as I discussed earlier in relation to Eszterhas, were framed in terms of both his and his star's earlier collaboration, its sexual content casting it as much of a straight up and down (as it were) erotic thriller as its predecessor. I do not dispute that *Sliver* is an erotic thriller.

However, for all its flaws as a film, it does present an interesting case of the parameters and forms of hybridisation the genre can take, without anyone really noticing or caring much. If *Basic Instinct* is a classic *noir* erotic thriller, *Sliver* is a female Gothic erotic thriller. The genre-shift focuses entirely on how we read the Stone character, as woman on the rampage or as woman on the run. Of course, we might see *most* women in Hollywood as on some level women on the run: even the intimidating Tramell is a woman on the run, if you think of the film's point of view as Nick's – he pursues her, she is pursued, the object of the law's gaze and energy, however slippery and skilfully she is in resisting this and turning the tables on Nick. Carly in *Sliver* perhaps simply makes overt what is covert in *Basic Instinct*, rendering explicit the old Hitchcockian voyeuristic story of how the male gaze catches women, and how they might sometimes reverse this or escape it (this too is Hitchcock). Catherine as dangerous dame and Carly as paranoid princess-in-a-tower present two reliable forms which the genre has taken, as well as two of Stone's career routes ('Nudity isn't difficult', Stone has said. 'Avoiding simpering traditional women's roles – now that's hard' [Goodman 1994: 32]) – like, presumably, her woman-in-peril in *Cold Steel*. Earlier, I discussed some of the common tropes and types of the mainstream genre – the *femme fatales* and dumb lugs at the *noir*ish end of the erotic thriller's development and the smart female heroines pursued by, but eventually outwitting, a range of *hommes fatals* at the female Gothic end of the erotic thriller continuum. Stone's career spans these character formations, encapsulating one version of the erotic thriller's potential as an ever-hybridising genre form. Along the way the question of Stone as devil or bedevilled focuses how we read some of the prevailing ambivalences (and misogynies) which still stick to the female star.

In *Sliver* Stone plays a formation of the good-bad girl, in the sense that she is both highly sexualised and actively sympathetic, but she is not a good-bad girl as developed earlier in this study. As a form of the 'divorcée back on the dating market' female sexual quest film *Sliver* replays some of the concerns of *9½ Weeks*, with Stone's Carly revisiting Basinger's Elizabeth (both films begin with their heroines walking towards the camera, and leaving the male love objects at the end; they are female point of view films). But *Sliver* also 'Gothicises' this sex in the city narrative, making Stone's character both the quester and the woman in peril. Her epistemological uncertainty drives *Sliver*'s sense of suspense, whilst Carly herself is paranoically positioned: as blonde she is always already a target, a replacement blonde for the murdered woman who occupied her apartment before her (Carly's resemblance to her predecessor marks her as the next in line). *Sliver*'s focus on Carly's predicament aligns it once again with the paranoid woman film I looked at in chapter 2; its visualisation of the modern spaces of the New York Sliver tower look more like Gothic horror than the characteristically anodyne California of the erotic thriller (the novel upon which *Sliver* was based is by Ira Levin, who also penned *Rosemary's Baby*, a demonic woman-in-peril tale, but set in the Gothic Dakota

Building rather than Carly's high-rise, see-and-be-seen contemporary panopticon). If since *Basic Instinct* Stone's star persona has been 'possessed' by the devil of Tramell, *Sliver* was an active act of exorcism,[99] and it certainly looked like the vehicle to achieve this, though its marketing pushed it as another hot little number starring that woman who showed you her genitals. However, in embracing a paranoid Gothic scenario, Stone had also to flirt with victimhood: the paranoid woman's film is predicated on the psychic targeting of women, making the problem of Carly, for Stone, that of how 'to play her so she is not simply a victim' (Hayward 1993: 8; though this quote appears under the sub-heading 'Man-Eater', suggesting that Carly isn't so far from Catherine, at least for copy-editors). Perhaps this simply bears out one formation of Hollywood's lingering patriarchal choices: you can be pursuer or pursued, devil or bedevilled, doer or done-to, never both.

Between *Basic Instinct* and *Sliver*, Stone may then simply be oscillating from one position to the other. But these are positions already mapped out in her early work – if *The Calendar Girl Murders* forms a prototype for *Basic Instinct*, *Scissors* forms a prototype for *Sliver*, in which a pursued woman is victimised by both the architecture of the building she occupies and the man who owns it. Both images, both films, engage in symptomatic sexualisation. It is hard to escape the 'sex star' charge when you have done a *Playboy* spread in conjunction with a consistently eroticised film portfolio, as Shannon Tweed and Kathy Shower have discovered to their cost. It is also probably easier to escape the glamour ghetto as an A-lister than a B-lister. But, public as Stone's attempt to diversify has been since the *Playboy* shoot in 1990, we might look back to one of her earliest film roles for a pre-*Playboy* shot at the magazine's legacy. *The Calendar Girl Murders* features Stone – eight years before her official employment by the Hugh Heffner empire – as glamour model Cassie Bascombe, who kills off a range of other glamour models working on a calendar for an organisation uncannily like *Playboy* itself (they are bumped off month-by-month – will cop Dan Stoner [Tom Skerritt] catch the killer before she reaches Miss December?). Paradise magazine is owned by Hefner-clone Richard Trainor (Robert Culp),[100] who has parties at the Trainor Villas (remarkably like those at the Heffner mansion), and is seen early in the film diversifying into 'tasteless adult programming' (a softcore *Playboy*-like cable channel – 'Paradise Magazine in your living room'). Cassie was once (and is no more) Paradise's 'Angel of the Year', and the film makes much of the fickleness (and dangers) of an industry predicated on two-dimensional sex (Miss February is killed off as her unseeing boyfriend reads magazine copy about her). *The Calendar Girl Murders* betrays a number of ambivalences about both Stone and the erotic thriller. More of a slasher set in the sex industry than an erotic thriller, like *Scissors* it cannot make up its mind about who are its victims and who are its villains – a dilemma which has also animated the history of readings of *Basic Instinct*. Stone is a natural focus for this, a figure who, it seems, can go either way. This is also true of the cultural history of blondes – undecidable figures who may be the worst kind of white devil, but may also be milk-white unblemished girls of fairy-tale. As *The Calendar Girl Murders* reaches its trashy dénouement, Cassie is revealed as a kind of hybrid victim-villain, briefly moving through a hit-girl/*femme fatale* incarnation, then collapsing into pitiful tears of culpability as her motives are exposed (revealed as her father, Trainor's double rejection prompted the daughter to eradicate her rivals for his love). This positions *The Calendar Girl Murders* in a tradition of sexy crime stories which play with psychoanalytic justifications for trauma-generated irrationality, featuring either revenge-acts on behalf of murdered parents – usually dead mothers – or adult derangement because of childhood torments. But the film also betrays one of the fascinatingly telling glitches which animates the B-quality erotic thriller. It is common to find lesser-known and cheaper movies (*The Calendar Girl Murders* was originally a TV movie) released in different formats and in different territories under different titles. *Basic Instinct* may be that particular film product's universal English-language brand-name, but this film has no such fame or distinction. Hence its distribution under (to my knowledge) at least three different titles. Throughout this book I pause on alternative titles when they reveal something about a distributor's marketing dilemma – as I said in chapter 1, title says all in a low-budget market when there is no cash spare to mount a big advertising campaign. *The Calendar Girl Murders* is its commonest moniker (website references cite it as this), and sells the film as a prime exploitation combination of sex and violence (nude women-in-peril). However the video version which I viewed was called *Victimized*, and features a cover-image of Stone looking sexually available, with her name and the title so close as to suggest that 'Sharon Stone [is] victimised'. The strapline above her image reads: 'She's insatiable . . . He's clinical' (in fact 'her' insatiableness is murderous; 'his' clinicalness is investigative). Who, then, is the victim here? Stone/Cassie or the objects of her jealousy and derangement? Another 'alternatively known by' title for this film is *Insatiable*, which, in combination with a smattering of knowledge about the plot, may suggest both excessive carnality and/or excessive crime (an insatiable killer or insatiable glamour models?). For the purposes of opportunistic video release after Stone herself had become the film's primary marketable commodity, jacket copy trades on her established image ('Sharon Stone (*Basic Instinct*), Hollywood's most desirable and insatiable leading lady, ignites our screens in this fast paced erotic thriller'). Yet betwixt and between these titles a confusion about Stone herself might be read: Victim or aggressor? Pin-up or revenger? Insatiable for *what*?

However differently these films position Stone's women on different sides of the doer/done-to divide, they still manage resolutely to sexualise her in fairly equal measures, and miss no opportunity to feature her naked. Stone's role as thriller-regular, and eroticised blonde, also signifies in a discourse which situates her in relation to the screen past. In particular, she is situated 'in the direct line of descent of Hitchcock women (Grace Kelly, Tippi Hedren, Janet Leigh)' (Johnstone 1992: 16), and her movies frequently claim some position in a tradition of the post-Hitchcockian thriller. Paul Verhoeven discusses *Basic Instinct* in the frame of *Vertigo*, whilst *Sliver* has been read as a kind of post-modern *Rear Window*. In this spirit we might read *Scissors* as *Marnie*, a con-fused little story in which Stone's Angie is rendered deranged by a scheming shrink who imprisons her in an apartment and terrorises her with a range of bizarre infantile fantasy-figures (mechanical toys and accusatory Mynah birds). This *Gaslight*-like tale is essentially 'about someone's campaign to drive the fragile Stone around the bend' (Variety 1991: 90), showing a woman-in-peril crumbling and then escaping (she has a lot to avenge, including a nasty rape, repeated male interrogation and being preyed upon by various masculine figures – chivalrous, misogynistic, violent, prurient and lunatic strangers). Whilst some critics, particularly post-*Basic Instinct*, chose to focus on the pres-ence or absence of nakedness (even when playing a frigid 26-year-old virgin [Angie] Stone must bare her breasts), *Scissors* did attract comments on perfor-mance (rare in the corpus of Stone reception material), which suggests a recog-nition of its genre-position, nudging the thriller format in the direction of the paranoid woman film (Stone 'overacts wildly, and the general tone is hysterical' [Kermode 1991: 59]; 'a palpably pained, involving performance' [Willman 1991: 12]). It also, through a post-Hitchcockian, pre-*Dead Again* motif of Angie's obsession with scissors, establishes her as an unreliable heroine, who may be doing more with her scissors collection than just mending dolls. The ambivalence about whether she is killer or victim also underpins the question of her sexuality. 'Like Brigitte Bardot,' enthuses Toby Young, Stone (not Catherine or Carly) 'breathes sex from every pore' (1993: 5). But the breast scene is also a key character-moment, primarily concerned with exposing her vulnerable state of sanity (she is scrutinised naked by a spooky pig-doll, her tal-isman throughout the film), and inaugurating a whole scenario in which woman is set up primarily to be surveilled. 'You're very very careless with your blinds,' says one of her male neighbours. 'I know more about you than your therapist' – a line which prefigures the visual predicament of Carly in *Sliver*. Thus ques-tions which come to characterise Stone's whole star profile – Sexual tigress or ice-maiden? Active self-controlling exhibit or victim-of-the-gaze? – are embed-ded even here, pre-*Basic Instinct*.

Post-*Sliver*, two Stone roles characterise the limits on a sex-identified per-former ('Can she really handle something serious without getting her kit off? [Dennis 1993: 27]). As Feasey has noted, Stone's most radical attempts to diver-sify have resulted in critical ridicule (*The Quick and the Dead, Last Dance*), though with a strong director she was rewarded for a nuanced performance in *Casino*. The *Casino* role was still, of course, sexually-inflected, but Stone's wild-child fatality was extended beyond its customary *femme*-formation into a gen-eralised self-destructiveness. Overall, Stone took the two routes which *Basic Instinct*/*Calendar Girl Murders* and *Sliver*/*Scissors* presented, developing the *femme fatale* of *Diabolique* and the asexual woman of *Intersection* or *Last Dance*.[101] *Intersection* goes so far as to make Stone's character's frigidity a prime plot-point, the cause of her marriage breakdown (Stone has said, 'I became a sex symbol, which was absurd especially as I symbolised the kind of sex I don't believe in . . . I want to play talkie roles, no cleavage, no legs' [Gray 1998: 6]). In *Diabolique* her costume provides as much dangerous signification as her performance: *Basic Instinct* made white the primary colour of Tramell's demonism,[102] whilst *Diabolique* deploys an overtly hellish palette. Stone's Nicole Horner moves through the film sluttishly smoking and posing in a range of wicked lady garments – skin-tight scarlet capri-pants or business suits, leopard-print bras, black cocktail dresses, deep-red lipstick emphasising her skin's pallor. This is not the wardrobe of a boarding school mathematics teacher (the unlikely premise of her character); it loudly declares both murder and sexual omnivorousness. It is almost as if the film's lack of confidence in its performances and screenplay compels it to underscore everything with an extra-lurid visual code echoed in the marketing – while Stone retains her trademark blondeness in the movie itself, the DVD sleeve photograph has been processed to present her as a 'dark lady' brunette, the flip-side of good girl Mia (Isabelle Adjani), to whose profile Stone's face is juxtaposed. Like Tramell before her, Horner (the name evokes a male sexual appetite) sleeps with women as well as men, and though *Diabolique* is a Hollywood remake of the classic Clouzot 1954 original, it revisits *Basic Instinct*'s suggestion that all women are really dykes and all dykes work together to destroy men (particularly in the dénouement, which sees private eye Shirley Voguel [Kathy Bates] upholding the alibis and justifications of Horner and Mia). Here, Mia is the paranoid woman, rendered so by her diabolical husband (Chazz Palminteri again), her own diabolical attempt to murder him and Horner's diabolical double-cross; unhinging Mia is the project of the movie. Stone therefore has simply to act hard-bitten, matching performance to costume. Good reviews and bad connected this to Stone's prior *femme* incarnations, and (at their kindest) to Stone as contemporary reincarnation of a classical Hollywood goddess – a comparison which, as we have seen, also damned Fiorentino with faint praise. Though such references may make both female performers essentially postmodern stars, marked by a critical nostalgia which condemns them to unoriginality however good they are at what they do, Michael Douglas, by contrast, is allowed to be himself, incarnating new versions of contemporary masculinity rather than reincarnating classic male icons; rarely is he read – as I have done above – in the frame of 1940s *noir*. Stone as Horner is, significantly, not Simone Signoret, who played the role in the French original, but 'evokes the high bitch style of Bette Davis' (Hinson 1996); 'she smokes cigarettes the way they used to, kind of angrily' (Shulglasser 1996). But (again like Fiorentino, unique in her repetition of classic icons) Stone is also condemned to be read as just 'back doing what she does well – the "Basic Instinct" siren' (Shulglasser): 'wickedly funny, dry as a poisoned martini, and sexy in her '50's movie magazine way';[103] 'Miss Stone does her Catherine-Tramell [*sic*] routine from her most famous film . . . cool, cynical, calculating, clever and bitchy, but [she] doesn't appear nude'.[104] This is read by

Foster Hirsch as central to Stone's star reinforcement strategy – if *Basic Instinct* made her a star, it makes sense to keep doing *Basic Instinct*: 'Sharon Stone tackles the role by showily . . . remaining Sharon Stone, glamorous movie queen. . . . [S]he keeps her focus securely offscreen, on her fans' (1999: 77). Essentially, what this material proves is not just that Stone is yet another actress who finds it impossible to shrug off a powerful role, but that what everyone said (herself included) was that she *was* that role, and therefore any future performance which echoes that role reinvigorates the notion that star image and singular performance work together to reinforce each other.

Though Stone has played fewer *femmes fatales* than we would like to think, it is the *femme fatale* which has stuck. And though she plays naked less than we would like to think, the sheer power of the crotch-flash ensures that nakedness is negatively present even when she is clothed (she 'doesn't appear nude' as a spectre of her availability to be as nude as mainstream cinema gets). Like a weird kind of reverse palimpsest, the bare crotch overrides the clothed body – when not nude the spectre of her nudity is still annoyingly present. This is particularly difficult for an actress in her forties attempting to cast off the minx as she moves into middle age.

In an attempt to keep secret the twist at the end of Clouzot's 1955 *Les Diaboliques* the credits charge the viewer thus: 'Don't be a devil . . . Don't tell them what you saw.' Stone's attempt not to be the devil is intimately bound to what we saw in her most famous film. An interview-profile in 1994 makes reference to two possible career-paths Stone might have taken: Plan A, 'in which you become successful by living and acting with a lot of integrity' and "Plan B", where you sell your soul to the devil'. When aspects of celebrity seem to take on a life of their own Stone admits that 'there's a part of me that keeps saying, "Did you step into Plan B and you didn't know it?"' (Campbell 1994: 58). This ambivalence suggests that Stone's stardom may be closer to the demonic celebrity of Catherine Tramell; any woman who poses for *Playboy* to get noticed quickly is unlikely to evade sexualisation that easily. Like other sexually inflected female stars of the 1990s, to be or not be the devil is out of control of the star, residing in the interplay between genre and audience.

NOTES

1 The watercooler quality of his stories in turn feeds into his salary excesses. Andy Spletzer writes for website Film.Com: 'Joe Eszterhas is the highest paid screenwriter of all time and for that I say, "More power to him." I wish he was the most talented screenwriter of all time, too, but you can't have everything. . . . Because of the additional media attention his "controversial" films stir up, he has become an indispensable part of the marketing campaign which justifies, from a business standpoint, his multi-million dollar salary' (http://www.film.com/film-review/1995/8885/3/default-review.html).

2 Monica Sullivan reviewing *Jade* for *Movie Magazine International* (http://www.shoestrong.org/mmi-revs/jade.html).

3 Eszterhas' pay cheques are legendary: $3 million for *Basic Instinct*; the 'handwrit-

ten synopsis for *One Night Stand* . . . snapped by New Line for $2.5 million'; a deal struck in just seven minutes in which $1.5 million was offered 'against $3.4 million (the maximum he'll get if the film actually gets made) to write up' another script (*Empire*, April 1995: 4); 'two million dollars and two-and-a-half million per two-page treatment (for *Showgirls* and *Jade*, respectively)' (Carrie Gorringe reviewing *Jade* for Nitrate Online film internet site, http://www.nitrateonline.com/rjade.html). Nicolas Kent has written: 'Though only a handful enjoy such rewards, it's not surprising that writers of highly desirable original screenplays may feel a brief, joyful rush of power' (Kent 1991: 117). What *is* surprising is that so much should be paid for a film such as *Basic Instinct*, which has already been made in a slightly different form several times over.

4 Direct-to-video reviewers recognise that this practice is still rife: 'Do you think that Hollywood producers just have a big hat of ideas where they pick out phrases and put them together to form a movie?' writes the reviewer at B-website 'Oh the Humanity!', before describing the formulaic bolt-together construction of Wynorski's *Sins of Desire* (http://www.ohthehumanity.com/reviews/rev20.html).

5 'Flat and Foul' by Andy Spletzer, for Film.com at: http://www.film.com/film-review/1995/8885/3/default-review.html.

6 An IMDb respondent wrote of *Jade*: 'The neck on the guillotine belongs to Mr Eszterhaus [*sic*], who has spent the past few years reshuffling the deck of cards from which he produced "Basic Instinct," recasting the characters, and retitling the scripts, then peddling them for astronomical sums to producers eager to duplicate the steamy sex of that earlier film' (http://us.imdb.com/CommentsShow?0113451).

7 Sean Means, 'Not Even Semi-Precious' for Film.com, at: http://www.film.com/film-review/1995/8885/27/default-review.html. By the time of *Jade*, most reviewers noted the repetitions, and *Premiere*'s formula of repeating the plotlines itself became a repeated point made in a number of reviews – a repetition of a repetition (see, for example, Leith, Billson, Johnston, all 1995).

8 *The Daily Mail*, a UK tabloid serving middle-class Middle England, saw *Jade* as another stage in its long-standing linkage of screen images with socially undesirable acts: 'The plot hangs around an unnatural sex act which has been used to make the film more accessible to perverts' (Bamigboye 1995: 41).

9 See Andy Spletzer, Film.Com, note 5 above.

10 This is also a swipe at the American MPAA ratings system, which has provoked much hostility from parents and moral guardians as it has relaxed its guidelines on what can be seen and heard in a PG-13-rated film (Bart 2002), despite the fact that the rating board consists entirely of parents 'who have themselves experienced the difficulties of determining their own youngster's moviegoing' (Gray 1994; see also Douglas 1999).

11 It is often characterised as the Eszterhas film it's OK to like: one internet reviewer wrote: 'Forget *Showgirls* and *Sliver*, and *Flashdance*, and *Basic Instinct*, *Jagged Edge* gave Big Joe his bones, his legitimacy' (Dr Bob-3 of Austin Texas, at http://us.imdb.com/CommentsShow?0089360).

12 This trope of confronting a woman with the spectacle of another woman's suffering in order to watch the first woman squirm (presenting a second spectacle of horrified female identification which is close to fear) was luridly explored in the nasty horror-thriller *The Bone Collector*. Here rookie cop Angelina Jolie is 'toughened up' into a forensics expert by Denzel Washington forcing her to absorb, record, photograph and narrate details of the mutilated body of a serial killer's female victim. Using a woman on-screen as a screen may also be a neat way of circumventing the censors: you don't have to show the corpse itself (risking a genre slide into body horror and perhaps a higher rating) because showing the distressed female witness to the corpse tells you what you need to know about how awful it is. She has absorbed the spectacle so that we can view her reflected version of it. A

version of this was played out in Jodie Foster's relationship to the female victims of Buffalo Bill in *Silence of the Lambs*.

13 Here Eszterhas manages to demonise both mothers and television: 'My mother was an actress on the soaps', Zeke says. 'She used to spend most of the year in LA. I used to take a cab home from school and watch her on TV. That was just about my life with her.'

14 See '"Sliver" Production Information', United International Pictures (UK)/ Paramount Pictures, pp. 5–6, p. 7, lodged at The British Film Institute Library, London.

15 However one judges the screenplay itself (in terms of how much it cost, or in terms of its similarities to other Eszterhas thrillers), it is hard to see it as solely responsible for the final product. Subject to extensive re-edits, the final sequence of *Sliver* in particular resulted from dire test-screenings (one journalist cites 'five different endings tried on for size' [Davenport 1993; see also Billson 1993; Errigo, 1993]).

16 He also uses the subliminal to insert what appears to be a Hitchcockian directorial signature-image, towards the end of the film, following the attack on Maria, the maid. Friedkin claimed to me when I interviewed him that he was unaware of this image.

17 Scoopy of Budapest at http://us.imdb.com/CommentsShow?0113451; Carrie Gorringe wrote for Nitrate Online: 'Whatever problems *Jade* has, they don't stem from Friedkin's visual style' (http://www.nitrateonline.com/rjade.html); James Berardinelli commented 'even a talented director and a promising cast can't redeem a moronic storyline' (http://movie-reviews.colossus.net/movies/j/jade.html). This is similar to the way in which the convolutions of *Basic Instinct* are laid at Eszterhas' door rather than Verhoeven's (e.g. Nigel Andrews' 'screenwriter Eszterhas piles on Mr V's shoulders one implausible plot twist after another'); whereas most invisible writers hide behind the celebrity of the auteur-director or star, who might consequently take the blame for a project, it is testament to Eszterhas' celebrity that he is picked over for elements of responsibility.

18 For instance Ebert's: 'If you made an inventory of "Jade", you'd find lots of standard thriller ingredients. The movie contains bizarre murder weapons, blackmails, adultery, criminals in high places, kinky sex, hidden cameras, a chase scene, nudity, knives, guns and even such reliable lines as "I'm taking you off this case!" The problem is that they're not assembled in a compelling order' (Ebert 1995). One IMDb respondent called *Jade* 'Basic Instinct part 2' and 'a barely competent erotic/thriller'; another called it 'the usual Eszterhas nonsense about a woman with kinky sex habits and possible homicidal tendencies' ('cygnus x-1' then 'bwaynef', both at http://us.imdb.com/CommentsShow?011345). Another wrote: 'I think Joe Eszterhas got out his first draft of *Basic Instinct* and gave this to the producers and they loved it. . . . The only problem is William Friedkin is not Paul Verhoeven, Linda Fiorentino is not Sharon Stone, David Caruso is not Michael Douglas and *Jade* is a very bad clone of *Basic Instinct*' (ibid.).

19 Film.com wrote of *Jade*, 'If I gave a damn, I might try to psychoanalyze Joe Eszterhas, starting with the question: What is this guy's problem with women? Looking at his script for *Showgirls*, one would think Eszterhas sees all women as bitch-goddesses who live to take off their clothes and contort in swimming pools like a caught marlin on "The American Sportman"' (Sean Means for Film.com, ibid.).

20 Monica Sullivan, reviewing *Jade* for *Movie Magazine International* (http://www.shoestrong.org/mmi-revs/jade.html). This is underlined by the *San Francisco Examiner*'s Barbara Shulgasser, making the inevitable comparisons with Fiorentino's *Last Seduction* character: 'Now let me get this straight. A woman with the self-esteem to get herself through school and set up a lucrative practice thought that a good way to repay her husband for his infidelity would be to subject herself to the humiliating sexual demands of numerous strangers? . . . What shared adolescent wet dream has led Eszterhas and Friedkin to believe that this is the way a

woman seeks revenge for her husband's philandering? I suppose rubbing hot peppers in hubby's condoms never occurred to them. That's certainly the approach that the Fiorentino character of "The Last Seduction" would have taken' (Schulgasser 1995). Hugo Davenport of the right-wing British broadsheet *The Daily Telegraph* even criticised the film on the grounds of its anti-feminism: 'In Friedkin's sleazy, misogynist picture, her sex drive leads her to be suspected of murder while her screen persona is subjected to the female equivalent of gelding' (1995: 26).

21 Eszterhas was horrified by protests against his script. Having met gay leaders during *Basic Instinct*'s production he says that the scales fell from his eyes regarding what he had written and, though at first he maintained 'an attitude of hurt innocence' ('How could he, Joe Eszterhas, champion of the underdog, whose scripts decry intolerance and bigotry, possibly write a gay-bashing piece?'), he soon was persuaded that 'the script *was* insensitive', and wrote to Verhoeven, 'When people feel they are being hurt, I think we have a responsibility as human beings and as filmmakers to listen' (all quotes Holub 1991). He responded by rewriting the screenplay so that the Douglas cop-role is a lesbian, and redressing the sexual balance of murder by having the bisexual female killers who populate the film kill women too. After this Eszterhas vowed that 'this entire Sturm und Drang over "Basic Instinct"' would have a politically positive result, promising to write a film which would present a good guy 'who just happens to be coincidentally gay', arguing that because 'I get the highest amount of money (for a screenwriter) in town, that I'm in a better position than most to try to do something different' (Grove 1992: 10).

22 He told the liberal British broadsheet *The Observer* in August 2000, 'I find myself with an immediate understanding of people who are on the outside, the Jews, whatever colour or creed they are. The showgirls, gays and outcasts' (Vulliamy 2000: 2).

23 '*Music Box* Joe Eszterhas Writes a Wrong', *American Film*, February 1990, p. 15.

24 One internet reviewer of *American Rhapsody* wrote, 'Eszterhas reminds me of Norman Mailer. He's a dirty old man who pretends to be preoccupied with sex for intellectual reasons .. when in fact he's just a lech. . . . He reminds me of Geraldo Rivera here: they both talk about all the women they used to sleep with, pretending to be ashamed and repentant, when the subtext the whole time screams, "Ain't I a stud!"' (review posted 16 August 2000 at http://www.amazon.com/exec/obidos/ASIN/03745411445/o/qid+9..../102–8766226–132490).

25 The Douglas–Clinton connection was consolidated in a rather more potent fashion in 1995's *The American President*, which Thomas Doherty, in his essay 'Movie Star Presidents', describes as 'a third liberal fantasy of what Bill Clinton would be like if he were only less like Bill Clinton and more like Michael Douglas' (2001: 155).

26 '[T]he only amusement, entertainment we could get were American movies,' he has said. 'So when I was a child of seven, eight, nine, I saw a lot of American movies . . . not what you would call A-movies, they probably were B-movies' (Shea and Hennings 1993: 5).

27 Despite popular American perceptions that European filmmakers have greater sexual freedom, Verhoeven had fallen foul of a funding system which effectively 'pre-censors' movies: '[I]n my case the problem was that they [the Dutch funding body] felt that the scripts that I was giving to them, that I wanted to be financed, they thought were too . . . let's use the words "decadent" and "immoral" . . . And so, what is bad about the system is that you start to censor yourself' (Shea and Hennings 1993: 9–10).

28 Verhoeven justifies this thus: 'God is male and female. And that's why I think the Devil is male and female, and that's why I think bisexuality is appropriate to Catherine's character' (MacGregor 1999: 19).

29 See, for instance, Thomas Austin's work on women viewers of *Basic Instinct* (2002: 68–77) and Moore (1992: 34).

30 Interview featured in the 2001 documentary *Blonde Poison: The Making of Basic Instinct*, directed by Jeffrey Schwarz, included in the Momentum Pictures 10th Anniversary Special Edition DVD of *Basic Instinct*. It was not only San Francisco gays who took offence at the film; protests extended to the UK. *The Daily Telegraph* reported that Outrage! were planning to demonstrate in London, Nottingham and Newcastle against the film in the week of its release in Britain. 'Protest at Film', *Daily Telegraph*, 7 May 1992, p. 3.

31 It might also be said that gayness is everywhere in this film, across positive and negative character-parings, and on both sides of the law. J. Hoberman argues that '[I]t is Douglas who is the movie's real love object', reading the relationship between Nick and his partner (George Dzundza) homosexually: 'That [Dzundza's] public tantrum was evidently shot at a gay-and-lesbian country-western bar called Rawhide II suggest that Verhoeven, at least, understood the implications of this scene' (2003: 17).

32 As Jon Lewis concludes in his discussion of the NC-17 category, 'Conventional wisdom in Hollywood today [since *Showgirls*] is that it is impossible to make money on an NC-17 title in theatres' (2002: 297).

33 *Showgirls*' musical composer, Dave Stewart, sold it in an interview as 'a big musical drama for adults with some eye-popping scenes, but it's classy glamour rather than sleazy' (Bamigboye 1995).

34 *Showgirls* production notes, Guild UK distributors, pp. 3 and 4, author's own copy.

35 Stone first denied that she even knew that her naked crotch was being filmed, before taking credit for it. 'Sharon Stone claims that "flash" scene in *Basic Instinct* was her idea,' reports Andrews (1994: 78).

36 *Showgirls* production notes, Guild UK distributors, p. 9, author's own copy.

37 Sexual encounters are, as I. Q. Hunter points out in his celebration of the film, always a form of sex-work (2000: 191).

38 As Hunter's essay (2000) and a round-table issue of *Film Quarterly* (2003: 56: 3, 32–46) attest.

39 *Empire* noted that he likes 'to poke fun at this awful monster, PC', to which Douglas replied, 'Well I *do*. It's a terrible thing. . . . But I've been scared to death about what we're *supposed* to be, versus what we *are*. I don't think it's conscious. I go on my emotions' (Dawson 1995: 89). One Newsgroup writer commented on *Disclosure* in 1994, 'You know that Angry White Male we've all been hearing so much about since the November election? Well, I've just figured it out: he's Michael Douglas. Ever since FATAL ATTRACTION in 1987, Douglas has seemed to be there every time a film exploded into an infuriating zeitgeist phenomenon, and Douglas himself has mastered the role of the somewhat-less-than-innocent-victim' (Scott Renshaw at: rec.arts.movies.reviews newsgroup).

40 Writing as *Basic Instinct* was in pre-production, Nicolas Kent reported that 'Michael Douglas has been signed to star. His fee is said to be $15 million' (1991: 85), though subsequent writers put payment for the film at 'only' $10 million (see, for example, Cooney 1992: 54–60).

41 One internet reviewer refers to 'the Michael Douglas sexy-mystery flick genre' in which the star rolls out 'his usual messed-up, white male schtick' (credited to Russell Fortmeyer and Kansas State University Student Publications Inc. at: http://collegian.ksu.edu/issues/v099B/sp/n137/a-e-disclosure-fortmeyer.html).

42 Schickel continues, 'Douglas, with *Fatal Attraction* and *Basic Instinct* behind him, knows all about playing male victimization without total loss of amour propre'. Internet writer James Berardinelli calls *Disclosure* 'a sort of *Fatal Attraction* of the workplace (Douglas has made a career out of getting involved with "dangerous" women)' (http://movie-reviews.colossus.net/movies/d/disclosure.html), and Julie Burchill called *Fatal Attraction* 'the latest instalment in the Poor Little Man as Victim big screen serial' (*Mail on Sunday*, 24 January 1988: 18).

43 The other 'Cain male' often cited for being 'helpless in the throes of desire and

attempting to escape the frustrations of his existing life' (Spicer 2002: 85) is the drifter-hero of *The Postman Always Rings Twice*, both versions of which are discussed elsewhere in this book. The men of *Mildred Pierce*, another frequently cited Cain adaptation, are more problematic because their weaknesses are filtered through the central perspective of Mildred herself: the flaws and masochism of Mildred's men are significant only in the way they impinge on the heroine's consciousness.

44 'And there is satisfaction in knowing he will be punished – if not for one crime, then for another; if not by the law, then by himself or by an accomplice. In any case the "postman," whatever symbol of fate or death or order in the form of a uniformed and familiar person, will "ring twice"; there is no escape' (Oates 1968: 128).

45 Oates writes: 'Everything is "past," finished, when the narrator begins; the stories themselves are no more than recountings of events, not intended to represent events themselves' (1968: 111).

46 Most reviewers saw the fire and butchery of the *mise-en-scène* as identifying Alex as succubus (though it was also noted that Manhattan's meat-packing district *circa* 1987 was oh-so-chic and said more about Lyne's attention to style than to Alex's hellishness). Lyne also uses it to associate Alex with the sexual fringes: of the 14th Street meat market where they filmed he said, 'It's Fellini down there. It functions as a meat market, but on the periphery, you have a motley crew living round the oil drums: transvestites, transsexuals, a mind-boggling collection' (Tanner 1987: 598). Alex's passion for *Madame Butterfly* (which Dan shares), strange stories around the death of her father, even overheard TV news reports about gruesome murders which play in the background as she gears up her intimidation campaign, all suggest sadomasochism, an equal potential for murderousness and self-harm.

47 Some reviewers not only sympathised with Dan but went so far as to endorse his doubt. Failing to note that Dan had got confirmation from Alex's gynaecologist, Alexander Walker wrote, 'That Douglas never demands proof from a woman whose previous mistreatment by men can be read like a fever graph, is one of the movie's major improbabilities.' For Walker, the pregnancy announcement was just the bait in 'the ultimate man trap' (Alexander Walker, *London Evening Standard*, 14 December 1988: 32–3).

48 Adrian Lyne discussing Douglas in his special introductory segment appended to *Fatal Attraction*, part of the Paramount Directors Signature Series, released in Britain by CIC Video.

49 Alex Walker also wondered that Dan 'can't see through to the back of her sociopathic mind which is sharper by far than his', whilst Duane Byrge saw intellect as one of Alex's weapons (*The Hollywood Reporter*, 14 September 1987: 11). Hoberman wrote that 'For a high-powered lawyer, he seems strangely fuzzy-tongued, ineptly explaining his whereabouts to his unsuspecting wife, and he's pointedly non-predatory. . . . Although she's the self-destructive one, he's set up to be the passive victim' (*Village Voice*, 29 September 1987: 68).

50 In another context Lyne has said: 'He's a vulnerable man, but he always played macho. In this he plays a loser and it was a real conflict for him to reveal that vulnerability' (Lawson 1993: 180).

51 Another change which took place in the rewrite-shift between versions of James Deardon's script from *Affairs of the Heart* to *Fatal Attraction* which has a bearing on Alex as arch-*femme fatale* is her name change. Though Alex started life as Eve Rubin (in *Affairs of the Heart*), she ends up Anglicised as Forest but also masculinised as Alex. The racial shift from Jew (Rubin) to WASP (Forest) has the effect of making her a less 'othered' monster: the story becomes that of WASP versus WASP, not WASP demonising and then dispatching Jew.

52 James Dearden, *Affairs of the Heart*, first draft script, pp. 123–4, author's own copy.

53 Adrian Lyne is obviously fond of female suicide as a dramatic conclusion or plot-point which sets the hero free. In the original ending of *9½ Weeks* Elizabeth (Kim Basinger) had been persuaded by John (Mickey Rourke) to kill herself, and in *Lolita* the eponymous heroine's mother tops herself too.

54 Adrian Lyne on the Paramount Directors Signature Series of *Fatal Attraction*.

55 Lauding the glowing Anne Archer, a female journalist in the *Daily Mirror*'s Mirror Women section (targeted at older women and wives) wrote, 'She's angry, sexy, intelligent and proves to be the strong one in the end' (Taylor 1988: 1).

56 She continues: 'Freud speaks in many of his works of the strange relationship between the impulse of destruction, how the sadistic impulse (see *Civilization and its Discontents*) may be an expression of Eros – but an Eros concerned with the self and its survival.' If *Fatal Attraction* plays out a dynamic between Eros and Thanatos, Alex might be said to manifest both.

57 Douglas's character Nick is also subordinated to other men, however – whilst his partner Gus is 'Pop', he is 'Son'.

58 Which might connect *Basic Instinct* quite closely to the interpretation of *Total Recall* as the dream/implant of Arnold Schwarzenegger's character.

59 'I just tried to avoid any script that was based on dialogue, because . . . [dialogue] cannot be your favorite thing when you go to a country where you know the language only partially. And so I avoided that and concentrated on films that have a strong visual impact' (Shea and Hennings 1993: 12).

60 *The Cool Surface*, a DTV erotic thriller rendition of *The Player* made two years after *Basic Instinct*, revisits some of these concerns with opposite gender positionings. Screenwriter Jarvis (Robert Patrick) writes a script based on his steamy affair with his neighbour (Teri Hatcher), who proofreads his work as it proceeds (he writes naked, at an Eszterhas-style old-fashioned typewriter). When she asks him what happens at the end he replies 'I kill you', provoking her question 'Do you fuck me to death?' At the end of the film, as he embarks on his next screenplay, he does kill her (though not through sex), then hooks up with a woman who looks just like her – his next subject, his next lover, his next victim.

61 J. Hoberman noted a theme of 'beleaguered patriarchy' also haunting *Fatal Attraction*: 'when Close and Douglas exchange family confidences, it's of troubled memories of their respective fathers' (*Village Voice*, 29 September 1987: 68).

62 Tom's failure to control women is in proportion to his reliance on them. One reviewer noted that 'After the assault, he's so clueless about office politics that he calls Susan to help him figure out what to do. And when he can't reach her, he goes to his secretary and asks what she thinks Susan would tell him to do' (Hinson 1994).

63 Michael Douglas as the edible object of the carnivore seems to be a resonant metaphor for his 'sitting duck' passivity. Reviewing *Fatal Attraction*, Alexander Walker notes that the pet rabbit of that film is 'stewed in its own juice, like Michael Douglas, but at an even higher temperature' (1988: 32).

64 The short, ominous scene which follows Tom's legal victory features Meredith reinforcing the 'no idea' line: 'You know I almost feel sorry for him. He has no idea does he?'

65 This scene, for Tasker, 'expresses a fear that the hero might be produced as object of (homo)sexual (as well as heterosexual) attentions' (1998: 133).

66 See also Tasker's reading of this scene as one in which offers 'a variant of liberal feminism'; 'Rather than oppose good women in the home to bad women at work, *Disclosure* opposed good, supportive women at work . . . with the aggressively sexual Meredith' (1998: 132).

67 'Fagel Attraction', Series 4, episode 22, of NBC's *Will & Grace*, first aired on 24 April 2002, directed by James Burrows.

68 Gershon is well aware that *Showgirls* has sealed her star persona: '[Gershon:] . . . that movie will follow me to my grave. [Interviewer Charles Isherwood:] Yeah, you'll have won your third Oscar – [Gershon:] And they'll say, can we talk a

little about Showgirls?' (Isherwood, Charles: 'Gina Gershon', *E-Online* interview, www.eonline.com/Celebs/Qa/Gershon/).

69 In her review of *Bound* Judith Halberstram criticises the casting of Gershon, not because the performance is poor but because of *Showgirls*' legacy: 'Everything [about the performance] is right except for, well, Gina. There's still a show-girl lurking beneath the grime and a vixen behind the lone wolf' (1997: 14, quoted by Noble 1998: 32).

70 Co-director Andy Wachowski reported to a group of gay journalists that they had hoped to have actresses 'lining up around the block to be in this movie', but when they read the sex-scene, 'the script would go flying out of the window' (Crockett 1997). Tilly also reported, 'You would not believe how many young actresses – B-list actresses – refused to come in and read for this movie because of the lesbian love scene' (Horkins 1997: 55). It may, of course, be that any hint of lesbian screen-willingness would ghettoise a B-actress in the kind of softcore flesh-fare lesbian-ism-for-men spectacles which she is striving to escape; far easier to commute into and out of lesbian roles when you are a hip A-lister like Gershon. However, Gershon has also said, 'As an actress, I have one rule for myself . . . F—— the rules' (Svetkey 1996). Nick Cassavetes (1997) asked her, 'Haven't you risked becoming a poster girl for nudity or lesbianism?' To which she replied, 'I'd be really proud to be the poster girl for lesbianism.'

71 Yet perhaps it may still only be possible to be a celebrity lesbian if you're not actu-ally one – see Susie Bright's 'Famous Lesbian Dilemmas' (1990: 145–9), which begins: 'Name a lesbian celebrity. Now name two lesbian celebrities. Getting stuck?' There may be more lesbian celebrities around post-Ellen DeGeneres and Anne Heche, but it is still far safer in Hollywood to be professionally lesbian and personally heterosexual.

72 See, for example, Gina Gershon: an unofficial tribute (http://www.geocities.com/Paris/LeftBank/7614/gershon/gina.html), The Gina Gershon Sanctuary (http://soft-butchdyke.tripod.com/index_m.htm) and The Gina Gershon Shrine (apparently a heterosexually convened site, in its subtitling 'The only woman I would give up all men for'; http://www.marianstuff.com/ginagershon.shtml). There are dozens of other websites dedicated solely to providing downloadable screensavers and other images of Gershon, reinforcing the fan obsession with body and an image which is visually available for both sexes. See also the eulogy to *Bound* at the Lesbian Flicks website (http://glweb.com/lesbianflicks/movies.html).

73 Paul McDonald discusses internet promotion of celebrity (2003: 29–44) in the context of contemporary star studies.

74 Foster Hirsch sees '*noir* and homosexuality [as] a negative match' (1981: 204–5), despite his observation that, in *noir*, homosexuality is 'disruptive and dangerous': 'On virtually every occasion in which homosexuality appears in *noir*, it has been branded as the narrative's *noir* element, the source of aberrant, criminal behaviour' (1987: 204). One would have thought that this would make homosexuality *noir*'s sexuality of choice, given the genre's obsession with aberration.

75 Gershon is explicit about the identificatory shift required when jumping into the male role: 'forget the lesbians. . . . You don't often get to play the hero. It's a tra-ditional male role. I get the girl. I get the money. . . . Corky reminded me of the guys I used to get obsessed with. I thought by playing her I wouldn't be so obsessed with them any more' (Iley 1997: 21).

76 Lisa Schwarzbaum, 'Girlie Movie: Gina Gershon and Jennifer Tilly are *Bound* to Please', *Entertainment Weekly*, 11 October 1996, p. 72, quoted by Kessler (2001: 22).

77 Of the 1998 Monique Parent vehicle *Dark Secrets*, the softcore review site 'This is Sexy?' writes: 'This film's one redeeming quality . . . is a fantastic scene with Julie Strain and Parent. Oh my goodness. Boys, pull down the shades and make sure the door is locked – this one's gonna get ya' (archived at http://www.thisissexy.net/).

78 This is not to say that lesbians cannot enjoy watching DTV erotic thrillers, or that the actresses involved did not enjoy what they were doing. But much lesbian porn marketed specifically for women themselves self-consciously appears under the 'by women, for women' rubric, using lesbian models, photographers, editorial staff. Nothing could be further from the values and images of the Axis brand, not to say the 'higher' lesbianism of *Basic Instinct*.

79 Brian Johnson, 'Killer Movies', *Macleans*, 30 March 1992, p. 50. Quoted by Holmlund (1994: 48).

80 www.askmen.com/women/actress_60/95b_gina_gershon.html.

81 For Lynda Hart, by contrast, *Basic Instinct* insists on 'erotic triads', playing with and playing out a *ménage-à-trois* which fulfils the vacillations of male desire, in which the male is partnered by a fantastically double feminine figure: 'one who's desire is "like" his (the "lesbian" in a masculine imaginary that can only think homosexuality as heterosexuality) and one who is different (the straight woman)'. Erotic thriller lesbians are also subject to this vision, set against straight women but also 'straightened' by the readings of the male (diegetic and cinematic) audience' (Hart 1994: 134). Kessler's argument shows that this is not the case with *Bound*, in which the potential for heterosexual male readings and authentically lesbian ones coexist and conspire to produce maximum box office.

82 Kessler, quoting Alan Frutkin, 'Bonnie and Bonnie', *The Advocate* 689, 5 September 1995, 55–7.

83 See online OED, http://dictionary.oed.com for full definitions of bitch as noun and verb.

84 Which Julie Burchill asserts is a devaluation of the term (2004: 3).

85 Farber continues: 'What the film seems to say . . . is that the obsessions of materialistic, success-oriented parents lead to violence and corruption; the fruit of ambition is murder' (1999: 54). We might also recall *Final Analysis*, in which Uma Thurman inherits the mantle of the *femme fatale* on the death of her sister.

86 Newman does, however, distinguish between what Fiorentino was given on the page and the subtleties she extracts from it in performance: 'Bridget occasionally overplays her sweetness act when manipulating lesser men, but Fiorentino always stirs in enough underlying contempt to signal the character's belief that the fools she dupes are not worth the effort of a really convincing imposture', adding that performance also enables *The Last Seduction*'s unique 'sympathy for the Devil' quality: 'It is entirely due to Fiorentino's performance that she is as fascinating as she is rotten' (1994).

87 Source uncredited, archived at The Unofficial Homepage of Linda Fiorentino, http://www.geocities.com/Hollywood/Academy/6215/Interview.html.

88 'Have you ever been screwed over by a guy? Did he cheat on you? Use you? Take your money? Then, welcome to The Last Seduction Club' (http://www.geocities.com/rodeodrive/2188/index.html).

89 As Warner points out, even blondes like Monroe embody a contradiction, part-'winsome dumb babyish' (her hair recalling 'the fluffy down of some children's heads, or baby chicks, or ducklings'), part-knowing sexiness (1995: 372).

90 This is discussed by Bram Dijkstra in chapter 5 of *Evil Sisters: The Threat of Female Sexuality in Twentieth Century Culture* (1996).

91 See, for instance, Gritten (1996: 32) and Davis (1991: 37), though there are many more.

92 Dyer writes: 'There is a considerable emphasis on narcissism in Monroe's image. She is often shown caressing herself. . . . Readiness and narcissism both work aspects of male sexuality into female sexuality' (1987: 53).

93 Describing the distress she felt performing the murder sequences in *Basic Instinct*: 'I cried, I fought with Paul and all the women on the show came and sat on the set with me. Lots of women came onto the set and we moved in a pack the entire day, and these women kept saying "Don't you get near her" to Paul. I mean, this female

energy just came out and they made a line around the side of the set to protect me' (Cooney 1992: 60).

94 An eighteenth-century reference presents glamour as a magical/demonic power which plays with what and how you see: 'When devils, wizards or jugglers deceive the sight, they are said to cast glamour o'er the eyes of the spectator.' Stone seems to understand this when she says, 'I've never really thought I was a great beauty, just a great magician. You can create an illusion of glamour' (quoted in Campbell 1994: 58).

95 Beau to Monroe's Cherie in *Bus Stop*: 'Look at her gleaming there so pale and white' (Dyer 1986: 45).

96 Biographical statement produced in the *Police Academy 4* press pack, archived in the British Film Institute Library, dated August 1987.

97 Stone's 'natural' style, a quality almost as indefinable as charisma, is discussed by Epstein (2000).

98 Numerous reports repeat this fact of stardom: see for instance, Miller (1996: 11), Jones (1995: 2), Mars-Jones (1993: 18), Goodman (1994: 32); 'Cover Up', *Sunday Telegraph*, 7 April 1996, p. 12.

99 Perhaps she also avenges Levin's Rosemary, exposing the secret goings-on of the apartment building which renders what ought to be safe (home) ultimately danger-ous. The paranoid woman's tale, Doane tells us, engages in 'a defamiliarization, a denaturalization of what is seemingly most familiar and most natural – the spaces and components of the home' (1987: 137). This defamiliarisation of home might also constitute a form of the uncanny for women's genres.

100 His name may also echo porn and sex-industry Svengali Chuck Traynor.

101 However, in a detailed reading of the nuances of Stone's performance style, Susan Knobloch (2001) reads all of her performances, not just the overt *femme fatales*, as inflected with active violence.

102 The pale palette choice bleeds into her personal style: one profile tells us, 'Stone is wearing white: white jodhpurs, an oversized white jacket and a white see-through blouse' (Andrews 1994: 78).

103 IMDB respondent 'moonspinner55' http://us.imdb.com/CommentsShow?0116095.

104 IMDB respondent 'Asokan Nirmalarajah', ibid.

INTERVIEW:
DIRECTOR PAUL VERHOEVEN

Linda Ruth Williams (LW): You made *Basic Instinct* and *Showgirls* with screen-writer Joe Eszterhas. Tell me about your relationship with him.

Paul Verhoeven (PV): Well, as you probably know, my relationship with Joe Eszterhas was very stormy on *Basic Instinct*. I was given *Basic Instinct* after Adrian Lyne had turned it down. He had just done *Fatal Attraction* with Michael Douglas, so he was the natural choice. But he probably felt that he had already done it in some way. So it came to me. And at first I felt that I had to change his script. And Michael Douglas felt so too; he felt that his character needed strengthening because in the original draft he was losing a lot of these verbal battles with Sharon Stone. She was winning them all the time. And that was somewhat annoying to him as an actor.

LW: But that is one of the things that fascinates me about Douglas's role choices. He made films like *Fatal Attraction* and *Basic Instinct*, and he then went on to do *Disclosure*, all *noir*ish films. It's interesting that a star like him should be willing to take on these loser roles.

PV: Well, you have to see that in the history of the family, because Kirk also made some very daring choices, notably *Ace in the Hole*. And he was also the one that put a blacklisted writer on *Spartacus*. So I think that in that family, both father and son have made those kind of choices. *Ace in The Hole* is very shadowy, very dark, and Kirk Douglas is a very dark character there. And I think Michael, growing up in a family where those kind of choices were made, has never been afraid of them. Also, having lived through many problems in his own life, with alcohol, womanising, whatever, I think he knew all about these things, and they are all elements of *film noir*. The diabolical force of the woman, and the man as victim; there's a lot of that stuff going on there. And I think that's something that he likes, that kind of danger. Now of course with

Catherine [Zeta-Jones] he has two kids and everything is nice and wonderful, so I don't know whether that still interests him. But I think the *film noir* side *was* very attractive to Michael, and it is to me because although I'm not an alcohol fan, and I'm not into drugs too much, never was, I too had many other demons. Certainly, with the women and the possibilities of my own thinking I always felt that this was a terrain that I knew very well. In fact, you could say that *Basic Instinct* is an Americanisation of *The Fourth Man*. It's not literally, of course, because Joe wrote it without thinking about *The Fourth Man*. But it is me choosing twice something where women is perhaps fatal, isn't it?

LW: So did you think that you were revisiting that *femme fatale*, or trying to redefine her?

PV: No, I was not trying; I was simply aware of the fact. I described it myself as like a Hitchcock for the 1990s. And *Vertigo* is kind of dark and sometimes other movies of his are dark, and I felt more in that kind of direction. I remember, [cinematographer] Jan de Bont and I sat round, and Jan said, 'Well this is a *film noir* in some way' and that's how we discussed it. How are we going to do that? Are we going to use all the black shadows on the walls, of the blinds and all that stuff? And then we said, 'No, let's go for Hockney, the painter, and perhaps a little bit of Hopper. So there's a lot of blue there, bright blues and whites. All this is effectively countering the *film noir* style by making '*film clair*'. In one scene we created shadows that are vibrating. And Jan did this by breaking a mirror, putting it in water, and putting a lamp on it. Then he would tremble it a bit, so the water would reflect on the wall, and it gave a feeling of unease. So we were all aware that we were working in *film noir* but we tried to make it look a little bit different. We said, 'OK how can we do a *film noir* that is basically a *film noir* of the 1990s?'

LW: Following on from that, I'm interested in what your relationship is to genre. Do you see it as a limit, or as something that is enabling?

PV: I would say that, for me, it has been enabling because of the need to survive. If you really look at the European movies, you'll see that there is no genre there at all. These are stories about people. Yes, *Spetters* is a little bit about AIDS. But *The Fourth Man* is not really a horror movie, it's not an occult movie either. In some ways it's also a funny movie. So in my work in Holland I never chose genre. I have never done so. If you look also at the basis of all these films, *all* of them are based on books, and all of them are to a high degree biographical. Now if you look at the American movies, with the exception of *Showgirls*, they are all based on fiction. They are all completely fictional. There is not a certain reality to the narrative. It's not based on anybody's life. It's not based on anything that happened. It's *influenced* by things that happened. But my feeling when I did all those Dutch movies was that I was talking about something real. Of course, what first brought me to the United States was the offer to do *Robocop*, which was a fantasy. I think by starting there I never got myself *outside* the genre too much. *Showgirls* is perhaps the most *un*-genre-like of my American films, and it was the worst received. With *Showgirls* I did very extensive research. Joe and I went out to Vegas three or four times, and every time we went there we stayed a week and we basically interviewed everybody. Strippers, showgirls from the big shows, managers, choreographers, producers everybody. And a lot of things that are in the movie are based on reality, although the big line, of course, is *All About Eve*. But I always thought that basically, to make that movie more successful, I should have just had a murder mystery and situated it in Vegas, and it would have been fine. If we'd done that, I think we would have got away with everything that people became so angry about. I should have protected myself better and gone back to genre.

LW: So, do you think *Showgirls* was misread and misunderstood?

PV: It is a very cynical film. And it was misread. Myself, I was amazed at the *violence* of the reviews. But it was similar to the reviews of *Spetters* in Holland. *Spetters* had the same fate, although it was more successful, it was also bashed throughout. The extravagance of *Showgirls*, of course, was built. Like the scene when she goes into the swimming pool and he puts on the lights and you have these kind of neon palms in the garden. Well, *that's* the movie, isn't it? Everything is like that, everything is over the top. Every*body* is over the top and every location is over the top, and all the lights are over the top, and so . . . it was like taking the cue from Vegas itself. I think that was probably misunderstood. Or that element of style was really probably too much identified with the movie, or they were holding that against the move. But I was continually thinking, 'If this is over the top, then let's do it!' That was the feeling even when you were writing the script – let's push it one more up, you know?

LW: It sounds like you're saying that it was a filmed in a manner which was deliberately *about* excess, but it was maybe read as simply excessive in a different way.

PV: Right. And if we didn't make that clear you could perhaps argue that we failed in what we intended to do because nobody read it. Although it's read better again now than it was then, but I still don't know if it will ever be read as we intended. It will always probably be vulnerable to attacks because of the flaws that are inherent in what we did. Perhaps I'll see it differently in five years' time. I see it more positively now than when it happened. But if you get *such* a negative press, you start to wonder how you could have failed so miserably. I still feel that the film was very elegantly made. There are beautiful camera moves, the fluorescent lights, the costumes, the colours. It's a kind of hyperreality, like those painters in Holland in the seventeenth and eighteenth centu-ries, who would paint an egg and they would show an egg that is *more* egg than any egg you have ever seen. So this kind of pushing was something that we tried to do. For the rest I'll wait for the judgement of history.

LW: Did you see *Showgirls* as a sex film, or a film about sex?

PV: I think I felt that *Basic Instinct* was more an erotic film, whilst *Showgirls* was really about the use and abuse of sex. That was always the idea. It's not erotic. And I think a lot of people were also pissed off *because* it was not erotic. On the contrary, it was like seeing sex as foul. Because the way they use sex in Vegas is really disgusting. I think that was always the idea. With the sex in *Showgirls* there's always a goal. There's always a purpose to anything that the characters do. Throughout the film, nudity and sexuality are always used by the people themselves to attain something else. So it's a tool.

LW: One of the target audiences for some of the films I'm looking at, the more generic material, is absolutely guys who want to masturbate but are afraid of renting a hardcore video. So any film that's got that quota of nudity in it is perhaps going to be misinterpreted as a film that ought to be delivering on that level. Is that a failing of the audience's perception?

PV: It's a failing also in the filmmakers for not seeing that. Perhaps we should have announced that more profoundly at the beginning, clarified what we were saying. And it is also that MGM propelled it with a campaign that said, 'You're going to see something you have never seen.' And that's true. I have never seen that much nudity ever in a film, or so many sexual symbols. Or so much sexu-ality – open sexuality. It still goes further than anything you have ever seen in an American movie, in fact. And some of the dances – like when she makes the lap dance on Kyle – this is extremely direct. But I think we should probably have announced that there was dramatic material, what it was really about.

LW: But did you want *Basic Instinct* to be arousing?

PV: Yes and no. Not the whole film, but a couple of scenes, yes. Certainly the two big scenes. The one between Sharon and Michael, the long scene. But still you have to notice that the scene, which is three or four minutes long, and which we shot for three days with full nudity, is still disguised. Or to put it another way, the nudity is only possible there because it's also a thriller scene. Because you are continuously reminded of the first scene which was a killer scene. And all the symbols of the scene, the tying up and mirror and the way the bed is, are continuously signalling to the audience that, yes, they're making love, but is she going to kill him or not? So I was able to include all the erotic elements *because* of the thriller elements.

LW: So in and of itself it's obviously highly choreographed but it's also the sex scene as story-telling. And that's what allows it to be arousing – because it has to be extended in order to maintain the whodunit thing?

PV: Basically, yes. I was wondering how we could make a really interesting sexual scene that doesn't use dissolves; that uses continuously hard cuts and that has several episodes to it. The first episode is he does her, orally. Then she does him. Then they do it together. Then she ties him up. Then she's maybe going to kill him. So there's four elements to it, and it's like a symphony a little bit. And I have to think this could only be done for a length of three or four minutes *because* it is a thriller scene. I mean, it was always the idea for me to make the ultimate sex-scene.

LW: I was talking to William Friedkin about the violent protests that surrounded *Cruising*, which effectively recurred with *Basic Instinct*. There was very little changed in the gay communities' responses to what you were and were not allowed to show.

PV: Yes, absolutely, clearly. And I know that when Friedkin did *Cruising*, which was after these very successful movies like *The French Connection* and *The Exorcist*, he got punished not only for the fact that he made a movie where homosexuals show their dicks or whatever, but also because he had been so successful in the past. But it's interesting that Friedkin had such enormous protest when he did *Cruising*. I think a lot of things in that film were changed or diminished or cut, and a lot of the darkness of the plotting was lost. The ending originally was to be *very* dark that the Pacino character would continue on the same path as the other killer. That was kind of the idea, that he would be sucked in. Much of that is no longer visible in the film. I think it was an extremely outrageous movie. And at that time, even me – being Dutch – thought it was a truly outrageous movie. Nothing like that is made any more.

LW: So how do you feel about what's happened since *Showgirls* in terms of the possibilities for sexual representations in American cinema?

PV: Well, in *Showgirls* I felt that I was not so much taking sexuality in a new direction, more like showing (or *thinking* that I was showing) the total cynicism and opportunism that was a metaphor for a lot of other things. After all my orientation in Vegas I had a feeling that *everything* was about money. And there was really nothing else there. It was all about 'What part of my body for how much money?' I felt it was this dark pit, where people creep into Vegas and they creep out, but they don't acknowledge it too much. And it was sort of a pleasure to expose this for what it really is. And on the other hand, Nomi was a kind of prototype of anybody who goes over dead bodies, basically.

LW: It seems to me that from *Basic Instinct* through to *Showgirls*, there was a pushing back of the boundaries of what you could show sexually on screen. And *since Showgirls*, that seems to have closed down.

PV: The whole window has closed down. That's true. But of course, you must realise that it's not me, it's the whole society. You cannot look at this government and think that this is Lewinsky any more. This total puritanism, this Christian attitude towards sex – the Bush administration, perhaps in reaction to what happened with Clinton, has gone completely the other way. And that drips down onto the studios. So there are basically no scripts at the moment that dare to go into any sexuality – they're really difficult to find. And if it's shown, then it just says 'And then they make passionate love'. No descriptions, nothing. Whereas if you read a script of Joe Eszterhas, these scenes with Sharon and Michael were described for four or five pages, you know. I mean there was a *lot* there on the page. And to a large degree I followed that. But you would never find anything like that nowadays. It's like the moment a script is coming to the sex or the nudity, the writers are already onto the next scene. Of course, this country was puritan from the start, and I've always had more problems here than in Europe regarding sexuality and nudity. And it's even worse now because of this government, and the rise of the fundamentalist Right. Ashcroft is extremely fundamentalist, Bush is a born-again, and I think they all think that God's on their side. And since God doesn't fuck, basically, then we shouldn't do it either. That's good for a title for your book: *God Doesn't Fuck*!

LW: So do you think that means that there's no possibility of using sexuality to tell stories now?

PV: No. Which some people might think is a great advantage because they are anyhow pornographic. But there has always been a tendency throughout the film industry that the moment you do sexuality or nudity, it's exploitative. And that might be partially true. But on the other hand, it denies you the possibility of taking sexuality seriously. Because as an artist basically if you look at the work of Rembrant, there are etchings of him and his wife fucking in bed. And look at all the Indian sculptures, with erections and penetration – all sculpted with much precision. And I think we need that openness, or willingness, to accept sexuality in the same way as anything else in life. To say that this is as much a part of life, more a part, than any of the power-games we play, or all the aggression. What's the problem that we cannot show sexuality?

LW: Do you imagine that this is cyclical – that it will change back?

PV: Yes, it'll cycle back. But not if this president is re-elected. Then it'll take another six years before we can go in another direction.

LW: One last thing about *Basic Instinct*: Why do you think it became the event movie that it did? Why has it has come to culturally signify so much?

PV: I don't know if there is one reason. Of course there is *one* reason, I don't know if it was the most important reason, which was, of course, that because of the attacks of the gay community, and because of their behaviour in San Francisco, which was on the television every night for weeks you know. Basically, when they were cutting our cables and shining lights, and all that kind of harassment. I'm sure that there was a certain awareness of the movie that you got for nothing because of the problems. Also, *Basic Instinct* is a really good title, isn't it? Then I would say that the openness and the amount of sexuality were very daring, and people were perhaps craving for something like that, the same as they are probably craving now but don't dare to say so. Also, don't forget that what Joe's script did with the detective story was kind of unusual because, in general, detective stories are really about who did it. You have all these different suspects and one of them is guilty. And I think it was pretty innovative to have here a movie where it was clear from the beginning that it's going to be her, and then you think it's *not* her, and then you think it's the *other* girl, and then you think it's *her* again – it is constantly flip-flopping.

LW: Regarding the infamous crotch-flash; does it piss you off that that became such a big thing?

PV: Well no, it doesn't piss me off. Basically, I think that without that shot the film would have been OK too, it would still have worked. And it's a little bit silly that it became so important, and that Sharon made it so important by basically saying that she didn't know I was filming it. On the other hand, I think that moment would never have worked if the scene had been not so good anyhow. Because the scene is *really* good. The power-game that she plays, because she plays it not only with her crotch, she plays it with waving her arms and showing her armpits, and her whole attitude. The cigarette, the power-play, the way she basically plays these men and reducing them to dwarves. I mean, in that perspective, that shot was the ultimate metaphor for the whole scene. Like, *this* is how I play you all, you drooling males! I also know that when we shot it we didn't even think that we were pushing the envelope. It was more just something that we thought would be nice because we know she's naked underneath and she talks about it later. And when I said to Sharon 'Shall we do that? Shall we show some shot like that?' she said 'Oh yeah that's *great*!' I remember that I told her at a dinner in San Francisco the story of a girlfriend of mine who did that – it's taken from reality, from my student years. And when I told her the story her eyes lit up with diabolical pleasure, because she saw that was such a great idea. And so I think she realised immediately what the power of that would be.

PART II

SUSPENSE IN SUSPENDERS: THE DIRECT-TO-VIDEO EROTIC THRILLER

INTRODUCTION

The direct-to-video erotic thriller occupies a unique space at the birth of a new set of viewing patterns which transformed cinema in the last quarter of the twentieth century. Its case reveals a complex and sometimes confused relationship to both genre and audience: part-porn, part-*film noir*, all 'B'-movie, a hybrid form dripping with the symptoms of our anxieties and pleasures. Yet not only does the genre remain the most under-discussed in film studies, its constituent elements of home viewing context and softcore content are also almost entirely ignored, despite the ubiquity of both. The importance of home video/DVD playback is usually discussed in film studies only in terms of video as a distribution option and as an alternative reception avenue. The influential British Film Institute publication *The Cinema Book* acknowledges the importance for film of the video market (providing the powerful statistic that by 1992 '$11 billion dollars was generated from this area as opposed to $5 billion from theatrical release' [Cook and Bernink 1999: 104]), but spends only a single paragraph (out of 406 pages) discussing home viewing.[1] One writer argues that 'In order to recoup massive production and marketing budgets, movies now have only one audience – the global audience' (Stables 1998: 165), a homogenising statement which may characterise the world of the blockbuster, but entirely ignores the fragmentation of audiences and niche markets which followed the development of video in the 1980s, and the proliferation of digital and other imaging systems which developed later. Television theorists read video as an alternative mode for delivering TV, whilst video artists enthuse about the revolutionary potential of independent, community and avant-garde video production (Cubitt 1991). The video rental and retail marketplace is rarely discussed as a factor in film form; indeed, even though the contemporary B-movie is also a form of independent movie-making, it attracts little of the art-house prestige of the American indie scene. Indeed, whilst the more hip indie companies in the 1990s, making offbeat or 'smart' movies, got absorbed in corporate takeovers, many B-movie production houses working off-Hollywood[2] remained truly independent. The case of Axis Films International will form one focus for this chapter, described by Gernert and Garroni above as almost a three-man show. Axis made successful (if not very 'indie-looking') erotic thrill-ers from 1989 to 1995, when Miramax (who produced some of the most indie-looking movies of recent times) were actually being absorbed into the Disney monolith. A further underdeveloped area is video (or, more recently, DVD and laserdisc) as a way of viewing movies; the direct-to-video film as a form in its own right is almost entirely left to fan enthusiasts, despite the fact that 'During the mid-1990s, DTVs became a seventeen-billion-dollar-a-year industry, involving more money than all the major studios combined' (Naremore 1998: 161). Softcore sex is equally under-discussed, although it too is culturally ubiq-uitous: softcore is (the academically more fashionable) hardcore's more nebu-lous sister. The DTV erotic thriller's proclivity for arousal threatens to marginalise it further. It is a genre perfectly fitted to the terms of its new viewing context, doling out sexual spectacles in regular dollops gauged precisely to the requirements of the home viewer's desire. Targeted at women and couples as well as young heterosexual men, the genre requires the privacy of the living room and the control of the remote to do its job best, and cuts its cloth to the constraints of televisual dimensions and the power over time and image offered by the VCR handset. At its most explicit the erotic thriller is unashamedly response-provoking, and is thus subject to all the scorn poured on both trash culture and masturbation itself. Laura Kipnis reads approbation against the two as part of the same political drive:

> The dismissal of popular cultural forms as 'masturbatory' has a certain tedious familiarity. It's a favourite chestnut of cultural elitists, with the guilt-by-association link between the two meant to prove, by implication, that popular culture too is mindless and self-indulgent, enjoyed mainly by adolescents, the intellectually feeble, and the lower echelons. The child-hood shame of guilty self-abuse is strategically annexed to confer shame onto mass culture and its audiences. (1996: 180)[3]

The films I will be discussing in this chapter are both overtly masturbatory (or copulation-oriented) and unashamedly mass-cultural, and whilst I will look at how these work together, I hope not to cast the same aspersions of class appro-bation which Kipnis laments. At its simplest this chapter maps out the history of the DTV erotic thriller, asking a series of questions, including, what are these films? (since we lack a map). Who makes them? (since the astonishingly pro-lific key players in the genre are almost entirely unrecorded by film history). Who watches them, and where? (since none of the above has yet been connected to what we now know about the home viewing market for sexual material). And, finally, what do they tell us about (our desire for) cinematic sex, its con-servative repetitions and surprising disruptions?

NOTES

1 Though there is a short section covering 'The 'New Technologies: Interactivity, Multimedia and Virtual Reality' (60–3), which covers more specialist forms such as interactive movies on CD-ROM.
2 Such as the companies detailed in hack director Fred Olen Ray's surprisingly scholarly tome, *The New Poverty Row: Independent Filmmakers as Distributors* (1991).
3 Roger Horrocks also discusses this infantilising of onanism, arguing that the shame of porn is bound up with the shame of masturbation because both bespeak need and lack: men are '"caught in the act", not the act of oppressing women, but the act of admitting to their own needs and their own lack of fulfilment. They are "wankers". That word is one of the great put-downs of men in our culture, hurled by car drivers at each other, and by politicians and academics at each other in private' (Horrocks 1995: 119).

4. SOFTCORE ON THE SOFA

First impressions of the erotic thriller in DTV form convey a deep and dubious conformity, reflecting US porn distributor Dick James' meditation on male desire: 'Go pick up a copy of *Playboy* or *Penthouse* and look at the women in there. This is what the average guy wants. He says he wants somebody with intellectual substance, someone more mature and all this kind of stuff. Naw, what he really wants is some 19-year-old hardbody girl that is sexually fun and won't give him the encumbering baggage' (Gaffin 1997: 36). Dave Lewis of Medusa Pictures, the leading distributor of erotic thrillers in Britain in the first half of the 1990s, said in interview in 1993 that DTV erotic thrillers 'are good quality B-movies: B for Beer, Biriani, and bonking. They are films which will appeal mostly to young guys aged between 18 and 30.'[1] The gender balance of the audience is something I will come to in a moment; what's interesting about this is not just that the B-movie status of these films is stressed at the level of distribution, it's that these are specifically marketed to be watched with a six-pack, a take-away and your mates or your girlfriend in your living room.[2] For what you can now do at home which you would formerly have had to do in a specialist cinema is respond overtly sexually to what you see on-screen.

It is hard to underestimate the seismic shift brought about by the rise of video and home viewing. Those film historians who do approach it are brazenly epochal: Douglas Gomery writes, 'The most important transformation in movie watching in the second half of the twentieth century has been the innovation of the video cassette recorder' (1992: 276);[3] he calls home video a revolution which 'would transform movie watching as nothing had since the introduction of the movie show itself' (1992: 275). Considering the attention film historians have paid to earlier cinematic revolutions, it is surprising that this massive shift at the heart of our cinematic moment has not been more extensively discussed.[4] Originally, Hollywood approached the advent of the VCR as an opportunity to sell tapes to consumers, and had no notion that the big market would be in video rentals.[5] Consumers soon showed that whilst perhaps they wanted to own some titles at an inflated price, they were generally more interested in renting a wider range more cheaply and for one night only. This is especially true of sexual and genre material, where the scope for repetition and the need for continual variation is high. The rental boom of the 1980s was a cinematic gold rush.[6] Tracking the rise of video rental chain Erol's in the 1980s, Gomery reports that the company went from seven stores in 1982 to 'nearly two hundred Video Clubs . . . and one million Video Club members, adding up to nearly a million rentals per week' by the end of the 1980s: 'Gross revenues for tape rentals increased from zero to $100 million in six years' (1992: 281). Revenue from video and DVD rentals now far exceeds theatrical box office: Stempel reports that the US figure for video rentals in 1998 was $8.1 billion, as opposed to $6.88 billion from cinemas – he also cites spending on video purchases as approximately $6.85 billion for that year (Stempel 2001: 172); Schatz quotes an increase in video sales between 1980 and 1990 as 6,500 per cent (1993: 25).

1: VIDEO VIEWING

Rather like car ownership, home viewing became instantly appealing because of its neat fit with a number of late capitalist leisure demands. The editor of one prominent genre video guide, Joe Kane, defines 'the homevideo credo' as '*Watch* what *you want*, when *you want*' (2000: x, original emphasis). No longer did you need to travel to a public place at a time designated by someone else to view a product in the company of strangers chosen from a small range of available titles which happen to be on general release as determined by studios and distributors. 'The viewer,' writes Sean Cubitt, 'remote control in hand, assumes a position of dominance over the flow of the screen' (1991: 5). Now you could watch in domestic privacy, at a time and place you yourself have determined, choosing a title from a plethora of proliferating products. 'Though subject to decay and fatigue,' writes Richard Dienst, 'the tape offers viewers a chance to rearrange, slow, duplicate, and even manipulate signals that once crossed through as irretrievable events' (1994: 23), a point confirmed by Tashiro, who reads the video viewer as active critic: 'Whether we like it or not, home video turns us all into critics. Instead of being engulfed by an overwhelming image that moves without our participation, we're able to subject film texts to our whims. . . . As home video allows us to meet the film text halfway, it does to film what film-makers have done to the world for years: turns it into an object for control' (1999: 367–8). This is the 'timeshifting' about which Cubitt writes so passionately ('the most poetic word to enter the English language in the last twenty years' [1991: 58]).[7] Here video becomes a liberating form which democratises media culture. 'Timeshifting . . . fast-forward, vision-rewind and freeze-framing reintroduce television to the qualities of writing' (1991: 58), an idea prefigured by Cahill:

> Home video has made the viewer a more active participant . . . home video recorders have made the relationship between the user and the software

more print-like and less television-like. The new video technologies allow the user to browse through video materials much as one might browse through a book. (1988: 147)

Gauntlett and Hill's study also confirmed that the VCR has given people some control over their own time (1999: 146–9), and there are areas in which consumers are able to access greater choice (it also may not finally be helpful to film history to understand this sense of control as merely a form of cultural false consciousness). The exponentially expanding back catalogues of a number of distributors is highly significant to genre fans; Kane insists that though the bucks still go to the distributors, the very fact of proliferating material has meant that ordinary viewers can now access 'a wealth of movie material that was once the private province of privileged film collectors' (2000: xi), and 'today's homeviewer can be his or her own creative programmer'.[8] This is, as Corrigan puts it, 'cinema as an adult toy (a domestic game rather than a public ritual' (1991: 28). Whilst video distributors go in and out of business as fast as you can say 'boom or bust', video titles stick around, by virtue of rental stores which hang on to tapes even when they've gone out of distribution, and the vast market for second-hand material, particularly on the internet. 'On video,' writes Kane, 'a title doesn't have to rack up instant powerhouse numbers; its potentially eternal shelf life grants viewers the chance to discover it at their leisure' (2000: xii). With home-viewing technology striving ever harder to catch up with the splendour of the movie theatre, even quality need not be sacrificed. Barbara Klinger is one of the few to investigate 'the impact of watching theatrically released motion pictures on television': 'Neither strictly cinema nor strictly television, the domesticated feature film is a hybrid form that falls between the analytical cracks' (1998: 4).[9] I hope here to fill in some of these cracks by looking at some films meant only for the home.

The individually determined, private space of video consumption had particular importance for the viewing of sexual material. Says New York pornography publisher Al Goldstein (who set up the adult cable channels, Midnight Blue [softcore] and Ecstasy Channel [hardcore]), 'Pornography is the real reason people bought VCRs before Hollywood filled the vacuum' (Gaffin 1997: 113). The VCR amplifies and individualises the association of movies with sex. Both Gray and Gauntlett and Hill note the almost secretive forms of behaviour people manifest in relation to their video players; Cubitt also writes that

video seems more likely to be used for solitary or slightly illicit viewing – by housewives during coffee-breaks, by teenagers late at night – which suggests to me a relation closer to that of the gambler to the game than of the nuclear family round the set. It is the use of the video as an alibi – not a surrogate for company but an alternative to it – for more or less intensively introverted pleasure. (1991: 42)

The VCR as a literal aid to onanism is thus only an intensification of its general significance as agent of solipsism.[10] Just as increased individual ownership of cars, especially by the young, provided a secluded space for sexual activity from the 1940s onwards, so the private ownership of the cinematic viewing space from the 1980s onwards enabled sexual material to be more widely consumed for openly sexual reasons. The highly publicised arrest and prosecution of Paul Reubens (aka children's entertainer Pee-Wee Herman) for masturbating in an adult cinema in Florida in 1991 highlighted the dangers inherent in sexual response in a public place, even if that place is widely assumed to be an appropriate location for such activity.[11] Video ensures that you need no longer brave a stag club to get your celluloid kicks (unless, of course, the semi-public condition of the darkened cinema and the possibility that you might be being watched by undercover police officers – as was Reubens – constitute part of the thrill). Bringing cinematic sex home with you in video form to enjoy on your sofa, perhaps with your partner, with the curtains closed, takes none of the risks presented by sexual response even in adult cinemas.[12] Gauntlett and Hill's study suggests that the video rental market corresponds almost exactly to the target audience for the erotic thriller – 'the 14–35s' (1999: 154):[13] the big market for movie rentals is also the biggest target audience for sexual material. The sofa here takes on particular significance as viewing-space, signifying domesticity and relaxation. The hotel room has a similar ambience, and many erotic thrillers have extended lives as pay-per-view fodder for international hotel chains, making the viewing space perhaps even more laced with the significations of secrecy (the hotel is precisely *away from* the home, and here porn may be used in different ways).

The temporal control offered by the VCR also has a sexual dimension. The confluence of control over time and control over location gave audiences the ability to mould the material to the determinants of desire in privacy, with liberal use of the fastforward and rewind functions. Tashiro sees the remote as a way of challenging the hegemony of cinematic time: 'Who, after becoming used to the flexibility of home video, has not wanted to fast-forward past bits of a boring or offensive theatrical film? . . . What we once might have endured, we now resent' (1999: 367). Armed with their VCR and their remote-control zapper, audiences ' "zip" . . . effectively skipping portions of the taped program . . .' (Friedberg 2000: 442–3): with sexual videos this often means skipping elements of plot to concentrate on sexual set-pieces. The freeze-frame and jog buttons have also had particular significance for some genre viewers; whilst horror and sci-fi aficionados use these to unpick the sleight-of-hand produced by tricky special effects nipping past the field of vision at normal film-running speed, porn viewers use it to isolate and highlight key images, as a focus for sexual consummation. Some research even suggests that the range of remote control buttons used by viewers is determined by genre.[14] 'I would say just fast forward through the movie and only watch the nude scenes with Diana Baron,' writes one DTV viewer,[15] and similar comments are commonplace on the web.

Freezing the unfolding movement of a sexual film when a pleasing image is identified has the effect of turning moving cinematic sex into something more akin to still magazine pornography. Perhaps, then, it is the video viewer who is emblematised by the geeky shop clerk of Jag Mundhra's *Wild Cactus*, caught reading 'Big Ones' before being hoodwinked by a *femme fatale* ('Wow! This is just like Penthouse Forum,' he says).

Video viewing has thus altered how porn is used. The man who would never have gone to a 'blue' cinema, offering straightforward satisfaction and a space for public masturbation, might now rent an erotic thriller, largely for the same reasons as the traditional porn punter – for sex, solitary or not – but for sex which can be had at home, in private. Phillip Brian Harper discusses cinematic pornography straddling an uneasy public/private divide: you may sit in the dark, but your response has to be measured against the fact that others surround you, that the images are shared, even though you might presume you have been rendered invisible by the darkness and the fact that your co-spectators' gazes are focused on the screen.[16] The rise of video has validated cinematic porn for a new audience who prefer the sofa to the stalls, and whose pleasures are no longer constrained by the fleetingly temporal nature of film *per se*: in the cinema, you cannot control or extend your response once the images you desire have passed by, moved on – once the next reel comes around. At home you control the time of the film and with DVD, laserdisc and CDI, you even control the sequence of narrative.

This has massive implications for how we understand the role of the viewer in the production of cinematic meaning, and it has profound implications for the metaphors with which we have traditionally understood the cinematic experience itself. It is ironic that as Metzian and Lacanian patterns of cinematic identification took their hold on film studies in the 1970s and 1980s (predicated on the likeness of the spectator in the darkened auditorium to the voyeur, fetishist or infant witnessing the primal scene in classic psychoanalysis), so different viewing patterns were being forged in the intimate, embryonic relationship between viewers and their brand new VCRs. Few would recognise their more active reading patterns, their control over the speed, sequence and duration of a narrative via their video controls, the social and sexual context of the living room, in spectator theory's images of the deliciously solitary and silent voyeur, pinned to his seat and defined by the dazzling screen. Yet it is not enough to look at audience without psyche, or psyche disassociated from audience: video sexual material speaks to and of both. The industry of fantasy has also driven technological change: 'The porn business was quick to recognise the potential of the new technology,' writes O'Toole, 'and was transferring its product onto cassettes in advance of mainstream Hollywood. In this way, porn was performing its regular duty as a key driver for the economic emergence of a new technology' (1998: 104). Video viewing is explicitly sexually active *and* implicitly psychosexual; both a socially and sexually shared activity *and* a solitary pleasure, facilitating actual sex and psychosexual fantasy. But all of these factors need to be read through the changing web of viewing technology, requiring film history to be dextrous and inclusive in the tools it uses to understand this history and these texts.

2: WOMEN AND OTHER AUDIENCES

DTV erotic thrillers are mechanically driven by the expectation of masturbation, which means that at regular intervals the narrative must be interrupted by the urgent need for thrill-delivering spectacle. There is therefore something interruptible built in to the softcore DTV form of the genre, which may also be present in the mainstream version but disavowedly so. Like the ad breaks which punctuate a made-for-TV movie, any film which flirts with the pornographic must accept that it will not be viewed all the way through in one go, if at all. The film will be interrupted if coitus (or masturbation) is to be uninterrupted. Television theorists describe the domestic viewing environment as characterised by disruption; failing to watch single-mindedly and reverentially has long been a hallmark of trash cinema. Klinger notes the different viewing behaviour associated with different viewing contexts:

> Art houses . . . recommend observant and deferential viewing habits associated with the 'art' experience, while the drive-in includes a host of 'unaesthetic' distractions associated with family life and courtship, from squalling children to concession-stand flirtations and backseat romances. The film remains the same entity, but the experience of it changes dramatically. (1998: 16)

The DTV home viewer is much more like the drive-in spectator than the art-house consumer (just as the DTV film is more drive-in B-fodder than auteur work, though later I will discuss some exceptions to this). Nevertheless, research has shown that doing something else in different viewing contexts other than single-mindedly watching seems to be anathema to male viewing habits: 'men state a clear preference for viewing attentively, in silence, without interruption,' writes Ann Gray (quoting David Morley); men 'spoke with dismay of their partner's tendency to be doing other things whilst the television was on, talking to other members of the family or interrupting them. This would suggest that there is a masculine mode of viewing which is concentrated and single-minded and a feminine mode of viewing which is distracted and lacking in concentration' (Gray 1992: 126). Though Gray goes on to warn against essentialising gendered viewing habits, one implication of this might be that men are only happy to do 'other things' whilst viewing when those other things are sexual. Sexual response or involvement might then be understood not as an interruption to the viewing experience (though the video itself might be rewound or freeze-framed) but as an extended, out-of-time interaction with it. From the other side of gender, and as if to bear this out, Greg Dark's DTV erotic thriller *Object of Obsession* shows Margaret (Erika Anderson), channel-surfing her way across some cable erotic thriller sex-scenes whilst eating chocolate or ice-cream, in the breaks around her boring telesales job.

If distributors market the erotic thriller towards their prime beer, biriani and bonking target audience, we might assume that this is because their representation of women begins and ends with the Playmate of the month, and their appeal to (most) women is limited. However, in that previously quoted interview Dave Lewis of Medusa Pictures qualifies the earlier point; 'Having said that,' he continues, 'these are also very appealing to women. You might say that they look at sex from a woman's angle.' We have no immediate reason to believe him, except that, the closer you look at the films narratively and textually, the more truth there seems to be in this. Jag Mundhra says in my interview below that his films 'have a very good following among women', and that he includes 'equal opportunity' spectacles, 'because the guys want to see breasts and the girls want to see bums'. Whirry has herself (rather hopefully) said, 'My films are not just male fantasies. I think they appeal more to women' (Salisbury 1994b: 64). Across a range of DTV erotic thrillers a number of female-focused positions on sex are explored in some surprising ways. One reviewer of *Killing Me Softly* (which despite A-list stars went DTV in the USA) praised it as a 'film that seems to play much better to ladies than it does to men', even though 'with most erotic thrillers you get the sense that a group of pissed menopausal men got together and worked out who should knock boots with whom' (Jameson 2002). Later I will challenge this 'sense' of the maleness of the genre in light of a number of interesting DTV examples. Writes Laura Kipnis

> There's been a lot of attention paid lately to the way pornography is transforming itself to appeal more to women viewers, and to the development of a new subgenre referred to as 'couples' porn, which focuses more on romance, foreplay, and mutuality. Just as the introduction of greater numbers of women into the work force has had a transforming effect on workplaces, the growing number of female pornography viewers has perhaps similarly 'feminized' porn. (1996: 223–4)

Williams bears this out: 'The pornographic marketplace,' she writes, 'is now almost as eager to address women as desiring consumers as it once was to package them as objects of consumption' (1990: 230).[17] This manifested itself in the magazine world with a (failed) relaunch of *Penthouse* in the UK as more of a style than a girlie mag, facing the competition of neo-men's magazines such as *Arena* or *Loaded* with an image that was 'devotedly sophisticated, tasteful – appealing to girlfriend as well as boyfriend – and fit for leaving out on one's coffee table' (O'Toole 1998: 137). The mid-to-late 1990s also saw publication of a spate of guides purporting to help novices negotiate uncharted territory, including *The Couples' Guide to the Best Erotic Videos* (Brent 1997), *The Wise Woman's Guide to Erotic Videos* (Cohen and Fox 1997) and *The Good Vibrations Guide: Adult Videos* (Winks 1998).[18] These invariably go out of their way to normalise the practice of watching sex films or using erotic films as part of a smorgåsbord of available sex aids in the post-video age. But even viewers writing in their thoughts to mainstream web forums have their fingers on the pulse of what constitutes good couples-friendly spectacle: 'This movie is sexy,' writes one Chicago woman to the IMDb of the DTV *Threat of Exposure*; 'This is a great movie to rent if you're going to spend a night at home with your boyfriend', whilst 'Mister Whoopee' tells Australian site EFilmcritic that *Sliver* is a 'Decent flick for a night of perving. Otherwise, it's a pre-sex date-movie.'[19]

Direct-to-video erotic thrillers have their place at the very softest edge of the pornographic marketplace, even as their distributors are successfully promoting them as ordinary feature films and placing them in the mainstream marketplace of Blockbuster Video. Changes in the fortunes of the porn video market in the late 1980s (Alvarado 1988: 4) resulted in the development of more specific audiences being identified as the market diversified. At the same time that the distinction between sexual and family markets broke down, softcore grew and penetrated the 'family' merchant, Blockbuster. Erotic thrillers are important here, as unique, sexually goal-oriented movies which are not hived off into the porn section of videostores. As Gernert and Garroni attest, getting Axis titles into Blockbuster was central to their campaign for a safe mainstream image. The films themselves also demonstrate an acute awareness of their role. When negotiating the TV movie-of-the-week being made about her life, the anti-heroine of *Body Chemistry 3* demands 'a woman writer . . . she wants a female point of view', in order to protect her screen image from victimisation. The movie-producer male lead of Jag Mundhra's *LA Goddess* sells his latest script (improbably penned by the film's female lead, ex-Playmate of the Year Kathy Shower) to his studio as an erotic film for women: 'It's new and it's fresh,' he says, 'it's from a woman's perspective.' This is undercut when the title's prospective director (fresh from directing the film-within-a-film which forms *LA Goddess*'s main story, an erotic western called *Frontier Foxes*) decides on this female-friendly film's first shot: 'Yeah! We can open on two big boobs!' he says.[20] Thus the industry parodies its own shortcomings and touches base with its contradictory audience base: any attempt to secure a female audience (women's stories, female-authored) must not threaten the established viewership of mainstream softcore: young heterosexual men. This is the terrain explored by Odette Springer in her documentary about the contemporary B-movie industry on the fringes of Hollywood, *Some Nudity Required*, which features fringe Hollywood marketing director Alex Kostich, referring to erotic B-movies as films which 'appeal to a male demographic between the ages of 16 to 40 and we just try to make it as erotic as possible within the bounds of good taste'. The same documentary features a male director arguing that exploitation B-feature softcore lets 'men look at women in a real safe way' – Scott MacDonald's essay on his enjoyment of pornography argues that 'Some of the popularity of pornography even among men who consider themselves feminists may be a function of its capacity to provide a form of unintrusive leering'

(1999: 195). Equally important (and underpinning what is happening in B-movie softcore) is the hardcore industry's increasing awareness of the power of female and couples audiences in the early 1990s. An Australian survey in the mid-1990s found that 70 per cent of those purchasing X-rated sex videos from mail order companies 'are ordering to share with a partner':

> What is offered for sale under the X-rating has, like adult products in general, evolved in recent years to meet a growing female audience. People are more likely to watch a video with a partner than on their own. With current prices for X-rated videos ranging from $20 to $80 it is understandable that they often become a joint purchase. (Patten 1997: 36)

Adult Video News cited the rise of the couples audience as one of 'The 25 Events That Shaped the First 25 Years of Video Porn', 'a boon for female performers-turned-directors'.[21] Candida Royalle makes porn for women and couples in a way which at first defied market definitions and predictions:

> In the beginning, the men in the business told me that there is no 'couples' market, and that women don't watch porn. 'Honey,' they said, 'you won't make a dollar.' . . . But I knew that a new market had opened up that no one was addressing.
> . . . Now people are saying 'Well, maybe she's right. Maybe there is a "couples" market', and they've started trying to make movies that are more palatable to women. (1993: 23–4)

Royalle has refused to include images patterned to a male hardcore rubric,[22] and has developed a pornographic style defined by 'a holistic approach' to sexuality 'instead of a collection of body parts' (1993: 31). Indeed, in the wake of HIV, some feminists have called for increased consumption of pornography as an alternative sexual practice and therefore a potentially life-saving preference (e.g. Carol 1993). Masturbation, writes Laqueur in his cultural history of the practice, is safe sex (2003: 413), and porn's primary purpose is masturbatory (Patten's 1997 statistic notwithstanding). Others see porn as an adjunct of woman-centred congress: Cohen and Fox subtitle their book '300 Sexy Videos for Every Woman – and Her Lover'. So is the erotic thriller part of a movement in erotic materials which openly play to women, couples and safe-sex practices? Even if the films' characters are rarely seen putting on a condom, perhaps the very existence of the genre as sofa-pleaser evidences a shift in mainstream sexual entertainment.

One view of women's traditional lack of interest in erotica has been given – by feminists and non-feminists alike – as their desire for plot-, narrative- and character-led pieces, so according to this position, hang your pornography on a ripping yarn and women will begin to watch. Winks, Brent and Cohen and Fox all sing the praises of plot-orchestrated sexual spectacle in their introductory material, and Brent even commits himself to the statement: 'men are turned on by looking at unfiltered physical sex, and women are turned on by experiencing the more emotional side of sex: candles, courtship, and romance' (1997: 20). The editor of *The Erotic Review*, a UK journal devoted to soft sex and literature, said that she still believes

> that the sexual desire of women is often triggered by a story or a romance, a suggestion rather than the actual act, which is why there had been such a phenomenal growth in our circulation. When we launched the magazine in 1997, 95 per cent of the subscribers were men; now 30 per cent are women, and I expect that to rise. (Reid 2000: 66)

Director Nancy Zala argues in *Some Nudity Required* that 'women are different sexually than men are. As you know, women like the spoken word. They like to be caressed.' Gernert and Garroni stress in my interview that they didn't make their films for women at all. *Die Watching*, a movie about a sleazy porn filmmaker who kills his models, features a video store assistant who says, of a punter who's just rented Greg Dark's hardcore video *Between the Cheeks 2*: 'You watch – next week he'll be in with his wife looking for something with Meryl Streep in it.' However, Shannon Whirry *does* consider women in the audience of the movies Gernert and Garroni produced featuring her, and has said that she has tried to inject some female-friendliness into her roles, emphasising character and caring, tastefulness and wide acceptability. Of her first reading of the screenplay Whirry thought her *Animal Instincts* character 'was a slut', but she performed her as 'a woman who was looking for love and perhaps didn't really know the correct way to do that and she was just trying to be acceptable and loved'.[23] When asked what she wouldn't do on screen, Whirry replied,

> Anything that I don't feel comfortable with or, I don't think the character would do. . . . [T]here is a point where you'd say this is above and beyond the line and I won't do it, things that I don't think are tasteful, that I think are repulsive, that I think are a man's fantasy and not a woman's . . . I don't mind being a male fantasy figure, I mind being a male fantasy figure that women go, 'Oh my God, no woman would ever do that.' (Salisbury 1996: 111)

Two DTV erotic thrillers *Body of Influence* and *Sexual Intent* try actively to address this by opening with a montage of women speaking to an off-screen interviewer about their sexual fantasies. *Body of Influence* (released in the UK as *Animal Instincts II*, though it bears no relationship to *Animal Instincts* except the same director and star) begins with four women telling a shrink about their variously active or passive desires, its first words setting a romantic agenda ('If a man is a good kisser, he can bring me to the brink of an orgasm without even touching anywhere else'). Other voices suggest male fear or hatred of women. One husband 'feels this fear before we make love. . . . I'm this dark void that he can't enter into without part of him being permanently changed. Sex is a very dark power.' Another woman tells of her husband's rejection: 'Is this conversation a conspiracy on your part to make me impotent?' *Sexual Intent*, on the other hand, begins with a series of what seem to be genuine vox-pops of women talking about how lousy men can be: 'I haven't had a relationship with a man for a while . . . I'm scared of men, scared of getting into that'; 'Men will always look at another woman while they're with you . . . they will always keep their subscription to *Playboy* after they move in with you. . . . Most men are so fully fixated on their own dick it's hard to compete'; 'All men are shit'. These voices, and faces, punctuate the film at significant intervals, giving extra-diegetic comment on the action and lending a sub-textual support to the actions of the women who band together in the story to get their revenge on a misogynistic conman. But pasted up-front and intercut with the credits, they form an immediate invitation to women, promising that this film will, in part, give credence to female perspectives on sexual conflict. This is something of a surprise given *Sexual Intent*'s video-box art, in the UK at least, which featured a model's near-naked body (not one of the film's characters) shot from behind, being disrobed by a non-specific male – a clear promise of softcore pleasures to come. This practice of using box art which features a glamour-body which never appears in the film is common in DTV distribution, selling a sometimes relatively non-explicit film as infinitely racier.

The offloading of sexual fantasy to an off-screen listener (in *Sexual Intent* it's a female sex therapist; in *Body of Influence* it's a male shrink; in the *Indecent Behaviour* films it's Shannon Tweed as a serial 'clinical sexologist') is a trope previously found in the more respectable Cannes prizewinning indie sex-melodrama *Sex, Lies and Videotape*, but whereas there the women's fantasies functioned solely to shore up the man's introverted sexual universe, in these forgotten DTVs the pseudo-vox-pop footage serves to foreground female desire. Whilst these sequences might function rather like the 'fronts' of legitimacy established when women allegedly pen letters about their sex lives to porn magazines, or even when women nominally edit those magazines (giving the guilty male punter the alibi that women are active participants, not just passive objects of their masturbatory desire), they also place female desire at the top of a film's agenda. Williams also points to pornography's increasing appeal to women as it leaves the cinema and arrives in the VCR. Whilst X-rated cinemas in the US are closing down,

> Hard-core videocassette rentals . . . are booming. . . . women now account for roughly '40% of the estimated 100 million rentals of X-rated tapes each year.' . . . women must be watching pornography in great numbers. (1990: 231)

As the erotic thriller developed in the 1990s this self-conscious re-orientation towards a female market split the genre further into specialist forms, developing erotic-romantic stories for women which were one or two removes from the neo-noir influences of darker stablemates.[24] A film such as *Night Eyes 3* minimises the *noir*ishness of its two predecessors, favouring a look more akin to a romantic TV movie-of-the-week. Here Andrew Stevens, the heterosexual woman's consummate DTV love object, plays a tough but protective security guard (Will Griffith) who also relishes doing his share of the childcare. Impeccably courteous, chivalrous, displaying an innate moral sense and with a super-honed butt, Will recalls Tom Berenger's policeman/bodyguard in *Someone to Watch over Me*, the working-class man protecting the more privileged but isolated woman in a nod to *Lady Chatterley's Lover* – a bit of rough, whose role in life is to serve, protect and display his assets. There are still regular sex-scenes (between Stevens and genre favourite Shannon Tweed as Zoë), but these are lit by candles, twinkling Christmas lights or roaring log fires, and accompanied not by the usual sleazy saxophone[25] but romantic piano and synthesised orchestral music. This is developed in *Night Eyes 4*, in which new Stevens-clone (Steve Caldwell as Jeff) romances the woman he is protecting (Paula Barbieri as Dr Cross) by casually playing her grand piano in a pseudo-sophisticated fashion: she then straddles him on the piano stool before they have romantic, firelit sex accompanied by non-diegetic classical music. In *Night Eyes 1* and *2* Will was single, but by *Night Eyes 3* he has an ex-wife and a daughter, whose presence lends a family-friendliness and enhances Stevens' profile as the housewife's choice: not only is his character here hunky and heroic, speaks a little French and shares custody of a well-balanced little girl, he *also* has enough time around the edges of running his successful business to have inventive and sensitive sex with the lonely Zoë.

If such a fantasy package has been put together to appeal to a popular notion of what women want from erotic cinema, it bears out the worst clichés bandied around about female desire such as those of Zala et al. cited above:[26] sex must be sensitive, justified by character and story, and above all it must fit in with family life. Nevertheless, the presence of prime beefcake in a heterosexual context supports the notion that the erotic thriller needs its female viewers; the genre regularly supplies 'something for the ladies'. Ex-model Stevens functions in this way in *Night Eyes 3*. By contrast, hack director/writer/producer Jim Wynorski (*Sins of Desire*, *Victim of Desire* and *Virtual Desire*) makes guy-films stuffed with laconic or macho, doughnut-eating cops, silicon-enhanced women, and marked by visual precision and a slick, over-illuminated look. Wynorski's 'by men, for men' philosophy means that he leaves the male beauties out of his casting: 'I don't believe guys at home drinking beers, watching television, want to see five good-looking studley guys in a movie. They wanna see themselves in a movie. So you don't put great looking guys, you put great looking girls, and you put guys that appeal to other guys . . . Everybody has a character they can relate to.' Everybody, that is, except the women in the audience. But Wynorski doesn't believe that women will be watching his flicks anyway. A successful self-distributor as well as director, Wynorski knows his market, but his genre films in general veer towards the T&A/horror end of the scale: 'I don't think some housewife is gonna go to the videostore and say "Oh – *Dinosaur Island*! I wanna rent that tonight!" No, they're gonna rent *The Way We Were* again.'[27] They might also rent something which takes the romantic elements of *The Way We Were* and eroticises them – such as *Night Eyes 3*. Germaine Greer argued in 2002 that what most women want in men is a good lover and someone to look after the children. But erotic thriller men should also suggest a bit of rough. In *Victim of Desire* (despite Wynorski's claim to offer little for women) Shannon Tweed deems cop Marc Singer 'the best of both worlds. You're an honest man who's just a little bit dangerous.' *Night Eyes*' Will fits this bill: Zoë says at one point that all she knows about him is that 'You have a beautiful daughter and you're a fantastic lover'; Will replies that this is all she needs to know (both know that he is also armed and voyeuristically inclined). Nevertheless, suspense in the film is partly achieved through the, more famil-iarly feminine, tension in Will's loyalties between being a good lover and being a good parent: employed to keep Tweed's house secure, he forfeits his own family time, leaves his home vulnerable and his daughter Natalie is snatched. (This is effectively a male version of the female melodrama trope, which teaches heroines such as Mildred Pierce that illicit sexual activity brings dire domestic consequences.) Despite the final tableau of Will, Zoë and Natalie – a pseudo-family unit looking out from Mulholland Drive over the nightscape of Los Angeles[28] – it seems that Will can't quite have it all, as both his job and his extra-curricular sex life have patently got in the way of competent fathering. This is a sentiment which may have a more acute resonance for older female viewers (torn between work and parenting but happy to watch a *male* character who recognises this) than the 18–30 single man targeted by traditional porn.

Romance notwithstanding, DTV erotic thrillers are still top-heavy with sex. The racy plots may arguably be there to give timid punters a more acceptable way in to sexual material, but the point is that in the end the extended sex-scenes are the point. As Kim Newman bluntly put it, 'these films can be rented out by punters who don't want the nice people at Blockbuster to think they like porn' (Newman 1996a: 112). Male, female and/or 'couples' viewers of softcore might then be more interestingly defined not by their gender or sexual orientation but by the fact that it's softcore rather than hardcore that they're after. A number of writers state the obvious point that the division between soft- and hardcore punters is not gendered: 'there are women who have said my films are too soft. Some women like regular hard porn, and think mine could be harder,' writes Royalle. 'On the other hand, there are also a lot of men who don't like hard-core, and feel more comfortable with mine' (1993: 31).[29] The softcore viewer is then defined by a desire to see images that tease rather than expose – cinematic foreplay, we might say. Or she might be defined by her desire to keep just 'this' side of the ratings. Or she might indeed appreciate softcore's disavowal of its pornographic nature. All of these responses are equally available to male and female video consumers, and allow us to avoid the discourses which, on the one hand, have it that men (in Dick James' words) want that 'nineteen-year-old hard-body', whilst women (in Nancy Zala's words) 'like to be caressed'. So who are these softcore viewers, and what do they want from their visual sex?

3: SOFTCORE: 'WHERE ADULT MEETS MAINSTREAM'

The trouble with softcore sex is that, like heterosexuality and whiteness, it is everywhere on display and all but invisible. Softcore sex is culturally ubiquitous, non-explicit but ever-revealing. It is also largely heterosexual and white and has acquired the veneer of 'normality', which pervades all expressions of white heterosexuality.[30] Any distinctive definition of softcore as a cinematic genre is particularly hard to delineate, because softcore sex is (almost) everywhere in cinema.[31] Richard Dyer has discussed the sinister invisibility of both heterosexuality and whiteness in two places. In an essay on 'Straight acting' in *The Matter of Images*, he writes, 'Heterosexuality as a social reality seems to be invisible to those who benefit from it. In part, this is because of the remorseless construction of heterosexuality as natural' (1993a: 133). Later, he discusses the perceived normality of whiteness: 'As long as race is something only applied to non-white peoples, as long as white people are not racially seen and named, they/we function as a human norm. Other people are raced, we are just people' (1997: 1). Softcore represents itself as 'just' normally sexual in a similar way: other sex is deviant, heterosexual softcore sex is just normal. It is not-seen because everywhere it peddles the notion that universal sexuality is (broadly) heterosexual (those lesbian scenes notwithstanding) and (broadly) non-deviant (bar the odd mild *frisson* of consenting bondage). Dyer's Freudian question 'What do heterosexuals want?' (which I tried to answer in part when looking at male heterosexuals and lesbianism above) seems to be answered by softcore, in its anodyne parade of nubile white girls and muscled men, none of whom ever get too messy or too anatomical. Softcore is the universal currency of western titillation. Perhaps, then, if we can answer the question What is softcore?, we can push forward the process of defamiliarising heterosexuality itself.

One definition of softcore as a spectacle might be that it is any representation of sex which is simulated; less rather than more explicit; which may or may not be there to arouse the viewer; and which is constructed in relation to the limit pitched by mainstream tolerance. The website *Softcore Reviews* defines softcore film as 'any movie that features simulated sex as an integral part of the storyline'.[32] Softcore is what mainstream audiences will swallow *en masse*; it can be anything from the aggressive, forced rear penetration of Jeanne Tripplehorn by Michael Douglas in *Basic Instinct* to the three-in-a-hot tub strip collections or flimsily plotted good clean American fun of *Playboy*'s products. Consequently, softcore can seem almost limitless, indefinable as well as indefinite. Royalle reports that 'In some parts of Europe, they don't know what to do with my movies because my work falls between super hardcore and nonexplicit softcore. They haven't yet recognized a market for them. Here [in the US] I created the market' (1993: 32).[33] Al Goldstein has said that he believes 'the real porno money is in soft-core': 'Hard core will never be a real player in the big game stakes in our lifetime' (Gaffin 1997: 112).[34]

Sometimes the perception of mainstream tolerance is articulated as a classification barrier: a film containing nothing hotter than softcore sex will receive an R or NC-17 rating in the US, a 15 or 18 in the UK. What is permitted with an 18-certificate in the UK also changed significantly in 2000, with the BBFC (British Board of Film Classification) extending its smorgåsbord of 18-rated images to include actual (consensual) sex and erections. Sometimes, as a result of a film's classification, the relative 'softness' of its sex will be reflected in where it can be obtained. Rent your videos at Blockbuster, and most of the sex they contain will be 'soft'; find your videos in the back room of an independent video store in the US, or a sex shop anywhere, and the sex will provide 'harder', 'realer' pleasures (the language of opposition used here to distinguish hard from soft – strong/weak, real/fake – loads the dice of preference in favour of hardcore). Blockbuster Video actively promotes a family-friendly image, so in the US will stock films with an MPAA (Motion Picture Association of America) rating only. The UK equivalent (introduced in the wake of the Video Recordings Act) is the requirement that all videos carry a BBFC rating of 18 or under if they are to be available in high street video stores or for sale at outlets such as Virgin or HMV – R18 films, the 'strongest' BBFC category, can be supplied by registered sex shops only. X-rated films in the US are hardcore only, but there is also the netherworld of the 'unrated' film, utilised by filmmakers whose spectacles exceed the R- or NC-17 ratings but are not necessarily hardcore (Brent refers to this category as 'Soft X'). Softcore sex cinema as a particular sub-genre might be said to be most at home in this netherworld – web and other reviewers urge punters to look for unrated versions wherever possible (in 1997 *Empire* urged viewers of the mainstream *Bound* to go for the uncut version, where 'you get a few more minutes of top shelf pervy lesbo action in the comfort of your own home' [Hemblade 1997: 132]). There is no UK equivalent of the unrated film, though 'uncut' may get an 18 certificate on video where cut achieved a 15 (*Bound* was 18 certificate in the UK in both versions).[35] Both unrated and X films can be obtained in the US at independent 'mom and pop' stores, the X titles separated into porn sections, but still in high street locations. One fact of the US video industry in the 1990s is that porn has enabled these stores to survive the dominance of Blockbuster, since they provide something Blockbuster will not. In effect, this means that the dividing line between hardcore and softcore, between what you get in sex shops or the backrooms of 'mom and pops', and what you get in Blockbuster and other mainstream chains, is determined by the sexual checklists of the MPAA or the BBFC.

However, in the US it is legal to sell unrated films. Why, then, do DTV filmmakers go to the expense of submitting their films for MPAA rating, even though they will never be shown in a cinema? Simply, in order to get acceptance at Blockbuster. Rame.net, 'The official website of rec.arts.movies.erotica', clarifies this, using the example of erotic thriller auteur Gregory Hippolyte (aka Greg Dark, more of whom later):

> Hippolyte films are released direct-to-video, and never see the inside of a movie theater. Therefore there is no need for him to spend good money just to have the MPAA Ratings Board rate his movie. But if you'll check, you'll see that his films come in two traditional flavors – 'R' rated, and unrated. Why is this? It's simple – if he doesn't edit his movie down to an 'R' rating, then Blockbuster won't buy it. . . . So who cut Hippolyte's film? Not Blockbuster – Hippolyte/Dark did it himself.[36]

The reason for this self-censorship is that in the video market, size matters. Rame.net cites a *Video Software Magazine* study which found Blockbuster to be five times the size of the next largest chain, 'bigger than all the other 94 chains combined'. With a market that huge 'you find out what their rules are, and beg for a chance to play by them. If the only version of your movie has no rating, then you've excluded a HUGE portion of your market.' Blockbuster and its competitors stock R-rated erotic thrillers on the feature film shelves (notwithstanding Garroni's discussion with me about Axis' ability to get unrated versions of its movies into Blockbuster); 'mom and pop' corner video stores will stock unrated erotic thrillers alongside the main bulk of mainstream products, and 'harder' products in their specialist 'through the door' back room of pornography proper. In the UK, erotic thrillers are universally categorised for video at 18 or lower, and can therefore be obtained anywhere. But since erotic thrillers as a genre are designed for the mainstream softcore market, even their US unrated versions usually go no further than is legitimised by an 18-certificate in the UK. In effect, the erotic thriller has done for cinema what *Playboy* did for print porn in the 1950s, as argued by Richard Dyer:

> *Playboy*'s greatest success was to get itself sold in the most ordinary newsagents and drugstores, taking a sex magazine out of the beneath-the-counter, adult bookshop category. . . . What *Playboy* succeeded in doing was making sex objects everyday. (1986: 39)

What the erotic thriller had done is locate a dedicated cinematic sex product in mainstream locations. With the DTV erotic thriller, the masturbatory moving spectacle becomes ubiquitous.

Much of this definition through reference to a border, a limit, is the result of hardcore calling the shots, hardcore being the measure by which softcore is judged. Hardcore is perceived as the most sexual of sexual materials and markets, because in it you see the most. A number of conventions which are the bread-and-butter of hardcore (cum shots, multiple penetration shots) have been traditionally deemed off-limit for mainstream audiences, consigned to pro-scribed distribution pathways and specialist market sectors. In one sense, then, softcore sex is defined as sexual spectacle which is anything other, or rather less, than hardcore. However, increasingly hardcore and softcore films are now merely longer or shorter versions of each other. Though it would be odd to call the BBFC-sanctioned version of *Deep Throat* softcore (the film was released on video in 2000 with an 18 certificate, shorn of hardcore images; an R18 version was also released),[37] more recently filmmakers have actively worked with two markets in mind: to avoid the censor and maximise audiences, films will be shot in different versions for different classification bands and different marketing outlets. Viewers are canny to this.[38] Discussing director Paul Thomas's filming of two versions of the sex film *AD 6969* (one for hardcore audiences, the other for distribution in more respectable outlets), Laurence O'Toole writes:

> The soft-core version means there'll be no erection, no penetrative sight-ings, no ejaculation, just backside to lap, lots of humping, face spasming and strategically placed cutaways. 'Woman's legs in the air, it's soft-core', says PT [Paul Thomas]; 'legs on the floor, it's hard-core.' Legs in the air the woman's genital area is obscured, and therefore so is any kind of actual genital contact between performers. Legs on the ground, the viewers see a whole lot more. (O'Toole 1998: 211)[39]

One sex production convention is to film a scene with two cameras, one 'hot' (positioned to record as much explicit detail as possible), the other 'cold' (dis-cretely set back from the action). However, as O'Toole goes on to argue, the trick sometimes risks a confusion of genre styles, which comes close, perhaps, to a definition of what differentiates soft- from hardcore. When a hardcore film essentially 'contains' a softcore film, the joins begin to show:

> In the hard-core version the couplings switch uneasily between coy mid-distance views and close-up shots of genital detail . . . This juxtaposition of euphemism and explicitness, even with the deftest transitional edit, can be jolting, like switching between different television channels and two distinct porn subgenres. A singularly made-for-hard-core movie doesn't need to finesse in this way, and a singularly made-for-soft-core is all finesse, and both therefore can possess a visual unity and harmony that the high-end, hard-soft shuffle struggles to emulate. (1998: 211)

O'Toole's 'different but equal' distinction between hard and soft notwith-standing, 'softcore' is also generally used as a pejorative term, from both sides of the wire. On the one hand, it is the term used to mock forms of sexual spec-tacle which don't have the courage of their desires, which fall short of the 'hard' finishing post – softcore, then, as a kind of *coitus interruptus* of visual sex, or an elaborate ritualised ellipsis which is defined by a refusal to show and tell.

But 'softcore' is also used in mainstream discourse to deem sexual spectacle smutty. It is a shorthand way of suggesting that the erotic has slipped into the pornographic, used by those who believe that there is a distinction, and would prefer eros to porno. Sex, they might say (in what sounds like a caricatured female voice), is fine as long as it's justified, integral to plot and character, non-exploitative, etc. Pornography is riskier, since whether hard or soft, it's probably there to arouse rather than entertain, inflame rather than inform. Softcore, it seems, may be everywhere, but it pleases no one. By this account, mainstream detractors think softcore is too close to pornography, hardcore-aligned detractors think it's too scared of pornography.

The unprecedented academic interest in pornography since the 1980s has concerned itself almost totally with hardcore pornography, save the few feminist writers who argued that *all* sexual representations of women are pornographic, therefore exploitative, therefore violent – therefore all pornography amounts to the same thing. Hardcore has had a racy sexual prestige which eludes its softer sister; it has offered intellectuals and journalists the opportunity to walk on the wildside. By contrast, softcore seems the Cinderella of sexual theory.[40] The obsession with hardcore has also meant that softcore is somehow defined as secondary, neither as interesting nor as primary – that is to say, culturally important, generically definitive – as hardcore, and (like the most considerate of partners) always coming second. And softcore is tainted by the stigma of simulation. If hardcore really does it, softcore merely fakes it. If hardcore hangs on the authenticity of the real view (that adolescent shock of seeing people *actually getting off*), softcore holds back, cannot show, kisses but finally does not tell. Whether or not softcore actors are (like their hardcore counterparts) really doing it as the cameras roll, they may as well not be for all we see. Does this sound like a feminine characterisation? Critiqued for being both oversexed and insufficiently sexual, softcore it seems (like women) pleases no one and everyone.

What, then, of softcore's ubiquity? The problem with positing hardcore as the primary defining form of sexual spectacle against which all other forms of cinematic sex are deemed 'soft' is that it belies the dominant trajectory of cinema's relationship with sex. The history of sexual cinema is not primarily 'hard'. Hardcore cinema has a limited and specific story, which has been well documented, from stag films to smokers to short loops and peep shows, through to the blossoming of the adult feature and 'porno chic' in the 1970s, growing to gargantuan proportions in the video age. For the most part it is, however, a story acted out in the shadows and at the fringes of the mainstream. Softcore has historically had a much more central role, and is intimately bound up with mainstream, mass audience cinema. Since its inception, cinema in general and Hollywood in particular have pushed image-making to the very limit of public acceptability. Stories of Howard Hughes' obsession with framing Jane Russell's breasts or Hedy Lamarr skinny-dipping in *Ecstasy* are no different from Paul Verhoeven's insistence on the fleeting flash of Sharon

Stone's unknickered crotch or Gregory Hipplolyte's passing view of a starlet's labia in *Night Rhythms*, both in 1992. Neither of the latter examples, when they were first exhibited in cinemas and on video respectively, were strictly speaking 'legitimate': mainstream cinematic big releases did not deal in beaver shots, nor had UK or US classification bodies by this point legitimised frank views of female genitalia.[41]

We might read that view of Stone's genitals as a moment where hardcore images are incorporated into mainstream, image-making – a shifting of the goalposts of the explicit, a moment when hard turns soft. We might also say that mainstream sexual representation – which is another term for softcore – is all about going as far as you dare, just to find out how far you're allowed to go. The Los Angeles Police Department Administrative Vice Division carries complete runs of *Playboy*, *Penthouse* and *Hustler*, as (so they say) a way of teaching rookie vice officers 'how the line of acceptability has changed over the past two decades' (Gaffin 1997: 115). This line is being pushed from the mainstream outwards, formed by a constantly moving boundary slowly inching open what we can and cannot see in multiplexes and on certificated video. There is also, of course, a constantly moving boundary in legal hardcore too, which also wants to present its audiences with the new and the novel within the realms of a genre which strives to show everything, so must incessantly reinvent that 'everything'.[42] We might therefore see these two limits, or lines in the sand of tolerance (between what's mainstream and what's hardcore, and what's hardcore and what's 'beyond' it), as shifting in parallel. But for all the moral panics and implausible, unproven statistics testifying to the massive-scale 'problem' of porn consumption, beside the vast sea of mainstream cinema hardcore is a small if significant current of commercial sexual representation, and it would be wrong to view it as the dominant form which calls the shots of cinematic sex. It is mainstream cinema, with its opportunistic appetite for incorporating the possibilities of more explicit representation, which pushes the envelope of sexual representation and acceptability for the majority of audiences. Why, then, has softcore sex been so disregarded? Why has that which is seen so frequently by all kinds of audiences been subject to such a marked critical oversight? Because it is so universal? The DTV erotic thriller has also often been criticised for being neither fish nor fowl (as in one critic's judgement that 'the erotic thriller is disreputable . . . an orphan too tame for "adult", too strange for six-pack Seagal's and too everything for discerning "art" audiences' [Rivett 1998]). Yet particularly in its DTV form, the erotic thriller has been phenomenally successful. In chapter 5 I will ask why this is the case, by looking at some of those responsible for its success. I will then move on to textual discussions which pinpoint some of the pleasures and surprises of the genre in its DTV form. Questions of pleasure and permission are implicit in my discussion of production and text below.

NOTES

1 See chapter 1 above, note 49.

2 Viewer responses posted on websites and quoted throughout this book testify that this is an international mode of consuming the erotic B-movie: only the choice of takeaway would change.

3 Though this is necessarily culture-specific. Despite global capitalism's best efforts, the experience of television or video is not (yet) universal. A 1980 United Nations report on information availability stated: 'In most developing countries, the number of [television] sets approaches that of households. In the developing countries, however, only a small minority of households can afford a television set – in some 40 countries, only 10 per cent of households have a receiver – and programmes are available chiefly in cities' (quoted by Cubitt 1991: 10). This is borne out by the international studies included in Alvarado (1988), which was also carried out in conjunction with UNESCO. Cubitt adds that by 1991 'the distribution of VCRs and computers in underdeveloped nations is even more sluggish than that of TVs' (1991: 11), despite the fact that underdeveloped nations are responsible for the cheap manufacture of the equipment upon which Westerners view films. The penetration of the UK market up to 1999 is described by Gauntlett and Hill, (1999: 141–72), who report that in 1996 21 per cent of UK households remained videoless (1999: 155).

4 Though perhaps this is an effect of how quickly we have become used to it. Even those in the West old enough to remember a time when movie viewing was determined by theatrical programme times and TV schedules had by the 1990s normalised the experience of owning and renting films on video or DVD; to those born after the mid-1970s owning copies of movies, whether on video, DVD or laserdisc, always has been a fact of leisure life.

5 Though whilst the British Film Institute's longitudinal five-year Audience Tracking Study (which forms the basis of Gauntlett and Hill's book) testifies that the biggest use of the VCR in the home remained by the end of the twentieth century the practice of 'timeshifting' – recording broadcast programmes off-air – this discussion is concerned with the delivery of movies on VCR. One implication of Ann Gray's analysis (1992) of women's relationships with their VCRs is that, since women are more temporally restricted and their TV viewing is likely to be more disrupted by domestic life, the timeshifting potential of the VCR could provide them with more control over their televisual viewing.

6 Barwise and Ehrenberg note that there were 'more video shops than bookshops' (1988: 78), and that the video rental and sell-through industry was 'the fastest-growing part of the television market' (1988: 79). Gray suggests that the video rental outlet at first occupied an uncertain place in consumers' lives, describing the hastily constructed new stores as occupying 'the 'twilight zones' of shopping, attracting the impulse buy or an unplanned extra when going to buy a pint of milk or filling the car with petrol' (1988: 218).

7 Dienst refuses to see this as liberating, since, despite this apparent control, 'who profits from the new and immense expansion in the volume of overall televisual time' is still finally 'paranational electronic manufacturers and entertainment conglomerates' (1994: 166); Cubitt also argues that 'the entire medium can now be considered as largely devoted to the distribution of Hollywood cinema films' (1991: 18).

8 DVDs offer even greater control of film form than videos, effectively enabling viewers to re-edit works and review them in a preferred form – perhaps this is the 'browsing through a book' activity Cahill describes. Examples include *Memento*, which plays in reverse time from the narrative's conclusion to its inception: on DVD there is now the option of playing it in forward-flowing chronology.

9 Klinger shows how home theatre systems advertising campaigns sell home viewing as a high-end experience, characterised by privacy, exclusivity and audio-visual

quality tailored to your specific interior, equating 'ownership of these systems with elite class status' (1998: 12).

10 Cubitt suggests a Kleinian analysis for understanding the psychological magic of video pleasure: 'these tiny manipulable figures on the video screen can be made to suffer, to repeat, to stand still for minutes on end, to be inspected, judged and spurned. Through video, the predestined and predetermined flow of the outside world, of the televisual Symbolic, of civilisation, can become subject to the subject. As such, they are voided of their "real" referents and become instead manifestations of internal states. Through video, you can play with yourself, renegotiate the terms the world has imposed through your entry in to the social, invoke the time before time was so ineluctably uni-directional, play among signifiers freed, at least partially and for a moment, of the social necessities of signifying something for someone' (1991: 42). Though Cubitt discusses video as sex aid only briefly, the resonances of this for analysis of an overtly sexual relationship to video material are profound, and require further work.

11 Phillip Brian Harper discusses the Reubens case in relation to a range of sexual liminal spaces hovering between public and private, such as bath houses and cars. He also focuses on the scene in *Dressed to Kill* in which Kate (Angie Dickinson) is pleasured by a stranger in the back of a taxi, observed by the driver in his rear-view mirror. Debates pinpointing De Palma as sexist exploitation filmmaker have suggested that Kate is killed as a punishment for her sexual activity. Harper's suggestion takes this further: Kate endangers herself because she misapprehends 'an effectively public space – the back seat of the taxicab – as a fundamentally private one' (1992: 98). Real-life Reubens also failed to negotiate this distinction, assuming – perhaps along with the rest of us – that 'one's very entrance into a theatre that screens sexually explicit triple-X features might well be construed as implicit consent to copresence in the sexual encounters that likely take place therein' (1992: 104). MacDonald (1999) also discusses the experience of the porn theatre.

12 The 'video on demand' innovations in the early twenty-first century takes this further. Participants in a *Playboy* broadband trial were 'able to bypass embarrassing conversations at their local videostore', accessing 'at any time a huge variety of adult TV material instantly and anonymously' (Hayes 2002: 40).

13 Though this statistic is rather catch-all: Cahill (1988: 134) reports that 'the cinema and home video audiences are drawn from different demographic pools. The median age of the core filmgoer in the United States is 18–25 years, somewhat younger than those who generally purchase home video software and hardware' (which he cites as the 30–39 age group).

14 Barwise and Ehrenberg write that 'many VCR users touch no more than half of the buttons, perhaps because of the low-involvement nature of most television viewing. The feature used most is fast-forward, especially to avoid seeing commercials. Replay and slow-motion facilities are sometimes used for sport' (1988: 79).

15 Derrick Dunn, advising on how best to view Jag Mundhra's *Sexual Malice*, 'IMDb user comments for Sexual Malice', http://us.imdb.com/Comments/Show?0111138, original typos corrected.

16 For Harper, Reubens misreads the line between public and private (though his defence attorney argued that 'Florida's indecent exposure laws did not apply to pornographic theatres. The statute in question says it is unlawful to expose sexual organs except in a place set aside for that purpose' (Harper 1992: 104, quoting Larry Rohter, 'Pee Wee Herman Enters a Plea of No Contest', *New York Times*, 8 November 1991: A12). Reubens is also victim of a shift from spectator to spectacle brought about by the presence of the police disrupting the dark anonymity of the adult cinema (Harper 1992: 105–6): though there to watch, and respond to what he watched, instead he was surveilled and caught. David Denby asks the cogent question 'how do you "expose" yourself, indecently or otherwise, in a darkened theatre? And if you did, and there was enough light to see you, who in the world would be

looking? We're talking about a heterosexual porno house, so the other patrons – men, presumably – would be looking at the screen. Answer: No one would be looking; except the police' (David Denby, 'Movies', *New York*, 19 August 1991, 50–1, quoted by Harper 1992: 110–11).

17 See also O'Toole on couples porn (1998: 106). Not all media theorists agree, however. Gauntlett and Hill note that TV sex is viewed more favourably by men, and 'Women in particular seemed either unhappy about sex and nudity on television, especially satellite and cable programmes, or dismissive of the type of men who enjoy seeing such images, or both'. The women they quote 'are dismissive of the need for showing sex scenes on television, and regard men's tastes in erotic material with some suspicion' (1999: 277). Gray makes brief mention of women viewing 'blue movies', reporting that both men and women hire them, sometimes to watch with partners, sometimes 'with friends, for a laugh' (1992: 105): 'I wouldn't hire one a week, not to that extent. But sometimes we might have one of a Saturday night and I'd watch it, just out of curiosity. I think they're funny' (1992: 105–6). A major source of conflict or embarrassment in Gray's study comes from women watching sexual material in the company of their fathers (1992: 116–17); women are also concerned about bringing rental material which is not suitable for children (1992: 220–1) – a major issue underpinning the UK Video Recordings Act. Gray also reports that the women in her study hire films with an understanding of what their partners like to watch, whilst their partners rarely take into account the women's tastes when video hiring (1992: 217–37).

18 Winks writes that 'Good Vibrations was in the right place at the right time to represent the erotic tastes of consumer group largely ignored by the mainstream adult industry: women, male/female couples and lesbians' (1998: vi). Brent – who goes to great lengths to prove he and his wife's suburban 'ordinariness' – promises to provide 'a guide for a regular man or woman who rents the occasional adult video for recreational purposes' (1997: 8).

19 See Stacey Crowley's comments on the IMDb user comments page for *Threat of Exposure* (http://www.imdb.com/titl/tt0276877/usercomments) and 'Mister Whoopee' on the *Sliver* page at http://efilmcritic.com/hbs.cgi?movie=781

20 Here *LA Goddess* might almost be referring to Hippolyte's *Undercover*, which does 'open on two big boobs' but is also sympathetically voiced from its female protagonist's point of view. Images of a woman getting dressed or in the shower frequently accompany erotic thriller credit sequences; if she's getting dressed (as in *Deadly Surveillance*) it means that the film can start with an image of her naked and then dress her in anticipation of the narrative starting. If she's in the shower (as in *Night Eyes 4*) her image will be cross-cut with an unfolding crime which imperils her. *Deadly Surveillance* also cross-cuts its credit sequence images, alternating between *femme fatale* Rachel (Susan Almgren) putting on underwear to a saxophone score, with scenes of a shoot-out in a warehouse. This promises more sexuality than the 15-certificate movie delivers. Axis-produced *The Pamela Principle*, on the other hand, simply opens with a close-up of a woman's rear, from the point of view of a male onlooker.

21 'The theory was that the fairer sex claimed to loathe porn but secretly craved it every bit as much as men. And if the inherent misogyny in facial popshots and genital ECUs were removed and replaced with soft-focus sex and romantic storylines, maybe it would appeal to the distaff side. Taking the theory a step further (since 'nice girls' don't watch porn, let alone rent or buy it by themselves), the idea was that men would buy or rent these tapes and bring them home – or maybe couples would even shop for tapes together' (Ehrlich 2002a).

22 Furthermore, Royalle's idea of making films for couples does not involve one member of the couple intimidating the other. One distributor, she reports, said to her '"I know who watches these films . . . It's the husbands who buy these movies, to show their wives what they want them to do."' Royalle continues: 'I was hor-

rified. I thought, do you realize who you are talking to? Here I am, a woman wanting to make movies from a woman's point of view, and you're telling me to make something that the husband can bring home and talk their wives into doing. . . . [A]fter that I started my own distribution . . . People in the porn business recognize now, though, how large a part of the market women are, and a lot of filmmakers are changing their films to reflect this' (1993: 30).

23 Whirry's gloss on her softcore work must also be seen in the context of the fact that by the mid-1990s she was trying to secure more mainstream, less sexual roles.

24 I discuss erotic dramas like *Two Moon Junction, Zandalee* or *The Red Shoe Diaries* franchise in my conclusion, and more extensively in 'Looking for Mr Goodbar? Softcore romance and the female sexual quest film', paper presented to the SCMS Conference, Atlanta 2004 and forthcoming.

25 The parody *Fatal Instinct* plays with this trope by featuring a sax-player actually generating the film's score within the diegesis, revealed lurking behind doors or walking a few paces behind the hero in key scenes.

26 The audience-targeting of this film for a couples/female audience seems to have paid off though: at least one female viewer has reported on the IMDb user comments list for *Night Eyes 3* that 'My boyfriend rented this one for us to watch', though she reports spending most of the movie 'either making fun of it (When Tweed says the line "I'm not even Zoë Clairmont" I replied with, "No, you're Shannon Tweed!") or pointing out the huge potholes. I didn't even think the sex scenes were that erotic' (Lori Ann Chauvette writing on the IMDB user comments list for *Night Eyes 3*, at http://us.imdb.com/CommentsShow?0107680).

27 Wynorski interviewed in Odette Springer's documentary *Some Nudity Required*.

28 This revisits *Fatal Attraction*'s final family photo shot, which unites the family in closure following defeat of its greatest threat, a single woman. In *Night Eyes 3* the single woman (Tweed) is incorporated into the family as a step-figure, and together this reformulated unit is explicitly framed looking out on a landscape which symbolises the *noir*ish danger they oppose. The implication is that as long as they stick together it doesn't matter that the danger still lurks out there in some other form. Lack of closure also keeps open the possibility that a sequel will continue this struggle (though Stevens' character spends *Night Eyes 4* in a coma, and no mention is made of his daughter or, indeed, Tweed's character).

29 One female porn user reports that 'Among the heterosexual women I know, there is a consensus that mainstream porn just doesn't deliver. A lot of what's on offer is far too romantic, or it's tits and bums stuff. The people who make it assume that all women are part of a couple. There's a real need for porn for single women. We want erections, attractive men, things that don't look fake' (Reid 2000: 65). Porn performer Nina Hartley sees women enjoying porn alone as an adjunct of couples viewing: 'A lot of women want to watch movies, but they want to have their first reactions alone without worrying about what he wants, what does he expect, what's he going to think' (Gaffin 1997: 100).

30 There are significant exceptions to this, which I will be looking at in my conclusion, particularly the development of the black erotic thriller in the early twenty-first century, including DTV titles such as *Trois, Pandora's Box, Uninvited Guest* and *Playing with Fire*, each following the DTV erotic thriller blueprint which I will lay out here, but with an all-black cast.

31 The exception to this is where there is no sex at all (as with some family films) or where there is sex and nothing else (as in some hardcore – although even hardcore has its softcore moments: all is not revealed always and throughout).

32 Website Softcore Reviews FAQ section, http://www.sreviews.com/faq.htm.

33 This is further confused by the perception of different markets suggested by other porn filmmakers: 'What about the plot? Is it really necessary? Again we turn to Joe. 'America, it wants the sex,' he says. 'The rest of the world, it wants the story' (Harris Gaffin talking to filmmaker Joe D'Amato, 1997: 197).

34 Arguably the most popular sex website is a softcore one. Danni Ashe, CEO and star of Danni's Hard Drive, 'holds the Guiness World Record as the most downloaded woman on the web': 'Danni's niche is what is known as soft core. No male–female sex is shown. Instead, model Shauna O'Brien will earn $750 for a little wiggle, a little jiggle and a little giggle' (*American Porn*, TV programme aired on 7 February 2002 as part of the US PBS 'Frontline' series, transcript archived at http://www.pbs.org/wgbh/pages/frontline/shows/porn/etc/script.html).

35 Brent (1997: 17–19) also discusses how US categorisation impinges on representation from a consumer's point of view.

36 Http://www.rame.net/faq/part9.html, accessed 04.09.00.

37 Also released around the same time were softcore versions of 'classic porn' titles such as *The Devil in Miss Jones* and *Night Dreams*. However, in these cases the distinction between hardcore as real sex and softcore as simulated begins to break down – these releases contain reframed and/or shorter edits of exactly the same 'real' sex-scenes. There is no question around whether Linda Lovelace is 'really doing it' in the 2000 UK video release of *Deep Throat* – the distinction of actuality and simulation has no meaning here (of course she is). But whilst we don't see all of the act, we don't call it softcore – in this case, softcore is a different genre altogether.

38 All the sex in *LA Goddess* is lumped together in one lengthy montage sequence at the centre of the film, perhaps making it easier to cut if censors required it. One Kathy Shower fan noted on-line of *LA Goddess*, 'if you intend to buy this treasure, get the unrated version, at the beginning of the film Kathy Shower gets out of the shower naked, and in the R-Rated version she covers herself with a towel. That and many other reasons.' Michael Joseph Chrush, IMDB user comments for *LA Goddess*.

39 This is a curious version of the infamous Hays Code dictum that in bedroom scenes all actors should keep their feet on the floor, for fear of inflaming too much if both parties were fully to occupy the bed. Paul Thomas has also directed some softcore erotic thrillers, including Axis' *The Pamela Principle* (though originally credited as Toby Phillips) and the voyeuro-saturated *Killer Looks*.

40 It is also the Cinderella of popular culture: 'Softcore Reviews' writes in self-justification: 'there is already an abundance of information available on [hardcore] films. We believe that softcore fans would also like more information about the movies before they buy or rent them, as well as information about the stars they love to watch. Often online resources (such as the IMDb) are incomplete, inaccurate, and lacking when it comes to user reviews and updates.'

41 Verhoeven saw to it that such could now be viewed under the respectable umbrella of BBFC and MPAA certification, even though explicit views of female genitals were otherwise beyond the pale until the late 1990s, even when safe sex for lesbians was at stake: *Well Sexy Woman: A Lesbian Guide to Sexual Health* could not show female genitalia even when demonstrating safe sex techniques. The BBFC had, however, been happy to certificate safe-sex videos for gay male and heterosexual audiences which contained erections (for example, *Getting it Right: Safer Sex for Young Gay Men* and *Seriously Sexy: Safer Sex for Young People*, both 1993), and had also, in a limited way, long certificated films which displayed erections for distribution to middle class audiences in art house cinemas (such as *Ai No Corrida*). For a fuller discussion of these classification conundrums and inconsistencies, see Linda Ruth Williams (2002).

42 Susie Ehrlich in the August 2002 *Adult Video News* roundup of 'The 25 Events that Shaped the First 25 years of Video Porn' described the Extra-Hard movement of the 1990s: 'Anal and d.p. became a requirement; soon it became the "airtight" trick (a cock in every hole), the ultimate-in-homoerotic-denial position (double-anal), mega-gangbangs, choke-fucking, peeing, bukkake . . . even vomit for a brief, unsavory period. We can only wonder what'll hit next' (2002b). A discussion of the close affinities between hardcore gross-out and horror gross-out may be in order.

INTERVIEW:
DIRECTOR GREGORY DARK

Linda Ruth Williams (LW): How did you get started making erotic thrillers?

Gregory Dark (GD): I was making very unusual hardcore films. I graduated in art, and I was trying to do conceptual art, and I figured a medium that I could use where people would leave me alone was pornography. And so my goal was to do pornography that was completely anti-erotic, where human beings were just disgusting pieces of meat but people did almost stage plays that were similar to Alfred Jarre, things of that kind – sort of surrealistic plays on video. When I came up with the idea of 'erotic' films I had originally gone to people other than Gernert and Garroni. The Samuel Goldwyn company set me in an office and investigated the potential of making these kind of movies, and they decided that they weren't actor-driven enough. Then I went to Heritage Entertainment and pitched the idea to them and they put me in an office as well, in the Directors' Guild building, and they set to work investigating the same sort of stuff. Finally, because I really wanted to get this off the ground, I went to Gernert. The original idea for me was to make movies like the early Roger Vadim movies, the French erotic movies that were more character-driven studies – that were in my opinion a bit better written scripts than we ended up working with.

LW: Was your impulse to explore this area artistic or financial?

GD: To me it was something that we hadn't really seen in the US before. There was the Zalman King stuff which was OK; I *did* like *9½ Weeks*. And I thought, maybe it's a place to try and explore some things. I learned a great deal from doing it. But it's very difficult to cast these movies in the United States because in the US there's such a taboo on nudity, eroticism – it's a very puritanical country. Despite what happened in the 1960s and all that, in Hollywood it's still somewhat puritanical unless it's driven by a major studio. I think Paul

Verhoeven probably had the same problem with *Showgirls*. And we face this continually.

LW: But from my reading of that period it seemed that up to *Showgirls* there was an increasing desire to go up to the wire, but Verhoeven really got burned. The boundary between softcore and what was beyond was blurring, and then *Showgirls* was such a critical and financial failure that *that* was the point when it . . .

GD: Stopped! Yeah. What happened was that there is a difference between what I consider erotic movies and erotic thrillers. Erotic *thrillers* are movies that studios make. Perhaps *9½ Weeks* portrayed that a bit, I think that was maybe a bit more. Softcore is where there are softcore sex scenes, simulated sex, that go on for two or three minutes in the movie and ultimately destroy the progression of the story from a structural point of view. This was my problem with the genre generally. And I've made a lot of these movies. And as soon as the softcore sex-scenes would start, the movie would stop. And you would watch these people who weren't really having sex, who were just moving about like this and that, and you're thinking you might as well watch your dog out on the lawn taking a leak. And that's what disillusioned me in the genre. I started trying to do things that were odder, we could say. I did a movie called *Animal Instincts 3* where the guy was a blind knife thrower, and stuff like that was more interesting potentially but it just never developed.

LW: But that film has some very avant-garde techniques running through it which is surprising.

GD: The DVD movie is becoming the place where you can explore things. The studio feature, you know, is a place that they want guaranteed money-makers. Whereas the DVD movies can be a little more avant-garde. It's becoming that way again in the US. That's why, in the US, there's a resurgence of the erotic thriller. The big agencies, such as ICM, or William Morris, or CAA, are becoming interested in DVDs, and they never were before. And there's a situation at the moment where the studios want to make an erotic thriller very badly. But the problem is casting. How do you cast in the US? If you're Lars von Trier, you cast with your theatre group, you cast a very different way than you would here. Here, you're screwed. You're left with the agencies, the managers, who say, 'What good is this going to do my actress, how's it gonna propel her career forward?' The problem with the erotic thrillers that I was making was that the acting was not good enough for them to be character-driven pieces so that the sexuality would come from the characters. They were in a sense imposed upon the movie as a formula, not unlike the Roger Corman movies of the mid-1980s. This is what we did. Now, my stuff looked a little better, I tried to make it a little more avant-garde but it still had the same flaws.

LW: Why did you move away from hardcore, where it seems to me that as long as you delivered the sex, you could do whatever you found interesting?

GD: Well, the budgets are very limiting in hardcore, and they were getting slimmer and slimmer. And there was too much . . . the stuff was just product. There was not any sort of artistic integrity to it anymore. And I then said to myself 'You know, I've got to be in a different business'. Even though I was an extremely big porno director. One of the top three perhaps. And that's sort of why I left. Also I needed more shooting days to do what I wanted, I needed better crews, I couldn't get them, and you're only as good as the people that you surround yourself with. And the people that do hardcore are oftentimes not the most talented people in the world. And so that was very frustrating.

LW: So did you see erotic thrillers as a way of moving into bigger budgets and better talent, that that would give you the opportunity to do more of what you wanted?

GD: Yeah, I think that it enabled me to *try* to do more of what I wanted. I had done a couple of action-*noirs*, science fiction *noir* movies between hardcore and softcore – *Dead Man Walking* and *Street Asylum*. It enabled me to work with slightly bigger budgets, better potential crews. The cinematographer that I worked with, Wally Pfister, has gone on to make really big movies.

LRW: And did you know at the time that these guys were going somewhere?

GD: Yeah, they were good. Of course. You can tell when you work with people that some of them are talented, some have ideas, and some are just showing up and collecting a pay cheque. Peter Denning was a relatively well-known cine-matographer who had already worked for David Lynch, Wally had worked for Corman, he'd done about eight or nine movies for him, and eight or nine movies for me. And you could tell that guy was smart. It's always a great joy to work with people who care about their work and are good at it. It's a partner-ship, a learning experience.

LW: Did Axis function like Corman's studio?

GD: It was very similar. I designed the company. Garroni was producer, I was head of production, but I kind of produced the first few films as well because I knew how to put stuff together, so he kind of sat back and watched me for the first three. I thought to myself that I had put together a company that could do that. The problem I had was finding directors that were any good, unless you could pay them. Good directors cost money.

LW: So was that how you became the Axis house director?

GD: Well, I brought the concept to Gernert originally and so I was allegedly a partner in the company at one point which caused some of our rift. But it's hard to find talented filmmakers to work in certain genres because it doesn't move their career forward. Now it's different when a cinematographer practises shooting. It's just photography. You can shoot naked girls, you can shoot car chases, you can shoot this and that, it doesn't matter. But a director gets tarred and feathered.

LW: But different genres have ups and downs. The most discredited exploitation horror films of the 1970s are now considered important.

GD: Oh, of course, like Dario Argento movies, if that's what you're thinking of. And it's also the case with erotic movies. Roger Vadim to me was again one of my other heroes.

LW: So why, then, do we revere Roger Vadim and not Zalman King?

GD: I think like if you look at *And God Created Woman*, it's a very interesting character-driven piece, with a fascinating young Brigitte Bardot as an actress. It was like people that were interested in acting, and again the eroticism came out of character. And sex came out of the character's need, rather than sex just being I'm gonna throw some naked girl in here getting banged in the shower. Even though Roger Vadim was certainly making exploitation movies in his time, and I think he would have admitted that . . .

LW: And been proud of it probably . . .

GD: Yeah, and been proud of it. So there's an interesting character dynamic to create the sexuality which to me makes things more sexy. That's why Playboy Channel stuff is like wallpaper. There's no connection to the viewer, no subtle, psychological or visceral connection to the work.

LW: What about women viewers? Do you agree with the idea that women will watch porn if it's got a good story and it's packaged in a particular way?

GD: I think that women watch porno if they want to see nasty shit, just like men do. I think it has nothing to do with women or men – the whole packaging of it is bullshit, in my opinion. To me, you know, I was just curious to see what women would say to each other when they're having sex; it had nothing to do with couching it in softness. 'Softness' is just people saying that women only like 'soft' things, and that's ridiculous. That's ghettoising women. I did a series for *Playboy* called 'The Profession', maybe three years after I stopped working for Axis, stopped doing erotic thrillers. And it was very hard – they hired me originally and then they didn't like what I did. My pitch to them was too aggressive and hard, too unpleasant. I wanted to do a series about call-girls and their tricks and their lives and what it was about. And I wanted to use real stories, and real research, and real people that I knew and see what this was about. I didn't want to make this romantic; if it's soft and subtle and beautiful at times then that's wonderful, or if it's about some crack-whore beating her up, that's fine too. But I wanted to make it about all these things. They went for it. And then they looked at some of these things and said 'Oh my God this is not *Playboy*, we want *Red Shoe Diaries*, we don't want to have some crack-whore springing her pimp. And there was nudity in these things, softcore-simulated scenes and whatnot. I made two of them for them.

LW: And was the problem that the sort of nasty contextualisation was going to put people off in terms of what they were supposed to be doing with the sex, or just that the whole thing seemed wrong?

GD: I think that as a piece of product it lost a masturbatory fantasy element because it became too real, and I think that's what scared them.

LW: So reading back through that to what you were doing under the Axis label, were there not the constraints that you had to deliver these regular dollops of softcore like songs in a musical?

GD: Quite frankly I was so busy shooting these things, developing scripts, looking at post, that I didn't stop. 'Cos I went for five straight years doing this stuff. Producing and directing I think I did about thirty of them. Whatever. But I do find that what you just said is so. It was like dollops of these sort of erotic interludes which sort of stopped everything.

LW: So why did you keep doing it for those five years?

GD: I don't know why. I don't really have an answer for why I kept doing them. I really was looking at trying to do other things. And I guess I hoped the company would elevate itself to a different . . . not 'elevate', that sounds like sort of a moralistic judgement, but *transition* into a variety of other things, and it never did. I had hoped that we would make erotic thrillers sometimes, just softcore movies sometimes, sometimes horror movies, different kind of genres. Very specific genre-oriented movies, but having the company develop a number of things. In the end, I left and started making music videos, and also working for *Playboy*. I don't know if Axis ended up doing much of anything else. I was the guy who was a star of a one-man studio so to speak, who could edit, shoot and produce – everything.

LW: Jag Mundhra said to me that after he made *Night Eyes*, everyone thought it was so massively successful that this genre would be a great idea. Is that so?

GD: No, no. Look, I worked with Walter in hardcore, and I knew that I could get the company financed that way. Around that time, *Night Eyes* came around. But I had been to other people, like the guy who was the executive producer of that dolphin series on TV, *Flipper*, I went to him originally because he was the owner of Heritage entertainment. So I went to him as a precursor to Axis. I think that in light of the erotic film business probably Jag and myself are the best known guys, though I think I did a lot more of it than him.

LW: **What Mundhra said was that, on the one hand, you had sex as explicit as you could do within an R-rating, and, on the other hand, you've got a thriller plot. Axis were telling him to push it in the sex direction as far as he could, and he was trying to pull it in the opposite direction as much as possible.**

GD: I believe he's right. I believe he's right.

LW: **So did you see those parameters in that same way?**

GD: Yes. I think that Jag is really correct in his analysis. I think he was trying to push it more towards the thriller aspects although the actors and the shooting time period were often not accommodating that all that well. Because, you know, Walter Gernert was basically a guy who started a porno company. He's a smart guy. But that was his understanding – pornography. Flesh sells. And that's the direction he kept trying to push the company in. I took a stance which was a little bit away from Jag – although I understand what he was doing – and a little more straight towards exploitation. Again, a little more *Belle de Jour*. The French erotic movies, those were the things that really interested me so in my head that's where I was at.

LW: **So did you feel at all constrained by the fact that you had to deliver a thriller plot – that there was a genre commitment that you had to make because you knew they were going to have this label on them at the end?**

GD: I didn't deliver thriller plots a lot, though. I mean, they weren't thriller plots. I did kind of what I wanted to do with them. You know, *Animal Instincts* 1 and 3 are not really thrillers at all. A lot of them aren't *film noir*ish.

LW: **But they've all got that look about them . . .**

GD: Yeah, and I like Melville's films, you know, French *film noir*. I like those French police procedurals with Alain Delon, that kind of stuff. And they have those moments in there. I love *his* films because nobody *talks* in them!

LW: **But you know you've got an audience who are not going to let you do that, for the Axis films anyway. Yet sex is also so much at the heart of the intrigue that's going on in 1940s *film noir*.**

GD: Well, those films like *Double Indemnity* are interesting because the sex is always the underpinning that drives the movie. Take *Body Heat* for example. There are no softcore sex scenes in *Body Heat* that go on for very long.

LW: But it was received as a hot, on-the-edge affair when it was released.

GD: Yes it was. But *Body Heat* is a great script – it's almost a perfect structural thriller. There's this seething eroticism that underpins the whole movie, and that's interesting. That's *not* what I was trying to do. That might have been what Jag was trying to do. I was trying to do *And God Created Woman*, *End of the Game*, *Belle de Jour* – things like that. That's where I was going.

LW: And if you felt that you weren't able to do that, was that because you were let down by what the audience needed at regular intervals. Or was it the budget constraints, or the scripts, or the performances?

GD: I think that the big problem was script. I mean coming to this thing today, knowing what I know now, the development of the scripts was extremely shoddy. You know, I tried to fix a lot of things when I was shooting, and sometimes I succeeded and sometimes I didn't. And then again, acting talent is difficult too.

LW: One last trivial question. As a hardcore director, you were credited as one half of 'The Dark Brothers'. Was there actually another Dark Brother?

GD: There was Walter in the hardcore. Because to be honest with you, I was out of graduate school and I needed a job. So I said, how can I get this guy to invest in my bizarre visual plan? Well, I'll make him my partner, call him my brother. He's a salesman and a distributor, but this is going to give him some kind of avant-garde cachet. But I know that people generally think that 'The Dark Brothers' was all me – me and my *alter-ego*.

5. THE BAD AND THE BEAUTIFUL: KEY PLAYERS IN THE DIRECT-TO-VIDEO EROTIC THRILLER

The high cost of moviemaking is rather like the membership fees to country clubs and golf courses: it is designed to keep out the undesirables, the upstarts.

Thomas Elsaesser (2001: 17)

The direct-to-video film is a late twentieth-century form of the B-movie. Strictly speaking, the B-movie ceased to exist when exhibitors stopped showing their products in double bills consisting of an A-feature – the main picture, usually a big budget, big star, full-length product – paired with a B-film – a shorter, supporting feature, usually much more cheaply and quickly produced. B-feature production developed during the studio era of vertical integration, particularly during the period of peak production in the 1930s and 1940s, when studios needed products to fill the bills of their own cinemas and please increasingly demanding audiences. B-films were low-budget, often genre films, which sat next to the feature-length A-picture, contributing to an evening of entertainment which might also feature newsreels and cartoons. The big studios all had their B-production arms, though there were some independent 'Poverty Row' studios (so called because of their very restrictive budgets) which specialised in B-production, as well as serials and series films. With less money at stake, B-features could be less stringently supervised than A-productions, sometimes providing a context for riskier material.[1] B-movie history provides a particularly interesting slant on debates around *film noir*. Lyons (2000) traces an honourable history of fascinating *film noir* B-production which includes some key texts which now form part of the *film noir* canon, whilst Silver and Ward, in one of the few print discussions of recent low-budget B-films (an account of 'neo-B' – neo-*noir* B-movies), see the flowering of neo-*noir* in B-production as 'a return to the roots of the cycle' (1992: 420). Discussing contemporary *noir* as 'the darling of low-budget filmmakers' (its basic co-ordinates can be done on the cheap) Lyons reports that 'Direct-to-video companies Vestron, Promark, Concord, and Vidmark have found *noir* to be a natural for their $1 million plus budgets, as have cable companies such as Showtime, which showed forty made-for-cable movies in 1995, half of which were *noir*' (2000: 163).

The post-B form of B-production which developed in the 1950s bears strong comparison to today's world of DTV and made-for-cable. Even though exhibition forms are different, both are audience-led and opportunistic. As the B-film as supporting feature ceased to be, the B-film as low-budget teen-pic came into being. Sam Arkoff, often called 'The Godfather of B-Movies' and co-founder the independent American International Pictures (AIP), grasped the moment when the newly identified youth market emerged as an exploitable sector. 'We came along at a particular juncture and that is the 1950s' says Arkoff:

> The older people were staying at home, raising their kids, paying off their mortgages and watching television. So who did you have left? You had the young people who had to get out of the house.[2]

Arkoff's production, and later that of his protégé Roger Corman, presents an interesting precedent for the 1990s DTVs. The sex-and-violence or creature-feature themes continue to be standard exploitation fare. The optimal viewing context of a private car at a drive-in has been replaced by a private sofa and a VCR.[3] Thus it is hardly surprising that Corman has become a major producer of DTVs. Other markets for products which might formerly have been classed B-films included television. In the 1960s and 1970s the 'made-for-TV' film took on an identity which the DTV film was to inherit. Compared unfavourably to glossy theatrically-released films, both made-for-TV and DTV have been viewed as cheap and formulaic filler products (bulking out TV schedules and video store shelves respectively).[4] They have in common their small-scale sense of scope; both are downsized in production because their exhibition destiny is the living room television (though there are honourable exceptions to this, films destined for home viewing which won a theatrical release).[5] What often differentiates them is their self-censorship regarding subject matter, cutting (in pre- or post-production) to fit the strictures of exhibition context. The popular notion of a 'made-for-TV' film is a bland, family-friendly product, perhaps a melodrama or light comedy – a film made for screening to a broad audience base, which deliberately guards against any possibility of offence – what Rapping refers to as the 'disease of the week, disaster of the week, social issue of the week, whitewashed history of the week' (1992: 33).[6] The popular notion of a DTV film is a product not worthy of a theatrical release, but which might contain scenes, particularly sexual scenes, which would offend a mainstream theatrical audience – in quantity if not in quality. In reality, the two categories have a more fluid interrelationship. Films at the cheaper end of the production scale, which either never expect a theatrical release or gain only a very limited one to showcase a product whose real market is video, are frequently released in different versions for different markets and distinct audiences. This has become particularly marked since the rise of specialist cable and pay-per-view TV channels. Just as the DTV film was created in answer to a demand for more rentable movies, so cable and pay-per-view answered the audience's desire to watch different kinds of movies at home: 'the pay-cable industry', writes Gomery,

> has grown and thrived for one reason – its ability to deliver uncut, uncensored, uninterrupted screenings of feature films. Indeed with all the technological change and skilled marketing, the most important point is that the true demand rests not with new technology but with interest in seeing feature films. (1992: 275)

Thus the categories 'made-for-TV' and 'DTV' begin to blur into each other, and the erotic thriller is a prime example of this marketplace fluidity. The same film might be shot with scenes which can be included or cut depending on the target audience, released in one version for terrestrial television, a more explicit version for cable television, and different cuts might then be released on video or DVD.[7]

1: B FOR BAD

This brief history might be all but meaningless to younger, contemporary audiences (the DTV target 18–30 sector), who may have no notion that 'B' ever stood for anything other than 'Bad'. Fuelled by a strong injection of postmodern irony, the 1990s saw a new veneration of movies 'so bad they're good', drawing on the enthusiasms of existing fan cultures and cult movie aficionados, particularly those with a fondness for rejuvenated genres such as horror. This is the subject matter of Jeffrey Sconce's discussion of 'paracinema', the movement which has grown up around sleazy, excessive or poorly executed B-movies which venerates them over and above A-features, a counter-cultural valorisation of 'all forms of cinematic "trash"' (1995: 372). Sconce's focus is the fanzine, particularly the horror and/or sci-fi fanzine, and some of the more established journals which have developed from fanzines. Since the mid-1990s, however, much of this activity has transferred to the internet. B-movie is now a term unselfconsciously bandied around on websites as well as in wider fan culture, an abbreviation of 'bad', drawing in a wide brief connoting all things cult. The few internet sites devoted to celebration of B-movies in the original, studio-era sense of the term (such as oldb-movies.com or B-Movie Central, which acknowledges the debt classic B-movies owe to the home viewing market)[8] are far outnumbered by a plethora of sites 'devoted to bad movies' (Oh, the Humanity!.com),[9] which eulogise 'more unsavoury cinematic tastes', as badmovies.org puts it (which calls itself 'A website to the detriment of a good film').[10] Though there is a heavy preference for horror and science fiction on contemporary B-sites (perhaps because their target audience and authorial remit is young, white and male; the beer, biriani and – if they're lucky – bonking brigade), many sites proclaim a generic omnivorousness: Bad Cinema Diary boasts, 'We've got horror, sci-fi, classic "B" films, trashy exploitation, and my personal favourite, the downright unexplainable', whilst Oh, the Humanity! claims that it is 'continually reviewing bad movies from all genres and updating our site to promote only the highest standards in crap'. *The San Francisco Examiner* identified the wide parameters of the contemporary B: 'Now the term can be applied to nearly anything – made-for-TV movies, straight-to-video movies, low-budget movies, indie movies and even big-budget genre movies. Just about the only movies safe from B-movie classification are the celebrated and bloated films that win Oscars' (Anderson 2002). The B-Hive reviews 'bad movies of all kinds',[11] whilst the B-Movie Film Vault cites its territory as 'Creature Features, Zombie Movies, Classic B-Movies, Cult Films, and movies that are just . . . plain . . . *bad*!' Thus 'bad movies' aren't just *bad* movies, they are bad movies of a particular type, a sub-genre of a sub-genre, or set of interconnected sub-genres. There is considerable interest in softcore films on these sites, but many narrative genre films which contain ropey exploitation made-on-a-shoestring content augmented by significant fleshly spectacle are welcomed into the contemporary B-pantheon. One site's definition of a B-movie is partly predicated on softcore content: 'Women's clothing becomes a nuisance or non-existent (though Hollywood A-list films play this game as well)'.[12] The B-movie movement has also spawned its own film festivals.[13]

Though the world wide web is now by far the most fruitful arena for circulating the shared knowledge of B-fans, print media still forms a significant site of exchange. Again, the vast bulk of this is concentrated at the sci-fi/horror end of the market, with publications such as *Video Watchdog* and (the now defunct) *Gorezone* in the US, or *Shivers* and *The Dark Side* in the UK, giving sometimes preferential treatment to low-budget fare (long-time editor of the biggest selling horror magazine *Fangoria*, Anthony Timpone, contributes briefly to Cook et al.'s *The B-Movie Survival Guide*). The niche market for review collections is also ripe, though specialist guides cast their nets beyond B for Bad to include C for Cult, G for Genre and W for Weird. The brief of these books is to act as trusty guide for the overwhelmed consumer through the jungle of a proliferating market: 'Major and smaller studios, independent filmmakers, "outlaw video" auteurs, cable-TV and direct-to-video suppliers, among others, have all upped their volume with "product" that, sooner or later, finds its way to home-video . . . [meaning that] you have an annual output that reaches into the thousands' (Kane 2000: ix). Rather like the erotic video guides cited above, *The Phantom of the Movies' Videoscope* defines its mission as 'search[ing] out quality (usually low-budget) genre flicks that often get lost in the celluloid shuffle', which involves focusing on 'lower profiled titles that proliferate on homevideo but receive little or no review coverage in the mainstream media' (Kane 2000). It only reviews films which have been or are available on home video, though since the ancillary market of video release is now central to a film's profitability, that includes pretty much everything.[14] As Sconce would point out, these judgements and preferences might be negotiated with reference to Pierre Bourdieu's classic study of taste, *Distinction: A Social Critique of the Judgement of Taste*. I, however, am not particularly interested in how the valorisation of the films under analysis here as good-because-bad or bad-because-good is achieved. More significant to this study is the fact that these paracinematic materials constitute one of the few places where DTV films are given any space at all.

This new B-movie culture runs on the convoluted equation that cheap means bad which means good. Such products garner far more respect from fans because they manage to press the same buttons on one million dollars (or less) rather than one hundred million (or more). A mock-heroism pervades the discourse of the intrepid reviewer, who 'has sacrificed more than a few of his own brain cells so that you might preserve your own' (Kane 2000: x); Kim Newman's Video Dungeon in British film magazine *Empire* runs with the by-line 'Braving DTV hell so you don't have to . . .'. The fan-passion which underpins much of the review material is driven by a sharp awareness of quantity (the sheer amount of product released means that small-scale promotion and viewing choices get swamped) and an inverted attitude to quality: the web-based Bad Cinema Diary site advertises itself as 'A movie guide for those who believe lower budgets mean better films'.[15] All the aforementioned guides trade on the privileged knowledge acquired when high becomes low, when modes of judgement for valuing prestige products and that tricky sign of worth, 'high production values', are inverted. This celebration of the cheap is almost universally carried out in conscious opposition to the unnecessarily expensive excesses of mainstream Hollywood. For the purposes of entry submissions, The B-Movie Festival 'defines a "B-Movie" as a low-budget film which provides a level of entertainment and/or artistic value which rivals or surpasses big-budget mainstream pictures'.[16] Apel's *Killer B's* promotes '"buried treasures," or unknown little films that are just as entertaining as any big budget, high profile, famous film' (Apel 1997: 2).[17] Sconce reads similar tendencies in print-fanzine culture as potentially radicalising for those involved (1995: 393), in the 'pitched battle' that they wage 'between a guerrilla band of cult film viewers and an elite cadre of would-be cinematic tastemakers' (1995: 372). B-websites also take a certain cinema-historical pride in unearthing hitherto overlooked treasures – 'mostly ignored film atrocities' as Oh, The Humanity! puts it – a sense of specialist and privileged knowledge which defines the fan culture of cult cinema. To give a Terriblemovies example, everyone knows who Ben Affleck is; only the privileged few can appreciate Tim Thomerson's talents. In erotic thriller terms this would be to value now-faded video star Delia Sheppard far above globally famous Sharon Stone.

These anti-Hollywood sentiments are fuelled by a number of impulses. The postmodern valorisation of trash culture has manifested itself in a widespread anti-aesthetic, particularly in youth culture, particularly amongst young males whose interest in genre cinema has developed into an underground passion for exploitation and nostalgia works. Yet it is unlikely that there is a serious counter-corporate feeling fuelling these diatribes against the multinational studio owners, even though these comments appear on the democratising world wide web in the No Logo era of anti-capitalist protest. Valorisation of bad movies also seems to go hand-in-hand, for these young male writers, with an unreconstructed, distinctly non-ironic appreciation of B-movie female flesh. The feelings which animate this cyber-paracinematic culture might seem a long way from academia (though film nerds share with academics the same traits of meticulous scholarship and respect for historical minutiae, and Sconce recognises a relationship with academic counter-cinematics), yet in many ways these sentiments share the same interest in exploitation creativity as that manifested by scholars such as Carol J. Clover and the editors of *Unruly Pleasures* (Mendik and Harper: 2000). Sconce also notes that trash cinema is now fruitful terrain for graduate student projects.

The softcore DTV film has its own smaller paracinematic culture, a more limited string of review websites and review publications which form a branch of contemporary B-culture. Print film guides such as the aforementioned couples guides (Brent 1997; Cohen and Fox 1997; and Winks 1998) generally focus on X/R18 movies, rather than softer feature films, though all emphasise the importance of story. Foremost websites are *This is Sexy? Your Guide to DTV Eroticism*, *Softcore Reviews* and (the now defunct) *Nos Darkly's Reviews*, sites which overlap with some of the couples-oriented film guides on the market today and replicate some of the 'bad is good' discourse of wider B-sites.[18] *This is Sexy?* argues that 'for most in search of decent DTV eroticism, the map is largely undrawn. We here at *This is Sexy?* are striving to be your amoral compass. . . . what we do hope to accomplish is the creation of a decent resource for the discriminating videophile in search of just the right combination of soft-core porn, overwrought plots and atrocious acting.' *Nos Darkly* refuses to deploy a star-rating system because the films 'are simply never that good' (the site consequently trades in fractions of a star), but, true to the mainstream nature of softcore, promises that 'nothing will be reviewed on these pages that can't be found at any Blockbuster or Hollywood Video location around the United States'. *Softcore Reviews* deals in 'the late-night flicks you see on cable channels like Cinemax, the direct-to-video erotic thrillers you see on the shelves of your local videostore, and basically anything else that can be considered softcore erotic entertainment'. King of softcore reviewers (and related para-cinematic products) is, however, Joe Bob Briggs, the voice of 'Joe Bob's Drive-In', archived on the web, syndicated by *The New York Times*, and anthologised in various volumes of writings.[19] The Joe Bob persona is a right-wing and horribly funny Texas Good Old Boy who 'seems to be making fun of both the establishment and the Bible Belt yahoos' (Naremore 1998: 161). His reviews of a wide array of DTV erotic thrillers, however, demonstrate a meticulous insider's appreciation of the joys of ripe Playmate T&A as well as the absurdities of a cheap plot. Like both Hosoda's *The Bare Facts Film Guide* (which tells you how many tits, and *where*) and – for the opposite reason – kids-in-mind.com, Joe Bob provides young men looking for softcore eye candy the reasons to rent, or not (and provides readers like me with some of the funniest moments when researching a book like this). Whether his is the voice of ironic genre playfulness or market-canny sexism is questionable; perhaps it depends on who's reading. These websites are important because they provide the only secondary material available on some of the films I am discussing here, and though they usually confine their discussions to burning issues such as 'First appearance of the nipple', they are marked by a canny genre-awareness which is entirely absent when DTV erotic thrillers are discussed in more mainstream locations. As one crucial context for the reception of the DTV erotic thriller, I refer to them readily.

2: THE PRODUCERS

In the post-video era, 'B' is no longer opposed to or seen as supplementing 'A'; it no longer stands for 'supporting', though it still connotes budget work. DTV and made-for-TV films have followed the original B-movie precedent in that they owe their existence to gaps in the market or new markets in search of product. If the studio era B-movie was invented to fill the bill of studio-owned theatres, post-studio-era B-movies exist to provide product for TV and cable programmers, and to bulk out the limited blockbuster fare at the video store. Just as new Hollywood was concentrating more and more resources on fewer and fewer (more ludicrously expensive) films in the early 1980s, so home viewing was developing as an area of exhibition which could not possibly be satisfied by the slim corpus of expensive A-listers. The opportunistic B-producer recognised that video sales of theatrically-released films would never fill the shelves of proliferating video stores, and so the direct-to-video film was born, a factor which a number of writers and fans see as keeping indie production afloat: 'the relatively new but rapidly expanding video (and cable TV) aftermarket made it easier for small filmmakers to raise the money necessary to produce little films' after 1980 (Apel 1997: 4). As a result of this proliferating market, self-distribution of DTVs has often been the starting-point for low- or no-budget filmmakers, with horror and sci-fi (as in Corman's early days) being the entry-level genres of choice largely because it is possible to find some kind of audience and distribution opening for cheaply made films of this kind: fan and genre audiences are not only more tolerant of the foibles of cheap production, the small-screen context of viewing is more forgiving to shaky effects and home-made monsters.

Like the original B- (supporting feature) film, the contemporary B-film in its DTV form also hails from the lower end of the scale of production, and though budgets are a tightly guarded secret, DTVs can cost anything from no-budget to low-budget. Viewers accustomed to mainstream Hollywood fare would call the DTV erotic thriller low budget. Filmmakers with an understanding of no-budget work, or most pornographers limited to two-day shoots, would call DTV erotic thrillers which end up in Blockbuster mid-budget. *Empire* reported that erotic thriller director Gregory Hippolyte is involved in making (as writer, director and/or producer) on average five films a year, which 'usually take between 13 and 20 days to shoot and cost anywhere from $350,000 to a million dollars'. Jag Mundhra cites a budget of below $1.2 million as standard. Video erotic thrillers are conventionally produced, and though costs seldom rise higher than the low millions, they are kept low by limiting pre-production and script development. Pre-production information on *Night Rhythms* gave its budget as $1,250,000, which compares well to a TV drama budget for an equivalent 90-minute slot. There are generic distinctions here too; erotic thriller DTVs are usually low-budget, whilst many no-budget first features are horror or sci-fi projects, as discussed in Lindenmuth's series of interviews (2002).[20]

The most regular players in the production of the DTV erotic thriller during the 1990s also tended to be reliable low budget producers across a wide spectrum of B-genres. As we saw with Gershon, Fiorentino and Stone, it is said that in B-movies you're either on your way up or on your way down,[21] and the expanding video market (like exploitation production in the 1950s and 1960s) has offered a springboard into more mainstream work for a number of players. Perhaps the biggest career move from a DTV start is Ashok Amritraj's, who graduated from erotic thriller and other genre filmmaking to the top of Hollywood's production tree in the mid-1990s: he now commands budgets of up to $80 million for big-star vehicles such as *Bandits*, *Antitrust* and *Battlefield Earth*, is on the board for Foreign Films at the Academy of Motion Picture Arts and Sciences, and – as one of India's most illustrious ex-patriots – has won 'Pride of India' and 'Spirit of India's Man of the Year' awards. This is after arriving in America as a top tennis player in the 1970s (he played at Wimbledon and the US Open, with his brother Vijay), and setting himself up at the bottom end of film production. Between 1985 and 2003 he produced or executive produced seventy-three films, only a handful of which were theatrically released. Before hitting the mainstream he was particularly prolific in his collaborations with fellow Indian ex-pat erotic thriller director Jag Mundhra, producing or executive producing Mundhra's *Last Call, Night Eyes, Illicit Behaviour, Tropical Heat*, and – for other directors – *Sexual Response, A Woman Scorned* and its sequel, *Victim of Desire*, and the three *Night Eyes* sequels. Amritraj has done small walk-on parts in a number of these films. He has had a close working relationship with Andrew Stevens, whose star also rose from acting to production through the 1990s and who collaborated with Amritraj producing action films on limited budgets towards the end of the decade.[22] But this softcore back catalogue is often glossed over or conveniently forgotten when the now A-list producer's résumé is outlined, particularly by Indian writers,[23] even though Amritraj has effectively followed the same trajectory from B- to A-production as the likes of directors Scorsese, Demme and Cameron. Whilst all these directors are proud to acknowledge Corman as their mentor, Amritrajs erotic thriller heritage is rarely mentioned. When 'the home video market began to boom; the cable TV had just blossomed,' he says; he 'started by making medium budget films',[24] before shifting up a gear into bigger budgets and theatrical releases following the success of his 1992 Jean-Claude Van Damme vehicle *Double Impact*. Yet well after this release he was still producing low-to-medium budget erotic thrillers for cable and video, a much more recent involvement with softcore which perhaps sits awkwardly with his Academy acknowledged respectability (though it might have prepared him well for his role as one of the judges at the 2001 Miss World contest). That said, Amritraj executive-produced with his company Hyde Park Entertainment the 2001 mainstream, big-star erotic thriller/costume drama *Original Sin*, which – tellingly – a number of critics noted would have been DTV fare if it weren't for the presence of Antonio Banderas and Angelina Jolie.

As in A-production, the money in DTV comes from distribution, which is why key DTV and cable director-producers (Fred Olen Ray, Jim Wynorski, Zalman King) have their own distribution arms.[25] Discussing the 'food chain' of indie film production, James Schamus argues that to survive companies must try

> holding on to long-term ownership interests . . . when [they] can and grab-bing as much control of the revenue streams as is feasible, for example, when [they] sell the international distribution rights to [their] films them-selves. (These days, controlling the means of production is not the issue – controlling the means of distribution is). (1998: 103)

Ray, maker of a number of erotic thrillers (*Mind Twister, Illicit Dreams 2, Masseuse*, though he's not fussy about the genres he exploits), saw the new DTV industry as 'a ready outlet for new independent production. It has also created an innovative means for independents to re-enter the distribution arena with less cash being risked and more secure returns' (Ray 1991: xii). Amritraj's large-scale success can partly be attributed to the fact that he has distributed as well as pro-duced, and though independent, by 1998 was heading what looked very much like an old studio-style mode of production: 'We are very much a vertically inte-grated company,' he said of his Trademark Films in 1998. 'We have our own development and production staff in-house, editing for post-production – and our own distribution network outside the US. In America we distribute through the major or mini-majors.' Commenting on how hard it is to compete for a share of the American market with the major studios, he justified his move to 'join them in the domestic area and do my own thing everywhere else' (Melwani 1998).

But independent producers of sex-themed cinema are not merely competing with studio products, they are also competing with multi-media giants such as *Playboy*, which manifests its own form of contemporary vertical integration by being able to connect and sell through products from different areas of its empire. Softcore cinema is a logical next stage for aspiring *Playboy* models (as well as women featured in other 'prestige' softcore such as *Penthouse*, as it was in the early 1990s at least). *Playboy* also commissions its own feature films, usually either sex dramas or erotic thrillers, made by Indigo Entertainment and released on its bunny-branded Eros label as DTVs, or for screening on *Playboy* cable TV. In the move from glamour modelling to feature films, a model-turned-actress need never leave Heffner's empire, finding her way into a gentleman's living room in a number of electronic and print forms. Web softcore reviewers target Eros/Indigo products as providing a particularly uncluttered (by complex plots or unnecessary character development) form of spectacle, and one website showcases an interview with Eros regular director John Quinn, who notes that for his first co-funded foray, *Fallen Angel* (a sex-*noir* set in 1940s Los Angeles), *Playboy* 'coached us as to how much nudity and eroticism we should put into the script'.[26] With its reputation for strict control of image and explicitness, there is no margin for error on what you can get away with in *Playboy* products. Films such as *Testing the Limits* features ample soft-lesbian hot-tub cavorting (like magazine *Playboy*, going no further than breasts and pubic hair) – the tension comes from the repetition, the question of 'how will they do the same thing in a different way next time?', making it in many ways a pure genre product. *Testing the Limits* foregrounds sex over any semblance of plot for far longer than even an Axis film would attempt (it is ages before the primary characters meet each other; far longer before the film opens its 'psycho-on-the-loose/kidnap' story). In the mainstream, Eros seems to lead the way in pushing the envelope of softcore representation, particularly in its representation of lesbian sex, with relatively graphic views of female genitalia and apparently unsimulated girl–girl cunnilingus surreptitiously moving from hard- to softcore as the 1990s closed. For Eros' UK distributors Medusa Pictures, this was an unparalleled product. However Medusa's distribution brand in the UK – high-end DTVs, pioneering the glossy erotic thriller market – was fashioned much earlier 1990s when they picked up one of Axis International's first films, *Animal Instincts*. Quickly, Medusa recognised a new kind of product – not cut-down porn, but films that were designed to go as far as possible within classification constraints. They then bought a further six Axis titles (including *Night Rhythms*, *Secret Games* and *Mirror Images*), which became some of the most lucrative erotic thriller DTVs in the UK market in the 1990s. The names of Axis' key players are as recognisable in the video store as any other aspect of genre-as-brand: here the 'name above the title' is usually a combination of three key players: producer-director Gregory Hippolyte, and producer/indie-video moguls Walter Gernert and Andrew Garroni. Axis occupy similar fringe Hollywood territory as the indie producer/distributors discussed by Ray (1991), rooted in B-production rather than porn (though Gernert comes from hardcore). But both porn and B-movies exist at the margins of the Hollywood mainstream, sometimes literally in the geographical sense (much of US porn is based in the San Fernando Valley, adjacent to Hollywood but cheaper), and figuratively as Hollywood's poorer relations.[27] Key player in the valley-based porn industry is Vivid, a top-end company which pitches itself at the mainstream and includes women and couples in its audience base.[28] Vivid is a sex-production house which moves across the hard/softcore boundary to attract as wide an audience as possible, and looks remarkably like an old-style studio. It has a vertical structure, producing and distributing in-house, and a star system: in 1984 Ginger Lynne was signed up as the first 'Vivid Girl', with an exclusive contract which made her synonymous with their brand (there have been many 'Vivid girls' since, though only Lynne has come close to crossing over into the mainstream; see Gaffin 1997: 21). Vivid's market, writes Gaffin, 'lies where adult meets mainstream':

> they provide 80 per cent of the Playboy Channel movies, have the softcore market lion's share, create CD-ROMs, interactive CD-ROMs, video games and compilation videos. . . . They put out 6,000 boxes or more for many of their videos, then quickly drop prices to 'catalogue', thus reaching a mass market. They're flooding the market all by themselves. . . . Much of their product is considered too soft for the hard-core market. (1997: 22)

However, although some Vivid products target the same audience as Axis ones, Axis's narrative feature films are far more mainstream and very generically defined, despite the fact that their prime auteur (Dark/Hippolyte) was also a hardcore director in the 1980s and 1990s. Renting an Axis film you could just about pretend that you were more interested in the plot than the sex. This would never be so with a Vivid film, or for that matter a *Playboy* film. Vivid's budgets are also lower – Gaffin cites a $10,000 budget for a hardcore film called *Head to Head*, shot over only two days. In its softcore production, Vivid makes porn stars out of strippers or glamour models and may move them into spectacle-based softcore, whilst Axis and its mainstream competitors take *Playboy* centrefolds, TV stars and a sprinkling of has-been names and feature them in narrative-based softcore feature films. *Night Rhythms*, for instance, features *Playboy* and *Penthouse* models Delia Sheppard, Traci Tweed – sister of Shannon – and Deborah Driggs, plus ex-*Kung Fu* star David Carradine and emergent scream-queen Julie Strain. So who are the DTV erotic thriller's most regular performers; how does genre function in the construction of their stardom, and what have they done to (and for) the genre?

3: VIDEO STARS AND MOVING CENTREFOLDS

When I started out I was so in love with acting. I wanted to *be* Meryl Streep. Then you compromise and you compromise a little more. And pretty soon people think you're some fucking bimbo who got fished out of a pile of eight-by-ten glossies. And you spend the rest of your career doing things you can't stand.

Zoë (Shannon Tweed's B-actress character) in *Night Eyes 3*

You either want to work or you don't. For all the ten to fifteen actresses you see in the A-list movies, there were 2,000 of us working regularly.

Shannon Tweed on being a B-performer[29]

I'm a real actress. I may not be good, but I get hired!

Julie Strain[30]

This book has referred on several occasions to the old adage that in B-movies you're either on you way up or on the way down. The direct-to-video movie shows that this is not entirely true, and here I want to pause on the profiles of some stars who stayed resolutely where they started, in contemporary B-culture's netherworld of small-scale fame and employment longevity. Names such as 'the two Shannons' – Tweed and Whirry – plus Andrew Stevens, Delia Sheppard and Martin Hewitt became well known amongst DTV erotic thriller audiences after appearing in numerous titles in the 1990s. Smaller careers were carved by any number of centrefold names entering B-moviemaking in the 1980s and 1990s, perhaps hoping for something bigger, lending their physical wares to a range of genre exposures including horror and action as well as erotic thrillers. Perhaps the most public of contemporary B-movie stars are the scream-queens of fringe horror such as Brinke Stevens and Linnea Quigley, better known than other genre performers because horror has spawned prominent glossies such as *Fangoria*, *Cinefantastique* and *Femme Fatales* which have promoted these star images, whilst the women themselves have enthusiastically participated in horror conventions. Hardcore porn has a similar paracinematic culture, with film stars featuring in specialist video industry journals, and gracing porn conventions and erotic dancing circuits to further promote themselves. The erotic thriller has no such paracinematic culture, though its stars are well-known genre players – at least to home viewers of popular movies. Foster Hirsch argues that neo-*noir* is distinguished from classic *noir* by the absence of genre stars: 'Neo-*noir*'s long history hasn't produced actors who have become specifically identified with the genre. There have been potent performances in individual films, but no actor has emerged with the iconographic impact of a Stanwyck or a Bogart' (1999: 20). Perhaps this is further evidence of the critical establishment's almost exclusive concentration on theatrically-released films. DTV actors may lack the universal iconographic status of those Hirsch cites, but performers such as Tweed or Stevens are exclusively identified with the genre and have honed a characteristic 'look'. Stevens is so prominent that softcore review website 'This is Sexy?' gives as its strapline, 'Welcome to the world of direct-to-video eroticism – better known as the reason Andrew Stevens can still afford groceries'.

It is, however, particularly difficult to research some of these figures in terms of the conventional strategies of star studies. Frequently budget, script and personal talent do not facilitate performances which reward intensive analysis, though there is clearly work to be done on genre-related performance style in low-budget moviemaking. Studies of cult stardom have yet to catch up with this area: Danny Peary's *Cult Movie Stars* has not been updated since its first 1991 imprint, and pre-dates the wave of erotic thriller production which brought the Tweeds and the Stevenses to prominence. Individual pieces such as Joanne Lacey's (2003) analysis of made-for-television stardom are useful, though academic star studies in general have been slow to focus on this proliferating area. Only B-movie websites and fansites (the source of Lacey's material), or the few dedicated print-columns such as *Empire*'s 'Video Superstars', show sustained interest in DTV performers *per se*. These stars are also rarely celebrities; their private lives do not feature in the pages of *Hello* or the *National Enquirer*, nor are their faces used to endorse products (except the videos themselves), so it is difficult to engage in the kind of public/private analysis which facilitated my studies of Gershon, Fiorentino and Stone. Is it then possible to read DTV performers as stars at all?[31] One erotic thriller performer with some extra-textual fame is Nick Cassavetes, truly a DTV curiosity. The son of indie godfather John Cassavetes, his small-scale celebrity is not due to proliferating star gossip but a serious filmic pedigree. Despite this Cassavetes Junior starred in one of the ropiest of bottom-line erotic thrillers (Wynorski's *Sins of Desire*) as well as two of the genre's more interesting texts.[32] Yet (as with Ashok Amritraj), Cassavetes' more recent biographical statements make no mention of his erotic thriller back catalogue. The career overview which accompanied the 2004 release of *The Notebook*, which he directed, covers critical accolades and Cannes awards for previous directorial outings, his co-star roles with A-list performers, but makes no mention of *Sins of the Night* or *Body of Influence*.[33] Cassavetes aside, only Tweed and Stevens have attracted significant extra-textual attention on the basis of marriages and connections. As Playmate of the Year in 1981, Tweed's sexual fame preceded her film career, and was augmented by her longstanding partnership with Kiss musician Gene Simmons and reported one-time liaison with Hugh Heffner. Still, the resounding fact of Tweed's star identity on dedicated websites is attributed to her regularity as the most prolific erotic thriller actress. Her name is now synonymous with this form: 'A Shannon Tweed film' means one thing; Playboy.com calls her the 'queen of the erotic thriller' and 'the grande dame of the video market',[34] demonstrating the tight adherence of stardom to genre, and vice versa. Tweed featured in both *Falcon Crest* (1982–3) and the long-running US daytime soap *The Days of Our Lives* (1985–6), both of which gave her some familiarity with female audiences. Andrew Stevens is also a veteran of popular US television, appearing in *Dallas* from 1987 to 1989. He started as a model, but became known in mainstream movies (e.g. Brian De Palma's *The Fury*) and was something of a pin-up in the 1970s and 1980s. (He is also cited as having posed nude for *Playgirl* and *Cosmopolitan*.) He has some celebrity cachet as son and ex-husband of more famous women: he was married to Charlie's Angel Kate Jackson, and is the son of 1960s star Stella Stevens (herself an ex-Playmate of the Month who re-emerged in a number of 1990s erotic thrillers in sexy char-

Figure 11: Prime Beefcake Andrew Stevens (here with Tanya Roberts) provides 'something for the ladies', and a glamorous surrogate for male viewers, in *Night Eyes*. Amritraj-Baldwin/The Kobal Collection.

acter roles).[35] Some of this star-fodder will nourish readings of Stevens' erotic thriller performances. Though he is prime DTV beefcake (cameras linger on his muscular torso and buns), his primary role is to serve (and service) a movie's main spectacle for its target male audience – the naked starlet (Fig. 11). His men are, then, central to the action, glamorised spectacles, but simultaneously displaced by ubiquitous female nudity. Stevens (and his other male genre counterparts, Marc Singer or Jay Richardson or Gary Hudson, as well as Hewitt) must then function as the sofa viewer's surrogate in the action. Interestingly, Stevens' ecstatic face as he is pleasured by a woman-on-top is a frequent focus in his sex-scenes, providing a curiously feminised view of male pleasure. His role of choice is the caring but arousing good guy who protects the heroine, or powerful but respectable *hommes fatals*. As a rather bland straight guy, he is no DTV Cain male, and doesn't seem to relish the degraded male persona in which Michael Douglas has specialised. Andrew Stevens doesn't do dirty or depraved, instead veering towards more romanticised roles as deceiving or deceived.

Tweed and Stevens have also starred in some surprisingly self-reflexive films which read off the performers' own career trajectories. In *Night Eyes 3*, for instance, Tweed plays a B-movie actress and star of a noirishly sexy TV female-detective show *Sweet Justice*, who repeatedly laments the downhill trajectory of her career and complains about lines which would have been 'great in the fifties'. 'It's ridiculous, isn't it,' she asks Stevens (who co-stars), 'becoming that famous on a show that bad?' However, as the quotes which open this section evidence (one from Tweed herself, the other from her *Nights Eyes 3* character), between role and star lies an ambivalence about B-performance: the roles may be formulaic but at least they are *work*. *Body Chemistry 3* also features Stevens as Alan Clay, 'a TV producer who specialises in women-as-victim pictures'. The TV movie he sets up here is the story of the central character of all four *Body Chemistry* films, the multiply-careered serial killer Claire Archer (first a sex-research scientist at UCLA, then a radio shrink, then a sex-TV presenter). 'A woman who gets sexually involved with two men who die trying to kill her – now is that a movie-of-the-week?' asks network head Bob Sibley (Robert Forster), recounting the stories of the first and second films as fodder for the third. (The answer, by the way, is yes, as long as its an erotic thriller.) *Body Chemistry 3* finally turns in on itself when Alan (who has become sexually involved with Claire) is shot by her, his wife (a soap actress) is cast as Claire in the movie (which Claire produces), and Bob opines to the wife, in one of the genre's most preciously hammy moments, 'If there's a screening room in heaven – and I think there is – Alan's up there saying "You made it to the A-list Beth! You're a star!"'

Body Chemistry 3 is, then, a B-movie about a B-movie, replaying the stories of two prior B-movies (*Body Chemistry 1* and *2*) in the plot of a third. Complicated as this is, it is nevertheless one of the few places where rising from B to A is fairly straightforward. Perhaps the on-her-way-up Beth is Sharon Stone *circa* 1990. None of my real-life DTV subjects have had such luck. Because of this, information about them is restricted, so that repeat-performers at home within the constraints of their genre such as Tweed or Stevens, Sheppard or Hewitt, are best discussed using the texts as the primary analytic framework. This is not unlike Richard deCordova's model of early cinema's 'picture personality', whereby knowledge of a player is restricted – in the absence of starrier, celebrity fodder – 'to the textuality of the films they were in. . . . The site of interest was to be the personality of the player as it was depicted in the film' (1991: 25). When I come to look at the key themes and issues which dominate the DTV erotic thriller I will show how Shannon Tweed, Delia Sheppard and Shannon Whirry have branded themselves as incarnations of the DTV good-bad girl, the *femmes fatales* and the revenging woman (Tweed is adamant that she never plays victims),[36] (Fig. 12) whilst Andrew Stevens and Martin Hewitt regularly provide 'something for the ladies', as well as variations on the *homme fatal*, tortured artist or philandering powerbroker. These per-formers' star-images are heavily inflected by genre; we might say that they are 'genred'. The closer a star is identified with their genre, the more intensely they will reflect on, and be a reflection of, that genre (at its simplest, Sharon Stone's crotch-flash did as much for the erotic thriller as it did for Stone's star identity, but the price she paid for this is that the genre became a trap). For a genre 'repeat offender' such as Tweed, there is no escape from the constraints of *femme fatale* or good-bad girl, no cinematic or paracinematic world into which

Figure 12: DTV diva Shannon Tweed (here in *A Woman Scorned*): 'I've never played a prostitute. I've never played a dumb blonde either.' Prism Pictures/Scorned Productions/The Kobal Collection.

one can avoid sexualisation (at least Stone has high fashion to flesh out her celebrity three-dimensionality). DTV stars are also more typecast than their A-list counterparts; they are known quantities by virtue of how fast they stick to genre, and how fast those genres sell. It therefore makes sense to discuss the formulaicness (as well as the occasional innovativeness) of text and star together. Performers are the primary element in a movie's marketing at the video store and in TV listings: in one website diatribe, William Martell, the screenwriter of Wynorski's *Victim of Desire*, discusses how his thriller-plot was systematically watered down by Wynorski so that star names (and bodies) such as Julie Strain's could be showcased: '[I] was told that nobody cares about plot holes, they care about cast.'[37] Yet, like the DTV film itself, the video star is doomed to be negatively defined in contrast to the riches of the theatrically-released mainstream movie. This is where the 'on your way up or down' model is strongly maintained. A brief mention of Jean-Claude Van Damme in Nick Lacey's book on genre states that 'Like Steven Seagal and Cynthia Rothrock, he ha[d] not (by 1999 at least) successfully "crossed over" to mainstream films' (2000: 12). Video stardom is, then, that which is *not* mainstream stardom, but which is doomed, like the desires these stars represent, to occupy a position of lack in relation to the mainstream's presumed plenitude.

Figure 13: The has-been star as prime selling-point for the dtv movie: David Carradine and friend in *Animal Instincts*. Courtesy of Upcoast Film Consultants, Inc.

But the DTV can only sell through a DTV-only star when he or she has done a lot of work establishing a brand identification – Lacey's examples of Rothrock or Seagal as action/martial arts exponents are useful. Stars are the prime 'presold' element of a film, making it easier to market, which accounts for the number of near-has-been or faded stars in the armoury of a DTV. Remind your distributor that your leading man was once Shaft (Richard Roundtree) or a Charlie's Angel-turned-Bond Girl (Tanya Roberts), and you give them a strong handle with which to sell the film to audiences. The phrase '. . . and featuring David Carradine' (or Jan-Michael Vincent, C. Thomas Howell or Stella Stevens, for that matter) towards the end of a credit sequence gladdens the heart of a regular DTV viewer: it tells you that you are on solid ground with a film which has dredged up an ex-star down on their luck and hoping to bring some semblance of fame to a starless production (Fig. 13).[38] What is comforting about this to a genre viewer is not the qualities a Michael Ironside or a Robert Davi might bring to the role and the film, but the regularity and predictability of the casting strategy.[39] The importance of the former A-list actor as a selling-point of the DTV erotic thriller cannot be underestimated. A vaguely recognisable name makes an unrespectable genre more acceptable to renters. Another familiar strategy is to feature actors who sound like the bigger stars who are actually their siblings – Patrick Swayze's brother Don, Julia Roberts' brother Eric, Tom Hanks' brother Jim.[40] Shannon's sister, Traci Tweed, also counts here, though the tendency is to allude to big-screen casting whilst still paying B-salaries.

Stars can also be helpful if they are already established in another form; Wyatt discusses those who are renowned elsewhere before entering movies (1994: 163). This might account for some of the successes of ex-glamour models in DTV softcore filmmaking, which probably could not exist without them. Female B-movie stars are a particularly interesting focus for the question of how stars exploit (but also try to distinguish themselves from) the repetitions and demands of genre. Many of them have found wide exposure in the 'show-casing' opportunity of high-end glamour modelling. The question of how erotic thriller stars function within the industry therefore needs to be developed with an awareness, not only of the differences between the A- and B-movie worlds, but of the close connections between, and casting opportunities offered by, the movie and modelling industries. As the title of Odette Springer's documentary indicates, 'some nudity' is required off-Hollywood, and glamour modelling is one form of preparation for this. Directors Mark Burchett and Michael D. Fox, who brought us the erotic-horror cheapies *Evil Ambitions* and *Vamps: Deadly Dreamgirls* (a vampire strip-flick with the inimitable tag-line 'Tonight Heather will be lap-dancing for her soul!') have said of the genre and casting require-ments of their work:

> Given our emphasis on pretty images (and pretty women), and the expec-tation on the part of the B-movie audience that there would be a certain level of nudity in their low-budget fare, we were faced with how to cast some of these 'key' roles. As we needed women who were physically attractive and who were comfortable enough with their bodies not to balk at nudity, we networked with local models and exotic dancers. We were lucky that many of them harbor desires to be actresses. We were even luckier that some of them could act. (Lindenmuth 2002: 66)

Softcore cinema has an intimate relationship with the magazine world in that it is the logical next career step for any number of glamour pin-ups, moderately budgeted and reasonably plotted erotic thrillers being a more prestigious career development for Penthouse Pets or Playmates of the Month than harder film pornography or the strip circuit. Though some *Playboy* models go into hardcore (despite the company's squeaky-clean desire to differentiate itself from real screen sex [Gaffin 1997: 166]), the drift into B-movie acting is common. Hardly an issue of American *Playboy* went by in the 1980s which didn't feature Shannon Tweed, Kathy Shower or Tanya Roberts (Tweed was Playmate of the Year in 1982; Shower in 1986). Julie Strain (*Carnal Crimes, Virtual Desire, Lethal Seduction*) and Joan Severance (*Illicit Behaviour, Criminal Passion, The Last Seduction 2*) garnered important exposure through glossy, high-end soft-core magazine spreads. As an article on 'Playmates in the Movies' at Playboy.com attests, 'Video may have killed the radio star, but it proved a real boon to Playmates in the Eighties, who played a not insignificant role in that decade's video revolution.'[41] Delia Sheppard and Kira Reed (like Nomi in

Verhoeven's film) started as showgirls – Sheppard in Paris, Reed as a topless dancer working her way through a UCLA degree in Theatre, Film and Television.[42] However for all the twenty-something starlets whose assets grace these films, two of B-cinema's most prolific names – Shower and Strain – didn't start glamour modelling until they were in their thirties (Strain was Penthouse Pet of the Year aged thirty-one; Shower was Playmate of the Year aged thirty-three), with film careers proceeding on from this. It is, then, possible to maintain a B-movie career well into your forties (as Strain and Shannon Tweed have done), as long as you continue to embody the standard nubile female form. Furthermore, these women usually carry their movies (Tweed in erotic thrillers, Strain in sexy horror-inflected vehicles), playing assertive, non-victim roles. Both have been hugely prolific: Strain appeared in nearly 100 feature films between 1990 and 2004 (though only ten or so are erotic thrillers); Tweed featured in around sixty feature films between 1982 and 2004 (the majority being erotic thrillers, sold on her presence). These statistics may amount to a 'Never mind the quality, feel the width' assessment of a B-performer's importance. Even so, the very fact of being so astonishingly prolific must surely guarantee more serious critical attention for the DTV star in the future. Though Tweed and Strain may have survived only because of their willingness to strip, it is also true that no A-list actress has worked with such a consistent ability to sell a movie.

Willingness to meet the nudity requirement has also been viewed as one of the essential differences between A- and B-list performers but, as with other aspects separating these movie realms, this too constitutes a fluid distinction. New technology in particular means that it is increasingly difficult to distance oneself from past 'indiscretions'. A-list female performers like Stone may start with nude roles and then spend the rest of their career trying to escape them (some actresses manage to maintain 'no nudity' clauses in their contracts for their entire careers). Changes in exhibition practice and digital technology mean that it is now increasingly difficult to escape one's own past nudity, even if one is clothed in the present. The interchange between magazine and moving image has become more intimate. Video and DVD enable moving images to be fixed as glamour stills; and the web facilitates the global dissemination of these stills. Discussing *The Cool Surface* with its star Teri Hatcher in an article about screen nudity, David Handelman notes:

> unlike the old days, when mis-steps like *The Cool Surface* would have quickly disappeared, they now linger on cable and video, generating still frames for the Internet and magazines like *Celebrity Skin*, and earn citations in *The Bare Facts Video Guide*, a popular book listing all such movie moments. 'If you choose to do nudity in a film,' Hatcher says, '99 per cent of the time with any legitimate actress, it's because they feel comfortable with how that scene works in the context of the film and the character. But if you lift it out of context, it's like doing a spread for Playboy, which 99 percent of actresses wouldn't do.' (1997: 32)

Whilst this begs the question of whether non-glamour actresses remain legitimate whilst ex-glamour ones will always be illegitimate (as well as whether *The Cool Surface* is a mis-step), it also shows the uneasy boundaries at work (or failing to work) in softcore, moving or still. The interchange between modelling and B-acting threatens to close the gap between 'posing' and 'picture performing' which characterises one development in early cinema history. DeCordova discusses the 'struggle between a photographic and a theatrical conception of the body' (1991: 19) which was resolved by the development of early movie acting. Erotic acting by those established previously as erotic models will always threaten some notion of skilled movie acting, partly because of some performers' lack of skill, partly because their (as it were) 'still' lives overshadow their moving performances. The after-life of a movie, achieved through erotic video-grabs on nude celebrity websites reinforces the notion that performers have struggled from glossy magazines into moving pictures only to be fixed again into still (masturbatory) images by the pause button. This is compounded by the fact that much of the sexual substance of B-acting involves little more than posing in a manner that recalls a female star's other work in magazine spreads. The grinning, wooden Kathy Shower seemed to step onto the film set with little apparent awareness that it required a more diverse performance repertoire than a magazine shoot;[43] Tweed and Roberts have adopted limited performance styles which cover grim-faced determination or dour nonchalance fairly convincingly (lacking range, but this hardly matters when your stock-in-trade is *femme fatale* or revenging woman), and Tweed has shown some comic potential. Translating these efforts back into still-form by freezing the moving image (as do countless pin-up websites, such as those discussed by Paul McDonald [2003], and film-specific sites such as Softcore Reviews) reminds viewers that erotic stars may be purchased still as well as moving, by shifting across media.

Yet perhaps subtle or mobile performance skills are not the point in this genre. Dyer discusses 'authenticity' as a key element of a star's charisma:

> There is a whole litany in the fan literature surrounding stars in which certain adjectives endlessly recur – sincere, immediate, spontaneous, real, direct, genuine and so on. All of these words can be seen as relating to a general notion of 'authenticity'. It is these qualities that we demand of a star if we accept her or him in the spirit in which she or he is offered. . . . Authenticity is both a quality necessary to the star phenomenon to make it work, and also the quality that guarantees the authenticity of the other particular values a star embodies. (1991: 133)

As pin-up and sexual commodity, the B-actress fosters the notion that her authentic sexuality pervades real life into non-fictional glamour spreads, and then back into the fictional characters she performs, as consistent as the words in a stick of seaside rock. But as an actress seeking a wider work portfolio, she also needs to project a 'reality' of self which suggests more than sex whilst not negating it. Tweed's extra-textual profile makes much of her vulnerable girl-friend position in relation to Simmons, father of her children and allegedly a serial philanderer who refuses to marry her[44] – a view which may be mitigated by her forthcoming book *Kiss and Tell: The Care and Feeding of a Rock Star*. Kim Dawson's website tells the story of a life struggling to rise above nudity, writing and producing more humane new roles for herself and her skin-flick friends.[45] These may be small-scale versions of the A-listers' efforts to differentiate themselves from their sexual personae, but they are also attempts to establish some form of extra-textual star branding. Stardom can constitute a pin-up as something more than a moving centrefold, and may even pave the way to recognition as a performer with a wider repertoire. Kira Reed may currently accept a career solely in R-rated or unrated erotic movies, though she tends towards dramas rather than thrillers (including a number of movies in the 'Passion and Romance' franchise, and some *Playboy*-labelled Eros titles). But her ambition is to move into genres in which nudity is *not* required (rather than from B- to A-list – though this would, presumably, be welcome). 'I will continue my acting career as I grow out of being The Queen of Skinemax and into more mature roles in other genres,' she has said, in terms which are careful to avoid alienating her male fan-base. Here, then, lies the conundrum for successful video stars, who have usually established themselves in body genres like sex or kickboxing movies. The subtext to Lacey's observation about Seagal and Rothrock 'failing' to cross over is a more complex story which requires detailed further work about video stars wedded to B-movies because they are fixed to their own physicality. Dolph Lundgren, Jean-Claude Van Damme or Seagal himself may be brilliant martial artists, but their failure consistently to hit the A-list is underpinned by their failure to move into non-action genres. By contrast, Arnold Schwarzenegger succeeded in crossing over into movie stardom because early on he tried non-action roles, and kept body-genre work and comedy roles simultaneously in play across his Hollywood career.[46] The glamour model-turned-actress may also excel in the body genre of erotic B-movies, but unless she can deliver a line in a straight drama she will never cross over into mainstream role diversity.

So reading the DTV erotic thriller as a body genre featuring star bodies not actorly performances, we might ask whether the worlds of softcore still photography, softcore narrative film and mainstream mass-market cinema are really so far apart. The star images constructed in the conjunction of these worlds merit closer examination. Starting with Monroe, a good number of mainstream stars have used glamour shoots as a publicity and role-enhancement strategy. Here *Playboy*, with its pretensions of serious, prestige journalism, is the show-case of choice. Almost without exception all the performers discussed in this book, A-list or DTV, feature in Playboy's annual roundup in each December issue entitled 'Sex stars of . . .' the year in question. Profiles or interviews will follow key sex-inflected films (Mickey Rourke was interviewed in February

1987 following 9½ *Weeks*), and any star of any significance has done a *Playboy* '20 Questions' at some point. Perhaps the only tenable remaining distinction between 'glamour' modelling and 'legitimate' acting (like that between B- and A-list) is between a star who does *Playboy* as a calculated career move (whether an interview or a photo-shoot) and a previously unknown Playmate, who then moves into movies. But if Sharon Stone's *Playboy* spread enhanced her chances of landing the lead in *Basic Instinct,* why should this not also be true of Delia Sheppard (whose website reports that she read for the Tramell role)? This is part, I would argue, of a wider drift between sexual representation in main-stream culture and dedicated softcore sex. The happier mainstream cinema is to work within the strictures of softcore, the closer sexual simulation will be identified with other practices of the sex industry, with *Playboy* positioned at the softest edge. Glamour models move into acting; legit films move towards softcore. There is a large crossover area: at one extreme lies real sexual specta-cle, performed by actors working at sex; at the other extreme are mainstream films with little explicit sexual content. In between lies a zone which includes all kinds of simulated sexual spectacle, performed for mainstream, cable and DTV, by actors and models-turned-actors willing to go up to the wire of public acceptability in their simulations. The softcore world includes real strippers being brought in to do their turn in Verhoeven's big budget *Showgirls,* and any number of DTV erotic thrillers and strip-flicks.[47] McDonagh even calls Jim Wynorski a panderer (1995: 3), since he pedals naked women for the visual consumption of the marketplace, soliciting audiences with his lurid sleeve designs – but then, isn't this what all softcore marketing come-ons are doing, including that *Showgirls* poster I discussed earlier?

I now want to sketch out overviews of the work of two directors who have been particularly prolific in the genre, bringing a number of the performers cited above to prominence, before looking more closely at the films themselves, and how they have used their star genre-players, in chapter 6.

4: GENRE AUTEURS: GREGORY HIPPOLYTE AND JAG MUNDHRA

I'd like to help along the moral downfall of the United States. . . . I wanna do stuff so that if some Christian-right person turns on the TV and sees it, he'll want to kill himself.

Gregory Dark[48]

For seven highly productive years in the 1990s, writer-producer-director Gregory Hippolyte (who now directs and likes to be known as Gregory Dark) dominated the low-budget fringes of the genre. As my interview with him (above) attests, he is something of an all-purpose filmmaker, making erotic thrillers and science fiction (*Dead Man Walking, Street Asylum*) under the names of Alexander Hippolyte, Alexander Gregory Hippolyte or A. Gregory

Hippolyte; and hardcore pornography as Greg Dark and as one of the Dark Brothers, all for cable TV, pay-per-view and DTV. If only single-genre, softcore productions are taken into account, Dark/Hippolyte was not quite as prolific as other directors (in August 1996 *Time Magazine* reported that 'superhack' Fred Olen Ray was already on his sixth film that year, although 1997 seems to have been his most prolific, with ten releases).[49] But 1993 and 1994 were astonishingly productive years for Dark as erotic thriller and hardcore director, with six titles released in 1993 and seven in 1994.[50] During the first half of the 1990s his output was so consistent that he became known as 'undisputed king of the direct-to-video "erotic thriller"' (Salisbury 1994a: 66)· When I discuss his DTV erotic thrillers I use the name 'Hippolyte' in order to give this identity confusion some consistency, and because 'Hippolyte' has become something of a one-man erotic thriller brand. Despite the irony, the vying of critics to deploy the most exalted auteurial comparisons speak volumes about the level of consistency and recognition Hippolyte had attained by mid-decade: Salisbury called him 'the Steven Spielberg of the soft-core set', whilst Kim Newman called him 'the Martin Scorsese of the erotic thriller' (Salisbury 1994a; Newman 1996).

If the DTV erotic thriller is the 'purest' form of the genre, Greg Hippolyte's films are the genre's distilled essence. Whilst I am only half-seriously using such terms here, the sheer driven efficiency with which DTV erotic thrillers do what they do commands a certain admiration – there is nothing peripheral to clutter up the sense that a genre's gotta do what a genre's gotta do in this world of fast turnaround and proficient thrill delivery. It may also seem absurd to discuss such characteristically formulaic work in terms more appropriate to an auteur study, but the consistency with which certain names are attached to the low-budget erotic thriller (Hippolyte, Jag Mundhra, Andrew Stevens, Jim Wynorski), coupled with a cohesive regularity of style and narrative focus across the genre in its DTV form, supports an approach which takes directorial moniker as a kind of genre brand-name. Affluent suburban Los Angeles is to Hippolyte what Manhattan is to Woody Allen; the basque and the G-string are for Hippolyte what the Stetson is to John Ford; the voyeuristically inflected sex-scene is to Hippolyte what the production number is to Minnelli; Shannon Whirry is to Hippolyte what Dietrich was to Von Sternberg. We recognise directorial motifs partly because they emerge in relief against a backdrop of generic consistency. Yet few directors are as repetitively consistent as Hippolyte, who has seen through more of the sequelled, extended series than any other single director, providing the genre with some of its most characteristic titles: *Animal Instincts 1, 2* and *3*; *Mirror Images 1* and *2*; *Secret Games 1, 2* and *3*; plus the singular *Carnal Crimes* (Hippolyte's first attempt at the genre), *Night Rhythms* ('reckoned by connoisseurs to be the ultimate top shelf video title' [Newman 1996: 112]), *Object of Obsession, Stranger by Night* and *Undercover*. The director even claims to have invented the erotic thriller full stop in my interview above, and here, in *Empire* magazine: 'It occurred to me that there weren't really erotic movies in this country,' he said, 'so I thought it would be really interesting to create a genre that expressed a lot of eroticism which was integral to the stories' (Salisbury 1994a: 66). In discussion he doesn't explicitly relate his erotic thrillers to *film noir* (though films such as *Body of Influence* are saturated in chiaroscuro lighting and knowing narrative references), but does claim high intellectual ground – French surrealism, Balzac – as the basis for his narratives (see Barth 1996: 81). Nevertheless, he recognises the centrality of sex: 'The first film I made had a certain amount of erotic scenes and nudity and I've sort of stuck to that. . . . There's usually a certain amount of tease in the first little bit. I try to make them as hot as I can.' As a key player in Axis Films, Hippolyte also co-produced Jag Mundhra's *The Other Woman* and *Sexual Malice*. Despite this success with the formula, he gave up erotic thrillers in 1996, claiming in one interview that he would be concentrating on hardcore, and citing thwarted artistic ambition as the reason for this shift. This means that the work of the genre's key DTV director exactly coincides with the high point of erotic thriller production. As Greg Dark, he casts himself as an experimental porno-auteur: 'With triple-X' he told *TIME* magazine in 1996, 'I can explore video imaging, different film stocks and all sorts of weird underground stuff as long as I have the obligatory pornography. When I made erotic thrillers, they wanted things that look like movies of the week' (Corliss 1996). Indeed, as a hardcore director his work has been recognised for its formal innovation; David Flint writes that the Dark Brothers' films of the 1980s 'have a stylish, punk-video look and an outré sexual attitude (with much emphasis on anal sex) and were head and shoulders above the standard of most shot-on-video hardcore of the time' (1998: 46).[51] By 1996, when he was making *Animal Instincts: The Seductress*, he was, however, claiming to be challenging both the US Christian right-wing (see epigraph above) and 'making the anti-Axis show' (Barth 1996: 92).

The confusion of names attached to Greg Dark/Hippolyte has also reinforced a separation of his work into different filmmaking identities, promoted to different audiences and sectors of the popular market. Most recently he has turned to directing music videos (for Ice Cube, Counting Crows, Vitamin C), and his video for Britney Spears' 'From the Bottom of my Broken Heart' attracted press because of the clash between Spears' wholesome image and Dark's unwholesome back catalogue. The résumé amnesia which marked A-list Amritraj's failure to remember his B-list history has also affected Dark's/Hippolyte's public profile. The British tabloid newspaper the *Sunday Sport* reported Spears' spokeswoman as saying: 'As far as I'm aware the director just does music videos. This is a video for young teenage girls and not sexy at all.' Of course, the *Sport* concentrated its gleeful report on exposing Dark's hardcore file, never mentioning his more mainstream erotic thriller identity or his work in other genres.[52] But equally the press notes released by Axis films for a number of Hippolyte erotic thrillers fail to mention the director's hardcore work. Those for *Animal Instincts* and *Night Rhythms* reprint the same text which begins (with that wonderful sense of the ludicrous for which the Axis films came to be known) 'Alexander Gregory Hippolyte brings a cultural sensitivity to the films he makes'. Here the director's Stanford education and his wide-ranging directorial experience are cited (not something the *Sunday Sport* would be interested in), but – strangely – the *Devil in Miss Jones* sequels, the *New Wave Hookers* series and *Black Throat* are conspicuously absent. Though Dark himself has never been reticent about his multiple identities and wide sexual-directorial expertise, as an erotic thriller player he is marketed by Axis with an eye to mainstream audiences, who might be deterred by the idea of viewing work directed by a hardcore veteran.

Dark/Hippolyte designs his work for the dimensions of the living room, giving his films a characteristic DTV look. 'High production values' is the phrase which sticks, usually signifying convincing, genre-aware performances, enhanced by sometimes elaborate musical scoring (though usually synthesised, it is well matched to the image and film-specific), and efficiently edited, with a good sense of the basics of thriller pacing.[53] It cannot have harmed the Hippolyte 'look' that his regular cinematographer was the now celebrated Wally Pfister. Pfister shot *Secret Games*, *Secret Games 3*, *Night Rhythms*, *Animal Instincts*, *Animal Instincts II*, *Stranger by Night* and *Object of Obsession*, but has since gone on to wow critics with his work on *Memento* (2000), *Insomnia* (2002) and *The Italian Job* (2003), amongst other high-profile projects.[54] One wonders if, when he collects his best cinematography Oscar (as one day he surely will), he will thank Gernert and Garroni for giving him his break, or whether his erotic thriller back catalogue will be as buried in his résumé as in the cases of Amritraj and Cassavetes.

Hippolyte also benefits from the sometimes surprising 'cleverness' of Axis screenplays (the result, it seems from my interviews with Gernert and Garroni, of intense script discussions). These are desperately quotable and rather more self-consciously referential than one might expect, given the lowest common denominator image which prevails of the DTV audience. *Body of Influence* – an entertainingly daft *noire*sque romp about psychoanalytic transference and the evils of repression – contains such lines as the semi-Lawrentian 'Someone told them sex was bad so they murdered their sex. But when you murder your sex it doesn't die. It just becomes plain old murder'; and the Cronenbergian sentiment 'The body has its own morality . . . listen to the flesh'. That this is 'classy' schlock is reinforced by the choice of character and locale: the upper-middle-class social standing of most of the characters and opulence of the *mise-en-scène* means that the aspirations of sex and money can be prettily tied together in one neat Beverly Hills parcel. What Laura Kipnis calls 'the upwardly mobile professional-class fantasies that fuel the *Playboy* and *Penthouse* imaginations' (1996: 130) and the 'sleek, laminated' bodies of those magazines (1996: 133) also characterise this form of the genre. The class of the bodies which populate Hippolyte's erotic thrillers and the 'classiness' of his look are frequently foregrounded in overt discussions about who our heroine should be bedding.

Joanna in the second *Animal Instincts* film describes one sexual partner as 'very wealthy, very perverse', whilst Cindy in *Undercover* masquerades as a high-class prostitute with clients who are 'so far up the social ladder they get nose bleeds'. Sexual technique, it is said, improves the higher up you get.[55] If the background to this is a long history of the (perhaps dangerously, usually European) sexually experimental aristocrat, it enables a set of *mise-en-scène* choices which can make a cheap American film look expensive. Sets and locations emphasise luxury and wealth to spare, and one characteristic costume trait visible across a range of Hippolyte's films is the naked woman cavorting whilst still wearing her jewellery: fetish this may be, it also tells us that she'll willingly take everything off except the pearl choker. Kim Newman's tongue-in-cheek characterisation of auteurial motifs is quite useful in this context:

> By now the field was thriving and it was possible for the discerning to spot the difference between the directorial style of a Jim Wynorski (*Body Chemistry 3* and *4*, *Sins of Desire*) – flat lighting, enormous breasts, some jokes – and a Jag Mundhra (*Last Call*, *Tropical Heat*, *Improper Conduct*) – complex plots, unusual sex locales, near has-been 'stars'. . . . [P]roducer-director Hippolyte makes and remakes dark fables in which glamorous but unfulfilled women explore their own neuroses (usually by having sex with dangerous men and women). (Newman 1996: 112–13)

This woman-centred concern makes Dark/Hippolyte one of the most interesting of contemporary schlock directors, as well as arguably a genre-bender in addition to being a genre-initiator. As erotic thriller director Gregory Hippolyte, he is king of suave style and satisfying endings, but as hardcore director Greg Dark he works at the edge of disturbing and difficult imagery. Gaffin calls Dark 'a director who thrives on a performer's misery and anxiety' (1997: 35), characterising his work as 'like an X-rated version of *Pygmalion*. Women start out looking sweet and innocent and become wild and untamed. He calls that "maximising a performer's potential"' (1997: 72). If hardcore enables him to experiment technically, it also allows him to push the envelope of aggressively directed performance: 'My problem is to show the disintegration of the humanism of the female, or the male, and show the pure animal nature which is pornography. Sex is animalistic. I want to see a beautiful woman, maybe a young woman who doesn't look like she's going to do that, and then she goes to the other end of her mind' (Gaffin 1997: 71). This is a formidable rubric, uncompromising but also promising some kind of subjectively challenging project, confirming Kipnis' argument that pornography might be politically provocative because it can shock bourgeois sensibilities by actively opening up a culture's 'sore spots'.[56] The utopianism of a form of sexual representation which claims to show 'pure animal nature' aside, it is also true that what the hardcore Dark describes as his directorial aim here is not what the softcore Hippolyte could ever deliver for Blockbuster's customers. Softcore never strives to display the physical manifestation of subjective disintegration, and its spectacles are not even particularly animalistic. In *Hardcore* Linda Williams read some Dark Brothers films as self-conscious exaggerations of misogyny (1990: 162); Dark himself told me that he made these films as anti-pornographic exercises in extremity – picking at the scabs, perhaps, which Kipnis identifies. Nevertheless, as Williams concludes,

> As one enthusiastic male aficionado of the Dark Brothers puts it, these films make one think that 'neither the sexual revolution nor the women's liberation movement had ever happened.' That, precisely, is their utopian appeal to some male audiences. (1990: 64)

But it also underpins Dark/Hippolyte's sexual-political ambiguity, as he straddles different forms of popular cinema, appeasing or offending audiences, in particular struggling with different manifestations of the modern sexual woman. One might think that nothing could be further from Dark's hardcore work than Hippolyte's DTV erotic thrillers, but this would not be entirely true. I have suggested that in many ways the mainstream erotic thriller is like an anodyne remake of the sometimes edgier DTV form, but I also want to suggest that if the mainstream erotic thriller is a diluted form of the DTV erotic thriller, the hardcore Dark tackles some of the issues which also emerge in the softcore erotic thriller. Dark's dehumanising hardcore project might also be seen as underpinning Hippolyte's choice of a softcore form which flirts with *noir*, perhaps the prime mainstream genre also to experiment in showing 'the disintegration of the humanism of the female, or the male'. This is why certain key issues continue to dominate the organisation of Hippolyte's narratives and frames, which I will develop further when I look, in the next chapter, at the dominant issues and formulae manifested in a wider range of DTV erotic thrillers, including the question of how softcore exploitation deploys the female protagonist and the woman's story. *Pygmalion* may be Gaffin's preferred image for Greg Dark as Svengali-director, but *Rebecca* or even *Jane Eyre* might be better templates for Greg Hippolyte's women's stories, which revolve around tales of frustrated or deceived women investigating or even avenging the death of other women, or finding out the dark secrets of the man she thought she knew.

Earlier, I discussed *Killing Me Softly* and *A Kiss Before Dying* as late twentieth-century forms of the 1940s 'paranoid woman' film. Hippolyte also explores this territory, though on a smaller budget and with sometimes more interesting results. The focus on female disappointment and isolation, followed by a quest for fulfilment which takes the heroine to a point of abandonment and then self-awareness, means that Hippolyte's erotic thrillers in particular flirt with the conventions of the woman's film. That these realms of high seriousness are also tempered by 'sly humour, a refusal to let plot get in the way of sex, Beverly Hills lifestyle locations and Frederick's of Hollywood costuming' (Newman 1996:

113) means that Hippolyte's soft porno-feminism has a more sexually alluring packaging in which to deliver women's stories (as well as women's bodies) to its perceived mixed audience. Hippolyte's films demonstrate that flagrant exposure and exploitation of the female body does not automatically exclude some sympathetic exploration of female subjectivity and fragmentation. I will also look at the related issue which is both a genre motif and an area of subjective problematisation, the trope of a character going undercover to investigate a crime or adopting someone else's identity to solve a mystery. This *noir* staple finds its feet in the DTV erotic thriller when glamorous female cops moonlight as strippers, or bored housewives pretend to be call-girls, or a repressed twin takes on the identity of her liberated sister in order to solve a crime and experience sexual ecstasy. Hippolyte's cinematic obsession with voyeurism is also important, a focus for how the apparatus of surveillance enables elaborate forms of mediated sexual and cinematic reflexivity. It is, of course, also received as prime masturbatory fare, though Dark/Hippolyte insists, perhaps disingenuously, that – as with his hardcore work – he doesn't 'want to give the viewer an erotic experience' (Barth 1996: 92). This was the aspiration of Hippolyte's final erotic thriller, *Animal Instincts: The Seductress* – softcore filmmaking which would follow its female protagonist through an anti-erotic, anti-humanist journey in which 'What she learns is that people are fucked and should die' (Barth 1996: 80). After this, Dark gave up making erotic thrillers, and the genre has never followed through this interesting set of propositions – even if Dark's words seem to preclude the loftier ambitions of Kubrick in *Eyes Wide Shut*.

Jag Mundhra is another DTV director who has reinvented himself since leaving behind the American erotic thriller, most recently making more serious, bigger budget work in his native India as Jagmohan Mundhra. Mundhra moved from an engineering background,[57] to postgraduate research in advertising and marketing, culminating in a PhD on the Marketing of Motion Pictures from Michigan State University in 1973. He then worked as a university professor in Los Angeles, whilst simultaneously managing three cinemas (pioneering the screening of Hindi films to enthusiastic LA audiences [Verma 1997]), and studying filmmaking in the evenings, since 'his heart – like any real Indian's – was in films' (Melwani 1998). Though not as prolific as the Fred Olen Rays or Greg Hippolytes of his trade, Mundhra has stuck fairly closely to the erotic thriller rubric when other DTV directors have jumped across genre boundaries like the hired hands of the studio system. Though his directing career started with Hindi work, his American filmmaking has progressed almost solely through the erotic thriller. During the 1980s and 1990s he made over twenty feature films, four in Hindi and the rest in English, almost all of the English products being erotic thrillers, save a few forays into horror and straight thriller work. By far the most successful was one of the first, the Tanya Roberts/Andrew Stevens vehicle *Night Eyes*; one correspondent reports that 'His 17 erotic thrillers have grossed over $170 million worldwide, while costing just $45 million to make'.

Mundhra is also an erotic thriller signature director: his is the other name (alongside Hippolyte's) which DTV aficionados will drop into discussion of the genre's early genesis. His films frequently begin with the auteurial 'above the title' phrase, 'A Jag Mundhra Film'. In an online interview (one of many web-pieces focusing on Mundhra's Indian origins) Verma credits the director with 'sparking off' the erotic thriller, which 'walked the thin line between pop and pornography, between the hackneyed and the horrifying' (1997). '*A film by Jag Mundhra*', writes Verma, 'is a brand name in the video circuit the world over, synonymous with sensuality and titillation. It highlighted sex – sex shot beneath multicoloured lights, sex shot in the glow of candles, sex with wax, sex in the swimming pool'.[58] The director's professional collaborations map out a mini-history of the DTV format genre, notably with rising producer Amritraj, on *Eyewitness to Murder*, *Last Call*, *Legal Tender*, *Night Eyes* and *Tropical Heat*, plus *Illicit Behaviour* with Mundhra as writer. Mundhra also cast Karen Elise Baldwin (now credited as Karen Baldwin, a highly successful producer of big-budget titles such as *Sudden Death* and *Ray*) in *Night Eyes*, *Last Call* and *Eyewitness to Murder* (for which Baldwin also got a story credit). Mundhra's production company Everest Pictures made some key genre titles, including *Irresistible Impulse*, *Tainted Love* and *Improper Conduct*. Mundhra has also directed a couple of films for Axis (*The Other Woman* and *Sexual Malice* were also co-produced by Hippolyte). Mundhra doesn't seem to have muses, though his stars include the DTV erotic thriller's A-list of dedicated genre faces: half of erotic thriller pin-up girl Lee Anne Beaman's twelve films were directed by Mundhra; other faces include the ubiquitous Andrew Stevens, a sprinkling of ex-*Playboy* or *Penthouse* models-turned-actresses, and mainstream actors on the downhill slope (Steven Bauer, Sam 'Flash Gordon' Jones, David 'American Werewolf in London' Naughton).

A certain unevenness of product is common in quickly produced DTVs, and perhaps only Hippolyte manages to maintain some kind of quality control when rolling out his slick identikit movies. Mundhra's erotic thrillers range in standard from shakily executed cheese marked by rough sound quality and outlandish plot twists to energetically engineered works of suspense. Sometimes it's hard to distinguish between weakly performed sequences and deliberately parodic stylised genre moments. In the spirit of B-culture's cele-bration of films 'so bad they're good', Mundhra sometimes seems to be having a joke on his audience. I thought the opening flashback scene of *Last Call* was postmodern pastiche, a caricatured piece of *noir*esque knowingness, featuring a 1970s couple flinging gloriously hammy slices of hardbitten dialogue at each other ('Faking it? You've been faking it as an actress for years! Nothing but a washed-out B-movie slut!') beneath a veneer of period monochrome, whilst simultaneously ignoring the man's gigantic stuck-on sideburns. But then I real-ised that this was *Last Call*'s primal scene, justification for the heroine (Shannon Tweed)'s revenge (the 'B-movie slut' is her character's doomed mother). Perhaps the truth lies somewhere in between: Mundhra takes his genre seriously enough to allow his parodic moments also to function as plot junctions. He is not above explicitly referencing other films (*Irresistible Impulse* features a woman-on-staircase-in-bathrobe homage to *Double Indemnity*, the death of a pet fish called Wanda, and a roll-in-the-surf nudge to *From Here to Eternity*). The difference between Mundhra's homage and his original inspiration is that, this being a 1990s erotic thriller rather than a 1940s or 1950s *noir* or drama, the salesman climbs the stairs and follows the *femme* into her bedroom (in the first example) and (in the last) the shore-line tumble is conducted nude.

Mundhra is also capable of psychologically complex work, and even his cheapest films are marked by intricate *noir*ish plots, frequently featuring at least one character changing sides or deploying some kind of embezzlement double-cross or con scenario ('Frankly, I was shocked,' says the icy widow of *Tropical Heat*. 'I didn't know he took out that much life insurance'). Even the characters can't believe how complicated it all is. (Don Swayze says in *Sexual Malice*: 'That's one hell of a story, lady. Who needs movies for entertainment?') *Improper Conduct* mixes the moral and talking-point themes of *Disclosure* and *The Accused* with the sexual spectacle of softcore: starting as a sexual-harassment-in-the-workplace story, it mutates into a courtroom drama, which pins the blame for near-rape on the female victim, then twists again into a female revenge thriller complete with the honeypot props of two-way mirrors and lacy underwear. Mundhra (who frequently gets a story credit in his movies) sometimes loses a clear sense of who is doing what to whom in the complication of sub-plots and over-abundance of half-sketched characters, which is partly an effect of his genre melding: of *Improper Conduct* Joe Bob Briggs writes, 'We've got way too much plot gettin [*sic*] in the way of the story, but it's basically a feminist revenge flick disguised as an erotic thriller.'[59] But Mundhra also brings a vague if rather likeable liberal confusion to his films. More humane and less cynical in tone than some of his DTV stable-mates, the sex is soft and so are the issues, touching on feminism, human rights, a critique of corrupt power politics, which may account for a certain ideological contradiction regarding the use of exploitation cinema to facilitate liberal opinion-making.

If Hippolyte is more sex than thriller, Mundhra is more thriller than sex. He attests in my interview below that his struggle with Axis was to push the balance of elements towards complex plot/characterisation and away from explicitness, in the face of producers who were trying to do the opposite. Despite being termed by one online writer 'the sultan of soft-porn',[60] compared to Hippolyte, who is fuelled by a hardcore back catalogue into pushing the envelope as far as the conventions of the genre and the Blockbuster 'family viewing' rules will allow, Mundhra's sex is rather coy, primarily motivated by showcasing the softcore wares of whichever *Playboy* centrefold is starring, though experimental in terms of location and other elements of *mise-en-scène* (which can be delivered cheaply). Mundhra's sex does meet genre requirements in terms of regularity,[61] though he delivers this through tricky camera and editing experimentation (as far as budget allows). A sweeping tracking shot which zooms in on sexual detail is a characteristic Mundhra move, as is the soft-porn library music (wailing saxophone, synthesised rhythm). *Last Call* features one of the most astonishing pre-coital undressing sequences ever committed to celluloid: Tweed and her leading man, William Katt, sit entwined, circling around and around on a revolving chair, and at each turn they are briefly masked by a wipe, which repeatedly reveals them in progressive states of undress, from no trousers to even less underwear to completely nude. Their first sex-scene involves a 360-degree circle around the room, leaving them as they get under way, taking in Tweed's trendy Little Tokyo loft conversion, then finding them again fully at it on a pony-skin rug. The scene progresses through lots of fades and dissolves between different views of the bodies. Soft S&M features only briefly in Mundhra, rather than as a regular set-piece charged with an experimental *frisson* in Hippolyte, and usually signifies negative violence rather than risky sexual pleasure. Bondage contextualises one character's sex-fuelled death in *Last Call* (he is tied up before he has a heart attack), and enables a killer to get his victim in a position from which she can't resist suffocation in *Wild Cactus*. Meanwhile, Nikki's disturbing rape fantasy in *Night Eyes* (she makes the nice Will, Andrew Stevens' otherwise polite character, force himself on her) turns out to be a means of setting him up as fall-guy.

Mundhra's generally unremarkable vanilla sex is occasionally spiced up by novel settings: sex on a roof pressed against a skylight shot from below, sex on a stair-rail shot from above, sex in a boutique changing-room, sex on a pool table (a Mundhra favourite). *Indecent Behaviour* also foregrounds sex with a pregnant woman (the very unpregnant-looking Kathy Shower): Shower's husband asks, before penetrating her, if it will bother the baby, a reminder of the biological consequences of sex which will perhaps alienate some of Shower's fan-base. There is also *lots* of sex in water: though most erotic thriller DTVs feature the obligatory shower scene (alone or with a lover, most films' glamour-starlets at some point *have* to get wet),[62] the conjunction of water and nudity is a Mundhra trademark, perhaps his 'wet sari scene'. Like a softcore Johnny Weismuller, Rick Rossovich's character in *Tropical Heat* seems capable of having sex only in water (in a swimming pool, under a rocky waterfall naked except for his shoes, then in the bath). *Sexual Malice* features sex standing in knee-high surf, and sex in a hot-tub at the base of a waterfall. *LA Goddess* also at first sites its nudity in watery locations (Kathy Shower – appropriately – in the shower, in the bath, in the hot-tub) before moving to more conventional locations. Everyone in *The Other Woman* seems to be constantly getting in or out of the shower, which also established this not as a place to cool down overheated ardour, but as Mundhra's short-hand for masturbation prompted by sexual frustration (spurned by his wife, the frustrated husband of *The Other Woman* says, 'In that case I'd better get back in the shower'; by *Wild Cactus*, however, Mundhra is no longer euphemising about the shower's function, when the frustrated wife adamantly protests to her bookish husband that she's going in the shower 'to masturbate!'). Mundhra also has a fondness for food and breasts: in *Improper Conduct* champagne is poured on them, in *Wild Cactus* maple syrup is poured on them, whilst in *The Other Woman* – in a too-close-for-comfort conjunction of softcore and lactation[63] – milk is poured on them (in all cases the food is also consumed).[64]

Issues of influence also mark out Mundhra's work, rather more literally than in other cases. Viewing a Jag Mundhra film is very often an explicit exercise in ticking off the scenes or images which either came before or will follow, a point of which Mundhra himself is acutely conscious. His films can be seen as pivoting at a switch-point of influence, taking from 1980s antecedents as much as they lend to 1990s descendants. Certainly he is not afraid to borrow liberally from his genre predecessors: compare fellatio in the lift *circa* 1990 in *Last Call* with fellatio in the lift *circa* 1987 in *Fatal Attraction*, or the opening stranger-danger break-in by a rapist in *Jagged Edge* with the rape scene which opens *Night Eyes*. *Improper Conduct* – released shortly after *Disclosure* – is explicitly marketed as reflecting 'the timely issue of sexual harassment'.[65] Sexual harassment has always existed, so is always 'timely'; what makes it particularly 'timely' in 1994 is *Disclosure* itself. But equally Mundhra could be forgiven for being peeved at the unacknowledged plagiarism by his more expensive followers: I discussed in chapter 1 some key Mundhra images which were taken into mainstream films. When Mundhra doesn't get there first, however, he's still pretty quick to respond: the hack director who features in *LA Goddess* (made the same year as *Basic Instinct*) promotes his script as 'so hot it's going to knock *Basic Instinct* out of bed. It's called "Terminal Passion" and it's my definitive work, my masterpiece'. The film never gets commissioned.

None of this is lost on Mundhra. Though on returning to India to make the more realist *Bawandar* Mundhra strove to downgrade his erotic portfolio and reinvent himself as the respectable craftsman of suspense thrillers, he nevertheless staunchly defends his work in terms dear to this study's heart: 'Some people mistake me as a porn moviemaker but let me correct this myth,' he told one on-line entertainment site. 'I make movies which are more on the erotic fantasy lines with an intrinsic message to society. It's just that when a similar movie has Sharon Stone or Demi Moore in its cast, people grade it as an erotic thriller and categorize it in a different way.'[66] This was reiterated in an interview with *The Hindu* newspaper in 2001. When asked whether 'These "Night Eyes" kind of films [are] simple soft porn,' he replied rather defensively:

> Replace my cast with expensive stars like Michael Douglas and Glenn Close and your perception will change. It will be 'Fatal Attraction'. Mine are mid-budget, quick-time and effectively crafted films. Sure, I would like to direct films with bigger budgets and stars. That is no reason, though, to belittle my hard work.[67]

However, as Elsaesser states in this chapter's epigraph, budget is *every* reason to belittle (or applaud) a work in Hollywood. In chapter 6 I will look closely at a number of films by these directors (and others) which, though limited in terms of the kinds of spectacles they *can* present, nevertheless produce some interesting interventions, particularly on issues of gender, for contemporary cinema.

NOTES

1 There is an interesting history of B-films which turned out to be as textually and historically important as their counterpart A-features. Val Lewton's horror productions with RKO in the 1940s are often cited as the shining example of B-features which are now central pillars of the academic canon (Hayward 2000: 50), though Kim Newman argues that 'Lewton's horror films were always intended to be modestly-budgeted A features and to go out at the top of double bills' (Newman 1999: 7). Writes McDonagh, 'A 1990s viewer could be forgiven for thinking *film noir* was a major cinematic movement, since so many major directors of today have copied its distinctive look. . . . It's a safe bet that more people have rented Edgar G. Ulmer's unnerving *Detour* in the last decade than ever saw it when it was released to cinemas in 1945' (1995: xiii).

2 Sam Arkoff, interviewed in Odette Springer's documentary *Some Nudity Required*.

3 Though indie filmmaker Tim Ritter writes that 'It's common knowledge that the independent exploitation video market killed the drive-in movie experience' (Ritter, in Lindenmuth 2002: 217), the death of the drive-in is also attributed to the rise of the blockbuster. But as the B-movie's customary exhibition outlet declines, new markets for low-budget products are secured.

4 Gomery (1992: 247–62) discusses the impressive successes of made-for-tv series such as NBC's 'World Premiere' movies and the 'ABC Movie of the Week', some of which garnered Emmys and other attention: 'When President Richard M. Nixon declared *Brian's Song* one of his all-time favorite films, ABC reaped an unexpected publicity bonanza' (Gomery 1992: 253). No president has yet declared a fondness for the DTV erotic thriller, though Eszterhas' image of Clinton's liking for *Basic Instinct* comes close. By the end of the 1970s, reports Gomery, the made-for-TV movie constituted 60 per cent of all movie screenings on TV; and 'It must be repeated that a successful made-for-television film can attract an audience of from forty to seventy million, while only twenty to thirty million persons attend all theatrical screenings of a movie in an average week' (1992: 254).

5 Blandford et al. note that 'Though made-for-TV movies and theatrical movies generally lead very separate lives, there can be some crossover: Steven Spielberg's first feature, *Duel* (1972), began life as a made-for-TV movie but later enjoyed a successful theatrical release. The increasing involvement of television companies in film production, especially in Europe, has led to much more movement between small and big screen' (2001: 141).

6 In Rapping's history of the US 'movie-of-the-week', though she argues that the genre is far more complex than this categorisation.

7 Shooting alternative takes for TV screening is also common in mainstream cinema – no-swearing and non-nudity versions, for instance.

8 'Thanks to the home video market, we're finally able to enjoy these B-movie classics in all their restored glory' (www.bmoviecentral.com/bmoviecentral/content.html). See also The B-movie Memory Bank (www.badmovieplanet.com/links/).

9 See www.ohthehumanity.com/mission.html.

10 See www.badmovies.org. The number of websites devoted to cheap, genre and exploitation material continues to proliferate. When accessed on 19 June 2002, www.badmovies.org/links listed thirty-three of the best 'bad movie sites'. When

accessed on 18 October 2002 the B-Movie Central Low-Budget Links page listed forty sites, including production companies, magazines, specialist merchandise and VHS stores, and fan sites.

11 See The B-Hive at http://personal.nbnet.nb.ca/mcnally/bhive/index.html.

12 'B-Movie Cinema' at http://www.videoflicks.ca/features/Bmovie/.

13 Most importantly, The B-Movie Film Festival, funded by B-movie distributor Sub Rosa, which takes place annually in Syracuse and presents awards (known as the B-movie Oscars), as well as New Orleans' annual Worst Film Festival, B-Fest in Chicago and the B-Movie Explosion Festival in Ottowa. See www.b-movie.com for details of Sub Rosa's Syracuse B-Movie Theatre Film Festival. Chicago's B-Fest takes place annually at Northwestern University (www.b-fest.com); The Ottowa B-Movie Explosion Film Festival has been running since 2001 (www.angelfire.com/film/bmovieexplosion/).

14 Scott Apel's *Killer B's: The 237 Best Movies on Video You've (probably) Never Seen* cites its terrain as 'little-known films that never got the publicity, distribution or attention they needed to allow their audience to find them', though Apel also distinguishes himself from the inverted judgement system which values '"so bad they're good" trash movies as trash: '*Killer B's* is devoted to *good* movies,' he writes (Apel 1997: 12, 13).

15 Bruce V. Eswards, Bad Cinema Diary, at www.cathuria.com/bcd/index.html.

16 See Call for Entries page at www.b-movie.com/hof/fest.html.

17 *Oh, the Humanity!'s* terrain is squarely 'only real B-movies, movies that in a way, were meant to be bad' ('the films here will all be pure B-movies, not just A-movies that are really bad,' they write). Terriblemovies.com's justification for 'Why are we doing this?' includes this snub: 'We . . . want those who scoff at B movies to learn that the Bs aren't funded by some big monster studios, and so they aren't the same old re-hashed cheesy poop starring really poor actors with dull personalities' (www.terriblemovies.com/why.html).

18 *This is Sexy?* can be found at http://www.thisissexy.net/; Softcore Reviews can be found at http://www.sreviews.com.

19 See 'Joe Bob Briggs Drive-In Movie Critic of Grapevine, Texas', http://hotx.com/joebob06–02–96/bio.html for a biographical statement.

20 See Lindenmuth (2002: 167) on funding options for independent work; Merritt also discusses the indie 'micro-budget movement' (2000: 365–73), whilst Springer's interviewees illuminate the sometimes exhilarating context of fast and furious filmmaking .

21 Though in *Some Nudity Required* Springer argues that the direction of progression is entirely gender-determined, making the point that whilst male performers have readily moved from B- to A-productions (Jack Nicholson's rise to mega-star status following his early mentoring by Roger Corman being the most celebrated example), female actresses in B-features seldom climb any higher up the ladder.

22 The Amritraj/Stevens company Franchise Films specialises in making 'blockbusters on a budget' to compete with more expensive studio pictures, films which are often pre-sold to foreign markets to cover their costs so that they are in profit before they are released (for example, *The Whole Nine Yards*). As one commentator puts it, 'Not only does Ashok have access to hundreds of millions of foreign funding, he also knows how to make films at a cost that guarantees a profit . . . something that studios seem to have forgotten' (Martell 2000). These successful ex-B-producers thus carry the lessons of low-budget production with them into higher-stakes filmmaking.

23 In her report on 'The Hollywood Wallahs', Lavina Melwani (1998) notes that 'In the 80s the video market was booming and Amritraj established himself with action-packed films for the direct to video market' and that 'he made over 70 low-budget films in 17 years', but mentions involvement in only horror and action thrillers. Another Indian on-line magazine reports that 'Most Amritraj productions feature superstars' (Honeycutt 2001) – clearly, they haven't seen *Scorned 2* or *Night Eyes 4*.

24 'Ashok Amritraj – A Multi-faceted Personality – A Press Meet', ChennaiOnline, archived at http://www.chennaionline.com/eevents/ashok.asp.

25 Cubitt has argued that video has given studios the opportunity to reintroduce a new form of the vertical integration which was disbanded with the Paramount decrees: 'Vertical integration returns in control over electronic distribution, for example in Ted Turner's purchase of MGM or Murdoch's purchase of Fox, in which TV networks' ownership of studios' back catalogues allows them enormous power over releasing, pricing and marketing strategies. This consolidation of the US industry, allying film, TV and video distribution in single companies, works to maintain a solidly homogenous market' (1991: 18). However, Ray's collection of profiles of indie distributors is testament to his introductory statement, 'Some filmmakers decided that the only way to make the pictures they wanted and to receive the money they earned was to become distributors themselves. In this way they could control both the artistic and the business end of the product. To accomplish this the producer had to be artist as well as entrepreneur' (Ray 1991: x)

26 'A Conversation with John Quinn', Softcore Reviews website, archived at http://www.sreviews.com/johnquinn1.html.

27 Porn in particular, writes Harris Gaffin, 'moved west from New York because the mainstream movie industry was here. Moonlighting mainstream professional cameramen, lighting gaffers and technicians were available as well as actors and actresses who realized they weren't going to make it big time. The porno business was a natural offshoot. First set up in Hollywood and West Los Angeles, it then migrated to the Valley because property values were much cheaper' (1997: 20).

28 'Who do we appeal to?' Vivid president Bill Asher told the Frontline *American Porn* programme-makers: 'Well, a large portion is couples. There's women. There's men. I mean, that is our niche. That is our area. And it's really more, like I said, the mainstream.'

29 Quoted in Playboy.com's feature 'Playmates in the Movies', at http://app2.playboy.com/playmates/feature/movies/80s/05.html.

30 From 'Julie Strain "Queen of B-Movies"', interview by Jason Morris, www.rockhardplace.com/horror/interviews/juliestrain.htm.

31 Lacey (2003: 191) asks a similar question of her subject, Melissa Gilbert.

32 In Jim Wynorski's *Sins of Desire* – so ludicrous that it is considered by some webwriters to be a spoof – Cassavetes gets one of the best lines in the genre. (Aficionados enjoy the genre's screenplay absurdities. The 'Can you repeat that? section of reviews on the This is Sexy? website contains some gems.) Already shot in one leg in a previous scene, Cassavetes now apprehends the sheer awfulness of Tanya Roberts having to succumb to lesbian sex with Delia Sheppard in order to protect Cassavetes, by saying, 'I would rather they'd shot me in the other leg than let that happen!'

33 See Publicity Information, *The Notebook*, Entertainment Film Distributors Ltd, pp. 24–5 (author's own copy, also archived at the BFI Library, London).

34 These are common labels, especially on softcore websites. Playboy.com's article 'Playmates in the Movies' dedicates a whole section to Tweed's profile in this respect (http://app2.playboy.com/playmates/feature/movies/80s/05.html).

35 Stella Stevens has featured in *Last Call*, *Body Chemistry 3* and 4, *Illicit Dreams* and *Hard Drive* – the third and fourth of these with the 'Fred and Ginger' of the genre, son Andrew and Shannon Tweed, the first also with Tweed and the second with Andrew and Delia Sheppard.

36 Tweed reports that she primarily plays 'doctors or lawyers . . . I've actually never played a prostitute. I've never played a dumb blonde either,' she told Playboy.com; she emphasises that her role in the spoof *Cannibal Women in the Avocado Jungle of Death* was a professor of feminist studies.

37 Martell's discussion is an interesting insight into DTV screenwriting, and is incorporated into the review of *Victim of Desire* at the Cold Fusion website, http://www.coldfusionvideo.com/v/victimofdesire.html.

38 Joanne Lacey discusses the potency which 'used to be' women who now crop up in made-for-television films (Farah Fawcett, Donna Mills, Linda Carter) bring to their roles, arguing that the appeal 'of an actress who has struggled and survived in "real life" playing her part in a struggle and survival narrative is significant' (2003: 193). The publicised troubles of David Carradine and Jan-Michael Vincent have none of this tragic cachet for the erotic thriller, suggesting that male tragedy, and a shift of genre from melodrama to thriller, differently inflects how we read the present significant of a star's past. In a different vein and as part of a discussion of the role of a star's death in the story of their celebrity, Mikita Brottman discusses on-screen ageing (2000: 109).

39 Carradine has, of course, been rehabilitated of late courtesy of Quentin Tarantino, with his stint as a DTV regular liable to be forgotten in his twenty-first-century résumé.

40 Joe Estevez, Martin Sheen's brother and Emilio's uncle, is also a hugely prolific DTV performer, featuring in well over a hundred films since the mid-1980s. Robert Mitchum's two actor sons, Christopher and James, have also had successful DTV careers following small roles in A-movies in the 1960s and 1970s.

41 Felicia Feaster, 'Playmates in the Movies', at http://app2.playboy.com/playmates/feature/movies/80s/.

42 See biographical information at Shepperd's website, http://www.deliasheppard.com and interview with Kira Reed at Glamourcon website, http://www.glamourcon.com/interview/kira.html.

43 One viewer of a Shower flick noted that 'Most of the film is a Playboy softcore shoot . . . Clearly fake sexuality with Photo Shoot smiles all round' ('paw-8' in the IMDB user comments on *LA Goddess*, http://us.imdb.com/CommentsShow?0107353).

44 See, for instance, 'This Much I Know' by Gene Simmons, *The Observer*, 16 May 2004, archived at http://observer.guardian.co.uk/magazine/story/0,11913,1216044,00.html ('The first thing I did when I met Shannon, or Cher, was say . . . "This is who I am. Take it or leave it"').

45 See the section entitled 'Kim's Personal Life for the First Time' at http://www.kim-dawson.com. By 2004, however, this website seems to have become an agent for the sales of Dawson's own-design handbags and her work in animal charities. ('Kim Dawson is Awesome', ibid.).

46 Interestingly, Lundgren, Van Damme and Schwarzenegger are all European, and strong non-US accents may also hamper the crossover process. Schwarzenegger has battled with this throughout, though has made something of a virtue of his Austrian accent in comedy.

47 Exotic dancers are regular background eye candy in the B-movie. Jim Wynorski said of *Sorority House Massacre II*, '[Corman was] shooting some *Stripped to Kill* movie at the time, and he said, "Here's a couple more bucks – go get some strippers and put them in your movie." So we wrote in a couple of scenes of the police investigating this stripper who was accosted by this guy. . . . It was just a shameless excuse to get a stripper into the movie' (McDonagh 1995: 12).

48 Interviewed by Jack Barth (1996: 80).

49 Corliss (1996). In 1991 Ray – who also found the time to edit a useful study of independent cinema – wrote of his company American Independent Productions, Inc., 'We have extended our shooting schedules from five or six days to seven. Our budgets have risen from $60,000 to $80,000 to $125,000 to $150,000' (1991: 197), though his record is shooting 'all twenty-seven pages of script in one twelve-hour day'(1991: 191).

50 According to the IMDb, *Between the Cheeks 3*, *Body of Influence*, *The Creasemaster's Wife*, *New Wave Hookers 3* (all as Greg Dark) *Secret Games 2: The Escort* and *Sins of the Night* (as Alexander Gregory Hippolyte and Gregory Hippolyte, respectively) were released in 1993; 1994 saw the release of *The Devil in Miss Jones 5: The Inferno*, *Hootermania*, *New Wave Hookers 4* (all as Greg Dark),

Mirror Images II, *Animal Instincts II* (both as Gregory Hippolyte), *Secret Games 3* (as Alexander Gregory Hippolyte) and *Stranger by Night* (as Gregory H. Brown) came out in 1994.

51 So even in his hardcore production Dark has been noted for his favouring of interesting technique and high production values. Of the director's work on the *Devil in Miss Jones* series, David Flint writes: 'After Greg Dark quit porn to make mainstream "erotic thrillers" like ANIMAL INSTINCTS (1992) under the name Gregory Hippolyte, the series lay dormant until his triumphant return to the genre in the mid-nineties. The re-emergence of high-end production values made it possible for him to create the most extravagant film of the series so far' (1998: 46).

52 It wrote: 'Dark is one of the world's greatest porn directors with a string of sizzling hard-core skin flicks under his belt, including *Psycho Sexuals*, *Between the Cheeks* and *Hooter Mania* to his name' (*Sunday Sport*, 20 February 2000, p. 26).

53 High production values may be another distinguishing feature between hard- and softcore, though as a hardcore director Greg Dark also prides himself on 'quality' filmmaking. Other hardcore producers – including here John 'Buttman' Stagliano – argue that 'There's no point to production value unless they enhance the sexual value of the film . . . People who rent a porno tape don't want to see conflict or crying or a love affair gone wrong. They want to see sexual build-up. If it doesn't work for the sexuality of the film, it shouldn't be there' (Gaffin 1997: 188). IMDb respondents do comment on the quality of the score or the look of Dark's films, however: 'As stupid as it may sound, "Animal Instincts II" . . . is quite a beautiful film, or, at least, it's very nice-looking and it has a gorgeous, haunting soundtrack (Seriously . . .). Rent it out and you'll see what I mean. (Just tell the guy behind the counter in the video shop that it's for somebody else.) The movie doesn't look cheap, and it certainly doesn't look like soft-core porn in disguise as something else' (credited to 'Glyn Ingram', http://us.imdb.com/Details?0109131).

54 Pfister also worked as a second-unit dp on *Body Chemistry*. His website lists his more major achievements, though of his Axis films only *Stranger by Night* (a relatively chaste Hippolyte product) is mentioned, another example of selective résumé amnesia (http://home.earthlink.net/~wallyp/index.html).

55 *Madame* Mrs V. says, 'With these gentlemen love-making is an art – it borders on the theatre . . . These gentlemen love to be entertained.' Sex as power is also overtly foregrounded in a range of different ways, but in *Undercover* a friend of the murdered woman says at one point (in true sex-*noir* mode), 'She'd talk about power. She'd get turned on just talking about it. And I'd get turned on just listening.'

56 '[P]ornography can provide a home for those narratives exiled from sanctioned speech and mainstream political discourse, making pornography, in essence, an oppositional political form' (Kipnis 1996: 123). '[I]nstead of seeking to suppress the pornographic, we might instead regard it as performing a social service: one of revealing these cultural sore spots, of elucidating not only the connection between sex and the social, but between our desires, our "selves," and the casual everyday brutality of cultural conformity' (1996: 121).

57 He is celebrated on the Indian Institutes of Technology at Bombay's Distinguished alumni site; see http://www.alumni.iitb.ac.in/dist_alu_2002.htm.

58 IMDb respondents are confident in the communal knowledge produced by this director-brand: 'This shoddy excuse for erotica-thriller is probably exactly what you'd expect from Jagmohan "Jag" Mundhra,' writes Badman5 of New York in response to *Tropical Heat*, though the inimitable sleaze-reviewer Joe Bob Briggs applauds 'veteran Indian director Jag Mundhra, for doing it the drive-in way' (Joe Bob Briggs: '"Improper Conduct"': On a Mission to Act Awful', at *Joe Bob's Drive-In* 19 October 1997, archived at http://hotx.com/joebob10–19–97/drivein.html).

59 Briggs, ibid.

60 Siliconeer (2002): 'Karisma Trying to Get Pregnant', *Siliconeer*, US-based South Asian online magazine, February 2002, http://www.siliconeer.com/feb2002.html.

61 One excited viewer of *Night Eyes* posted the user comment on the IMDb: 'I swear, I think (referring to UNRATED version here) that this is the biggest amount of sex scenes I've ever seen in a movie!!! . . . Will and Nikki have wild passionate sex from there on out every 7½ minutes of screen time.' A viewer of *Wild Cactus* responded, 'This was made by Jag Mundhra, who is not exactly a character-motivated director. But at least he knows what sells: lots of rampant well-proportioned female nudity. Now THAT'S entertainment.'

62 Andrew Garroni admits in my interview that he often asked at story conferences, 'Couldn't she have this conversation in the shower?' Any plot juncture looks better, it seems, if the heroine is naked as it unfolds. Kurt MacCarley's *Sexual Intent* even features a born-again Christian character who sings 'Kumbaya' whilst soaping herself in the shower.

63 Lactation's place in sex cinema has been confined to specialist hardcore films. See Krzywinska (2000) for a discussion of this.

64 Indeed, food sex is one way in which the DTV erotic thriller rings the changes, with Mundhra innovating. *Night Eyes 4*, part of the franchise which he started, features sex on a kitchen counter involving peach juice. Eroto-gastronomy's high point in the mainstream was, of course, the refrigerator sex in *9½ Weeks*; *Another 9½ Weeks*, aka *Love in Paris*, features a sex scene with honey.

65 Jacket blurb for *Improper Conduct*, Monarch Home Video, R-rated version (MHV 7483).

66 See 'Jag Mundhra strikes back with "Bawandar"', Interview with Jag Mundhra, *netGuruIndia.com* entertainment section, http://www.calonline.com/entertain/jag-mundra.html.

67 From 'In the World of Films, by Choice', interview with Jag Mundhra, *The Hindu: Online edition of India's National Newspaper*, 4 March 2001, http://www.hindu-onnet.com/thehindu/2001/03/04/stories/13040612.htm. The class point Mundhra is making here is underlined elsewhere: 'So much sexual steam did he generate that Mundhra might even have paved the way for films like . . . *Basic Instinct*.'

INTERVIEW:
DIRECTOR JAG MUNDHRA

Linda Ruth Williams (LW): Tell me about *Night Eyes* and how you first become involved in making erotic thrillers.

Jag Mundhra (JM): When I started out doing movies here in America, initially it was horror. Blood, guts, some guy with a chainsaw – it's easy to scare people. And they're cheap to make. But they became so much about blood and gore that it was also turning off a part of the audience. Then I thought about comedy, but comedies don't travel well around the world – what is funny here may not be funny in Japan or England. Action sells well in the Far East and so on, but then you have to compete with the *Beverly Hills Cop*s and the *Lethal Weapon*s. The studios keep raising the bar on action, and the little guys cannot compete. Science fiction too, they cannot compete, because after all the studios keep doing special effects which you cannot do with the budgets you have. But where you *can* compete with *anybody* is with a good erotic thriller. Take the script of *Fatal Attraction*. One house – Michael Douglas' house. One apartment – Glenn Close's apartment. And one lift where they make love. Two or three locations. Five or six characters. If you had the same script, but instead of Michael Douglas you had Andrew Stevens, and instead of Glenn Close you have Tanya Roberts – attractive people but not as famous – the exact same script can be made for half a million dollars, or one million dollars without compromising on the quality of telling the story. But these kind of movies are still interesting because the script is a thriller. And then the erotica is always a part of it, because no matter what people say, that is the main attraction for people to see an R-rated film – they want to see some erotica. And you can have interesting *femmes fatales*, *film noir* elements, and that genre doesn't cost very much. Ninety per cent of *Night Eyes* was shot in one beautiful Malibu mansion. So we shot for three weeks in a house in Malibu, the production values are great, and still the film can be done within a short amount of time and with a limited amount of money. I don't mean to brag, but *Night Eyes* became almost like a watershed movie. At that time, I had directed for Roger Corman, for all these other independents. I had done two horror movies, two cop stories, and suddenly we hit upon *Night Eyes*. And the reason we did was exactly this logic. Ashok Amritraj the producer, Andrew Stevens the writer/actor, and me as director – we sat down and we talked about this. I said, 'Without compromising on quality of production, what can you make?' And we came up with the idea of the erotic thriller. *Night Eyes* was done for $750,000 dollars, and it did twenty million worldwide.

LW: Do you know how that compares to imitators and later films?

JM: Yes. When something becomes a hit, different people try to imitate. But in this case they thought it became a hit because of the sex, not because of the story, and how it was shot, and how the script worked. And sex is cheap to shoot. There are 200,000 girls in LA who, for $150 dollars, will take their clothes off to be in the movies. Very pretty girls. So a lot of imitators decided to a *Bikini Car Wash*, or whatever – they didn't care about the script as long as there was T&A. And that really brought down the standard of these movies and the price of these movies. I was making them between $600,000 and $1.2 million. So it had to have a story, it had to have a good script, and I was not really interested in just doing T&A. But the others thought, 'Well, those movies are only selling because of the sex-scenes so we should make some that hardly have a story, just any reason for people to take their clothes off' – which is how the porno industry works. So they were like a soft version of the porno industry. And their costs were nothing. So the prices came down. And the market became glutted with this kind of product.

LW: Was that in the mid-1990s?

JM: Yes, around 1996. My last good sale on a movie like that was *Irresistible Impulse*. And after that I did *Shades of Gray*, which for me was better than some of the others but didn't do as many sales because of the fact that the prices came down.

LW: And was that because of market saturation?

JM: Market saturation, exactly. If somebody else is giving you a T&A movie for $50,000 for Germany, and I'm asking $300,000, and I need that because it cost $300,000 to make my movie while the other guy's film only cost $50,000, you can see what happens. So I couldn't cover my costs, and by putting out that kind of product eventually the market just crashed. And a lot of the direct to video companies went out of business, like Prism – a lot of the companies I directed for. They all went out of business because suddenly the prices came down. Personally, I stopped making them after *The Perfumed Garden*, which I directed. And that was not really an erotic thriller, but more a sort of a reincarnation erotic story. But it had a mixture of the exotic with the erotic. That's another thing I keep telling people who want to make these movies – either you make a good thriller with erotic elements in it, or you make an erotic film in an exotic background. Then you have something new to offer other than what these other guys are doing.

LW: So do you think that some formation of the genre, in a mixture of those terms, is still alive?

JM: I think it's ready for a revival. For three or four years I went back to my original love: I did a film called *Sandstorm* which was completely different, a social issue drama, which opened here in LA to very good reviews, and I had to sort of reinvent myself. But even in the erotic thrillers I made I never used a woman as a victim. I would never show rape as a sexual thing. Rape is about power, about subjugation, not sex. I will never show a woman as a victim in those movies. She's in charge of her sexuality. If she wants to she can be the *femme fatale*, or it could be a great moment of love and affection. But I will not show that she is victimised by somebody for sexual purposes. Except in *Improper Conduct* where I had a story about sexual harassment. But there also the sister comes in and she's on the top. So that's why I was told by my buyers that my films have a very good following among women. And I never shot nudity as gratuitous. There *is* nudity, there is no question, and I was always very open with my actors and actresses from the beginning. I'd say, 'Look, let us be straight about the fact that we don't have Michael Douglas and Sharon Stone to sell it, we have you guys to sell it. We don't have Robin Williams. So what is going to sell is sex. But as long as you are clear about it, you have to trust me that I will shoot it very aesthetically. It will not be like some kind of a cheap vulgar way of shooting it. And then I don't want any trouble on the set that you will not show this or that. And it has to be equal opportunity, because the guys want to see breasts and the girls want to see guys' bums.

LW: And were your performers in general co-operative?

JM: Yes, all of them. And most of them worked again and again with me. Because I care as a filmmaker about how the shots are taken, how the lighting is done, even if its an erotic thriller.

LW: Did you think of your films in terms of a genre-literate audience?

JM: I always thought of them as good stories. And knowing the budgetary parameters of these films, I knew that I could tell a good story with twists and turns, and there is a sexual tension. Because in most thrillers something has to motivate whatever happens. What are the biggest motivators? Sex and greed. And infidelity.

LW: Did your work in the erotic thriller genre pre-date the launch of Axis?

JM: Yes, it did. They had their own in house director, Gregory Hippolyte. I met Walter Gernert to discuss projects. They wanted to make films which had proper stories, but they also wanted to make sure that there would be a certain number of sex scenes and attractive girls, and so on. So I said, 'Let me try and find stories for you which have that kind of focus'. That's how I did *The Other Woman* and *The Other Man* for them. *The Other Man* was then released as *Sexual Malice*. And actually, within the genre of erotic thrillers, *Sexual Malice* is my favourite film. There's *lots* of sex in it, more than any other movie I've shot. But it had a very interesting story, and good actors who did the job.

LW: So when you were working with Axis, was there a general encouragement for you to push more toward the limit of what you could show sexually within an R-rating?

JM: They wanted to go to the edge of . . . not porn, but as hard as I could get. That was their thing. And one other thing was that they *had* to have a lesbian scene. They always wanted a girl–girl scene, it was their own fantasy. So when they told me you have to have a girl–girl scene in *Another Woman*, I said, 'OK, if you want a girl–girl scene at least let me give you textures within it. I want a black woman with a white woman.' The idea that a woman suspects her husband to be having an affair, and then she ends up having an affair with that woman that she suspects her husband to be having an affair with, was interesting to me. So I said, 'If you want me to have a girl–girl scene, let me bring it into the story in this manner.'

LW: And they were happy about that?

JM: Oh yes, that movie did very well for them. And then they gave me *The Other Man/Sexual Malice* to do and they still wanted a lot of sex in it. So I said 'Let me think of a story of a sexually repressed woman.' I once went with a friend of mine, a famous actress from India, to visit one of these Chippendale-type clubs. They wouldn't let men in, but I somehow managed to get in the back, and I saw how the women behaved. The women are raunchier than guys in a strip club, you know. Really. It's amazing once they are not answerable to any outsiders, and they can be left to express their sexuality without having to be a mom or a grandma or a hundred other things which society puts on them. How they behaved was incredible. It was an eye-opener. So when we were planning this movie, I said, 'You guys always want me to have a scene in a strip-club. Well fine, but I would like to shoot a scene like *this*.' But of course, since *Night Eyes* was such a success, nobody ever thought to give me any other kind of work. You get pigeonholed: 'He has a good eye for sex, so give him erotic thrillers.'

LW: Your last two erotic thrillers are based on an interesting premise – they are cultural hybrids on some levels. *Monsoon*, for example, is about past and present; Christianity and Hinduism. And presumably you had an Indian and American crew working together?

JM: Yes, and one thing I decided after that was that if I ever shoot in India I will *never* again take an American crew!

LW: Really?

JM: Never! And *Perfumed Garden* didn't have *one* American crew member. With *Monsoon* I was shooting for the first time on super-35, and my Indian crew didn't have any experience with that. But they were learning on the job and doing it. Meanwhile, my sound guy was saying, 'Oh, it's raining and I'm wet and I'm not comfortable'. I said, 'Look you signed up for a movie called *Monsoon*, what did you expect?' So, all my American crew were giving me a very hard time, and the work was all done by the Indian crew anyway. Because the Americans were always complaining they were sick, sometimes they had a Delhi-belly, they didn't want to work on a Sunday. But when you are shooting outdoors, you have to shoot *then*. In India we have the same length of history of cinema, and we have people who have worked for years in cinema, and they can't speak English but they are very good workers. And they are as good as anybody in the world.

LW: So with *Perfumed Garden*, the sense that this is a multinational co-production is in the funding, and the American cast members . . .

JM: . . . and not in the crew. Exactly. In that one there was no crew that is American. I need somebody who is comfortable in a foreign environment and who doesn't expect that there has to be hamburger round the corner and French fries. You have to adapt to where you are, rather than bitching and moaning and complaining.

LW: Were those films still primarily targeted at an American audience, or an international audience?

JM: In fact, the main part of the revenue comes from foreign sales. From sales to countries like Germany and Korea. Korea used to be very big for these kind of movies. Also Japan, and some parts of Europe. That's where we'd get 40–50 per cent of the revenue. In the US the revenue comes mainly from HBO, Showtime, Cinemax, Cable, and then DVD. And DVD also initially we used to do very big numbers. But now, Blockbuster don't want to carry a film unless it has had a theatrical run. For example, for *Night Eyes*, we received $400,000 dollars from video rights. But for *Monsoon*, I got only $50,000 dollars. That's how far the market has gone . . .

LW: And are there territories in the world that you would never think of marketing this towards?

JM: I was very fortunate that all my movies I was able to sell, even to Saudi Arabia. The reason being whenever I shot love scenes, I shot them in three different ways. It was very modular. And the length of the movie will not change – the love scene is coming here, right? Now I'll set up the camera moves and set up everything, and then I'll shoot one with a very tight lens so you don't see much. If I am shooting with a wider lens you can see more. Then if you go with a longer lens you can see above the waist, OK? Then if you go with an even tighter lens you have the same camera move around the body but you are not really seeing the body; you are seeing the shoulders and all that. It's implied. So that was the television version, which didn't change the length of the move – the background score, mix, everything was the same length as the other shot.

LW: So you would cut in different versions of the same scene?

JM: Yes, different versions, same scene. The DVD people always wanted the harder 'R'. The television, HBO and all wanted the softer 'R'. And all these other countries like Saudi, they wanted the movie but they wanted it with *suggestive* sex. So it was a clean TV version. So we sold to them, and that was why it was so very important that the film should have a story. Because if it only had sex scenes and no story, then what would you sell them? So in my films, out of the 95 minutes of length, maybe the total number of sex-scenes would be never more than nine or ten minutes. The other eighty minutes is solid story. And the scenes were interspersed in such a manner that I was also able to sell it to Turkey, Saudi and Moslem countries. But the real buyers at that time used to be Korea. Korea always wanted the raunchiest version and they paid good money for it at that time. In some cases, such as *Perfumed Garden*, since the producer was a selling company, August Entertainment, they pre-sold the title on the basis that Jag Mundhra was directing it, and it was shot in exotic India.

LW: And within those countries, is the target audience roughly the same kind of person? Because I was very interested in what you were saying about not wanting to exploit women, and it doesn't surprise me that the audience for those films would include couples.

JM: Well, remember what the women's movement originally said about Russ Meyer's movies like *Ultravixens*. It's funny how time changes perception. When I was here in the 1960s, the women's movement used to say that he objectified women. Then three years ago, they had a Russ Meyer retrospective in Cannes, and this same guy was heralded as the one who has given women's sexuality a voice. It's amazing how the same person, same movies can be perceived differently later on than they were then. But the bottom line is that as you grow older, as you become more mature, you are more comfortable with yourself, and are able to express yourself. So what's the big deal? OK, it's erotic and it turns me on and I like it. Are you going to shoot me? Am I a bad person because of that?

LW: Another thing I was going to ask you about was the possible influence of your films on mainstream cinema. For example, there's a scene in *Last Call*, where they're making love on a bed of dollar bills, which is later reproduced in *Indecent Proposal*, and then there's the candlewax scene in *Night Eyes* which is reproduced in *Body of Evidence*. I wondered what you felt when you saw that in a big-budget film.

JM: Well, I'm glad you noticed all that! And I'm telling you, one of these days one of those big-budget films is going to shoot a love-scene on a skylight, which I did in *Last Call!*

LW: You've worked with people from the Penthouse Pets and Playboy Playmates stable. What is it like directing women who come in from that glamour magazine world and have never worked in cinema before?

JM: One thing is they're very insecure – as women they're very insecure, and the prettier they are the more insecure they are, it's really amazing. Secondly, they want to prove themselves beyond just being a sex object. They may be limited in experience and talent, but they want to work hard, they remember the lines, they'll do all that. On my sets, they were always treated with respect. I never made them feel that they were less of a human being, or less smart or intelligent because they had done this. They wanted to be known as actresses and get some acting opportunities. They knew very well that they were taken because of their bodies and I never lied to them. I was always upfront about it. I'd say, 'They'll hire me because *Night Eyes* ran, and they wouldn't hire me if it was a flop. So I know where I stand, and you should know where you stand. You were hired because you have a good body, and because you have a following among men, you know. So as long as we don't disappoint that core audience, let's try to make the best damn movie we can.' For example, on *Tropical Heat* I came up with a story which was quite clever, about insurance fraud. A man dies, and his wife, who is American, claims money. So this investigator is sent to verify the claim, and she starts ensnaring him, and so on. When I came up with the story, my concept was about faking one's death; that was my concept. And you can do that in a third world country very easily because you can buy a medical examiner, corruption is rife. And so you set it up in this regal palace with elephants, and so on. They liked my story idea, but then the script that was written was so *bad*. I always felt that if you're using an elephant in a story, there should be a pay-off to all this! But no. And I said, 'What is the use of the characters we have created if they are not paying off in any way?' But they are in a hurry, they've already signed Miriam d'Abo and Rick Rossovich and they're supposed to shoot in India, which was always an attraction to me. So I just started rewriting on the set. Whatever I could fix I just rewrote the whole thing on the set. And the producers only looked at the dailies when there was nudity: 'Did you shoot the love scenes well or not? Did you do nudity?' That was the thing they wanted to see, they didn't care about the rest of it. So, it's like I'll give you what you want, but at least let me fix the story the way I want it. The scriptwriter got upset with me later on, but I said, 'Look, if you want your script to be made exactly the way you want it, *you* become the director.'

LW: Do you differentiate between the work you do in the erotic thriller genre, and your 'social issue' films like *Sandstorm*?

JM: Well, I have created two brand names. 'Jag Mundhra' is for erotic thrillers and 'Jagmohan' is for my social issue films. So *Sandstorm* was done under 'Jagmohan', for example. And I realise there is still a brand recognition for 'Jag Mundhra' movies. When I was at the American Film Market this year, the first time after an absence of three years, I thought that by now things must have changed. But it's the same usual suspects, you know. All these buyers came up to me and said, 'There's no good erotic thrillers left in the market'. Jim Wynorski has stopped doing them, David Wexler has gone somewhere, there were four or five guys who did it and they've stopped. And these buyers said, 'Yours were always some of the most popular ones. So why don't you do one another one and we can all make some money?'

LW: And would you see that as a way of funding films like *Sandstorm*?

JM: Absolutely. I could only fund *Sandstorm* because of the money I made on these other movies. I couldn't do it otherwise. So now my resources are depleted because I did *Sandstorm*, and I haven't worked on any of these movies for three years. So now I need to do another one.

LW: I wanted to ask you about some of the regular names on your credits, like Carl Austin, your screenwriter. Who is he?

JM: He is the first cousin of John Singleton, who did *Boyz N the Hood*. He's a black street-kid, lives in South Central, very shy. *Wild Cactus* was the first time I met him. He was just a kid from South Central LA, and he sat in my office, like you're sitting there, and I didn't think he was getting what I was saying at all. I was trying to tell him the story of *Straw Dogs* and how I was inspired by that to do the story of *Wild Cactus*. He wasn't taking any notes, and I was thinking 'Are you not following me because of my accent or what?' So he said, 'OK. I'll see you in a week.' And after a week, he gave me a script and I couldn't put it down! He had absorbed *everything* I said, added elements of his own, given it nice twists and turns, within the genre. And I thought, 'Wow, this is good.' His dialogue is very street-smart; very crisp and distinct. He wrote *Improper Conduct, Tainted Love, Shades of Gray* and *Wild Cactus*.

LW: The other name I was interested in was Lee Anne Beaman.

JM: She came from the Midwest and really wanted to be a serious actress. She had done all sorts of lessons, voice lessons and so on, but she was not really getting anywhere for some reason. And in order to support herself she started working in a strip club. And I met here when I was doing films for Axis, like *The Other Woman*. I found her to be very serious about her craft, and when she told me her story it really moved me a lot. She was working as a stripper, but she was a lot smarter than what you would think a stripper would be. That also is another preconceived notion.

LW: So are you ultimately proud of your work in the erotic thriller genre?

JM: I am, but it's funny how little respect it gets. When Paul Verhoeven makes a film like this, or Michael Douglas, that's fine. But when *we* do it, they say, 'Oh he makes these *porno* films'. In India, that is what they used to say. But I said, 'I've never made a porno film'. I've never shot a movie in which body parts are going in each other. I've never done any of that. I've done erotic thrillers. But this whole attitude of people, especially in India, has been very strange. They'll all go to see *Basic Instinct,* and they'll talk about Sharon Stone. But when it comes to respect for my work as a filmmaker, it was always like this. That's one of the reasons why I also wanted to make *Sandstorm,* because I wanted to show them 'Look, I can do this as well as anybody else'. When I'm making a film, if my mandate is to do something then *that's* what I'm trying to do – whatever's possible.

6. UNCOVERED AND UNDERCOVER: ISSUES IN THE DIRECT-TO-VIDEO EROTIC THRILLER

The erotic thriller poses a number of confused challenges to questions of gender and genre, some of which can be revealed through a closer look at the cheaper end of their production. During the 1990s the DTV form adopted a distinct quality which made a virtue of restricted budgets, rather like the drive-in fodder which characterised Roger Corman's work with AIP in the 1950s. The DTV erotic thriller has prided itself on what it has been able to achieve with limited funding, and has developed a characteristic style. If hardcore focuses more on explicit sexual content than complex context (scripts, acting skills, *mise-en-scène*), the softcore aesthetic has often been defined in terms of expensive-looking illusion, which marries simulated sexual content with decent scripts, passable performances, the occasional action sequence and varied sexual scenarios (*Body Chemistry 4* boasts sex on a pool table, sex on a courthouse table, sex on the bonnet of a car). However, perhaps above all it is concerned with that elusive quality 'high production values' (apparently beloved of female audiences), reflected in sumptuous locations, costumes and overall good looks. Of all the prominent exploitation genres, the erotic thriller has become expert at getting 'the most production value for the dollar' (Lindenmuth 2002: 82). In his account of the independent filmmaking world, James Schamus suggests that since 'a film's mode of production bears some relation to its mode of representation', a specific aesthetic emerges from a particularly stringent budget. That the look of a film speaks volumes about its economic genesis is most obvious in higher-budget films, the sheer extravagant excesses of which narrate one episode in the 'poetics of late capitalism' (Schamus 1998: 91). But the DTV erotic thriller tells another, important side of this story.

The most manifest softcore hallmark played out by the erotic thriller is protracted sexual spectacle, spun out often over approximately ten sex scenes and ninety or so minutes, as a specific kind of tease. Softcore erotic thrillers are exercises in cinematic foreplay: it's not that they fail to get to the 'point' of actual intercourse, but they frequently spend as long as possible arriving at that point in each sexual scenario, and the thriller content facilitates even more erotic detours. Narrative (thriller as delay) therefore affects sexual pacing. Both sex and scenario are as much about delay as they are about display: the scene from *Animal Instincts: The Seductress*, which is most written-about on the web, consists of one woman (Wendy Schumacher, the star) seducing another in front of her supposedly blind boyfriend (she thinks he can't see her, but puts on the show for him anyway) whilst two maids scrub away at the bathroom fixtures, peering in on the scene. The original pair of women move into the bathtub in the background, whilst the maids begin to fondle each other in the foreground. Then the man joins his girlfriend and her partner in the tub. The scene builds up in terms of who is doing what variety of stroking to whom, involving lesbianism, heterosexual sex, voyeurism, exhibitionism and (arguably) prostitution (since the maids are paid to stay and watch). 'Pink shots' (labia, anuses, graphic views of genitalia) are not included, nor do we see erect penises, so the scene conforms to the checklist of softcore. But it is arguably the climax in the film's own build-up of soft sexual possibilities, preceded by single scenes featuring each of the individual elements which are then put together here.

We might, then, figure the erotic thriller's sequence of sex scenes as perverse detours, stops which the sexual tourist makes in her journey towards solving the problem of unfulfilment. This is, of course, a genre in which the detours are more important than the primary goal, a list of acts or sexual possibilities ticked off as the heroine progresses through her odyssey. This might cast the erotic thriller as perverse, by which I mean perverse in the sense that Freud uses the term in the *Three Essays on the Theory of Sexuality*, to mean a straying from the norm, lingering on and at moments one should properly pass through and over. For Freud, 'normality' in sexual practice is quite strictly circumscribed. The 'normal sexual aim', he writes, 'is regarded as being the union of the genitals in the act known as copulation'. Nevertheless there is 'perverse' normality – forms of sexual play which delay the 'union of the genitals' (foreplay, looking, oral sex). These activities effectively provide detours on the journey to copulation, extending pleasure beyond the scope of intercourse through exploration of other areas of the body. Perversions, for Freud, are (amongst other things),

> sexual activities which either (a) extend, in an anatomical sense, beyond the regions of the body that are designed for sexual union, or (b) linger over the intermediate relations to the sexual object which should normally be traversed rapidly on the path towards the final sexual aim. (1977: 61–2)[1]

Because softcore cannot manifestly present 'the final sexual aim' it must (perversely) linger on intermediate pleasures: softcore elaborates a journey towards rather than arrival in a sexual goal, and then – as if to be even more perverse – it 'fails' to display that arrival when it gets there.

The softcore sex film thus has to make do with euphemism; just as hardcore titles parody mainstream ones (*The Sperminator* or – in the spirit of this book – *The Postman always Comes Twice*), so softcore parodies the conventions of hardcore as well as conventional cinema's strategies of concealment, and laughs at (or with) its own inability to show what hardcore revels in. The softcore equivalent of the cum-shot is the popped champagne cork – expensive, aspirational and ejaculatory – which releases a blast of foaming bubbly in full view of the camera: as temptress Kay (Lee Anne Beaman) straddles her partner in Jag Mundhra's *Improper Conduct*, she fires the cork and fizzes the juice over her breasts and face, swallowing it and challenging us to see the shadow of what we're not seeing. These are 'placeholder' moments, where what we witness is metonymic of what we cannot see (Wallace notes this strategy at work in the mainstream *Bound*, in which 'Violet's finger inserted between her open lips' is 'a softcore placeholder for that earlier wetted finger pressed to unseen depths' [2000: 377]). *Those Bedroom Eyes* conflates sex, death and censorship when it cuts from the shooting of a man in a torrent of Jacuzzi foam to a train going into a tunnel (and this in a film whose hero is a psychology lecturer with a cat called Freud). The 'beaver shot' is also not part of the softcore repertoire, but the erotic thriller jokes about it (better perhaps to laugh at your inability to show something than to laugh at the thing itself). After sex with Kaitlin in *Mirror Images* Gina (Julie Strain) skips into the kitchen and declares, 'You've gotta come to my place – I have an amazing pussycat to show you!' This apparent non-sequitur becomes even more absurd when it emerges as a prime murder clue later in the film: the pussy turns out to be not the female genitals we wouldn't be permitted to see here anyway, but a model cat which contains the crime's solution.[2]

The erotic thriller also 'lingers' in a number of ways, mostly in skimming its camera-eye across peripheral parts of the body (when hardcore would squarely focus on the genitals). It is obsessed with female pleasure – which must be kept in the foreground through female sexual quest narratives if women's bodies are to be centre-stage – even though it is restricted in what it can represent. Linda Williams has famously argued that one of hardcore's central contradictions is its 'inability to make the invisible pleasure of woman manifestly visible and quantifiable', which becomes its 'most vulnerable point of contradiction' (1990: 56–7). Some female pornographers have tried to capture 'authentic' (unfaked) female orgasm, but acknowledge that this requires a shift in visual expectation which challenges the conventions of the genre.[3] However, Dyer (1987: 55) argues that Hollywood sexuality is in any case more focused on the diffuse all-encompassing sexuality it ascribes to women, which means that their pleasure is manifest simply in their corporeal visibility. This is particularly true of a highly sexualised form such as Marilyn Monroe's, a body so intrinsically eroticised that it needs no further visual proof of its arousal. Whether film can show the climax of female pleasure *per se* is irrelevant to softcore (and to

Hollywood sex), since it cannot show 'real' climaxes anyway. There is no female version of the popped champagne cork. This is compounded by the fact that the most ubiquitous sexual signifier there is across the whole spectrum of mainstream and porn is the woman's ecstatic face. The DTV erotic thriller has got round this by activating female visual desire, deflecting the point of spectacle away from genital contact, and I want to look at this next. Seen almost as often as the ecstatic female face is the gazing female face as signifier of desire.

1: SEXUAL SURVEILLANCE AND FEMALE VOYEURISM

'What are you, an expert in bedroom-window ethics?'
Riker (Johnny Williams) in *Victim of Desire*

A mainstay of feminist theory since the 1980s has been discussion of the impossible position from which the woman looks in classical cinema. Yet on one simple diegetic level the DTV erotic thriller not only has no problem with female voyeurism, it actively dramatises women as viewers of sexual material, endlessly foregrounding and fixating on a range of imagistic variations on the visual theme. In this sense it is a sexual intensification, and visual literalisation, of 'how the cinema in Hollywood and elsewhere has represented and played to women's pleasure in looking, including their gaze at men' (Cowie 1997: 194). The theatrically-released erotic thriller has had some limited interest in the sexiness of looking women (*Sliver* being the foremost example, or *Blink*'s suggestion that sexual obsession can be described – as it is by Madeleine Stowe – as having your eyes 'filled' by someone), but in its video form the genre is positively obsessed with it, befitting filmmaking so consciously influenced by Hitchcock. (My epigraph – a casual reference to a more famous line from *Rear Window* – bespeaks the video genre's playfulness as well as its aspirations.) But Hitchcock's murderous or eroticised gaze was problematically male. Numerous DTV erotic thrillers present (primary) scenes of women looking on from a position of eroticised exclusion, at a (secondary) sexual spectacle which is often less erotically charged than the image of the female voyeur's aroused gaze itself, raising in turn a number of questions. What is it about women looking at women looking which is so erotically charged? Why has the spectacle of the seeing woman become one of the video erotic thriller's most characteristic interpretations of female pleasure? What is this female pleasure which enjoys sexual spectacle from both sides of the diegetic camera?

Above I described softcore's habit of 'failing' to show 'the final sexual aim', its preference for lingering over 'intermediate relations', as a perverse strategy born of the classification choices it has made. These are moments of sexual spectacle which hesitate on the brink of manifesting the full presence of sexual fulfilment (if such a thing were possible). The most common form of DTV voyeurism usually functions as such a detour, one stop in this journey from desire to desire. Women looking thus themselves transgress the model which says that they shouldn't (as only perverse women look), but they also produce some significant moments when the action hesitates for a sexual encounter to take place. If perversion is a kind of deferral of action, the suspense involved in the thrills of the thriller and the thrills of the skin flick comes ever closer. Almost all DTV erotic thrillers contain at least a glimpse of the voyeuristic, a trace of self-reflexive pleasure taking its place in the list of wares offered in a film's sexual smörgåsbord. Even a hybrid sexy-actioner like the made-for-cable *Deadly Surveillance* (a cop-buddy story which plays with judgements of the *femme fatale*) contains a *Blue Velvet*-inflected scene of star Michael Ironside, trapped in a cupboard, surveying its semi-naked anti-heroine through a blind. One might think with a title like this that *Deadly Surveillance* would be chock-full of voyeuristic titillation, but the surveillance of the alluring suspect is mostly aural. We do at one point hear her having sex, however, via Ironside's listening equipment, a kind of auditory voyeurism. As if to redress this loss of visuals, *Victim of Desire* has Marc Singer placing bugs in Shannon Tweed's home (a prelude to sex-scenes when we both see with an omniscient narrating camera and hear with the listening stake-out cop), intercut with views of Shannon herself undressing down to her designer underwear, the two separated by a *Double Indemnity* staircase. Screenwriter Jarvis (Robert Patrick) in *The Cool Surface* also only hears before he sees. He bases his erotic thriller-style script (with 'some neat twists – lust, violence. I wanted to write something with commercial appeal') first on the sounds of violent passion coming from the neighbouring apartment, and then on the affair he has with the woman next door.

But these examples of withholding visual information are rare. The Axis-produced and Wynorski-directed *Sins of Desire* features Delia Sheppard as a sex therapist (iconic in a white lab coat revealing an ample cleavage) who 'cures' one of Wynoski's 'guys that appeal to other guys' (a fat, naked slob) by having two sexy girls cavort in front of him. She watches and makes notes, whilst beyond the inevitable two-way mirror Tanya Roberts also watches. The sex clinic run by Shannon Tweed in *Indecent Behaviour* also features staged scenes where 'sick' clients undergo sexual healing in 'the pleasure centre' set up behind a two-way mirror, beyond which the pseudo-clinical onlooker views the action. (Tweed is thrown through the mirror in the film's climax.) The viewers are invariably women: Tweed in best professional mode, or her attractive assistant, who is rather more prone to putting her clipboard down and watching for pure enjoyment's sake when Tweed isn't there to police her style of viewing. 'There's a difference between watching and *watching*,' Tweed counsels. 'You have to remain detached.' However, the film's sexual pretext and its criminal subtext all concern how women fail to remain detached. A characteristic DTV shot features a camera slowly closing in on someone watching a video. In *Body of Influence* Lana (Shannon Whirry) strokes herself whilst holding a gun, as she watches a woman performing fellatio. Jessica in Mundhra's *The Other Woman* secretly watches a lesbian photo-shoot through binoculars, the scene producing a provocative layering of lenses as it cuts between her view of the shoot, the (female) photographer's view, the (two female) subjects' reverse view of the photographer, and Mundhra's camera-view of the whole scene.

But sometimes voyeurism is more thematically central, driving the narrative's primary engine as well as fleshing out its erotic contemplations, its Mulvey-esque 'frozen moments'. In these movies *about* looking (pleasurable renditions of horror's 'murderous gaze' staple) scopophilia is articulated around a part-nership of the voyeur and the exhibitionist, the first either male or female, the second usually female. Hippolyte's *Animal Instincts* series (three films between 1992 and 1995) sits intriguingly alongside another DTV series, the four *Night Eyes* films, directed by Jag Mundhra (one), Rodney McDonald (two and four), and Andrew Stevens (three) between 1990 and 1995. The *Animal Instincts* movies are sequences of sexual trysts revolving around stories of avowed voy-euristic contracts between couples, and as a whole the series is something of a low-budget extension of the obsessions of *Sliver*, both pre- and post-dating Joe Eszterhas' big-screen voyeuro-*fest*. In the first film, Joanna (Shannon Whirry) is a frustrated housewife who turns to Primak, an antidepressant with aphro-disiac side-effects,[4] when husband David (Maxwell Caulfield)'s sexual interest in her wanes. David can only get excited by watching Joanna have sex with other men via a video link, and the film's sexual set-pieces involve Joanna with a parade of partners, and a blackmail/murder plot resulting from filming these exploits with powerful men. But Joanna also looks back, replaying (and playing to) the footage of herself with other men when she later has sex with David. At its dénouement *Animal Instincts*, which understands its own narrative silliness and accepts that its main asset is Whirry's body, slips into self-parody when an attorney regales the press with a justification of Joanna and David's marriage-saving solution in a mode recalling the doctor-with-clipboard speeches which book-ended (and excused) Scandinavian pornography for UK and US audiences in the 1960s. 'Joanna Cole suffers from excessive sexual desires, nymphoma-nia, a medical condition induced by the use of the drug Primak,' he says:

> If this was a wasting illness David Cole would have been praised for sup-porting his wife's needs – he would have been called a hero and she would have been called a saint. She took her treatment, her therapy in a safe envi-ronment, a clinical environment, entirely under the supervision of her husband. . . . The camera was David's way of assessing her wife's condi-tion. It was as clinical as an X-ray or an MRI.

One can only imagine the atmosphere at Axis' script meeting when this speech was concocted. Whilst sending up an attorney's ability to justify *anything*, it neatly encapsulates the genre's mélange of salacious voyeurism rendered pseudo-clinically, sex as cure for sickness, and experimentation as remedy for marital malaise (more of which later). The *Animal Instincts* franchise contin-ues in this voyeuristically obsessed mode, but the second film foregrounds female pleasure: Joanna (also Whirry) is by now living alone, and whereas in the first film she was a housewife/hooker, here she gets a job as a stylist for a porn photographer. The plot intersects with the *Night Eyes* films when her male neighbour secretly plants cameras around her house, which Joanna discovers and plays up to, looking back at the camera-gaze (and us) as a way of signalling to her viewer/visual-invader that she knows he's looking. The third film, *Animal Instincts: The Seductress*, is by far Greg Dark's most stylistically daring erotic thriller, featuring whip pans, abrupt edits and artful black-and-white footage, wrapped around with an almost Brechtian disconcerting to-camera confession by the (sighted) male protagonist who pretends he's blind ('you'd be amazed at what people allow you to see when they think you can't see them at all').[5] There are numerous voyeuristic set-ups, scenes when exhibitionist Joanna (now played by Wendy Schumacher) thinks she can't be seen but is, but also – in keeping with the genre's interest in women who are 'seen-to-be-seeing' (as well as imbued with 'to-be-looked-at-ness') – significant moments when Joanne is made to look rather than show. This is Dark/Hippolyte's genre swansong, perhaps best signalled by the postmodern gesture of having Joanna write a book called 'Animal Instincts'.

The first three *Night Eyes* films all feature Andrew Stevens as Will Griffith, a security technician whose company (called 'Night Eyes Security') specialises in installing observation devices in glamorous rich women's houses; invariably Will gets sexually entangled with them whilst in the process being caught by the very video equipment he has installed, which is usually also used to catch the criminal, and observe people having sex from the safe distance of the control room. *Night Eyes 4* follows the same company, but with Jeff Trachta [Steve Caldwell] as its new hero. Crime and its solution, and sex and its complications, are intimately bound by the web of security devices which Will/Jeff mastermind, are seduced through, and become victim of by turns (the first film's tag-line runs, 'He was hired to watch, now he's tempted to touch . . .', whilst vision and desire are conjoined in the third: 'The more he watched . . . the more he wanted'). The films pass up no opportunity to celebrate visual sex once Will/Jeff's affairs with the various women to whom they function as personal bodyguard get under way: in *Night Eyes* one scene is first seen from outside a window as if through the eyes of a stalker, then seen again inside, duplicated by mirror-reflections. Indeed, both Will and Jeff are customarily introduced to the naked beauty of the female lover-to-be via a half-glimpsed mirror image. One bizarre, non-explicit sex scene in *Night Eyes 2* comes in a scene when rich Marilyn (Shannon Tweed) takes the rather humbler Will shopping: in the aisle of a bookshop Will fondles Marilyn to the point of orgasm, and her face is viewed by another bespectacled customer in the next aisle through a gap in the shelves.

The technology of surveillance is itself also fetishised: early in each *Night Eyes* film there is an 'installation montage', repeated in subsequent films, when Will/Jeff, perhaps aided by whatever (inevitably doomed) buddy-partner he has secured for the duration of the story, climbs through the house erecting cameras, positioning infra-red beams, setting ultrasonic traps and other bits of techno-gobbledygook, finally flicking lines of switches on the master control-board – a panopticon power-position – from which banks of monitors display and record the sexual-suspense story of the house. Other films fetishise the equipment of vision in relation to sex in various ways, such as sex on a photographer's light-box in *Body Shot*, or sex leaning against shelves of video equipment and then in front of a TV playing video-firelight in *Lipstick Camera*, or the compliment paid to the protagonist of *Die Watching* 'You do have a lot of equipment! Video equipment that is . . .'. But the *Night Eyes* films specialise in the 'tooling-up' montage, when the sex-and-crime location is visually prepared for action. There will be some plot-point discussion about whether one or other camera is badly positioned, and the villain will inevitably find a way round the technology (often hiding in the gaps between two cameras' surveillance terrains), so the failures of these prosthetic eyes are as foregrounded as their potency. The *Night Eyes* films occasionally pause to discuss the morality of looking: in the first, Will is employed to spy on Nikki (Tanya Roberts) not protect her; he is decent enough to balk at this, but not so decent that he won't peek as she gets undressed (a failing the *fatale* Nikki uses to her advantage).

In general, the *Night Eyes* films rewrite liberal suspicions about the intrusion of surveillance by making the professional voyeur always the good-natured, impeccably polite, good guy. By contrast, some erotic thrillers develop a tradition of films which self-reflexively demonise the technology of looking, more familiar as a horror trope, from *Peeping Tom* to Marc Evans' *My Little Eye*. The hard-boiled voiceover of the paparazzo hero of *Body Shot* Mickey Dane aligns the visual with the violent ('Did I say shoot her?' he asks; 'I meant take her picture'). This is a film in which an active desire to be seen ('she always found the lens,' says Mickey) is tempered by the ability of the technology of seeing to become the technology of both death and the frame-up (a key character dies by plunging into a super-trooper spotlight, and the hero's addiction to photographing one particular woman turns him into a patsy). But even as it is sexually exploited, voyeurism is also made to underpin the genre's punishment scenarios. Literally *dozens* of erotic thriller criminals get caught when video recordings of their illicit sexual performances are discovered, making the VCR an agent of the law as well as a tool of licentiousness, and an agent of narrative as well as one of spectacle. A common Jag Mundhra shot first shows whatever sexual encounter is under way, then allows the shot to slide away from the primary focus to show us a hidden surveillance camera watching (and recording) the scene with us. The scene which follows the credit sequence in Hippolyte's *Undercover* displays a sexually dominant woman fucking a man whilst a hidden photographer takes pictures (this sets in motion a predictable blackmail/murder plot). The killer, it turns out, is himself a voyeur, which places *Undercover* in a loose canon of films which self-reflexively critique their own cinematic processes by demonising the diegetic looker. As Jeff in *Night Eyes 4* does, so he is done to, photographed having a surreptitious blow-job. *Die Watching*, as its title suggests, takes its cue from *Peeping Tom* by featuring a serial killer who makes his (sexualised female) victims watch on a TV monitor a video-relayed image of themselves as they die (he himself commits suicide only when he knows he is being watched). Sex here is the motivation for murder, though via a familiar pseudo-psychoanalytic backstory which functions as *Die Watching*'s primal scene: as a boy he had filmed his father, caught in bed with two women, shot by his mother, who then shoots herself. *Die Watching* is a thriller about a sex killer, and though salacious it is not geared at the arousal market – its voyeuristic focus has a horror function. *Lipstick Camera* is similarly genred, but reverses the male-view of *Die Watching* by featuring a young camera-woman heroine who turns the tables on the photographer/sex-murderer *homme fatal* by filming his final confession (though as her photo-journalism mentor he insists on directing her camerawork, until she hits him with the camera and gouges his eyes – she then sells her film to a news network).

These horror-thriller-weighted examples aside, the erotic thriller's obsession with the look usually relies on its diegetic role as a pornographic prop. But what of women looking? Trailing Traci (the woman she supposes is her husband's lover), Jessica in *The Other Woman* is part-stalker, part-pervert, part-private dick. But looking at Traci comes to reflect back on *her*: 'At work I couldn't shake [Traci] off,' says Jessica in voiceover. 'It was as if she was there all day watching me.' One scene from *Secret Games* features a masturbating woman (Delia Sheppard), on the dominant side of the surveillance equipment. On the screen-within-the-screen, a man and a woman are having sex, watched over by a video link-up camera. In a room elsewhere, Sheppard watches and enjoys. Compare this to *Sliver*'s Carly, who is shown lying in the bath masturbating from two positions, neither of them hers – the editing cuts between two particular views. First, she is seen through the invisible eye of a conventional set of camera-sweeps, moving round the bath in order to take in the spectacle of solitary female pleasure loaded with a voyeuristic legitimacy of the 'male' camera-gaze focusing on the 'to-be-looked-at' woman's body. Second, she is seen through the eye of a secret, silent diegetic voyeur, peering down through the surveillance camera positioned behind the (two-way) bathroom mirror. Thus she is seen on-screen, and on the screens-within-a-screen, yet not through the woman's own view, in counter-shots taken from the bath, as the editing techniques of classical Hollywood would bring us to expect. We see her, and we see with someone else seeing her. But although it is her solitary pleasure, coupled with her ignorance of its voyeuristic context which charges the scene, even her narcissism only signifies because of the fact that when she looks in the mirror in this film, she unwittingly presents herself for our view.

A spectacle such as this is relatively rare in the DTV erotic thriller. More in favour is the surreptitiously seeing woman. One of Cindy's johns in *Undercover* says to her, 'When I am alone I like to pretend that someone's watching me – it makes being alone a little more bearable', a speech shot as a reflection in a wardrobe door mirror, the wardrobe concealing the john's wife, who is indeed watching. Here, then, one permutation of the identity-pretence scenario of

Undercover – which I will move on to shortly – involves a man who likes to pretend he is being viewed pretending that doesn't know he's *actually* being viewed. As he speaks, he is being watched by two women in the story, and any number of women in the film's audience. When women watch, particularly when they watch women, they are expected sexually to respond. Perhaps this is another version of men liking lesbianism because it relieves their performance anxiety: female voyeurism is lesbianism-for-men in a near-perfect form, expressed without the participating women even touching each other. Hippolyte's *Mirror Images* is full of films-within-films, often using video or surveillance technology to do the imagistic repetition, as well as – as the title suggests – overtly signalled mirrored images which split and refract as well as duplicate the glamorous twins who form the film's subject-matter. At one point, Kaitlin (Delia Sheppard) watches her twin Shauna (also played by Sheppard) doing an on-video striptease, which presents the narcissistic spectacle of Sheppard watching herself as sister-watching-sister (the film stops short of making this voyeuristic knot an overtly desirous one: though Kaitlin is clearly interested in what she sees, the video of her sister sends her to sleep. Hollywood B-movies aren't 'out there' enough to contemplate conscious incest as a soft-core masturbatory delight).[6] Later in the film Kaitlin watches an incriminating sex video, in which a political candidate-turned-murdering drug-smuggler has sex with two women, one of whom masturbates as she looks at the others (here, then, Kaitlin watches a video of a woman watching a man and a woman having sex). The 1994 female revenge erotic thriller *Sexual Intent* begins with, and is punctuated by, a sequence of women in various viewing relationships with each other: this is *Sex, Lies and Videotape* twisted towards a voyeuristic lesbianism and given a darker tone. In one scene a female shrink becomes aroused by videotaped women describing their sexual fantasies. The layering of looks involves the speaking woman watched by a camera, the monitor screen on which her image plays being viewed by the shrink, the shrink in turn being watched by a man who is watching her watch the recorded woman speak.

So what is it about the woman taking voyeuristic pleasure which constitutes the central erotic focus of these films? Visual pleasure is partly about the narcissism of distorted reflection, the screen mirroring of self seen on screen (or rather a more glamorous, available and precocious version of self). If the sexiest thing in these films is the spectacle of the woman enjoying video footage (often of other women), remote control device in her hand as she cues, reviews and freezes the film to the images she's most interested in, who's pleasure is she representing? Clearly on one level this offers just another variation on 'T&A' heterosexual spectacle for the beer, biriani and bonking male, a libidinous affirmation of what the man on the sofa is doing with that woman's image. As she watches, the on-screen woman will frequently loosen her clothing or take it off, fabricate facial formations of desire, present herself as a sexually responsive creature – in other words, although it's looking which has done this to her, the spectacle of female sexual availability and responsiveness is the same. But what the image is doing might also be used to assuage male guilt about using porn: if on-screen the women are also using recorded porn (or enjoying performed live action), then surely it's OK to use it yourself, and surely its doubly OK to get off on the vision of that woman's own visual enjoyment. The thought that women do it too may then offload male guilt about their own viewing predilection and visual objectification of women. T&A spectacle is thus adjusted and augmented through the suggestion that the on-screen woman is driven by a sexual agency which is also voyeuristic. Her diegetic sofa is a surrogate location for the place of the audience.

But this would be to see the primary process of sexual identification as passing between the (simulated) voyeurism of the on-screen woman and the sexual response of the man on the erotic thriller's viewing sofa. The woman's desire, as it were, comes to stand for the man's. But as I have argued, this is the genre which embodies most overtly that moment when porn – enabled by the new technologies of home viewing – opened its doors to women, and women walked through. The on-screen voyeuristic woman is therefore a very clear image of and for an embryonic female audience, a reference within the film to the way in which the video itself might subsequently be viewed within the home, by women. 'Active scotophilia remains a powerful drive for women, as it does for men, nor can this be seen as a failure to be feminine,' writes Cowie (1993: 194), outlining the Freudian precedents for understanding female visual pleasure. The DTV female viewer may provide more grist to the psychoanalytic mill, but she also suggests a diegetic canniness about audiences. These scenarios represent women on-screen taking pleasure in exactly the kind of video footage which women off-screen are presumed to be watching. The self-referential quality of the erotic thriller thus tells a story about audiences, with the genre imagining its anticipated audience as a female home viewer.

A coda to this is the way in which the erotic thriller generally validates seeing as not just sexy but also *safe*, with its counterpart blindness being figured as downright dangerous.[7] The genre demonstrates a significant thread of interest in the visual spectacle of the blind woman:[8] the theatrically released 'sexy thriller' *Blink* featured Madeleine Stowe as a blind musician, whose eyesight is restored early in the film, though reliable vision comes on only intermittently – she is the only eyewitness who can verify the appearance of the killer, yet a bizarre post-operative tick (she sees things in a delayed way, out-of-context and after she has actually apprehended them) means that though she sees, she is still unreliable. As a sensory witness, the woman is discredited, even though she seems to be more sensorily tuned in than anyone else in the movie – even when sight is restored, Emma retains the blind person's heightened sense of hearing and smell, so can identify the particular soap the killer uses. Yet the cops' comment, that 'We got an eye witness . . . [and] we got an ear and smell witness' doesn't seem to have any bearing on Emma's reliability. Her restored vision is also the reason she becomes a target victim: the killer, it turns out, is popping off anyone who received organ donations from a dead woman he was fond of, and Emma has her eyes. Emma, in turn, blames the organs themselves for her visual unreliability, like Peter Lorre given the murderous hands of a killer in *The Hands of Orlac* ('Who's eyes are these anyway?' she asks. 'They don't work'). When vision fails her she retreats into darkness, an element she trusts and which constitutes safety for her.

Visually disenfranchised blind heroines might make more sense in a feminist framework which sees female visual prowess as punishable. But the requirements of genre demand danger and tension, and female blindness provides the pretext for these: put simply, *Blink*'s blind heroine is sometimes more insightful because of her visual impairment, but she is also at greater risk; her blindness provides the central pretext of thriller tension, and it is also exposed as a highly dangerous condition for women. The erotic thriller promotes a specular epistemology: favouring and enabling visual prowess as a driver of female desire, the genre also sees visual knowledge as a safe space for women. If arousal comes from (sometimes covert) sexual seeing, awareness and the advantage needed to overcome adversity comes finally from overt 20:20 vision.

2: WOMEN'S STORIES AND LOUSY HUSBANDS

'Ken hasn't given me an orgasm since Noriega ran Panama.'
Sandy (Catya Sassoon) in Secret Games

If to many people's minds filmic sleaze equals political dubiousness, we might assume that the lower and cheaper the erotic thriller is, the less positive its representation of women becomes. This is not true. The sexually strong women who populate the DTV genre may offer an easy focus for the submissive or masochistic fantasises of male viewers, but they might equally offer a point of identification, desire or wish-fulfilment for women in the audience. Murray Smith reads the 1940s woman's film and *film noir* as 'two sides of the same coin'; separate but equal, one a male genre, the other a female one (1988: 64). Here I will argue that, in its DTV formation at least, the erotic thriller makes contemporary women's issues a principal element of neo-*noir*, even if this is an epiphenomenon of the fact that women's bodies have to be centre-stage in sexual genres. Though marketed as films for a male heterosexual audience, what is surprising about the contemporary erotic thriller is the way in which issues more associated with the woman's film emerge through it. Elizabeth Cowie asks, simply, 'Who's story does the film tell? On which character does the narrative centre? . . . Does it tell a man's or woman's story?' (1993: 137). In the films discussed below, the answer is female.

Avedon Carol has suggested that in feminism as well as in sexual representation 'female sexual ethics have to go back to the original demands of the women's liberation movement: that women should have both the right to suggest or accept sex, on the one hand; and that women have the right to refuse sex, on the other' (1993: 150). Broadly speaking, this is the sexual ethic which animates the DTV erotic thriller. Depictions of rape (date or otherwise) such as Nick's attack on Beth in *Basic Instinct* seldom violate the DTV form (Mundhra, as we have seen, refuses to show titillating sexual violence). Nor is non-sexual femininity propounded as a positive stereotype as in a number of mainstream examples of the genre. Indeed, unlike mainstream erotic thrillers such as *Fatal Attraction* or *Body of Evidence*, the low-budget versions seldom penalise women for simply possessing erotic or economic power – here the 'good' women are as sexually voracious as the *femmes fatales*; it is not the fact of desire which divides them. Indeed, the echoes of *noir* notwithstanding, what divides the female good from the bad is no more a reflection of legitimate sexuality than it is for men. Here the DTV erotic thriller, in all its (at times pernicious) confusion, does seem to be doing something genuinely unique. Kate Stables argues that 'straight-to-video titles, produced rapidly to feed the market frenzy, were low-budget affairs, with a heavy male slant' (1998: 170) – cheap they were, but 'male-slanted'? The traditional division between bad girls and good girls as an effect of their desire, on the one hand, or lack of it on the other, has no place here. Perhaps more generically straightforward cinema does indeed maintain this Madonna/Whore division along the lines of sexual response; as Williams argues:

> Like the slasher film, sadomasochistic pornography is still caught up in the cultural law that divides the 'good' girls from the 'bad'. The slasher film kills off the sexually active 'bad girls,' treating them as the victim-heroines who cannot save themselves, and reserves heroic action to the sexually inactive 'good girl' victim-hero. Sadomasochistic pornography, in contrast, combines the 'good' and 'bad' girls into one person. The passive 'good girl' still needs to prove to the audience of the superego that her orgasms are not willed; but the active 'bad girl' is author and director of the spectacle of coercion designed to fool the superego, and part of her pleasure lodges in the very fact that this superego knows she enjoys it. (1990: 226)

However, these 'devious and indirect forms of subversion/perversion' are *not* present in the good girl/bad girl dynamic of the erotic thriller. At the moment of sexual spectacle these films are supremely uninterested in how characters are ethically aligned, nor do they ethically align women according to their sexual response. Certainly, there are bad girls (Delia Sheppard built a whole career on them), but the division of the good from the bad, necessary as long as you are working through a basic set of thriller narrative co-ordinates, does not take place across attitudes to sex. Good and bad, women and men, all want sex in the DTVs and all are equally applauded for it. The *femme fatale* is *fatale* for reasons other than her desire: heroes and villains who function on a level of plot are not the same as good girls and bad whose meaning is imbued at the level of patriarchal master discourses. These films are certainly not seamlessly radical – they are far too ideologically confused for that – but it is remarkable that here, whilst women can be villains, they are not demonised for their sexuality. If thriller plots demand on some crude level a morally containing dénouement, this is not an effect of, or an opportunity for, sexual punishment.

Another point of attraction for female audiences might be the DTV erotic thriller's interest in women's friendships. These films repeatedly flirt with the possibility of becoming female buddy movies, as women turn to each other for support, sexual advice or a partner in revenge. This is partly facilitated by the generic promiscuity of the erotic thriller (*noir*, revenge and buddy-movie by turns), but the simple point is that women aren't necessarily rivals in the DTVs. Here women have buddies to look out for them. This is rare in the blockbusters:[9] the move from low to high budget loses women their friends. Whilst Glenn Close's character in *Fatal Attraction* has no other contact with women except when she is notoriously dispatched by Archer as righteous wife, the videos tell a different story, of female loyalty to mitigate the isolation. Demi Moore might negotiate each of her choices in *Indecent Proposal* entirely alone, and *Body of Evidence* might pit all three women completely against each other in a triangle of hate (Madonna, Dafoe's wife, and Anne Archer replaying her *Fatal Attraction* role as the now faithful secretary). But in the DTVs women actually *like* each other, and of these simple scenarios some forms of female cinematic pleasure are made.[10] It is true that often the plot function of these friendships is to draw for our heroine a series of erotic vignettes and intrigue, so female friendship functions also as an agent of female spectacle. The benefit of sexual healing is central to the lore which circulates between DTV women, where it is the best friend's role to prescribe a specific sexual cure for the ills of marriage. *Mirror Images*' Kaitlin is urged on by other women, as is typical for the genre: 'You've gone this far,' says lesbian Gina, 'why not keep going?' Disappointed by her husband, Kaitlin is changed by the satisfaction she finds with other men and women – this is signalled, in the simple signification of the erotic thriller, by Kaitlin's renewed interest in her post-coital breakfast: after her first bout of satisfying sex, she ravenously tears at her toast, moaning a little as she swallows.[11] In *The Other Woman* the formerly uptight but now post-coital Jessica arrives at work glowing, with her hair down, wearing casual clothes. *Mirror Images* closes with a freeze-frame of its heroine's face fixed in an expression of sexual satisfaction. It is often best mates who urge our heroines towards this bliss. Elise's chum in *Carnal Crimes* encourages her affair and dismisses all guilt, whilst battered wife June in *Sexual Intent* is told by her friend Kath, 'Sometimes you just have to go for it – listen to your gut for a change.'

In the move from 'low' video to 'high' blockbuster these female friends are lost. Though pre-dating it, *Secret Games* is the mirror-image of *Indecent Proposal*, with women actively choosing high-class, Beverly Hills prostitution, bringing pleasure and profit, in preference to the institutionalised prostitution of marriage. Compare the best friend's cry of *Secret Games*, 'I'm tired of watching you live your life as Mark's prize museum piece', with Demi Moore's astute but impotent, 'You collect things, don't you?', spoken *to* her collector, *as* she is collected in *Indecent Proposal*. In *Secret Games* the discourses of the sexual marketplace are writ large, and capitalist sexual liberation is the starting-point from which other questions may be posed. In both films women are 'bought', but in *Secret Games* women *actively* sell themselves, combining commodity and profiting entrepreneur in one body. Whilst each film is firmly pitched in the world of sexual contract, the difference is finally one of control: better to sell yourself than to find yourself being bought and sold. An even starker image of cashing in your powers comes in the metaphorics through which women take revenge on men. One three-way exchange between women in *Night Eyes* focuses on what a lousy creep Nikki's husband is; a sympathetic police officer says, 'Personally, I'd like to nail the creep', to which Nikki's friend Ellen (Karen Elise Baldwin) retorts, 'Yeah, I'd like to make a gelding out of the little shit.' After a series of airbrushed sex-scenes in *Sexual Intent*, the women get together to dispatch the *homme fatal* John who has conned them all, played by veteran DTV actor Gary Hudson, the bad guy of *Wild Cactus* and *Mind Twister* (who also does a turn as cop-falling-for-suspect in *Indecent Behaviour*). *Sexual Intent* is a mixed-genre confusion of sleaze and feminism, allegedly made for $200,000[12] and featuring a cast of regulars and unknowns. Whilst John is seducing his conquests and visiting his sexy shrink Barbara (Michele Brin) it is an erotic thriller; when prime-conquest June (Sarah Hill) enlists fellow victims it becomes a female-revenge movie, culminating in perhaps the most spectacular and protracted male death in the whole genre, when John is kidnapped by June's cronies, shot and then (accidentally) run over by Barbara.

One way of explaining the appearance of these sentiments is that old-fashioned virtues of female friendship on-screen might offer a way in to a film whose pornographic content might otherwise be problematic for, or exclusive of, women audiences. This doesn't negate the fact that these remain sometimes positive images, which have implications for male viewers as well as female. How, then, do we position the male viewer *vis-à-vis* these messages? Just as these different emphases open doors to women as viewers, so the erotic thriller's 'natural' audience (heterosexual men between eighteen and thirty) might find that straightforward pleasures are troubled by contradiction, and sometimes a political discomfort supplants the glossy sexual thrill.

Building on this is the consistent motif comprising the lousy husband/ neglected wife story which, next to the regular sex- and shower-scenes, is the genre's most reliable staple. 'Have you ever been married?' asks Lara Flynn Boyle of Nic Cage in *Red Rock West*. 'It does strange things to people.' Indeed, the erotic thriller, from cheap exploitation to prestigious art-flicks such as *In the Cut*, is a hotbed of critiques of the institution of marriage, especially in its implications for women. Husbands are neglectful or downright duplicitous, lovers are exciting but dangerous, and the woman's predicament, trapped between these possibilities, is foregrounded. Madonna's line in *Body of Evidence*, 'I never know why men lie – they just do' is the faint, mainstream echo of many angrier voices in the videos. Interestingly, both publicity blurbs and reviewers formulate this as the 'bored housewife' syndrome; reviewing Mundhra's *Sexual Malice*, the softcore website *This is Sexy?* offers in its 'What's Passed Off As Plot' section, 'Once more, bored housewife finds comfort – and murder – in the loins of another man'.[13] The jacket blurb for Dark/Hippolyte's *Carnal Crimes* tells us that this is 'the tense, chilling story of Elise, a beautiful but bored Beverly Hills socialite who becomes a sordid slut to escape the frustration of marriage to her rich, fat husband'.[14] Erotic thriller 'housewives' are, however, more actively rejected than passively bored, more sinned against than sinning. They stray only after months of sexual neglect: all Alex's academic husband can think about in *Wild Cactus* is work, causing her to protest, 'No time is playtime in this marriage!' *Animal Instincts*, as we have seen, offers a pharmaceutical twist on this 'male indifference causes female infidelity' theme, when Joanna is prescribed antidepressants to cope with rejection by her money-obsessed husband, which double as an aphrodisiac and cause her to stray. Women's romantic fiction has long been interested in the intense uncertainty of courtship, the period leading up to the closure of marriage – a happy ending when all questions are answered, when unknowns become known. Ros Coward (1986: 230–1) characterises Mills and Boon romantic novels as stories in which 'the heroine invariably finds material success through sexual submission and marriage'. Elsewhere, she points out that the nineteenth-century novel is largely predicated on the expression of the consciousness and desires of heroines, whose 'choices were for a brief moment before marriage of crucial importance, socially and sexually' (Coward 1984: 178). Earlier, I discussed some erotic thrillers as forms of the paranoid woman's story, especially in their deployment of the female hero/*homme fatal* story. Deborah Jermyn has described female Gothic as a genre in which 'the heroine is typically a young woman either on the brink of marriage or a newlywed' (1996: 264). For the heroines of stories which 'end with a marriage', the legitimisation of the marriage contract resolves sexual uncertainty. For the typical erotic thriller heroine (and some female Gothic protagonists – the second Mrs De Winter in *Rebecca*, or the aforementioned 'hasty marriage' victims), marriage creates a whole new set of sexual problems. The erotic thriller continues the romantic heroine's story, after marriage and into the bedroom, first charting her sexual frustration before following the sexual odyssey she undertakes as solution to her problems.[15]

This heroine's most regular rival is man's obsession with his work, a thread beloved of Axis screenplays: the synopsis which features in the press pack of *Secret Games* includes the detail: 'In a futile attempt to seduce her husband, [Julianne] finds Mark more interested in his architectural plans than her.'[16] Male materialistic obsession makes our heroines acutely conscious of their objectified role as prize possession (the synopsis continues: 'Mark in reality treats Julianne more as a possession than a wife. Showering her with expensive gifts designed to show off his "prize", Mark ignores her emotional and physical needs . . . and controls how she dresses, who she sees and what she reads').[17] Kaitlin's husband Jeff in Dark/Hippolyte's *Mirror Images* won't even touch her, he 'just married me for show' she says.[18] Coward's formulation about fiction as a focus for feminine consciousness finds echoes here too; trash flicks these may be, but in their focus on the female experience of sexual neglect as the flipside of emotional control they make Elise, Julianne and Kaitlin the softcore sisters of a number of nineteenth-century heroines. Of course, the fact that their quests are also the prime pretext for sexual display shifts the film's focus of attention from experience to body. However, female experience is not marginalised by the woman's body: one confusing but inclusive image in Mundhra's *The Other Woman* features a naked Jessica (Lee Anne Beaman) crying in the shower, eliciting simultaneous sympathy and arousal. A brief mirror-scene in *Sexual Malice* shows the lonely heroine Chris (Diana Barton) appraising herself in the mirror, fondling her breast, watched by a hidden man. These are images which – perhaps confusingly and incompletely – try to show that it is possible to look both *with* and *at* the woman. Attempting to appeal to male and female audiences, these images – to speak in the terms of 1970s feminism – objectify and subjectify the woman at the same time, and it would be a mistake to assume that this genre privileges the former over the latter. This conflation of looking and looked-at flirts with the dynamic which finds exhibitionism implicated in voyeurism. In looking as the woman *and* as the man, the viewer bears out the multiple spectatorial perspectives of the cinematic fantasist, but she also bears witness to the female protagonist's final control over where the story goes. In a sense, these women's stories form the meeting point between a woman's view of herself (seeing herself, she is both voyeur and exhibit), her willingness to be viewed, and – as protagonist – her identity and quest as focus for the whole film's point of view (her story drives the narrative; frequently her voice provides the voiceover; she is the conduit of sympathy and empathy). She is the site where view (voyeuristic) and point of view (subjective, cohering, empathic) collide.

But these images are not solely images about looking relations and the imagistic self; they are also about agency and who carries the story. Male hostility and indifference to women here also underpins the economic relationship which constitutes the film's backstory, which is sometimes complicated by other anxieties about female power and control over the Symbolic. If men here prefer money (and the work needed to generate it) over their wives, they also dislike women for a whole slew of other finance-related reasons. The *Carnal Crimes* press synopsis reads: 'Elise approaches Stanley in a sexy negligée, promising him a provocative, early anniversary present. Stanley rejects her proposition coldly, seemingly uninterested in her obvious charms. He reminds her that all they have is due to the fact that business must come first, ahead of all else.'[19] The *homme fatal* of *Sexual Malice* resents his wife's success but covets her cash ('I never loved her,' he says, 'but I did get to love her money'). The rock-dinosaur husband of Mundhra's *Night Eyes* thinks that his wife's humble origins should foster acceptance of his philandering, shouting 'Fuck off, bitch! You were a bloody secretary when I met you!' The film's surveillance of femininity is instigated by this man's insistence on a camera watching his wife's every private move. In *Night*

Eyes 2 Marilyn (Shannon Tweed) is rebuffed in a classic lousy spouse scene by a man who sponges off her private wealth: despite the fact that she's a Playboy pin-up modelling her best undies, her creepy diplomat husband says, 'Stop! I will not be obligated to perform for you!'

Lousy wives also feature in the erotic thriller, but they are treated differently. Because so many of these stories privilege a female point of view and are essentially the heroine's sexual quest story, when the tables are turned and the *woman* loses interest in sex with her husband because of her job, she is viewed far more sympathetically. Erotic thriller neglectful husbands are generally appalling and frequently criminal; erotic thriller neglectful wives are usually nothing worse than preoccupied workaholics, who always thaw out by the end. Perhaps, then, the primary problem the erotic thriller must solve isn't its thin whodunit pretext, but the problem of sexual deprivation – a problem solved by a visit to Dr Feelgood and some generous sexual healing. The Beverly Hills shrink-protagonist of *Body of Influence* (Nick Cassavetes as Jonathan Brooks) has a clientele which 'seems to consist exclusively of the frustrated wives of high-powered men' – he 'heals' them by encouraging them to act out their fantasies (which he conveniently videotapes – 'I find it a very useful therapeutic tool') (Fig. 14). Either way it is the woman's problem to solve: if she is deprived by her husband, she must go elsewhere. If she herself loses interest in sex, this too is the film's problem, for this is a genre in which women must be seen to perform sexually, so any woman who doesn't want to must be made to. Woman either *has* a sexual problem or *is* a sexual problem. The upside of this is that her pleasure is centralised, her role as narrative problem-solver foregrounded. A clear example is *The Other Woman*'s journalist Jessica, with too many deadlines to have sex with her writer husband. The film charts her journey of sexual discovery which takes place whilst he is away on a book tour, promoting his touchy-feely self-awareness book entitled *Letting Go*, something his wife cannot do until she has independently indulged in voyeurism, heterosexual and lesbian infidelity, and has been blackmailed by an incriminating video. Female work does not cuckold men; instead it desexualises women: in voiceover Jessica says that her newspaper workplace was 'The one place I could be the person I kept telling myself I was – brilliant, totally in control, about as feminine as a printing press'.

But just as female sexual problem-solving in this genre provides a pretext for female sexual display, it also offers an opportunity for audiences to enjoy the view of the heroine's sexual partners. The DTVs obligingly deliver ample portions of male beefcake to appeal to female heterosexual (and gay male) audiences. Jag Mundhra in particular reliably provides 'something for the ladies', his 'T&A' sequences usually featuring female 'Ts' and male 'As'. *Sexual Malice* even offers a strip-joint sequence in which an all-girl audience watches an all-male show (but not *all*-male: there are muscular buttocks aplenty but the pouches remain firmly in place. In this, the softest of softcore, not even flaccid penises are allowed). However, it is here that framing the heroine is first set up,

Figure 14: Shrink Jonathan Brookes (Nick Cassavetes) analyses a patient in *Body of Influence*. Courtesy of Upcoast Film Consultants, Inc.

suggesting that participation and surrender to the public spectacle of male flesh is a dangerous pleasure which might ultimately land you in jail. Men also function to 'service' women, as at the start of Hippolyte's *Night Rhythms*, a film which presents a mini-case history in the aural/visual confusions of the erotic thriller. Though driven by a male rather than a female protagonist, *Night Rhythms* sets up its hero Nick (Martin Hewitt) as someone who lives to solve women's sexual problems – he listens to them for a living (he is then framed for a murder, goes on the run and has sex with lots of women whilst trying to prove his innocence). Nick is a radio gigolo (clearly modelled on Clint Eastwood's character in *Play Misty For Me*) who's phone-in show gives women the space to complain about their love lives, and fantasise. As the women become aroused on air whilst talking to him, the phone-in becomes more like a sex chat-line. These are not conventional scenes of heterosexual fulfilment: this is broadcast phone-sex for girls, an aural spectacle. The male protagonist becomes the women's listener, his ears being initially his most important organ (his first words in the film are 'Talk to me, Linda'). As the sounds of women pleasuring themselves waft across from their private bedrooms to the public space of the airwaves, Nick's position becomes curiously complex, both marginalised by the women's pleasure and pivotal to it. Excluded from the physical action, his voice is also a key masturbatory aid, woven into the patchwork of sexual sounds because, as the anchorman, his voice ensures that the show goes on.

So how does the sex between these characters connect with the various relationships of sex which we might be able to construct between male or female viewers of the scene itself? Buried at the heart of one exchange is Elaine, a Playmate of the month spectacle, who is the audio-sexual consumer of the man's voice and is seen only by *us*. Dark/Hippolyte then proceeds to cut between three images: the masturbating Elaine, the speaking mouth of Nick and the ironic glances of Bridget (his producer, played by Delia Sheppard) in the control room. In the middle, Nick sees nothing, though he listens to women and services them with his voice. He's an aural voyeur of their heavy breathing, yet the encounter with Elaine, though spatially distanced, is replete with the metaphorics of vision ('I wish you were here to see them' / 'But I am baby – I'm right beside you' / 'look how wet you are'). Finally, Bridget, a cool observer of the sights and sounds of sex, watches Nick and listens to everyone, in a scene animated for the characters by an aural dynamic of speaking and listening, and animated for us viewers by a visual pattern of editing which keeps cutting from Nick's mouth to Elaine's body. To the diegetic characters female sex is a purely auditory experience; only Hippolyte's viewers see what the women are doing and wearing (or not) in the frequent cutaways to Nick's phone-in punters. *Night Rhythms* thus opens in a strange space as far as female spectacle and the issue of the female-centred narrative are concerned. Though the call-in women *sound* sexy they can't be *seen as* sexy to Nick and the film's other characters, separated as they are by the apparatus of radio. The protagonist consequently does not share the camera's point of view, experienced by the film's viewer in the cutaways which intrude on the private scenes of the women as they talk to Nick. Nick himself is left in the dark, as it were, about what they look like, sitting in his dimly-lit studio drinking his coffee and whispering into his microphone. The scene thus oscillates curiously between public and private, seen and not-seen, voice and spectacle, with the man 'having' them aurally but not visually. And as the scene (and the radio show) builds toward female pleasure as hetero-male-porn spectacle, it also frustrates this, constantly cutting away from naked Elaine and back to Nick's mouth and Bridget's disparaging glances (although it may be Nick's commentary, his voice, which allows the male viewer to insert himself into the scene). The only thing Nick does is speak and break his coffee mug (another softcore euphemism). When this happens, there's an exchange of shots between Nick's mouth, his lacerated hand and Bridget in the control room, all accompanied by the sound of Elaine's climax. It is both a montage of frustration and completion, comprising sex between separated bodies brought together by the voice. Somehow the visual dissonance is rather more interesting than the similar premise which establishes the serial *femme fatale* character Claire Archer in *Body Chemistry III*: here Archer helms a TV sex programme called 'Looking at You' in which viewers with video link-ups phone in and discuss their sex fantasies whilst performing them. All is seen, and seen by all, unlike in *Night Rhythms*, which separates out relationships of seeing and seen. And whilst the visuals display the aroused women's bodies for male heterosexual viewers, *Night Rhythms'* screenplay (giving the reasons why frustrated women phone in) also issues a relentless complaint against men. Male viewers will, then, not wholly have Nick as their surrogate (he sees nothing); instead, they access women's pleasure as secret voyeurs forced to pay for the view by enduring the message that men are sexually deficient. Nick also pays for his participation: one of his listeners comes into the studio and, as she and Nick have on-air sex, she is murdered (by Bridget, it turns out), with Nick being framed for a crime his women listeners apparently heard him commit.

Perhaps most surprising about these narratives, given their ambitions to appeal to softcore couples audiences, is their relentless critique of coupledom. Carl (J. K. Dumont)'s extra-marital affair in *The Pamela Principle* is intercut with footage of weeping brides-to-be at his bridalwear shop, suggesting the cheating and heartbreak to come. Early in *Object of Obsession* Margaret (Erika Anderson) throws her wedding-ring into the fire. If one target audience is that described by Steve and Elizabeth Brent in *The Couples Guide to the Best Erotic Videos* as 'just a normal couple interested in enhancing our sexual pleasure' (1997: 9; the Brents also tell us how many kids they have, and what they grow in their garden as part of a detailing of their 'normal couple' credentials), how do they respond to narrative critiques of marriage and faithful partnership as (to quote *Bitter Moon*) the 'matrimonial tomb'? This latter example, though an erotic melodrama dressed up as an auteur work, is particularly telling for what it learns from and bequeaths to the DTV film. It is essentially the story of two interconnecting relationships gone bad, the frigid, sexless marriage of uptight

Englishfolk Nigel and Fiona (impeccably played by Hugh Grant and Kristin Scott Thomas) and the oversexed experimentalism of Oscar and Mimi (Peter Coyote and Emmanuelle Seigner). Like some bizarre cinematic Scheherazade, Oscar must tell – and Nigel must listen to – stories of his sadomasochistic relationship of dependence with Mimi. Nigel wants what Oscar has, though eventually it is Fiona who fulfils Mimi. No couple in this quartet of extreme repression and ludicrous over-expression is seen to be happy or fulfilled. Though its dimensions are almost identical to the DTV movie which *Bitter Moon* would expect to rise above, its art-house credentials (respected European director, up-and-coming or veteran A-list performers, bohemian pretensions which would have it compared to Henry Miller or Anaïs Nin rather than Greg Hippolyte or Katt Shea) ensure that it will never play as a 'couples' fuck-film (it is also all talk and little action). Nevertheless, *Bitter Moon* is but an extreme example of the couples-critique which underpins the central narrative of the DTV erotic thriller: conventionally sanctioned relationships are stifling; sexual adventure can only be found outside, beyond. That this 'escape fantasy' is central to the desire landscape of couples sex-cinema is one of the genre's fascinating paradoxes.

What softcore women's stories do to and for male viewers is another question. Like Carol Clover's male horror spectators, whose presumed identification with the (male) monster shifts from sadistic to masochistic as the monster becomes the film's ultimate victim at the hands of the 'final girl', the aroused male who buys an erection at the expense of having to listen to a diatribe against the average guy's sexual neglect of women, or who has only lousy husbands, murderers and conmen with whom to identify, is in a difficult position. Michael Douglas's neo-Cain male has been seen as one risky symptom of the genre's gender crisis, and there are countless feckless weak men at the cheaper end of production too. In *Object of Obsession* Margaret is basically kidnapped by Blaze (Scott Valentine), who subjects her to various sexual experiments. However, she soon realises that the door isn't locked, frees herself, then returns, only to turn the sexual tables on Blaze, locking him into the sumptuous prison he has constructed for her (and numerous women before her, whom she avenges at the film's conclusion). The image these films deliver to their male audience is, then – for one respondent in Springer's *Some Nudity Required* – far more problematic than their image of women:

> I think the kinds of archetypes that get portrayed in B films are equally as damaging to young boys than the female archetypes. . . . What are the kinds of men in these films? The men are rapists, the men are murderers . . . the men are people who don't have much consciousness.[20]

DTV softcore is thus predicated on a conundrum for men: the need to show lots of female nudity ensures women's stories are foregrounded, but the genre goes further, all but demonising a large proportion of its male representations. The few exceptions to this may be the odd decent male protagonist, or the rare, sexually satisfying man who doesn't fuck over our heroine at the same time as he fucks her.

3: THE UNDERCOVER HEROINE

'You know what they say about broads in uniform, don't you?
They're either nymphos, lesbos or psychos.'

Officer Earnest Pitts (Carl Anthony) in Black & White

A development of the DTV's focus on female agency comes through the disguise/discovery scenario, whereby a heroine undergoes some process of existential self-awareness through going undercover, usually as a stripper, high-class hooker or some other sex industry worker. The fact that someone is not what they seem has long been a staple of *noir*ish sexual scenarios: in the mainstream *Palmetto femme fatale* Elisabeth Shue encourages Woody Harrelson's suspicion that she is a wired undercover cop by presenting him with her behind and inviting him to do a thorough search (he obliges). But as a narrative mainstay the DTVs may have taken a number of cues from mainstream models – the 'bored housewife moonlights as classy hooker' theme of *Secret Games* owes much to *Belle de Jour* and its 1980s homage, *Crimes of Passion*. Christine Gledhill has noted the propensity of *noir* thrillers to 'locate strong women in image-producing roles – night-club singers, hostesses, models etc.', a means by which heroines are created,

> whose means of struggle is precisely the manipulation of the image which centuries of female representations have provided. Thus, though the heroines of film noir, by virtue of male control of the voice-over, flashback structure, are rarely accorded the full subjectivity and fully expressed point of view of psychological realist fiction, yet their performance of the roles accorded them in this form of male story-telling foregrounds the fact of their image is an artifice and suggests another place behind the image where the woman might be. (1998: 30–1)

The 'undercover' stories I want to look at now are progressions of this model: narratively speaking they are female- rather than male-controlled, allotting their protagonists as much 'full subjectivity and fully expressed point of view' as the trash-DTV film will allow. They also, by virtue of making their protagonists diegetically step from straight heroine to performed persona (in often 'image-producing' roles) take issue with the various identities women inhabit. Uniforms enable all sorts of discoveries, as does taking them off and donning a 'foreign' uniform. Mainstream erotic thrillers sometimes do this too – *Black Widow*, for instance, features cop Debra Winger masquerading as a tourist in order to befriend, and perhaps trade identities with, the *femme fatale* of the title (Theresa Russell). But the DTVs seem positively obsessed with the issue. In *Sins of Desire* Gail Harris (Tanya Roberts) goes undercover as a sex-therapy nurse. In *The Other Woman* Jessica (Lee Anne Beaman) gets access to a softcore photo-shoot (entitled, appropriately for an erotic thriller, 'Crimes of Passion') by pretending to be a journalist investigating the adult industry. In *Cover Me* (one of Playboy's mid-1990s attempts to make mainstream movies) cop Holly Jacobson (Courtney Taylor) goes undercover as a topless model to catch a cross-dressing killer of glamour models. In *Black & White*, our first image of Gina Gershon's tough cop character is in deep cover: a whore is standing in the middle of the police station, presumably there to be booked. In fact, the thigh-high PVC boots, hot-pants and red wig connote a higher kind of authority, and in this garb she introduces herself to her new partner, a bemused, much younger rookie. But it is Gregory Dark/Hippolyte's films which betray a most insistent interest in disguise, identity challenges and role play. *Body of Influence* plays out a knowingly absurd tale of repressed Laura (Shannon Whirry) who creates a sexualised *alter-ego* Lana to do her 'dirty work' (as her shrink's voiceover tells it, 'Laura's problem was now clear: her sexual instincts were so severely repressed they had taken on an identity of their own – the bad girl Lana'). But when Whirry's double-character emerges as another *fatale*, the 'real' woman is crystallised as Lana, with Laura her good girl fabrication.[21] In *Mirror Images* (1991) this is refracted through the doubling and fragmentation of a twins sce-nario, which is, as we have seen, a common pairing for women in cinematic and literary *noir*.[22] Delia Sheppard plays the double role of twins Kaitlin and Shauna, replaying a mystery/thriller staple, the good twin/bad twin axis, which Brian De Palma had tried out in the proto-erotic thriller *Sisters*.[23] *Mirror Images* is terribly self-conscious about its own visuality, opening with photo-graphic and camcorder images of twin girls, and making constant play on the reflexivity of video, TV and films-within-films. If one Delia wasn't enough for you, this film gives you Delia in duplicate, then often doubled again by her own mirror reflection: 'You can't be in two places at once,' says Shauna's lover to her, but it seems that Delia can. In fact, the film's first image of Kaitlin is three-fold – the back of her auburn head as she sits at her dressing table, duplicated by two mirrored reflections. A fairly early Axis film, *Mirror Images* might act as a blueprint for what was to follow, particularly in the key period 1992–5. Kaitlin's husband is a louse: in the first few minutes we discover that he hasn't made love to her for months, he is repelled by her touch and he thinks more of his job as a political spin-doctor than he does of his wife, so the demure Kaitlin has to turn elsewhere for her favours.[24] When her twin sister Shauna, a raunchy rock-chick with big blonde hair, mysteriously leaves town, Kaitlin is able to insert herself into her place and her lingerie, and discover that there's more to life than political functions. This is the opening for a series of set-pieces: Kaitlin alone in her white lacy lingerie (Delia Sheppard's trademark uniform), playing with a chiffon scarf, or taking a shower; Kaitlin-as-Shauna stripping for and then having sex with LA rock-lover Joey; Kaitlin writhing in a moment of lesbian experimentation beneath a mirrored ceiling with Gina.

Like its Axis stablemates, *Mirror Images* and its sequel are unquestionably not what cinephiles would think of as 'good' films. Yet both know what they need to do as formulaic genre-pieces. That said, no individual film is ever *only* generically formulaic, and the *Mirror Images* films, for all their clunking predictability, gesture towards some interesting areas, as many 'twins films' do.[25] In particular, the accoutrements of masquerade, as one twin 'becomes' her other (courtesy of key elements of *mise-en-scène* such as clothes, makeup, hair), facilitate the heroine's problem-solving and lend themselves to comedic parody. Rebuilding herself as Shauna from the underwear upwards, Kaitlin tries out an adjacent, same-but-different identity, exploring the fact that (as one twin says to another in a dream sequence) 'It's not easy getting back through the looking glass'. This is partly approached through a good twin/bad twin story (Shauna dresses in black, Kaitlin in white), which is scuppered when the twins turn out to be the best of friends: 'Nobody messes with my sister,' says Shauna, as she rescues Kaitlin at the film's climax. She is, however, the locus of *Mirror Image*'s role as both erotic *and* a thriller. Through Shauna, suburban housewife Kaitlin finds sex, but through Shauna she also dabbles in crime. 'If only you could talk,' Kaitlin declares to Shauna's extensive wig collection (they don't have to, as the nefarious details of Shauna's life soon emerge). A daft drug-smuggling sub-plot and a murder later, Kaitlin-as-Shauna is donning a policewoman's uniform and coming on to handsome detectives, as the film briefly slides from the characteristic Axis overillumination to a more *noir*-ish lighting set-up which tracks the gun-toting Kaitlin as she searches for evidence.

Mirror Images II is not so much a sequel as a slightly varied remake. Instead of twin Delia Sheppards we have twin Shannon Whirrys, but this time the good and bad twins are terminally divided by a troubled family backstory, a motif reminding us of the problematic identity agenda through repeated flashbacks to the *noir*ish night that their father murdered their mother. It is perhaps the audience which is the greatest victim of this film's identity confusions, for Terrie and Carrie's role exchanges take place without forewarning, augmenting the sense that we are lost in a sea of conflicting motivations. Good (frigid) sister Carrie believes that bad (promiscuous) sister Terrie was killed in a fire following their father's death, when really the fiendish Terrie is alive and well and doing things like fucking Carrie's husband, fucking her maid's husband, fucking her shrink and fucking the private detective Carrie hires (and those in a position to compare miraculously discern no difference in sexual technique when the bad twin masquerades as the good). *Mirror Images II* is a reliable genre-piece because it manages to present a ludicrously complicated murder/corruption/double-crossing mystery, complete with confused identities, private detectives, oedipal sex ('Daddy's watching,' says Carrie's husband as she – or is it Terrie? – has sex with a woman) and a considerable helping of therapeutic psycho-babble, all mixed with a plethora of sex-scenes starring one of softcore's most recognisable stars. Its conclusion is also uncharacteristically nihilistic. Carrie and Terrie, having blurred the good girl/bad girl distinction by agreeing that they are exactly the same, shoot it out without men or cameras present. Having spent eighty-eight minutes identifying closely with Carrie against Terrie, we are left not knowing which twin has survived and which has died (there has been a sub-plot twist about exchanged dental records, so whoever survives either *is* Carrie or is able to *masquerade* as Carrie). Though the last thing this character says is that it doesn't make a bit of difference if she is really Carrie or Terrie, it does to the viewer, who is left not knowing whether their 'preferred' twin has survived. But this is also another effective deconstruction of the good girl/bad girl hierarchy of other cinemas, functioning rather like Jermyn's (1996) deconstruction of the victim-wife/female psychopath dyad in various contemporary 'bitches from hell' films. Jermyn argues that 'the feminist appropriation of the double' is 'an important act of critical resistance' (1996: 263) because of the figure's potential to resist the virgin/whore dichotomy. Of course, no one in a Hippolyte film is a virgin, and being a whore is, we might say, a virtue. Nevertheless both *Mirror Images* films begin with a 'good twin/bad twin' premise but refuse to choose the good over the bad: in the first through the friendship of the twins; in the second through the nihilistic refusal to say which twin survived. This is not to read Hippolyte/Dark as wholeheartedly critically resistant to dominant pernicious images, rather that we don't have to dig beyond text into subtext to find a reading of oppositional femininities, which is sometimes surprising.

In Hippolyte's 1995 film *Undercover* (released as *Undercover Heat* in the USA), some of these issues are pursued further, with one woman trying out different identities through an active sexual project. A number of 'undercover films' feature revealing 'disguise sequences', transformations which function like the action film's 'tooling up' scene. Here the heroine becomes her own sexualised *alter-ego* courtesy of a new wardrobe, in order to fulfil her investigative or revenging mission. In this genre disguise is another word for sexualisation: these sequences are the erotic thriller equivalent of the plain-Jane secretary letting her hair down and casting her spectacles aside. As with Kaitlin's adoption of Shauna's clothes, going undercover is a form of self-discovery, achieved via a sexual mask. Disguise, then, is usually not a form of physical putting on, but a way of getting naked: the serious professional woman undoes rather than covers up, though this becomes transformative. The disguise sequence of Mundhra's *Improper Conduct* is typical: dowdy Kay (Lee Anne Beaman again) takes revenge on her sister's boss (who was responsible for her death) by going undercover as his new PA: the camera catches the grieving Kay crying into the mirror, pans away, then pans back to find her fully sexualised in black lace, stroking her legs and ready to vamp it up for the unsuspecting villain. In *Undercover* Athena Massey plays Cindy, a cop who goes into deep cover at a brothel where a call-girl has been murdered. Predictably, Cindy comes to enjoy the tricks and casts off her inhibitions, describing this as 'getting lost' inside the character she's playing. Clearly, the driving force behind this narrative turn is the opportunity to display Massey in various scenarios, either without her clothes or kitted out in fetishistic sex-gear. But just as alternative identities enable sexual experimentation, so sexual experimentation enables characters to try out new personae. If the first is driven by the need for softcore spectacle, the insistence of the second across a range of Hippolyte's films means that sex also drives a more interesting set of possibilities for exploring alternative identities. In other words, this exchange of favours between lowest common denominator sex spectacle and more complex identity issues means that we need to rethink the question of priorities, of what drives what, in the erotic thriller. If – as is repeatedly said of these films – plot is a thin excuse for sex, sex can also frame and implement questions of subjectivity.

Undercover owes a lot to Kathryn Bigelow's *Blue Steel*, particularly in its interest in the woman (not just the body) underneath the uniform. Like Bigelow's film, it opens with its heroine getting dressed. This has the double effect of foregrounding the primary spectacle of Massey's body and introducing the secondary question of Cindy's self-uncertainty. As is often the case with the more interesting DTV erotic thrillers, what we see and what we hear splits the film in two directions. We *watch* a naked woman first putting on her white underwear, then donning masculine gear – jeans, heavy boots, gun. But we *hear* a woman's voiceover telling us of her desire for solitude, her overbearing family ('It wasn't just protection. It was more like house arrest'), her uncertainty regarding her own femininity ('I can finally act like a normal woman, whatever "normal" is' she says, as she picks up her cop's identity shield). As the clothes goes on (promising to softcore viewers that they will be coming off again later) so a backstory of female repression begins to unfold. Like *Sexual Intent*'s vox-pops, a woman's story begins to be told right at the start of the credit sequence. It would be easy to say that the spectacle is for the objectifying eyes of the male heterosexual viewer, and the voice/story is for the empathetic ears of the female audience (and just as easy to retort that it's a minor miracle that there *is* anything here for the female viewer at all). But unless you watched the film with the sound turned down (which probably has been done) it would be hard cleanly to extrapolate narrative from spectacle, female story from female body, voice from underwear. Both sides of the couples audience get both stories right from the start. And if the image–sound combination cannot be neatly divided into what the woman says and what she looks like, neither can the audience be separated into those interested in looking and those interested in hearing – the two come packaged together, so the audience must make some effort if it is to reject or accept one over the other. Roger Horrocks reads porn as a form in which the female body is 'put on' by the viewer, whether male or female (1995: 122). Is the arousal which is facilitated by this overt masquerade what makes these films particularly interesting?

Dressing up is also the context for the various kinds of sexual role-play which the film shows, and the issue of sex-as-theatre is foregrounded. The murderer in *Undercover* gets the victim to call on him by disguise and pretence, a motif which is repeated when the next girl calls on him; he is one of their regular johns

THE EROTIC THRILLER IN CONTEMPORARY CINEMA

THE EROTIC THRILLER IN CONTEMPORARY CINEMA

pretending to be a stranger, the known masquerading as unknown. In keeping with the 'classy' look of Dark/Hippolyte's *mise-en-scène*, brothel *madame* Mrs V says, 'This is the *crème de la crème*. . . . They come here for pleasure, for theatre. They come here either to be empowered, or to have power lorded over them. You must be an actress.' When Cindy insists to her police colleagues that despite the dangers she must continue with her assignment, one retorts, 'Don't be John Wayne'. That Wayne is embodied in this film by a woman in a brothel wearing designer underwear is intriguing in itself, but Cindy then comes to enact a double-masquerade when she 'entertains' a client with a police-show, 'arresting' then overpowering him in a PVC-fetish cop's uniform (breasts visible, however).[26] The scene also seems to be an ironic reversal of one in *Cruising*, in which Al Pacino's cop, undercover in the gay S&M scene, is thrown out of a club because he's the only one who *isn't* dressed in cop's uniform. Though still a cop, Cindy enjoys sex work because it gives her a chance – as she puts it – to sow a few wild oats, but it is only within the performance of sex-work that she can become a sexualised cop. Gina Gershon's cop character in *Black & White* only dates fellow cops because 'civilians' either want 'to see your gun or they don't want you to carry a gun or they want to put your gun somewhere where it doesn't belong', recalling Ron Silver's fetishisation of Jamie Lee Curtis's weapon in *Blue Steel*. To recall the epigraph to this section, Cindy becomes a nympho-psycho only in donning her cop playwear; the real uniform had done exactly the opposite for her. Here is a cop masquerading as a prostitute masquerading as a cop. That the first is a professional masquerade and the second is a sexual one only shows that the two sides of Cindy's persona (work and sex, voice and body) are interdependent: through sex Cindy can act out a sexual version of the cop-persona she has abandoned. Only when she is back at work and pulled off the case does she articulate how sex-work had enabled her to connect the masculinity of police work with the femininity of her sexuality. Asking her partner how being taken off a case made him feel he says, 'Like the guest of honour at a gelding', to which Cindy replies, 'Well I don't have the same props that you have, but I do have the same feelings'. Costume (and the lack of it) as a way of developing this double emphasis on sexuality and power (or its lack) is a common Dark/Hippolyte trait.

When *Showgirls* and *Striptease* came out *The Guardian* proclaimed that the Hollywood wardrobe departments ought to be in fear of their jobs given the ratio between slivers of cloth and acres of flesh in the neo-sex film (Katz 1995: 5). However Hippolyte and his erotic thriller stablemates are as fond of the lacy or mildly fetishistic accoutrements of vanilla sex as they are of nakedness itself. In *Undercover* seasoned prostitute Rain (Rena Riffel, who moved into A-list films with small roles in *Showgirls*, *Striptease* and *Mulholland Drive*) shows Cindy how to strip seductively for her clients, embellishing the scene with the aura of lesbianism (she's diegetically stripping for Cindy's pleasure as well as her instruction, whilst the wider audience watches one watching the other). Cindy then repeats this in a later show for one of her own clients (Rain plays a seductive stripper; Cindy then plays Rain playing a seductive stripper, and becomes one herself at two removes). This is prefigured by a rather less theatrical show of girlie post-shopping dressing up: after taking the undercover assignment Cindy returns to her flat with bags full of purchases, and her new identity is paraded for our pleasure when she tries everything on in front of the mirror. This again is accompanied by a self-deprecating voiceover, but here even her body is split: from the neck down she's a lingerie model, in her lacetop stockings and PVC boots; from the neck up she performs unconvinced puzzlement as her thoughts run, in voiceover: 'Look at this! . . . Is that me? Nah – can't be me – I am looking at someone else here!' (Fig. 15) We too are sharing her point of view of the mirror-image rather than looking directly at Cindy herself. This would not be surprising in more critically debated costume-change works such as Sally Potter's *Orlando* or Mike Nichols' *Tootsie*; that softcore schlock bothers to articulate identity quandaries suggests the possibility that here Dark/Hippolyte's interest in clothes goes beyond their removal. I now wish to develop some of these identity observations by looking at a sub-genre of the erotic thriller which has specialised in the 'undercover' motif: the striptease film.

4: THE STRIP-FLICK

Striptease films are as old as cinema – for as long as bodies have been filmed, they have been filmed in the process of becoming naked. Early peep-show flicks featured fleshly beauties captured by the voyeuristic cinematograph in the act of disrobing. There has always been a market for cinematic striptease, from early 'smokers', through the burlesque films of the 1940s and 1950s, to nudie-cuties and stag films. Striptease has also featured in more respectable mainstream films (even in classical Hollywood: think of *Gilda*, *Pal Joey* or *Gypsy*). But the 1990s saw an unprecedented revival of the striptease film, in both mainstream and DTV forms, in the wake of a wider popular cultural interest in different ways for women to take off their clothes. In the UK in particular, this was the decade when pole-, table- and lap-dancing clubs moved into respectable locations, and became the business entertainment venue of choice. Where popular sex culture led, cinema followed – even respectable Mike Figgis features a scene in a lap-dancing club in *Internal Affairs*. Huge budget star vehicles such as Verhoeven's *Showgirls* or Andrew Bergman's *Striptease* exploited the form, as did art-house and indie works such as Atom Egoyan's *Exotica*, Michael Radford's *Dancing at the Blue Iguana* or Ice Cube's *The Players Club*. Even Peter Cattaneo's *The Full Monty*, a humanised strip-flick, exploits the market which developed around female-focused 'hen party' male acts such as The Chippendales and The London Knights.

But the strip-flick proper was made for home viewing. Indeed, the majority of contemporary examples resemble pornographic showcase collections (such as *Playboy*'s centrefold portmanteaux) but with added narrative. Around eight or ten 'dance' sequences are strung out along the story functioning like the

Figure 15: 'Is that me? . . . I am looking at someone else here':
Cop Athena Massey masquerades as a hooker in *Undercover*.
Courtesy of Upcoast Film Consultants, Inc.

sex-scenes in a conventional erotic thriller. If sex-scenes are, as Williams has said, a sex film's version of the musical's production number (1990: 120–52), strip sequences are both sex-scenes *and* production numbers, since they are choreographed and played out to music. Erotic thriller sex-scenes, however gratuitous, do sometimes have a narrative and character function; by contrast strip-scenes are usually narratively insignificant. Typically, the star will perform several times, but her co-strippers – perhaps five or six of them – will also each take the spotlight once, often accompanied by pop songs with excruciatingly literal lyrics, in an attempt to show strip as an externalisation of self. Many sexually-inflected films will ring the changes with perhaps one scene set in a strip-joint: *Black & White*, for instance, contains a stark exploitation edit, from a well-mannered conversation at a police station to close-ups of breasts and gyrating lap-dancers at a strip-joint, which just happens to be where a witness is available for questioning. But though *Black & White* has a full quota of sex/crime intrigue, this is the film's only example of graphic nudity, as if it had been edited in to please the DTV softcore aficionado expecting something more from a Gina Gershon thriller. Nevertheless, the gesture is common enough, even in highbrow auteur works like *In the Cut*, which contains a similar exploitation cut to a strip-joint, over which one of its key characters (Jennifer Jason Leigh) just happens to live. Jim McBride's 1986 film *The Big Easy* flirts with erotic thriller conventions by situating an entrapement scene setting up morally lax cop-hero Remy (Dennis Quaid) in a strip-club: an iconic image features Remy taking his packet of filthy lucre whilst topless girls cavort on stage in the background. *Sexual Intent* contains several strip-joint scenes justified by the profession of one of the characters, as does *Night Rhythms*, which features David Carradine as a gangster strip-joint owner (in one iconic genre-shot in that film, Martin Hewitt and Deborah Driggs hold up Carradine with guns whilst strippers are viewed through a gap in the curtain). But for the strip-flick proper, the world of the club is the world of the film.

Here A-list stars slum it in order to take the next career step; DTV stars define their genre identity through the strip-flick. Demi Moore was paid an alleged $12 million for getting her kit off in *Striptease*, just another stage in a highly body-focused career. 'Demi bares all' was *Striptease*'s unabashed tag-line, and stories of her relentless workouts to get the film's central commodity – that body – to the peak of profitable perfection circulated in the publicity. Daryl Hannah similarly prepared for her *Blue Iguana* role (which involved building up rather than down – she was too skinny at first, poor thing), and – in a curious real-life twist on the undercover-stripper flicks – went undercover herself, training and then stripping for real disguised by a wig. If Hannah's method-driven research sounds spookily like a DTV plot (respectable actress just *has* to take her clothes off for real to prepare for the right role), then look no further than *Lap Dancing*, which features an aspiring actress who finds work in a 'gentleman's club' to prepare herself for work in erotic films: life imitates B-movies. But whilst Moore and Hannah dipped in and out of the genre, the DTV strip-flick has regular stars and directors who have defined themselves through the genre: they include Maria Ford, Kim Dawson and Tane McClure (Doug's daughter: from Trampas to tramp in one generation), whilst a number of contemporary B-directors have had a go, including Fred Olen Ray and (most regularly in this sub-genre) Mike Sedan. Veteran exploitation maestro Roger Corman is also fond of setting films in strip-joints, capitalising on the genre's ample potential for remakes and sequels, though Katt Shea discusses below how at first she had to work hard to persuade him of the merits of this in *Stripped to Kill*. Connoisseurs of DTV soft-core, discussing the genre on internet film sites, use 'high' (expensive, respectable) or 'low' (cheap and trashy) versions of the same films as a benchmark. *Lap Dancing* is the DTV version of *Showgirls*;[27] *Confessions of a Lap Dancer* the DTV version of *Striptease*. Originality is not at issue, only how many interesting quirks and variations on the theme have been injected into a standard formula on a minuscule budget. Makers of DTV strip-flicks aren't fussy about whether their inspiration comes from films which were successful in the first place: the expensive *Showgirls* flopped on a grand scale, whilst the cheap but energetic *Showgirl Murders* succeeded in its own little world. Where the big-star *Striptease* was generally considered to have failed on the big screen, the micro-budget *Stripteaser*, *Stripteaser 2* and *Stripshow* worked for home viewers on video. The B-feature's trump card was to add murder to the mix, turning mainstream melodramatic cheesecake such as *Striptease* into quickie 'suspense-in-suspenders' fare. But fans know the genre rules and scorn any violations: 'Now please get this straight,' writes exploitation commentator Joe Bob Briggs; 'male psychos kill centrefold models. Female psychos kills strippers. Violate these rules, and you end up with garbage like "Showgirls".'

The queen of the genre is Katt Shea (formerly Katt Shea Ruben), whom we have to thank for the archetypal stripper-in-peril film *Stripped to Kill* and its sequel. These are particularly good examples of the 'undercover' staple, in which an attractive female professional (here a detective) pretends to be a stripper in order to the catch a killer preying on the girls, and just *has* to strip herself to be convincing – uncovering whilst undercover – thus discovering her sexual potential as she simultaneously solves the crime (the first film gives rise to a fine 'I'm taking you off the case' line of dialogue, when the female detective-turned-stripper is told 'you can hang up your G-string'). In a rare critical discussion of striptease movies (which focuses on how the films conform to whilst simultaneously challenging Mulvey's model of female to-be-looked-at-ness), Jeffrey A. Brown formulates this storyline as 'dance, be stalked, kill the stalker' (2001: 57). In *Stripped to Kill* the story runs more like: go undercover, dance, catch the killer, discover your sexuality, go back to normal life transformed. As Shea attests in my interview, she was most interested in showing how the strip-scene context provides a location for some level of self-expression as well as the opportunity for considerable assertiveness (her heroine says of the stripping experience, 'It is interesting. It's more than just going out there and turning them on. It's like something's cutting loose'). Other psycho-at-large-in-the-strip-joint flicks include *Midnight Tease* (which, like *Stripped to Kill 2* before it, injects a supernatural stripper-dreams-the-murders-so-did-she-do-it? slant to the format) and *Midnight Tease 2* (another undercover story), but the DTV strip-flick is also willing to hybridise in any genre direction it can. The 'Titty Twister' sequence in *From Dusk till Dawn* is Disney compared to a tributary of the strip-flick, the vampire-stripper film, which marries flesh with blood in a neat hybrid of film sensation. The Shea-directed and Corman-produced *Dance of the Damned* (vampire and stripper philosophise about life) was remade by Corman (never afraid of using the same idea twice) with more money as *To Sleep with a Vampire*, and as *Dance with Death* (directed by Charles Philip Moore, but based on Shea's story). Shea's *Dance of the Damned* co-writer Andy Ruben went on to make the far less cerebral *Club Vampire*, which was not just vampires *and* strippers, but vampires *as* strippers. Whilst both *Vamps: Deadly Dreamgirls* and the Grace Jones vehicle *Vamp* cast pretty vampires as strippers all the better to lure their male bait, *Night Shade* rings the changes when a man discovers his dead wife is now working as an undead stripper.

Stripper-thrillers, stripper-horror – there are also stripper-melodramas. This, essentially, is where the mainstream strip-flick goes, in an attempt also to woo female audiences. As with the female-friendly DTVs discussed above, *Blue Iguana* and *Striptease* may entice women into watching by the (sometimes thin) female-centred narrative, driven by (sometimes strong) female protagonists. Once again, it seems occasionally that the narratives are there just to keep women interested so that the boys can get their fill, it may also be that with stripper-melodramas heterosexual men end up watching an interesting women's film decorated with T&A. This is achieved through a 'strippers are real people too' movie-of-the-week message. For this to work the 'dance' sequences must be balanced by moving scenes which show us the girls as both sexy *and* sensitive; troubled souls who just happen to trade in titillation. Lacing the porn with some poignant profundity is an attempt to justify the erotic through recourse to the emotive. Backstories of 'real lives' are transplanted wholesale from melodrama and focus particularly on showing how maternal they are. In *Blue Iguana* Daryl Hannah's character strives to foster a child and fantasises about being pregnant, whilst Jennifer Tilly's character leaves the abortion clinic with her foetus intact and determined to prove that tramps make good mothers too (she later warns her private clients about her lactating breasts). But thwarted mothers weep tears aplenty in *Blue Iguana*'s forebears: in *Striptease* Moore's character is driven to disrobe to support the custody battle over her daughter, a dilemma shared by Erica, heroine of *Confessions of a Lap Dancer* (1997), whilst in *Dance of the Damned* the kidnapped stripper is suicidal because she is denied access to her child. The spectre of unfit, and unfulfilled, motherhood haunts these women's every turn around the pole.

So too does the possibility that they're as dumb as they look, so concealed mental agility is as compulsory for some celluloid strippers as manifest physical talent. The family-focused heroine of *The Players Club* strips to fund herself

through college, whilst Sandra Oh's Jasmine in *Blue Iguana* goes to poetry readings and reads her own work to a disillusioned porn star. Akin also to the backstage musical, a strip-film staple is the communal dressing-room scene, with
barbed personal chit-chat carried out over the cheap costumes and coiffure,
spiced up by the occasional catfight. The resounding 'feel good' message is that
you have seen and survived the squalid underbelly of the sex industry and discovered a solid camaraderie amongst the low-lifes, more genuine than the
passing affections of their hypocritical punters. A portmanteau style often suits
this message, with the wages of sin presented as a variety of punishments as
characters' individual stories scatter them onto the skids: not only might you
lose your child, you might fight or succumb to drug addiction, the threats of
psycho-johns, the killer on the loose. And here beats the contradictory heart of
the exploitation film: whilst purporting to show us pseudo-realistically how
exploited these women are in the backstage scenes, strip-films exist to exploit
them afresh in the 'dance' numbers.

5: SEQUELS AND REPETITIONS

'Give us the same film, only different.'

Jim Wynorski (McDonagh 1995: 14)

One last word on the DTV film, and that is repetition. Many DTV erotic thrillers replicate the plot-lines and sensational motifs of mainstream fare (and vice
versa). Fred Olen Ray refers to this as 'deli platter' filmmaking – a particular
genre menu, guaranteeing optimum performance in foreign markets, is ordered
by the companies who employ him (1991: 182). The DTV sequel is, however,
a form of lucrative self-generating self-cannibalism. DTVs manifest an intensified form of new Hollywood's propensity to repeat itself in the form of
sequels, and the erotic thriller is as prone to this as any other exploitation genre
– perhaps more so. Kate Stables asks why the contemporary *femme fatale* survives at the end of the film, when her forebears were killed off in a sweep of
moral closure. Is the survival of Bridget at the end of *The Last Seduction* or
Catherine at the end of *Basic Instinct* telling us 'that the combination of poly-
semic narratives and the enigmatic figure of the *femme fatale* is producing films
that cannot achieve closure? That ideology no longer requires the suppression
of self-determining female sexuality? Or that postmodern cinema works an ultimately dominant feminist discourse into its construction of the *femme fatale*?'
(Stables 1998: 171). Or perhaps that the film's producers, realising that she is
the most marketable character, need her for the sequel? Whilst I am rather glad
that the death of Rebecca precludes *Body of Evidence 2*, *The Last Seduction 2*
went DTV in 1999. The 1990s *femme fatale* is a franchise, primarily surviving
in sequel form for the DTV market. Yet whereas in mainstream sequel production there will be some sort of thematic or character consistency between instalments of the same title (making them look rather like big screen episodes in a

cinematic series), DTV sequels show no desire to conform to the requirements of consistency. The titles thus function more like franchises than umbrellas; modes of repetition rather than arcs of coherence. There may be nothing about the titles in series such as the *Illicit Dreams* or *Poison Ivy* films which links the second to the first 'instalment'.[28] No characters survive between films; there are no story-arcs which connect elements of the overall series as there are in mainstream sequel machines such as *Die Hard* or *Back to the Future*. Greg Hippolyte's two *Mirror Images* films have no relationship with each other except a set of common repeated themes. The *Animal Instincts* films (all variations on a voyeurism theme) feature a heroine with the same name, and in the first two she is played by Shannon Whirry, but the connection ends there. Sequels are often isolated episodes which function in the same way as the previous series' instalment, with little story or character development between films (thus challenging their claim to be sequels). Confusingly, some actors pop up again and again in the same franchise, making no reference to who they were when you saw them in the last film of that title. There is, in other words, no 'previously on' aspect to *Secret Games*, *Animal Instincts* or most of the more sequelised DTVs. This means that there is no limitation posed by prior events or resolutions, but nor is there the opportunity to push an idea or character further than the duration of each 90-minute atomised narrative: each film starts afresh with a blank canvas of suspense potential. A kind of narrative amnesia thus spookily pervades these films: remember enough of the first *Secret Games* to know that you want to rent another film like it, but forget that you ever saw Martin Hewitt in it because by *Secret Games 2* he has changed identity and profession. Forget too the lessons learned and the mistakes made in the first film of a series, because similar hurdles will inevitably be negotiated in the second and third.

The exceptions to this rule of forgetfulness make viewing even more confusing. Like the *Emmanuelle* series of films (which itself became a cable franchise), two erotic thriller film sequel-series in particular look more like feature-length instalments in an erotic cable TV series (a sister genre to the feature-length erotic thriller). The four *Night Eyes* films and the first three *Indecent Behaviour* films present events in the life of the same protagonist, whom viewers can thus expect to see in each sequel. In the *Night Eyes* films Andrew Stevens' surveillance company ('Night Eyes Security') prospers enough to survive into each sequel: in *1* he is an employee saving up to travel; by *2* he owns the company, and by *3* it is the security company of choice for the residents of Beverly Hills, but by *4* Will is in a coma for most of the film, leaving his partner Jeff to take over the action. Thus Will is there enough to reassure audiences that they are in roughly the same narrative universe, and at the conclusion he engages in an explicit franchise handover as if *Night Eyes* were some formation of *Star Trek*. The company's growth between films is achieved despite the fact that it is the failures of Will's security systems which allow the villains to imperil the heroine. Though a bachelor in *Night Eyes* and *Night Eyes 2*, by the third film (made a year after its predecessor) Will has had time to get married, divorced and have a (now eight-year-old) daughter. Between 2 and 3 a certain forgetfulness also sets in. The heroine of both sequels, for whom Will falls, is Shannon Tweed, but playing different characters – a diplomat's wife in 2 and a TV actress in 3 (working, appropriately, on a sexy *noir*ish B-series – a series within a series, we might say – called *Sweet Justice*). It is impossible to watch 3 without asking *why* Will doesn't recognise his love-object as the woman he had an affair with last time round. Whilst it may be acceptable to cast Martin Hewitt in two *Secret Games* films which don't pretend to have any relationship to each other, maintaining some similarities but striking other marked differences (Stevens is the same, Tweed is different) exposes the astonishing carelessness (or perhaps blithe carefreeness) of the DTV genre (imagine Al Pacino turning up as two different characters in *The Godfather* trilogy). The first three *Indecent Behaviour* films are more consistent, but still marked by the compulsive amnesia which afflicts erotic thriller characters: each stars Shannon Tweed (again) as the same sex therapist character, with the same name, but (like Will) learning nothing from the lessons of previous films. However, if *Indecent Behaviour 1–3* were essentially different outings for her therapist character, *Indecent Behaviour 4* – marketed in some territories as *Human Desires* – is a completely different premise: still Tweed, but now she has another name and runs a modelling agency. The name-change here – of the character, and the film itself – indicates that by 4 the *Indecent Behaviour* franchise had succumbed to the fact that it was just another Tweed vehicle.

In each of these cases the production companies have hit on a marketable idea and brazenly repeated it: the same with difference.[29] If you rented the first, you might just rent the second to experience a similar set of viewing sensations. There is the reassurance of reliability for the potential viewer, as well as the possibility that another director might handle similar material differently. Some series are auteur works, some not: Hippolyte directed all the *Animal Instincts* films, whereas none of the four *Indecent Behaviour* films has the same director. Jim Wynorski has a reputation for being the B-sequel genre director, with *Sorority House Massacre 2*, *Bare Wench Project 2* and *3*, *Munchie Strikes Back*, and *Ghoulies IV* amongst his multiple mixed-genre DTV follow-ups, though of the six erotic thrillers he has directed, only *Body Chemistry 3* and *4* are sequels. Wynorski balks at the regular call from producers to 'Give us the same film, only different' (McDonagh 1995: 14),[30] which is interesting given his reputation as the DTV 'sequeliser', carrying with it the assumption that he doesn't really care much about what he's doing so long as it comes in on or under budget.[31]

DTV sequel-series thus appear to be the supreme American genre product: recognisable instances of alike substitutions, repetitions which ring a few character and plot changes but retain a brand identity. They offer the safety of the known, the reassurance of the typical, but promise a modicum of differentiation and variety because each sequel is not *exactly* the same film (though often near enough). Sequels provide an intensified form of the repeat-buying which characterises the consumption of erotic thriller (or any other) genre material. In my conclusion I will look at some more diverse formations of genre's 'sameness with difference', thinking about ways in which the erotic thriller has spread beyond the US, beyond cinema, beyond its constituent generic elements, beyond whiteness and beyond these ambivalent masculine imaginings. The same, but perhaps *not* the same.

NOTES

1 I first discussed this model of perversion as delay in *D. H. Lawrence* (1997: 98–9).

2 Jane Campion's rather more highbrow *In the Cut* makes what seems to be a rather more vulgar joke on this premise: after the camera has watched Meg Ryan quietly masturbating, the scene cuts to a shot of her giving milk to her cat.

3 Kristine Imboch describes – and tries to capture through genital close-ups in her female-focused films – the full range of female orgasmic responses, but says that these differ from the 'Hollywood orgasm version'. See Gaffin (1997: 182–3).

4 Another fictional movie drug is sexologist Shannon Tweed's Extremis in *Indecent Behaviour*, which 'helps' sexually dysfunctional patients by making their orgasms more intense through oxygen deprivation. The criminal plot revolves around death resulting from its misuse.

5 *Love in Paris (Another 9½ Weeks)* features a visual male-masochistic scene in which Mickey Rourke is blindfolded whilst two women engage in a lesbian romp in front of him. The prime heterosexual male fantasy (two women together) is denied him as it is acted out.

6 Though the Hong Kong Category III film *Erotic Ghost Story* does feature two sister-fairies in a lesbian clinch. Perhaps supernatural beings are not subject to the incest taboo.

7 There are some exceptions to this, of course, the most cinematically reflexive being the 'returned gaze' moment, which seems generally to signal a reference to the moment in *Rear Window* when Raymond Burr looks back at James Stewart (and us), thus betraying the fact that Burr knows that Stewart knows. This is replicated in *Scissors*, when Sharon Stone sees her ostensibly wheelchair-bound neighbour walking, and he sees that she sees through their adjacent apartment windows. *Flinch*, briefly discussed above in relation to Gina Gershon, also plays with the voyeur-exhibit dynamic to some effect. Here Gershon and Judd Nelson are shop window 'living mannequins', who have to stay stock-still all day. They witness a murder, but at first are 'hidden' from the sight of the murderer by the fact that they are on display, and proficient at playing the unseeing mannequin. But later the murderer returns with, as it were, point blank vision: he stands in front of their shop window display stage and *looks*. They cannot 'flinch' away from his gaze.

8 The voyeur films also sometimes feature scenes focusing on the come-on of denied looking, which is interesting when read in connection with blindness films. In *Night Eyes* hero Will has to witness Nikki having sex with another man, but denies himself a view of it. First, he is an unwilling aural witness (overhearing the sounds of sex from another room), then from the refuge of his master-control 'lookout' station he refuses to turn on a bedroom camera, instead pacing around his surveillance room deliberately *not* looking. The sex-scene (which we eventually do see, and which Will eventually succumbs to, to the point of recording and replaying it) is therefore first played out off-screen. Listening to sex scenes is also common in stake-outs, when police 'keep an eye on' (by listening in via bugs) a suspect. This occurs in *Victim of Desire*, when the listener does not realise that he is hearing the sounds of the suspect having sex with his own cop partner.

9 Although Chris Straayer argues that indie mainstream erotic thriller *Bound* is remarkable because it underscores lesbianism with trust: 'Through its narrative, *Bound* suggests that, in contrast to the heterosexual failings of classic film noir, women can trust one another' (1998: 160).

10 Lynda Hart's account of female buddy films uses Virginia Woolf's suggestion that representations of female friendship function as covert signals of same-sex desire (see 'Chloe Liked Olivia: Death, Desire, and Detection in the Female Buddy Film', 1994: 65–88). In the erotic thriller 'Chloe likes Olivia' in a way which sometimes spills over into the customary lesbian scene, sometimes functions as a gesture towards the feel-good chick-flick.

11 Food is also signalled as a rival to sex when Shauna and Kaitlin meet in *Mirror Image*'s reconciliatory conclusion: 'I'm ravenous,' says Shauna, woman of many appetites. 'From now on, when I think of men I'm going to think of food instead.' If in the sex-food scenes discussed above men want women *as* food, here women want food *instead of* sex.

12 According to a report in the IMDb User Comments section for this film – see http://uk.imdb.com/title/tt0111137.

13 This is developed through a call to abandon the adultery pretext altogether: 'I believe it's about time someone comes up with a new stock storyline. Okay sure, we all know that many spouses wander. But if their situations ended up like DTV writers would have us believe, the murder rate in L.A. alone would quadruple.' Review of *Sexual Malice* at 'This is Sexy?', archived at http://www.thisissexy.net/.

14 Video jacket blurb for *Carnal Crimes*, distributed in the UK by Medusa Communications Ltd.

15 Wager proposes that 'film noir, and Weimar street film before it, is concerned with the forced immobility of the woman placed in the role of wife, and with exploring options that forced immobility outside and inside the family' (1999: 13). By the 1980s and 1990s thriller cinema recognised that few of the same 'forces' were in operation to fix women into this position of domestic immobility, so this becomes a starting point from which the erotic thriller's heroines break away.

16 *Secret Games: Third of a 6 Picture Erotic Library*, press pack, Axis Films International, p. 3, author's own copy.

17 Ibid., p. 2.

18 Though in an interesting left-liberal twist, when he is at his most contemptible (finally dumping Kaitlin), he is framed next to a picture of Ronald Reagan, suggesting a visual critique of Reaganite politics through the framed conjunction of the president and an erotic thriller lousy husband (this guy *must* be bad, says the image, because not only does he abuse his wife, he's also a Republican).

19 *Carnal Crimes: Synopsis*, press pack, Axis Films International, p. 1, author's own copy.

20 Chuck Moore in *Some Nudity Required*.

21 The names evoke *noir* heroine Laura in Otto Preminger's film of the same title, as well as *noir* performer Lana Turner.

22 Lee Horsley also discusses a number of examples of female good/bad girl pairings (the two-woman structure) in thriller cinema (2001: 137–45).

23 *Sisters*, aka *Blood Sisters*, could easily be marketed as *Psycho* meets *Dead Ringers*: Margot Kidder plays separated Siamese twins Dominique and Danielle, though by the time the film opens Dominique exists only as a murderous spirit inhabiting Danielle, since she died on the operating table when the conjoined twins were separated. Danielle owns duplicate sets of clothes for the identical women she is, sometimes speaks as Dominique (like Norman Bates performing his mother) and murders Danielle's sexual partner in the guise of Dominique. Mirrors, inevitably, work hard to formulate the psychological twists of the double woman: multiple mirrors propagate images of the self, or split it in two. The good/bad dyad is also seen as mutually reinforcing and defining: Danielle, says a medic commenting on the twins, 'who

is so sweet . . . so normal, as opposed to her sister, can only be so *because* of her sister'.

24 Like *Mirror Images'* framing of Jeff against an image of Ronald Reagan, *Undercover* also contains a brief moment of political critique, when Cindy says to the killer, 'I can't believe a man like you has made it into the government', to which he replies (extending the role-play theme), 'You're the one who said she understood leading a double life.'

25 Though not a twins film, the mainstream *Blink* utilises a number of mirror/identity visualisations once its initially blind heroine Emma has her sight restored. Since she lost her sight courtesy of a mirror – Emma's mother smashed her head against one when she was eight, rendering her blind – the mirror is a conduit of memory and identity, a reflection of and for trauma. As a newly sighted adult, she hallucinates her mother besides herself in the mirror: 'The last time I looked I was a little girl,' she says. 'And I blink, and I look like my mother.' Mirrors as trauma sites thus close the gap between vision and memory.

26 Though meant as a criticism, the fact that one of the few writers on this film found the sex scenes to be too obviously acted seems curiously appropriate. The review of the film on the 'This is Sexy?' website says: 'Even for simulated sex it seems, well, simulated'. (In a more self-consciously postmodern pastiche film this would be praise indeed.) Inadvertently, then, *Undercover* plays out the theme of play-acted theatricality and simulated identities even if it's striving to be authentic. That this makes it a failure in masturbation terms causes the writer to slip into *noir*ish discourse: 'for most [viewers] the movie will leave them searching for their real guns instead of the metaphorical ones they were hoping to get some use out of' (archived at http://www.thisissexy.net/).

27 Joe Bob's Drive-in site calls *Lap Dancing* 'the movie that "Showgirls" was TRYING to be. But "Showgirls" cost about 40 million bucks, and this movie cost about . . . oh . . . 40 bucks. My kinda flick' (www.hotx.com/joebob04–14–96/moviere-view.html). This is Sexy? also calls it 'the DTV-version of Showgirls' but uses this as a critique: 'There's just too much nudity. Strike that. Too much "empty" nudity. It's just breast after breast after breast. Don't these women have sex lives?' (archived at http://www.thisissexy.net/).

28 This is true of most B-genres. Jim Wynorski has said in interview that *Sorority House 2* was not a sequel to *Sorority House*, was written without a thought to the 'original' film, and given the working title 'Jim Wynorski's House of Babes' on the slate. Producer Roger Corman decided to make it a sequel when he released it, but because it is marketed in some regions as *Nightie Nightmare*, this means that it is both a sequel and not a sequel, linked to the first film by a title connection in some countries but not others ('The Jim Wynorski Interview' at The Old Hockstatter Place website, conducted by Tony, Webmaster, http://www.digivoodoo.net/oldhockstat-terplace/index.shtml).

29 Only rarely does a title franchise stay with the same production company for the duration of a series, largely because of the frequent turnover of company identities in B-Hollywood. Though a wide range of companies seem to be behind the sequelled titles I am discussing here – Axis Films International, Vision International, Prism Entertainment Corporation, Royal Oaks Entertainment – a small core of production personnel will be involved with these bodies.

30 '*Munchie* was a very big success. We offered Roger [Corman] a number of widely varied stories for the sequel, and in every case he would say, "Do that for part three, but for part two, I want something very much like the first movie"' (Jim Wynorski, quoted in McDonagh 1995: 14).

31 Wynorski is one of the most prolific graduates of the Roger Corman school of film-making, thought of as Corman's true heir, learning 'to work quickly and inexpensively, to value marketing, and to recognize that there's no such thing as an idea too outrageously dumb to sell' (McDonagh 1995: 4).

INTERVIEW: DIRECTOR KATT SHEA

Linda Ruth Williams (LW): How did you get *Stripped to Kill* off the ground?

Katt Shea (KS): I got a couple of acting parts in Roger Corman movies, and on the second film I also shot second unit, because they decided that I was good *behind* the camera, *better* probably, because I'm not such a great actress. Roger likes that – you come along with no pretensions about being a big actor. I would have carried cable around if they wanted me to. After that I came, back to the States, and I approached Roger with this idea for a movie. I had lost a bet with my then partner, Andy (Ruben), and he thought I was such a feminist that my punishment should be to go to a strip-club. So I go in and sit down and these strippers come out and they're putting on a show. It was like burlesque; as if they were artists and this was their only outlet for expressing their art. They were fantastic. There was a Southern belle who did her whole thing; there was this girl who came out as an *alien*, with neon antennae coming out of her head, and she had these big huge neon hula hoops which she would swing around against a black light, and she had neon nipples, so that was all you could see – just her nipples, and the ropes and the antenna. And that same girl did a show with a puppet in which the puppet stripped off her clothes while she was saying 'Stop it!' They were just so creative. And Andy was saying, 'OK, we can go now', and I just said, 'Oh no, we're not going anywhere.' I stayed until it closed. I just fell in love with what they did. They had artistry. It was like a little flower growing out of a crack in the cement. That's what it reminded me of. For me it wasn't about the nudity, which was basically, OK, thirty seconds or so at the end. But I just felt like they were expressing themselves, *and* they were getting paid. When we finally walked out of the club I said, 'We *have* to do a movie about this, because nobody really knows about it . . .' This was before you saw strippers in movies, or if you did, it was in the background. And you'd never seen a pole. The pole? They were swinging around on this pole like gymnasts, gravity-free. They were so athletic. So I thought, 'I know exactly who to take this to', because I can't imagine Roger saying 'No' to a movie about strippers. So we came up with kind of a skeleton of a plot and I 'accidentally' ran into him, and I described the poster to him. I said 'I can just see the poster with this pole and this girl hanging off of it'. And he just lit up and said, 'OK, come in Monday morning and pitch me the idea.' So I went in and pitched him the idea that one of the strippers has a twin, and the twin is a boy who kills the stripper and takes her place. But Roger was just not convinced that it could be done, and he said No. He said, 'A man cannot pull off being a female stripper in a G-string. I'm saying No.' And I said, 'No you're not, you're saying "Yes!"' This was very bold 'cos I'm like twenty something. And I don't know why that worked. But he said, 'OK, yes, OK'. I guess if I was that sure, it just over-whelmed him.

LW: It's strange, because Corman seems very sure of himself, not the kind of person who could be bamboozled like that.

KS: Yes, but he loved the idea, and I *knew* he loved it and I knew he wanted to say yes.

LW: How did you then cast the film?

KS: I used real strippers in almost all the roles. I thought it really gave the movie an authenticity. The guy who played the brother was not an actor, he was a female impersonator at a club called Le Cage Aux Folles. And then I held acting classes at my house, and so much of those girls' own experiences went into the script. Then we hired a choreographer, but I didn't want him to change them at all. We just had to know, from the point of view of filming, so I could cut it together and it would look really great we had to know where they were going to be on the stage. The choreographer took their act and said, 'OK, you're going to go from point A to B to C to D to E. That was all. Like the motorcycle girl, that was her act. She didn't *have* a motorcycle, but she would be real tough and do the motorcycle chic thing. We let them do their thing.

LW: What's most surprising about the film is that you expect it's going to be a guys' film with tits and that's it. And then suddenly you have women doing interesting things, in the context of that single rule that you have to give the audience thirty seconds of exposure.

KS: That was it. That was the whole thing. Like, they take off their top for thirty seconds at the end. OK, we can do that, if that's what it takes, all right.

LW: But are there still guys in the audience getting off on it?

KS: Yeah. But that's . . . for guys, you know. It's very incidental, it really is.

LW: How did the murder plot come about? Presumably, you needed something to drive the strip premise along.

KS: Right, yeah, that was basically it. I don't know why I got so obsessed by this thing about the brother coming along as a female. It's probably very psychological – experiencing this power of sexuality that women have over men. The obsession was so great.

LW: But it has spun off an entire genre of stripper films, hasn't it?

KS: Definitely, yes. And the first thing I thought was, 'Oh my God what have I started?' I didn't wanna see all these stripper movies! And from then on Roger had to have a stripper in every movie he did. It's kind of cool in a way – like I had big influence there. But what's funny is that when I'm interviewed by men, they always ask me if I was a stripper. That was the first thing. I was on the radio once, the first interview, and this guy said, 'So you were a stripper, right?' and I was just . . . silent. I was just so shocked.

LW: It's like asking John Ford if he'd ever been a cowboy.

KS: Yeah, really bizarre. I think that people from the outside often do these things really well, though, because we are so intrigued.

LW: *Stripped to Kill* also triggered off a vogue for films in which a sexy female professional goes undercover. What made you interested in that premise – the idea that you can discover something about yourself in this different world, even if you resist it?

KS: I think that character was me. Not that I ever went undercover as a stripper, but just her being in that world. The strippers saw me as this preppy college girl, with no experience. So I was the odd one out again.

LW: How did *Stripped to Kill* lead on to *Dance of the Damned*?

KS: It nearly didn't. Roger wanted 86-minute movies. Nobody told me. So when I was making *Stripped to Kill* I showed him a two-hour rough cut, and he nearly tore my head off. And then . . . well, you see how it's chopped. If there were any flowing qualities at all, he would just chop to make the movie fit that 86 minutes. But then the other thing was that he would look for *more* strip stuff. He'd say, 'Do you have any more on her breasts there?' So I hid all the trims, the breast trims and the butt trims, and I put them in boxes labelled 'Wheels turning on taxi-cab' or 'Hubcaps', because Roger would actually *look* for it. So Roger was *furious* at me after *Stripped to Kill*. He thought I had completely screwed up, it didn't make any sense. And then it made seven million dollars in France, like overnight.

LW: What was your budget?

KS: Around $600,000. So to make seven million dollars on a Corman film – it was just unheard of. And so he called me and asked me if I wanted to make another movie. He said, 'I have a haunted house set, and a nightclub set, can you come up with a movie, a story?' So Andy and I came up with this story for *Dance of the Damned*. You know, we were always trying to think of a classy idea, so that's what would come first. And then we'd go, OK, now how do we make it for the exploitation genre? The whole idea of being a filmmaker is that you take every element and shape it because you want to say something. I was very into that. It's incredible what we accomplished with the design team. My gaffer on *Dance of the Damned* was Janusz Kaminski who went on to shoot *Schindler's List* and has won two or three academy awards. And Phedon Papamichael was my DP, and he's become very big – he shot *Identity* recently. And Wally Pfister was one of the assistants. There were so many people came out of that . . .

LW: *Dance of the Damned* is an interesting hybrid of striptease and vampires, and horror and erotica. What were your genre parameters?

KS: I took it to Roger and said 'It's going to be about a waitress and vampire, and she's going to teach him all about the day, you know because he can't experience that because he's a vampire. They're going to do something for each other.' I was so into it with so much passion about all this psychological stuff that's so *deep*. And Roger says, 'You can do it if she's a stripper.' He loved the fact that I would aspire to these amazing lofty things. But he would still pull me right back to exploitation and say, 'OK, but she's got to be naked for ten seconds.'

LW: But does it also work the other way round – that as long as you do those things, press these buttons, you can do whatever else you want?

KS: Yes. As long as I came through and delivered on the erotic elements, I could basically do what I wanted. Within the confines of, in the case of *Dance of the Damned*, about a $350,000 budget.

LW: So the budgets were going down?

KS: Yes. If you exceed Roger's expectations, you get demoted. 'She did it for *that* much money? Let's see if she can do it for *this* much money!' And we did.

LW: What about *Stripped to Kill 2*?

KS: What happened was that Roger came down to the set on the last day of shooting *Dance of the Damned* and said, 'I want to use this set one more time. I want you to make *Stripped to Kill 2* using this club. And we're tearing it down in two weeks.' I said 'But Roger, there's no script, there's no *idea* . . .' But you can't turn down a filmmaking job. So a week later we shot scenes in the club. And I hired my assistant to be the leading man in the movie. He was an actor and he was *there*, so he got the job. And I just started shooting scenes. But there was no script. *And* it was a murder mystery, and I'm shooting scenes *about* the murder! It became almost like fun because I can't take this seriously. The movies I had made up till this point, *Stripped to Kill* and *Dance of the Damned* I took *so* seriously. I wanted so much for them to be *art*, fantastic films, and I aspired to be like Fellini, Bergman . . . and Katt Shea. But it was really funny with *Stripped to Kill 2* because I would almost be telling them what to say just before the scene; 'OK, you say this, then you say that, then you say this . . .' And the fact that they all just sort of rose to the occasion was incredible.

LW: How long did it take to shoot in total?

KS: Three weeks – fifteen days.

LW: And is that average for a Corman production?

KS: Yeah. I mean *Stripped to Kill* was thirty days, but after *Dance of the Damned* they were all fifteen days.

LW: The *Stripped to Kill* Films have a *noir*ish quality in that so many of these stories are sexualised murder stories.

KS: Well, the 1940s' *femmes fatales* were my favourites. When I saw those movies as a little kid I was just blown away by the power of these women.

LW: And with *Poison Ivy* and *Streets* and *The Rage* you're again dealing with these *femme fatale* figures, but as adolescent girls.

KS: It's such an interesting time. And it's funny with girls because we don't understand the power. All of a sudden we've got all this power. It's *power*. That's what I find really interesting.

LW: But importantly, your films are stories that are being told as girls' stories, rather than a stories of a sexy nymphet who's there for the use whatever guy comes along. In *Poison Ivy*, for example, so much of the film is to do with Sara Gilbert's *voice* and the role of dysfunctional families.

KS: I agree, and I was really disappointed with the way New Line was trying to sell it.

LW: So did you see it as a genre film?

KS: Well, the interesting thing about *Poison Ivy* is that it is actually based on real people we knew. I knew a girl who would have you coming and going, doing things for her, and screwing you and yet you would help her out again and get sucked in again. It's her sexuality to a certain degree, but it's also some kind of magnetism on top of that. And that sexuality works for either gender. It doesn't matter if you're gay or straight – know what I mean?

LW: It's also about the willingness to *be* manipulated.

KS: Yes, she finds the needy people. She will be that for them, and fill that void.

LW: Did you see *Poison Ivy* as something that would spawn sequels?

KS: No, no, not at all. I mean she died in the end! And I didn't see it as a film that teenagers would watch. It was so dark. But teenagers loved it and are its biggest fans still. It's about the battle for the father, for the love of the father between a sort of mother and daughter combination – because it's almost Cooper and Ivy are one person at times – the geek and the *femme fatale*. They're two separate entities, but sometimes they come together.

LW: And who did you think your audience was going to be when you made it? Do you work with an ideal viewer in mind?

KS: No, I made it for myself. I made a movie I'd want to see. But I guess that it works with teenagers because I didn't play down to them at all. In fact, I would have wanted to protect them from a lot of stuff that was in there. It never occurred to me that it was an R-rated movie.

LW: There is a sense in all your films that you're telling the other side of the story. You could call it feminist filmmaking – telling the girls' story, which is generally untold in mainstream Hollywood.

KS: There's a simple reason for that. It's because women are not the ones making the movies at the studios.

CONCLUSION:
THE EROTIC THRILLER'S HYBRID
CHILDREN

'Can I play too, or is it just for boys?'
Kelly Van Ryan (Denise Richards) in *Wild Things*

I have always liked the title of the seminal early 1980s collection on Women and Revolution, *The Unhappy Marriage of Marxism and Feminism*. Its content told of the then much debated relationship between Marxism and feminism (characterised by Heidi Hartmann as 'like the marriage of husband and wife in English common law' [in Sargent 1981: 2]) as well as meditating on the productive nature of conflict, the sparks spawned by opposition. There are many unhappy marriages in this book, not least those between DTV lousy husbands and bored housewives, the blockbuster's murderous *femmes fatales* dispatching their partners with sex, or the long-regretted hasty marriages of the genre's paranoid form. But the erotic thriller has also spawned some unhappy (if not dangerous) generic liaisons. When the carnal dominates the criminal, or vice versa, or other third parties get involved, do we either 'need a healthier marriage or . . . a divorce' (to borrow from Hartmann)? Are unhappy or mixed generic marriages in the end rather more interesting than genre purity?

In my introductory chapter I asked whether the erotic thriller should in itself be considered a hybrid form (amongst other cross-fertilised terms). Viewers will judge whether the marriage of the thriller and porn-flick works; the market has judged the success of the genre's multiple progeny. Many of my films are multiply-genred, and often more interesting (if more confused) for that. One internet respondent writing about *Acting on Impulse* finds the fact that it is 'attempting at once to be a stalker thriller, a murder thriller, a tale of loyalty and betrayal, and a steamy erotic thriller' problematic.[1] Leonard Maltin's description of it as a 'seriocomic movie-on-movies thriller' contains no pejorative connotation; nor does this study use multi-genericity as a term of criticism.

Cross-breeding has extended beyond these basic forms, with a range of mutant children born of market opportunity. The hybridised erotic thriller has even bled into television, a niche which deserves further scrutiny in light of the media's differences. I am not primarily referring to the fact that a number of DTV films first run on cable, but that series such as the sexy cop show *Silk Stalkings* (which first aired in the CBS 'Crimetime after Primetime' slot in the US, and featured an inordinate number of crimes of passion in its caseload) are televisual rather than cinematic products, delivering titillating genre fare in programmable chunks. Zalman King's films are popularly understood as prime 'T&A' works targeting young men – especially in their DTV form. King's cable franchise *Red Shoe Diaries* followed the success of his feature film of that title, originally running (from 1992 to 1999) on the American Showtime channel. TV instalments are produced as segments of around 25 minutes each, before being anthologised, three at a time, for DVD and video release. The *Red Shoe Diaries* format is internationally popular, television-based softcore: according to King, on the back of these sexual-portmanteau ex-TV flicks, 'the whole foreign market . . . is exploding for us' (McDonagh 1995: 66).[2]

The opportunities of the video market in the 1980s and 1990s, combined with an increasing readiness to push the sexual envelope, also produced some further filmic cross-fertilisations. One of the most obvious sub-sub-genres is the action-adventure sexy thriller (*Red Blooded, Deadly Surveillance*), but sexual spectacle of some kind is commonplace in much of action cinema, from James Bond to *Charlie's Angels*. Women-in-prison films are also a thriving and long-standing exploitation genre, with a fixed formula facilitating action sequences, suspense, sexual abuse and lesbian spectacle. This is a form with a long history, particularly in Italian exploitation cinema, and the history of the form since the 1970s in low-budget cinema runs parallel to the related but distinctly more *noir*ish erotic thriller. 'Caged' or 'chained' is a strong titular genre signifier, but it is often paired with what now looks like erotic thriller-inflected terms ('heat' – with all the connotations of female sexuality I outlined in chapter 2 – is common). Jonathan Demme's *Caged Heat* is perhaps the American genre prototype, after which came *Chained Heat, Caged Seduction, Caged Hearts* – but there are numerous others. *Caged Women*, an Italian movie from 1992, was marketed by Rio Pictures as 'A powerful erotic prison thriller', whilst *Caged Fury* is targeted at video dealers as an 'adult thriller'.[3] Science fiction hybrids also traded on the mainstream successes of the erotic thriller, sometimes weaving sci-fi motifs into conventional erotic thriller narratives, suggesting new blood in old bodies. Futuristic gadgets are often the key to this. The Italian serial killer-thriller released under the English title *A Taste for Fear* is set in an indeterminate future, but rings the changes with sci-fi weapons and vehicles. *Virtual Voyeur*'s sexploitation plot revolves around the development of a virtual reality sex-machine (remember Woody Allen's orgasmatron?). Other films cash in on the new technology of the 1990s. *Hard Drive*, for instance – fairly early in the life of the world wide web – explores the alienating effects of internet obsession and virtual sexual encounters, marketing itself as a 'Hot, Sexy, Techno-thriller'.[4] More chemically-focused sci-fi inflected thrillers also traded on the genre's success. The Canadian/US co-production *Dangerous Desire* develops a literal 'animal instinct' story by featuring a hero who is 'cured' of a disease by having feline DNA injected into him, which then turns him into an oversexed and deadly human tomcat (its alternative title, *Tomcat: Dangerous Desires*, might not have played well in the UK, a nation where cats are the principal pet). The Pamela Anderson vehicle *Naked Souls* also mixes genres by combining a mad scientist mind-swap story with ample views of Anderson's assets.

There are even erotic musicals. Earlier, I mentioned that one of the problems with *Showgirls* is attributable to its split-generic identity. Verhoeven's suggestion that a murder may have solved its box office and critical problems is interesting as a validation of the erotic *thriller*'s success, but the legacy of the musical would remain, and perhaps continue to function as an irritating generic glitch. Split between an allegiance to Busby Berkeley and Larry Flynt, *Showgirls* plumps for both; a murderous gesture towards James M. Cain may compound the confusion. Yet perhaps the Berkeley connection is the most interesting aspect of the film in its guise as rags-to-riches tale – Nomi's (Elizabeth Berkeley's) climb from dirty dancer to star sex-hoofer parodies the backstage musical. From her earliest words ('I'm gonna dance'), Nomi is set on a path trodden by all the Ruby Keelers of showgirl history, dragged from understudy obscurity to top billing with one twist of her star-rival's ankle ('The show goes on. The Stardust is never dark'). The message is not so much 'gotta dance' as 'gotta lap-dance', for unlike the other hybrid genres which have blossomed in the margins of the musical (skating musicals, horror musicals, roller-disco musicals), the porno musical will only ever be camp or cult fodder. Even that famous backstage musical trope, 'Show me your legs' (delivered to chorus-line hopefuls as a staple device to bypass the strictures of the Hays code by offering a narrative justification for the brief flash of a starlet's thighs), has mutated here to 'Show me your tits' when Nomi auditions for the Stardust. The body of the showgirl has come a long way.

Another example comes from De Palma. Aside from the issue of whether sex-scenes themselves function like production numbers, the Frankie Goes to Hollywood turn in *Body Double* is a production number. 'Relax' accompanies the film's hero's first foray into hardcore acting, then the action stops and segues from narrative to film-within-a-film, laced with backstage musical qualities (except that this backstage musical is set in a sex club). A number of reviewers saw the film's skit on the sex industry as parodic (Ellis 1984; Hogan 1985); Justin Wyatt also reads this as a point when the feature film mutates into the music video (1994: 42–3). Strip-flicks too have an uneasy relationship with the musical, just as stripping does with dancing. Many of the strip-flicks discussed in Chapter 6 – especially high-end offerings like *Striptease* and *Dancing at the Blue Iguana*, with A-list stars performing the numbers – have choreographic pretensions, and the sequences, though intended also to be visually stimulating, are, if not 'show-stopping', then action-stopping non-narrative spectacular pauses, set to music. They are also often intensely character-driven, with song lyrics commenting on the action, and dancers using the space to demonstrate something of their subjective dilemmas. This tendency is perhaps set in motion by the prototype of the genre, Katt Shea's *Stripped to Kill*, in which the 'dance' sequences really do function like pop video-inflected musical numbers, with athletic action and striking musical choices taking precedence over sexual spectacle (tits only, no pubic revelations). *Kiss me a Killer*, a Hispanic district remake of *The Postman Always Rings Twice*, substitutes a Latino bar for the obscure roadside café of the previous two films, giving ample opportunity for pauses in the action when the band play and glamorous couples dance out the venue's changing fortunes. Here the lover-murderer figure (John Garfield in the first film; Jack Nicholson in the second) is a charismatic singer and guitarist played by Robert Beltran, prompting one reviewer to call it 'The *Caballero* Always Rings Twice'.[5]

Another interesting development in the erotic thriller's recent history is further off-Hollywood, targeting specific audiences in a rather different way. Throughout this book I have worried away at the fact that this genre peddles supremely white American sexualities, melding Hollywood genres into slick vehicles for blonde Playmates of the Month. Cultural difference and national sexual tastes will be accommodated by what's left in or out of a grab-bag of images which can be reformed to constitute a number of possible cuts, depending on what a particular market will swallow. Though Mundhra insisted on mixed-race and Indian pairings in his stories, the building-blocks of the average movie remain erotically WASPish. Susie Bright has gone some way to identifying the bland building-blocks of 'white sex', but acknowledges that 'White sex is commonly referred to simply as "sex"' (1995: 108). Thus it is remarkable that a new incarnation of the erotic thriller should emerge around the new century in an African-American form. If white, mainstream erotic thrillers are neo-sexploitation it would be tempting to term black erotic thrillers neo-blaxploitaiton,[6] though – if one can generalise – some manage to be both sleeker, slicker entities than many of their white counterparts, and also inject some element of realism into their sex/crime/melodrama sagas of infidelity, blackmail and the pleasures of walking on the wild side. This may be because, as low-budget movies (some with limited theatrical releases), they come after ten or fifteen years of fringe Hollywood development of the formula, enabling latecomers who start making cheap erotic thrillers around the turn of the century to pick and choose what will work. Eric Lott argues that *film noir*, for all its whiteness, is rooted in racial anxieties; it is 'a sort of whiteface dreamwork of social anxieties with explicitly racial sources'.[7] But a number of reviewers of *Devil in a Blue Dress*, Carl Franklin's innovative mid-1990s neo-*noir*, saw the central Denzel Washington character Easy Rawlins as putting 'the *noir* back into *film noir*' (Dargis 1996: 38). White classical Hollywood's *film noir* may, as Wager argues, be black-inspired as it disavows race, but neo-*noir* has facilitated a more assertive avowal of racial issues (1999: 124–7).

Yet erotic thrillers like *Trois* and *Pandora's Box*, both directed by Atlanta-based, straight-out-of-film-school protégé Rob Hardy, seem to have picked up wholesale the white B-movie prototype and rearticulated it with an African-American emphasis, and with a mostly black cast and crew. 'I wanted to see African Americans in a situation that you typically see mainstream white Americans in the movies,' he says on the DVD featurette about *Trois*. The similarities to other erotic thrillers are as interesting as the differences in the frame of this book. Like his white DTV predecessors, Hardy ups the glamour factor by focusing on beautiful people in sexy suspense situations. His characters are successful professionals with showcase homes (his heroines work, unlike the bored housewives of the Axis-style films), who spend their leisure-time in sophisticated pursuits. If fringe Hollywood casts ex-Playmates, Hardy casts a former Miss USA (Kenya Moore, who won in 1993) in the main role of Jasmine in *Trois*. The men provide eye-candy too; there are ample shots of highly worked-on muscular torsos and thrusting butts. *Pandora's Box* also engages in a sameness-with-difference take on the genre. Familiar motifs include a steamy opening sex-in-the-shower sequence which is swiftly curtailed by violence, and a therapist-protagonist (Monica Calhoun as Mia) for whom the analytic situation sparks sexual challenge in her own life. Mia's broker-husband is such a work-obsessed lousy specimen he even brings his laptop into bed, giving Mia ample incentive to visit the secret sex-club Pandora's Box. Experimental sex takes place in a number of locations: in a restaurant, in a courtyard overlooked by office buildings (and a secret video camera), in the ladies' toilet. But Hardy rings the changes too: the scene-of-the-crime scene contains a stark shot from the perspective of the corpse, looking up as the white cops bear down, and his set-piece orgy scenes at Pandora's Box provide inventive displays of bodies in different locales and atmospheric lighting set-ups on the cheap. Other similar black-cast thrillers, such as Roy Campanella's *Playing with Fire*, may not focus on sexual themes but trade on erotic thriller motifs and marketing. Diane Wynter's *Intimate Betrayal* contains a couple of non-explicit sex scenes, but is most interesting as a thriller for its investigative heroine, also played by Calhoun (who featured, incidentally, in Ice Cube's black strip-flick melodrama *The Players Club*). Timothy Folsome's *Uninvited Guest* deploys the yuppie-couple-in-peril theme of more mainstream thrillers with some R-rated sexual sequences contributing to its story of an affluent marriage threatened by a seductive stranger.

What, then, sets these movies apart? One Net review called *Trois* 'essentially a direct-to-video erotic thriller' and 'a FATAL ATTRACTION knockoff . . . distinguished by its African-American cast and crew' (McDonagh 2000), but there are differences. Couple-reinforcing happy endings are rare for a start. *Trois* concludes with the married couple estranged, its heroine in a wheelchair following the violent dénouement, whilst *Pandora's Box* concludes, like *Body*

THE EROTIC THRILLER IN CONTEMPORARY CINEMA

Heat, with its heroine $20 million (legitimately) better off and not a man in sight, relaxing at an exotic location with her female friend. Both films are also set away from California, in Atlanta. And for all the aspirational lifestyle quota evoked by the generally high production values of these movies, their screenplays talk turkey in a franker fashion than their Hollywood stablemates – and I don't mean the forensic vulgarity or sexual bravura of Eszterhas. *Trois* focuses on Jermaine's fantasy of a *ménage-à-trois* with his wife (Jasmine) and another woman (Jade). The romance/sex axis which, as I discussed above, separates women from men in popular discourse (and in discussions around pornography) is opened up here through parallel conversations between Jasmine and her friend, and Jermaine and his. Here the women talk about wanting slow caresses whilst the men talk about anal sex. Friedkin's *Jade* may allude to its heroine 'taking it any way', but it is none so open as this. When Jade and Jasmine dance in a nightclub the lesbianism-for-men euphemisms of other screenplays are thrown out of the window as a man hands them his card for future reference, just in case they 'want some dick in there'. Jasmine's unease about the *ménage-à-trois* as legitimisation of her man 'sexing another woman' is not forgotten in the film's heady lipstick lesbianism, but Jasmine and Jade become friends. After the three-way sex, the film also pauses to discuss whether her participation means that Jasmine really is gay. This is, in my experience, a unique reflection on the significance of lesbian experimentation for the female characters; DTV scenes of lesbianism-for-men usually operate with the understanding that women's participation in such scenarios constitutes no real threat to their men. Indeed, it seems to confirm both women's and men's heterosexuality. However ubiquitous the lesbian scene in the erotic thriller, actual homosexuality is hardly mentioned. There is even some discussion of Jermaine – as it were – returning the favour and participating in a two men, one woman *ménage-à-trois*. This is the only way in which *Pandora's Box* (which Sony renamed *Trois 2: Pandora's Box* to maximise market awareness when they took on its DVD distribution deal) touches base with its predecessor – a brief scene in which this takes place. Mainstream erotic thrillers would risk a lot to include such a fantasy (their male audiences, for a start). Here it turns out to be only a (woman's) dream, so *Pandora's Box* also disavows what it briefly indulges.

Hardy's translation of the genre blueprint is also reaching different audiences. Most fringe Hollywood DTVs are set in Beverly Hills because it's cheap to film just down the road, so if you are based in the South it makes budget sense to do the same. But Hardy's road is not the same road. Southern locality is also key to distribution, which is perhaps the most interesting story to be told about *Trois* and *Pandora's Box*. Though made on a tiny budget (*Trois* cost $200,000, *Pandora's Box* $800,000), Hardy's films look gorgeous, as do their cast. Yet *Trois* couldn't find a distributor in Hollywood, so Hardy, producer William Packer and co-producer Gregory Anderson distributed it independently with their company Rainforest Films. Packer, in a strategy which 'harkened back to the 1930s and Oscar Michaeux's similar methods' (Persall 2002), negotiated directly with exhibitors and got the movie shown, primarily to African-American audiences, resulting in its becoming 'the second highest-grossing independently distributed black film ever, and the fastest to earn $1 million' (Holman 2002). After *Trois*, Rainforest Films became a 'boutique division' of Sony, through which it hoped to target black audiences with genre products. It is also very South-East US-focused, getting huge audiences for *Trois* in Charlotte and Jacksonville. The regional appeal of these films is, then, not primarily that they are erotic thrillers, but that they are black erotic thrillers, with genre and race reinforcing each other. Hardy has said that he does not see the erotic thriller as 'ethnic-specific' even though it usually features 'mainstream actors such as Michael Douglas or Sharon Stone'; his move is simply to replace white performers 'with people who happen to be of color' (Holman 2002). Genre-bending through race is then crucial to Rainforest's place in the market: 'Just to generalize the African-American audience for a second: We support comedy, and we support action. . . . That's just about it. That's what we support, so that's what we get. Just a thriller with African-American actors is unheard of, but an erotic thriller? You're not going to see much of that' (Persall 2002). The success of delivering to a new market niche is thus bound up with the kind of film you target at that niche. But this reinflection of genre has also given Rainforest Films a platform from which to develop into a significant distribution company. One viewer of *Uninvited Guest* calls it 'like *Basic Instinct*, *Fatal Attraction*, and *Soul Food* (beautiful people) all rolled into one'.[8] Take the co-ordinates of a narrative usually (though not intrinsically) populated by white performers, and flesh it out with attractive African-Americans, and you have a black genre movie with legs.

Yet for all their fascinating market and textual innovations, these works are still resolutely American (even if they celebrate other Americas), and to some extent are limited variations on a dominant theme. This book has largely concentrated on American-produced erotic thrillers and has deployed reception sources from the US and the UK, yet the international export of the erotic thriller is clearly crucial to its distribution success. Detailed work on sales patterns and consumption of American made-for-cable/DTV genre movies in non-US markets would tell us much more about what happens to American genres in other reception contexts. Questions about international and transnational sexuality as peddled by softcore need extensive discussion beyond the bounds of this book. Marguerite Duras called EuroDisney 'cultural Chenobyl' (quoted by Miller et al. 2001: 196),[9] and one question which has nagged me throughout this research is whether there is a sexual version of EuroDisney, and whether the erotic thriller might be it. Walter Gernert quipped to me in interview that Axis movies did well 'wherever the Allies had occupied during World War II'. The global ubiquity of a 'universal' form of American softcore in international hotel chains indicates that the narrow visions of sexuality this book seeks to understand have become globally dominant in one form at least. The

Axis producers report that in the dissemination of their products across the globe, Korea and Germany were their biggest markets, taking the 'strongest' cuts of the films.

But other forms of the erotic thriller have also sprung up in different territories and within America, and Janet Staiger's essay on genre, 'Hybrid or Inbred: The Purity Hypothesis and Hollywood Genre History' might help us understand both these forms and those discussed above. Following Homi Bhabha's model of cultural hybridity as something which 'ought to be reserved for truly cross-cultural encounters', Staiger argues that hybridity can only be 'true' (a curious notion in itself) if it is the meeting of unrelated elements. Are, she asks, 'the breedings of genres occurring in Fordian and Post-Fordian Hollywood [her preferred terms for classical and post-classical/New Hollywood] truly cross-cultural? Truly one language speaking to another? I seriously doubt that the strands of patterns that intermix in Hollywood filmmaking are from different species. Rather, they are in the same language family of Western culture' (1997: 16–17). What some genre theorists call hybridity Staiger refers to as '*a case of inbreeding*' (1997: 17, her emphasis). However we term these second-generation erotic-thriller-action-romance-sci-fi-musicals written in the language of Hollywood's classical form with MPAA judgements in mind, they are, in Staiger's account, not hybrids, but rather examples of the interbreeding of slightly differing conventions as part of the production imperative to ring the changes.

So what happens when the erotic thriller emigrates? What other forms of softcore 'sexandviolence' have sprung up internationally? European cinema has produced some interesting if sporadic examples, including recent French feminist films such as Catherine Breillat's *Romance* or Virginie Despentes/ Coralie Trinh Thi's occasionally hardcore road-movie *Baise-moi*, both of which have set precedents for other developments in art-cinema. Euro sex-thrillers like *Suite 16* would be interesting to discuss in this context, though its disparate origins in different national cinemas make it a hybrid form on its own terms (it is a UK/Belgian/Dutch co-production with a trans-European cast and a confused sense of narrative). Another interesting departure is brand-name director-producer Jag Mundhra, who moved production back to India when he filmed the erotic (or 'exotic') thrillers *Monsoon* and *The Perfumed Garden*. These are Indian/US co-productions, which hybridise story-lines (Indian myths with twentieth-century twists concerning contemporary sexual dilemmas), and cast internationally to facilitate the focus on inter-racial desire and Americans in India. But the interest in reincarnated identities and love stories across time, and the incorporation of traditional Indian erotic lore into the fabric of Western filmmaking, make both films uneasy as thrillers, and may require a different critical frame for thinking about their mythological focus. A more consolidated example of erotic thriller obsessions manifested in a quite different national cinema comes in some examples of the Hong Kong Category III film, which raises interesting possibilities for transnational genre hybridity.

1: SEX, ZEN AND VIDEOTAPE: HONG KONG CATEGORY III FILMS

Perhaps the most significant non-US relation of Hollywood's erotic thriller is the sexual formation of the Hong Kong Category III film, though it could not be called an émigré erotic thriller, rather a distinct outcrop of softcore thrills which has sprung from the fertile soil of extreme Hong Kong cinema. Throughout the 1980s and 1990s increasingly violent and explicit forms of filmmaking developed in the region, which became legitimised (and then encouraged) by the introduction of a new ratings system in Hong Kong in 1988. This system includes three advisory categories relating to a film's suitability for children, and the legally enforceable Category III. Often referred to as the equivalent of the US NC-17 or the UK 18 category – available only to those 18 or over, commonly on account of their softcore quotas and/or intense violence – Cat III legitimised an extreme exploitation/sexploitation strain in Hong Kong cinema. What is different from the US NC-17 is that the Cat III industry in Hong Kong is huge (whereas NC-17 is almost defunct). 'In Hong Kong', wrote Richard Corliss in *Time* in 2002, 'movie people saw the new rating not as an inhibition but as a liberation'. Cat III also operates like the UK 18 certificate in that many mainstream films can attract the category if they contain some excessively violent scenes or other 'transgressions' (both *Wild Things* and *Eyes Wide Shut* were Cat III in Hong Kong). But unlike the UK's 18, there is also a distinction about this label, which functions as a come-on as well as a warning (the classification symbol which appears on video boxes is three vertical bars, rather like prison bars, in a black triangle). Following its establishment, which effectively legalised explicit (though not hardcore) sexual spectacle in mainstream Hong Kong cinema, an extensive industry making films for this category grew up, with its own dedicated stars and studios. NC-17 it ain't. Darrell W. Davis and Yeh Yueh-yu, in their excellent overview of the category, write:

> Porn films are Category III, but not all Category III is porn. Category III is marked out as 'other', not suitable for children; and yet, it is not stigmatized, segregated, or shunned by mainstream audiences. (2001: 14)

The Category III violence/sex/comedy/shocker mélange is, then, one of the most prolific of Hong Kong sub-genres (if such it is). *Pretty Woman*, for instance (resolutely *not* the Julia Roberts flick, but rather a famous vehicle for Cat III diva Veronica Yip), is often cited as the exemplary Cat III sexual monster-hit, making HKD 30 million (Davis 2001 and Yueh-yu: 14). Yet despite this, it is still a relatively under-researched area: Logan's *Hong Kong Action Cinema* (1995) doesn't discuss Cat III films; Teo's extensive study gives the phenomenon one paragraph, though he does acknowledge that 'Category III films have now become such a commercial proposition that producers, distributors and exhibitors have chosen to specialise in them as a genre'(1997: 244). However, Davis and Yueh-yu argue that it would be wrong to think of Cat III as a distinct form (the image which is given by numerous B-websites, dedicated to its goriest, most body-horror inflected manifestation). 'There are so many of these films that classifications of style (exploitation/cult film, art cinema, adult film) or genre (horror, gangster, marital arts) fail to cover them' (2001: 12). Like the up-to-the-wire erotic thriller DTVs I discussed earlier which producers strived to get into Blockbuster, Cat IIIs happily sit alongside mainstream films on video store shelves and in theatres in Hong Kong. Indeed, though they may look like DTV fare, and, as Davis and Yueh-yu acknowledge, viewers may prefer to watch many of these films at home, the congested nature of Hong Kong's domestic space may make the anonymity of theatrical viewing preferable. Given their limited audience (like Hollywood erotic thrillers, excluding the lucrative family and younger teenage markets), Cat III films occupy 'an inordinate amount of screen time' (Davis and Yueh-yu 2001: 13). Straightforward violent/action movies are common in the category, representing mainstream Hong Kong action fare as well as extreme 'classic' shockers such *Dr Lamb* or *The Untold Story*. Davis and Yueh-yu divide Cat III films into three groups, which is useful here: quasi-pornographic, genre films ('Almost any Hong Kong genre can be revisited with an adult Category III treatment' – they include gangster, crime, horror and detective films) and 'porno-violence' ('the most appalling and sensational Category III films' containing alarming 'cruelty and raw misogyny' [2001: 18]). This last form is perhaps what international cult film viewers laud as the 'real' Cat IIIs – the cannibalistic *Dr Lamb* and *The Untold Story* are in there, and many claim to be based on true stories or police files. Rape-revenge stories (such as *Her Vengeance* and *Malevolent Male*), which take their cues from *I Spit on Your Grave* or Abel Ferrara's *Ms 45*, are also common, and rape in general is spectacularly present, evidenced in the English-language titlings of the four films sparked by *Xiang Gang qi an zhi qiang jian* (1993), which is usually translated as *Raped by an Angel*. The notion that rape can be both pleasurable and consensual for its victim runs throughout the various strata and genres of Cat III films; Davis and Yueh-yu propose that these texts are ripe for thorough-going feminist analysis – they would surely benefit from further discussion in the context of work on the rape-revenge movie undertaken by Carol Clover and Jacinda Reed (2000). These rape scenarios, as well as other components of more extreme Cat III films (not least those dealing with real animal cruelty), mean that many titles never make it into foreign markets. The BBFC retains a strict policy on pleasurable images of sexual violence as well as infringements of UK animal cruelty legislation, so on these grounds Hong Kong Cat III does not automatically translate into UK 18. But there is also clearly scope here for extensive work on transnational configurations of consent.

Films which suggest some interesting interfaces with the Hollywood erotic thrillers might come from the first two of Davis and Yueh-yu's categories. Their 'genre films' are a loose designation, but thrillers dominate, and the cocktail of sex and crime which marks a number of prominent titles bears strong comparison particularly with American DTV and mainstream titles. *Evil Instinct* is widely read as Hong Kong's answer to *Basic Instinct*, even including a leg-cross-ing sequence. *Naked Killer* is a kind of erotic thriller *Nikita*-story about rival female assassins, containing strip-joint scenes, voyeurism, lesbian scenes (all four of its leading hit-women demonstrate lesbian tendencies at the very least), another *Basic Instinct*-style interrogation scene, and a deadly sex ethic ('We are women: our body is a weapon,' says hitwoman-coach Sister Cindy). *Pretty Woman* contains Veronica Yip in a *ten-minute* shower scene – evidence, if it was needed, that the Cat III sexploitation-thriller is the Hollywood erotic thriller turned up to eleven. The sci-fi-action hybrid *Robotrix* (an erotic-comedy retake on *Robocop*) also has one of its action heroines going undercover to catch a prostitute-killer, and features her having sex in the presence of a surveillance camera which effectively stimulates the watching cops. Some plot and theme co-ordinates thus align such movies with Western erotic thrillers, but these are also distinct Hong Kong products. Extreme attitudes to (and affirmation of) female violence (particularly *Naked Killer*'s retributive acts of castration) are highly post-Hollywood, far beyond anything which could be marketable on main-stream American theatrical screens. There is also more graphic female nudity (even a brief medium-shot 'beaver shot' in *Erotic Ghost Story*, though no male equivalent), whilst the violence is more casual and intense (as well as sometimes funnier). *Robotrix* features all three of its heroines kicking ass and having steamy sex by turns, two of them as cyborgs who just *have* to experience human sex in order to carry out a convincing simulation of humanity. Both films' martial arts-inflected action sequences are elaborately executed and choreo-graphed, showcasing their often silicone-enhanced softcore actresses as also acrobatically physical performers. Reviews of *Naked Weapon* praise its slick Matrix-style wire-work, as well as its nubile heroines. Davis and Yueh-yu also celebrate some Cat III films as actively soliciting 'female or gender-ambiguous audiences' (2001: 17), particularly when the quota of female-initiated action supersedes the sex. There is also an almost Shakespearean requirement to lighten the tone, particularly following really nasty death scenes, with a little bit of semi-slapstick, usually at the expense of oafish authority figures. This looks like genre confusion when sat alongside the po-faced psycho-sexual seriousness of Hollywood products, but is commonplace in some Hong Kong thrillers. Quite nasty violence routinely erupts cheek-by-jowl with comedy, including (in *Naked Killer*) a joke about a male cop inadvertently eating the castrated 'evi-dence' in place of his breakfast sausages at the scene-of-the-crime scene. Not only, then, do women shoot men's dicks off, the film enacts a secondary – culi-nary – revenge on men through comedy. Even Ezsterhas wouldn't go that far. Violence is frequently intrinsic to comedy (and vice versa) in a way that far out-strips the cool humour of Tarantino. Producer-director Wong Jing, a prolific figure across the genres of popular Hong Kong cinema, is known for his ener-getic gambling films and his sexually-inflected violently comedic formula films (his huge output as writer-director – though largely as producer – aligns him closely with figures such as Roger Corman or Ashok Amritraj). One source cites his movies as accounting for some 30 per cent of Hong Kong box office takings in the mid-1990s, but laments that 'regardless of his impressive list of credentials, the one genre Wong Jing is perhaps most famous for (in the eyes of Western fans of Hong Kong cinema) is the erotic thriller'.[10] This is, of course, the frame through which I would read him: Jing masterminded *Naked Killer* (which he produced and wrote, and cast his then-girlfriend Chingmy Yau in), as well as a spate of sexy-action/exploitation fare with English titles which have clearly learned something from the off-Hollywood DTV (*Deadly Dream Woman; Body Weapon*). *Naked Weapon* – tag-line: 'They will seduce you – just before they kill you!' – takes off from *Naked Killer* by focusing on a female Svengali-assassin trainer who kidnaps twelve-year-old girls talented in martial arts then spends years training them to become seductive killers, mixing *Charlie's Angels* with women-in-prisons motifs, whilst relying on the *Body of Evidence* stalwart, that female bodies are deadly in themselves. The gender politics of some Cat III films magnifies victim-aggressor-revenge patterns a hundred-fold: if women are tortured to extremity, they also wreak extreme forms of revenge, with the effect that both sides of violence collapse into each other as the form ups (its own) ante in an economy of ludicrous excess.

As with *Evil Instinct*'s overt referencing of *Basic Instinct*, some films deliberately signal their debt to the Western form of the erotic thriller, if primarily to cash in on its established box office success. One web authority reports that *Naked Killer*'s emergence at the time when 'Paul Verhoeven's massively over-rated "Basic Instinct" was box-office champ in Hong Kong cinemas' prompted Wong Jing to rush 'this project into theatres to capitalise on that film's success'.[11] Yet it would be hard to prove that Cat III sexploitation films rose in the wake of (and were directly influenced by) Hollywood's erotic thriller; the histories are coterminous through the 1980s and 1990s. Other Cat III films, however, constitute a unique branch of erotic mainstream filmmaking, drawing on Chinese mythology and history, and building sometimes preposterous sexual scenarios around traditional and supernatural stories. The films which Davis and Yueh-yu call 'quasi-pornographic' Cat III films are often 'loosely based on Ching dynasty Chinese literature and utiliz[ing] the generic iconography of a period or a costume film (e.g., the trope of the itinerant scholar)' (2001: 14). The *Erotic Ghost Story* series and the *Sex and Zen* films are incomparable to Western forms – presenting strong heroines in sexual and action scenes framed by supernatural and historical narratives, which mean that pretty much anything can happen. Wong Jing is again responsible for some of the key titles in this mode of historic-erotic fables, including *Sex and Zen II* and *III* and *Sex and the Emperor*. *Erotic Ghost Story* is a fine example of the Category III film's simultaneous overlap with and marked separation from Hollywood softcore formats. Funny and horrific by turns, it can be an unsettling view, hilariously mocking oafish predatory bandits cheek-by-jowl with a sequence in which a woman is raped by a three-headed demi-god. The story (of three fairies who must stay pure for 36 days in order to ascend to the next level of Being, but just can't help themselves) is a strange mix of art-film and sex-comedy – the special effects come straight out of cheap 1980s gore-horror, the sex scenes are romps showcasing female anatomy, whilst the fight sequences present the flying hero-ines as supreme beings. This is more erotic costume drama than erotic thriller, but the combination of sex and action may mean that it plays to the same market niche as derivative Hong Kong erotic thrillers such as *Naked Killer* and *Evil Instinct*. Despite the sexual quota, it will not be quite such comfortable sofa viewing for the average erotic thriller punter whose expectations have been constructed around the Hollywood format. For all the close-up obsession of the camera with Amy Yip's breasts, it is also remarkably refreshing to see supernat-ural action heroines so resolutely winning.

As a broad classification band, Cat III may cover titles across a wide spec-trum of mainstream and fringe tastes, and adult audiences may dip in and out of both. Whether these films are the true expressions of a distinct national cinema incorporating, changing and exposing the absurdities of the genre's original American form, further examples of sexual colonisation – the USA's infiltration of the world's erotic fantasyland – or an 'original' form which has traded on Hollywood successes in foreign markets, requires more detailed his-torical work. Cat III is significantly different from its American lookalike in that its audience component and production histories are not marked by the class stratification which divides Hollywood from fringe-Hollywood, where A- and B-list worlds are kept distinctly separate. In Hong Kong filmmaking there is considerable fluidity between different kinds of work, with actors (male ones, at least) commuting easily between (what in Hollywood would be perceived as) exploitation and mainstream, with no stigma attached to their careers. A prolific action figure such as Anthony Wong, for instance, is able to star in the exemplary Cat III violent shocker *The Untold Story* (a Sweeny Toddesque tale of everyday cannibalism – he even got a Hong Kong Film Award for the role) or the classically-inflected sexploitation *Erotic Ghost Story 2*, as well as international hits like John Woo's *Hard-Boiled*, and Andrew Lau and Alan Mak's psychological cop-thriller *Infernal Affairs* (and its sequels). Anthony Hopkins may have built a career on his Oscar-winning turn as psycho Hannibal Leckter, but it would be hard to imagine his career surviving a role such as the character called 'Human Milk Drinking Doctor' (a rapist who targets lactating women), forcefully played by Wong in Wong Jing's *Raped by an Angel 4: The Raper's Union*. But the situation is not the same for women and looks remarkably similar to the 'Some Nudity Required' fringe-Hollywood B-movie world. Amy Yip, for instance – whose name was almost synonymous with the softcore end of Cat III production until her retirement – featured in *Erotic Ghost Story 2* alongside Wong (she was also in the 1987 original *Erotic Ghost Story*), as well as *Sex and Zen* and *Robotrix*, but did not make the transition to mainstream fare like Wong.[12] Actresses who *have* diver-sified, such as Chingmy Yau and Carrie Ng, are still identified through their softcore profiles: one website refers to Yau as 'one of the queens of Category

III' but ruefully notes that 'Despite her attempts to diversify her acting portfolio, she is still best known for her roles in ultra-sleazy exploitation flicks such as *Raped by an Angel*.[13] Both Yau and Ng have made around fifty films; only seven of Yau's and nine of Ng's are Cat IIIs, though these do include titles such as *Naked Killer* (Yau and Ng together), *Evil Instinct* and *Sex and Zen* (Ng) and *Street Angels* (Yau). This is surely a pattern which genre-branded Hollywood and off-Hollywood stars such as Sharon Stone at one end of production or Shannon Tweed at the other would recognise. Your career may thrive despite playing the rapist of lactating women, but show your breasts in Hong Kong movies and you risk a similar fate to your sisters who do the same across the Pacific in Hollywood.

2: SEXUAL MELODRAMA

Closer to the erotic thriller's Hollywood and off-Hollywood 'home', an important sub-genre to develop in the genre's wake (as well as parallel to it) is the erotic melodrama or romance. It has much in common with the history this book charts, visible in theatrically-released and DTV markets, willing to push sexual spectacle to a softcore limit, keeping a keen eye on the couples market, but containing little criminal *noir*ishness. As with the male Cat III stars, performers in Hollywood or off-Hollywood softcore melodramas have more easily moved across and between mainstream and dtv filmmaking: baring all seems to attract little of the stigma which has ghettoised the Tweeds and the Whirrys to the erotic thriller, perhaps because erotic melodramas take romance as their prime co-ordinates and erotic thrillers are tainted by porn. Typical plots concern a female sexual quest, foregrounding infidelity or choices more akin to popular romantic fiction, and with crime usually signifying only in terms of how these affect the heroine's predicament. The term 'melodrama' is, however, (almost) never used in an erotic film's marketing (perhaps its association with the domestic makes it the least sexy of labels) – I have seen countless DTV films labelled 'Erotic Dramas', but not one labelled 'Erotic Melodrama', even though many of the 'dramas' (particularly from the Zalman King stable) have much in common with the 1940s woman's film and contemporary romantic fiction. Steve Neale (2000) stresses the problems surrounding the historical status of the woman's film, a category he finds almost as slippery as *film noir*. Various critical discussions posit an emphasis on female suffering and familial relationships, the dichotomy between bondage and freedom, domesticity and choice, and the undermining or reinforcement of stereotypes. However, the contemporary erotically-charged female sexual quest film replaces suffering with desire, overlapping with romance in its focus on the dangerous enticements of unknown sexual pleasures. In the mainstream films such as Adrian Lyne's *9½ Weeks* or *Unfaithful*, Sam Pillsbury's *Zandalee* or Zalman King's *Two Moon Junction* and *Wild Orchid* are prime sexual melodramas, nourishing erotic thriller tropes in the non-*noir*ish landscape of romance. In a book on contemporary sex cinema it is also worth briefly logging the importance of Just Jaeckin to the form. Running alongside the development of 'porno-chic' in the 1970s was a parallel history of hip, high-profile softcore, perhaps starting with Jaeckin's *Emmanuelle* in 1974, which flirts with both comedy and melodrama in their exploitation of female self-discovery in the universe of the zipless fuck. After *Emmanuelle*, with erotic adaptations such as *Lady Chatterley's Lover* and *The Story of O*, Jaeckin might be credited with creating an international audience for popular 'arty' softcore, laying the ground for the couples audience. Pre-AIDS, Jaeckin's films encapsulate stories which foreground women discovering sex without consequences.

Adrian Lyne is positioned at the racier end of mainstream Hollywood production: *9½ Weeks* (which was also written and produced by King), *Fatal Attraction* or *Indecent Proposal* are, as we have seen, scandal films predicated on sexual-political issue-led spectacle (*Lolita* was also marketed on the basis of how it reinflects for the 1990s the scandal of Nabokov's book and Kubrick's earlier film version). Yet *9½ Weeks*, *Indecent Proposal* and *Unfaithful* are all also species of the 'will she/won't she' female sexual quest tale, and are so consistent in foregrounding the heroine's point of view that they might suggest Lyne as a primary director of the contemporary Hollywood woman's film. *Unfaithful* is in many ways a fascinating 'answer' to the problems posed by *Fatal Attraction*, and – particularly following Diane Lane's Oscar nomination – was read as the story of Connie (Lane)'s fulfilment in the arms of glamorous wild lover Paul (Oliver Martinez). This is despite the fact that it mutates into a murder-melodrama when Connie's husband Ed (Richard Gere) kills the lover. In chapter 2 I suggested that here Gere occupies a position similar to Anne Archer's role in *Fatal Attraction*. Both dispatch the rival lover. But whereas in *Fatal Attraction* Archer's trigger-pulling bolsters the film's *noir*ishness, in *Unfaithful* Gere's killing becomes subordinate to Connie's romance story, instigating her mute grief and appalled decision to stand by her man – the man's crime of passion becomes subsumed in the story of the woman's choices. This is not just an effect of Lane's powerful performance, but of the way that Lyne has reinflected some of his earlier film's terms towards melodrama.

9½ Weeks can also be read as a woman's film, opening with Elizabeth (Kim Basinger) walking towards the camera through crowded streets, and ending with her walking away from it. Whilst this might position us with John (Mickey Rourke) as Elizabeth's spectator, it also positions Elizabeth's movements as beginning and end-points of a drama focused on how she meets him then how she leaves him. Jeanine Basinger identifies melodrama's 'bliss montage' as the brief interlude in a woman's cinematic story between 'after she meets the man' and 'before he lets her down' (1993: 8). This Happy Interlude splices good-time scenes of unalloyed pleasure (dancing, picnicking, winning at the races), compressing perhaps a few weeks of satisfaction into two minutes before things start to go wrong. The narrative of a female sexual quest film overlaps with but also extends this, in the process revealing retrospectively how much like a sex-scene the Happy Interlude always was. *9½ Weeks* is a feature-length montage of varying sexual encounters between Elizabeth and John, including those in which John positions Elizabeth as the subordinate or maso-chistic party. Still, the structure of the film moves her from the position of a confused divorcée to that of a woman in control of her choices. If in the woman's film the Happy Interlude of love/sex with a man is a briefly anoma-lous moment of bliss in a story of despair, in the female sexual quest film sexual experience frequently enables escape.

Elizabeth's 'No' to John which concludes *9½ Weeks* also resonates through its (female-directed) DTV sequel, despite the fact that the point of view shifts to Mickey Rourke's John. Essentially here director Anne Goursaud gives us an extended story of male torture provoked by Elizabeth's absence (it turns out she is dead, though he experiences this as one long rejection). *Another 9½ Weeks'* alternative title, *Love in Paris*, also gives a sense of its generic preferences: there are no murders, just a series of sexual set-pieces indulging the power of Lea (Angie Everhart), the new woman on the scene, to torment John. Essentially, Lea *becomes* John, the role-reversal making plain the sado-masochism of the first film's relationship, and perhaps suggesting *Love in Paris* as male tragic-roman-tic fiction. This is an interesting premise for an erotic drama marketed on its erotic thriller credentials, but Goursaud, in my interview below, counsels caution for any female director, particularly at the low-budget end of produc-tion, who embraces sexual material. She also directed the sequel to Katt Shea's *Poison Ivy*, and the first two *Poison Ivy* titles present interesting forms of female-directed erotic melodramas. *Poison Ivy* itself, with its UK poster/video box art campaign featuring a vivaciously sexual Drew Barrymore as Ivy, looked very much like an erotic thriller. Shea reported that she was hired 'by New Line Cinema to come up with a teenage *Fatal Attraction*' (Norman 1993: 41), and it certainly works on one level as a *femme fatale* revenge story. However, it also develops Shea's wider interest in the psycho-sexual power of adolescent girls, and is articulated as the fantasy/nightmare of Coop (Sara Gilbert), who provides the voiceover and primary point of view. Lolita figure Ivy infiltrates Coop's life, first moving into her house, then seducing her father, then killing her mother, and finally killing herself. The film's erotic thriller credentials are significant, but its analysis of female friendship is perhaps more powerfully read in the frame of melodrama. As much a story of the ambivalence of adolescent desire as it is the revenge of poor white trash against bourgeois abundance, *Poison Ivy* is a complex transgeneric work. Indeed, it is its sexuality and its interest in displaced femininity that allows it such generic leeway (sexual women are central to both genres, and here they wilfully migrate back and forth, shifting the tone of the film). Goursaud's sequel touches base with Shea's story, with its heroine (Lily) fixated on the traces Ivy left behind (diaries and memorabilia), so the female con-nection is mapped out via artifacts between the living and the dead. But Lily is older, an art student, so is more manifestly pitching into adult femininity, an active-passive figure. Her attempted seduction of a professor, leading to his death and her acceptance of an equal relationship with a boy her own age, seems to resolve the *Poison Ivy* stories' uneasy oedipality (until Kurt Voss's mark 3 comes along, that is). Goursaud's films are stylish-looking and seemingly directed with a view to how powerfully they will edit (she is an established editor of a number of big-budget mainstream productions, many with Francis Ford Coppola); budget limitations are manifest in sometimes shaky performances and the obligation to meet genre requirements in regular sex scenes (*Love in Paris* revisits, and sometimes unpicks, a number of *9½ Weeks'* original sexual premises). By contrast Shea directs with a guerrilla energy appropriate to her training in the Corman school, though following her spate of stripper-killer films *Poison Ivy* is a slick studio production. Her interest in girlhood on the cusp of womanhood has developed in subsequent movies.

Zalman King is one of the most significant figures in popular sexual melo/drama/romance, a powerful 'brand name' producer-director who delivers consistent couples products.[14] However, behind his porno-auteur profile there lies some significant female writing production: much of the credit for his sex-melos must be attributed to his writing/production partner (and wife) Patricia Louisianna Knop. He also collaborates with his writer-producer daughters, and employs a number of other female writers because his company is 'telling stories from a woman's point of view' (McDonagh 1995: 68). This is not to say that the presence of women in the credits guarantees feminism in the text, but that female fantasy-production runs insistently if sometimes invisibly through these films, the women on-screen perhaps acting as surrogates for those off. The original, feature-length *Red Shoe Diaries*, though book-ended by the story of David Duchovny's grief about his dead girlfriend (Brigitte Bako) and marketed as man-friendly T&A, actually tells that woman's secret love-story, laid out in her diary discovered after her death and manifest in the film text as her governing voice-over. *Two Moon Junction* is even closer to romantic fiction, the story of a Southern heiress torn between rich fiancé and working-class lover providing ample opportunities for softcore. Sam Pillsbury's *Zandalee* was similarly positioned in the market, and shadows the *Red Shoe Diaries* story, ticking off a number of erotic thriller motifs in the process but resolving itself as an erotic melodrama. Erika Anderson plays the eponymous sexually frustrated wife of New Orleans poet-turned-businessman Thierry Martin (Judge Reinhold), who succumbs to the wild passions of Johnny (Nicolas Cage). When Thierry inherited his father's business a year before he also lost his sex drive ('paralysed' as he puts it, 'a paraplegic of the soul'), positing *Zandalee* as a 1980s reworking of *Lady Chatterley's Lover*, the animalistic lover supplanting the damaged husband. In the film's first scene, *Zandalee* dances naked round the bedroom whilst her husband talks business-talk to himself in the bathroom mirror. Johnny articulates their affair as a function first of her desire: 'You want it – and I want to give it. Perfect relationship.' This, then, overtly sexualises the motifs of women's romantic fiction. King's *Wild Orchid* – marketed as a follow-up to *Red Shoe Diaries* – follows a similar blueprint. First it foregrounds the story of its initially uptight heroine (Carré Otis as Emily) as sexual quester, aided and abetted by the older man and woman figures of Wheeler (Rourke) and Claudia (Jacqueline Bisset). Wheeler conforms fairly closely to the romantic fiction staple of enigmatic powerful male who eludes the heroine until the final scene: this figure in the female sexual quest film is little more than a kind of sexed-up Darcy (or 'tall, dark and handsome' Mills and Boon/Harlequin hero), promising sexual ecstasy in place of 'Reader, I married him'. But Wheeler is also a kind of damaged roué-initiator, like Mario in *Emmanuelle* or Sir Stephen in (Jaeckin's rendition of) *Story of O*: he pushes Emily into sexual experimentation because he can't do it himself (until Emily melts him, he is phobic about touch). *Wild Orchid* then traces a double narrative of sexual awakening: as Emily becomes sexually confident, she is able to 'cure' Wheeler of his frigidity. The Austensque ends-with-a-marriage dénouement is replaced by Wheeler and Emily riding into the sunrise on his Harley Davidson after a climactic night of passion.

Wild Orchid also features numerous moments when the woman as sexual consumer (visual and economic) is foregrounded: as Emily and Claudia pass a hunky man early in the film, Claudia asks the younger girl 'Do you like what you see?' Despite the fact that she's supposed to be a high-powered international lawyer brokering a major property deal with some Chinese businessmen, Emily also spends a lot of her time standing on her balcony in Rio looking longingly at basketball players on the beach. Later, Claudia and Emily summon a beach-boy to their room, and as Claudia seduces him Emily acts as translator: Emily's words mediate Claudia's desires in a scene which features fully-dressed women and a naked man. 'Ask him', says Claudia, 'if he understands what tremendous pleasure women get looking at naked men.' As with *Night Rhythms*, Emily also does a lot of dirty talking, with Wheeler encouraging her fantasies of confessed voyeurism: Emily watches people having sex (sometimes via a mirror), then tells Wheeler what she's seen. She is also made to watch sex whilst Wheeler watches her: he consumes the image of her uncomfortably looking whilst she consumes the image of sex. At these points in which views are being traded, it's hard to read who is doing what to whom.

Other recent films by women present alternative female desires which may be saying no to traditional romance, but yes to its (perverse) reinscription. Based on Barbara Gowdy's short story 'We so Seldom Look on Love', Lynne Stopkewich's *Kissed* is a necrophiliac fable, featuring a woman who goes to work in a mortuary to facilitate her love for just-dead male bodies (Sandra is sexually compelled: 'I need to do it – I have no choice,' she says). On the one hand, *Kissed* justified itself through its role-reversal; 'A male director might be accused of exploitation if he showed female bodies being violated, or a woman offering her life for a lover', one (female) critic argued (O'Sullivan 1988: 48). The same is true of Lizzie Borden's *Love Crimes*, a classic erotic thriller narrative in which an undercover female DA discovers masochistic desires at the hands of an *homme fatal*. Borden thought that because 'The slight element of consent in the relationships makes this dangerous territory' (Hartl 1992) it could only be directed by a woman. In *Kissed*, Matt is the first and only live man Sandra has sex with. Through his love he comes to identify so strongly with his (dead) rivals that first he tries to pose as a corpse in their sex-play, then kills himself in order to take the relationship forward to the stage of post-mortem bliss Sandra can only experience in conjugation with the dead. This necrophiliac post-romance makes man the consummate sex object/abject. Though on one level Sandra is a rather quirky indie-cinema heroine, she is also perhaps the most *fatale* of *femmes* in her total immersion in the sex of death, an acceptable figure of desire for a Canadian female-auteur work, though not perhaps for the popular genre mainstream.

This book has investigated a number of key players in the theatrical and DTV erotic thriller, which may mean that it has sporadically subscribed to an auteurist mode of practice. One form in which the erotic thriller has persisted in the public eye untainted by some of the pejorative connotations of the genre term is as an auteur product. As we have seen, its history is peppered with films singled out (and separated from the genre morass) as 'unique visions'. Critical reception of De Palma's films, or auteur-helmed works such as Polanski's *Bitter Moon*, Lynch's *Lost Highway* or *Mulholland Drive* or Abel Ferrara's *Blackout* or *Fear City* bear out the truth that the author is alive and well and thriving in popular film genres. *Bad Timing* and *Full Body Massage* look like art-house erotic melodramas when read in the frame of this book, but their promotion foregrounded their director, Nicolas Roeg. I now want to look briefly at a set of films that shed light on some of the transnational questions I opened up above, looking at three erotic thrillers which were marketed and received as auteur works, US-produced films which forged fraught relationships with American culture. Spanning the period 1985–2003, they also tell of the vicissitudes of US and UK censorship, particularly across the theatrical/video divide, demonstrating the fickleness of these different marketplaces. *Eyes Wide Shut* was directed by an American (Kubrick) who spent much of his life in the UK; it was shot largely in the UK. *Crimes of Passion* was directed by a British 'national treasure' (Ken Russell) in Hollywood, but looks rather like an anti-Hollywood exercise in guerrilla shock tactics. *Wild Side* was directed by another Brit in Hollywood (Donald Cammell), and was released in two versions – a DTV version, which makes the perfect partner for the DTV movies I discussed in Part Two, and a re-edited art-film, seen as the fitting epitaph to Cammell's troubled career. My Afterword concludes with a reading of *In the Cut*, the American genre product of New Zealand's foremost female auteur, Jane Campion, promoted both as woman's film and a neo-*noir*, though viewed in the frame of this book it emerges as an exemplary erotic thriller for contemporary cinema.

3: THE EROTIC THRILLER AND THE AUTEUR

'B-movies have always been my inspiration.'

China Blue (Kathleen Turner) in *Crimes of Passion*

And then there are the established genre auteurs like Jonathan Demme, Martin Scorsese, David Lynch, and Woody Allen who, like Ford and Hitchcock and the other top studio directors of old, are the most perplexing and intriguing cases – each of them part visionary cinéaste and part commercial hack, whose best films flirt with hit status and critique the very genres (and audiences) they exploit.

(Schatz 1993: 35)

Is the auteur dead? Yes, if you read some formations of contemporary film theory; no, if you read popular film journalism and trace the director-dominated manoeuvres of film publicity. The vicissitudes of film studies which followed auteurism's high-water mark in the 1950s and 1960s saw the director's sovereign position threatened by structuralist neo-auteurism (Wollen) and reader/audience-empowering 'death of the author' theory (Barthes). However, in certain quarters the director-as-author has never had a day off sick, let alone died. Key New Hollywood figures such as De Palma and Stanley Kubrick, both of whom have directed prominent erotic thrillers, have fostered hyper-controlling directorial profiles which have become useful hooks for the marketing of their movies. Yet we have seen that particularly in its cheaper form, the erotic thriller is prime drive-in work, often branded more by a producer's mark than by directorial style. Gernert and Garroni, Amritraj, Hong Kong's Jing Wong, know how to squeeze their particular brand of sexploitation from a limited budget. As an aspiring studio executive early in his career Roger Corman 'asked for total control and considered this non-negotiable' (Corman 1998: ix), yet some of the auteur figures under discussion here also require it, even when they are following a genre recipe rather than a singular inspiration.

The fierce promotion of individualised 'visionary' filmmaking has been amply rewarded in popular review and journalistic responses. The most prominent name directors working in Hollywood since the 1980s operate in a positive feedback-loop of auteurial self-regard: statements such as De Palma's 'One is a director because one want to be the master' (Pally 1984: 14) have been fed into the system of reception. PR bodies have used these (like the promise of generic repetition) to promote a guaranteed, standardised product (Kubrick's control is so strong that you can be sure his next film will live up to his last), which has then been rewarded when reviewers have constructed their reading of a film wholly within the context of a pre-existing directorial profile. If you want to kill the author, ask popular film magazines and websites to delete all references to a director's name. Regardless of the variable adherence to generic moulds which the auteurist erotic thrillers below demonstrate, in reception they are read almost universally as divine emissions of directorial drive. However much these films have in common as genre products, individually they are seen as unique examples of a single man's vision.

The genre auteur is a concept derived from a collision of auteur theory and genre production, and is perhaps crystallised by the work of Mundhra and Hippolyte, discussed above. But the auteur who seeks to rise above genre whilst directing vehemently genred works is another matter, as is the auteur whose products are so stylistically standardised that they begin to look something like a genre. De Palma in particular has, as one critic noted, 'self-consciously created for himself the role of auteur: he has single-mindedly promoted himself as someone known by the general public for a certain sort of film' (Hugo 1989: 56). Here we might see how categories such as art and popular cinema come to bleed into each other. When exploitation genres such as the erotic thriller trade on the pretensions and promises of auteurial consistency, each risks contamination by the other: the erotic thriller risks losing its marketable distinctiveness (and its audience), the auteur risks the dilution of his 'vision' in a welter of formulae, his unique selling point giving way to the marketability of genre. De Palma has been successful because name and a particular film form have become synonymous, straddling popular and art-house cinemas. However, it is significant that in the interviews I conducted, the A-list auteur figures tended to disavow genre discourse by propounding the message that they make Great Films rather than genre flicks, whilst those working at the cheaper end of production seemed happier to discuss the productive constraints of genre on their filmmaking. Further questions need to be posed in relation to the auteur-helmed erotic thriller include: Has the fact that a number of key erotic thrillers have been helmed by respected auteurs of art cinema made any difference to this form? How do genre films contribute to (or undermine) their directors' auteur profiles? How are auteur profiles used to market genre products?

Eyes Wide Shut, Stanley Kubrick's last film, is essentially an erotic thriller, even if it is a lot of other things too. Perhaps no film exemplifies the possible extremes erotic thriller filmmaking can take more than this. Whilst Gary Graver's *Sexual Roulette* was made on a shoestring in a matter of weeks, *Eyes Wide Shut* took two years with a budget of $65 million. No one has heard of Graver (despite the fact that he was at one time Orson Welles' cameraman); everyone has heard of Stanley Kubrick. Graver's stars (Tane McLure, Gabriella Hall) are perhaps destined to work on the B-movie treadmill before retiring out of the film world, or going into production like Andrew Stevens or Karen Baldwin have done. *Eyes Wide Shut*'s stars Tom Cruise and Nicole Kidman are household names and will never be out of work; Kidman is an Oscar winner, Cruise an Oscar nominee. Nevertheless, their film bears many of the hallmarks of a DTV production. Kubrick has long played with genre, emulating and exemplifying the pinnacles of trash genres through meticulously rendered works of cinema art. What *2001, The Shining* and *Full Metal Jacket* did for science fiction, horror and the Vietnam film respectively, *Eyes Wide Shut* does for the erotic thriller, which is to say it is both generically formulaic and challenging, deploying but also developing the codes of sex and thriller cinema in the 1990s. It was also received as the consummate example of 'The strange authority of Kubrick's vision' (Gross 1999: 23).

Alice and Bill Harford are bored with their marriage and beginning to look elsewhere for sexual excitement. Spurred by jealousy at his wife's confession of a fantasised infidelity (which gives rise to a series of video-like monochrome mental replays of the image of her with another man), Bill goes on a sexual odyssey into a secret world of high-class orgies which ends (probably) in murder. Alice's fantasised encounter has led Bill to try to take revenge through sex with other women, but despite being (as *Sight and Sound*'s reviewer put it) '[p]resented with a queue of obliging fantasy women – a needy patient's daughter, a nice prostitute, an underage shopkeeper's daughter, a perfect-bodied masked orgyer – he fails at consummation every time' (Whitehouse 1999: 38–9). Alice didn't have sex with someone else, she only wished it; Bill looks for sex with other women, but never quite gets his trousers off. This then is a sex story which is finally monogamous in deed if not in thought. And what of the crime? A woman dies following her participation in the orgy, Bill suspects foul play, and so goes on a detective quest, which parallel's his sexual quest, to find out whodunit. Eventually, however, he is told that she was just a junkie who had simply OD-ed. It is, then, also a murder story which (perhaps) lacks a murder victim. These generic 'failures' are only the start of its problems. *Eyes Wide Shut* promises treats in its marketing which it fails to deliver through its diegesis. The DVD package blurb is worthy of any cheaper erotic thriller title: 'Cruise plays Dr. William Harford, who plunges into an erotic foray that threatens his marriage – and may even ensnare him in a lurid murder mystery – after his wife's (Kidman) admission of sexual longings.' By pushing particular genre buttons ('erotic foray', 'murder mystery'), *Eyes Wide Shut* quite specifically targets this particular niche. But the film itself stops short in its presentation of both sex and death. Its erotic intrigue is resolved through a monogamous pact between the central couple, and its thriller mystery is resolved by the substitution of suicide for murder. Thus it manages to be a sex film with hardly any sex (with sex, in fact, as pure fantasy) and a murder mystery in which someone dies but no one is killed. In between is left the search, or the desire, but not the arrival or the dénouement. Like the porn hero, Bill Harman is involved in a sexual quest, but unlike the porn hero, he fails to have sex. And, like the hero-detective, Bill Harman is involved in a search for the criminal truth, but unlike the detective he finds that there is no killer. A film which promises dicks of both kinds – private eyes and private parts – finally gives us neither.

If you ever suspected that Kubrick was a dirty old man masquerading as an auteur, this film confirms it. The first shot features Nicole Kidman stripping, and from then on in when she isn't mothering her daughter she is often in a state of undress. That a mainstream American film would present its female lead as only mother or lover is clearly nothing new, and is not redeemed by

Alice being given the last word ('Fuck', uttered as an invitation to Bill that they renew their relationship through sex). Kubrick's women have always looked most at home in the kitchen or the bedroom: as co-writer Frederic Raphael has said in his study *Eyes Wide Open*: 'What [Kubrick] wants is the naked woman at the refrigerator door as she remembers to put the chicken away before she goes to bed.'[15] The orgy sequence is a soft-porn rendition of a Sadean set-piece which looks more like the work of Just Jaeckin than of Stanley Kubrick (echoing the ponderous art pretentions of Jaeckin's 1975 film of *The Story of O*. The scene also duplicates a masked orgy/public sex scene from the Zalman King skinflick *Wild Orchid*, and prefigures the much cheaper debauchery in Rob Hardy's *Pandora's Box*.) *Eyes Wide Shut*, as the title suggests, presents its voyeurism, its sexual quest and its hints of lesbianism-for-men in a way that is indistinguishable from lower-end softcore, and marries these to a narrative of intrigue, murder and sexual power which has been more extensively handled in much cheaper films. But unlike King's or Hardy's films, it is resolutely a male point of view film, even when a performer as interesting as Kidman co-stars.

Why, then, was it received as the consummate auteur work? Not only because Kubrick is *Kubrick*, but because, it seems, the traditional belief that one's dying breath contains the soul as it leaves the body has also infected film reception. This is Kubrick's last film and so might contain his directorial essence: one reviewer, noting that it was 'delivered, as it were, from his deathbed', calls it 'in many ways the summation of his life's work' (Williams 1999). Reviewers desperately stress that, despite the nudity quota, *Eyes Wide Shut* 'is personal filmmaking as well as dream poetry of the kind most movie commerce has ground underfoot' (Rosenbaum 1999). Even a negative review, which saw it as 'a woeful exit for a talent who deserved a far sturdier cinematic headstone', still asserts that 'The real star of a Stanley Kubrick outing . . . is Kubrick himself' (Schneider 1999). In chapter 1 I said that an index of the erotic thriller's cultural capital was that one might know one without ever having seen one. Such is the stardom of the contemporary auteur, personal branding has eclipsed critical knowledge; as Tim Corrigan writes, 'An auteur film today seems to aspire more and more to a critical tautology, capable of being understood and consumed without being seen' (1998: 50). This is auteur branding as the logical conclusion of high-concept movie-making. One may know *Eyes Wide Shut* as a Kubrick film without having seen it; but art-house viewers lacking the cinematic omnivorousness which might have led them to popular genre works may not know it as an erotic thriller however many times they see it (they may instead read it as a classy, sexy, but essentially 'Kubrickian' piece, adapted from a respected novella – Arthur Schnitzler's 1926 *Traumnovelle* – but still somehow a unique work). Yet it *is* an erotic thriller, as the narrative co-ordinates and textual obsessions sketched above evidence. It is tempting, given this auteurial reverence, to argue the film into a genre corner ever more thoroughly. However, a more productive approach would be to think further on how auteurs have worked with genre traits in art-house contexts to produce more complex contemporary formations.

Crimes of Passion is a rather different case: a hybrid genre/auteur work, marked by the determinants of the developing erotic thriller, but clearly identifiable as a Ken Russell film. It also gave rise to a very early press use of the term 'erotic thriller' (Hunter 1985: 6).[16] Russell has consistently revisited the garishly transgressive, often bringing sex and religion into play in a mix of hysterical excess. His films are colourful, frequently ludicrous, usually immensely entertaining fantasies of desire and outrage. He does not purport to produce finely crafted realist dramas, but nor does he make genre films in the strict sense of the term: *Lisztomania*, *The Music Lovers*, *Savage Messiah*, may be loosely termed biopics, but they were marketed as Ken Russell films, and whilst they strive to produce a version of historical personae, Russell is hardly known for his fastidious drive to accuracy. *Crimes of Passion* foregrounds a range of lurid Russellesque concerns: sex, blasphemy, madness. Though the director was once a committed Catholic, he also enjoys provoking certain castes of fundamentalist Christian: *Crimes of Passion* picks up where savage investigations of Christian orthodoxy such as *The Devils* left off. The film begins with a dirty joke about God and features Anthony Perkins as an oversexed, over-repressed, murderously evangelical street-corner preacher (Peter Shayne) with a bag full of sex toys. His prey is China Blue, a $50 hooker by night, enthusiastically played by Kathleen Turner, who is by day respectable besuited designer Joanna Crane. At one point China dresses as one of Russell's favourite icons, a rampant knickerless nun, who sings 'Onward Christian Soldiers' whilst leaping on Shayne. Between divine insanity and profane eroticism Russell inserts Bobby (John Laughlin), an everyman figure who is having trouble with his marriage (a prototype neglected spouse). China beds various men in a variety of ways (incurring the wrath of the censor in the process, particularly when she sodomises a policeman with his truncheon), until Bobby comes her way and Shayne closes in for the kill, armed with a menacingly pointed steel vibrator with which he hopes to exorcise 'demons'. *Crimes of Passion* thus plays rather like *Belle de Jour* meets *Psycho*, the split identity of China/Joanne echoing Catherine Deneuve's recreational hooker. The combination of Barry Sandler's arch fast-talking screenplay and Russell's stylised red light district resembles Oscar Wilde on acid. But it is also the missing link in the mediation of Buñuel's film – so influential on the erotic thriller, from Axis's *Secret Games* series to Friedkin's *Jade* – from French art cinema to popular US genre.

The film's concern with the sex industry, with double identities, and with fantasy as an escape from the ordinary problems of the sexual everyday form its rough genre co-ordinates. And it is not only De Palma who reveals Hitchcock's work as a fruitful seed-bed for the erotic thriller: here Russell makes full use of Perkins' most famous cinematic *alter-ego*, Norman Bates. Indeed, for all its heady humour, *Crimes of Passion* is a more inventive reading of *Psycho* than *Dressed to Kill*. When Perkins' character is not peering in on gyrating hookers and fantasising their bloody deaths, he is holed up in a small room bedecked with porn and pictures of Christ, spying on China as she satisfies her customers through a peep-hole remarkably like that through which Norman Bates views Marion Crane (China's *alter-ego* and masculinised daylight self is, of course, also named 'Crane'). In the final attack sequence, Bobby arrives at Joanna's flat to find Shayne dragged-up in China's gear, in memory, perhaps, of Norman tarted up as his mother, with Joanna dressed in priest garb as Shayne. But here – unlike *Psycho* and *Dressed to Kill* – the sexual woman is not punished by death for her erotic excesses; instead, the death of Shayne – killed in self-defence by China/Crane wielding the steel vibrator – forms a moment of exorcism allowing China/Crane to integrate the whore and the working woman, building her two identities back into one, courtesy of a loving *and* erotic relationship with Bobby.

Crimes of Passion is a surprising film for a number of reasons, not least because whilst it undoubtedly relishes going too far, it also shows considerable sensitivity to the everyday subtleties of marriage breakdown.[17] It is as interested in the emotional context for fluctuations in desire as it is in representing the extremes of purchased sex. Still, it was yoked with De Palma's *Body Double* as an equal partner in crime and further evidence of a wave of nastiness spreading through celluloid. Cinemas were picketed by the UK feminist group Women Against Violence Against Women, who explicitly connected mainstream sexual representations and commercial pornography;[18] tabloid newspapers also called it 'soft-porn' as a term of abuse (Christie 1985; Johnstone 1985; Walker 1985; Watson 1985). Manchester police chief James Anderton was deeply offended by it. According to Russell, Turner was dubious about taking on China Blue, worried that it 'was degrading and would be injurious to her career'. Since *Body Heat*, she had concentrated on forging a more wholesome star identity. Whether it was feminism or a desire for more family-friendly roles which caused Turner's anxieties about playing a hooker, Russell reports that she threw herself into it with professional relish.

Crimes of Passion was funded by a post-Corman New World Pictures, and Russell predicted that it would do better in the embryonic video market than in theatrical release (it did).[19] But it was here that it proved potentially most problematic for UK audiences. The newly passed Video Recordings Act proscribed violent and sexual representations for consumption in the home, and Russell's film, replete with Shayne's fantasies of slashing naked prostitutes into a pool of blood (and then acting these fantasies out on blow-up sex dolls), plus images of China participating in rape fantasies, fed into a climate of anxiety about cinema as harmful. New World's contract required Russell to deliver an R-rated film, and – more than any specific act or individual scene – it was the generalised sense of extremity exuded by the film which suggested X material, rather than any actual image. Erections bulge *under* denim not *out* of it, all sex (including the rape fantasy) is simulated and consensual sex-play (Russell [1989: 243] describes Turner choosing lemon yogurt for her sperm-swallowing), discussion of sexual violence is crisp but mocking (of Shayne's steel vibrator China says, 'What's this? Cruise missile or Pershing? . . . What are you gonna do – fuck someone to death?'). Russell is adept at giving the impression of explicitness whilst not technically crossing any lines, which meant that the MPAA censors hardly knew where to start when asking for cuts.[20] The delirious sense of the explicit is further reinforced by repeated cuts from China's sex room to classic line drawings of penetration and erections – Aubrey Beardsley and Japanese erotic art – images which, if they were photographic low art rather than pen-and-ink high art, would be squarely hardcore. These serve primarily as exteriorisations of China/Joanne's fantasies (decorating her smart apartment; one – a brief flash of Waterhouse's Ophelia – seems to prefigure her doom). They also function as surreal subliminal shots directed by Russell straight at the viewer, not narratively contextualised, just presented in oblique commentary, perhaps eliding what Russell cannot show on-screen. They are also overt provocations to the censor. If mainstream cinema in 1984 was unable to show hardcore images, Russell seems to be asking whether such images, when lifted directly from classic artworks, would be more acceptable. In this he also tackles head-on the question surrounding the relationship between high art and low porn provoked by the Minneapolis Ordinance, which had infused American reactions to *Body Double*.

How, then, to market such a generically messy mix of auteur-signature and scandalous content? The trailer promotes a work which is at best a rather slippery example of an erotic thriller as a dependable genre product, trading on *Crimes of Passion*'s mixed profile as both an auteur/star vehicle and a piece of sexual controversy. First the voiceover reminds us of key elements of Russell's cv, whilst his name is displayed on screen: 'In *Women in Love* he crossed forbidden boundaries', we are told; 'In *Altered States* he explored the unknown powers of the mind. Now he explores the most provocative power of all.' The voiceover then moves efficiently from auteur to genre, suggesting resonant genre plot-points, but in terms so vague that they could be describing anything from *Basic Instinct* to any Gregory Hippolyte film: 'A woman who lives in two worlds. A man who must lose himself to possess her. They are strangers. They are lovers. They are outlaws. But their crimes are *Crimes of Passion*.' The genre message is reinforced by the pervasive sense of sado-masochistic promise (self-loss, sexual possession) which infuses this discourse, intensified by the sleazy saxophone underscore.[21] Finally, the star–genre axis is evoked when we are told that *Crimes of Passion* features 'The star of *Body Heat* . . .'.

If the trailer were to tell us all we need to know about *Crimes of Passion*, we would receive it as a reliable genre product reinforced by the guarantees of consistency which genre and star names can provide. However, critical reception – which was enthusiastic in castigation or praise – tended to split these attributes into distinct elements, privileging star, or director, or scandalous content, as rhetorical devices for judgement. Whereas promotional strategies aim to maximise audiences by pinpointing different elements which will attract distinct sectors,

CONCLUSION: THE EROTIC THRILLER'S HYBRID CHILDREN

reviewers frequently focus on single aspects of the film. For instance, the auteur message is reinforced by *The Hollywood Reporter*'s headline for a brief piece on the film: ' "Crimes of Passion" evidence of Russell as master director' – no problems with auteurism there then (Knight 1984: 3). *The Guardian* directly aligned director and text, and reinforced the image of Russell as a national treasure ('The whole positively glistens with virtuosity . . .'; 'that is Russell, take him or leave him . . .'; *Crimes of Passion* 'ought, like Russell himself, to be cherished' (Malcolm 1985b: 11). Some writers followed the trailer in promoting *Crimes of Passion* as the next step beyond Turner's *Body Heat* performance, even though her family-friendly work in *Romancing the Stone* and the comic *femme fatale* of *The Man with Two Brains* had functioned to create distance from her darker sexual incarnations.[22] Negative criticism was generally attributed directly to the influence of Russell as controlling force, although both positive and negative reviews deploy similar language. Hibbin (1985a: 4) calls it 'a typically overblown Russellian delve into the problems of sex'; Davis writes that Russell's 'talent could pass for an uncheckable lava flow' (1985: 20), Perry calls it 'another over-the-top foray by the outrageous Ken' (1985: 38) – and these are the *good* reviews. Even the promotional programme notes hedge their bets, calling 'Russell's notorious gift' ' "excess" and "bad taste" if you don't like it, "flair" and "pyrotechnics" if you do'.[23] The Edinburgh Film Festival clearly didn't know what to make of the film at all, since it included two reviews in the programme notes, one (according to Malcolm 1985a) 'lambasting it for "deep-riven misogyny," the other praising it as "the funniest and most scathing portrait of America" '. Critical discourse was infected by the film's overblown qualities, as if the outrageous marriage of director and genre had spawned its own sensational form of response.

However, as with De Palma's films of sexual violence (*Body Double* was released in the UK a week after Russell's film), *Crimes of Passion* was caught in a wider debate about sexual spectacle on mainstream screens, in its pre-release censorship and through debates over its status as pornography. The (female) *New York Times* reviewer called it Russell's 'most aggressively sexual film' (Maslin 1984: C23) (which is not the same as saying it is sexually aggressive), whilst in the UK Clancy Segal argued that it 'purports to be about women's sexual fantasies but is in fact an expression of the crudest masculine view of what a woman is supposed to fantasise' (1985: 33). Nevertheless, *Spare Rib*, then the UK's foremost popular feminist journal, separated itself from protests such as those from WAVAW ('porn is repulsive and aims to intimidate and terrify women, and *Crimes of Passion* didn't have this effect on me' [Bishop 1986: 32]). The familiar critical tactic of increasing the scandalous cachet of a film by bagging it together with a range of like-minded bedfellows dogged, or boosted, *Crimes of Passion*'s audience figures: in this way film scandals are generated in the public arena largely by referencing them in terms of each other. (Did you see *Body Double*? Well here's another one like it.)[24] Nigel Horne reported in *The Sunday Times* (1985: 39) that the film had had

its run in one London cinema extended three times, and promotion capitalised on scandal ('Crimes of Passion is "Ken Russell's most controversial film",
according to the tantalising marquee signs at the Odeon Haymarket'). The
film also attracted audiences seeking sexual material, but unwilling to find it
in conventional pornography; Russell's name on the marquee adds a certain
legitimacy to the hoped-for sexual image. 'We are perhaps attracting some
people who wouldn't want to be spotted going into a Soho peep-show but
don't mind being seen going to the cinema' a Rank spokesman told Horne,
whilst the manager of a chain of independent London cinemas added, 'There
is no doubt that the whiff of erotica can bring in a matinée audience of gentlemen, which helps increase the total audience at the end of the day.' The
mark of respectability or quality which even a maverick name such as Russell's
brings to a project can then protect audiences from any implication that they
are seeking smut when they buy *Crimes of Passion*. 'In the foyer stands the
manager, immaculate in a penguin suit, assuring wary customers that his
establishment is the very epitome of respectability,' wrote *New Society*. '"The
idea that we're showing porn in a top West End theatre is preposterous," says
a clocking-on projectionist. "Ken Russell is an artist. Anyway, it's a very
upmarket film"' (1985: 441).

If Russell's notorious auteurial authority – however eccentric – can rescue
his film from the opprobrium of scandal, my next case shows the director
wielding control from beyond the grave. Donald Cammell's last film takes a
number of threads and weaves them into an interesting genre case. *Wild Side*
is another *Belle de Jour*-inflected story of banker Alex (Anne Heche) who
turns tricks on the side, falls in love with Virginia (Joan Chen), the ex-wife of
her money-laundering client Bruno (Christopher Walken), and then – as with
Bound – gets away with the girl. A textually fascinating exercise in genre
fodder rendered as art film, *Wild Side* is also notable for the fact that its production company, Nu Image, took Cammell off the case when they perceived
his cut was *not* going to be the commercial sexploitation fare they were
expecting.[25] The film was released, direct-to-cable in the US, minus Cammell's
name, with its lesbian sex quota augmented and presented in one extended
scene. Cammell committed suicide. Tartan Films in the UK then bought the
rights to the film and produced, with original editor Frank Mazzola (a long-
time Cammell collaborator) and co-writer China Kong (Cammell's widow), a
posthumous 'director's cut'. This played theatrically in the UK, and now has
a strong reputation as a true Cammell work, available on DVD in a cut with
'his signature on it. It's his again' (in Mazzola's words [Le Cain 2001: 46]).
Reception materials about the film uniformly discuss the Nu Image version as
an act of 'butchery' (Pendreigh 2000: 12) and 'a cable TV time-waster'
(Newman 2000: 57); it 'goes through the motions of a bargain basement erotic
thriller' (Le Cain 2001: 12), and is 'the sort of trashy sex thriller that turns up
late at night on Channel 5' (Pendreigh 2000: 12). Frank Mazzola, a deeply
spiritual man, told me that he felt Cammell working through him in the

editing suite as he re-formulated the footage,[26] and enthusiastic reviewers of what is called in the end credits '*Wild Side* – The Director's Cut' take the auteurial authority of the dead director for granted (the National Film Theatre programme notes say that it has been restored 'according to its maker's original intentions', quoting Mazzola as saying its 'a movie only Donald could have made').[27]

I do not dispute that the Nu Image version is 'notable for its incoherence and general tawdry awfulness' (Kermode 2000: 59). However, tawdry awfulness has not stopped me looking at a number of films as interesting genre works in this book. That we have two versions of *Wild Side* in existence provides a fascinating insight into the pervasive discourses of auteurism which run through popular film reception (a readiness to judge genre negatively against artistic integrity), concerning which films suit what audiences/locations (cable for Nu Image's version, London's National Film Theatre for Cammell's). But Cammell's *Wild Side* is not *only* an auteur work (whether the auteur is finally Cammell or Mazzola); it is a genre work too, and all the stronger for this. Back in chapter 1 I cited Barry Keith Grant's image of genre movies as the 'Model T's' of cinema (Grant 1986: xi), reproducible popular models 'with interchangeable parts'. Kermode uses a similar vehicular metaphor in his review of the Cammell/ Mazzola *Wild Side*. 'Cammell's last feature bears all the stylistic hallmarks of an arthouse extravaganza,' he writes,

> But combining this with the nuts-and-bolts ingredients of a meat-market erotic thriller creates something far more enticing than any esoteric exercise. As if transposing a chugging American V8 truck engine into a funky European run-around, editor Mazzola conjures a generic hybrid which rips along at a roaring pace; noisy, unstable and dangerous, but irresistible. (2000: 59)

Judgements which therefore choose between auteur-inflected art film *or* debased genre flick miss the possibility that the power of *Wild Side* mark 2 is as a fascinating hybrid of both. Cammell/Mazzola's is a remarkable film, combining non-linear narrative story-telling with a sophisticated, coded use of colour (fades to blue and red) and a pervasive dreaminess, particularly in the lesbian seduction scenes. Mazzola argues that the movie 'sees the man's world through the eyes of a woman' (Le Cain 2001: 47), and it played well to lesbian audiences.[28] It also revisits some of *Crimes of Passion*'s residual conflation of sex/guilt, which eroticises atonement and sin through sex games (Alex makes Bruno 'confess' through performing cunnilingus; 'with me you can fuck your guilt away,' she says). But this is also complicated through a further discourse about sex and money which runs through the film; early on Bruno and Alex discuss financial institutions as temples, but the 'dirtiness' of circulating money is also manifest (as Bruno bows out he laments that he is 'too old to be chasing money like it was snatch'). Kong's/Cammell's clever, at times hardboiled,

Figure 16: Lesbian romance in the auteur-framed erotic thriller: Joan Chen and Anne Heche in Donald Cammell's *Wild Side*. Mondofin/Nu Image/Wild Side Prod/The Kobal Collection.

screenplay foregrounds philosophical discussions about the nature of love, sex and power (love is at one point called 'an obsessive-compulsive neurosis'; Alex and Virginia discuss the word 'visceral' as they fall in love). Thus *Wild Side* stays true to its genre co-ordinates: Alex is called 'the crème de la crème of female con-bitches'; and there is a neat body-*noir* motif (also visited in De Palma's *Blow Out*) of bodily functions sabotaging surveillance equipment (sweat makes bug-wires short out). Edginess about who is setting up whom pervades the exhilarating paranoia of the piece. But although women may function also as currency at key moments in the film, in the end they circumvent the economy of money/hetero-sex, instead driving through Mexico in each other's arms with nothing but legitimate funds (Fig. 16).

Cammell/Mazzola's use of techniques such as non-synchronised sound and what Mazzola refers to as 'jazz editing' – spasmodic, disconcerting cuts which reinforce the film's insistent themes of synchronicity and reflection – were cut from the Nu Image version. In rearranging the edit so that the heist story and lesbian sex are foregrounded, and removing Cammell's stylistic ticks, Nu Image effectively removed auteurist traces from a genre film. But this did not make it somehow *more* of a genre film (merely a less interesting one). Nor does Cammell's presence in the fabric of the director's cut make *Wild Side* any *less* of a genre film – merely a fascinating kind of transnational hybrid of the contemporary erotic thriller.

NOTES

1 'David Neilson' writing in the IMDB user comments section on *Acting on Impulse*, http://us.imdb.com/CommentsShow?0106216.

2 'The Europeans really like the show, the Asians love it . . . it's a worldwide thing', and he attributes its success to a look which is pitched 'somewhere between high-end commercials and rock videos' (McDonagh 1995: 66).

3 Jacket blurb for UK video edition of *Caged Women* (originally titled *Caged – Le prede umane*), distributed by Rio Pictures 1992; *Caged Fury* (1989) distributed by RCA/Columbia International Video, 1990.

4 Jacket blurb for US video edition of *Hard Drive*, distributed by Triboror Entertainment Group, 1994.

5 Review of *Kiss me a Killer*, archived at www.tvguide.com/movies/database/show-movie.aso?MI=35054.

6 The DVDVerdict.com reviewer asks 'Is *Trois 2: Pandora's Box* indicative of a neo-blaxploitation movement? Here we have a primarily African-American cast and a black director and producer, shooting an indie film on a very low budget, which then gets distributed by a major label. Sounds eerily familiar . . .' (archived at http://www.dvdverdict.com/reviews/trois2.shtml).

7 Eric Lott, 'The Whiteness of Film Noir', quoted by Wager (1999: 124).

8 'MT from Columbia, SC USA' writing at the Amazon 'Spotlight Reviews' section for *Uninvited Guest*, archived at http:/www.amazon.com.

9 One Australian source also quoted in this detailed critique of American cinematic cultural imperialism argues that 'MGM is mightier than the CIA' (Miller et al., 195).

10 'Biography for Jing Wong' by Neil Koch and Joseph Kuby at the IMDb entry on Jing Wong, archived at http://uk.imdb.com/name/nm0939147/bio.

11 See M. C. Thomason's review of *Naked Killer: Director's Cut*, at the Sex-goremutants review website, http://www.sexgoremutants.f9.co.uk/nakiller.html. One profile of Carrie Ng, who plays the princess in *Naked Killer*, argues that she took the role (even though she wanted to avoid more bad girl parts) 'because of recent mega-hits like BASIC INSTINCT (1992) which did very well in Hong Kong and actually convinced many moviegoers to view the cinematic "villainess" in a less prejudicial light'; Ng reports that her performance was inspired by Stone's ('Lethal Hong Kong Lolita Carrie Ng', at http://www.handsoftime.com/she/carrie/html).

12 As Corliss puts it, 'Because Cat III films were allowed to coexist with tamer fare in the same theatres, they didn't have the toxic tinge that attaches to sexy and ultra-violent films elsewhere. In the U.S. and Europe, "ultra" films are separate and lesser industries; for Hong Kong movie people, the line between mainstream and murky backwater is blurrier. Actors like Anthony Wong, Simon Yam, Danny Lee and Kent Cheng shuttled with impunity from one category to the other. . . . Appearing in adults-only Hong Kong movies was tougher for actresses, who might be quickly and permanently typecast once they had bared all, and for whom Cat III was not so much a calling card for stardom as a brand of shame' (2002).

13 See 'Chingmy Yau,' at http://www.hkfilm.net.chingmy.htm.

14 '[W]hat you really need to do to cement an audience is to have a franchise. I'm using my name, but it could be yours or anybody else's . . . What you're doing is creating the kind of identity that the major studios used to have' (McDonagh 1995: 67).

15 Frederick Raphael, *Eyes Wide Open*, quoted by Whitehouse (1999: 39).

16 In the same issue of *Films and Filming*, reviewer Sally Hibbin also calls it 'a thriller about sex' (35).

17 Though this is almost wholly articulated from the point of view of the frustrated husband Bobby, yoked to frigid wife Amy. Female-focused DTV erotic thrillers usually privilege the wife as victim of sexless marriages, and shows her quest to find 'love' beyond the arms of her husband sympathetically. Two deleted scenes in *Crimes of Passion* contained on the 'Unrated. Uncensored' DVD do, however, show that

Russell was interested in a different view of Amy, allowing her to explore her own feelings about desire and its constraints. One also contains a sympathetic encounter between Amy and Joanna which does not fall into the familiar 'women as sexual rivals' trope. Other elements, such as China's sympathetic treatment of an elderly terminally-ill man who is 'given' China as a present from his wife, take the film towards melodrama.

18 The WAVAW leaflet which, according to a *New Society* report, was distributed at the London Haymarket, bore the title 'Ken Russell's Jerk Off', ('Ken's Crime' (unattributed), *New Society*, 27 September 1985, pp. 440–1).

19 Despite heavy cuts to ensure an R-rating in the USA, Russell retained the right to release an uncensored version of the film on video, which went platinum and did '$4 million worth of business' in the first few weeks of release (Hunter 1985: 8).

20 Anthony Perkins reported that to the MPAA ratings board 'The whole thing looked X-ish . . . They told us, "This is an extremely explicit film about explicit matters, and we don't know what you can do about that"' (Maslin 1984: C8). See also on the UK situation 'Censors Clip away at Ken's Comeback' (unattributed), *The Standard*, 21 September 1984, p. 10, and Tony Raynes' interview with Russell ('Preacher's Pet', Raynes 1985: 17).

21 This runs through the trailer, but not the film, which contains an almost entirely electronic keyboard score by Rick Wakeman, very uncharacteristic of the genre.

22 See in particular Davis (1985), 'Now the Body Heat Girl Gets Even Hotter'.

23 Programme notes to *Crimes of Passion*, distributed by Rank, quoting a Gavin Millar article from *The Listener*, archived at the BFI Library, London.

24 See Edelstein and Corliss (both 1984) for comparisons with *Body Double* and Clint Eastwood's *Tightrope*; William Russell (1986) compares *Crimes of Passion* favourably to *9½ Weeks*.

25 'Although initially committed to an art product that would upgrade their image,' wrote Le Cain, 'the company soon got cold feet. When shooting began, the producer would repeatedly visit the set, demanding more nudity' (2001: 46).

26 Interview between author and Frank Mazzola, Los Angeles, August 2003.

27 London's National Film Theatre Programme text on *Wild Side* (unattributed), February 2000, p. 6.

28 See review on the Lesbian Flicks website, http://www.glweb.com/lesbianflicks/wild-side.html.

INTERVIEW: DIRECTOR AND
EDITOR ANNE GOURSAUD

Linda Ruth Williams (LW): You are a very well-known and highly respected editor. So how did you start directing?

Anne Goursaud (AG): Not the way I expected to. I went to film school at Columbia, and I always wanted to direct, and I had the idea of directing a little film – not very ambitious. I come from a small town in France and I thought I'd do my own little personal film. And then I became an editor because I real-ised I had a talent for it, and that I could survive doing it. And that went so magnificently well, that that's what I did. Then finally one day I said, 'Oh I'm *never* going to direct'. So I did a little short that I wrote which got not much attention, and then I went back to editing *Bram Stoker's Dracula* for Francis Ford Coppola, and another film as well. And then out of the blue somebody contacted me because they needed somebody with a French passport to direct a *Red Shoe Diary* episode. So suddenly I found myself doing an erotic TV series, and then erotic movies. I was hired one after the other. I developed none of these movies, they were not stories that I worked on – although obviously I had to work on them when I got them because they were mostly horrible. So, you know I was basically a hired gun for three movies in a row, and then I decided I had to stop because that's not really the kind of movies I want to spend my life doing.

LW: So what happened when you got to the end of that period – was there not the opportunity to direct stuff in the area that you wanted?

AG: There was no opportunity. That's the thing about doing these kind of movies, in this country, it's not a good *carte de visite* [calling card].

LW: Of the run of films that you made, how did they differ in terms of success levels?

AG: In terms of success I would say *Embrace of the Vampire*, which was made for $500,000 dollars in thirteen days (which is pretty amazing) has been the most successful. Only a few years ago it was still the top of the video sales for Yahoo, it has made maybe $15 million for a movie that cost half a million. So that was the most successful. *Poison Ivy 2* has done very well too. Probably the least successful was *Another 9½ Weeks*, although in France it plays on cable all the time. I know from the residuals. So somebody's watching it – I don't know who, but . . . It was a difficult movie in the sense that the script never happened, I didn't pick Angie Everhart who was not a serious actor, and Mickey [Rourke] looked like Quasimodo. So there were a lot of things to overcome. But, you know, I'm very proud of the work in it. I think it's a beautiful film. We only had thirty-five days, we had two cities, Vienna and Paris, which we had to make connect – because the story only takes place in one place but we are constantly switching locations. Mickey I think is always very good. But he just didn't have enough to do . . . And we couldn't delay the start because the rights were going to expire.

LW: **But as it happens, the role is very much a beaten-up role, isn't it? So it's not entirely inappropriate. He's not *meant* to be a matinée idol who's romantically successful.**

AG: Well, that's true to a certain extent. But when he arrived he looked so bad that I changed the whole shooting schedule so I could do crowd scenes first, which was a real nightmare for production. Because I was trying to delay going to the scenes where I would have to see him close up. But Mickey was wonderful. And once he got there he was really into it, and he was the one who suggested Angie Everhart. Then once he got to know her, two days into it, he realised she was not going to be great. But Mickey was very helpful, certainly with the big sex-scene with the flowers and the honey – he was very very helpful with that.

LW: **In terms of how to go about doing it?**

AG: How to be at ease, and to do it.

LW: **And presumably he must have been helpful in getting the other actors?**

AG: Only Angie. The other actors I got.

LW: **What about Stephen Berkoff?**

AG: He was wonderful. I really wanted him, and I think his only regret is that he wanted the film to be better than it was – didn't we all! You know how much better it would be if you have an actor who could give you that mystery, and

Angie had no mystery. And this is a movie where you *need* mystery – where things are not what they seem to be. When I did the scene by the subway at night, where I had her in this strapless dress, and I was telling her 'Gilda'. And, you know, she had never heard of *Gilda*. So of course I rented it for her, but when you are dealing with people who don't have that kind of knowledge – I mean, *Gilda*! I think all great actors have knowledge of the ones who came before them. Same with directors, and painters. You're stealing from the best and going from that to building your own thing.

LW: It's interesting that no one I've talked to so far has expected that kind of cultural capital to be present in what their performers are doing. The directors all say 'Of course I'm doing *film noir*', but they haven't talked to me about drawing that out of their performers.

AG: Well, I was trying to give it content. Mickey came with it. Also because he came from the original movie he understood already the whole history of the story. But with Angie, I had to give her everything. And maybe I didn't do enough. I guess that as a teacher, you may have a brilliant student, but then you have one when you know you are going to have to spoon feed. It's hard to have the same excitement for both.

LW: The only other thing I know her from is *Jade*. What else has she done?

AG: Well, you could say that we're in the same boat. We didn't bring each other luck.

LW: So was the screenplay already in place at the point when you got involved?

AG: There was something, but we did a lot of work on it to make it a little more believable, not so preposterous. It was not just about 'We're going to have couple of people who are going to fuck'. Because in this genre often the producers are pushing just that – they want enough of that so that they can sell the movie, and they just want you to get on in your merry way. So to try to make it more legit., more serious – I mean I'm a very serious person. So it's always a struggle for me because I always try to deepen the meaning, to give it *gravitas*, or make it *about* something, I don't do anything gratuitous. I always try very hard to say 'what is this about, what is the effect I'm looking for here?' And I hope it will work the way I imagine it. This was a man who was troubled, and in love, and searching. And I tried to communicate that through, for example, the lighting.

LW: It's interesting that the power structure of 9½ *Weeks* is mirrored or reflected back onto the female character in your film. It's *her* story, but it's also absolutely *not* her story; it's about her impact on him, because she's got the power.

AG: Right, until he has it and turns it on her.

LW: And this is in the context of a template of sexual explicitness which you _had_ to deliver.

AG: And which we didn't do very well in that film. I think it's very suggestive. I think that in the other movies I came up with scenes that were more interesting maybe, because in the other films I had actors who absolutely trusted me. In _Poison Ivy 2_, I also did the power thing where _she's_ the one who undresses _him_ first in the bathroom, and seduces him, so that we would use _his_ nudity. And he had the most beautiful back. So I just said, 'Let's shoot this back _for ever!_' I love actors, and need to have trust with them, which is essential to the sex. And when you've got that trust, they give you things you don't expect. Like in _Embrace of the Vampire,_ when the girls kiss, and one puts her hand in the other's crotch. They did it. Let me tell you, I was a little . . . you know; 'God that was a little much for me, you know, to ask them to do it'. But like, wow! They did it.

LW: Because they took it in the direction you wanted it to go in without articulating it?

AG: Totally. You know they absolutely did what that scene required and they delivered it. And that's what I feel I didn't quite get with _Another 9½ Weeks._ I feel we get almost there, but we don't quite get there – sexually, I mean. But I think that visually its my best, the mood, and the use of location which I'm very pleased with.

LW: Within the terms of you wanting to do something different with the sex-scenes and the sexuality of that film, was there nevertheless a demand that you deliver something for a particular kind of young male audience to enjoy the spectacle?

AG: Well, I know that when you do this kind of movie you have to deliver a certain amount of sex, otherwise you have not done your job, and the people who are going to distribute your film are counting on it. It's like if you do an action movie, you _have_ to have action. So definitely those are your set-pieces, your meat and potatoes; you _have_ to deliver that. Do I think about a male audience? No. I think about myself. I'm the audience and it's what I think would be interesting, what would turn me on. And also it's a progression in the movie, so if we did this here, we should do something different here. You have to keep inventing and coming up with new ways of blocking the scene, or shooting it. Because I think what's really important in those type of scenes is how you shoot them. The gritty, ugly approach doesn't really appeal to me. If I had to deliver it for a specific dramatic story, I definitely would do it. But my natural tendency is to see beauty and to need beauty. You know, I love Fellini and Visconti, and of course Francis Ford Coppola – people who always put images of beauty in their work. I will always try to search, to do something to make it more mysterious, more meaningful, and ultimately maybe more sexy, I hope. And I don't like to repeat myself within one movie. So if you look at *Embrace of the Vampire,* you'll see that one scene is bright white, which is kind of the innocence of the two women, kind of young girls, and then when it gets a little more deranged, and she's turning more into a vampire, we have very different lighting – very dark, very red. It gives you a different feel. So I will always try to vary what I'm doing, including with the sex – because very often in those scripts it's not indicated what they are doing. You have to invent it.

LW: In what sense?

AG: Well, like it just says, 'They make love'.

LW: So all the variety is coming from you?

AG: Definitely. Very often the sex, just like action, is described in a very simplistic way, and then it's up to the director and actors to develop the idea and see what are they going to do here. In the script for *Another 9½ Weeks,* there was nothing about honey and flowers, you know. We did that. And I don't think that's unusual. I have edited movies, and I have seen the script that the director brings. Maybe in *Basic Instinct* that was exactly described because it's so precise when she opens her legs and she has no underwear.

LW: The big set-piece sex-scene was several pages long in Eszterhas' script, detail by detail.

AG: So he *had* described everything? Well, I think that is very unusual.

LW: Did you have a sense of the audience for the *Poison Ivy* sequel?

AG: Again, I always use myself as the audience, it's the only thing I know. Imagine yourself as the audience. But for the sex stuff, obviously I do think about the producers. (laughs) *That's* my audience. That I have to deliver enough.

LW: And did you feel that about pressure with *Poison Ivy 2?*

AG: The most. Because *Embrace of the Vampire* was a maiden journey for me and Alyssa Milano, and we had a lot of fun doing it. Then with *Poison Ivy 2* it was a little bit like 'Oh God, do we have to do that again?' And I think that she thought it would not be as daring as *Embrace*. But luckily we had a guy who is absolutely gorgeous, and every time he took his shirt off we all gasped! So I said, 'Well, this is lucky, because now I can use *him* as the sexual object more than her.' Take the burden away from her, which as a woman I like, obviously. And so that's how I tried to modulate all those different audiences.

LW: But was more of the guy going to satisfy your producer?

AG: Well, they didn't seem to have a problem with it! Nobody ever brought it up. Those movies are watched by young people. More boys, of course, but I think girls too. *Poison Ivy* definitely had a following with girls. So if you put a gorgeous guy in the frame, I think it's good.

LW: And it's absolutely a girls' story – about adolescence cusping into adulthood – which is going to be very attractive to that audience.

AG: Totally. *Exactly*. So a male sex-object who was really gorgeous was not a bad thing, and we lucked out by getting him. Also, the great orgy scene in *Embrace*, those were all college students from around there that I collected. There is not one professional actor except for our actors. And I got them all to do this. When I look at it, it's amazing. And that's what I'm talking about, being a cheerleader, getting people to trust you and being fun. Creating this atmosphere where I got all these kids to take off their clothes and take a position and do this and do that – we shot it fairly fast because I knew I couldn't keep that going. It would not have worked over two days – they go home, tell their parents . . . I thought we would have the police after us because we were in Minnesota! But I've got a lot of pride in the fact that I got them to loosen up and do it. That's quite an accomplishment for a director. I think that's where being a woman really helps. With a guy it gets immediately a little bit dirty, a little bit voyeuristic. With a woman who comes on like me, it looks like 'Let's have some fun. What's the big deal? Let's be loose, let's not feel bad about sex.' I don't literally say that, but I think this is the message I send out. Because I don't have this kind of guilt. I used to, but I worked on it. So it's like 'This is no big deal, let's just have fun.'

LW: And that approach worked with the guys as well as the girls?

AG: Totally. One of the ideas that we had – I'm not sure if it was me or one of the assistants – was that we paired a lot of girlfriends and boyfriends. So then it was OK for them to be smooching, kissing, hanging, doing whatever they were doing. They didn't feel so uptight.

LW: In your opinion, is overtly sexual material still considered to be a male province?

AG: Well most of us have to struggle to free our sexuality. Most of us are not raised to be truly sexual. In this country, 95 per cent of people believe in God and go to church, so how can women be free? Sexually? That's impossible. I think that a lot of women struggle with their sexuality. We want to claim it, but from the moment we worry about our virginity, should we give it or not, what is the proper thing to do. . . ? We spend so much time thinking about being attractive, being chosen. For me, having done all this work has freed me so totally that I couldn't care less. I'm over it. And I've come to realise that the interest comes from the taboos. Once you get rid of that, you wonder what the big deal is. It's just sex! There are so many more interesting things in life really. Because when you are directing, you realise that you can only do it in so many different ways with so many different lights, positions, partners, whatever. Ultimately, it's still just sex.

LW: But aren't you then saying thanks to the Christian Right for creating all those interesting taboos?

AG: Oh definitely, the fun comes from the fact that we make such a big deal of it because it is *so* forbidden. Because if it were not we would move on very quickly and do other things. But because we have become so obsessed with it – 'Oh God, what's that? What's this image? Should we go there?' – it's so exciting.

LW: So where do you think the possibilities for cinematic sexual expression are in America at the moment? Particularly post-*Showgirls*?

AG: Well what did Paul Verhoeven say? He's not American.

LW: He said, 'God doesn't fuck so we shouldn't either'.

AG: Ha! He's right. I think with the kind of government we have now, the sort of people in power . . . of course, we have never had so much pornography. Repression and pornography seem to go together.

LW: Have your films ever been accused of being pornographic?

AG: Not to my face.

LW: But anything with any sexual representation, however chaste, is going to be unacceptable for some viewers.

AG: Well, look, it has not helped my directing career.

LW: The subject matter?

AG: Definitely. Definitely. It's not a good way to get noticed in this country. Definitely not.

LW: So with the films you've done, do you think that if they had been from a different genre, things would have gone differently? Is it about you being a woman director associated with these films . . .

AG: Certainly. It's very hard to direct, it's harder for a woman, and it's harder still for a woman who is French by birth. So all those things don't work in my favour. But ultimately those kind of movies can't really establish anything. If I had been given *Last Tango in Paris*, or *Basic Instinct* – a film with sexual content but written by wonderful writers – maybe it would be different. In the end, you know, I tried to make very mediocre material into the kind of movies that I would like to see. That was a big challenge.

AFTERWORD ON *IN THE CUT*: NEW CENTURY, OLD SEX?

God doesn't fuck . . . so we shouldn't either. That's good for a title for your book!

Paul Verhoeven

Hollywood doesn't do sex like it used to. A pervasive puritanism infiltrated the industry in the new century, particularly after the election of George W. Bush, putting the erotic back in the closet along with a range of other so-called 'progressive' cinematic concerns. Clinton's Hollywood-friendly America, it is said, was a warm petri-dish in which sexual images could blossom or – to some minds – fester (remember Joe Eszterhas' view of the sexually incontinent Clinton, immortalised in *American Rhapsody* as the number one fan of the film genre which Eszterhas helped to create). By the new century the picture looks different, with British classification statistics telling a story of the decline of explicit mainstream sexual representations and story-lines. 'There are no scripts that dare to go into any sexuality – they're really difficult to find,' says Verhoeven. An 'openness, or willingness to accept sexuality as anything else in life' is important to figures like Verhoeven, for artistic as well as the box office reasons which have concerned other producers I have looked at. Genuinely 'adult' films for adult viewers (mainstream films which don't pander to family audiences rather than *adult* films) are in decline. The trend seems to counter the impression UK audiences have had since the BBFC liberalised its classification guidelines in 2000, that explicit, sometimes hardcore images are increasingly acceptable in 'serious' contexts, like European auteur-helmed pieces such as Gaspar Noé's sensation works. It may be that whilst Europe, in the form of (albeit a few) scandal-pics, is going in one direction, Hollywood is going in another. But look elsewhere – such as the Hong Kong Category III film – and the picture is less puritanical. As this book goes to press in the early twenty-first century, mainstream Hollywood sex scenes are rare, fully naked sex-scenes even rarer; sex-scenes which actually do something subjectively interesting are almost non-existent. In chapter 4 I quoted Italian porn filmmaker Joe D'Amato as saying 'America, it wants the sex. . . . The rest of the world, it wants the story' (Gaffin 1997: 197). Whilst this may be true in hardcore, it is certainly not true in the mainstream, where perhaps the opposite pertains. Major studios now largely refuse to release NC-17-rated movies, meaning that even acclaimed international art-house films such as Jane Campion's *In the Cut* are cut in the US for an R-rating. Bernardo Bertolucci's sexually explicit *The Dreamers* was threatened with censorship in 2004, but eventually its studio agreed to an NC-17 rating – the first major release under that category since *Showgirls*, and evidence, perhaps, of a small climate shift. However, *Eyes Wide Shut* – by then beyond the reach of the dead Kubrick – had digital bodies inserted in post-production to obscure the view of copulating couples in order to secure its R-rating. In the UK all of these films had national releases, uncensored at 18, and adult audiences saw no problem in watching them in their entirety (those digital figures were not there to protect British sensibilities). It may be that the 'sexual Chernobyl' which I mooted may spread from Hollywood in the form of the MPAA-sanctioned erotic thriller is actually a rather puritanical sexual fantasy, compared to some of the visions which other cinemas encourage on mainstream screens elsewhere.

I want to conclude this study with a brief look at *In the Cut*, the 2003 high-profile scandal film which reinvented Meg Ryan as a sex star, mindful of this classification context. Campion's rewriting of the erotic thriller as woman's film provides further evidence of the genre's saleability and malleability, though at its core this is essentially an exalted, star-driven revision of a number of discredited DTV works. A woman's sexual romance produced by a woman (Nicole Kidman) and based on a woman's novel (Susanna Moore's novel of the same name; Moore also gets a writing credit), *In the Cut* is an American independent film directed by a New Zealand auteur with strong non-American sensibilities, though it was likened to the long tradition of US urban-*noirs*. But it is also foreshadowed by a spate of edgy, hardcore-inflected and female-centred sagas emerging from France around the turn of the century, such as Breillat's *Romance* and *À ma Soeur!*, and Virginie Despentes/Coralie Trinh Thi's *Baise-moi* – each of which deserve more extensive discussion as sexually edgy genre movies. Like these films, *In the Cut* explores the stresses under which both women and heterosexuality are put when self-awakening stories are probed open – part-female sexual quest film, part-contemporary urban melodrama, it plays out a number of contradictions textually and cinematically: a theatrically-released art-house film, a star vehicle for romance-branded Ryan, a woman's film with a (simulated) hardcore sequence, a censorship scandal and an auteur-helmed exploitation story. But it is crucially also an anti-romantic romance, investigating the troubling but compelling heritage of marriage for heterosexual women (the dream/family romance sequences of skating parents, the sister's obsession with marriage, the hesitant proposals from the cop-lover).

So if God doesn't fuck, can anyone in American movies? *In the Cut* suggests that they can. It is a complex film, taking on race and class and urban politics as well as sex, but its story will be familiar to readers of this book. Bluestocking teacher Franny (Ryan, like Theresa in *Looking for Mr Goodbar* and Marie in *Romance* before her) embarks on a sexual quest with blue-collar cop Malloy (Mark Ruffalo) who may be investigating her, but may be the murderer. She is also in danger of becoming the next victim, as her sister does halfway through the film. There are a number of scenes when Franny revels in Malloy's frank sexual talk and expert sexual techniques (whilst audiences revel in parts of Ryan never seen before), but the film's prime erotic set-piece is a scene early on when Franny surreptitiously peeps in on a shadowy man getting a blow-job. The scene is remarkable for a number of reasons. The camera's close-up enjoyment of an erection (albeit prosthetic) which has been so absent from so many of the films in this book is wonderfully salacious. The woman (soon to be a murder victim) who is pleasuring the man is hardly visible, just her lips and fingers. The intense focus on the male organ seen from the point of view of a secret viewer mixes a genre commonplace (female voyeurism) with a cinematic rarity: it is almost as if Campion is, in one astonishing sequence, trying to redress the long history of cinema peeping in on women's bodies. Here, the image says, this is the sexualised, fetishised body for your delectation – but not the body you are used to seeing. At the same time the charged eroticism of the scene challenges male heterosexual viewers to be turned on by the close-up of another man's penis being pleasured. And it makes men see their organs through the diegetic woman's eyes, and through a woman's camera-eye. That Campion claimed the penis was a prosthetic is hardly material to the scene's visceral affect (it is indistinguishable from the real thing). From this moment, though the film unfolds as a familiar erotic thriller, a potentially new erotic landscape has been suggested.

In the Cut is Campion's most American film, and – for all the talk about it as a *noir* – is situated squarely within the most successful (and explicit) modern rendition of *noir* which this book has explored. The 'Poetry in transit' which Franny dwells on whilst subway riding at one point – a Dante line, 'I found myself in a dark wood. For I had wandered off from the straight path' – is a neat art-movie device for uniting the concerns of *noir* with those of sex (the dangerously seductive possibilities of straying down another alley). The look of the film is, of course, different from the bland over-illuminated DTV 'look' which strives for glamour; Campion runs her version of *noir* through some experimental uses of colour (sepia-drenched nostalgia, oversaturated black and bleached-out tones). She also both signals and defuses the impact of forensic views of dismembered women by switching from colour to monochrome (though the horror of this does not, ironically, present such a censorship quandary as the close-up blow-job does). But this is resolutely a 'cop and copulation film' (Franny copulates with a sexy cop and kills a murderous one) – there is even a scene in a strip-joint. When other actresses are buttoning up, Campion persuaded Ryan to undress; when other Hollywood films dealing with sex and sexual violence are refusing to show, Campion makes the spectacle (a woman watching a woman giving a blow-job) a talking-point. But the fact that only Campion could do this and get away with it in the US cinematic climate of the film's production ironically also militates against its genre-branding. *Variety* was referring to it as an erotic thriller even in pre-production reports, yet by the time of its release it was being marketed as an edgy auteur work. The image of Campion as one of the most prominent female directors on the planet functioned in reception, as with Kubrick and Russell before her, to diminish the impact of her film as a genre work. But some genres are more equal than others. If *In the Cut* resisted its erotic thriller label, this was so that it could be promoted as a woman's film in production (the product of a female team led by a singular woman's vision). It is not, then, that *In the Cut* refuses genre *per se*; rather that in its promotion as a feminist film, a female film, an art-film, other genre categories – perhaps more credible and politically palatable ones – supplant discredited ones such as the erotic thriller.

Nevertheless, in presenting such an explicit film to classifiers (even if it never reached US theatres in that form) Campion became a singular exception to the pre-censoring rule of the moment. *In the Cut* thus bears out and challenges the image of Hollywood's increased puritanism; it tries to do, within American cinema, something Verhoeven laments people 'don't dare' to go near any more. The erotic thriller is by this account both alive and dead; a form which has consolidated itself into a safe, known product, which has performed both well and badly at various levels of the market, and one which perfectly exploits the contemporary cinematic afterlife of video and DVD. Where it will go when sex-cinema, as Verhoeven predicts, does cycle back again, will form the next (unwritten) chapter on the erotic thriller in contemporary cinema – a genre certainly not 'just for boys'.

BIBLIOGRAPHY

Aaron, Michele (ed.) (1999), *The Body's Perilous Pleasures: Dangerous Desire and Contemporary Culture*, Edinburgh: Edinburgh University Press

Ackroyd, Peter (1985), 'Bright Lights, Bright People', *The Spectator*, 28 September, pp. 34–5

Aitken, Will (1981), 'Straight Men: Dressed to Kill', *Gay News* 209, pp. 21–2

Alloway, Laurence (1963), 'On the Iconography of the Movies', *Movie* 7, pp. 4–6

Altman, Rick (1993), 'A Semantic/Syntactic Approach to Film Genre', in *Film Genre Reader*, ed. Barry Keith Grant, Austin: University of Texas Press, pp. 26–40

Alvarado, Manuel (ed.) (1988), *Video World-Wide: An International Study*, Paris and London: UNESCO/Libbey

Amidon, Stephen (1993), 'Sliver', *Financial Times*, 2 September, p. 15

Amiel, Barbara (1988), 'Anti-Femme Fatale', *The Times*, 15 January, p. 11

Anderson, Jeffrey M. (2002), 'B-plus', *The San Francisco Examiner*, 3 November, archived at http://www.examiner.com/ex_files/default.jsp?story=X0311DIGIT

Andrew, Dudley (1993), 'The Unauthorized Auteur Today', in *Film Theory Goes to the Movies*, ed. Jim Collins, Hilary Radner and Ava Preacher Collins, New York: Routledge, pp. 77–85

Andrews, Nigel (1985), 'Knaves, Nasties and Knives', *Financial Times*, 20 September, p. 27

——(1992), 'Injuries Inflicted on Basic Intelligence', in *Financial Times*, 7 May, p. 21

——(1995), 'Jade', *Financial Times*, 2 November, p. 15

Andrews, Suzanna (1994), 'Wits out for the Lads!', *Empire* 59, May, pp. 76–81

Apel, D. Scott (1997), *Killer B's: The 237 Best Movies on Video You've (Probably) Never Seen*, San Jose, CA: Permanent Press

Applebaum, Stephen (1997), 'Bound over', *Film Review*, April, pp. 74–6

Asselle, Giovanna and Gandhy, Behroze (1982), '"Dressed to Kill": A Discussion', *Screen* 23, 3/4, Sept/Oct, pp. 137–43

Austin, Thomas (2002), *Hollywood, Hype and Audiences: Selling and Watching Popular Film in the 1990s*, Manchester: Manchester University Press

——and Martin Barker (2003), *Contemporary Hollywood Stardom*, London: Arnold

Bailey, James (1988), '"Fatal Attraction" Suicide Version Finds Takers at Japan Screens', *Variety*, 16 November, p. 10

Bamigboye, Baz (1995), 'Vile Film Left Me Jaded', *Daily Mail*, 15 September, p. 41

Barkley, Richard (1985), 'Fatal Allure', *Sunday Express*, 22 September, p. 22

Bart, Peter (2002), 'Rate for "R" for Raunchy', *Variety*, 4 August, archived at www.variety.com

Barth, Jack (1996), 'Darkman', *Premiere*, August, pp. 78–81, 92

Barwise, Patrick and Ehrenberg, Andrew (1988), *Television and its Audience*, London: Sage Publications

Basinger, Jeanine (1986), *The World War II Combat Film: Anatomy of a Genre*, New York: Columbia University Press

——(1993), *A Woman's View: How Hollywood Spoke to Women 1930–1960*, London: Chatto & Windus

Baxter, Brian (1985), 'Body Double', *Films & Filming*, 372, September, p. 36

Belton, John (1994), *American Cinema/American Culture*, New York: McGraw-Hill

Berardinelli, James (1998), 'Palmetto', http://movie-reviews.colossus.net/movies/p/palmetto.html

Berens, Jessica (1997), 'Going it Alone', *Daily Telegraph* (Weekend Magazine), 12 July, pp. 40, 43

Berger, John (1972), *Ways of Seeing*, Harmondsworth: Penguin

Bergson, Phillip (1985), 'Now you see it . . .', *What's On*, 19 September, p. 437

Berk, Philip (2000), 'Michael Douglas and Catherine Zeta Jones', *Hello* 601, March, pp. 56–8

Berry, Joanna (1997), 'Bridget Is Just too Bad to be True', *The Box* 2, June/July, p. 19

Bilbow, Marjorie (1980), 'Dressed to Kill', *Screen International* 261, 4 October, p. 17

Billson, Anne (1992), 'Revenge of the Killer Bimbos', *New Statesman and Society*, 8 May, pp. 29–30

——(1993), 'Shameless Peeping on the Hoof', *Sunday Telegraph*, 5 September, p. 7

——(1995) Review of *Jade*, *Sunday Telegraph*, 5 November, Review section, p. 10

Bishop, Marla (1986), 'Crimes of Passion', *Spare Rib*, February, p. 32

Blandford, Steve, Grant, Barry Keith and Hillier, Jim (2001), *The Film Studies Dictionary*, London: Arnold

Boorman, John and Donohue, Walter (eds) (1996), 'Emotion Pictures: Brian De

Palma talks to Quentin Tarantino', in *Projections 5: Film-makers on Film-making*, London: Faber, pp. 25–39

Bordwell, David (1989), *Making Meaning: Inference and Rhetoric in the Interpretation of Cinema*, Cambridge, MA: Harvard University Press

Bourdieu, Pierre (1984), *Distinction: A Social Critique of the Judgement of Taste*, trans. Richard Nice, London: Routledge and Kegan Paul

Brent, Steve and Elizabeth (1997), *The Couple's Guide to the Best Erotic Videos*, New York: St. Martin's Griffen

Brien, Alan (1980), 'A Love Affair with Violence', *Sunday Times*, 28 September

Bright, Susie (1990), *Susie Sexpert's Lesbian Sex World*, San Francisco: Cleis Press

——(1995), *Sexwise*, Pittsburgh: Cleis Press

Britton, Andrew (1991), 'Stars and Genre', in *Stardom Industry of Desire*, ed. Christine Gledhill, London and New York: Routledge, pp. 198–206

Brosnan, John (1980), 'Dressed to Kill', *Starburst*, 28, pp. 14–15

Brottman, Mikita (2000), 'Star Cults/Cult Stars: Cinema, Psychosis, Celebrity, Death', in *Unruly Pleasures: The Cult Film and its Critics*, eds Xavier Mendik and Graeme Harper, Guildford: FAB Press, pp. 104–19

Brown, Geoff (1993), 'Sliver', *The Times*, 2 September, p. 35

Brown, Georgia (1995), 'Jade', *Village Voice*, 24 October, p. 80

Brown, Jeffrey A. (2001), 'If Looks Could Kill: Power, Revenge, and Stripper Movies', in *Reel Knockouts: Violent Women in the Movies*, ed. Martha McCaughey and Neal King, Austin: University of Texas Press, pp. 52–77

Brown, Joe (1994): 'Romeo is Bleeding', *Washington Post*, 4 February, archived at www.washingtonpost.com

Brown, Royal S. (1980), 'Dressed to Kill: Myth and Male Fantasy in the Horror/Suspense Genre', *Film/Psychology Review* 4, 2, Summer/Autumn, pp. 169–82

Bryant, Tony, and Pollock, Griselda (1981), 'Window Dressing – A Poster Competition for Dressed to Kill', *Framework* 15/16/17, pp. 25–8

Burchill, Julie (1988), 'Fatal Distrations of New Man', *Mail on Sunday*, 24 January, p. 18

——(2004), 'To Hell with Princesses – Give Me a Bitch Every Time', *The Times*, Review section, 7 February, p. 3

Burston, Paul (1998), 'So Good it Hurts', *Sight and Sound*, November, p. 24

Buscombe, Edward (1986): 'The Idea of Genre in the American Cinema', in *Film Genre Reader*, ed. Barry Keith Grant, Austin: University of Texas Press

Bygrave, Mike (1987): 'Mortal Friends', *The Guardian* 17 December, p. 11

Cahill, Paul (1988), 'United States of America and Canada', in *Video World-Wide: An International Study*, ed. Manuel Alvarado, Paris and London: UNESCO/Libbey

Campbell, Jeremy (1985), 'Stemming the Tide of Lurid TV', *The London Standard*, 3 July, p. 7

Campbell, Virginia (1994), 'Soft like a Stone', *Premiere* 2, 11, December, pp. 54–63

Carol, Avedon (1993), 'Porn, Perversion and Sexual Ethics', in *Pleasure Principles: Politics, Sexuality and Ethics*, eds Victorian Harwood, David Oswell, Kay Parkinson and Anna Ward, London: Lawrence & Wishart, pp. 149–56

Carroll, Noel (1990), *The Philosophy of Horror*, New York: Routledge

Cassavetes, Nick (1997), 'G Equals Generous, Glamour-Puss, and Going Somewhere . . . Gina Gershon', *Interview*, July, archived at http://www.geocities.com/Paris/LeftBank/7614/gershon/interv2.html

Chaudhuri, Anita (1993), 'Stone Unturned', *Time Out*, 14–21 July, p. 22

Christie, Ian (1985), 'Crimes of Passion', *Daily Express*, 13 September, p. 32

Christopher, Nicholas (1997), *Somewhere in the Night: Film Noir and the American City*, New York: Owl Books

Chute, D. (1981), 'Tropic of Kasdan', *Film Comment* 17, 5, pp. 49–52

Chutkow, Paul (1998), 'I Dream of Gina', *Cigar Aficionado*, October, archived at http://www.geocities.com/Paris/LeftBank/7614/gershon/cigarart.html

Clover, Carol J. (1992a), *Men, Women and Chain Saws: Gender in the Modern Horror Film*, London: British Film Institute

——(1992b), 'Getting Even', *Sight and Sound*, May, pp. 16–18

Cohan, Steven (1998), 'Censorship and Narrative Indeterminancy in *Basic Instinct*: "You won't learn anything from me I don't want you to know",' in *Contemporary Hollywood Cinema*, eds Steve Neale and Murray Smith, London: Routledge, pp. 263–79

Hark, Ina Rae (ed) (1993), *Screening the Male: Exploring Masculinities in Hollywood Cinema*, London and New York: Routledge

Cohen, Angela and Fox, Sarah Gardner (1997), *The Wise Woman's Guide to Erotic Videos: 300 Sexy Videos for Every Woman – and Her Lover*, New York: Broadway Books

Cohen, Mitchell S. (1974), 'The Actor: Villains and Victims', *Film Comment* 10, 6, Nov-Dec, pp. 27–9

Collins, Jim (1993), 'Genericity in the Nineties: Eclectic Irony and the New Sincerity', in *Film Theory Goes to the Movies*, eds Jim Collins, Hilary Radner and Ava Preacher Collins, New York: Routledge, pp. 242–63

Combs, Richard (1980), 'Dressed to Kill', *Monthly Film Bulletin* 47, 562, November, p. 213

Cook, Gary, Rochan, Debbie and Schmideg, Peter (1998), *The B-Movie Survival Guide*, Minneapolis, MN: Image

Cook, Pam and Mieke Bernink (eds) (1999), *The Cinema Book*, 2nd edition, London: British Film Institute

Cooney, Jenny (1992), 'Naked Hollywood', *Empire* 36, June, pp. 54–60

Corliss, Richard (1984), 'Dark Nights for the Libido', *Time*, 29 October, p. 36

——(1996), 'There's Gold in that there Schlock', *Time* 148, 10, 26 August, archived at http://www.time.com/time/magazine/archive/1996/dom/960826/shobiz.html

——(2002), 'That Old Feeling: Hong Kong Horrors!', *Time*, 13 November, archived at http://www.time.com/time/columnist/corliss/article/0,9565,3889 06,00.html

Corman, Roger, with Jim Jerome (1998), *How I Made a Hundred Movies in Hollywood and Never Lost a Dime*, New York: Da Capo Press

Corrigan, Timothy (1991), 'Film and the Culture of the Cult', in *The Cult Film Experience: Beyond All Reason*, ed J. P. Telotte, Austin: University of Texas Press, pp. 26–37

——(1998), 'Auteurs and the New Hollywood', in *The New American Cinema*, ed. Jon Lewis, Durham, NC and London: Duke University Press, pp. 38–63

Coward, Rosalind (1984), *Female Desire: Women's Sexuality Today*, London: Paladin

——(1986), 'Are Women's Novels Feminist Novels?', in *The New Feminist Criticism*, ed. Elaine Showalter, London: Virago, pp. 225–39

Cowie, Elizabeth (1984), 'Fantasia', *m/f*, 9, 71–104

——(1993), 'Film Noir and Women', in *Shades of Noir*, ed. Joan Copjec, Verso: London, pp. 121–65

——(1997): *Representing the Woman: Cinema and Psychoanalysis*, Basingstoke: Macmillan

Crane, Robert (1999), 'Gina Gershon Playboy's 20 Questions', US *Playboy*, December, archived at http://www.geocities.com/Paris/LeftBank/7614/ gershon/playboy.html

Crockett, Kenette (1997), 'Gina Gershon, Jennifer Tilly and the Making of "Bound"', *Girlfriends*, Jan/Feb, archived at http://www.geocities.com/Paril/ LeftBank/7614/gershon/gfriends.html

Cubitt, Sean (1991), *Timeshift: On Video Culture*, London: Routledge

Damico, James (1996), 'Film Noir: A Modest Proposal', in Silver and Ursini, pp. 95–105, originally published in *Film Reader* 3 (1978)

Dargis, Manohla (1996), 'Devil in a Blue Dress', *Sight and Sound*, January, p. 38

Davenport, Hugo (1993), 'Sliver', *Daily Telegraph*, 3 September, p. 16

——(1995), 'Jade', *Daily Telegraph*, 3 November, p. 26

Davis, Darrell W., and Yueh-yu, Yeh (2001), 'Warning Category III: The Other Hong Kong Cinema', *Film Quarterly*, Summer, pp. 12–26

Davis, Victor (1985), 'Now the Body Heat Girl Gets Even Hotter', *Daily Express*, 12 September, pp. 20–1

——(1991), 'Sex and Stardom in the Stone Age', *Mail on Sunday*, 15 September, p. 37

——(1993), 'Casting the Fast Stone', *Mail on Sunday*, 16 May, p. 39

Dawson, Jeff (1995), 'Everybody Gets Bumps and Bruises', *Empire*, April, p. 89

deCordova, Richard (1991), 'The Emergence of the Star System in America', in *Stardom Industry of Desire*, ed. Christine Gledhill, London and New York: Routledge, pp. 17–29

Deleyto, Celestino (1997), 'The Margins of Pleasure: Female Monstrosity and Male Paranoia in *Basic Instinct*', *Film Criticism* 21, 3, Spring, pp. 20–42

Denby, David (1980), 'Deep Threat', *New York*, 28 July, pp. 44–5

——(1984), 'The Woman in the Window', *New York*, 5 November, pp. 47–9

——(1987), *New York*, 5 October, pp. 116, 118

Dennis, Nik (1993), 'Sliver', *The Voice Now*, 14 September, p. 27

Derry, Charles (1988), *The Suspense Thriller: Films in the Shadow of Alfred Hitchcock*, Jefferson, NC: MacFarland

Dickos, Andrew (2002), *Street with No Name: A History of the Classic American Film Noir*, Lexington: University Press of Kentucky

Dienst, Richard (1994), *Still Life in Real Time: Theory after Television*, Durham, NC and London: Duke University Press

Dijkstra, Bram (1996), *Evil Sisters: The Threat of Female Sexuality in Twentieth Century Culture*, New York: Henry Holt

Doane, Mary Ann (1987), *The Desire to Desire: The Woman's Film of the 1940s*, Basingstoke: Macmillan

——(1991), *Femmes Fatales: Feminism, Film Theory, Psychoanalysis*, London: Routledge

Doherty, Thomas (2001), 'Movie Star Presidents', in *The End of Cinema as We Know it: American Film in the Nineties*, New York: New York University Press, pp. 150–7

Douglas, Kirk (1999), 'Letter to the Editor', *Variety*, 24 August, archived at www.variety.com

Duane, Paul (1994), 'The Last Seduction', *Film Ireland* 43, Oct/Nov, p. 33

Dyer, Richard (1986), *Heavenly Bodies: Film Stars and Society*, London and Basingstoke: Macmillan

——(1990), *Now You See it: Studies on Lesbian and Gay Film*, London: Routledge

——(1991), '*A Star is Born* and the Construction of Authenticity', in *Stardom Industry of Desire*, ed. Christine Gledhill, London: Routledge, pp. 132–40

——(1992): 'Don't Look Now: The Male Pin-up', in *The Sexual Subject: A Screen Reader in Sexuality*, eds John Caughie and Annette Kuhn, London: London: Routledge, pp. 265–76

——(1993a), *The Matter of Images: Essays on Representations*, London: Routledge

——(1993b) 'The Colour of Virtue: Lillian Gish, Whiteness and Femininity', in *Women and Film: A Sight and Sound Reader*, eds Pam Cook and Philip Dodd, London: Scarlet Press, pp. 1–9

——(1997), *White*, London: Routledge

——(1998), 'Resistance through Charisma: Rita Hayworth and Gilda', in *Women in Film Noir*, 2nd edition, ed. E. Ann Kaplan, London: British Film Institute, pp. 115–22

Dworkin, Andrea (1981), *Pornography: Men Possessing Women*, London: Women's Press

Ebert, Roger (1985), 'Jagged Edge', *Chicago Sun-Times* 10 April, archived at http://www.suntimes.com/ebert/ebert_reviews/1985/10/18170.html

——(1993), 'Guilty as Sin', *Chicago Sun-Times*, 4 June, archived at http://www.suntimes.com

——(1995), 'Jade', *Chicago Sun-Times*, 13 October, archived at http://www.suntimes.com/ebert/ebert-reviews/1995/10/1001611.html

——(1998a), 'Palmetto', *Chicago Sun-Times*, archived at http://www.suntimes.com/ebert/ebert_reviews/1998/02/022003.html

——(1998b), 'Wild Things', *Chicago Sun-Times*, archived at http://www.suntimes.com/ebert/ebert_reviews/1998/03/032005.html

Edelstein, David (1984), 'That Obscene Object of Desire', *Voice*, 10 November, p. 64

Ehrlich, Susie (2002a), '1990 – The Invention/Marketing/Phenom of Couples Porn'; and

——(2002b), 'Mid-1990s – Porn Turns Extra-hard'; both in *Adult Video News*, August, www.adultvideonews.com/cover/cover0802_01.html

Eisner, Ken (1993), 'Acting on Impulse', *Variety*, 28 June, p. 25

Ellis, John (1992), *Visible Fictions Cinema: Television: Video*, London and New York: Routledge

Ellis, Kirk (1984), 'De Palma Goes through Motions on Latest "Body Double" Thriller', *The Hollywood Reporter* 284, 5, 15 October, p. 3

Elsaesser, Thomas (2001), 'The Blockbuster: Everything Connects, but not Everything Goes', in *The End of Cinema as We Know it: American Film in the Nineties*, New York: New York University Press, pp. 11–22

Empire (1995), 'The Write Stuff: Joe Ezsterhas is in the Money Yet Again', *Empire*, April, p. 4

Epstein, Rebecca L. (2000), 'Sharon Stone in a Gap Turtleneck', in *Hollywood Goes Shopping*, eds David Sesser and Garth S. Jowett, Minneapolis: Minnesota University Press, pp. 179–204

Erickson, Todd (1996), 'Kill Me Again: Movement Becomes Genre', in *Film Noir Reader* eds Alain Silver and James Ursini, New York: Limelight

Errigo, Angie (1993), 'Sliver', *Today*, 3 September, p. 30

Eszterhas, Joe (2000), *American Rhapsody*, New York: Knopf

——(2004), *Hollywood Animal: A Memoir of Love and Betrayal*, London: Hutchinson

Evans, David (1995), *Glamour Blondes: From Mae to Madonna*, London: Britannia

Faludi, Susan (1992), *Backlash: The Undeclared War against Women*, London: Vintage

Farber, Stephen (1999), 'Violence and the Bitch Goddess', in *Film Noir Reader 2*, eds Alain Silver and James Ursini, New York: Limelight, pp. 45–55; originally published in *Film Comment*, Apr 1974

Feasey, Rebecca (2003a), 'Taste Formations, Cultural Distinctions and Sharon Stone', PhD thesis submitted to University of Nottingham

——(2003b), 'Sex, Controversy, Box-office: from Blockbuster to Bonkbuster', in *Movie Blockbusters*, ed Julian Stringer, London: Routledge, pp. 167–77

Film Comment (1984), 'Pornography: Love or Death?' 20, 6, Nov/Dec, pp. 29–49

Filmways Pictures/ITC Film Distributors (1980), 'Dressed to Kill Production Notes', London: British Film Institute Library, p. 9

Flint, David (1998), *Babylon Blue: An Illustrated History of Adult Cinema*, London: Creation Books

Frederick, Robert (1980), "Dressed To Kill" Hits Market; De Palma Stays with Suspense', *Variety*, 16 July

French, Philip (1985a), Review of *Crimes of Passion*, *The Observer*, 8 September, p. 17

——(1985b), Review of *Body Double*, *The Observer*, 22 September, p. 23

——(1995b), Review of *Jade*, *The Observer* 5 November, p. 11

——(1997), 'No End in Sight', in *Film and Censorship: The Index Reader*, ed. Ruth Petrie, London: Cassell, pp. 143–50

Freud, Sigmund (1977), *Three Essays on the Theory of Sexuality*, in *On Sexuality*, Pelican Freud vol. 7, Harmondsworth: Penguin

Friedberg, Anna (2000), 'The End of Cinema: Multimedia and Technological Change', in *Reinventing Film Studies*, eds Christine Gledhill and Linda Williams, London: Arnold, pp. 438–52

Fuller, Graham (1996), 'Unrestricted Viewing', *Interview*, August, pp. 40–1

Gaffin, Harris (1997), *Hollywood Blue: The Tinseltown Pornographers*, London: Batsford

Garber, Marjorie (2000), *Bisexuality and the Eroticism of Everyday Life*, New York: Routledge

Gauntlett, David and Hill, Annette (1999), *TV Living: Television, Culture and Everyday Life*, London: Routledge and British Film Institute

Gehring, Wes D. (ed.) (1988), *Handbook of American Film Genres*, New York: Greenwood Press

Gelmis, Joseph (1970), *The Film Director as Superstar*, Harmondsworth: Penguin

Geraghty, Christine (2003), 'Performing as a Lady and a Dame: Reflections on Acting and Genre', in Austin and Barker, pp. 105–17

Gibson, Pamela Church and Gibson, Roma (eds) (1993), *Dirty Looks: Women, Pornography, Power*, London: British Film Institute

Gill, Andy (1985), 'Double Trouble', *New Musical Express*, 21 September, p. 24

Gledhill, Christine (1998), 'Klute 1: A Contemporary Film Noir and Feminist Criticism', in *Women in Film Noir*, 2nd edition, ed. E. Ann Kaplan, London: British Film Institute, pp. 20–34

——(1999), 'History of Genre Criticism', *The Cinema Book*, eds Pam Cook and Mieke Bernink, London: British Film Institute

Gomery, Douglas (1992), *Shared Pleasures: A History of Movie Presentation in the United States*, Madison: University of Wisconsin Press

Goodman, Joan (1994), 'Steamy but Smart', *Evening Standard*, 22 September, pp. 32–3

Gordon, George (1987), 'Is This the Film that will Bring Fidelity back to Marriage?', *Daily Mail*, 29 December, p. 7

Gorfinkel, Elena (2000), 'The Body as Apparatus: Chesty Morgan Takes on the Academy', in *Unruly Pleasures: The Cult Film and its Critics*, eds Xavier Mendik and Graeme Harper, Guildford: FAB Press, pp. 157–69

Graham, Jefferson (1999), 'Gershon a Cybercool "Snoops" Sleuth', *USA Today*, archived at http://www.geocities.com/Paris/LeftBank/7614/gershon/usatoday.html

Grant, Barry Keith (ed.) (1986), *Film Genre Reader*, Austin: University of Texas Press

Gray, Ann (1992), *Video Playtime: The Gendering of a Leisure Technology*, London and New York: Routledge

Gray, Marianne (1997/8), 'Bound', *Film Review 22*, Yearbook, p. 21

——(1998), 'Stone Turned', *Evening Standard*, Hot Tickets, 5 November, p. 6

Gray, Thomas M. (1994), 'The Nuts and Bolts of Movie Rating', *Variety* 12 January, archived at www.variety.com

Green, Jonathon (1998), *Cassell's Dictionary of Slang*, London: Cassell

Griffin, Susan (1981), *Pornography and Silence*, London: Women's Press

Grimes, William (1995), '"Fleshdance": Back to Basic Instincts', *Sydney Morning Herald*, 25 February, p. 15A

Grist, Leighton (1994), 'Moving Targets and Black Widows: Film Noir in Modern Hollywood', *The Movie Book of Film Noir*, ed. Ian Cameron, London: Studio Vista, pp. 267–85

Gristwood, Sarah (1998), 'Whatever it Takes', *The Guardian* Weekend, 5 December, pp. 24–33

Gritten, David (1994), 'Sharon Stone', *Daily Telegraph*, Weekend Magazine, 10 March, pp. 32–4

——(1995), 'Linda Fiorentino', *Daily Telegraph*, Weekend Magazine, 28 October, pp. 33, 35 and 37

Gross, Larry (1999), 'Too Late the Hero', *Sight and Sound*, 9, 9 September, pp. 20–3

Grove, Martin A. (1987), 'Hollywood Report', *The Hollywood Reporter*, 23 September

——(1992a), 'Hollywood Report: Writer, Director Come Together on "Instinct"', in *The Hollywood Reporter*, 27 March, pp. 10–12

——(1992b), '"Instinct" Scribe's New Script Features Gay Hero', *The Hollywood Reporter*, 30 March, p. 12

Grove, Valerie (1988), 'Fatal Attraction of Passion in Society', *The Sunday Times*, 17 January, p. A12

Guthmann, Edward (1995), '"Jaded" is More Like it: It's got Sex, murder and it's all in San Francisco', *San Francisco Chronicle*, 13 October, archived at http://www.sfgate.com/cgi-bin/article.cgi?file=//chronicle/archive/1995

Halberstam, Judith (1997), 'Gangster Dyke', *Girlfriends*, Jan-Feb, p. 14

Hales, Barbara (1996), 'Woman as Sexual Criminal: Weimar Constructions of the Criminal *Femme Fatale*', *Women in German Yearbook*, 12, pp. 101–21

Handelman, David (1997), 'Nude Awakenings', *Premiere*, June, pp. 31–5

Hansen, Helen (2000), 'Painted Women: Framing Portraits in Film Noir and the Gothic Woman's Film of the 1940s', PhD Thesis, University of Southampton

Hansen, Miriam (1991), *Babel and Babylon: Spectatorship in American Silent Film*, Cambridge, MA: Harvard University Press

Hanson, Ellis (ed.) (1999), *Out-Takes: Essays on Queer Theory and Film*, Durham, NC and London: Duke University Press

Harmetz, Aljean (1987), '"Fatal Attraction" Director Analyzes the Success of His Movie, and Rejoices', *New York Times*, 5 October, p. C17

Harper, Phillip Brian (1992), 'Playing in the Dark: Privacy, Public Sex, and the Erotics of the Cinema Venue', *Camera Obscura* 30, May, pp. 92–111

Hart, Lynda (1994), *Fatal Women: Lesbian Sexuality and the Mark of Aggression*, Princeton, NJ: Princeton University Press

Hartl, John (1992), 'Borden Ventures into Dangerous Territory', Film.com website, archived at http://film.com/film-review/1992/9019/109/default-review.html

Harvey, Sylvia (1998), 'Woman's Place: The Absent Family of Film Noir', in *Women in Film Noir*, 2nd edition, ed. E. Ann Kaplan, London: British Film Institute, pp. 35–46

Hayes, Dawn (2002), 'The Bunny Turns Blue', *The Guardian*, 18 March, New Media section, p. 40

Hayward, Jeff (1993), 'Romancing the Stone', *Girl about Town*, 19 July, pp. 8–9

Hayward, Susan (2000), *Cinema Studies: The Key Concepts*, 2nd edition, London: Routledge

Heal, Sue (1988), 'Embrace of a Psycho Mistress is Enough to Spell the Death of Casual Sex', *Today*, 15 January, p. 26

Helmore, Edward (2003), 'Frankly, We Prefer Sex with Clothes on', *The Observer*, 15 June, archived at http://observer.guardian.co.uk/international/story/0,6903,977766,00.html

Hemblade, Christopher (1997), 'Bound', *Empire* 98, August, p. 132

Hensley, Dennis (1997), 'Everyone's Darlin'', *Movieline*, 8, July, p. 56, archived at http://www.geocities.com/Paris/LeftBank/7614/gershon/movieline.html

Hibbin, Sally (1985a), 'Kathleen Turner', *Films & Filming* 373, October, pp. 4–5

—— (1985b), 'Crimes of Passion', *Films & Filming* 373, October, p. 35

Hills, Matt (2002), *Fan Cultures*, London: Routledge

—— (forthcoming), 'Making Sense of M. Night Shyamalan: Signs of a Popular Auteur in the "Field of Horror"'

Hinson, Hal (1989), 'Sea of Love', *Washington Post*, 15 September

——(1990), 'The Hot Spot, *Washington Post*, 26 October

——(1994), 'Disclosure', *Washington Post*, 9 December

——(1996): '"Diabolique": Sharon Stone, Wickedly Good', *Washington Post*, 22 March, all archived at www.washingtonpost.com

Hirsch, Foster (1981), *Film Noir: The Dark Side of Hollywood*, New York: Da Capo Press

——(1999) *Detours and Lost Highways*, New York: Limelight

Hirschhurn, Clive (1993), 'Sliver', *Sunday Telegraph*, 5 September, pp. 44–5

Hoberman, J. (1984), 'Double is my Middle Name', *Village Voice*, 30 October, pp. 67, 105

——(1987), 'The Other, Woman', *Village Voice*, 29 September, p. 68

——(1992), 'Blood Libel', in *Village Voice*, 31 March, p. 55

——(2003), *The Magic Hour: Film at the Fin De Siècle*, Philadelphia: Temple University Press

Hoffmann, Alex (1993), 'Plot it Again, Joe', *Premiere*, July, p. 40

Hogan, David J. (1985), 'No Joy in the Film Universe of Brian DePalma' [*sic*], *Cinefantastique*, 15, 2, May, p. 45

Hollinger, Karen (1996), '*Film Noir*, Voice-over, and the Femme Fatale', in Silver and Ursini pp. 243–59

Holman, Curt (2002), 'Opening The "Box"', Creative Loafing website, 7 August, archived at http://charlotte.creativeloafing.com/newsstand/2002–08–07/film_feature.html

Holmlund, Chris (1994), 'Cruisin' for a Bruisin': Hollywood's Deadly (Lesbian) Dolls', in *Cinema Journal* 34, 1, Fall, pp. 31–51

Holub, Kathy (1991), 'Ballistic Instinct', *Premiere*, 4, 12, August, pp. 80–4/104

Honeycutt, Mira Aadvani (2001), 'Westward Ho! Indian Film-makers Make it big on the International Screen', in *The Week* on-line magazine, http://www.the-week.com/21dec30/enter.htm

Horkins, Tony (1997), 'Jennifer Tilly: Gangster's Paradise', *Empire* 93, March, pp. 54–5

Horne, Nigel (1985), 'Passion Pays at the Movies', *Sunday Times*, 13 October, p. 39

Horrocks, Roger (1995), *Male Myths and Icons: Masculinity in Popular Culture*, London: Macmillan

Horsley, Lee (2001), *The Noir Thriller*, Basingstoke: Palgrave

Hosoda, Craig (1992), *The Bare Facts Video Guide*, Santa Clara, CA: Bare Facts

Howe, Desson (1992), 'Final Analysis', *Washington Post*, 7 February

——(1993), 'Guilty as Sin', *Washington Post*, 4 June

——(1994), 'Disclosure', *Washington Post*, 9 December

all archived at http://www.washingtonpost.com

Hugo, Chris (1989), 'Three Films of Brian De Palma', *Movie*, 33, Winter, pp. 56–62

Hunter, Allan (1985), 'Ken Russell', *Films & Filming* 373, October, pp. 6–9

Hunter, I.Q. (2000), 'Beaver Las Vegas! A Fan-Boy's Defence of *Showgirls*', in Mendik and Harper, pp. 187–201

Hutchinson, Tom (1988), 'Dark Side of a Mistress is as Deadly as Any Iceberg', *Mail on Sunday*, 17 January

——(1992), 'On Backs to Basics', *Hamstead and Highgate Express*, 8 May

——(1993), 'Stone Unveils a Lack of Class', *Mail on Sunday*, 5 September, p. 40

Iley, Chris (1997), 'Lap of the Gods', *Sunday Times*, 30 November, Magazine section, pp. 18, 21, 23–4

Jameson, Fredric (1983), 'Postmodernism and Consumer Society', in *The Anti-Aesthetic*, ed. Hal Foster, Port Townsend, WA: Bay Press, pp. 111–25

Jameson, Jenna (2002), 'Killing Me Softly', *Loveprong* website, http://www.loveprong.com/exec/review?Killing-Me-Softly.htm

Jeffreys, Daniel (1995): 'Getting them off', *The Independent*, 28 July, section 2, p. 9

Jermyn, Deborah (1996), 'Rereading the Bitches from Hell: A Feminist Appropriation of the Female Psychopath', *Screen* 37, 3, Autumn, pp. 251–67

Johnston Sheila (1995), 'Jade', *The Independent*, 2 November, p. 11

Johnstone, Iain (1985), 'Crimes of Passion', *The Sunday Times*, 25 August, p. 33

——(1988), 'A Dark Destiny Shaped by Public Demand', *The Sunday Times*, 17 January, p. C6

——(1992), 'Emotional Cop-out', *The Sunday Times*, 10 May, section 6, p. 16

Jones, Alan (1985), 'Body Double', *Starburst*, 7, 10, June, p. 17

Jones, Mark (1995), 'Now You See it, Now You Don't', *Evening Standard*, 2 May, p. 2

Kael, Pauline (1980), 'The Current Cinema: Master Spy, Master Seducer', *New Yorker*, 4 August

——(1987), 'The Current Cinema', *New Yorker*, 14 October, pp. 106–7

Kane, Joe (2000), *The Phantom of the Movies' Videoscope: The Ultimate Guide to the Latest, Greatest, and Weirdest Genre Videos*, New York: Three Rivers Press

Kasindorf, Jeanie (1987), '*Fatal* Footage Bound for Glory?' *New York*, 3 August, p. 7

Katz, Ian (1995), 'The Naked Hunch', *The Guardian* G2 section, 5 September, p. 5

Kempley, Rita (1993a), 'Sliver', *Washington Post*, 21 May

——(1993b), 'Guilty as Sin', *Washington Post*, 4 June, all archived at http://www.washingtonpost.com

Kennedy, Barbara (1999), 'Post-feminist Futures in Film Noir', in *The Body's Perlious Pleasures: Dangerous Desire and Contemporary Culture*, ed. Michele Aaron, Edinburgh: Edinburgh University Press, pp. 126–42

Kent, Nicolas (1991), *Naked Hollywood: Money, Power and the Movies*, London: BBC Books

Kermode, Mark (1991), 'Scissors', *Sight and Sound*, September, p. 59

——(1995) 'Horror: On the Edge of Taste', *Index on Censorship*, p. 6

—— (1997), 'I was a Teenage Horror Fan: or, 'How I Learned to Stop Worrying and Love Linda Blair', *Ill Effects: The Media/Violence Debate*, eds Martin Barker and Julian Petley, London: Routledge, pp. 57–66

——(1998), 'Cruise Control', *Sight and Sound*, November, pp. 22–4

——(2000), 'Wild Side', *Sight and Sound*, August, p. 59

Kessler, Kelly (2001), '*Bound* Together: Audience Unification in Image Diversification', *Text, Practice, Performance* III, pp. 18–36

Kipnis, Laura (1996), *Bound and Gagged: Pornography and the Politics of Fantasy in America*, New York: Grove Press

Kirkham, Pat and Thumim, Janet (eds) (1993), *You Tarzan: Masculinity, Movies and Men*, London: Lawrence & Wishart

Klinger, Barbara (1998), 'The New Media Aristocrats: Home Theater and the Domestic Film Experience', *The Velvet Light Trap* 42, Fall, pp. 4–19

Knee, Adam (1993), 'The Dialectic of Female Power and Male Hysteria in *Play Misty for Me*', in Cohan and Hark, pp. 87–102

Knight, Arthur (1984), '"Crimes of Passion" Evidence of Russell as Master Director', *The Hollywood Reporter*, 17 October, pp. 3, 10, 12

Knobloch, Susan (2001), 'Sharon Stone's (An)Aesthetic', in *Reel Knockouts: Violent Women in the Movies*, eds Martha McCaughey and Neal King, Austin: University of Texas Press, pp. 124–43

Krutnick, Frank (1982), 'Desire, Transgression and James M. Cain', *Screen*, 23 1, May/June, pp. 31–44

——(1991), *In a Lonely Street: Film Noir, Genre, Masculinity*, London: Routledge

Krzywinska, Tanya (2000), 'The Dynamics of Squirting: Female Ejaculation and Lactation in Hardcore Film', in Mendik and Harper, pp. 30–43

Lacey, Joanne (2003), '"A Galaxy of Stars to Guarantee Ratings": Made-for-Television Movies and the Female Star System', in Austin and Barker, *Contemporary Hollywood Stardom*, London: Arnold, pp. 187–98

Lacey, Nick (2000), *Narrative and Genre*, Basingstoke: Macmillan

Lahr, John (1996), 'The Big Picture', *New Yorker*, 25 March, pp. 72, 74–8

Laqueur, Thomas W. (2003), *Solitary Sex: A Cultural History of Masturbation*, New York: Zone Books

Laurence, Charles (1987), 'When Sexual Obsession Becomes Lethal', *Daily Telegraph*, 11 November, p. 13

Lawson, Alan (1993), *Michael Douglas*, Long Preston, UK: Magna

Le Cain, Maximilian (2001), 'Donald Cammell's *Wild Side*', *Film West*, 44, Summer, pp. 46–7

Lehman, Peter (ed.) (2001), *Masculinity: Bodies, Movies, Culture*, New York and London: Routledge

Leigh-Kile, Donna (1987), 'Two's Company . . .' [interview with Michael Douglas], *Sunday Express*, Magazine, 13 December, pp. 12–13, 15

Leith, William (1995), 'Lust Action Hero', *Mail on Sunday*, 5 November, p. 38

Lewin, David (1988), 'The Adult Woman's View of Life, Love and Treachery . . .' [interview with Sherry Lansing], *Daily Mail*, 19 January, p. 13

Lewis, Jon (ed.) (2001), *The End of Cinema as We Know it: American Film in the Nineties*, New York: New York University Press

——(2002), *Hollywood v. Hard Core: How the Struggle over Censorship Saved the Modern Film Industry*, New York: New York University Press

Leydon, Joe (1995), 'Bodily Harm', *Variety*, 15 May, p. 102

Librach, Ronald (1998), 'Sex, Lies, and Audiotape: Politics and Heuristics in *Dressed to Kill* and *Blow Out*', in *Literature/Film Quarterly* 26, 3, pp. 166–77

Lindenmuth, Kevin J. (2002), *The Independent Film Experience Interviews with Directors and Producers*, Jefferson, NC and London: McFarland

Lippy, Tod (1996), 'Writing and Directing *Bound*: A Talk with Larry and Andy Wachowski', *Scenario* 3, 3, Autumn, pp. 92–5, 187–90

Lockyer, Daphne (1988), 'Sleeping around has Them Choking on their Movie Popcorn', *Today*, 16 January, p. 9

Logan, Bey (1995), *Hong Kong Action Cinema*, New York: Overlook Books

Logan, Brian (1997), 'A Fish called Gina', *The Guardian* Section 2, 7 November, p. 7

Lucas, Tim (1980), 'De Palma's Greatest and Most Confident Film to Date is also his Most Irritating', *Cinefantastique* 10, 3, Winter, p. 32

Lurie, Rod (1987), 'Glenn Close, Anne Archer and Michael Douglas Ignite in *Fatal Attraction*', *Spotlight*, November, pp. 68–71, 110–11, 126

Lyons, Arthur (2000), *Death on the Cheap: The Lost B Movies of Film Noir*, New York: Da Capo Press

Lyttle, John (1993), 'Sliver', *The Independent*, 30 April, p. 18

MacDonald, Scott (1999), 'Confessions of a Feminist Porn Watcher', in *Film Quarterly: Forty Years – A Selection*, eds Brian Henderson and Ann Martin, Berkeley: University of California Press, pp. 190–202, originally published in *Film Quarterly*, 36, 3, Spring 1983

MacGregor, Jeff (1999), 'Lips Like Mating Snakes', *Esquire*, September, archived at http://www.geocities.com/Paris/LeftBank/7614/gershon/esquire.html

Mackinnon, Kenneth (1981), 'Dressed to Kill', *Film Quarterly* 35, 1, Fall, pp. 41–6

Malcolm, Derek (1985a), *The Guardian*, 15 August, section 2, p. 8

——(1985b), 'Mistress of the Power Game', *The Guardian*, 12 September, section 2, p. 11

——(1985c), 'Stripping Yarns', *The Guardian*, 19 September, p. 23

——(1988), 'The Lovin' End', *The Guardian*, 14 January, p. 25

——(1993), 'Sliver', *The Guardian*, 2 September, section 2, p. 4

Maltby, Richard (1995), *Hollywood Cinema*, Malden, MA: Blackwell

Martell, William C. (2000), 'B as in Block-Buster: AFM 2000', at Script Secrets website, archived at http://www.scriptsecrets.net/articles/afm2000.htm

Mars-Jones, Adam (1992), 'Mad, Bad and Dangerous to Know, *Independent*, 8 May, p. 18

—— (1993), 'The Distorting Effects of Starlight', *The Independent*, 3 September, p. 18

Martin, Angela (1998), "Gilda Didn't Do Any of Those Things You've Been Losing Sleep Over!': The Central Women of 40s Films Noirs', in *Women in Film Noir*, 2nd edition, ed. E. Ann Kaplan, London: British Film Institute, pp. 202–28

Maslin, Janet (1984a), 'Crimes of Passion', *New York Times*, 8 November, p. C23

—— (1984b), 'And Two Versions of the Same Film', *New York Times*, 12 October, p. C8

Mather, Victoria (1994), 'Now, They Really Knock 'em Dead', *Daily Telegraph*, 12 August, p. 11

Matthews, Peter (1997), 'Bound', *Sight and Sound* 7, 3, March, pp. 42–3

Matusa, Paula (1977), 'Corruption and Catastrophe: De Palma's *Carrie*', *Film Quarterly* 31, 1, pp. 32–8

Maxfield, James (1996), *The Fatal Woman: Sources of Male Anxiety in American Film Noir 1941–1991*, London: Associated University Presses

Mayer, Geoff (1993), 'A Return to Form – Russian Formalism and Contemporary Film Practice', *Metro: The Media Magazine*, 93, Autumn, pp. 18–29

Mayne, Judith (1993), *Cinema and Spectatorship*, London: Routledge

McArthur, Colin (1972), *Underworld U.S.A.*, London: Secker & Warburgh

McBride, Joseph (1997), *Steven Spielberg*, London: Faber

McCarty, John (1973), 'Sisters', *Cinefantastique* 3, 1, Autumn, p. 28

McDonagh, Maitland (1995), *Filmmaking on the Fringe: The Good, The Bad, and The Deviant Directors*, New York: Citadel Press

—— (2000), 'Two Girls and a Guy', Cinebooks Movie Database review, archived at http://www.tvguide.com/movies/database/SHowMovie.asp?MI=42352

McDonald, Paul (2003), 'Stars in the Online Universe: Promotion, Nudity, Reverence', in Austin and Barker, pp. 29–44

McGregor, Alex (1992), 'Sex Crimes', *Time Out*, 22 April, pp. 18–21

—— (1993), 'Peek Viewing', *Time Out*, 14–21 July, pp. 20–1

McLean, Adrienne L. and Cook, David A. (eds) (2001), *Headline Hollywood: A Century of Film Scandal*, New Brunswick, NJ and London: Rutgers University Press

Melwani, Lavina (1998), 'The Hollywood Wallahs', *Little India* online journal, March http://206.20.14.67/achal/archive/mar98/hwood.htm

Mendik, Xavier and Harper, Graeme (eds) (2000), *Unruly Pleasures: The Cult Film and its Critics*, Guildford: FAB Press

Merck, Mandy (1992), 'From Minneapolis to Westminster', in *Sex Exposed: Sexuality and the Pornography Debate*, eds Lynne Segal and Mary McIntosh, London: Virago Books, pp. 50–62

Merritt, Greg (2000), *Celluloid Mavericks: A History of American Independent Film*, New York: Thunder's Mouth Press

Miller, Sasha (1996), 'Sharon Stone's Girl Talk', *Mail on Sunday*, 18 February, pp. 10–11

Miller, Toby, Govil, Nitin, McMurria, John and Maxwell, Richard (2001): *Global Hollywood*, London: British Film Institute

Mitchell, Ben (1997), 'Join the Plots: The Inventive Storylines of Joe Eszterhas', *Neon*, December, p. 17

Mitchell, Juliet (1984), *Women – The Longest Revolution: Essays on Feminism, Literature and Psychoanalysis*, London: Virago

Mooney, Deirdre (1992), 'Sharon Just Likes to Get Back to the Champagne Basics', *Evening Standard*, 13 May, p. 3

Moore, Suzanne (1992), 'Basic Instinct', *The Guardian*, 7 May, p. 34

Mulvey, Laura (1999), 'Visual Pleasure and Narrative Cinema', in *Feminist Film Theory: A Reader*, ed. Sue Thornham, Edinburgh: Edinburgh University Press, pp. 58–69, originally published in *Screen* 16, 3, 1975, pp. 6–18

Murrey, Donald (1985), 'News about Columbia Pictures: "Body Double" Product Information', nine pages, archived at the British Film Institute Library

Nadelson, Regina (1988), 'Fatally Yours', *The Guardian*, 7 January, p. 1

Naremore, James (1998), *More than Night: Film Noir in its Contexts*, Berkeley: University of California Press

Neale, Steve (1983), 'Masculinity as Spectacle', *Screen* 24, 6, Winter, pp. 2–16

——(2000), *Genre and Hollywood*, London and New York: Routledge

——(2003), 'Hollywood Blockbusters: Historical Dimensions', in *Movie Blockbusters*, ed. Julian Stringer, London: Routledge, pp. 47–60

——and Smith, Murray (eds) (1998), *Contemporary Hollywood Cinema*, London: Routledge

Nelmes, Jill (1996), *An Introduction to Film Studies*, 2nd edition, London: Routledge

New Society (1985), 'Ken's Crime', 27 September, pp. 440–1

Newman, Kim (1994a), 'The Last Seduction', *Sight and Sound* 4, 8, August, p. 44

——(1994b), 'Color of Night', *Sight and Sound*, October, in *Sight and Sound Film Review Volume January 1994 to December 1994*, London: British Film Institute, p. 216

——(1996a), 'Flesh and Bone', *Empire*, October, pp. 112–13

——(1996b), 'Exploitation and the Mainstream', in *The Oxford History of World Cinema*, ed. Geoffrey Nowell-Smith, Oxford: Oxford University Press, pp. 509–15

——(1999), *Cat People*, BFI Film Classics, London: British Film Institute

——(2000), 'Donald Cammell's Wild Side', *Empire*, September, p. 57

——and Crook, Simon (1994), 'The Ultimate Guide to Deliriously Bad Movies', *Empire* October, pp. 62–6

Noble, Jean (1998), '*Bound* and Invested: Lesbian Desire and Hollywood Ethnography', *Cineaction*, 45, February, pp. 30–40

Norman, Neil (1993), 'Katt Shows Her Claws', *Evening Standard*, 11 March, p. 41

Oates, Joyce Carol (1968), 'Man under Sentence of Death: The Novels of James M. Cain', in *Tough Guy Writers of the Thirties*, ed. David Madden, Carbondale and Edwardsville: Southern Illinois University Press, pp. 110–28

Orr, John (1998), *Contemporary Cinema*, Edinburgh: Edinburgh University Press

O'Sullivan, Charlotte (1998) 'Kissed', *Sight and Sound*, January, pp. 47–8

O'Sullivan, Michael (1981), 'Dressed to Kill', *Films* 1, 3, February, p. 31

O'Toole, Laurence (1998), *Pornocopia: Porn, Sex, Technology and Desire*, London: Serpent's Tail

Paglia, Camille (1994), *Vamps & Tramps*, New York: Vintage

Pally, Marcia (1984), '"Double" Trouble', *Film Comment* 20, 5, Sept/Oct, pp. 12–17

Palmer, R. Barton (1994), *Hollywood's Dark Cinema: American Film Noir*, New York: Twayne

Palminteri, Chazz (1995), 'The Fire in Fiorentino (interview with actress Linda Fiorentino)', *Interview*, March, archived at http://www.findarticles.com/cf_dls/m1285/n3_v25/16678904/p2/article.jhtml?term=

Palta, Lisa (2000), 'Catherine Zeta Jones and Michael Douglas', *OK!*, 25 August, pp. 127–35

Pappas, Nickolas (1990), 'A *Sea of Love* among Men', *Film Criticism*, Spring, pp. 14–26

Pasquariello, Nicholas (1992), 'Primal Urges Propel *Basic Instinct*', *American Cinematographer* 13, 4, April, pp. 44–51

Patten, Fiona (1997), 'The Economy of Pleasure and the Laws of Desire', in *Sex in Public: Australian Sexual Cultures*, ed. Jill Julius Matthews, St Leonards, NSW: Allen & Unwin, pp. 31–49

Peary, Danny (1991), *Cult Movie Stars*, New York: Simon & Schuster

Pendreigh, Brian (2000), 'A Cut above', *The Guardian*, section 2, 14 January, pp. 12–13

Perry, George (1985a), Review of *Crimes of Passion*, *Sunday Times*, 15 September, p. 38

—— (1985b), Review of *Body Double*, *Sunday Times*, 22nd September, p. 38

Persall, Steve (2002), 'Three Black Filmmakers Work to Make History', *St Petersburg Times*, 6 December, archived at http://www.sptimes.com/2002/12/06/Floridian/Three_black_filmmaker.shtml

Pidduck, Julianne (1995), 'The 1990s Hollywood Fatal Femme: (Dis)Figuring Feminism, Family, Irony, Violence', *CineAction*, 38, September, pp. 64–72

Place, Janey (1998), 'Women in Film Noir', in *Women in Film Noir*, ed. E. Ann Kaplan, London: British Film Institute, pp. 47–68

Postlewaite, Jeff (1988), 'First British Reaction to Fatal Attraction', *Today*, 16 January, p. 9

Powers, Bill (1999), 'I Dream of Gina', *Bikini*, September, archived at http://www.geocities.com/Paris/LeftBank/7614/gershon/bikini.html

Prince, Stephen (2000), *A New Pot of Gold: Hollywood under the Electronic Rainbow, 1980–1989*, Berkeley: University of California Press

Queenan Joe (1995), 'All that Glitters', *The Guardian, The Guide*, 28 October–3 November, p. 4

Rabin, Nathan (2003), 'Killing Me Softly', in *The Onion A.V. Club*, http://www.theonionavclub/review.php?review_id=6378

Rapping, Elayne (1992), *The Movie of the Week: Private Stories, Public Events*, Minneapolis: University of Minnesota Press

Ray, Fred Olen (1991), *The New Poverty Row: Independent Filmmakers as Distributors*, Jefferson, NC and London: McFarland

Raynes, Tony (1985), 'Preacher's Pet', *Time Out*, 5 September, p. 17

Reed, Jacinda (2000), *The New Avengers, Feminism, Femininity and the Rape-Revenge Cycle*, Manchester: Manchester University Press

Reid, Sue (2000), 'Porn Brokers', *Marie Claire*, May, pp. 59–66

Rich, B. Ruby (1998), *Chick Flicks: Theories and Memories of the Feminist Film Movement*, Durham, NC and London: Duke University Press

Ritter, Tim (2002), 'Theatrical Exhibition for Video Movies', in Lindenmuth, pp. 217–24

Rivett, Adam (1998), 'The Erotic Thriller, or How I Learnt to Love the Erotic Thriller' (review of *Wild Things*), *In Film Australia* website, archived at http://infilmau.iah.net/features/erotic/

Roberts, Glenys (1980), 'The Movie that Set New York's Streets on Fire', *Sunday Times*, 15 June

Rodley, Chris (ed.) (1997), *Cronenberg on Cronenberg*, London: Faber

Rogerson, Gillian, and Elizabeth Wilson (1991), *Pornography and Feminism: The Case against Censorship by Feminists against Censorship*, London: Lawrence & Wishart

Romney, Jonathan (1993), 'We've Been Framed', *New Statesman & Society*, 20 September, p. 35

Rosenbaum, Jonathan (1999), 'In Dreams Begin Responsibilities', Chicago Reader website, archived at http://www.chireader.com/movies/archives/1999/07239.html

Royalle, Candida (1993), 'Porn in the USA', *Social Text* 37, Winter, pp. 23–32

Rubin, Martin (1999), *Thrillers*, Cambridge: Cambridge University Press

Russell, Ken (1989), *A British Picture: An Autobiography*, London: Heinemann

Russell, William (1986), 'Fairly Good Week for Russells', *Glasgow Herald*, 17 May, p. 10

Ryall, Tom (1975/6), 'Teaching through Genre', in *Screen Education* 17, pp. 27–33

Ryan, Tom (1981), 'Looking in on Dressed to Kill', *Cinema Papers* 31, March–April, pp. 20–5

Salisbury, Mark (1996), 'Video Siren: Shannon Whirry', *Empire*, October, p. 111

——(1994a), 'Mammarymeister', *Empire*, October, 66

——(1994b), 'Video Vixen', *Empire*, October, 64

Sargent, Lydia (ed.) (1981), *Women and Revolution: The Unhappy Marriage of Marxism and Feminism*, London: Pluto

Schaefer, Eric (1999), *Bold! Daring! Shocking! True! A History of Exploitation Films, 1919–1959*, Durham, NC: Duke University Press

Schamus, James (1998), 'To the Rear of the Back End: The Economics of Independent Cinema', in *Contemporary Hollywood Cinema*, eds Steve Neale and Murray Smith, London: Routledge, pp. 91–105

Schatz, Thomas (1993), 'The New Hollywood', in *Film Theory Goes to the Movies*, eds Jim Collins, Hilary Radner and Ava Preacher Collins, New York: Routledge, pp. 8–36

Scheers, Rob van (1997), *Paul Verhoeven*, trans. Aletta Stevens, London: Faber

Schickel, Richard (1992), *Double Indemnity*, London: British Film Institute

——(1994), 'Sex! Controversy! Box Office!', *Time*, 19 December, 144, 25, archived at http://www.time.com/time/magazine/archive/1994/941219/941219.cinema.disclosure.html

Schlosser, Eric (1997): 'The Business of Pornography', *U.S. New and World Report*, 10 February, pp. 42–50, archived at http://www.usnews.com/usnews/home

Schneider, Steve (1999), 'Eyes Wide Shut', *Orlando Weekly*, archived at http://www.orlandoweekly.com/movies/reviews.review.asp?movie=431

Schrader, Paul (1972), 'Notes on Film Noir', in *Film Noir Reader*, eds Alain Silver and James Ursini, New York: Limelight, 1996, pp. 53–63

Schulgasser, Barbara (1995), 'This "Jade" isn't Even Semiprecious', *San Francisco Examiner*, 13 October

——(1996), '"Diabolique" Remake Strays', *San Francisco Examiner*, 22 March, all archived at http://www.sfgate.com

——(1998), '"Palmetto" Should Have Been Intriguing', *San Francisco Examiner*, 20 February

Schwartz, Ronald (2001), *Noir, Now and Then: Film Noir Originals and Remakes (1944–1999)*, Westport, CT: Greenwood Press

Sconce, Jeffrey (1995), '"Trashing" the Academy: Taste, Excess, and an Emerging Politics of Cinematic Style', *Screen*, 36, 4, Winter, pp. 371–93

Sen, Somanth (2000), 'We Have Arrived', *hollywoodmasala.com*, 1.1.2000, originally published in *India Journal* magazine, http://www.hollywoodmasala.com/content.asp?cat+news&index+40

Shea, Chris and Hennings, Wade (1993), 'Paul Verhoeven: An Interview', *Post Script: Essays in Film and the Humanities*, 12, 3, Summer, pp. 3–24

Sigal, Clancy (1985), 'Moving Madonna', *The Listener*, 12 September, p. 33

Silver, Alain and Ursini, James (eds) (1996): *Film Noir Reader*, New York: Limelight

Silver, Alain and Ward, Elizabeth (eds) (1992), *Film Noir: An Encyclopedic Reference to the American Style*, 3rd edition, New York: Overlook Press

Smith, Murray (1988), 'Film Noir and the Female Gothic and *Deception*', *Wide Angle* 10, 1, pp. 62–75

Sorensen, Holly (1997), 'The Sex Bomb Who Can't Get a Date', *The Scotsman*, 2 August, pp. 8–10

Spicer, Andrew (2002), *Film Noir*, Harlow: Pearson

Stables, Kate (1998), 'The Postmodern Always Rings Twice: Constructing the Femme Fatale in 90s Cinema', in *Women in Film Noir*, 2nd edition, ed. E. Ann Kaplan, London: British Film Institute, pp. 164–82

Staiger, Janet (1989), 'Reception Studies: The Death of the Reader', in R. Barton Palmer (ed.), *The Cinematic Text, Methods and Approaches*, New York: AMS Press

——(1993), 'Taboos and Totems: Cultural Meanings of *The Silence of the Lambs*', in *Film Theory Goes to the Movies*, eds Jim Collins, Hilary Radner and Ava Preacher Collins, New York and London: Routledge, pp. 142–54

——(1997), 'Hybrid or Inbred: The Purity Hypothesis and Hollywood Genre History', *Film Cirticism* XXII, 1, Fall

The Standard (1984), 'Censors Clip away at Ken's Comeback', 21 September, p. 10

Stanfield, Peter (2002), '"Film Noir Like You've Never Seen": Jim Thompson Adaptations and Cycles of Neo-Noir', in *Genre and Contemporary Hollywood*, ed. Steve Neale, London: British Film Institute, pp. 251–68

Stempel, Tom (2001), *American Audiences on Movies and Moviegoing*, Lexington: University Press of Kentucky

Stoddart, Helen (1995), 'Autuerism and Film Authorship', in *Approaches to Popular Film*, eds Joanne Hollows and Mark Jancovich, Manchester: Manchester University Press, pp. 37–57

Straayer, Chris (1998), '*Femme Fatale* or Lesbian Femme: *Bound* in Sexual *Différance*', in *Women in Film Noir*, 2nd edition, ed. E. Ann Kaplan, London: British Film Institute, pp. 151–63

Stratton, David (1994), 'The Last Seduction', *Variety*, 28 February, p. 70

Strauss, Bob (2000), 'Professional Player', *The Guardian* (*The Guide*), 7–13 October, p. 15

Summers, Sue (1988), 'Producing a Modern Fable of Infidelity', *The Independent*, 15 January, p. 14

Sunday Mirror (1984), 'Debbie is a Dubbed Turn-off', *Sunday Mirror*, 30 December, p. 5

Sunday Telegraph editorial (1996), 'Cover-up', *Sunday Telegraph*, 7 April, p. 12

Svetkey, Benjamin (1996), 'Gina Grrrrrrshon', *Entertainment Weekly*, Summer, archived at http://www.geocities.com/Paris/LeftBank/7614/gershon/entwkly.html

Tanner, Louise (1987), 'Adrian Lyne and Patricia Rozema', in *Films in Review*, December, pp. 597–9

——(1995), 'Accents and Umlauts', *Films in Review* 46, 1/2, Jan/Feb, pp. 34–5

Tashiro, Charles Shiro (1999), 'Videophilia: What Happens When You Wait for it on Video', in *Film Quarterly: Forty Years – A Selection*, eds Brian Henderson and Ann Martin, Berkeley: University of California Press, pp. 352–71, originally published in *Film Quarterly* 45, 1, Fall 1991

Tasker, Yvonne (1998), *Working Girls: Gender and Sexuality in Popular Cinema*, London: Routledge

Taylor, Noreen (1988), 'Is This the End of One Night Stands?', *Daily Mirror* (Mirror Woman section) 15 January, p. 1

Teo, Stephen (1997), *Hong Kong: The Extra Dimension*, London: British Film Institute

Thompson, Bob (1995), 'The Next Seduction: Linda Fiorentino Talks Tough about being a woman in Hollywood', *Toronto Sun*, 1 October, archived at The Unofficial Homepage of Linda Fiorentino, http://www.geocities.com/Hollywood/Academy/6215/Interview.html

Thompson, David (1995): 'Follow the Money', *Film Comment* 31, 4, July/Aug, pp. 21–5

Thompson, John O. (1991), 'Screen Acting and the Commutation Test', in *Stardom Industry of Desire*, ed. Christine Gledhill, London and New York: Routledge, pp. 183–97

Todorov, Tzvetan (1999), *Genres in Discourse*, Cambridge: Cambridge University Press

Tony, webmaster of *The Old Hockstatter Place* website: 'The Jim Wynorski Interview', http://www.digivoodoo.net/oldhockstatterplace/index.shtml

Travers, Peter (1990), 'After Dark, My Sweet', *Rolling Stone*, archived at http://www.rollingstone.com/reviews/movie?id=5948035

Trower, Marcus (1994), 'Linda Fiorentino the Last Seductress', *Empire*, 66, December, p. 59

Tudor, Andrew (1986), 'Genre', in *Film Genre Reader*, ed. Barry Keith Grant, Austin: University of Texas Press, pp. 3–10

Variety Editors (1999), *The Variety Insider*, New York: Perigee

Variety staff (1996), 'Fear', *Variety*, 1 January, archived at http://www.variety.com

——(1991), 'Scissors' review, *Variety*, 25 March, p. 90

Vega, Mark (1996), 'Sunset Films International', part of report on 'The American Film Market' at hollywoodNetwork.com website, http://www.hollywoodnetwork.com/AFM/sunset.html

Verma, Suparn (1997), 'Porn in the USA', *Rediff On the Net*, 20 October, http://www.rediff.com/entertai/oct/20jag/htm

VerMeulen, Michael (1988), 'Manhattan Transfers', *Sunday Telegraph*, 7 February, p. 21

Video Business (1985), 'A Sexy, Surreal Driller Thriller', *Video Business* 5, 22, 29 July, p. 24

Vulliamy, Ed (2000), 'The Hollywood Hitman', *The Observer*, 20 August, Review Section, pp. 1–2

Wager, Jans B. (1999), *Dangerous Dames: Women and Representation in the Weimar Street Film and Film Noir*, Athens, OH: Ohio University Press

Walker, Alexander (1985a), 'The Porno-nest Hatches Laughter' (Crimes of Passion), *The London Standard*, 12 September, p. 26

——(1985b), 'Drill M for Murder', *The London Standard*, 19 September, p. 26

——(1988), 'Husbands Beware', *London Evening Standard*, 14 January, p. 32

——(1993), 'Sliver', *London Evening Standard*, 2 September, p. 23

Walker, Michael (1992), 'Film Noir: An Introduction', pp. 8–38 'The Big Sleep: Howard Hawks and Film Noir', pp. 191–202, both in *The Movie Book of Film Noir*, ed. Ian Cameron, London: Studio Vista

Wallace, Lee (2000), 'Continuous Sex: The Editing of Homosexuality in *Bound* and *Rope*', *Screen*, 41, 4, Winter, pp. 369–87

Warner, Marina (1995), *From The Beast to the Blonde: On Fairy Tales and their Tellers*, London:Vintage

Watson, Don (1985), 'Forbidden Fruits?', *New Musical Express*, 7 September, p. 26

Waymark, Peter (1985), 'Guilt, Gore and Two Girls with Glamour', *The Times*, 24 August, p. 17

Whitehouse, Charles (1999), 'Eyes without a Face', *Sight and Sound 9*, September, pp. 38–9

Williams, Evan (1999), 'Eyes Wide Shut', Entertainment News website, archived at http://archive.entertainment.news.com.au/film/archive/90807a.htm

Williams, Linda (1990), *Hard Core: Power, Pleasure, and the 'Frenzy of the Visible'*, London: Pandora

——(1991), 'Film Bodies: Gender, Genre and Excess', *Film Quarterly* 44, 4, Summer, pp. 2–13

Williams, Linda Ruth (1997), *D. H. Lawrence*, Plymouth: Northcote House/British Council

——(2002), 'Sex and Censoriousness: Pornography and Censorship in Britain', in *The Media: An Introduction*, 2nd edition, eds Adam Briggs and Paul Cobley, London: Pearson, pp. 477–95

Williams, Raymond (1974), *Television: Technology and Cultural Form*, New York: Schocken

Willis, Ellen (1987), 'Sins of the Fathers', *Village Voice*, 15 December, pp. 85–6

Willman, Chris (1991), 'Scissors', *Hollywood Reporter*, 22 March, p. 12

Winks, Cathy (1998), *The Good Vibrations Guide to Adult Videos*, San Francisco: Down There Press

The Wolf (2002), 'Killing Me Softly', iofilm.co.uk website, http://www.iofilm.co.uk/films/k/killing_me_softly.shtml

Wood, Robert E. (1993), 'Somebody Has To Die: *Basic Instinct* as White *Noir*', *Post Script* 12, 3, Summer, pp. 44–51

Wood, Robin (1986), *Hollywood from Vietnam to Reagan*, New York: Columbia University Press

Wurtzel, Elizabeth (1998), *Bitch*, London: Quartet Books

Wyatt, Justin (1994), *High Concept: Movies and Marketing in Hollywood*, Austin: University of Texas Press

Young, Neil (2002), 'Killing Me Softly', *Jigsaw Lounge* website, http://www.jigsawlounge.co.uk/film/killingmesoftly.html

Young, Toby (1993), 'In on the Acting', *Sunday Times*, Section 9, 25 April, pp. 4–5

FILMS CITED

À ma Soeur! aka *Fat Girl* (Catherine Breillat, France 2001)
The Accused (Jonathan Kaplan, USA 1988)
Acting on Impulse (Sam Irvin, USA 1993)
After Dark, My Sweet (James Foley, USA 1990)
After Hours (Martin Scorsese, USA 1985)
Ai No Corrida (Nagisa Oshima, Japan 1976)
All About Eve (Joseph L. Mankiewicz, USA 1950)
Along Came A Spider (Lee Tamahori, USA 2001)
American Gigolo (Paul Schrader, USA 1980)
Among the Living (Stuart Heisler, USA 1941)
The American President (Rob Reiner, USA 1995)
Angel Heart (Alan Parker, USA 1987)
Animal Instincts (Gregory Dark, credited as A. Gregory Hippolyte, USA 1992)
Animal Instincts II (Gregory Dark, credited as Gregory Hippolyte, USA 1994)
Animal Instincts: The Seductress (aka *Animal Instincts 3*) (Gregory Dark, credited as Gregory Hippolyte, USA 1996)
Antitrust (Peter Howitt, USA 2001)
The Apartment (Billy Wilder, USA 1960)
Back to the Future (Robert Zemeckis, USA 1985)
Bad Timing (Nicolas Roeg, UK 1980)
Baise-moi (Coralie Trinh Thi/Virginie Despentes, France 2000)
Bandits (Barry Levinson, USA 2001)
The Bare Wench Project 2: Scared Topless (Jim Wynorski, USA 2001)
Bare Wench III: The Path of the Wicked (Jim Wynorski, USA 2002)
Basic Deception (Ivan Passer, USA 1992)
Basic Instinct (Paul Verhoeven, USA 1992)
Batman (Tim Burton, USA 1989)
Batman Returns (Tim Burton, USA 1992)
Battlefield Earth: A Saga of the Year 3000 (Roger Christian, USA 2000)
Bawandar (aka *Sandstorm*) (Jagmohan Mundhra, India 2000)
Beach Beverly Hills (Jonathan Sarno, USA 1993)

Belle de Jour (Luis Buñuel, France/Italy 1967)
Betrayed (Costa-Gavras, USA 1988)
Between the Cheeks 2 (Gregory Dark, USA 1990)
Between the Cheeks 3 (Gregory Dark, USA 1993)
The Big Easy (Jim McBride, USA 1986)
Bitter Moon (Roman Polanski, USA 1992)
Black & White (Yuri Zeltser, USA 1998)
The Blackout (Abel Ferrara, USA 1997)
Black Rain (Ridley Scott, USA 1989)
Black Throat (Gregory Dark, USA 1985)
Black Widow (Bob Rafelson, USA 1987)
Blindfold: Acts of Obsession (Lawrence L. Simeone, USA 1994)
Blink (Michael Apted, USA 1994)
Blonde Poison: The Making of 'Basic Instinct' (Jeffrey Schwarz, USA 2001)
Blood Simple (Joel Coen, USA 1984)
Blow Out (Brian De Palma, USA 1981)
The Blues Brothers (John Landis 1980)
Blue Steel (Kathryn Bigelow, USA 1990)
Blue Velvet (David Lynch, USA 1986)
Bodily Harm (James Lemmo, USA 1995)
Body Chemistry (Kristine Peterson, USA 1990)
Body Chemistry II: The Voice of a Stranger (Adam Simon, USA 1992)
Body Chemistry III: Point of Seduction (Jim Wynorski, USA 1994)
Body Chemistry 4: Full Exposure (Jim Wynorski, USA 1995)
Body Double (Brian De Palma, USA 1984)
Body Heat (Lawrence Kasdan, USA 1981)
Body Language (George Case, USA 1995)
Body of Evidence (Uli Edel, USA 1992)
Body of Influence (aka *Animal Instincts 2* and *Indecent Advances*) (Gregory Dark, credited as Gregory Hippolyte, USA 1995)
Body of Influence 2 (Brian J. Smith, USA 1996)
Body Shot (Dimitri Logothetis, USA 1993)
Body Weapon, originally titled *Yuen chi miu hei* (Aman Chang, Hong Kong 1999)
The Bone Collector (Phillip Noyce, USA 1999)
The Bonfire of the Vanities (Brian De Palma, USA 1990)
Boogie Nights (Paul Thomas Anderson, USA 1997)
Bound (Andy and Larry Wachowski, USA 1996)
Bram Stoker's Dracula (Francis Ford Coppola, USA 1992)
Business for Pleasure (Raphael Isenman, USA 1996)
Bus Stop (Joshua Logan, USA 1956)
Caged Fury (Bill Milling, USA 1989)
Caged Hearts (Henri Charr, USA 1995)
Caged Heat (Jonathan Demme, USA 1974)

Caged Seduction (Karen Arthur, USA 1995)

Caged Women originally titled *La prede umane* (Leandro Lucchetti, Italy 1992)

The Calendar Girl Murders aka *Victimised* (William A. Graham, USA 1984)

Cannibal Women in the Avocado Jungle of Death, (J. F. Lawton, USA 1989)

Carnal Crimes (Gregory Dark, credited as Alexander Hippolyte, USA 1990)

Casino (Martin Scorsese, USA 1995)

Chained Heat (Lutz Schaarwächter, USA/West Germany 1983)

Charlie's Angels (McG, USA 2000)

China Moon (John Bailey, USA 1994)

Chinatown (Roman Polanski, USA 1974)

Citizen Kane (Orson Welles, USA 1941)

Club Vampire (Andy Ruben, USA 1998)

Cold Steel (Dorothy Ann Puzo, USA 1987)

Color of Night (Richard Rush, USA 1994)

Confessions of a Lap Dancer (Mike Sedan, USA 1997)

The Cool Surface (Erik Anjou, USA 1994)

Cover Me (Michael Schroeder, USA 1995)

Crash (David Cronenberg, USA 1996)

Crimes of Passion (Ken Russell, USA 1984)

Criminal Passion (Donna Deitch, USA 1994)

Cruising (William Friedkin, USA 1980)

Dance of the Damned (Katt Shea Ruben, USA 1988)

Dance with Death (Charles Phillip Moore, USA 1992)

Dancing at the Blue Iguana (Michael Radford, USA 2000)

Dangerous Desire aka *Tomcat: Dangerous Desires* (Paul Donovan, Canada/ USA 1993)

Dangerous Indiscretion (Richard Kletter, USA 1994)

Dangerous Touch (Lou Diamond Phillips, USA 1993)

The Dark Mirror (Robert Siodmak, USA 1946)

Dark Secrets (John T. Bone, USA 1998)

Dead Again (Kenneth Branagh, USA 1991)

Deadly Dream Woman, originally titled *Nu hei xia huang ying* (Jing Wong and Taylor Wong, Hong Kong 1992)

Deadly Surveillance (Paul Ziller, USA 1991)

Deadly Weapons (Doris Wishman, USA 1974)

Dead Man Walking (Gregory Dark, USA 1988)

Dead Ringers (David Cronenberg, USA 1988)

Debbie Does Dallas (Jim Clark, USA 1978)

Deceptions (Ruben Preuss, USA 1989)

Deep Throat (Jerry Gerard also known as Gerard Damiano, USA 1972)

Devil in a Blue Dress (Carl Franklin, USA 1995)

The Devil in Miss Jones (Gerard Damiano, USA 1973)

The Devil in Miss Jones 5: The Inferno (Gregory Dark, USA 1994)

The Devils (Ken Russell, USA 1971)

Diabolique (Jeremiah S. Chechik, USA 1996)

Les Diaboliques (Henri-Georges Clouzot, France 1955)

Dial M for Murder (Alfred Hitchcock, USA 1954)

Dick Tracy (Warren Beatty, USA 1990)

Die Hard (John McTiernan, USA 1988)

Die Watching (Charles Davis, USA 1993)

Disclosure (Barry Levinson, USA 1994)

Dog Day Afternoon (Sidney Lumet, USA 1975)

Double Agent 73 (Doris Wishman, USA 1974)

Double Indemnity (Billy Wilder, USA 1944)

Double Impact (Sheldon Lettich, USA 1991)

Double Jeopardy (Lawrence Schiller, USA 1992)

Double Jeopardy (Bruce Beresford, USA 1999)

The Dreamers (Bernardo Bertolucci, Italy/France/UK/USA, 2003)

Dressed to Kill (Brian de Palma, USA 1980)

Dr Lamb, original title *Gao yang yi sheng* (Danny Lee and Hin Sing 'Billy' Tang, Hong Kong 1992)

Ecstasy (Gustav Machaty, Czechoslovakia 1933)

Embrace of the Vampire (Anne Goursaud, USA 1994)

Emmanuelle (Just Jaeckin, France 1974)

The Erotic Adventures of The Three Musketeers (Paul Norman, USA 1992)

Erotic Ghost Story originally titled *Lia zhai yan tan* (Ngai Kai Lam, Hong Kong 1987)

Erotic Ghost Story 2 originally titled *Lia zhai yan tan xu ji zhi wu tong shen* (Peter Ngor, Hong Kong 1991)

E.T. the Extra-Terrestrial (Steven Spielberg, USA 1982)

Evil Ambitions (Mark Burchett and Michael D. Fox, USA 1995)

Evil Instinct originally titled *Ji dou shou xing* (Barry Chu, Hong Kong 1997)

Exception to the Rule (David Winning, USA 1996)

Exit in Red (Yurek Bogayevicz, USA 1996)

The Exorcist (William Friedkin, USA 1973)

Exotica (Atom Egoyan, Canada 1994)

Eyes of Laura Mars (Irvin Kershner, USA 1978)

Eyes Wide Shut (Stanley Kubrick, USA/UK 1999)

Eyewitness to Murder (Jag Mundhra, USA 1991)

Face/Off (John Woo, USA 1997)

Fallen Angel (John Quinn, USA 1997)

Falling Down (Joel Schumacher, USA 1992)

Farewell, My Lovely (Dick Richards, USA 1975)

The Fashionistas (John Stagliano, USA 2002)

Fatal Attraction (Adrian Lyne, USA 1987)

Fatal Deception (Robert Dornhelm, USA 1993)

Fatal Encounter, original title *Duo ming jiechu* (Ng Doi-Yung, Hong Kong 1994)

Fatal Exposure (Peter G. Good, USA 1989)

Fatal Exposure (Alan Metzger, USA 1991)

The Fatal Image (Thomas J. Wright, USA 1990)

Fatal Instinct (John Dirlam, USA 1992)

Fatal Instinct (Carl Reiner, USA 1993)

Fatal Past (Clive Fleury and Richard Ryan, Australia 1993)

Fatal Proposal aka *I Can Make You Love Me* (Michael Switzer, USA 1993)

Fatal Pursuit (Eric Louzil, USA 1998)

Fatal Secret (Mats Helge, Sweden 1988)

Fatal Temptation (Beppe Cino, Italy 1988)

Fear (James Foley, USA 1996)

Fear City (Abel Ferrara, USA 1984)

Feminine Chemistry, originally titled *Alcune signore per bene* (Brunno Gaburro, Italy 1990)

Femme Fatale (Brian De Palma, USA 2003)

Final Analysis (Phil Joanou, USA 1992)

F.I.S.T. (Norman Jewison, USA 1978)

Flashdance (Adrian Lyne, USA 1983)

Flinch (George Erschbamer, USA 1994)

Forest Hump, aka *Foreskin Gump* (Mitch Spinelli, USA 1994)

The Fourth Man, originally titled *De Vierde Man* (Paul Verhoeven, Netherlands 1983)

The French Connection (William Friedkin, USA 1971)

Friday the 13th (Sean S. Cunningham, USA 1980)

Fried Green Tomatoes (Jon Avnet, USA 1991)

From Dusk Till Dawn (Robert Rodriguez, USA 1996)

From Here to Eternity (Fred Zinnemann, USA 1953)

Full Body Massage (Nicolas Roeg, USA 1995)

Full Metal Jacket (Stanley Kubrick, USA 1987)

The Full Monty (Peter Cattaneo, UK 1997)

The Fury (Brian De Palma, USA 1978)

Gaslight (George Cukor, USA 1944)

Ghost Busters (Ivan Reitman, USA 1984)

Ghoulies IV (Jim Wynorski, USA 1994)

Gilda (Charles Vidor, USA 1946)

Greetings (Brian De Palma, USA 1968)

The Guilty (John Reinhardt, USA 1947)

Guilty as Sin (Sidney Lumet, USA 1993)

Gypsy (Mervyn LeRoy, USA 1962)

Halloween (John Carpenter, USA 1978)

The Hand that Rocks the Cradle (Curtis Hansen, USA 1992)

The Hands of Orlac (Karl Freund, USA 1935)

The Handmaid's Tale (Volker Schlöndorff, USA 1990)

Hard-Boiled, originally titled *Lashou shentan* (John Woo, Hong Kong 1992)

Hard Drive (James Merendino, USA 1994)
Henry and June (Philip Kaufman, USA 1990)
Her Vengeance originally titled *Xue mei gui* (Ngai Kai Lam, Hong Kong 1986)
Hi, Mom! (Brian De Palma, USA 1970)
Hidden Obsession (John Stewart, USA 1992)
High Crimes (Carl Franklin, USA 2002)
Hollow Man (Paul Verhoeven, USA 2000)
Home Alone 2: Lost in New York (Chris Columbus, USA 1992)
The Hot Spot (Dennis Hopper, USA 1990)
Human Desires (aka *Indecent Behaviour 4*) (Ellen Earnshaw, USA 1997)
Identity (James Mangold, USA 2003)
Illegal Entry (Richard W. Munchkin, USA 1998)
Illicit Behaviour (Worth Keeter, USA 1992)
Illicit Dreams (Andrew Stevens, USA 1995)
Illicit Dreams 2 (Fred Olen Ray, USA 1998)
Improper Conduct (Jag Mundhra, USA 1994)
Impulse (Sondra Locke, USA 1990)
In the Cut (Jane Campion, USA 2003)
Indecent Behaviour (Lawrence Lanoff, USA 1993)
Indecent Behaviour II (Carlo Gustaff, USA 1994)
Indecent Behaviour III (Kelley Cauthen, USA 1995)
Indecent Proposal (Adrian Lyne, USA 1993)
Indiscreet (Stanley Donen, USA 1958)
Infernal Affairs, aka *Wu jian dao* (Andrew Lau Wai-Keung and Alan Mak Siu-Fai, Hong Kong 2002)
Insomnia (Christopher Nolan, USA 2002)
Intersection (Mark Rydell, USA 1994)
Intimate Betrayal (Diane Wynter, USA 1999)
Intimate Stranger (Allan Holzman, USA 1991)
Irreconcilable Differences (Charles Shyer, USA 1984)
Irresistible Impulse (Jag Mundhra, USA 1996)
I Spit on Your Grave aka *Day of the Woman* (Meir Zarchi, USA 1978)
Internal Affairs (Mike Figgis, USA 1990)
The Italian Job (F. Gary Gray, USA 2003)
Jade (William Friedkin, USA 1995)
Jagged Edge (Richard Marquand, USA 1985)
Jaws (Steven Spielberg, USA 1975)
Junior (Ivan Reitman, USA 1994)
The Juror (Brian Gibson, USA 1996)
Killer Looks (Paul Thomas, USA 1994)
Kill Me Again (John Dahl, USA 1989)
Killing Me Softly (Chen Kaige, US/UK 2001)
A Kiss Before Dying (James Dearden, USA 1990)

Kissed (Lynne Stopkewich, Canada 1996)

Kiss Me Deadly (Robert Aldrich, USA 1955)

Kiss Me a Killer (Marcus DeLeon, USA 1991)

Kiss of Death (Henry Hathaway, USA 1947)

Kiss the Girls (Gary Fleder, USA 1997)

Klute (Alan J. Pakula, USA 1971)

L.A. Confidential (Curtis Hansen, USA 1997)

Lady Chatterley's Lover (Just Jaeckin, UK/France/Germany 1981)

The Lady from Shanghai (Orson Welles, USA 1947)

L.A. Goddess (Jag Mundhra, USA 1993)

Lap Dancing (Mike Sedan, USA 1995)

Last Call (Jag Mundhra, USA 1990)

Last Dance (Bruce Beresford, USA 1996)

The Last Seduction (John Dahl, USA 1994)

The Last Seduction 2 (Terry Marcel, USA 1999)

Last Tango in Paris (Bernardo Bertolucci, Italy/France 1972)

The Last Temptation of Christ (Martin Scorsese, USA 1988)

Laura (Otto Preminger, USA 1944)

Legal Tender (Jag Mundhra, USA 1991)

Lethal Seduction (Fred P. Watkins, USA 1997)

Lethal Weapon 3 (Richard Donner, USA 1992)

Lipstick Camera (Mike Bonifer, USA 1994)

Liquid Dreams (Mark S. Manos, USA 1992)

Lisztomania (Ken Russell, UK 1975)

Lolita (Stanely Kubrick, USA/UK 1962)

Lolita (Adrian Lyne, USA 1997)

Looking for Mr. Goodbar (Richard Brooks, USA 1977)

Losing Control (Julie Jordan, USA 1997)

Lost Highway (David Lynch, USA 1997)

Love Crimes (Lizzie Borden, USA 1992)

Love in Paris aka *Another 9½ Weeks* (Anne Goursaud, USA 1997)

Malevolent Male originally titled *Ren rou tian fu luo* (Chin Wei Lin, Hong Kong 1993)

Malicious (Ian Corson, USA 1995)

The Maltese Falcon (John Huston, USA 1941)

Manhunter (Michael Mann, USA 1986)

The Man with Two Brains (Carl Reiner, USA 1983)

Marathon Man (John Schlesinger, USA 1976)

Marnie (Alfred Hitchcock, USA 1964)

Masseuse (Fred Olen Ray, USA 1996)

Matador (Pedro Almodóvar, Spain 1986)

Memento (Christopher Nolan, USA 2000)

Men in Black (Barry Sonnenfeld, USA 1997)

Midnight Tease (Scott Levy, USA 1994)

Midnight Tease II (Richard Styles, USA 1995)

Mildred Pierce (Michael Curtiz, USA 1945)

Mind Twister (Fred Olen Ray, USA 1994)

Mirror Images (Gregory Dark, credited as Alexander Gregory Hippolyte, USA 1991)

Mirror Images II (Gregory Dark, credited as Gregory Hippolyte, USA 1993)

Mission: Impossible (Brian De Palma, USA 1996)

Mission to Mars (Brian De Palma, USA 2000)

The Moderns (Alan Rudolph, USA 1988)

Monsoon, aka *Tales of the Kama Sutra 2* (Jag Mundhra, USA 1998)

Motel Blue (Sam Firstenberg, USA 1999)

Ms. 45 (Abel Ferrara, USA 1981)

Mulholland Drive (David Lynch, USA 2001)

Mulholland Falls (Lee Tamahori, USA 1996)

Munchie Strikes Back (Jim Wynorski, USA 1994)

Murder My Sweet (Edward Dmytryk, USA 1944)

A Murderous Affair (Martin Davidson, USA 1993)

Music Box (Costa-Gavras, USA 1989)

The Music Lovers (Ken Russell, UK 1970)

My Little Eye (Marc Evans, UK 2002)

Naked Killer originally titled *Chiklo gouyeung* (Clarence Fok Yiu-leung, Hong Kong 1992)

Naked Obsession (Dan Golden, USA 1991)

Naked Souls (Lyndon Chubbuck, USA 1995)

Naked Weapon, originally titled *Chek law dak gung* (Siu-Tung Ching, Hong Kong 2002)

New Wave Hookers (Gregory Dark, USA 1985)

New Wave Hookers 3 (Gregory Dark, USA 1993)

Niagara (Henry Hathaway, USA 1953)

Night Class (Sheldon Wilson, USA 2001)

Night Eyes (Jag Mundhra, USA 1990)

Night Eyes 2 (Rodney McDonald, USA 1991)

Night Eyes 3 (Andrew Stevens, USA 1993)

Night Eyes 4 (Rodney McDonald, USA 1996)

Night Rhythms (Gregory Dark, credited as A. Gregory Hippolyte, USA 1992)

Night Shade (Fred Olen Ray, USA 1997)

Nikita (Luc Besson, France/Italy 1990)

9½ Weeks (Adrian Lyne, USA 1986)

The Notebook (Nick Cassavetes, USA 2004)

Object of Obsession (Gregory Dark, credited as Gregory Hippolyte, USA 1995)

Obsessed (Jonathan Sanger, USA 1993)

Obsession (Brian De Palma, USA 1975)

Obsession: A Taste for Fear, originally titled *Pathos – segreta inquietudine* (Piccio Raffanini, Italy 1988)

An Occasional Hell (Salome Breziner, USA 1996)

Oklahoma! (Fred Zinnemann, USA 1955)

One Night Stand (Mike Figgis, USA 1997)

Open House (Jag Mundhra, USA 1987)

Original Sin (Michael Cristofer, USA 2002)

Orlando (Sally Potter, UK/Russia/France/Italy/Netherlands 1992)

The Other Woman (Jag Mundhra, USA 1992)

Over the Line aka *Out of Control* (Ovidio G. Assonitis, credited as Oliver Hellman, and Robert Barrett, USA 1992)

Out of the Past (Jacques Tourneur, USA 1947)

Pal Joey (George Sidney, USA 1957)

Palmetto (Volker Schlöndorff, USA 1998)

The Pamela Principle (Paul Thomas, credited as Toby Phillips, USA 1992)

Pandora's Box (Rob Hardy, USA 2002)

Peeping Tom (Michael Powell, UK 1960)

The Perfumed Garden, aka *Tales of the Kama Sutra* (Jag Mundhra, USA/India, 2000)

The People vs. Larry Flynt (Milos Forman, USA 1996)

A Perfect Murder (Andrew Davis, USA 1998)

Play Misty For Me (Clint Eastwood, USA 1971)

The Player (Robert Altman, USA 1992)

The Players Club (Ice Cube, USA 1998)

Playing with Fire (Roy Campanella II, USA 2000)

Poison Ivy (Katt Shea Ruben, USA 1992)

Poison Ivy 2: Lily (Anne Goursaud, USA 1995)

Poison Ivy: The Next Seduction aka *Poison Ivy 3* (Kurt Voss, USA 1997)

Police Academy IV: Citizens on Patrol (Jim Drake, USA 1987)

The Postman Always Comes Twice (Jim Travis, USA 1986)

The Postman Always Rings Twice (Tay Garnett, USA 1946)

The Postman Always Rings Twice (Bob Rafelson, USA 1981)

Powerplay (Chris Baugh, USA 1998)

Pretty Woman originally titled *Qing nem jia ren* (Yeung Chi Gin, Hong Kong 1992)

Psycho (Alfred Hitchcock, USA 1960)

The Quick and the Dead (Sam Raimi, USA 1995)

The Rage: Carrie 2 (Katt Shea, USA 1999)

Raising Cain (Brian De Palma, USA 1992)

Raped by an Angel, aka *Naked Killer 2*, originally titled *Xiang Gang qi an zhi qiang jian* (Wai Keung Lau, Hong Kong 1993)

Raped by an Angel 4: The Raper's Union, originally titled *Jiang jian zhong ji pian zhi zui hou gao yang* (Wong Jing, Hong Kong 1999)

Ray (Taylor Hackford, USA 2004)

Rear Window (Alfred Hitchcock, USA 1954)

Rebecca (Alfred Hitchcock, USA 1940)

Red Rock West (John Dahl, USA 1992)

The Red Shoe Diaries (Zalman King, USA 1992)

Robocop (Paul Verhoeven, USA 1987)

Robotrix originally titled *Nu ji xie ren* (Jamie Luk, Hong Kong 1991)

The Rocky Horror Picture Show (Jim Sharman, USA 1975)

Romance (Catherine Breillat, France 1999)

Romancing the Stone (Robert Zemeckis, USA 1984)

Romeo is Bleeding (Peter Medak, USA 1993)

Rosemary's Baby (Roman Polanski, USA 1968)

Saturday Night Beaver (USA 1986)

Savage Messiah (Ken Russell, UK 1972)

Schindler's List (Steven Spielberg, USA 1993)

Scissors (Frank de Felitta, USA 1990)

Scorned 2 (Rodney McDonald, USA 1997)

Scream (Wes Craven, USA 1996)

Sea of Love (Harold Becker, USA 1989)

The Secret Beyond the Door (Fritz Lang, USA 1948)

Secret Games (Gregory Dark, credited as Alexander Gregory Hippolyte, USA 1992)

Secret Games II: The Escort (Gregory Dark, credited as Gregory Hippolyte, USA 1993)

Secret Games 3 (Gregory Dark, credited as Gregory Hippolyte, USA 1994)

Sex: The Annabel Chong Story (Gough Lewis, USA 1999)

Sex and the Emperor, originally titled *Man qing jin gong qi an* (Sherman Wong, Hong Kong 1994)

Sex, Lies, and Videotape (Steven Soderbergh, USA 1989)

Sex and Zen originally titled *Rou pu tuan zhi tou qing bao jian* (Michael Mak, Hong Kong 1992)

Sex and Zen II originally titled *Yuk po tuen III goon yan ngoh yiu* (Aman Chang, Hong Kong 1998)

Sexual Intent (Kurt MacCarley, USA 1994)

Sexual Malice (Jag Mundhra, USA 1994)

Sexual Roulette (Gary Graver, USA 1996)

Shades of Gray (Jag Mundhra, USA 1997)

Shaving Ryan's Privates (Christopher Hull, USA 1999)

The Shining (Stanley Kubrick, UK 1980)

Showgirl Murders (Dave Payne, USA 1996)

Showgirls (Paul Verhoeven, USA 1995)

Silence of the Lambs (Jonathan Demme, USA 1991)

Single White Female (Barbet Schroeder, USA 1992)

Sins of Desire (Jim Wynorski, USA 1993)

Sins of the Night (Gregory Hippolyte, USA 1993)

La Sirène du Mississipi (François Truffaut, Italy/France 1969)

Sister Act (Emile Ardolino, USA 1992)

Sisters (Brian De Palma, USA 1973)

Sleepless in Seattle (Nora Ephron, USA 1993)

Sliver (Phillip Noyce, USA 1993)

Snuff aka *American Cannibale* (Michael and Roberta Findlay, Argentina/USA 1976)

Some Nudity Required (Odette Springer, USA 1998)

Someone to Watch Over Me (Ridley Scott, USA 1987)

Sorority House Massacre 2 (Jim Wynorski, USA 1990)

The Specialist (Luis Llosa, USA 1994)

The Sperminator (USA 1985)

Spetters (Paul Verhoeven, Netherlands 1980)

Stardust Memories (Woody Allen, USA 1980)

Starship Troopers (Paul Verhoeven, USA 1997)

Stella Dallas (King Vidor, USA 1937)

The Story of O (Just Jaeckin, France/West Germany 1975)

The Strange Love of Martha Ivers (Lewis Milestone, USA 1946)

Stranger by Night (Gregory Dark, credited as Gregory H. Brown, USA 1995)

Straw Dogs (Sam Peckinpah, USA/UK 1971)

Street Angels originally titled *Hong deng qu* (Dion Lam, Hong Kong 1996)

Street Asylum (Gregory Dark, credited as Gregory Brown, USA 1990)

Streets (Katt Shea, USA 1990)

Stripped to Kill (Katt Shea Ruben, USA 1987)

Stripped to Kill II (Katt Shea Ruben, USA 1988)

Stripshow (Gary Dean Orona, USA 1996)

Striptease (Andrew Bergman, USA 1996)

Stripteaser (Dan Golden, USA 1995)

Stripteaser 2 (Karl Ernest, USA 1997)

The Substitute (Robert Mandel, USA 1996)

Sudden Death (Peter Hyams, USA 1995)

Suite 16 (Dominique Deruddere, UK/Holland/Belgium 1994)

Sunset Boulevard (Billy Wilder, USA 1950)

Suspicion (Alfred Hitchcock, USA 1941)

Tainted Love (Jag Mundhra, USA 1995)

Taking Lives (D. J. Caruso, USA 2004)

Tales of the Kama Sutra, aka *Perfumed Garden* (Jag Mundhra, USA 1998)

Tales of the Kama Sutra 2, aka *Monsoon* (Jag Mundhra, USA 1998)

A Taste for Fear originally titled *Pathos – segreta inquietudine* (Piccio Raffanini, Italy 1988)

Taxi Driver (Martin Scorsese, USA 1976)

Testing the Limits (Brigitte Berman, USA 1998)

Thelma and Louise (Ridley Scott, USA 1991)

This World, Then the Fireworks (Michael Oblowitz, USA 1997)

Those Bedroom Eyes aka *A Kiss to Die For* (Leon Ichaso, USA 1993)

Threat of Exposure (Tom Whitus, USA 2002)

Three Men and a Baby (Leonard Nimoy, USA 1987)
Tightrope (Richard Tuggle, USA 1984)
Titanic (James Cameron, USA 1997)
To Sleep With a Vampire (Adam Friedman, USA 1993)
Total Recall (Paul Verhoeven, USA 1990)
Touch of Evil (Orson Welles, USA 1958)
Trois (Rob Hardy, USA 2000)
Tootsie (Sidney Pollack, USA 1982)
Tropical Heat (Jag Mundhra, USA 1993)
Twelve Angry Men (Sidney Lumet, USA 1957)
Twin Sisters (Tom Berry, USA 1992)
Two Moon Junction (Zalman King, USA 1988)
2001: A Space Odyssey (Stanley Kubrick, UK/USA 1968)
Undercover, aka *Undercover Heat* (Gregory Hippolyte, USA 1992)
Unfaithful (Adrian Lyne, USA 2002)
Uninvited Guest aka *An Invited Guest* (Timothy Wayne Folsome, USA 1999)
Unlawful Entry (Jonathan Kaplan, USA 1992)
The Untold Story, originally titled *Ba Xian fan dian zhi ren rou cha shao bao* (Danny Lee and Herman Yau, Hong Kong 1992)
Vamp (Richard Wenk, USA 1986)
Vamps: Deadly Dreamgirls (Mark Burchett and Michael D. Fox, USA 1995)
Vertigo (Alfred Hitchcock, USA 1958)
Victim of Desire (Jim Wynorski, USA 1994)
Virtual Desire (Jim Wynorski, USA 1995)
Virtual Voyeur (Richard Gabai, USA 2001)
Wall Street (Oliver Stone, USA 1987)
Warm Texas Rain (Daniel Rogosin, USA 2000)
War of the Roses (Danny DeVito, USA 1989)
Wayne's World (Penelope Spheeris, USA 1992)
Weekend in Vegas (Gary Graver, USA 1997)
Where Sleeping Dogs Lie (Charles Finch, USA 1992)
Wild Cactus (Jag Mundhra, USA 1993)
Wild Orchid (Zalman King, USA 1990)
Wild Side (Donald Cammell, USA 1995/2000)
Wild Things (John McNaughton, USA 1998)
Wildfire (Zalman King, USA 1988)
Wonder Boys (Curtis Hansen, USA 2000)
Woman of Desire (Robert Ginty, USA 1993)
A Woman Scorned aka *Scorned* (Andrew Stevens, USA 1993)
Zandalee (Sam Pillsbury, USA 1989)

INDEX